READINGS IN
FAMILY THEORY

READINGS IN
FAMILY THEORY

THOMAS R. CHIBUCOS
RANDALL W. LEITE
WITH DAVID L. WEIS
Bowling Green State University

SAGE Publications
Thousand Oaks ▪ London ▪ New Delhi

DEDICATION

David Weis and I started to develop the conceptualization for this book a number of years ago in discussions about the need for greater attention to theory in the education of both undergraduate and graduate students. Subsequently, I asked David (I was David's school director at the time) to consider teaching a graduate theory course in a manner that included both family theories and developmental theories. He decided to do it under the condition that I work with him to fill in the developmental information. Following a relatively successful teaching of the theory class in a more interdisciplinary and integrated manner than it had been previously taught (it had previously been taught as either family or developmental theory), we began discussing more pointedly what was eventually to become this book. Subsequent discussion with James Brace-Thompson at Sage, and with James White and David Klein, reinforced and further prompted our serious attention and commitment to the book. We wrote the prospectus for the book in late spring 2003, and received six reviews of our proposal in late summer. We began work on the book in earnest in mid-August 2003. While I was at a conference September 3–5, 2003, David received our book contract from Sage and left me a typically Dave phone message: "Where the hell are you, Chibucos? We got the book contract!" I returned home late on September 5 and learned immediately that David had died earlier in the evening. In late 2003 I asked Randy to join me in writing/editing the book, both because I needed support and because I knew his contributions would be high-quality ones. Dave would have loved the choice! Although David did not live to write much that wound up between the covers of the book, his creative role in its development, his work on defining the kinds of readings to be included, and his overall intellectual impact and vision were and remain ubiquitous.

—Thomas R. Chibucos

*We dedicate the book to David L. Weis: a colleague, friend,
humorist, academic, husband, father, son, and a person who unfailingly
spoke truth to power. David lived the ethical and caring life to the fullest.*

—Thomas R. Chibucos and Randall W. Leite

For information:

Sage Publications, Inc.
2455 Teller Road
Thousand Oaks, California 91320
E-mail: order@sagepub.com

Sage Publications Ltd.
1 Oliver's Yard
55 City Road
London EC1Y 1SP
United Kingdom

Sage Publications India Pvt. Ltd.
B-42, Panchsheel Enclave
Post Box 4109
New Delhi 110 017 India

Library of Congress Cataloging-in-Publication Data

Readings in family theory / [edited by] Thomas R. Chibucos, Randall W. Leite with David L. Weis.
    p. cm.
Includes bibliographical references and index.
ISBN 1-4129-0570-2 (pbk.)
  1. Family. 2. Family—Research. I. Chibucos, Thomas R. II. Leite, Randall W. III. Weis, David L.
HQ728.R37 2005
306.85—dc22

2004014909

Printed on acid-free paper in the United States of America.

05   06   07   08   09   10   9   8   7   6   5   4   3   2   1

Acquisitions Editor:	Jim Brace-Thompson
Editorial Assistant:	Karen Ehrmann
Production Editor:	Tracy Alpern
Copy Editor:	Brenda Weight
Typesetter:	C&M Digitals (P) Ltd.
Indexer:	Sylvia Coates
Cover Designer:	Edgar Abarca

CONTENTS

Preface   x

Acknowledgments   xi

1. **Theory: What It Is and Why It Is Important**   **1**
   Notable Differences Between Everyday Life and Family Research   4
   Example of Theory Building and the Research Process   6
   Defining *Family*?   8
   Issues for Your Consideration   9
   Further Reading   10

2. **Family Life Course Theory**   **11**
   The Readings   13
   Issues for Your Consideration   13
   Further Reading   13
      Involuntary Celibacy: A Life Course Analysis   14
       Denise Donnelly, Elisabeth Burgess,
       Sally Anderson, Regina Davis, and Joy Dillard
      Life Course Transitions, the Generational Stake,
       and Grandparent-Grandchild Relationships   30
       Robert Crosnoe and Glen H. Elder, Jr.

3. **Life-Span Developmental Theory**   **39**
   The Readings   40
   Issues for Your Consideration   41
   Further Reading   41
      The Influence of Context, Timing, and Duration of
       Risk Experiences for the Passage from Childhood to Midadulthood   42
       Ingrid Schoon, John Bynner, Heather Joshi,
       Samantha Parsons, Richard D. Wiggins, and Amanda Sacker
      Marital Status Continuity and Change Among Young and
       Midlife Adults: Longitudinal Effects on Psychological Well-Being   68
       Nadine F. Marks and James David Lambert

4. Social Learning Theory   **95**

The Readings   97

Issues for Your Consideration   97

Further Reading   97

    A Social Learning Theory Model of Marital Violence   98

      Sharon Wofford Mihalic and Delbert Elliott

    Intergenerational Transmission of Constructive Parenting   118

      Zeng-Yin Chen and Howard B. Kaplan

5. Social Exchange Theory   **137**

The Readings   139

Issues for Your Consideration   139

Further Reading   139

    Costs and Rewards of Children: The Effects of

      Becoming a Parent on Adults' Lives   140

      Kei M. Nomaguchi and Melissa A. Milkie

    Equity and Social Exchange in Dating Couples:

      Associations With Satisfaction, Commitment, and Stability   165

      Susan Sprecher

6. Social Conflict Theory   **183**

The Readings   185

Issues for Your Consideration   185

Further Reading   185

    A Conflict Theory of Family Violence   186

      David D. Witt

    Status and Income as Gendered Resources: The Case of Marital Power   194

      Veronica Jaris Tichenor

7. Feminist Theory   **209**

The Readings   211

Issues for Your Consideration   211

Further Reading   211

    Feminist Visions for Transforming Families:

      Desire and Equality Then and Now   212

      Katherine R. Allen

    Do Gender Role Attitudes Matter? Family Formation

      and Dissolution Among Traditional and Egalitarian Men and Women   225

      Gayle Kaufman

8. Symbolic Interactionism   **237**

The Readings   239

Issues for Your Consideration   239

Further Reading   239

    The Symbolic Origins of Conflict in Divorce   240

      Joseph Hopper

    "They Think You Ain't Much of Nothing":

      Social Construction of the Welfare Mother   258

      Karen Seccombe, Delores James, and Kimberly Baffle Walters

 9. **Family Systems Theory**   **279**
     The Readings   280
     Issues for Your Consideration   281
     Further Reading   281
         Relations Between Identity Formation
             and Family Characteristics Among Young Adults   282
             Ronald L. Mullis, John C. Brailsford, and Ann K. Mullis
         Structural Family Therapy   293
             Arlene Vetere

 10. **Ecological Theory**   **303**
     The Readings   305
     Issues for Your Consideration   305
     Further Reading   305
         Balancing Employment and Fatherhood: A Systems Perspective 306
             Judy O. Berry and Julie Meyer Rao
         The Social Ecology of Marriage and Other Intimate Unions   317
             Ted L. Huston
         Getting Dinosaurs to Dance: Community
             Collaborations as Applications of Ecological Theory   345
             Daniel F. Perkins, Theresa M. Ferrari,
             Martin A. Covey, and Joanne G. Keith

 11. **Discussion and Conclusions**   **359**
     Overview of Developments in Family Theory   359
     Thoughts on Future Directions   360

References   **364**

Index   **366**

About the Editors   **386**

PREFACE

The purpose of this book is to introduce students to theoretical approaches that deal with family and human development issues. We do this first by discussing theory as part of the overall process of developing scientific knowledge and understanding. This approach reflects our strong belief that student learning about theory is facilitated by providing a context into which theory fits. This seems to be particularly the case when students are in their family studies and human development classes at the basic level, in the position of being "forced" to pay attention to theory. We present relatively brief descriptions of the theories as well as explicit uses of the theories in the published literature. We have included the particular theories in this book because they have withstood the test of time and have demonstrated their usefulness for understanding family and developmental issues. In the latter case, theories have been included that are not usually emphasized in books on family science (social learning, life-span development, and ecological). We included them because of their great potential for contributing to understanding families and also because they provide key links between family and human development specializations, links that are too often not taken advantage of—at some scientific cost, we think.

Our general experience (and particularly our teaching experience over many years) tells us that, for most students, the issue of often-quite-noticeable weak connections between family science and human (or child) development that they see in too many classes and writing is not really understandable. In fact, they seem to share this perspective with many nurses, teachers, fathers, mothers, and others. Likewise, for many professors and researchers, the issue looms quite large, indeed. For historical disciplinary reasons, for reasons of organizational structure in universities and colleges, and for reasons having to do with disciplinary identification and specialization (not to mention university personnel procedures related to tenure and promotion!), it is the case that family science (also known as family studies) and human development still suffer from a surprising degree of compartmentalization.

The book is intended for possible use in two ways: (a) as a supplement to White and Klein's (2002) book, *Family Theories* (2nd ed.), or, perhaps, as a supplement to other such books on family theory or on human development theory; and (b) as a stand-alone text. We realized at the beginning that putting such a book together would not be an easy task. It was not. However, we believe we have gotten close to hitting the right balance as we tried to make the material accessible and palatable to students who have not had much experience with "theory."

To make both of these potential uses possible, we tried to write brief explanations, or summaries, of the theories to give students a "good enough" grasp of them so that they can be understood and distinguished one from the others. Interested students can pursue the various additional readings we have listed if their appetites are whetted. Also, as noted, we attempted to put the concept of theory in an overall scientific context because we believe that students typically learn about theories without being exposed to their roles in the overall process of knowledge development and understanding. We made no attempt to be complete in describing the assumptions, scope, concepts, and so forth. We do realize that much is left out: We left it out intentionally! Some may view this choice in a less than kind way—that the book is a watered-down version of what should be presented in an academic book. But our primary goal was to get new students interested in theory and to provide ready examples of scholarship building on theory. The fact seems to be (if student comments and the comments we received from reviewers of our book prospectus are accurate indicators) that most treatises on the subject of theory, although helpful and appropriate for practicing scholars and advanced graduate students, simply do not appeal to the interests of students who are relatively naïve about both theory and the areas of family science and human development.

To Students

The nine core chapters of the book include (a) relatively brief introductory descriptions and discussion of each of the theories; (b) introductory commentary on the articles (The Readings)

that were guided by the respective theories; (c) Issues for Your Consideration, which can be used to guide and inform your thinking as you read and contemplate the articles; (d) suggested Further Reading, which can help fill in your understanding and provide more in-depth coverage as well as different perspectives of some of the issues; and (e) the actual readings.

We offer this book as a contribution to broadening the appeal of theory to you, or, at minimum (like much of what teaching is about!), as an attempt to not turn you off to it. If you are interested in pursuing these (and other) theories further, if you come away with an overall understanding of what theory is and its role in developing scientific understanding, and if you develop some sense of how useful theories are, we believe we will have done our job with the book.

Finally, we hope that you and other readers enjoy the book and find it a productive introduction to thinking about family theory. Remember: Theories are simply attempts to explain and understand things. Theories, therefore, are just another version of what people do throughout their lives. Here's to understanding!

ACKNOWLEDGMENTS

We wish to thank J. B. T. and Karen Ehrmann at Sage, whose work, dedication, and support was essential in getting this project completed. Thanks also to these Bowling Green State University colleagues: Sue Bigaila, for her assistance on many aspects of preparing the book and for her understanding; and Judy Maxey and Sherry Haskins, for their expertise and professional commitment in preparing the manuscript. Thanks to James M. White, University of British Columbia; David Klein, University of Notre Dame; Marilyn Helterline, State University of New York College at Oneonta; Anisa M. Zvonkovic, Oregon State University; Elaine Wethington, Cornell University, Department of Human Development; Bill Rose, Villa Julie College; and one anonymous reviewer for their time and helpful comments at early stages in the development of this book.

Thanks to Pam, Thomas, Marcus, Elise, Elizabeth, Theresa, Matthew, Caitlyn, and John, family members all, who have made and make our families so meaningful, important, time-consuming, and special to us. Each of these people, whose ages range from 15 to 33 (spouses not included in the age range—chivalry lives!), is testament to the following fact: Although families are more than the sum of their parts, they, in fact, would not be what they are without every individual in them. From an individual development perspective, each is unique, each is special; from the family sciences perspective, life without any would be something, but it wouldn't be the same, nor would it be as meaningful and complete as it is.

Finally, thanks to Pamela for proofreading!

READINGS

Chapter 2

Chapter 3

Chapter 4

Chapter 5

Chapter 6

Chapter 7

Chapter 8

Chapter 9

Chapter 10

1

THEORY: WHAT IT IS AND WHY IT IS IMPORTANT

I f you were asked what is the ultimate goal of research in any discipline or subject matter, what would you say? What do geologists, psychologists, family scientists, medical researchers, experts in human development, chemists, political scientists, sociologists, biologists, astronomers, plant pathologists, and anthropologists have in common? No, the answer is not that they all have pointy heads and wear white lab coats. What they share is a common goal: the desire to increase understanding of their subject manner. They want to find out how things work and why they work the way they do. Why? Two major reasons: (a) to know for the sake of knowing and (b) to figure how some problem or issue can be better dealt with.

How do the study habits of students with good grade point averages (GPAs) differ from those of students with not-so-good GPAs? Why do they differ? What makes some families seem more resilient to stress than other families and how do they become this way? What makes some families less likely to reach out for help? Is exposure to successful parental behavior a way for new parents to learn how to be good parents? What particular teaching approaches work best with which student predilections for learning?

To make progress on these kinds of intellectual and practical questions, individual researchers (and, indeed, the entire research enterprise) operate in two distinct but highly related worlds: the abstract (the world of concepts/ideas) and the concrete (the empirical/observable world). What scientific theories do is link these two separate domains and, in so doing, provide descriptions, summaries, integration, and explanations about what is known from research as well as guidance for additional research and practice that will increase further understanding.

Theorizing, then, is the process of systematically developing and organizing ideas to explain phenomena, and a theory is the total set of empirically testable, interconnected ideas formulated to explain those phenomena[1] (Doherty, Boss, LaRossa, Schumm, & Steinmetz, 1993; White & Klein, 2002). It is extremely important to be clear that if one deals only with the conceptual, or idea, level without testing those ideas against independent empirical information (empirical means "available to the senses"), or if one deals only with observable information without trying to systematically explain it, then scientific theory development is not possible. It also must be understood that the process is not linear in nature.

1

For example, one can start with observations of some aspect of family life and then try to explain those observations (e.g., the children in a family seem to be less patient with one another when their mother or father has had an "adult temper tantrum" at some point in the day than when this has not occurred), or one can start with an explanation and then make empirical observations (e.g., what children come to know about how to be parents results from *modeling*—that is, from observing and re-creating the behavior of their parents).

We wrote this book to help increase your appreciation of how important theory is to the advancement of knowledge in family science and human development (as it is in every field of scientific inquiry) as well as to the practical application of ideas. Indeed, the level of theoretical development is one yardstick indicating the maturity and usefulness of a discipline such as family science (Marx, 1969; Weis, 1998). Is research in a given area conceptualized and carried out to test predictions from a theory? Is the development and implementation of practice (e.g., educational efforts or therapeutic interventions) fostered and supported by theory? If so, then there is likely to be a relatively strong knowledge base in the area of study. Contrary to the view that theory is "dry" or "not relevant" or "not needed" or "not important for the average person," it is simply the case that summarizing, organizing, testing, relating, reevaluating, and attempting to explain and understand things (which is what theories do) is absolutely crucial for all humans in virtually every facet of our lives. A famous thinker and psychologist, Kurt Lewin (as cited in Marrow, 1977) once said that there is nothing so useful as a good theory. This is true in regard to scientific theory as we have just defined it (and which is the focus of this book). But *theory building*—the process of accumulating, evaluating, linking, testing, retesting, and explaining information on an ongoing basis—is also an essential feature of everyday living. Of course, there are some clear distinctions between how this process works in everyday life and in scientific research.

As a way to begin to understand these distinctions, let us first introduce Professor S. Canon, who does research on the development of families over the life course. Canon may work in a university, a government research agency, a private company, or a foundation. Assuming that she is well trained in the ways of scientific research and is inclined to ethical behavior in her research (e.g., Nosek, Banaji, & Greenwald, 2002), she follows a fairly specific set of rules for the overall process of discovering and explaining. These "rules of the game" have been defined and refined over many years by researchers, theorists, and philosophers of science. They comprise the integrated processes of information gathering and explanation building and characterize how researchers operate back and forth in the concrete and abstract worlds. This way of "knowing," or developing understanding, must be understood so that you can appreciate the specific roles of theory and theory development in knowledge building, including the development of concepts and their relationships, the testing of predictions, and the uses of research results to modify, support, or not support theoretical explanations (e.g., Babbie, 2003; Miller, 1992; Sadler & Hulgus, 1989).

The following outline of important parts of the scientific research process is presented for your review (but be careful—the process only rarely proceeds in the kind of linear fashion that a list might suggest) along with how a family researcher such as Professor Canon might proceed to use the process:

1. Canon develops an interest in some general area of family studies or human development through reading, thinking, and talking with colleagues and students and by casual or planned observations (e.g., Benson & Piercy, 1997). Let us assume that she is interested in how families facilitate or inhibit the development of friendliness and concern for others; perhaps, phrased somewhat negatively, she is interested in the development of individual as well as family arrogance and self-indulgence.

2. Canon assesses the current state of knowledge and ideas about these family issues that have piqued her interest by examining

- prior scientific research,
- personal experience,
- practice,
- theory,
- advice/suggestions from a colleague or a teacher,
- armchair ideas.

3. Using the kinds of information identified above, Canon identifies and refines a problem or a set of problems she wishes to investigate. Depending on how she sees the state of knowledge of the phenomena in which she is interested, she may wind up testing very specific hypotheses, doing exploratory data gathering, or doing qualitative research that helps generate other ideas and/or gives voice to usually unheard perspectives.

- Canon refines the problems (one can't study everything).
- She carefully defines all major variables; for instance, what do the terms *arrogant, self-indulgent,* and *concern for others* specifically mean?
- Canon clarifies the *what* (i.e., specific questions or hypotheses), the *why* (i.e., the rationale for the research in terms of increasing understanding or with regard to important implications for practice or policy), and the *how* (i.e., the approach and methods to be used to answer the questions) of the research.

4. To address the identified problem(s), research questions, or hypotheses, data/input/information/facts/observations (DIIFO) of two general types are collected:

- DIIFO directly experienced by the researcher/theorist—either intentionally sought as part of planned research or not intentionally sought
- DIIFO indirectly received from someone or something else—again, either intentionally sought or not intentionally sought by the researcher/theorist

5. Canon uses already-developed ways to measure all major variables in her study (or invents new ways to measure them). All available and relevant DIIFO is

- assessed as to its reliability and credibility (the quality of all DIIFO is systematically assessed and is not simply assumed);
- summarized and integrated;
- evaluated as to its importance relative to other DIIFO, and all procedures that produce DIIFO are systematically described, organized, and evaluated.

6. Canon integrates and explains the obtained results. The interpretation of her empirical findings may or may not link directly to an already-existing theory about the phenomena. Even in this case, however, she will consciously (and, one hopes, conscientiously) link her research findings to other empirical research on the same issues. In so doing, Canon's results become part of the ever-developing knowledge base on family issues.

- Although the study may or may not have been generated by a specific theory, the results of the study can still be used to test a theory or theories (another example of how the whole process is anything but neatly linear). For example, do Canon's results tend to support the symbolic interaction theory of family functioning (Chapter 8), or do they support social learning theory (Chapter 4), or neither, or both?
- Depending on the nature of the results of her study, Canon (and other researchers, since research is a public process) may conclude that they provide strong or partial support (or nonsupport) of a theory or theories. This can then lead to modifications of the theory or to restudying the same issues to check if they were reliably investigated.
- Implications of the data and explanations generated may include specific suggestions of additional research that needs to be done to further test and enhance the explanation(s), and/or may produce specific ideas about practical interventions or practice.

7. The process continues as other researchers and theorists question, repeat, refute, refine, and so forth, the work that Canon has done. Others are able to evaluate Canon's work because she

has followed the rules of scientific research, including, in particular, the public nature of the research and theory-building process.

Within this overall process of information gathering and explanation developing, steps 6 and 7 are the ones that most directly emphasize theory or explanation of phenomena (which is not to say that all the other steps are not influenced by researchers' theoretical predilections—to one extent or another, they may well be). We hope we have been clear that theory development depends on an intricate process of ongoing empirical research that both generates and tests theoretical ideas, which in turn gets reflected back on additional research and practice in an ongoing iterative manner. It is instructive and essential to remember that scientific research is a collective enterprise. It therefore follows that a single study of any family issue is almost never definitive, either in regard to the research (empirical results) or in regard to explanation. Theory building and the testing of theoretical concepts through empirical research is not solely the prerogative of Canon or of any other single researcher. Although we have talked about this process in reference to Canon's research, many other researchers will use her work to inform their own and will integrate it with other research to reach both empirical conclusions (i.e., about what the facts are on a given family issue) and to explicate family theory (i.e., why the research facts are what they are).

NOTABLE DIFFERENCES BETWEEN EVERYDAY LIFE AND FAMILY RESEARCH

As noted previously, there are many similarities between scientific research and everyday life in the process of gathering data and developing explanations. The overall quests to seek information, to summarize it so that we can handle it, to check out its reliability and validity, and to explain what we see are quite similar overall. Humans have to do these things to live as well as to research. But there are also some truly key differences in how this process works in the world of science compared to how it typically works in everyday life. Here are several of the most important differences between scientific theory development and the development of understanding in everyday life, and between scientific information gathering and the gathering of information in everyday life.

First, the process in scientific theory development is consciously public. All steps, from problem definition (including why it is important to study this or that family issue, for example) to the methods of gathering information, to the reporting and interpretation of results, are open to scrutiny, testing, and refutation by other researchers. Second, clarity in definition and communication in all aspects of the research process, such as unambiguous definition of variables being studied and clear articulation of all procedures used, including data analysis decisions and choices, is fundamental in scientific theory building. Third, all concepts and the relationships between them (the "guts" of theory) must be testable in the empirical world (philosophers of science say they must be capable of disproof). Fourth, there is ongoing effort to keep personal or other biases out of the research process (certainly this is not always successful, but it is a value inherent to scientific research). White and Klein (2002, pp. 5–9) provide a relevant overview of the last point in their presentation of different philosophies of science. It is important to recognize, however, that one theoretical approach, feminist theory (Chapter 7), has made significant contributions to understanding families, particularly conceptions of gender development and power structures within families, by emphasizing research methodologies that are *value committed*—that is, research that acknowledges and builds upon the values of those who conduct it, a reflection of the belief that research cannot be truly value-free. The key issue for us is that although the practitioners of scientific research are not valueless or bias-free, the entire enterprise is structured so as to identify and police the interference of such intrusions on research or, as in the case of feminist theory, to integrate those values into the research process itself. One implication of all this, because the entire enterprise is public, is that research findings that are assessed by other researchers to be biased are, at minimum, open to attempts at replication and, at maximum, likely to be completely discounted (the most egregious example of the latter being cases of fraud, which regrettably do occur).

We will demonstrate some of these distinctions by taking a close look at how Mr. H. C. T. Judge's approach to studying family issues differs from that of Canon. Judge (who, in a move toward greater discretion, recently changed his last name from Judgmental) is a person who seems to be quite active in his pursuit of information and in reaching conclusions about other people's lives and how they got to be how they are. Leaving aside for a moment how it is that Judge got to be how *he* is (a question primarily of individual development), at first glance Judge seems to follow the same kind of process that Canon does when the latter pursues her research on the development of individual and family characteristics. For example, Judge observes things (sometimes on purpose, sometimes not), evaluates, integrates and summarizes information, reaches generalizations, makes informed (or not-so-informed) guesses about important things to look for, has unresolved questions, moves from the realm of observation to attempted explanations, tests one explanation against another, may or may not share all the previous with other observers, and may or may not test the reliability of his observations.

Judge sees his neighbors, the Hubris family (husband, wife, and two teenage children who are the offspring of the husband and wife), as self-indulgent and arrogant. He sees the Friendly family (husband, wife, and three children, ages 4, 10, and 12, from the wife's prior marriage) as having a giving nature and as possessing down-to-earth characteristics. What kind of information did Judge use to arrive at his conclusions? Do his conclusions and the bases for them match those of the family members themselves or those of other people outside the families? Given the

information he has about the families, are his conclusions reasonable, or are they based on some bias of his? In general, observations or facts or information about the families could have come to Judge's attention directly (he experienced them himself, whether intentionally or not)—for instance, Judge tried to listen or observe something or he happened to see something when he was walking his dog—or indirectly (someone or something else conveyed information to him—again, either intentionally or not)—for instance, he asked a neighbor for some information or a neighbor offered some information.

Let us conjecture about how Judge may have reached his conclusions about his two neighbor families. Some kind of direct or indirect observations, DIIFO, of the families must have occurred. For example, Judge may have witnessed Mrs. Hubris or one of the Hubris children being haughty to the mailperson (or someone else may have told him that this occurred) and seen Mr. Friendly being very nice to a Girl Scout delivering cookies. A number of these kinds of experiences over time (not all of which were necessarily equally supportive of his conclusions) may have occurred. Of course, in general, in everyday life we constantly take in information of many kinds. The taking in may be deliberately sought out, it may be whimsical, or it may be purely incidental and it likely will be from multiple sources. Judge may have deliberately tested his conclusions about these two families, perhaps by asking each to do a favor for him or another neighbor.

There is much involved with the taking in of information. For example, it seems to be the case that, after a while, humans have a tendency to prefer information that is more rather than less consistent with prior conclusions, and, because our brains can handle only so much information, we have built-in processes that help us selectively tune in only certain kinds of information (consider, for example, how hard it would be to successfully drive a car if the driver paid equal attention to all sources of input at any given moment). On the other hand, family researchers routinely try to build in protections to guard against selective attention and against ignoring information that does not fit preexisting theoretical ideas or personal predilections.

In any case, at some point in time, Judge had enough information (from his perspective) to reach conclusions about the two families. In fact, a function of theories, whether of the everyday variety or the family research variety, is to help summarize information. Instead of Judge listing in detail each of the 10 or 35 or 200 observations he had made of the Hubris family, he *induces* (from a bunch of specifics to a general statement) that a good summary is to describe his observations as depicting haughtiness in the Hubrises.

Now, perhaps you can imagine some reasons that Judge's conclusions may or may not be right on. He may be haughty himself, for example. Or maybe his interactions with and observations of the Hubrises always occurred on days when he was feeling insecure or perhaps his interactions with and observations of the Friendly family always occurred when he was feeling very positive. Perhaps he relied too heavily on second-hand information from someone who had a personal bias against the Hubrises. With regard to the latter, Judge may, at some point, have heard from a friend something fairly outlandish about how one of the Hubrises had talked to the friend about some local issue. Although it seemed to fit his own conclusions, he may have checked it out himself, for example, by asking Mr. Hubris what he thought of the new school budget proposal. If he did this, their discussion may have either supported or been inconsistent with the friend's assertions. If the former, then another "fact" to support his prior conclusion about the Hubrises would have been gathered; if the latter, then perhaps Judge might have begun to question his prior conclusions, or he might have simply ignored this information since it did not fit his prior perspective.

The next step for Judge might well be to reach some conclusion about *why* and *how* the two families he has been thinking about came to be as they are: Judge builds a personal theory to explain what he has observed. This is similar to what Canon does, and both of these information gatherers and theory builders may well have been generating explanations all along the way—that is, rarely do regular people and researchers wait until all the information is in before at least tentatively reaching some conclusions about why and how. But Canon's approach will follow the rules of the game we specified previously (she does have a well-developed and specific set of rules to follow, after all). In particular, Canon will deliberately test her theory by deriving hypotheses and research questions from it and putting them to empirical test. Judge may or may not do something like this, but if he did, rarely would it be systematic, well-defined, ongoing, and public.

In the next section, we present a brief synopsis of what a scientific theory looks like. We hope to reinforce your understanding of how theories develop, how they are tested, how they increase scientific understanding, and how they therefore provide a foundation for practice such as educational and therapeutic interventions.

EXAMPLE OF THEORY BUILDING AND THE RESEARCH PROCESS

Recall that a family theory is the empirically testable interconnected ideas that explain some phenomenon. Let us consider the issue of family violence and develop a very basic theory. First, assume that (a) we, the editors of this book, have some professional experience with families involved with family violence (we do), (b) there are some published research studies on family violence (there are many), and (c) our general awareness of various theories on family issues leads us to favor *social learning theory* as a generally strong theory for explaining parental and child behavior (certainly true for one of us!). If we did some thinking about all this information we might think that a number of concepts are important for understanding family violence: a person's own family history, overall family and individual stress, emotional support both within and outside the family, personal and family risk factors such as alcohol and substance use, personal experience with different models (parents and others) of how adults might deal with children's issues and behaviors, and personality characteristics of individual family members—to name a few possibilities. (As a brief aside, please note that it is entirely possible that a similar or different group of concepts of presumed importance to understanding family violence could be developed by, say, your grandmother, the person who delivers your mail, or a novelist. The *source* of a theory about families or children, the so-called context of discovery [White & Klein, 2002, p. 4], is not particularly important.)

Second, to be considered a scientific theory, the concepts (ideas or abstractions) within it must be capable of being represented at the empirical level (otherwise communication would be impossible—for example, 10 different thinkers might each mean something different by "emotional support"), and they must be specifically related to one another is some fashion (*propositions* in theories are simply statements of how one concept relates to another). How does one empirically represent a concept? It's easy; we say exactly how the concept can be measured. For example, emotional support might be a score received on a pencil-and-paper assessment that is developed for the purpose of measuring the concept. Or it might be ratings given on the quality and quantity of listening behavior exhibited by family members having a discussion about something.

Using previous information (other studies, observations from clinical practice, etc.), the following propositions might make sense to us: "The greater the culture of extrafamilial violence experienced as a child (*a*), the more family violence experienced as a child (*b*)" and "The more violence experienced in the family of origin (*b*), the greater the level of violence produced in the family of procreation (*c*)." We can deduce (i.e., logically conclude) from these two propositions a third one: "The greater the culture of extrafamilial violence experienced in childhood (*a*), the greater the production of violence in the family of procreation (*c*)."

It is important to observe that the three propositions are logically related. If the process stops there—with "mere" logic—then we do not have a scientific theory. With due respect to philosophers and other thinkers, we may have a perfectly reasonable set of propositions, but from a scientific perspective this is inadequate. Scientific theories must be empirically testable for them to be taken seriously. That is, the propositions and their relationships spelled out in the theory must be amenable to disproof through research. (This is a great distinction between everyday and scientific use and understanding of what theory is.) As things stand to this point, we have done conceptual (abstract) work only. Can we do research to test the theory? Well, you won't be surprised to discover that the answer is "yes," or we would not be going on like this!

First, we get out of our "thinking" chair and try to *operationalize* the major concepts in our proposition. Operationalize simply means to choose a good way to measure the concept (note that this does not mean that what we choose is the only way to measure the concept, nor does it mean that the measurement equals the concept). We need to change our conceptual hypothesis (the proposition we developed by linking the concepts *culture of extrafamilial violence* and *violence in the family of procreation*) to a measurement hypothesis. Let's say we operationalize *culture of extrafamilial violence* to mean the number of police reports filed over a given period that concern neighborhood assaults and armed robberies, and we define *family violence in the family of procreation* as the number of police calls over the same period to investigate within-home acts of violence alleged to have been committed by parents against each other or against their children. Perhaps you can think of better ways to operationalize these concepts.

There are lots of important, and often quite "messy," methodological details (e.g., taking account of age, race, ethnicity, and education levels of parents) that would have to be addressed to adequately test what has become a testable measurement hypothesis. This process of refinement helps define one of the other distinctions between scientific and everyday information gathering and explanation developing. For the former, specific research designs are developed and carried out to help answer questions. And, although unexpected things happen all the time throughout the research and theory-building process, the point is that the information gathering is systemized and matched in the best ways possible to provide information directly on the question(s) of interest.

It is very important to note that the outcome of the research process is, in fact, determined in large part by the carrying out of all the messy details. That is, results that are either consistent or inconsistent with a given theory or theories must be evaluated in regard to how well the study was done. For example, the researcher may have done a poor job in measuring variables, in sampling, or in ignoring contradictory information. To the extent that methodological problems influence results, judgments about the theory must be tentatively made.

Nonetheless, the point for theoretical development is that whatever the outcome, there will be implications for our theory—and for other theoretical approaches that may seek to explain the same phenomenon. For example, perhaps one or more of our propositions is simply wrong. Perhaps adding several propositions related to age and other family history variables would lead to a different hypothesis and outcome, and so on. None of this potential theoretical refinement, or change, or even discarding of the entire theory and starting over (which almost never happens) would be possible without the ability to bring the abstract/conceptual ideas to the level of concrete/empirical operations that allow research to be conducted. This is how the link between empirical work and theoretical explanation occurs, and it is what contributes to an ongoing process of scientific discovery and knowledge refinement.

In addition, as mentioned previously, the practical impacts from ongoing theoretical explanation are often extensive. For example,

assuming reasonably consistent empirical results that support our little theory, what would be some of the implications for the prevention and treatment of family violence from the above basic theory? What policy recommendations might follow? Family and human development theories almost always have strong implications that are very practical, even if the research studies undertaken to test them may not have been designed with particular practice or policy issues in mind.

This concludes our presentation of what theory is and what it is good for. We hope it is clear that the goal of researchers, to increase understanding of this or that phenomenon by developing conceptual linkages (theories) and testing those against empirical reality, is also something that people do in everyday life. We all seek to understand things, and we do this by observing, or collecting, and integrating information, by assessing the strength of our information, by reaching tentative or strong conclusions and explanations, and so forth. Although it is true that there are, indeed, extremely important differences between the realms of research and everyday life in the pursuit of information and explanations, it is good to keep in mind that these differences are often in emphasis, degree, or articulated sophistication, and that theory building in science and theory building in everyday life are really quite similar in their basic content and nature.

DEFINING *FAMILY?*

Before you begin to peruse the readings and the commentary we have developed on each of the theories presented in this book, we want to bring an important issue to your attention. The history of attempts to define *family* presents an interesting paradox for family researchers and theorists, particularly since (as we have noted earlier in this chapter) the rules of scientific research place a premium on the careful definition of terms. In a very informative discussion of this matter,

White and Klein (2002, pp. 18–23) present a list of 19 characterizations (Box 1.3, p. 22) and ask, "Which of These Is a Family?" They also suggest four major ways in which families differ from other social groups. Families last longer, are intergenerational, contain both biological and "affinal" (e.g., legal, common law) relationships, and are part of a larger kinship network. Families are a particular kind of social group, *but* "the distinctiveness of family groups tends to be only a matter of degree" (p. 21). After reading White and Klein's very thorough discussion, we are left with the feeling that we have some understanding of what families are, but remain frustrated at the apparent difficulty inherent in precisely defining family.

Family researchers and theorists, as well as the public at large, demonstrate an amazing ability to talk about families, to identify families, to do research about families, and to theorize about families without actually defining them! This is not a new conundrum. Although there may be other reasons for this state of affairs, we think two contribute mightily. First, we think that some of the difficulty family researchers and theorists, and others, have in defining family occurs because one can immediately think of existing groups of individuals who think of themselves as families, but who do not fit the definition being developed. Second, we believe that there is a general reluctance to define family in a way that seems inconsistent with important legal definitions that relate to family, such as the legal definitions of marriage.

This all sounds reasonable, but we are left with the same question: *What* is a family? We all live in, or lived in, or will live in families. Is the concept restricted to legally sanctioned heterosexual couples who procreate? We think not. Does family include a single parent living with his or her child? We think so. You may note that the difficulty in defining family to everyone's satisfaction provides another example of how everyday life and science often seem to deal with the same issues—simply in different ways.

Unfortunately, from a scientific perspective, this difficulty with definition has deep historical roots in family science. There has been a consistent lack of consensus regarding a common functional definition of families as definitions of families have evolved throughout the twentieth century. In the 1930s, families were simplistically defined as parent-child relations of some duration (Nimkoff & Ogburn, 1934). From that relatively superficial perspective, modern definitions must attend to the complex and varied nature of families. For example, Seccombe and Warner (2004) recently suggested families may be defined as a relationship by blood, marriage, or affection, in which members may cooperate economically, may care for any children, and may consider their identity to be intimately connected to the larger group. While this is certainly not the only recently stated definition of families, it does reflect increased scientific (and public, we think) awareness of the complexity involved in defining family.

Although we like Seccombe and Warner's (2004) definition of family, you may decide another is more appropriate. Rather than suggest one appropriate definition of families, we bring this issue to your attention to encourage you to consider it as you read this book. Although all of the possible structural representations of family types simply could not be included in one volume, you will note as you progress through the book that a wide range of family types or structures is evident. As you read, think about how the various authors choose to define the subject of their scholarship. Ultimately, we may not be able to do much better in defining families than the supreme court justice who said about pornography, "I know it when I see it!"

ISSUES FOR YOUR CONSIDERATION

1. Write a short theory about any individual or family development issue that interests you. Include four to five concepts and several propositions. Is your theory testable?

2. Why is it correct to say that a theory is never proven? Why is it more correct to say that a theory is supported or not supported by the research results to varying degrees?

3. What are the major ways in which scientific theory building and everyday life theory building differ?

4. Does the absence of particular types of families from this book (perhaps a type of family from which you come, which you belong to right now, or which you have friends in) mean that that combination of individuals does not compose a family?

5. Given the focus of this chapter on the interplay between theory and research, what might be the impacts of ongoing definitional problems on family research and theory development? Will theory testing and development be hindered?

FURTHER READING[2]

Babbie (2003), Miller (1992), Sadler and Hulgus (1989), Seccombe and Warner (2004), White and Klein (2002).

Notes

1. A wide variety of other terms indicate the same general idea as the term *theory* (Thomas, 2001). Such terms as *model, paradigm, conceptual framework,* and *explanatory scheme,* like *theory,* all indicate an attempt of one kind or another to explain phenomena. What is important for purposes of this book is to realize that, whatever term is used by researchers, the attempt to explain is tested against data and that the offered explanation is repeatedly assessed with respect to how the empirical world supports or does not support the explanation.

2. The complete citations for all publications listed under the Further Reading sections in each chapter are in the References section at the end of the book.

2

FAMILY LIFE COURSE THEORY

As detailed by Bengston and Allen (1993) and by Elder (1996), as well as by White and Klein (2002), a number of streams of thought have come together to produce current family life course perspectives. There are ongoing arguments and scholarly treatises on every aspect of this theory, including whether some theorists overemphasize family life cycle issues (e.g., becoming a parent or a grandparent, children leaving home) at the expense of paying attention to influences on the family from outside the family. In our view, the most important thing to focus on with regard to family life course theory is seeking to explain changes in *families* (not individuals) over time. Elder (1996, p. 31) maintains that the *(family) life course* refers to "age-related life patterns imbedded in social structures and cultures that are subject to historical change." Essentially, this definition integrates three of the conceptual distinctions provided by Elder that we have found to be useful in helping to clarify thinking about what life course theory is and is not.

Consider first the concept of the *life cycle.* The family life cycle concept essentially defines how families go through their lives by specifying a procreative life cycle—one is born, one develops in the family of origin, one moves into a separate abode, one chooses an occupation, one marries (creating the empty nest for one's parents), one procreates (creating an extended family as well as a new family of origin), one ages, one becomes a grandparent, one dies—that has mutual and reciprocal influences across time. But, how relevant is this perspective to many subgroups in American society? Or, indeed, how relevant is it cross-culturally? *Life history* is simply a chronology of salient life events of an individual or group. Life histories are recorded autobiographically or biographically. *Life span* refers to the description of and explanations for age-related biological and behavioral changes from birth to death (see Chapter 3 for a discussion of life-span developmental theory).

As we just indicated, family life course theory seeks to explain changes in families; that is, the specific social group, the family, is the focus of analysis. Although it is not easy to discern in the many discussions of theories that currently focus on families per se, White and Klein (2002) cogently note that life course theory is the only theory that was developed to specifically deal with families! All of the other theories described in White and Klein and, indeed, in the present book began with other focuses and were extended or modified to deal with families. For example, systems theory has its roots in general systems theory, feminist theory has strong roots in philosophies concerning societal structures and functioning, and social learning theory, like other incarnations of learning theory, emphasized individual behavior change before its concepts extended to include families and other groups.

Given the absolute centrality of this defining feature of family life course theory, it is important to explicate what *family as the unit of analysis* or *focuses on the family* really means. Consider the birth of a second child into a family. This event obviously provides an opportunity to study the ontogeny (i.e., individual development) of a new human being. But what life course theory does is focus on and interpret the new arrival's particular consequences for the family group, including how the group functions, sees itself, adjusts, and so on. It's also important to recognize that life course theory, like ecological theory, examines and tries to explain not only the new person's impact on the rest of the family but also the family's influence as a social system on the new person. The child's development as an individual, although clearly impacted by many family variables, is not the focus of family life course theory. Rather, the study of ontogeny is within the purview of the theory described in the next chapter, life-span developmental theory. Similarly, family life course theorists are interested in the overall impact of broad historical and time period changes—major events over different epochs— on families. To the extent that family life course analyses focus on individuals, it is to try to discover the mechanisms of change. For example, the increase in family violence during periods of extensive national economic distress may be mediated by men's reactions to lack of opportunity to provide for their families.

In family life course analysis and theory, then, the family is not simply the sum of its parts. Rather, the family is seen in much the same way that biologists view any single organism. Just as each of the human body's various systems influences the others, and as their ongoing interactions produce outcomes that are not reducible to a mere summation of their separate individual functioning, so it is with families.

Elder (1996) specifies four themes that characterize family life course theory:

1. the interplay of human lives and changing historical times and places,

2. human agency in choice making and social constraints,

3. the timing of lives,

4. linked or independent lives.

The first theme concerns the particular physical places (immediate environments as well as geographical locations) and the historical epoch in which individuals live, interact, and develop. Family development, just like individual development, is impacted by intimate within-family events as well as many historical events— wars, economic dislocation, the availability of educational opportunity or the lack of it, and so forth. Family life course theory places high importance on the timing of all those factors. For example, when parents claim with complete sincerity that they treated each of their children exactly the same, they state what never was and never could be! Why? Besides the fact that each child is different to begin with (and may differentially interpret what may seem to be objectively similar parental behavior), within-home environments cannot be exactly the same for individuals at a given time, let alone over time. For example, the parents are relatively younger (or older) when each of two siblings is 4 years old, for instance, Johnny in 1997 and Suzy in 2002. In addition, national events will differ, and so forth.

The second theme concerns the effects that individual choices and experiences have on the future options and experiences of families. "Individual differences and life histories interact with changing environments to produce behavior outcomes and their correlated constraints" (Elder, 1996, p. 38). The spouse's/parent's choice of a particular job, the decision by an 18-year-old to pursue or not pursue higher education, and a pregnancy (whether planned or unplanned) all impact future directions for individuals and their families.

The third theme, the idea of timing of lives, is very similar to the concept of family life cycle. It refers to the social timing of events in relation to normative expectations. For example, socially speaking, there are "appropriate" times for child bearing or marriage. It must be noted that the very definition of what is normative timing is itself highly influenced by changing cultural mores and values and many other variables. The age at first marriage, for example, has risen sharply for both men and women over the last 35 years. Why? We will let you ponder that one. We simply add a caution that, although the timing of major life events can be as important as the events themselves in impacting the life course, in many instances whether social roles and events seem to violate expectations will be strongly influenced by historical changes in expectations.

The fourth theme that Elder identifies as being important for family life course theory, linked lives, probably comes the closest to what laypersons have in mind when they think about the importance of families. At the most basic level, this concept includes the direct and immediate impact on other (nuclear or extended) family members of any one member's fortunes. A child with a life-threatening illness influences many family members, both those in direct daily contact and others. If Uncle Harold hits the lotto, a number of family ripple effects are likely to occur, and they are likely to extend in time for the same immediate family and even across generations! Many strong hereditarily determined personal factors have such "extended-in-time" impacts. Other examples with similar impacts include the family's resilience to broad historical/societal events (e.g., wars or economic depression) or personal events (e.g., divorce or job loss). As Elder (1996, p. 39) says, "The principle of linked lives extends beyond the notion of interdependent lives to the interlocking trajectories of individuals and their sequence of transitions, both social and developmental."

THE READINGS

The readings in this chapter use family life course ideas to guide research on grandparent-grandchild

relationships (Crosnoe & Elder, 2002) and on involuntary celibacy (Donnelly, Burgess, Anderson, Davis, & Dillard, 2001). Donnelly et al. performed Internet research on 82 participants to try to understand how people become and "remain involuntarily celibate." In addition to their interesting findings and conclusion, Donnelly and her colleagues differentiate family life course theory from scripting and developmental theories as explanations of sexual behavior. They also discuss specific aspects of family life course theory such as the importance of timing and sequencing, and the changing nature of normative expectations for human behavior. Crosnoe and Elder's (2002) research is cross-generational and, therefore, emphasizes one of the important themes of family life course perspectives we discussed above, linked lives. This theme is researched in terms of grandchildren's entry into higher education, an interesting approach in that it enhances the taking of a longer-term perspective, which allows the examination of generational stakes in regard to one context-specific type of linked lives.

ISSUES FOR YOUR CONSIDERATION

1. Think about the concept of linked lives in relation to the article on involuntary celibacy. How might the concept apply to interpreting the findings of Donnelly et al.?

2. After you read the articles below and read the chapter on life-span developmental theory, discuss with a fellow student the differences between how life course and life-span developmental theories might explain the findings from any study in this book.

3. Do you think significant societal level historical events are more, less, or similarly influential than more direct family variables in impacting the family life course?

FURTHER READING

Bengston and Allen (1993), Elder (1996), White and Klein (2002).

Involuntary Celibacy: A Life Course Analysis

Denise Donnelly, Elisabeth Burgess,
Sally Anderson, Regina Davis, and Joy Dillard

Abstract

Using a life course perspective, we explored the development and maintenance of involuntary celibacy for 82 respondents recruited over the Internet. Data were collected using an open-ended electronic questionnaire. Modified grounded theory analysis yielded three groups of involuntary celibates, persons desiring to have sex but unable to find partners. Virgins were those who had never had sex, singles had sex in the past but were unable to establish current sexual relationships, and partnereds were currently in sexless relationships. These groups differed on dating experiences, the circumstances surrounding their celibacy, barriers to sexual activity, and the perceived likelihood of becoming sexually active. They were similar, however, in their negative reactions to celibacy. Pervasive in our respondents' accounts was the theme of becoming and remaining off time in making normative sexual transitions, which in turn perpetuated a celibate life course or trajectory.

In an era when sex is used to sell everything from toothpaste to transmissions, the idea that large minorities of adults might have little or no sexual contact with others seems incongruous to many people. Yet, one researcher found that as many as 16% of married couples had not engaged in sexual intercourse in the month prior to a representative national survey of U.S. residents (Donnelly, 1993). Another group of researchers reported that 14% of men and 10% of women in the U.S. had not had any sexual activity involving genital contact in the past 12 months, and that 3% had none since their 18th birthdays (Laumann, Gagnon, Michael, & Michaels, 1994).

Certainly, some persons are celibate because they have chosen this lifestyle for religious or personal reasons. Others, however, would like to have sex but lack a willing sexual partner. For them, celibacy is not a choice. Since involuntary celibacy is a relatively new area of inquiry within the field of sex research, few studies have dealt with the dimensions, etiology, and consequences of this phenomenon.

In this research, we define the involuntary celibate as one who desires to have sex, but has been unable to find a willing partner for at least 6 months prior to being surveyed. The 6-month mark reflects the reality that people often go without sex for weeks or months (Laumann et al., 1994), but after a certain length of time, begin to worry. We realize, however, the arbitrariness of choosing a specific length of time, and suggest that what is really important is whether or not persons define themselves as involuntarily celibate. As Thomas (1966) pointed out, "situations we define as real become real in their consequences" (p. 301). Thus, for our purposes, length of time without sex is less important than self-defining as involuntarily celibate. Involuntary celibates may be married or partnered persons whose partners no longer desire to have sex with them, unpartnered singles who have never had sex, or unpartnered singles who have had sexual relationships in the past, but are unable to currently find partners. Involuntary celibates include heterosexuals, bisexuals, homosexuals, and transsexuals.

We used a life course perspective to understand the process by which persons become and remain involuntarily celibate. In doing so, we compared and contrasted three groups of involuntary celibates, exploring the transitions and trajectories by which involuntary celibacy developed and was maintained.

Literature Review

Extant celibacy research tends to focus on persons who are celibate by choice, such as those who are celibate for cultural or religious reasons (Abbott, 2000; Goergen, 1974) or those who fear HIV, other sexually transmitted diseases, or pregnancy (Netting, 1992; Siegel & Raveis, 1993; Sprecher & Regan, 1996). Some research has focused on *voluntary virgins,* persons in their teens and twenties who choose to wait until marriage to become sexually active (Sprecher & Regan, 1996), and the religious media has introduced the idea of *secondary virgins,* persons once sexually active, but who are now celibate by choice (Stafford, 2001). The scarce research focusing on involuntary celibacy, however, tends to be limited to certain groups, such as celibates in ancient times (Abbott, 2000), married celibates (Donnelly, 1993), persons with chronic diseases or disabilities (Greenblat, 1983; Kiernan, 1988), and the elderly (Mulligan & Palguta, 1991; Quinnan, 1997; White, 1982).

While not focusing specifically on involuntary celibates, Kiernan (1988) found that celibates (defined in her British study as nonmarried persons) were more likely to be introverted and ambitious, and to have parents who married at later ages. In addition, celibate women were more likely to have attained high educational levels and occupational statuses, while celibate men were more likely to be lower class and unemployed.

Other researchers (Donnelly, 1993; Medlicott & Waltz, 1993) investigated persons in sexually inactive marriages. While not distinguishing between voluntarily and involuntarily celibate marriages, Donnelly (1993) found that unhappiness with marriage, plans or desires to leave the relationship, lack of shared activity, increased age, the presence of preschoolers, and poor health were significant correlates of sexual inactivity in marriage. Additional reasons for sexual inactivity include pregnancy, recent childbirth, or acute illness or injury (Greenblat, 1983). Some persons also experience relatively permanent physical problems such as chronic illness or handicaps that hinder sexual activity (Greenblat, 1983; Kiernan, 1988).

Even though celibacy increases with age (Laumann et al., 1994), not all older persons stop having sex (Mulligan & Palguta, 1991; White 1982). In fact, most elders who are in good health and who have available partners remain sexually active (Marsiglio & Donnelly, 1991; Starr & Weiner, 1981). Because women live longer than men, however, elderly women tend to have fewer potential partners than elderly men (Moen, 1996).

Not only is research on involuntary celibacy scarce, it is fraught with conceptual and methodological problems. For example, Kiernan (1988) equated singlehood with celibacy, and used the terms interchangeably in both defining and measuring celibacy. Other researchers (Donnelly, 1993; Marsiglio & Donnelly, 1991) failed to distinguish between the voluntarily and involuntarily celibate in their analyses. Even when focused specifically on involuntary celibacy, samples have been restricted to a few small groups, such as the institutionalized elderly (White, 1982) or gay men in large metropolitan areas (Siegel & Raveis, 1993). Finally, in many studies, little explanation was given for why respondents became celibate, how long they had been this way, or their feelings on celibacy (Donnelly, 1993; Laumann et al., 1994; Marsiglio & Donnelly, 1991). Therefore, given the lack of knowledge about noninstitutionalized involuntary celibates, coupled with the limitations of extant research, we focus here on describing the transitions and trajectories by which one becomes involuntarily celibate and maintains this status over time.

Theoretical Framework

Contemporary researchers have drawn upon a variety of theoretical perspectives, including scripting theory (Gagnon & Simon, 1973) and developmental theory (Freud, 1953; Lancaster, 1994), to explain sexual behavior. While these perspectives provide a sound basis for examining some aspects of sexuality, their linear focus and attention to developmental stages and sexual scripts fail to adequately address the complexity of adult socialization and the interactions of social context and individual and cultural change over time.

Thus, we posit that the lives and circumstances of involuntary celibates can be best understood when viewed through a life course perspective. This perspective emphasizes how age-based transitions are "socially created, socially recognized, and shared" (Hagestad & Neugarten, 1985, p. 35) and acknowledges that change over time can occur on multiple dimensions (Bengtson & Allen, 1993). Despite the prevalence of life course perspectives in research on families and aging, few researchers, with the notable exception of Rossi (1994), have integrated the life course perspective into the study of sexuality.

Our study of involuntary celibacy emphasizes transitions and trajectories—two elements central to the life course perspective (Hagestad, 1990). Transitions are brief events that mark chronological movement from one state to another. First sexual intercourse and commitment to a monogamous relationship are two examples of transitions. Trajectories are more complex measures, not unlike careers, which measure the long-term processes and broader patterns of events in an individual's experience in specific life spheres over time. Sexual histories and marital relationships are examples of trajectories.

Cultural expectations suggesting that certain events and patterns are normative for different age groups exist in all societies. According to Hagestad (1996), these expectations can be examined along four key dimensions: (a) *timing,* or when life transitions occur; (b) *sequencing,* or the order in which events occur; (c) *duration,* or how long life events last; and (d) *prevalence,* or how many persons experience these transitions. We suggest that involuntary celibates may experience each of these dimensions differently than the voluntarily celibate or the noncelibate.

Most industrialized societies have normative expectations about sexual transitions, assuming that persons will begin to date in their teens or early twenties, experiment with and initiate sex at some point thereafter, and eventually marry or partner in a long-term relationship which includes an active sexual component (Gagnon & Simon, 1973; Thorton, 1990). As people reach late adulthood, ironically, the expectation *is* that interest in sexual activity will level off or decline (Marsiglio & Donnelly, 1991). For the majority of persons in Western societies, dating, sexual experimentation, and mating take place sequentially, with individuals progressing from one to the other in a somewhat linear fashion. Moreover, although the timing and duration of these initial transitions may vary, the majority of adults are presumed to have completed these life events, at least once, by the mid to late twenties. This can be thought of as the normative sexual trajectory. Persons (unless celibate for religious reasons, handicapped, or chronically ill) are expected to follow this trajectory and remain sexually active for major portions of their adult lives. Expectations for regular adult sexual activity are reinforced by a variety of social agents, including family members, peers, and the media. Individuals use these normative expectations to measure the progress of their own lives, judging themselves and others as "on time" or "off time" by these standards (Hagestad, 1996).

In contemporary Western societies, the timing of many life transitions has become less important, as people marry, divorce, remarry, and have children at increasingly diverse intervals (Coontz, 1992). In these cases, being off time has few consequences. In other areas, such as sexual activity, cultural expectations seem to be more rigid and have greater consequences (Lawrence, 1996). With the exception of those who choose celibacy, adults who have never had sex, or who go for long periods of time without a partner, may begin to feel off time in regards to sexuality. Once the person begins to feel different from others, it may become more difficult to interact and establish intimacy, and chances for sexually intimate relationships may be reduced. This may be particularly true when the person wants a sexual relationship and feels that everyone else his or her age is more experienced at and knowledgeable about sexual matters.

The same dynamic probably takes place with partnered involuntary celibates. They are expected to have sex with their partners, except when the partner is ill, disabled, or late in pregnancy (Donnelly, 1993). Thus, they may begin to feel off time and experience themselves as different from other partnered persons. The longer the relationship goes without sex, the harder it may be to reestablish this component. The norm may become sexual inactivity, and research suggests that the longer it lasts, the longer it is likely to last (Donnelly, 1993).

In summary, we theorize that involuntary celibacy is more than one event, it is a combination of the timing, sequencing, and duration of sexual behavior. A life course perspective suggests that persons who become off time in regards to life transitions involving sexuality begin to feel as though they are no longer traveling the same path as their peers (Hagestad, 1996). Once this happens, it may be difficult (but not impossible) to conform to the normative sexual trajectories that their age peers are following.

Based on a life course perspective on sexuality, we focus on four research questions:

1. What social factors inhibit initial transitions to sexual activity for involuntary celibates?

2. At what point do the sexual trajectories of involuntary celibates become off time?

3. What is the process by which involuntary celibates become off time in regards to sexuality?

4. What factors keep involuntary celibates off time and inhibit the establishment and maintenance of sexual relationships?

Methods

Background and Procedure

In September 1998, one of the members of an online discussion group for involuntary celibates approached the first author via e-mail to ask about current research on involuntary celibacy. As discussion ensued, it became apparent that little information was available. At this point, several members of the discussion group volunteered to be interviewed and a research team was put together to study involuntary celibacy. Because the initial respondents discussed the project among themselves and with the first author, this may have influenced the ways in which questions were answered. As feminist methodologists (Reinharz, 1992) argue, however, this sort of interaction can actually enhance understanding between the researcher and the researched, and often leads to higher return rates in survey research, since the persons being studied feel a sense of "ownership" in the project.

Initially, a questionnaire was e-mailed to the 35 on-line discussion group members who agreed to participate in the study, with a return rate of 85%. It was later posted to a web page to make it more easily accessible to potential respondents. These later respondents found the survey through links on web pages for involuntary celibates or web-based search engines, or obtained the web page address from prior respondents. We were unable to determine the return rate for the web-based respondents, since counters measured each visit to the site and there were multiple visits by our research team, our colleagues, and others curious about the on-line survey.

All respondents read an informed consent form, and were asked to complete and return the questionnaire if they agreed to participate in the study. Identifying information was removed from transcripts before distribution to the research team, and no records were kept of the respondents' e-mail addresses or identities. Because of the open-ended nature of the questionnaire, completion times reported by the respondents ranged from 1 to 4 hours.

In order to ensure that there was only one response per person, the web page was set up to accept only one completed survey from an e-mail address. To guard against one person answering the survey from two or more separate email addresses, we compared responses to demographic questions using SPSS to make sure that no two surveys were completely identical. Questionnaires were read and screened during the week in which they were received. If they were incomplete or seemed fabricated or outlandish, they were marked for full review by the research team. Six questionnaires were discarded because they contained little or no usable information, and four because the responses were obviously made up. In each case, we had 100% agreement by the research team regarding the disposition of the questionnaire.

Participants

The 82 persons who comprise our sample (60 men and 22 women) are described in more detail in Table 2.1. Sixty-three percent were age 34 or younger (the modal category was ages 25–34). Twenty-eight percent were married or living with a long-term partner. Only 5% had not completed high school, while 89% had attended or completed college. Professionals and students were the two largest occupational groups in the sample, with 45% identifying their occupational status as professional and 16% identifying as students. Eighty-five percent of the sample was white. Eighty-nine percent were heterosexual, 5% bisexual, 3% homosexual, and 4% identified as confused or unsure. Seventy percent resided in the U.S., with 30% of respondents living outside the U.S. (primarily Western Europe, Australia, or Canada).

Because we recruited respondents online, the sample characteristics are reflective of the group of persons most likely to have access to computers (Taylor, 1999). The majority are young, male, white, well-educated persons who hold professional jobs and enjoy middle-class lifestyles. They are skilled in computer usage and spend substantial amounts of time on the computer. Moreover, 30% of our respondents were from outside the United States. While sexual norms tend to be fairly similar across the U.S. and Western Europe, we recognize that some aspects of involuntary celibacy may differ depending on culture (Widmer, Treas, & Newcomb, 1998). In general, we found no national differences between respondents in terms of their sexual transitions and trajectories, with one exception— persons growing up in Western Europe were more likely to have received sex education as children, both from their parents and from other sources. This is consistent with what other researchers (Berne & Huberman, 1999) have noted. Contrary to Kiernan's (1988) finding that female celibates had higher education and income levels, however, the males in our sample were more likely to have graduate or professional degrees than the females.

Our sample is nonrandom; thus, results cannot be generalized to other groups (Marshall & Rossman, 1989). Rather, the utility of our research lies in the rich descriptive data obtained regarding the lives of involuntary celibates, a group about which little is known. In addition to allowing us to begin theory building (Strauss & Corbin, 1998), this information is useful for the respondents themselves, persons working with involuntary celibates, and researchers interested in designing more representative studies in this area.

Measures

The questionnaire contained 13 categorical close-ended questions assessing demographic characteristics such as age, sex, marital status, living arrangement, income, education, employment type, area of residence, race/ethnicity, sexual orientation, religious preference, political views, and time spent on the computer. Fifty-eight open-ended questions were used to investigate areas such as past sexual experiences, current relationships, initiating relationships, sexuality and celibacy, nonsexual relationships, and the consequences of celibacy. Consistent with a modified life history approach (Wallace, 1994), the questionnaire was organized so that demographics appeared first, followed by chronologically organized open-ended questions. We started by asking about childhood experiences, progressed to questions about teen and early adult years, and finished with questions about current status and effects of celibacy. Because this paper is part of a larger project on involuntary celibacy, the questionnaire is too large to include here. A copy is available upon request from the first author.

Analysis

Data were analyzed using both quantitative and qualitative methods. A coding sheet was developed for basic demographic data. Descriptive statistics such as frequencies and modal categories were then calculated for each variable. For qualitative data analysis, we used a modified grounded theory approach borrowed from the work of Strauss and Corbin (1998), blending our techniques with theirs to come up with useful ways of analyzing the data that were uniquely suited to our research questions (see Strauss & Corbin, 1998, p. 9, for a discussion of this technique). Unlike many qualitative researchers who begin with the data and build theory from it (an inductive approach), we began with research questions suggested by previous literature and theory (a more deductive approach) and used the research questions to guide and focus our analysis. We then used the results of our analysis to refine the original theory and to add to the literature in new ways. This interplay of deduction and induction (Marshall & Rossman, 1989; Strauss & Corbin, 1998) formed the basis of our analysis.

In analyzing the data, we looked for instances in the transcripts that addressed one of the four research questions, and used continuous coding to identify emergent themes within these answers. Themes represented similar ideas or ways of viewing celibacy that emerged over and over again in the responses. At biweekly meetings, we relied upon notes made during coding ("memos" in the language of Strauss and Corbin) to inform our discussion of emergent themes. Once we agreed upon the major themes, we developed a number of categories pertaining to each. Categories represented the variations themes took for individual respondents. As analysis continued, some categories were combined, some dropped, and others developed into two or more new categories (Lofland & Lofland, 1995). All five researchers read and coded each transcript, and four of the five (80%) had to agree upon the set of themes and coding categories to be used, as well as upon the ways in which each category was coded. Once a fairly stable set of themes and categories were in place, the most representative quotes were chosen to illustrate each. These quotes are presented in the sections that follow in the original language, spelling, and punctuation of the respondents. Final themes included celibate status, teenage experiences with dating and sex, becoming celibate, barriers to sex, and the consequences of celibacy. The underlying concept running through our research was that of becoming off time sexually.

Results and Discussion

Celibacy Status

In determining the celibacy status of our respondents, we examined two dimensions—whether they were currently partnered and whether they had any past experience. Our respondents fell into three categories (see Table 2.1), which included 34 virginal celibates, 25 single celibates, and 23 partnered celibates. *Virginal celibates* were not currently partnered and had never had sexual experience. *Single celibates* were not currently partnered, but had past sexual experience. *Partnered celibates* were currently partnered and had past sexual experience. None of the respondents was currently partnered and had never had sexual experiences, so a category was not created for this group.

Table 2.1   Descriptive Statistics of Respondents

	Virgin		Single		Partnered		Total	
	%	N	%	N	%	N	%	N
Sex								
Male	76	26	80	20	61	14	73	60
Female	24	8	20	5	39	9	27	22
Age								
18–24	41	14	24	6	—	—	24	20
25–34	44	15	40	10	30	7	39	32
35–44	12	4	32	8	44	10	27	22
45–54	—	—	4	1	17	4	6	5
55–64	3	1	—	—	9	2	4	3
Race								
White	85	28	96	23	86	19	85	70
Hispanic	—	—	—	—	5	1	1	1
African descent	—	—	4	1	9	2	4	3
Asian	6	2	—	—	—	—	2	2
Multiracial	6	2	—	—	—	—	2	2
Education								
Less than H.S.	6	2	8	2	—	—	5	4
H.S. degree	9	3	4	1	6	1	6	5
Some college	29	10	24	6	35	8	29	24
College degree	21	7	32	8	26	6	26	21
Some graduate school	6	2	8	2	9	2	7	6
Graduate degree	29	10	24	6	26	6	27	22
Residence								
Within U.S.	71	24	64	16	68	17	70	57
Outside U.S.	26	9	32	8	22	5	27	22
Sexual Orientation								
Heterosexual	86	29	83	20	100	23	89	72
Bisexual	9	3	4	1	—	—	5	4
Homosexual	3	1	4	1	—	—	3	2
Other	3	1	4	2	—	—	4	3
Total	**42**	**34**	**31**	**25**	**28**	**23**	**100**	**82**

As shown in the first column of Table 2.1, *virginal celibates* tended to be younger than the other two groups, and to have never (or rarely) dated. Seventy-six percent of the virgins in our sample were male, and 24% were female. The information on *single celibates* is presented in the second column of Table 2.1. This group included those who had dated or lived with a partner in the past, as well as a small group of males who had previously used the services of sexual surrogates or prostitutes. Eighty percent of the singles in our sample were male, and 20% were female. The *partnered celibates,* shown in the third column of Table 2.1, had been sexually active with their partners at one time, but because of problems in the relationship or a lack of interest by themselves or their partners, they were no longer sexually intimate. This group as a whole tended to be older than either the virgins or the single celibates. Partnered celibates had the highest proportion of women responding, with 61% of the sample male, and 39% female.

Teenage Experiences With Dating and Sex

While varying somewhat by gender and religion, by the time they reach adulthood many U.S. adolescents have masturbated, dated, and experimented with sex with partners (Janus & Janus, 1993; Laumann et al., 1994). Similar to their age peers, 78% percent of our respondents had discussed sex with friends and 84% had masturbated as teens. The virgins and singles differed from national averages, however, in their experiences with dating and interpersonal sex.

The majority of virgins (91%) and singles (52%) never dated as teenagers. As one virginal male, aged 18–24, writes, "I have never even had a date." A virginal female in the 18–24 age group says simply, "Never, not ever." Traditional gender role norms appeared to influence our sample, with males reporting hesitancy in initiating dates, and females reporting a lack of invitations by males. Even for those who dated, experiences tended to be very limited. As a single male in the 18–24 age group notes, "I didn't date all that much as a teenager. I dated a total of two females during high school. I was always shy, bashful and quiet."

Only 29% of the virgins in our sample reported first sexual experiences that involved other people (kissing, petting, etc.). Frequently, they reported no sexual activity at all, except for masturbation. As a male virgin in the 24–35 age range noted, "Unless you count masturbation (I don't), I haven't had any sexual experiences."

Singles were more likely than virgins to have had initial sexual experiences that involved other people (76%), but they tended to express dissatisfaction with these encounters, as the experience of a single male in the 25–34 age group illustrates:

I was 18. It was not satisfying. I had sex with a girl that I didn't care about, that I didn't find attractive, and we didn't use a condom. Luckily, she didn't get pregnant. We did it in my car and, later in a motel room. It was cheap, it was sleazy and I felt really dirty afterwards. I slept with her because she was easy and I was really messed up emotionally. I needed to feel wanted and loved by someone, ANYONE.

Seventy-eight percent of partnered respondents recounted initial activities involving other people (kissing, petting, oral sex, intercourse). One partnered male, aged 45–54 described this, "I was 16 when I first felt a girl's breasts (I had kissing-only relationships before that) which eventually led to oral sex." His response illustrates more adherence to the normative trajectory of dating and increasingly intimate forms of interpersonal sexuality than do those of the virgins (and many of the singles) in our study.

In summary, while most of our sample had discussed sex with friends and experimented with masturbation as teens, most of the virgins and singles did not date. Singles were similar to partnered persons in terms of first sexual experiences, while the majority of virgins reported first sexual experiences that did not include another person. As the data illustrates, virgins and singles may have missed important transitions, and as they got older, their trajectories began to differ from those of their age peers. As Thorton (1990) noted, patterns of sexuality in young adulthood are significantly related to dating, steady dating, and sexual experience in adolescence. It is rare for a teenager to initiate sexual activity outside of a dating relationship. Thus, persons reaching young adulthood without dating may have missed an important opportunity for sexual experience. While virginity and lack of experience are fairly common in teenagers and young adults (Sprecher & Regan, 1996), by the time many of our respondents reached their mid-twenties they reported feeling left behind by age peers. We suspect that this is especially true for gay, lesbian, and bisexual youth. In fact, all eight of the non-heterosexual respondents in our sample were either virgins or singles. As previous researchers have shown, a major reason for becoming off time in making sexual transitions is the process of coming out to oneself and others (Gonsiorek & Rudolph, 1991). Even for the heterosexuals in our study, however, it appears that lack of dating and sexual experimentation in the teen years may be precursors to problems in adult sexual relationships (Thorton, 1990).

Becoming Celibate

Many of the virgins in our sample reported that becoming celibate involved a lack of sexual and interpersonal experience at several different transition points in adolescence and young adulthood. They never or rarely dated, had little experience with interpersonal sexual activity, and had never had sexual intercourse. Singles were more likely to have dated and experimented sexually, but had difficulty in finding and maintaining relationships. They tended to go for long periods of time between sexual partners. Consistent with traditional sex role expectations, 20% of single men reported that their only sexual encounters had been with paid sex workers, although no single women reported this type of activity.

Partnered celibates generally became sexually inactive by a very different process (Donnelly, 1993). All had initially been sexually active with their partners, but at some point stopped. At the time of the survey, sexual intimacy no longer (or very rarely) occurred in their relationships. Because partnered celibates are different both from other partnered persons and from other celibates, we discuss them in more detail here.

The majority (70%) of partnered celibates started out having satisfactory relationships, but slowly stopped having sex as time went on. They described the process of becoming celibate as an evolutionary one. A woman in the 25–34 age group who had been married three years said, "[It was] not a conscious decision—just evolved and now it seems to be our way of life and neither likes it." A man in the same age group noted, "We started out active, but by the time of the wedding (18 months) it had already

decreased to near nothing. She has no desire for it. She doesn't seem at all interested."

Thirteen percent of the partnered celibates reported that one partner had been sexually reluctant from the beginning of the relationship. Illustrative of this group was the woman in the 35–44 age group who had been married 21 years and had one child:

> Within the first month he started avoiding sex and me. Generally sex happened once every 2–3 months. This was the norm for 16 years. Five years ago, after a 9-month abstinence, I approached him and he pushed me away and told me to leave him alone. I am hurt and could care less. I have not had sex with him or anyone else in 5 years.

Another man noted that there were danger signals from the beginning of his marriage. This respondent is in the 35–44 age group, and has been married for 20 years. He and his wife have two teenage children.

> Before we were married, we lived together for two years. We had fundamental sex twice a week at the time. My wife was very conservative and responded that she wanted to "save something for our married life" when I suggested less conservative activity. Once married, the only change was the frequency of sex tapered off. When I was "allowed" sex, it was at her convenience, and always followed the same pattern, I stimulate her to orgasm, then I can enter her (in the missionary position). The past ten years has seen us in bed together a total of three times.

Seventeen percent of partnered respondents reported one partner making a conscious decision to suspend sexual activity. This often occurred in the context of pregnancy or childbirth. As a woman in the 35–44 age group noted, "My husband made this decision two years ago. It seems that it was a conscious decision after I became pregnant with my second child." In another case, reported by a man in the same age group, his partner "stopped 6 years ago, shortly after our last child was born. She has no drive, now feels sex is dirty, doesn't want . . . to be touched." When a partner decides to stop having sex, often there is little that the other can do about the situation. There were no male-female differences among partnered persons, since all were not having sex and unhappy about it.

Thus, the trajectories by which each group of celibates arrived at their present condition varied greatly, with virgins becoming off time in their teens and early twenties, and never experiencing a transition to sexual activity. Single celibates showed some signs of difficulty as adolescents, but appeared to have been at least somewhat similar to their age peers in establishing sexual relationships. Similar to partnered celibates, they tended to get off time as adults, when they were unable to maintain sexual relationships. Partnered celibates were unique, however, in that they were currently in relationships that had over time become nonsexual.

Barriers to Sexual Relationships

Once respondents felt off time in their sexual trajectories, they suspected that several factors kept them from having sexual relationships. Similar to other researchers (Jackson, Soderlind, & Weiss, 2000; Joiner, 1997) we found that shyness was a barrier to developing and maintaining relationships for many of our respondents. Virgins and singles were more likely to report shyness (94% and 84%, respectively) than were partnereds (20%). The men in these two groups were more likely to mention being shy than were women (89% vs. 77%). In addition, 41% of virgins and 24% of singles reported an inability to relate to others socially. As one male virgin said,

> The biggest barrier to developing a relationship is my lack of social/dating skills. At my age (34), people are expected to have already gone through several real relationships, while I remain a perpetual teenager in terms of relationships potential.

Thus, the lack of social skills was seen as a barrier keeping this respondent who was chronologically approaching middle age trapped in a situation more common to persons half his age. Feelings of being off time worsened as respondents aged. One male virgin said, "I'm thirty

years old, for Christ's sake, everyone I know is married with kids."

Still celibate as adults, this group of respondents often felt like the single woman in the 35–44 age group who was, "nervous, unhappy, depressive, lost." Similar to another single man in his late fifties, some even worried that they might no longer be considered sexual beings. "[Being a celibate adult] has contributed to my bouts of depression. It has also caused me major anxiety. I am concerned that I am no longer a sexual being."

For virgins and singles, another barrier to establishing ongoing sexual relationships is body image. Researchers (Trapnell, Meston, & Gorzalka, 1997; Weiderman & Hurst, 1998) suspect an indirect link between body image and sexual experience. They suggest that persons with negative body images tend to avoid social situations, and by doing so miss out on sexual opportunities. Consistent with their hypothesis, one third of our respondents reported considering their weight, appearance, or physical characteristics as obstacles to attracting potential partners. Virgins (47%) and singles (56%) were more likely to mention these factors than partnered persons (9%). For example, this bisexual male virgin in the 35–44 age group said,

> I am terribly over-obese. I have a terrible set of teeth, a huge nose, bad skin on my body (lots of stretch marks . . .). No one likes to think of "Frankenstein" in a sexual way. I move uneasily and have problems with personal hygiene as a result of the excess weight (bathing is a real workout). The rest is self-evident.

This respondent felt that because of his physical appearance people would not want to be around him, and he thus avoided social situations. Although we chose his words to illustrate this theme, in general, the women in our sample were more likely to mention being overweight as a problem, while men mentioned being underweight as more of an issue. This is consistent with media and cultural images that demand that women be thin and men be toned and muscular.

Living arrangements, work arrangements, and lack of transportation all probably contributed to the self-perpetuating nature of celibacy for virgins and singles. Twenty percent of virgins and 28% of singles reported these barriers. A virginal female in 18–24 age group noted, "Where I'm living right now, there aren't a lot of extracurricular activities that I'm interested in, and most of the people I meet are older and already married." Another single male in the 25–34 age group illustrated the cumulative nature of structural constraints by saying:

> Well, the fact that I live at home is a pain in the ass, but not insurmountable. Being unemployed is a HUGE barrier that seems rather difficult to scale and not having a car is just horrid. I'm lucky to leave the house as much as I do, but meeting people without my own form of transportation just doesn't work.

Virginal and single men were more likely to be in sex-segregated occupations than their female counterparts, and to see this as a barrier. One virginal male in the age 35–44 age group noted, "I work in a male-dominated field, and other than church activities, don't get out that much." Another male virgin in the 25–34 age group reported, "Lack of social circle through which to meet women—working in a primarily male environment."

In all likelihood, the relationship between these barriers and involuntary celibacy is reciprocal, rather than unidirectional. While shyness, lack of social skills, poor body image, living arrangements, and sex-segregated occupations contribute to involuntary celibacy, it is also likely that celibates are shyer, less confident in social situations, view their bodies more negatively, and are less likely to leave housing or job situations that isolate them from potential partners.

For partnered celibates, children (50%), commitment to marriage (32%), and finances (27%) seemed to be the biggest barriers to leaving current relationships. Even though 82% had thought of leaving, 86% reported no plans to do so. As

one partnered male respondent in the 45–54 age group lamented, "Currently, establishing another relationship is impossible because I am in a committed relationship with many responsibilities." Another woman in the same age group noted, "we have a child, we own a house together—those things mean a lot." Moreover, most persons in this group planned to stay in their current situations, but because of concerns about their families, moral constraints, or lack of opportunities, were reluctant to establish extramarital sexual relationships. Thus, the barrier, to establishing sexual relationships appeared to be very different for the partnered and the nonpartnered.

The Consequences of Celibacy

Thirty-five percent of celibates expressed dissatisfaction, frustration, or anger about their lack of sexual relationships, and this was true regardless of their partnership status. As the quotes presented below illustrate, partnered persons tended to express dissatisfaction over not having sex with their spouses or partners, while singles and virgins were unhappy about the lack of sex with any partner. As one bisexual virginal male in the 25–34 age range put it, "I feel very bad about it. I feel as if I am not seen as an adult functional human being because of it. I feel very unwanted and feel like spending a lot of time crying and lonely as hell."

While many virgins and singles reported unhappiness about the lack of sexual contact, some expressed a greater sadness about not having love or a relationship. As this virginal male in the 35–44 age group explains,

> My lack of any sex has had some very serious effects upon me. Obviously, I could get a prostitute any time, but I haven't done that. It would be no different than glorified masturbation. It is the fact that no woman has ever wanted to be sexual with me (and as far as I can tell, even considered sex with me) that I find so painful. It makes me feel sexually worthless. And the fact that no woman has loved me or cared for me enough to have sex with me is tremendously damaging to my self-esteem. It makes me feel like a freak, an unloved person who is not

worth anything to anyone. I know intellectually that these feelings are to a large extent misleading and wrong, and that in fact they are damaging to me. Nonetheless, this is the visceral feeling in my gut that I get when I think about this—and I think about it every day, every hour. Sometimes every minute.

Consistent with the life course perspective we employ in this analysis (Hagestad, 1990), one major correlate of involuntary celibacy for virgins and singles was feeling off time, as though opportunities had passed them by, and their sexual development had somehow stalled in an earlier stage of life. Largely due to perceptions that "everyone else" was having sex, 44% percent of virgins and 56% of singles said that they were different from their peers. One female virgin expressed her frustrations as follows,

A sense of immaturity—a lack of completion. The great divide between childhood and adulthood hasn't been leaped despite my being almost thirty years old. Also, let's face it, men think it's a bit strange when they date me and I have no history whatsoever.

And indeed, lacking sexual experience probably not only leads to a feeling of being off time, but also to suspicions that they may never catch up with their peers. As another virginal female in the 25–34 age group put it,

It makes me feel like everyone else is going through some mythical gates into "grownup land" while I sit out in the courtyard with the children. So it makes me feel resentful sometimes and I feel childish and inadequate at times.

A male virgin in the 18–24 age group felt that he was so off time that people were unnerved when they learned the extent of his celibacy. His quote suggests a sense of both despair and resignation over the situation.

I feel it is important to highlight the extent to which I have not had a romantic relationship. Outside of [manually stimulating a female friend to orgasm], and a kiss a couple of months earlier, there has

been no non-platonic activity in my life. I have had crushes, and have frequently been attracted to someone, but never in a way that was reciprocated. No sex. No intimacy. No dating. Over the past year, I have been able to flirt, but it has been at the harmless, very unserious level. Most people assume some experience, and get unnerved [by my lack of experience].

For partnered persons, the issues were different. Unlike the others in our sample, they had successfully made the transition to sexual activity, and many had experienced a relatively normative sexual trajectory until the sexual components of their relationships dwindled. Many in this group reported feeling different from other partnered persons, and were frustrated by their partner's lack of interest. When they tried to initiate sex, they were often met with rejection, as this female in the 25–34 age group describes:

I would like to have sex with my partner. He doesn't want any physical contact in terms of touching, kissing, and sex. Yes, I tried, but every time I was brutally refused with a very serious warning not to do this. . . . Talking about sex, or us having sex is out of the question.

These refusals and rejections seemed to occupy the thoughts of many partnered celibates, and even went so far as to cause problems in other areas of their lives. A partnered male, age 55–64, probably describes it best, when he says:

It has a deleterious affect on my overall life. I dwell on sexual thoughts and fantasies. My depression is intertwined to this situation. My professional life is impacted because of the time I devoted to trying to understand my circumstance and deciding how to deal with it.

There was also a sense of being off time, but rather than feeling late in making the transition to sex, they reported being dissimilar to their age peers in that they were no longer having sex, something expected only of the sick, handicapped, and elderly in our society (Marsiglio &

Donnelly, 1991). Many mentioned frustration at being stuck (possibly for the rest of their lives) in sexless relationships. A married woman in the 25–34 age group who had no plans to leave her husband lamented, "He's prepared to live with me like this is not problem—I can't accept this as a way of life." Another woman (aged 35–44) had resigned herself to the situation, describing it as "[Lots of] hurt, tears. Knowing it will always be this way and missing intimacy. Forever."

Regardless of celibacy status, however, our respondents overwhelmingly perceived their lack of sexual activity in a negative light. In all likelihood, the relationship between involuntary celibacy and unhappiness, anger, and depression is a reciprocal one. Involuntary celibacy can certainly contribute to negative feelings, but these negative feelings probably also cause persons to feel less self-confident and to be less open to sexual opportunities when they occur. In fact, the longer the duration of the celibacy, the more likely our respondents were to view it as a permanent way of life. Virginal celibates tended to see their condition as temporary for the most part, but the older they were, the more likely they were to see it as permanent. For single celibates, the longer they were without a partner, the more likely they were to feel that celibacy was a permanent status. Partnered celibates, on the whole, saw their situations as unlikely to change unless their current relationships ended.

Conclusion

As our data indicate, the experience of being off time appears to be different for virginal, single, and partnered celibates. Although we discuss issues of timing, duration, and sequencing as they relate to multiple dimensions of sexual history, the theme of sexuality becoming off time permeates the stories of our respondents. It is important to recognize that while all three groups reported being off time with regard to their sexual behavior, they are celibate for different reasons and with different consequences. For virgins, the issue of timing is more evident because they have not met the cultural deadline of sexual intimacy with a partner. The duration of virginity has gone longer for them than for many of their peers, and they have not followed the same sequence of dating, relationships, and sexual activity. Though singles have met the cultural deadline of initiation to sexuality, the timing and sequencing of dating and long-term relationship formation is different from the normative trajectory. Moreover, they report worrying about the duration of their celibacy. Partnered celibates have followed the normative sequence for sexuality, but have stopped having sex at an age when most of their peers are still sexually active. These celibates have made a transition that generally is acceptable socially and culturally only for older persons, and they expect the duration of their inactivity to be much longer than that of their peers. Thus, as a group, all involuntary celibates appear to have difficulty with the timing and maintenance of culturally sanctioned age-based norms of sexuality. This is consistent with a life course perspective, which emphasizes the significance of multiple transitions and trajectories (Hagestad, 1996).

Although the timing of celibacy was significantly different by partnership status, the experience of being celibate appeared remarkably similar. Despair, depression, frustration, and a loss of confidence were commonly reported. Developing a sense of being off time appeared to negatively affect the ways in which respondents viewed themselves, and they seemed less likely to take the steps necessary to initiate sexual activity. The longer the duration of the celibacy, the more they may have despaired of ever having a "normal" sexual relationship. One final quote, by a male virgin in the 25–34 age group, who is unsure about his sexual orientation, aptly illustrates this trajectory:

> I learned about sex by hearing older friends talk about it. My parents gave the very scientific, antiseptic explanation of the whole sex act. [They] basically said that I should not even approach it until finishing high school. When I finished high school, I was very goal oriented and was scared that I would either catch a deadly disease from sex,

or have it hamper my career and choices. The longer I waited, the more intimidated I became about the whole process, and just never had the courage to pursue a sexual relationship.

Cultural expectations about masculinity and femininity also appear to have affected our respondents in several ways. For example, the men we interviewed were more likely to have graduate or professional degrees than the females, to work in sex-segregated jobs, and to spend more time on the computer. By following traditional male trajectories that emphasized the importance of an education and directed them toward certain jobs, their "maleness" became a barrier to meeting and dating available women. Similarly, traditional feminine scripts affected the females in our study. Women were less likely to report being shy than men, but were more likely to feel that their bodies were a real barrier to establishing a sexual relationship and to feel constrained by gender role norms which influenced them to act in traditional ways. Moreover, the males in our sample often mentioned feeling trapped by traditional expectations that they should take the initiative in relationships, while females felt that they should not initiate dates or sexual activity.

While there seems to be a trend among some segments in our society toward choosing virginity or celibacy (Sprecher & Regan, 1996; Stafford, 2001), this was not the case for our respondents. Their stories and their use of the label *involuntary* indicate that these are not persons saving themselves for marriage or consciously reclaiming their virginity. Instead, these are individuals who deeply desire a sexual relationship, who feel left behind by their age peers, and who are truly troubled by their lack of sexual intimacy.

Unlike others who use the Internet to fill sexual needs by viewing pornography, engaging in sexually explicit chatting, or having cyber sex (Maheu, 1999), less than a quarter of our sample (22%) reported engaging in these behaviors. In fact, they appeared to be using the Internet more to find moral support than for sexual stimulation.

For most, the Internet was used to create a sense of community and to fill emotional needs. Just as they were hesitant to begin sexual relationships in real life, our sample tended to be hesitant about establishing sexual connections online as well.

While our project represents a start toward understanding involuntary celibacy, additional research is needed. Groups such as females, elders, persons of color, and the poor and working class were underrepresented in our sample. This is probably because the data were collected using the Internet. Other possible reasons may be due to the nature of these groups. For example, it is possible that women see celibacy as less problematic than men. Sprecher and Regan (1996) note that males are more troubled by lack of sexual experience than are females, since they are socialized to be sexual aggressors and to expect to have plenty of sexual partners. Moreover, all of our respondents were younger than 65, so we learned little about older adults. We suspect that elders may not have responded to our survey because they felt they should not be worrying about lack of sex at their age. Persons of color may have been hesitant to respond because they have been socialized to believe that talking about sexual activity (or a lack thereof) is particularly shameful (Wyatt, 1997). Because our survey was computer based, we had few persons from the lower end of the socioeconomic ladder. We also recommend that future investigations include adequate numbers of this group in their samples, since their transitions and trajectories may differ from the educationally and materially privileged. Finally, although the proportions of gays, lesbians, and bisexuals in our sample are similar to those found by Laumann et al. (1994), larger samples are needed to learn more about the causes and consequences of involuntary celibacy for this group.

Probably the most important next step is to conduct studies of nationally representative samples of adults, in order to determine the true prevalence of involuntary celibacy in the U.S. and in other nations. Using the groundwork that we have laid in this paper, hypotheses about the causes and consequences, transitions and trajectories, of involuntary celibates can then be adequately studied. In conclusion, until the phenomenon of involuntary celibacy has been fully investigated and the results disseminated, it will remain a taboo topic, cloaked in mystery and ignorance, and untold numbers of persons will continue to suffer in silence and isolation.

The authors would like to thank Dawn Baunach, Alana Boltwood, Kirk Elifson, Frank Whittington, and three anonymous reviewers for their helpful comments and critiques. We would also like to thank the Department of Sociology at Georgia State University for providing space on their web page for our survey.

Please address correspondence to Denise Donnelly, Department of Sociology, Georgia State University, Atlanta, GA 30303; e-mail: socdad@gsu.edu.

References

Abbott, E. (2000). *A history of celibacy.* New York: Scribner.

Bengtson, V., & Allen, K. (1993). The life course perspective applied to families over time. In P. Boss, W. Doherty, R. LaRossa, P. Schumm, & S. Steinmetz (Eds.), *Sourcebook of family theories and methods: A contextual approach* (pp. 469–499). New York: Plenum Press.

Berne, L., & Huberman, B. (1999). *European approaches to adolescent sexual behavior and responsibility.* Washington, DC: Advocates for Youth.

Coontz, S. (1992). *The way we never were: American families and the nostalgia trap.* New York: Basic Books.

Donnelly, D. (1993). Sexually inactive marriages. *The Journal of Sex Research, 30,* 171–179.

Freud, S. (1953). Three essays on the theory of sexuality. In *Complete psychological works, standard edition* (Vol. 7, pp. 135–245). London: Hogarth.

Gagnon, J. H., & Simon, W. (1973). *Sexual conduct: The social sources of human sexuality.* Chicago: Aldine.

Goergen, D. (1974). *The sexual celibate.* New York: Seabury Press.

Gonsiorek, J., & Rudolph, J. (1991). Homosexual identity: Coming out and other developmental events. In J. Gonsiorek & J. Weinrich (Eds.), *Homosexuality: Research implications for public policy* (pp. 161–176). Newbury Park, CA: Sage.

Greenblat, C. (1983). The salience of sexuality in the early years of marriage. *Journal of Marriage and the Family, 45,* 277–288.

Hagestad, G. (1996). On-time, off-time, out of time? Reflections on continuity and discontinuity from an illness process. In V. Bengtson (Ed.), *Adulthood and aging: Research on continuities and discontinuities* (pp. 204–222). New York: Springer.

Hagestad, G. (1990). Social perspectives on the life course. In R. H. Binstock & L. George (Eds.), *Handbook of aging and the social sciences* (3rd ed., pp. 151–168). New York: Academic Press.

Hagestad, G., & Neugarten, B. (1985). Age and the life course. In R. H. Binstock & E. Shanas (Eds.), *Handbook of aging and the social sciences* (2nd ed., pp. 35–61). New York: Reinhold.

Jackson, T., Soderlind, A., & Weiss, K. (2000). Personality traits and quality of relationships as predictors of future loneliness among American college students. *Social Behavior and Personality, 28,* 463–470.

Janus, S., & Janus, C. (1993). *The Janus report on sexual behavior.* New York: Wiley.

Joiner, T. (1997). Shyness and low social support as interactive diatheses, with loneliness as mediator: Testing an interpersonal-personality view of vulnerability to depressive symptoms. *Journal of Abnormal Psychology, 106,* 386–394.

Kiernan, K. (1988). Who remains celibate? *Journal of Biosocial Science, 20,* 253–263.

Lancaster, J. B. (1994). Human sexuality, life histories, and evolutionary ecology. In A. Rossi (Ed.), *Sexuality across the life course* (pp. 39–62). Chicago: University of Chicago Press.

Laumann, E., Gagnon, J., Michael, R., & Michaels, S. (1994). *The social organization of sexuality: Sexual practices in the United States.* Chicago: University of Chicago Press.

Lawrence, B. S. (1996). Organized age norms: Why is it so hard to know one when you see one? *The Gerontologist, 36,* 209–220.

Lofland, J., & Lofland, L. (1995). *Analyzing social settings: A guide to qualitative observation and analysis* (3rd ed.). Belmont, CA: Wadsworth.

Maheu, M. (1999). Women's Internet behavior: Providing psychotherapy offline and online for cyber-infidelity. *Proceedings of the 107th Annual*

Conference of the American Psychological Association, USA, 107, 236–251.

Marshall, C., & Rossman, G. (1989). *Designing qualitative research.* Newbury Park, CA: Sage.

Marsiglio, W., & Donnelly, D. (1991). Sexual relations in later life: A national study of married persons. *Journal of Gerontology (Social Sciences), 46,* S338–S344.

Medlicott, J., & Waltz, D. (1993). *Celibate wives, breaking the silence.* Boston: Lowell House.

Moen, P. (1996). Gender, age, and the life course. In R. H. Binstock & L. George (Eds.), *Handbook of aging and the social sciences* (4th ed., pp. 171–187). New York: Academic Press.

Mulligan, T., & Palguta, R. (1991). Sexual interest, activity and satisfaction among male nursing home residents. *Archives of Sexual Behavior, 20,* 199–204.

Netting, N. (1992). Sexuality in youth culture: Identity and change. *Adolescence, 27,* 961–976.

Quinnan, E. (1997). Connection and autonomy in the lives of elderly male celibates: Degrees of disengagement. *Journal of Aging Studies, 11,* 115–130.

Reinharz, S. (1992). *Feminist methods in social research.* New York: Oxford University Press.

Rossi, A. S. (1994). *Sexuality across the life course.* Chicago: University of Chicago Press.

Siegal, K., & Raveis, V. (1993). AIDS-related reasons for gay men's adoption of celibacy. *AIDS Education and Prevention, 5,* 302–310.

Sprecher, S., & Regan, P. (1996). College virgins: How men and women perceive their sexual status. *The Journal of Sex Research, 33,* 3–16.

Stafford, T. (2001). A second chance at virginity? *Campus Life, 59,* 38.

Starr, B., & Weiner, M. (1981). *The Starr-Weiner report on sex and sexuality in the mature years.* Briarcliff Manor, NY: Stein and Day.

Strauss, A., & Corbin, J. (1998). *Basics of qualitative research* (2nd ed.). Thousand Oaks, CA: Sage.

Taylor, H. (1999). The Harris Poll #76: On-line population growth surges to 56% of all adults. Rochester, NY: Creators Syndicate. Retrieved December 22, 1999, from http://www.harris interactive.com/harris_poll

Thomas, W. I. (1966). The relation of research to social process. In M. Janowitz (Ed.), *W. I. Thomas on social organization and social personality* (pp. 289–305). Chicago: University of Chicago Press.

Thorton, A. (1990). The courtship process and adolescent sexuality. *Journal of Family Issues, 11,* 239–275.

Trapnell, R, Meston, C., & Gorzalka, B. (1997). Spectatoring and the relationship between body image and sexual experience: Self-focus or self-valence? *The Journal of Sex Research, 34,* 267–278.

Wallace, J. (1994). Life stories. In J. Gubrium & A. Sankar (Eds.), *Qualitative methods in aging research* (pp. 137–154). Thousand Oaks, CA: Sage.

Weiderman, W., & Hurst, S. (1998). Body size, physical attractiveness, and body image among young adult women: Relationships to sexual experience and sexual esteem. *The Journal of Sex Research, 35,* 272–281.

White, C. (1982). Sexual interest, attitudes, knowledge, and sexual history in relation to sexual behavior in the institutionalized aged. *Archives of Sexual Behavior 11,* 11–21.

Widmer, E., Treas, J., & Newcomb, R. (1998). Attitudes toward nonmarital sex in 24 countries. *The Journal of Sex Research, 35,* 349–358.

Wyatt, G. (1997). *Stolen women: Reclaiming our sexuality, taking back our lives.* New York: Wiley.

LIFE COURSE TRANSITIONS, THE GENERATIONAL STAKE, AND GRANDPARENT-GRANDCHILD RELATIONSHIPS

ROBERT CROSNOE AND GLEN H. ELDER, JR.

Abstract

Drawing on past research and prominent theoretical orientations, this research note suggests new approaches to intergenerational dynamics. For 316 grandparent-grandchild pairs, we found that the transition of grandchildren to higher education, controlling for other transitions, improves the quality of the grandparent-grandchild relationship. For grandparent mentoring, however, we see evidence of a generational stake, with grandparents overestimating their mentoring role, compared to grandchildren, during this transition. This generational stake reflects the importance of grandparent education, with increased mentoring for the college-going grandchildren of college-educated grandparents. These findings indicate that the intergenerational literature can be significantly advanced by taking a long-term perspective, incorporating multiple points of view, and examining contextual variation. Moreover, greater understanding of these intergenerational ties will benefit research on families and individual development.

The changing demography of the United States (e.g., decreasing mortality and fertility) has magnified the grandparent role (Uhlenberg & Kirby, 1998). Consequently, intergenerational dynamics have become a major research focus. Like other relationships, this intergenerational bond may be best understood as a developmental phenomenon—ebbing and flowing within social contexts (Silverstein & Long, 1998; Szinovacz, 1998). This research note pursues this developmental approach by applying a life course perspective to a specialized, but rich, longitudinal sample of mostly White and rural Midwestern families. The overarching purpose of this note is to promote avenues of future research that may lead to a fuller understanding of intergenerational dynamics and the ecology of children, adults, and the elderly.

Intergenerational Dynamics and the Human Life Course

Life course theory calls attention to the importance of family members' linked lives, which, like individuals, follow a developmental course. Transitions are strategic windows on such development (Elder, 1998). The lives of grandparents and grandchildren, like those of parents and children, are linked. Supportive relationships can be salutary by providing support and guidance to the young and serving as a source of assistance, meaningful activity, and pride for the old (Cherlin & Furstenberg, 1986; Elder & Conger, 2000; Hagestad, 1985). Unfortunately, the dynamic nature of this particular relationship is rarely studied. We do so here by examining how this relationship changes during the grandchild's transition from adolescence to adulthood.

Specifically, we ask the following: Does the grandparent-grandchild relationship (grandparent mentoring and relationship quality) change when grandchildren enroll in higher education? This transition can represent adolescents' entry into adult life, navigation of new social contexts, and opportunity to establish themselves as individuals independent of their families (Arnett, 2000). Focusing on transitions, including this one, addresses one void in the intergenerational literature (Silverstein & Long, 1998). Past research has rarely crossed life stages (typically examining old age or childhood) or examined key life transitions (grandparent or grandchild), but doing so provides a rich perspective.

Investigating this question brings up two issues. First, past research (e.g., King & Elder, 1995; 1998) has identified predictors of grandparent-grandchild relationships, some of which (grandparent gender, education, health, marital status, closeness with the grandchild's parent, and proximity) are particularly relevant to studying how this relationship changes during the grandchild transition to higher education and should be controlled. Second, we recognize that other grandchild transitions may also occur during this time period (e.g., marriage, parenthood, employment). Although we control for these potential co-occurring transitions, our specific focus is on grandchildren starting college, which may represent a test to the strength of family ties.

Our second research question is a twist on the first: Does the nature of the change in the grandparent-grandchild relationship during the transition to higher education depend on whether the point of view of the grandparent or grandchild is taken? To answer this question, we compare grandparent and grandchild reports of mentoring and relationship quality when examining the relationship over time. This question is derived from the concept of the generational stake—the tendency for the young to emphasize autonomy and the old to emphasize continuity in relationships (Bengston, Schaie, & Burton, 1995). Thus the same transition may be experienced differently. For the grandchild, enrollment in higher education may be a time to break free of family ties and establish an adult identity (Arnett, 2000), which

might lead them to distance themselves from their grandparents. In light of this distancing, grandparents may maintain some continuity by placing more value on the relationship and on their role in the grandchild's life. Our sample of rural Iowa families provides a vantage point for viewing these dynamics because such families are typically tightly knit and because higher education has become such a crucial pathway to adult success (which might entail leaving the area) in this region (Elder & Conger, 2000; Elder, King, & Conger, 1996).

This question addresses another important void in the intergenerational literature (Silverstein & Long, 1998). Like other relationships, the grandparent-grandchild bond is subjectively experienced by each participant. Intergenerational research typically focuses on one actor or the other, but we argue that taking the perspectives of both is a better test of the life course concept of linked lives and provides more valuable information about family dynamics. Our examination of the generational stake is an attempt to do so.

The Context-Specific Nature of Grandparent-Grandchild Relationships

Life course theory also asserts that linked lives are embedded in sociohistorical context (Elder, 1998). Relationships and their development are not monolithic across time and place. Intergenerational research does not typically bring in the moderating role of context, but studies that do, such as research on rural/urban or racial differences in grandparenting (Burton & Bengston, 1985; King, Silverstein, Elder, Bengston, & Conger, 2003), have been informative. Investigating such moderation could identify new aspects of the continuity and change in intergenerational relationships.

Our third research question addresses this potential contextual variability: Is the link between grandchild enrollment in higher education and grandparent mentoring moderated by grandparents' educational history? This question is based on findings that educated grandparents mentor adolescents more (Cherlin & Furstenberg, 1986; King & Elder, 1998), which might extend to this specific transition. A college-educated grandparent would have experience to draw on in mentoring a college-going grandchild, and this shared experience would increase common ground between generations. Thus grandchildren's transition to higher education might enhance the mentoring role of the college-educated grandparents and weaken it among less educated ones.

Our fourth research question also addresses variability. Is the link between the grandchild's entry into higher education and the quality of the grandparent-grandchild relationship moderated by the grandparent's relationship with the grandchild's parent? This question is based on family systems theory (Cox & Paley, 1997), which holds that any relationship cannot be divorced from the larger family system and past findings that the gatekeeper role of the middle generation links young and old and affects relationship quality (King & Elder, 1995; Rossi & Rossi, 1990). In families where grandparents and parents are not close, enrollment in higher education, which might entail freedom from parental constraints, could allow young people to build stronger ties with grandparents.

Method

Sample

The Iowa Youth and Families Project, which began in 1989, is a longitudinal study of 451 families (parents, focal adolescent in 7th grade in 1989, and a near sibling) in North Central Iowa. In 1994 and 1998, grandparents were also surveyed. Not all adolescents had a grandparent participate, and some had all four grandparents participate.

To select our study sample, we chose the 1994 survey (when focal adolescents were seniors in high school) as the starting point and the latest survey (1997 for adolescents, 1998 for grandparents) as the end point. Although these two end points differ, we believe they are close enough to each other and within the normative span of the adult transition to he useful. A total of 411 adolescents and 592 grandparents participated at both time points. This attrition is not negligible, but past

studies of the sample have shown no strong attrition biases (King & Elder, 1999). In order to match grandparent and grandchildren reports, we had to focus on specific grandparent-grandchildren pairs. Rather than having a single grandchild appear in the data multiple times (with the analytical problems this repetition poses), we selected one grandparent for each focal child who had a grandparent interviewed through a process of random assignment. The final study sample contains 316 grandparent-grandchild pairs.

Measures

For each of two intergenerational relationship characteristics, we create grandparent (based on grandparent reports on the focal adolescent in 1994 and 1998) and grandchild (based on grandchild reports about that grandparent in 1994 and 1997) versions. All other variables are based on 1994 data. From this point on, we refer to 1994 data as Time 1 (or pretransition) and 1997/1998 data as Time 2 (or posttransition).

Grandparent mentoring. Grandchildren assessed how often (1 = *never* to 4 = *often*) their grandparent gave advice or helped with problems *(M = 2.45, SD = 0.93 in 1994; M = 2.54, SD = 1.02* in 1997). For grandparents, we take the sum of their assessments (1 = *yes,* 0 = *no*) of whether to the last month they gave advice to the grandchild, served as a voice of experience, served as a source of family history, and talked to the grandchild about their own childhood *(M = 3.07, SD = 1.04* in 1994; *M = 3.18, SD = 0.94* in 1998).

Quality of grandparent-grandchild relationship. Grandparents assessed the quality of relations with their target grandchild (1 = *poor* to 4 = *excellent),* how close they felt to the grandchild (1 = *not at all* to 5 = *very*), and how much the grandchild made them feel loved and appreciated (1 = *not at all* to 4 = *a lot*). These items are standardized and averaged, with the absolute value of the minimum added to each case to ease interpretation *(M = 4.00, SD = 0.83 in 1994; M = 5.00, SD = 0.81* in 1998). For grandchildren, we take the mean of their assessments of how happy they were with their relationships

Table 2.2   Means (Standard Deviations) for Grandparent-Grandchild Relationships by Grandchild's Educational Status

	In College	*Not in College*
Grandparent mentoring[a]		
Grandparent report (Time 1)	3.05	3.10
	(1.03)	(1.03)
Grandparent report (Time 2)	3.29*	2.98
	(0.84)	(1.10)
Grandchild report (Time 1)	2.44	2.47
	(0.94)	(0.92)
Grandchild report (Time 2)	2.49	2.64
	(0.95)	(1.13)
Relationship quality[b]		
Grandparent report (Time 1)	4.12*	3.78
	(0.67)	(1.02)
Grandparent report (Time 2)	5.14*	4.76
	(0.65)	(0.97)
Grandchild report (Time 1)	3.50*	3.27
	(0.62)	(0.83)
Grandchild report (Time 2)	3.55*	3.26
	(0.59)	(0.86)
n	199	116

a. Mentoring ranges from 0 to 4 (low to high) for grandparents and 1 to 4 (low to high) for grandchildren at both time points.

b. Quality ranges from 0 to 5.65 (low to high) for grandparents at Time 1 and 0 to 4.71 (low to high) for grandparents at Time 2, and from 1 to 4 (low to high) for grandchildren.

*Differences in means between two groups significant at $p < .05$, as determined by one-way ANOVA.

with the grandparent (1 = *very unhappy* to 4 = *very happy*) and how often (1 = *not at all* to 4 = *a lot)* their grandparent made them feel loved and appreciated *(M* = 3.42, *SD* = 0.71 in 1994; *M* = 3.44, *SD* = 0.72 in 1997).

Grandchild transitions. We created binary measures for whether the grandchild had enrolled in a 2- or 4-year college, gotten married, become a parent, or started full-time employment between 1994 and 1997.

Control variables. Analyses control for grandparent gender (1 = *female,* 73%); grandparent education (1 = *attended college,* 24%); grandparent self-reported health (1 = *poor* to 4 = *excellent; M* = 3.03, *SD* = 0.77); grandparent marital status (1 = *married,* 69%); grandparent self-reported relationship with grandchild's parent (1 = *poor* to 4 = *excellent; M* = 3.72, *SD* = 0.51); and changes in residential proximity (1 = grandchild lived within 50 miles of grandparent at Time 1 but not Time 2, 26%).

Plan of Analyses

Our empirical analyses are conducted with Amos 4.0, a structural equation package that allows us to account for measurement error and estimate missing data with full information maximum likelihood (Arbuckle & Wocthke, 1999).

Results

Nearly two thirds of grandchildren enrolled in higher education between Times 1 and 2. They and their grandparents reported higher quality intergenerational ties than other youth who did not enroll in college (Table 2.2). According to their grandparents (but not themselves), they also received more mentoring.

Table 2.3   Results of Models Predicting Grandparent Mentoring[a]

	Grandparent Report		Grandchild Report	
	b	β	b	β
Control variables				
Grandmother	0.16	0.08	−0.10	−0.04
Grandparent education[b]	−0.07	−0.03	0.08	0.03
Grandparent health[c]	−0.01	−0.01	−0.15*	−0.11
Grandparent marital status[d]	0.14	0.19	0.06	0.03
Grandparent-parent closeness[e]	−0.02	−0.01	0.28**	0.14
Decrease in proximity[f]	0.02	0.01	0.06	0.03
Prior mentoring	0.44***	0.48	0.50***	0.46
Grandchild transitions[g]				
Higher education	0.36***	0.19	−0.19	0.09
Married	−0.04	−0.01	−0.21	0.06
Parenthood	0.15	0.05	0.12	0.04
Employed	−0.12	−0.06	0.03	0.01
R^2	0.27		0.28	
N	316		316	

a. Mentoring ranges from 0 to 4 (low to high) for grandparents and 1 to 4 (low to high) for grandchildren.

b. Attended college = 1.

c. Health ranges from 1 to 4 (poor to excellent).

d. Married = 1.

e. Closeness ranges from 1 to 4 (poor to excellent).

f. Grandchild lived within 50 miles of grandparent at Time 1 but not at Time 2.

g. All transition variables are binary, with 1 indicating that it occurred between Times 1 and 2.

$*p < .05. **p < .01. ***p < .001.$

Our first two research questions asked whether grandchild enrollment in higher education influences the grandparent-grandchild relationship and whether this influence differs depending on grandparent or grandchild point of view. Tables 2.3 and 2.4 present the results of regression analyses on two aspects of the grandparent-grandchild relationship.

Beginning with mentoring (Table 2.3), grandparents report mentoring more when their grandchildren are enrolled in higher education ($\beta = .19. p < .001$). Because the mean of grandparent-reported mentoring increases across time points, this regression coefficient represents a greater *increase* in mentoring than for other grandparents. The grandchild-based analysis reveals no enrollment effect. Thus we see evidence of an intergenerational stake—grandparents feel that their grandchildren's entry into higher education allows them to mentor more, but the grandchildren see no change. This apparent generational stake does not result from differences in the grandparent- and grandchild-reported measures of mentoring, as substituting a one-item grandparent-reported measure that matched the grandchild-reported measure did not change results.

Turning to relationship quality (Table 2.4), both grandparents and grandchildren report higher quality relationships when the grandchild is enrolled in higher education ($\beta = .14, p < .01$ for grandparents; $\beta = .16, p < .05$ for grandchildren).

Table 2.4 Results of Models Predicting Grandparent-Grandchild Relationship Quality[a]

	Grandparent Report		Grandchild Report	
	b	*β*	*b*	*β*
Control variables				
Grandmother	0.16	0.09	0.10	0.06
Grandparent education[b]	−0.15	−0.08	−0.04	−0.02
Grandparent health[c]	−0.00	−0.00	−0.01	−0.01
Grandparent marital status[d]	0.14*	0.08	0.12	0.08
Grandparent-parent closeness[e]	0.15*	0.10	0.21**	0.15
Decrease in proximity[f]	0.06	0.01	−0.00	−0.00
Prior quality	0.46***	0.47	0.39***	0.38
Grandchild transitions[g]				
Higher education	0.24**	0.14	0.24*	0.16
Married	0.08	0.03	0.10	0.04
Parenthood	0.02	0.01	0.10	0.04
Employed	−0.01	−0.01	0.08	0.05
R²	0.34		0.25	
N	316		316	

a. Quality ranges from 0 to 5.65 (low to high) for grandparents and 0 to 4.71 (low to high) for grandchildren.
b. Attended college = 1.
c. Health ranges from 1 to 4 (poor to excellent).
d. Married = 1.
e. Closeness ranges from 1 to 4 (poor to excellent).
f. Grandchild lived within 50 miles of grandparent at Time 1 but not at Time 2.
g. All transition variables are binary, with 1 indicating that it occurred between Times 1 and 2.
*$p < .05$. **$p < .01$. ***$p < .001$.

Again, because the mean grandparent- and grandchild-reported quality increases between Times 1 and 2, these coefficients indicate that the quality of college students' relationships with grandparents *increases* over time compared to non-college-going youth.

Our remaining questions deal with contextual variability in intergenerational relationships. Is the link between grandchild entry into higher education and grandparent-mentoring moderated by whether the grandparent ever enrolled in higher education? To investigate this, we included an interaction term (grandparent education X grandchild enrollment) in the mentoring model (Table 2.5). Again, point of view is important, with grandparents' educational backgrounds influencing grandchild-reported mentoring only. In the grandchild model, the main effect of grandchild enrollment ($β = −.31$, $p < .05$) indicates that it is inversely associated with grandparent mentoring when the grandparent had not attended college, but the significant interaction term ($β = .57, p < .05$) indicates that enrollment is directly associated with grandparent mentoring when the grandparent had attended college. Thus when viewing all grandparent-grandchild pairs as one group (refer back to Table 2.3), we saw no evidence of an association between grandchild enrollment and grandchild-reported mentoring, but splitting the sample into meaningful subgroups (Table 2.5) reveals two significant, although opposite, associations. College-going grandchildren report more mentoring from grandparents who have undergone this transition in their own lives and less from grandparents who have not.

Table 2.5   Results of Models Predicting Grandparent Mentoring[a], with Grandparent Education as a Moderator

	Grandparent Report	Grandchild Report
Grandparent education[b]	−0.22	−0.30
	(0.18)	(0.20)
Grandchild in higher education[c]	0.32*	−0.31*
	(0.11)	(0.13)
Grandparent education X grandchild education	0.22	0.57*
	(0.23)	(0.24)
R^2	0.27	0.29
N	316	316

NOTE: Unstandardized coefficients (standard errors). All models control for grandparent gender, health status, marital status, grandparent-parent closeness, decrease in proximity, and three grandchild transitions (marriage, parenthood, and employment).

a. Mentoring ranges from 0 to 4 (low to high) for grandparents and 1 to 4 (low to high) for grandchildren.

b. Attended college = 1.

c. Entered higher education between times 1 and 2.

$*p < .05.$ $**p < .01.$ $***p < .001.$

Is the link between the grandchild's entry into higher education and grandparent-grandchild relationship quality moderated by the grandparent's relationship with the middle generation? To investigate this, we included an interaction term (grandparent-parent relationship quality X grandchild enrollment) in the quality model. This interaction term did not reach statistical significance, indicating no such moderation.

Conclusion

Research on grandparent-grandchild relationships is in an early stage, but it can make a significant contribution to family studies, especially if it undergoes the type of evolution that has characterized the literature on parent-child relationships. The purpose of this research is to encourage such a revolution by mapping out potentially rewarding pathways of research in this area. We have done so by asking four questions built upon prior grandparenting research (e.g., Silverstein, King, Burton, and others) and drawn from family-related theoretical orientations (e.g., life course, family systems).

Clearly, intergenerational relationships do change when grandchildren transition into higher education, and this change seems to be positive. The importance of this transition is magnified when considering that other grandchild transitions (e.g., marriage, parenthood, and employment) do not influence grandparent-grandchildren relationships. The importance of these transitions might have been diluted by the broad time frame in which they were assessed, but our findings suggest that enrollment in higher education may be qualitatively different from other role changes in young adulthood. Entry into college may lead to a re-evaluation of relationships without moving the young person into a new family, as marriage and parenting would. More extensive research is needed to uncover the mechanisms behind such relationship development and the potential for life transitions to serve as turning points. In any case, this finding demonstrates the value of taking a long-term approach to intergenerational relationships.

These processes demonstrate a generational stake. Grandparents feel that their grandchildren's transition to higher education has enhanced their mentoring role, but their grandchildren do not. More so than relationship quality, mentoring refers to specific behaviors defined by each actor. Grandparents may be motivated to interpret their interactions with grandchildren positively if they feel they are losing their grandchildren to the adult world, but grandchildren entering new arenas may interpret these same interactions as interference. These findings reinforce the need to incorporate multiple perspectives when studying relationships. This can only enhance our understanding of intergenerational relationships (King & Elder, 1995), even more so when studying transitions that may differ in meaning for each participant.

Furthermore, these intergenerational processes vary by context. The generational stake discussed above does not hold for grandparents and grandchildren who have similar educational experiences. This common ground could grant more authority to grandparents. The stake does coincide with educational mismatches, which may convince grandchildren that their grandparents have no wisdom to share on this new arena and dissuade grandparents from offering advice on an unfamiliar domain. On the other hand, we found no such variation related to the strength of the grandparent-parent relationship. The gatekeeping role of parents may decrease before young adulthood, or its effects might be set well before this time. Still, these analyses, which draw upon contributions of family sociology (the potential moderation of social context) and family psychology (the embeddedness of relationships in a system of family ties) demonstrate pathways to illuminate grandparenting, and, by doing so, family dynamics as a whole.

Although our analyses have been specific, our suggestions are general—taking long-term perspectives, comparing viewpoints, and exploring contextual variability. For example, we have studied one grandchild transition, but we have focused exclusively on those who made this transition without exploring the lives of those who did not make it or who made other transitions instead. At the same time, we have ignored transitions in the lives of grandparents (e.g., widowhood, retirement) and of the parents who link the generations. Beyond transitions, modeling long-term trajectories (see Silverstein & Long, 1998) would offer a different approach to relationship development. Furthermore, qualitative research might be the best method for investigating the different perspectives of grandchildren and grandparents and for uncovering the seeds of the generational stake. Finally, in introducing context, we should think of both the proximate (e.g., family, community) and structural contexts (e.g., race, class) that shape the human life course.

Of course, future studies in this spirit should draw upon less specialized data. The Iowa sample is well-suited to our goals—rich enough to allow in-depth exploration of developmental and family processes, temporally broad enough to allow multistage analysis, and inclusive enough to combine multiple perspectives. Moreover, the dynamics addressed in this research may be more visible in this sample. In tight-knit, rural communities, where farm work has historically been more important for adult life than education, grandchildren's transitions into higher education may occasion more reflection and more reorganization of family ties. Although using this homogenous sample to put forward new possibilities for intergenerational research is a good start, more representative data are required to realize these possibilities.

Our main goal here has been to encourage new pathways of intergenerational research. We strongly believe that such research is valuable. First, demographic changes have increased the importance of the grandparent role on family and societal levels. The influence of these changes, which include decreasing mortality (which lengthens the duration of being or having a grandparent), decreasing fertility (which limits the number of grandchildren per family), and increasing divorce rates (which may lead to more active grandparenting), necessitates in-depth analysis. Second, the grandparent-grandchild relationship is not divorced from the larger family system, and so its study provides a broader understanding of families as a whole. For example, grandparent-grandchild relationships may interact with parent-child dynamics—undermining positive parenting, promoting resilience in troubled families, or opening new conduits of social capital. Third, these intergenerational relationships may help to structure the life course of both young and old, so that studying them promotes greater understanding of human development more generally. For these reasons, grandparent-grandchild relationships deserve the type of attention that has provided such insight into other areas of family life.

Note

The authors acknowledge support from the National Institute of Mental Health (MH 00567, MH 51361, MH 52429, MH 57549), a Spencer Foundation Senior Scholar Award to G.H.E., and the MacArthur Foundation Research Network on Successful Adolescent Development Among Youth in High-Risk Settings.

References

Arbuckle, J., & Woethke, W. (1999). *Amos 4.0 User's guide* [Computer software]. Chicago: Small-Waters.

Arnett, J. J. (2000). Emerging adulthood: A theory of development from the late teens through the twenties. *American Psychologists, 55,* 469–480.

Bengston, V. L., Schaie, K. W., & Burton, L. M. (1995). *Adult intergenerational relations: Effects of societal change.* New York: Springer.

Burton, L. M., & Bengtson, V. L. (1985). Black grandmothers: Issues of timing and continuity of roles. In V. L. Bengston & J. F. Robertson (Eds.), *Grandparenthood* (pp. 61–77). Beverly Hills, CA: Sage.

Cherlin, A., & Furstenberg, F. F. (1986). *The new American grandparent. A place in the family, a life apart.* New York: Basic Books.

Cox, M., & Paley, B. (1997). Families as systems. *Annual Review of Psychology, 48,* 243–267.

Elder, G. H., Jr. (1998). Life course and human development. In W. Damon (Ed.), *Handbook of Child Psychology* (pp. 939–991). New York: Wiley.

Elder, G. H., Jr., & Conger, R. D. (2000). *Children of the land: Adversity and success in rural America.* Chicago: University of Chicago Press.

Elder, G. H., Jr., King, V., & Conger, R. D. (1996). Attachment to place and migration prospects: A developmental perspective. *Journal of Research* on *Adolescence, 6,* 397–425.

Hagestad, G. O. (1985). Continuity and connectedness. In V. L. Bengston & J. F. Robertson (Eds.), *Grandparenthood* (pp. 31–48). Beverly Hills, CA: Sage.

King, V, & Elder, G. H., Jr. (1995). American children view their grandparents: Linked lives across three rural generations. *Journal of Marriage and the Family, 57,* 165–178.

King, V, & Elder, G. H., Jr. (1998). Education and grand-parenting roles. *Research on Aging, 20,* 450–474.

King, V., & Elder, G. H., Jr. (1999). Are religious grandparents more involved grandparents? *Journal of Gerontology, 54B,* S317–S328.

King, V., Silverstein, M., Elder, G. H., Jr., Bengston, V. L., & Conger, R. D. (2003, November). Relations with grandparents: Rural Midwest versus urban southern California. *Journal of Family Issues, 24,* 1020–1043.

Rossi, A. S., & Rossi, P. H. (1990). *Of human bonding: Parent-child relations across the life course.* New York: Aldine.

Silverstein, M., & Long, J. D. (1998). Trajectories of grandparents' perceived solidarity with adult grandchildren: A growth curve analysis over 23 years. *Journal of Marriage and the Family, 60,* 912–923.

Szinovacz, M. F. (1998). *Handbook on grandparenthood.* Westport, CT: Greenwood.

Uhlenberg, P., & Kirby, J. B. (1998). Grandparenthood over time: Historical and demographic trends. In M. E. Szinovacz (Ed.), *Handbook on grandparenthood* (pp. 23–39). Westport, CT: Greenwood.

3

LIFE-SPAN DEVELOPMENTAL THEORY

Life-span developmental theory concerns the study of individual development, or ontogenesis, from conception to death. A key assumption of this theory is that development does not cease when adulthood is reached (Baltes, Lindenberger, & Staudinger, 1998, p. 1029)[1]. Life-span researchers and theorists assume that each major period of life has its own developmental challenges and accomplishments, and that adaptive processes are at work within all periods of the life span. This theoretical approach is clearly focused on individual development rather than on family development. It is concerned with comparing an individual's development with that of others and with the individual's own status at various points in time. We include it in this volume on family theories for several reasons.

First, since the purview of the theory is "womb to tomb," it of necessity touches upon all of the family-related issues that characterize family life course theory, such as the birth of a child, the development of Alzheimer's disease, the macro-level political and economic slings and arrows that impact both individuals and families—the latter impacted either directly or indirectly through one or more of its members.

Of course, as noted, regardless of its study of development across the human life span, the focus is still on individuals rather than groups, and this makes the theory decidedly distinct from the family life course perspective that focuses on the family as the unit of analysis.

Second, we believe that this approach has much to teach others within subdisciplines of the family and human development sciences. For example, this theoretical approach is exceptionally rigorous in the way it links theory with methodology across the life span (you'll get a taste of this from the two readings we have selected for this chapter) as well as in the breadth of substantive issues that are studied ontogenetically. In addition, it has progressed from a largely descriptive focus on developmental stages (predominant 40–50 years ago) to a more recent focus (beginning in the 1970s) on trying to determine the mechanisms that determine developmental change or consistency. (Family life course theory is undergoing a similar transition as it has evolved from an emphasis on the family life cycle to a more comprehensive commitment to examining the causes of family development and change [cf. Chapter 3; Elder, 1996; White & Klein, 2002].) Overall, for the reasons mentioned as well as because it passes with flying colors most tests (White & Klein, 2002, p. 232, Table 9.1) of how to evaluate a theory's usefulness, life-span developmental theory can serve as an important model for new students as well as for scholars.

What does it mean to say that the focus of life-span developmental theory and research is the individual? Given the identification of a substantive focus (e.g., personality development or cognitive abilities), this approach aims to study one or more of the following things:

1. Normative developmental change (For example, what is the typical course of personality development, or of cognitive capabilities? What are the mechanisms for this typical course of development or developmental change?)

2. Interindividual differences in developmental change (For example, are there differences between people over time, within age periods or across age periods, in their outgoingness or in their visual acuity? What are the mechanisms that produce such differences between people?)

3. Intraindividual change and consistency in development (For example, what is the course of development for self-esteem or for the tendency to take personal risks? Are these things consistent in individuals over time or are they characterized by "plasticity"? [Developmental plasticity is a general term used in the study of ontogeny to indicate how malleable or changeable something is.] What are the mechanisms producing consistency or change?)

It is important to note that these three emphases apply to individual periods of the life span (e.g., infancy, adolescence, or old age) as well as to the life span as a whole. In asking the above questions, one also begins to get a flavor of the kinds of methodological implications of life-span developmental theory. How does one investigate developmental plasticity or consistency? Does one compare, say, a group of 9-year-olds with a group of 23-year-olds to see if interindividual changes in cognitive functioning

occur? Or, does one follow longitudinally the development of cognitive functioning over a protracted period of time? Further, if one substitutes the word *family* or *families* for *people* or *individuals* in the above questions, it becomes clear that life-span developmental theory and family life course theory are both fundamentally time-related theoretical approaches. (Do note, however, that *time* is really just a shorthand descriptor for all that happens during it. Like age, it doesn't explain anything.) This developmental perspective—what happens and why, over time—is an integral part of both conceptualizations, and it is one thing that distinguishes them from the other theoretical perspectives in this book. Although some of the other theories (e.g., social learning theory or social exchange theory) may imply or make assumptions about change over time, the concept of developmental change is not an integral component of these other perspectives.

THE READINGS

Schoon et al. (2002) use the life-span developmental perspective in combination with concepts from ecological theory (Bronfenbrenner & Ceci, 1994; Chapter 10) and *developmental contextualism* (Ford & Lerner, 1992) to examine the relationships between early and continuing social risk and academic achievement in childhood/ adolescence as well as between earlier risk and adult attainments. Developmental contextualism views human development as the dynamic interaction between a changing individual and a changing context. This reading uses fairly complex data analysis procedures (path analysis and multiple regression) to explicate a complex development trajectory over a significant portion of the life span. (You can safely ignore the statistical details since the article's text is very clear in stating what the analyses mean and how they can be interpreted.) Another key feature of the Schoon et al. reading is what we mentioned earlier in this chapter: the link between theoretical perspective and methodological choices. In this case, data were collected on the same individuals (longitudinal study) across a significant period of the life span to answer the specific research questions that the researchers had formulated. Without longitudinal data, the researchers' questions would not be as adequately addressed.

The other reading in this chapter concerns the longitudinal impact of change or continuity in marital status on the psychological well-being of adults (Marks & Lambert, 1998). The researchers' perspective on this issue is guided by both the life-span developmental and the family life course theories, which (as we have said previously) maintain that it is important to examine the sequelae of discontinuities and continuities throughout life, not just in early childhood. In their study, Marks and Lambert reflect on important life-span developmental concepts including the timing and sequence of life events, the context in which certain developmental outcomes occur (e.g., it is much less atypical in 2004 than it was in 1964 to be a divorced adult), and the developmental readiness of individuals to deal with positive and potentially negative change.

Note that, besides the overall theoretical approach, Marks and Lambert's research shares two features with Schoon et al. First, the use of longitudinal data to answer developmental questions was appropriately employed. Second, the analysis of these longitudinal data was, again, complex. We would urge you to examine the various data presentations, but not to be overwhelmed by them since the text is very clear in explaining things. Also, if you suspect a trend here—that longitudinal data require more complex statistical techniques—you are correct. But, the payoff is much greater when such data and analyses are employed in developmental research. They allow more direct answers to the research questions, which in turn allow more direct tests of theory (i.e., explanation and understanding of results). The nature of the data (same people over time) and the analyses take into account many possibly influential variables and connections among variables in a way that pays specific attention to sequencing and timing. This is simply not possible with nonlongitudinal (i.e., cross-sectional) information. This is another example of the usefulness of life-span developmental theory to guide research.

ISSUES FOR YOUR CONSIDERATION

1. Do you think developmental contextualism might be a useful concept for family life course theory? (Hint: The answer is "yes!") Why? How could it be integrated into the family life course perspective?

2. Discuss an individual developmental issue for a nonadult (any age under 18) that would likely impact the child's family and its functioning in positive or negative ways. Then, from the other direction, consider some discontinuity in family life that would be likely to impact one or more of the family's members. What theories might help you explain these impacts?

3. How do you think of different periods in the life span? Do you see them as preparatory for something later, as self-contained, or as being the result of earlier periods? If you had to make a guess, what are the relative degrees of continuity and discontinuity that might be normative across the life span? What do the readings in this chapter have to say about the last question?

FURTHER READING

Bronfenbrenner and Ceci (1994), Ford and Lerner (1992).

Note

1. This chapter relies extensively on Baltes, Lindenberger, and Staudinger (1998), and Goulet and Baltes (1970).

THE INFLUENCE OF CONTEXT, TIMING, AND DURATION OF RISK EXPERIENCES FOR THE PASSAGE FROM CHILDHOOD TO MIDADULTHOOD

INGRID SCHOON, JOHN BYNNER, HEATHER JOSHI,
SAMANTHA PARSONS, RICHARD D. WIGGINS, AND AMANDA SACKER

Abstract

This study investigated the long-term effects of social disadvantage on academic achievement and on subsequent attainments in adulthood. The study drew on data collected for more than 30,000 individuals born 12 years apart, following their development from birth to adulthood. The pathways that link social disadvantage to individual development across the life course were analyzed in a developmental–contextual systems model. The results showed that the influence of risk factors associated with socioeconomic disadvantage depended on the developmental stage of the individual, the experience of long-term or continuous disadvantage, and the overall sociohistorical context. Early risk had a moderate influence on the formation of individual competences. The greatest risk was associated with persisting and accumulating experiences of socioeconomic disadvantage throughout childhood and adolescence. Material conditions improved for the later-born cohort, yet pervasive social inequalities existed that affected outcomes during childhood and were consequently reflected in adult attainment.

Introduction

Children raised in socioeconomically disadvantaged families are at risk for a variety of adjustment problems, including increased risk for poor academic achievement (Bolger, Patterson, & Thompson, 1995; Campbell & Ramey, 1994; Duncan, Brooks-Gunn, & Klebanov, 1994; Felner et al., 1995; Pungello, Kupersmidt, Burchinal, & Patterson, 1996; Ramey & Ramey, 1990; Walker, Greenwood, Hart, & Carta, 1994) and adjustment problems in later life, as reflected in occupational attainment or social position (Blau & Duncan, 1967; Bynner, Joshi, & Tsatsas, 2000; Caspi, Wright, Moffitt, & Silva, 1998; Rutter & Madge, 1976; Schoon & Parsons, 2002b; Sewell, Hailer, & Ohlendorf, 1970). Socioeconomic background is one of the main predictors of cognitive development, which provides the underpinnings of academic achievement on which much success in later life depends. The experience of socioeconomic disadvantage may severely strain adaptational abilities of children, and is thus a potential risk factor for development. The consequences of growing up in a disadvantaged family environment can continue into adulthood or even into the next generation (Birch & Gussow, 1970;

42

Garmezy, 1991). Yet, most research on the influence of socioeconomic disadvantage on developmental outcomes has been cross-sectional in nature, and has assessed the impact of episodic rather than persistent economic difficulties. The aim of this study was to examine the long-term effects of socioeconomic disadvantage on academic achievement and consequent adult attainments. Taking a longitudinal perspective stretching from birth to adulthood, this study examined the impact of early and persistent social disadvantage (which was termed "social risk") on academic achievement during childhood and adolescence and on adult outcomes in a developmental-contextual framework.

Fundamental to the idea of risk is the predictability of life changes from earlier circumstances. As expressed through the concept of a "risk trajectory," one risk factor reinforces another, leading to increasingly restricted outcomes in later life (Rutter, 1990). In this study the question of the relation between early life experiences and consequent adjustment patterns was recast in terms of a testable model of continuities in social disadvantage and individual adjustment and their interactions over time. By analyzing data from two cohorts of children born in 1958 and 1970, the investigation also took into account the changing sociohistorical context.

Development and Context

The processes by which the socioeconomic background influences individual development are not yet fully understood. It has been argued that socioeconomic status (SES) at the time of the child's birth is an indicator of the social context, but may also reflect parental genetic characteristics, which are assumed to have some role in determining the level of academic functioning of their children (Plomin & Bergeman, 1991; Plomin & McClearn, 1993; Scarr, 1992). Proponents of behavioral genetics see the course of human development as a function of genetically controlled maturational sequences (Scarr, 1992). However, findings show that in no case is the genetic determination so strong that there is no room for environmental effects (Plomin & Daniels, 1987; Scarr, 1992). There is now increasing skepticism about the usefulness of approaches formulated within behavioral genetics, on scientific as well as social and ethical grounds (Baumrind, 1993; Hoffman, 1994; Jackson, 1993; Lerner & von Eye, 1992). Human development takes place in a social context, and is therefore influenced by a person's interactions within that context. Genetic factors are only one of a much larger series of possible explanations for human behavior. More recent developmental approaches have conceptualized genes and other biological variables as contributors to reciprocal, dynamic processes that can only be fully understood in relation to sociocultural environmental contexts (Bronfenbrenner & Ceci, 1994; Gottlieb, Wahlsten, & Lickliter, 1998; Horowitz, 2000). Human beings differ in their capacity for realizing individual talents, and it is important to understand under what circumstances individual potentials find expression.

This study was not designed to examine the heritability of certain traits, but rather to investigate the long-term effects of social risk on academic attainment and consequent adult outcomes in a changing sociohistorical context. Especially useful for this type of analysis are approaches developed by proponents of an ecological perspective of the life course that conceptualizes human development as the dynamic interaction between a changing individual and a changing context (Baltes, 1987; Bronfenbrenner, 1979; Elder, 1985; Featherman & Lerner, 1985; Lerner, 1984, 1996; Sameroff, 1983). For example, in their bioecological theory of nature-nurture effects, Bronfenbrenner and Ceci (1994) argue that the long-term interactions between children and their environments are a necessary condition for the expression of any trait. They differentiate between the proximal environment, which is directly experienced by the individual (e.g., the family environment), and more distal cultural and social value systems that have an indirect effect on the individual, and are often mediated by the more proximal context. Proximal processes constitute the basic mechanisms that produce effective developmental functioning. They reflect the immediate day-to-day experiences that most directly shape adaptation in the face of adversity. The form, power, content, and direction of the proximal processes that affect development very systematically as a joint function of the person, the environment (both immediate and more remote) in which the processes are taking place, and the nature of the developmental outcome under consideration.

Ecological explanations of the association between socioeconomic origin, educational achievement, and occupational attainment have emphasized the role of different opportunities and socialization processes that exist across SES levels. Individuals from more privileged homes have more educational opportunities, greater access to financial resources when they are needed (e.g., to pay for higher education), and more role models, occupational knowledge, and informal/kinship networks (Schulenberg, Vondracek, & Crouter, 1984). The same cumulative effect, in the opposite direction, can occur for those who are not born so lucky and who consequently acquire an enhanced likelihood of risk. However, early experiences, whether good or bad, do not determine an invariant life path. For example, in Werner and Smith's (1992) longitudinal study of high-risk children, one third had made satisfactory adjustments in adult life, despite being born into highly disadvantaged circumstances. Some individuals succeed despite the odds and break the vicious cycle (Clarke & Clarke, 2000; Elder, Pavalko, & Hastings, 1991; Pilling, 1990), whereas others from privileged backgrounds fail to succeed. Individual differences in response to adversity can lead to some form of intensification or increased vulnerability, or to the amelioration or protection against risk factors that could lead to maladaptive outcomes (Garmezy, 1985; Rutter, 1990; Werner & Smith, 1992). Thus, individuals are not passively exposed to experiential factors, but can become producers of their own development (Bronfenbrenner, 1979).

There is consistent evidence of three broad sets of variables implicated in the development of positive adjustment in the face of adversity, a phenomenon also referred to as resilience (Luthar, Cicchetti, & Becker, 2000; Masten, Best, & Garmezy, 1990; Rutter, 1990; Werner & Smith, 1992). These protective factors include (1) attributes of the individual (e.g., ability, temperament, and motivation), (2) characteristics of the family (e.g., parental interest and support), and (3) aspects of the wider social context (e.g., neighborhoods and social support system), thus lending support to the proposition that proximal processes are fueled by the joint function of the person and the context (both immediate and more remote), as suggested by Bronfenbrenner and Ceci (1994). Resilience is not a personality attribute, but a dynamic process of positive adaptation despite the experience of significant adversity or risk (Luthar et al., 2000; Masten et al., 1990; Rutter, 1990; Werner & Smith, 1992).

Recent discussions have raised questions regarding the multidimensional nature of positive adaptation or resilience, suggesting that it is necessary to differentiate between constellations of specific risks and specific outcomes (Bronfenbrenner & Ceci, 1994; Luthar et al., 2000). At-risk children can show considerable heterogeneity in functioning across different domains (i.e., academic, emotional, and behavioral adjustment), and successful adaptation in one domain does not imply positive adaptation in another (Cicchetti & Garmezy, 1993). The focus of this study was on academic adjustment, because of its importance as a context for adaptation in Western culture. Success or failure in school can have serious individual and social consequences, and lays the foundation for future careers.

Timing and Duration of Risk Experiences

There is evidence of great diversity in the temporal dimension of disadvantage: much socioeconomic disadvantage is short term, although a great amount lasts for most of the childhood years (Duncan & Rodgers, 1988). The experience of socioeconomic disadvantage does not always have an immediate impact, and vulnerabilities may emerge only later in life

(Clarke & Clarke, 1981). Early adversity may be overcome by improved circumstances, but may, nevertheless, leave the individual potentially more vulnerable to any disadvantage experienced at a later stage (Cicchetti & Tucker, 1994). Recent studies have shown that persistent socioeconomic disadvantage has stronger effects than intermittent adversity on individual outcomes (Ackerman, Schoff, Levinson, Youngstrom, & Izard, 1999; Bolger et al., 1995; Duncan et al., 1994; Pungello et al., 1996) and it has been argued that chronically stressful environments hinder the development of successful adaptation (Hammen, 1992). On the other hand, there is evidence that adversity during early childhood, as opposed to during later developmental periods, has a crucial impact on later adjustment, especially for academic attainment (Axinn, Duncan, & Thornton, 1997; Duncan, Yeung, Brooks-Gunn, & Smith, 1998; Haveman & Wolfe, 1994). There is, however, also evidence that current contextual adversity determines current adjustment (Campbell, Pierce, Moore, Marakovitz, & Newby, 1996; Feiring & Lewis, 1996; Tizard, 1976). Differences in findings can be explained by methodological variations in the studies that involve different developmental periods, different indicators of adversity and adjustment, and different analytical strategies. The relative contribution of early, concurrent, or persistent effects can only be elucidated by drawing on longitudinal studies, which provide detailed information of individuals followed over time.

Assessing Socioeconomic Risk

Socioeconomic disadvantage is associated with a variety of cofactors, such as poor living conditions, overcrowding, or lack of material resources that pose risks for adaptive development (Ackerman et al., 1999; Conger et al., 1993; Duncan & Brooks-Gunn, 1997; Fergusson, Horwood, & Lawton, 1990; Fitzgerald, Lester, & Zuckerman, 1995; Huston, McLoyd, & Coll, 1994).

Individual risk factors do not exert their effect in isolation, but rather in interaction with other influences. It has been suggested that it is the number of these factors and their combined effect that shape development (Sameroff, Seifer, Baldwin, & Baldwin, 1993; Rutter, 1979). The relation between any single risk factor and subsequent outcomes tends to be weak, and usually many variables are involved in determining an outcome (Ackerman et al., 1999; Rutter, 1990; Sameroff et al., 1993; Szatmari, Shannon, & Offord, 1994). Serious risk emanates from the accumulation of risk effects (Robins & Rutter, 1990). In comparison with single-risk models, multiple-risk models have been shown to be good predictors of individual outcomes (Ackerman et al., 1999; Caprara & Rutter, 1995; Fergusson, Horwood, & Lynskey, 1994; Sameroff et al., 1993). Most multiple-risk studies use a single index, summing the number of risk factors present. Summing the number of risk factors in a single index, however, gives equal weight to all risk factors and does not take into consideration the relative contribution or overlap in risk factors (Greenberg, Lengua, Coie, & Pinderhughes, 1999; Szatmari, Shannon, & Offord, 1994). There is now an increasing awareness that the processes that link socioeconomic disadvantage to individual development operate at varying levels of specificity, and that there is a need to distinguish between economic disadvantage per se and other associated aspects of environmental adversity (Ackerman et al., 1999; Duncan et al., 1994; McLoyd, 1990; Szatmari et al., 1994). Furthermore, Ackerman et al. (1999) argue that a single multiple-risk index aggregates a set of variables that may relate differently to child functioning, or that may function differently for advantaged and disadvantaged families, and that it does not distinguish between persistent and transitory experiences. Thus, they recommend the use of discrete groupings of indicators, narrowing the focus of the variables involved, or isolating specific factors that pose risks for individual adjustment. The usefulness of such an approach has been demonstrated in a number of studies (Ackerman et al., 1999; Deater-Deckard, Dodge, Bates, & Pettit, 1998; Szatmari et al., 1994) and was adopted in the present study. Instead of aggregating various cofactors of socioeconomic disadvantage, only indicators of the socioeconomic family background were included to assess the unique effect of socioeconomic disadvantage on individual development. The study drew on indicators of socioeconomic family status as well as indicators of living conditions and material resources available to the family. This approach thus went beyond studies that used social status or income as sole indicators of socioeconomic risk and more accurately reflected the everyday experiences within the proximal family context.

Effects of the Wider Sociohistorical Context

Another issue to be addressed concerns the impact of the wider sociohistorical context in shaping individual development. For example, Elder (1999) demonstrated the crucial impact of the Great American Depression and the outbreak of World War II on the developmental pathways of individuals born between 1920 and 1921 in Oakland, CA. The present study compared the development of two British birth cohorts born 12 years apart, thereby taking into account contextual effects that might help to explain differences in response to disadvantage. The study drew on data collected for two birth cohorts born in 1958 and 1970, respectively. Changes in social, economic, and education policies between 1960 and 1980 resulted in the cohort members growing up in very different environments. Between 1979 and 1986, and again between 1989 and 1993, the sharpest rise in unemployment since World War II took place in the United Kingdom. The mid-1980s saw the virtual disappearance of the youth labor market in Britain (Banks et al., 1992; Bynner, Elias, McKnight, & Pan, 1999). Many have argued that children born in the 1970s experienced a major shift in life expectations across the generations. This generation "X" grew up at a time when the prospects of achieving employment directly after leaving school and maintaining a continuing career were increasingly in question, especially for those young people without qualifications (Bynner, Ferri, & Shepherd, 1997; Schoon, McCulloch, Joshi, Wiggins, &

Bynner, 2001; Schoon & Parsons, 2002a). In response to the changing nature of labor markets and employment opportunities, young people are under increasing pressure to continue full-time education beyond the age of 16 years, and to acquire formal qualifications. Poor academic achievement, which presented no significant barrier to employment in the past, now predicts real difficulties in finding employment, and ultimately exclusion from the labor market (Bynner, Joshi, & Tsatsas, 2000).

A Developmental-Contextual Model of Cumulative Risk Effects

The aim of this study was to examine the extent of continuity of socioeconomic disadvantage from birth to midadulthood and the maintenance of academic adjustment in the face of that risk. To better understand the long-term effects of social risk, the extent to which risk effects persist and how they interact with individual adjustment was considered. Using Structural Equation Modeling (SEM; Bollen, 1989), the long-term influence of socioeconomic disadvantage on individual development was assessed, taking into consideration the influence of context, timing, and duration of risk experiences. The pathways through which the experience of socioeconomic risk influences the development and maintenance of individual adjustment (i.e., academic attainment) during childhood and adolescence as well as the pathways that link childhood conditions to adult outcomes were investigated. Figure 3.1 gives a diagrammatic representation of the developmental-contextual model for assessing the long-term impact of socioeconomic disadvantage. The model is an explicit developmental model that assesses the timing and the duration of the interactions between individual and context. The variables shown are all latent or unobserved variables.

The model specifies that conditions at birth (parental social class) influence the consequent experience of socioeconomic risk (i.e., low social class of parents and material disadvantage in the family home), as well as the level of individual

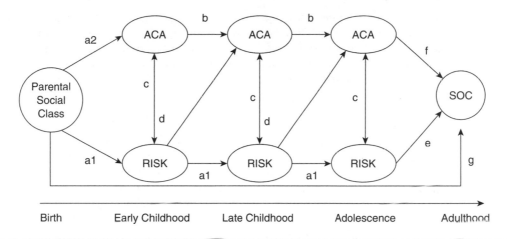

Figure 3.1   Developmental-contextual model of psychosocial adjustment. ACA = academic adjustment; Risk-socioeconomic risk; SOC = social position in adulthood. See text for further details.

adjustment (i.e., academic achievement). The path from parental social class at birth to consequent socioeconomic risk is labeled "a1," and the path from parental social class at birth to academic attainment is labeled "a2." It was hypothesized that socioeconomic disadvantage at one time point would predict the experience of socioeconomic disadvantage at a later time point. The arrows labeled "a1" that link the latent risk variables indicate this continuity of socioeconomic adversity over time. It was furthermore hypothesized that social class at birth would be an important predictor of academic adjustment (path "a2"), and that academic attainment at one time point would influence academic attainment at a later time point (paths "b"). It was also assumed that the experience of concurrent socioeconomic disadvantage would be associated with the development and maintenance of academic adjustment. These concurrent associations during early and late childhood, as well as during adolescence, are indicated as "c." The model thus tested the persistence of socioeconomic risk and the maintenance of academic adjustment in the face of that risk. The model furthermore assessed the cumulating effects of social risk on academic adjustment by estimating

the additional incremental risk effects at subsequent time points (early childhood, late childhood, and adolescence). The paths labeled "d" indicate these time-lagged effects of earlier risk on later academic attainment. The model furthermore examined the independent influence of social risk experienced during adolescence on adult social status (path "e"), as well as the influence of academic adjustment during adolescence on adult social status (path "f"). To establish whether parental social class at birth had an influence on an individual's adult social status, independent of intervening experiences, path "g" was included, which was an indicator of cohort effects not accounted for by the risk and adjustment levels carried forward in time. The model also considered the effects of a changing sociohistorical context, which is not shown in the diagram but was taken into account in the analyses by applying the model to two cohorts of young people growing up 12 years apart. The importance of the life-course developmental perspective for this study lay in its scope to integrate process and structure and to link individual time with historical time. The longitudinal approach had a number of methodological advantages with regard to the research questions:

reports of early life events were not influenced by knowledge of the subsequent personal history; the cohort included appropriate controls; and the conjoint impact of different factors experienced at different time points could be analyzed in a multivariate, multicausal model.

Method

This study used data collected for the National Child Development Study (NCDS) and the British Cohort Study (BCS70), two of Britain's richest research resources for the study of human development. The participants of the NCDS included all persons born in Great Britain between March 3 and March 9, 1958. In five follow-up studies, data were collected on the physical, psychosocial, and educational development of the cohort at ages 7, 11, 16, 23, and 33 years (Shepherd, 1995), and, most recently, at age 42 (Bynner, Ferri, Shepherd, & Smith, 2000). At each sweep between 1958 and 1974, wide-ranging information was collected from parents, teachers, school medical officers, and, at later stages, from the cohort members themselves via personal interviews. Satisfactory response rates have been reported for each sweep, and comparison of data has shown that the achieved samples did not markedly differ from the target samples, or from other survey samples of the British population (Shepherd, 1993, 1995).

The BCS70 has followed children born in the week April 5–11, 1970, from birth through to adulthood. Data sweeps took place when the cohort members were ages 5, 10, 16, and 26 years (Ekinsmyth, Bynner, Montgomery, & Shepherd, 1992), and most recently at age 30 (Bynner, Ferri, Shepherd, & Smith, 2000). In the birth survey, information was collected by means of a questionnaire that was completed by the midwife present at birth, and supplementary information was obtained from clinical records. In 1975 and 1980, parents of the cohort members were interviewed by Health Visitors, the cohort members themselves undertook ability tests, and the school health service gathered medical information on each child. This was supplemented at ages 10 and 16 by information gathered from head and class teachers who completed questionnaires. A low response rate at age 16 occurred because of a teacher strike, which coincided with the fieldwork. All school children were afflicted in the same way, and the demographic characteristics of the sample at age 16 remained representative of the target population (Shepherd, 1997). The follow-up study at age 26 was conducted via a mail survey. At age 30, data were collected by interview with the cohort members (Bynner, Ferri, et al., 2000). An analysis of response bias showed that the achieved samples did not differ from the target samples across a number of key variables (social class, parental education, and gender), despite a slight underrepresentation of the most disadvantaged groups (Butler, Despotidou, & Shepherd, 1997; Davie, Butler, & Goldstein, 1972; Shepherd, 1997).

Sample

The sample consisted of all individuals for whom complete data were collected at birth. The following analyses were based on a total sample of 16,994 cohort members for the NCDS and 14,229 cohort members for the BCS70. In both cohorts, there were 52% men and 48% women. Data collected between birth and age 16 were linked with data collected at age 30 (BCS70) and age 33 (NCDS) when the cohort members reached midadulthood. Potential bias due to missing variable information in both cohorts was addressed in the section on estimating the model.

Measurement of Socioeconomic Risk

Risk factors associated with socioeconomic disadvantage were indicated by parental social class and material conditions in the family household. The indicator variables were measured at ages 7, 11, and 16 for the NCDS, and ages 5, 10, and 16 for the BCS70.

Parental Social Class

In both the NCDS and the BCS70, social class was measured by the Registrar General's measure of social class (RGSC). The RGSC is defined according to job status and the associated education, prestige (OPCS, 1980), or lifestyle (Marsh, 1986), and is assessed by the current- or last-held job. The RGSC is coded on a 6-point scale: I, professional; II, managerial and technical; IIINM, skilled nonmanual; IIIM, skilled manual; IV, partly skilled; and V, unskilled (Leete & Fox, 1977). The occupational categories used in the U.S. census and other European countries are similarly based on the skills and status of different occupations (Krieger & Williams, 1997). Class I represents the highest level of prestige or skill and Class V represents the lowest. In cases in which the father was absent, the social class (RGSC) of the mother was used in the BCS70. The same applied to the NCDS at ages 7, 11, and 16; however in cases in which there was no father at birth, the mother's father's social class was used.

Material Conditions

Material conditions in the family environment were assessed on the basis of a summative index, in which the presence or absence of four indicator variables (listed below) is summed. The scale gives an overall score of material disadvantage that ranges between 0 and 4.

Overcrowding. This is a dichotomous variable based on the ratio of people living in the household to the number of rooms in the household. One or more persons per room was coded "1," and less than one person per room was coded "0."

Household amenities. This is a dichotomous scale based on the cohort member's family having sole use of a bathroom, toilet, and hot water. The same three questions were asked in both studies. Sole access to all of these amenities was coded "0," and shared use or no access to any of these amenities was coded "1."

Housing tenure. The tenure of the home was defined as owner-occupier (0) or other (1).

Receipt of state benefits. Receipt of state benefits is an indicator of financial hardship within the family environment (Fogelman, 1983). The assessed benefits include payment of unemployment benefit, income support, and housing benefit, but exclude payment of pension or child benefit. Parents were coded as either not in receipt of benefits (0) or in receipt of benefits in the last 12 months (1).

Individual Adjustment

Individual adjustment was measured by the child's academic attainment at each measurement point. To reflect the changing competencies of the growing child, academic attainment was assessed differently during early childhood (age 5 or 7), middle childhood (age 10 or 11), and adolescence (age 16).

Academic Attainment at Age 5 (BCS70) and 7 (NCDS)

The Human Figure Drawing Test used in the present study was a modified version of the Draw-a-Man test originally devised by Goodenough (1926) and developed further by Harris (1963). The Harris-Goodenough Test has good reliability (.94; Osborn, Butler, & Morris, 1984). It has been evaluated as a measure of intelligence and significant correlations, *rs* averaging between .4 and .5, with conventional IQ tests (Binet, Wechsler) have been reported (Scott, 1981). The scoring of the drawings produced by the children is based on 30 developmental items suggested by Koppitz (1968) and uses the Harris (1963) point system of scoring. One point is scored for each item represented in the drawing, giving a maximum possible score of 30. In both cohorts the children had to draw two figures. In the BCS70, however, only one figure was coded. Thus, the maximum score in the NCDS was 60, and in the BCS70 was 30. The achieved scores ranged from 0 to 53 in the NCDS, and 0 to 23 in the BCS70.

The Copy-a-Design test (Davie et al., 1972) assesses the cohort member's perceptual-motor ability. The ability to copy designs or geometric shapes is included as one element of assessment in many standard intelligence tests. The test used in the cohort studies assumed that children had reached a certain level of conceptual development to be able to recognize the principles governing different geometric forms and to reproduce them (Osborn et al., 1984). The test has satisfactory reliability (.70; Osborn et al., 1984). In the NCDS, test scores ranged from 0 to 12; in the BCS70, the range was 0 to 8.

The Southgate Reading Test (Southgate, 1962), a test of word recognition and comprehension particularly suited to identifying problems with reading in young children, was used in the NCDS. The test has good reliability (.94; Southgate, 1962). The range of scores in the NCDS was 0 to 30.

The English Picture Vocabulary Test, an adaptation of the American Peabody Picture Vocabulary Test (Brimer & Dunn, 1962), was used for the BCS70 cohort. The test has good reliability (.96; Osborn et al., 1984). It consists of 56 sets of four different pictures with a particular word associated with each set of four pictures. The child is asked to indicate the one picture that corresponds to the given word, and the test proceeds with words of increasing difficulty, until the child makes five mistakes in a run of eight consecutive items.

The Problem Arithmetic Test was used in the NCDS cohort only, because cohort members in the BCS70 were too young to have started formal training in arithmetic. This test has a satisfactory reliability of .85 (Pringle et al., 1966).

Academic Attainment at Age 10 (BCS70) and 11 (NCDS)

The National Foundation for Educational Research in England and Wales (NFER) constructed a reading comprehension test specifically for use in the NCDS (Fogelman, 1983). Good test reliability has been reported (.82; Goldstein, 1979), and scores range from 0 to 35. In the BCS70, a shortened version of the Edinburgh Reading Test, a test of word recognition, was used after consultation with the test's authors (Godfrey Thompson Unit, 1978). The

shortened test version contained 54 items that examined vocabulary, syntax, sequencing, comprehension, and retention. The test has good reliability (.87) and the items discriminate well between good and poor readers (Butler et al., 1997).

The NFER developed an arithmetic-mathematics test specifically for use in the NCDS (Fogelman, 1983). The scores range from 0 to 40. The test has good reliability (.94; Goldstein, 1979). The lack of a fully acceptable mathematics test appropriate for 10-year-olds also led to the development of a special test for the BCS70 cohort. It consisted of a total of 72 multiple choice questions and covered in essence the rules of arithmetic, number skills, fractions, measures in a variety of forms, algebra, geometry, and statistics. The test has good reliability (.92) and the items have adequate discrimination (Butler et al., 1997).

Academic Attainment at Age 16 (Both Cohorts)

Two measures of academic achievement in secondary school were considered: the highest level of secondary school examinations passed by the students at age 16, and the exam scores that students obtained when they were 16 years old (16 was the minimum legal age at which a child could leave school).

There are essentially two types of secondary school examinations that a student can pass at age 16: the Certificate of Secondary Education (CSE) examination and the ordinary (0 level) examinations within the General Certificate of Education (GCE) examinations. The GCE is the accepted examination for children of above average intelligence and caters to approximately 20% of the total age group, whereas the CSE examination is designed to cover a wider range of ability than does the GCE—an additional 40%—so that the two exams combined are intended for some three fifths of the population (Rutter, Maughan, Mortimore, & Ouston, 1979). Both the GCE and the CSE are subject based, and grades are awarded on the basis of performance with a range from 1 to 5 (or A to E). Generally, GCE grades of D and E are classified as failures. There is an accepted equivalence between the two examination systems with a grade 1 on the CSE examination being seen as equal to at least a grade C pass on the GCE examination. For both cohorts, the highest level of qualifications obtained at age 16 was recorded, ranging from none (0), CSE grade 2–5 (1), and CSE grade 1 or 0 level (2).

An overall "exam score" could also be calculated from the examination performance at age 16. The actual examination results of the NCDS cohort were collected from schools in 1978, whereas the BCS70 cohort members self-reported their examination results in a follow-up study in 1986. The examination system was the same for both cohorts, with the BCS70 being one of the last cohorts to sit the two-tiered examination structure of 0 levels and CSEs. A simple scoring technique was applied to the results, in which a score of 7 was given to a grade 10 level and a score of 1 was given to a grade 5 CSE. Scores ranged from 0 to 106 in the NCDS and from 0 to 97 in the BCS70.

Attainments in Adulthood

Adult attainment was indicated by two measures of social position: the RGSC and the Cambridge Scale (CS) assessed at age 30 for the BCS70 cohort members and at age 33 for the NCDS cohort members. The 6-point RGSC scale, developed by the Office of Population and Census Surveys (OPCS; 1990), was described above. For ease of interpretation the coding was reversed, so that a high score indicated a high social position. The CS was conceptualized as an indicator of general social advantage and lifestyle (Prandy, 1990). It is based on the analysis of friendship choices, judged to be the most accurate indication of perceived and experienced social distance between members of different occupations. The scale is measured on a 100-point continuum, whereby high scores indicate a higher level of social advantage.

Statistical Analysis: Modeling Cumulative Risk Effects

Structural equation modeling (Bollen, 1989) was used to formulate theoretically derived hypotheses about variable relations and to test postulated pathways between the variables and the assumed mediating processes involving latent variables with multiple indicators. Latent variables represent hypothetical concepts that cannot be observed or measured directly. Instead, a set of observed variables are hypothesized to be imperfect indicators of the latent variable. Because the study involved a cross-cohort comparison of data that had been collected for different surveys, some of the data were similar but not necessarily identical for the two cohorts. Great care was taken to define the latent constructs in as similar a way as possible in the two cohorts. Table 3.1 summarizes the selection of comparable indicator variables in both cohorts.

All analyses were carried out using the SEM program AMOS 4.01 (Arbuckle, 1999). The AMOS program uses maximum likelihood estimation that can be based on incomplete data, known as the full information maximum likelihood (FIML) approach. This approach is preferable to estimation based on complete data (the listwise deletion [LD] approach) because FIML estimates tend to show less bias and be more reliable than LD estimates, even when the data deviate from missing at random and are nonignorable (Arbuckle, 1996). In the LD approach, the complete data covariance matrix is the data source for the latent variable analysis. In the FIML approach, estimation is based on the many covariance matrices between observed variables for all patterns of missing data in the other observed variables. Thus, it is not possible to present a single correlation matrix for the observed variables. Instead, Appendices A and B give the FIML estimates of the correlations between the observed variables, the means and SDs for the observed variables, and the FIML estimates of means and *SDs*.

In line with current practice, several criteria were used to assess the fit of the model to the

Table 3.1   Variables and Observed Indicators in Both Cohorts

Variables	Observed Indicators
Socioeconomic risk (RISK)	
Parental social class	Father's social class
	Mother's social class
Material conditions	No housing tenure, overcrowding (>1 person per room), household amenities (shared use of bathroom), receipt of state benefits
Academic adjustment (ACA)	
Academic attainment	Ages 5 and 7: Human Figure Drawing, Copy-a-Design, Reading and vocabulary (NCDS and BCS70), and Arithmetic (NCDS only) tests
	Ages 10 and 11: Reading and mathematics tests (NCDS and BCS70)
	Age 16: Exam scores (NCDS and BCS70)
Social position in adulthood (SOC)	
Social position at age 30 (BCS70) and age 33 (NCDS)	Registrar General's measure of social class (RGSC) Cambridge Scale (CS)

NOTE: NCDS = National Child Development Study; BCS70 = British Cohort Study.

data. The x^2 statistic is overly sensitive to model misspecification when sample sizes are large or the observed variables are non-normally distributed. The root mean square error of approximation (RMSEA) gives a measure of the discrepancy in fit per degrees of freedom (Steiger, 1990). It is bounded below by 0, only taking this value if the model fits exactly. The RMSEA is useful because it encompasses the idea that a model is only expected to provide an approximation to the data rather than an exact fit. If the RMSEA is <.05, the model is considered a close fit to the data. Another advantage of the RMSEA is that confidence intervals may be calculated, which give further information on the reliability of the goodness of fit. The Consistent Akaike Information Criterion (CAIC) is a measure of parsimonious fit recommended for large samples (Bollen & Long, 1993). The CAIC considers both the fit of the model and the number of estimated parameters whereby smaller values indicate a more parsimonious fit (Bollen & Long, 1993; Bozdogan, 1987). The final index of choice was the comparative fit index (CFI) whose values are restricted to lie on a 0 to 1

continuum, with higher values indicating a better fit (Bentler, 1990). The CFI is a population-based index that compares the model to a "null model." The null model is a model in which there are no relations between any of the observed variables, but their variances are not constrained and are free to be estimated by the fitting procedure. The CFI of a model is normally tested against a minimum criterion value of .95.

Modeling Strategy

Four separate models were run for each cohort. Model 1 was the Full Developmental–Contextual Model, which included all paths indicated in Figure 3.1. In addition to Model 1 three other models were fitted to the data, to test the increase of fit depending on the pathways included, and to identify the most parsimonious model for describing the long-term influences of socioeconomic adversity on academic adjustment. Model 2 was the Developmental–Contextual Model without path "g" (which assessed the direct effect of parental social class on an individual's adult social status independent of the intervening variables). Model 3 was the Developmental–Contextual Model without paths "d" (which indicated the time-lagged effects from social risk to academic attainment). Model 4 was the Developmental–Contextual Model without the correlations "c" (which described the concurrent associations between social risk and academic attainment).

Results

The distribution of the risk indicator variables is shown in Table 3.2. Generally, material conditions improved for the later-born BCS70 cohort. In comparison with cohort members born in 1958, more families owned their home, there was less overcrowding, and fewer households had to share amenities. The percentage of families who were receiving state benefits had remained stable. Also noted was upward mobility among the parents of cohort members born in 1970, whereas

the social position of parents of the earlier born NCDS cohort remained stable over the years. If one compares the risk prevalence in the 1958 NCDS cohort at age 16 to the one in the 1970 BCS70 of the younger cohort at age 5, which were assessed at roughly the same time (i.e., 1974 and 1975, respectively), Table 3.2 shows that the distribution of social status of the parents was comparable in the two samples, as were housing tenure and shared use of amenities. Differences in the rate of overcrowding might be explained by different stages of family formation in the two cohorts.

In the next step, a set of nested alternative SEM models were run to test the increase in fit depending on the pathways included in the analysis, and to identify the most parsimonious model for describing the long-term influences of socioeconomic adversity on academic adjustment. The goodness-of fit indicators for the different models are shown in Table 3.3.

Table 3.2   Distribution of the Risk Variables in the 1958 National Child Development Study (NCDS) and the 1970 British Cohort Study (BCS70)

	Cohort (%)	
Risk Variable	*NCDS*	*BCS70*
Birth (1958/1970)		
Social class at birth (% in RGSC IV and V)	22	24
Age 7/5 (1964/1975)		
Social class (% in RGSC IV and V)	23	19
No housing tenure	55	44
Overcrowding (1+ person per room)	66	40
Shared use of amenities	19	7
Age 11/10 (1969/1980)		
Social class (% in RGSC IV and V)	23	18
No housing tenure	54	39
Overcrowding (1+ person per room)	51	30
Shared use of amenities	7	3
Family receives benefits	27	22
Age 16 (1974/1986)		
Social class (% in RGSC IV and V)	22	13
No housing tenure	50	28
Overcrowding (1+ person per room)	60	17
Shared use of amenities	7	1
Family receiving benefits	23	27

NOTE: RGSC = parental social position.

Table 3.3 Comparative Goodness of Fit of Structural Equation Models Run for the 1958 National Child Development Cohort (NCDS) and the 1970 British Cohort Study (BCS70)

	Goodness of Fit				Test of Close Fit		Step-Down Goodness of Fit		
	df	x^2	CFI	CAIC	RMSEA	90% CI	Δdf	Δx^2	p
NCDS									
Model 1: The full model	93	1,221.47	.998	1,866	.027	.025–.028			
Model 2: Excluding path "g"	94	1,229.10	.998	1,863	.027	.025–.028	1 (M2-M1)	7.63	<.01
Model 3: Excluding paths "d"	95	1,886.91	.996	2,510	.033	.032–.035	2 (M3-M1)	665.44	<.001
Model 4: Excluding correlations "c"	96	1,716.93	.997	2,329	.032	.030–.033	3 (M4-M1)	495.46	<.001
BCS70									
Model 1: The full model	77	723.73	.998	1,347	.024	.023–.026			
Model 2: Excluding path "g"	78	730.92	.998	1,344	.024	.023–.026	1 (M2-M1)	7.19	<.01
Model 3: Excluding paths "d"	79	848.12	.998	1,450	.026	.024–.028	2 (M3-M1)	124.39	<.001
Model 4: Excluding correlations "c"	80	1,022.88	.997	1,614	.029	.027–.030	3 (M4-M1)	299.15	<.001

NOTE: df = degrees of freedom; CFI = comparative fit index; CAIC = Consistent Akaike Information Criterion; RMSEA = root mean square error of approximation; CI = confidence interval.

In both cohorts Model 2 was judged to be the best model for describing the relations in the data. Because the x^2 statistic is overly sensitive to model misspecification when sample sizes are large, the x^2 statistic in conjunction with the CAIC were used to identify the best-fitting model for the data. Model 2 was run without path "g" suggesting that there were no cohort effects independent of intervening variables. Given that Model 2 was the most parsimonious in both cohorts, it is described in detail below.

Table 3.4 gives the standardized parameter estimates of the measurement model for both cohorts. The standardized regression weights of the indicator variables on their latent variable differed slightly for the two cohorts. Social class had a similar weighting in both cohorts, and was the most important indicator of socioeconomic disadvantage. Material deprivation gained more importance as the NCDS cohort members grew older, whereas for the BCS70 cohort there was a peak at age 10. The most important indicators of a child's adjustment in the NCDS were generally reading and math test scores, and at age 5 also the Human Figure Drawing and Copy-a-Design tests. The BCS70 cohort had slightly different indicators: at age 5 the Copy-a-Design test and the reading test were the principal indicators, whereas at age 10, the reading and math tests were the principal indicators. For both cohorts, test performance at age 10/11 was more crucial than earlier performance as a determinant of a child's adjustment. At age 16, the exam score was the key indicator of a child's adjustment in both cohorts, particularly so in the later-born cohort. Social status for the 33-year-old NCDS cohort members was slightly better identified by the CS than by the RGSC, whereas in the BCS70 at age 30 years, the RGSC was a better indicator than the CS.

Figures 3.2 and 3.3 show the pathways between the latent or unobserved variables, which represent continuities and interactions of social risk and academic adjustment, and give the standardized coefficients for the structural model, fitted separately for both cohorts. Several covariances between the error terms for the observed variables were included a priori to account for the autocorrelations over time. Parental social class and material deprivation were hypothesized to covary for the measurement points at consequent ages, as were the academic attainment scores. The variables shown were all latent or unobserved variables.

The hypothesized pathways were supported by the data, with the parameter estimates all being significantly different from 0, $p < .005$, and in the predicted direction. The effect sizes of the parameter estimates are described as small, $r = .10$, medium, $r = .30$, and large, $r = .50$, following Cohen's 1992 power primer. In both cohorts a stark chaining, or continuity of risk factors, was found: parental social class at birth predicted the experience of risk at subsequent ages, and the experience of risk at one time point increased the probability that risk would also be encountered at a later time point. Parental social class also had a moderate influence on academic adjustment. The experience of social risk at birth influenced the level of later academic attainment. Also observed were continuities in academic adjustment level over time. Academic attainment at one time point was a significant predictor of academic attainment at a later time point. Continuities occurred because current adjustment encompassed previous adjustment as well as earlier structural and functional change. The detrimental effect of experiencing disadvantage at one measurement point was carried forward into the future via decreased individual adjustment levels.

The model also shows concurrent associations between social risk and academic attainment. In the NCDS, these current associations (coefficients "c") were of moderate size at age 7 and 16, and were only of small size at age 11. In the BCS70, the concurrent association between social risk and academic attainment at age 5 was of moderate size, whereas at age 10 and 16 the associations were only small.

In addition, there were small time-lagged risk effects (paths "d") which indicated the added negative influence of social risk on subsequent attainment not accounted for by the risk carried

Table 3.4 The Measurement Model. Estimated Standardized Regression Weights for the National Child Development Study (NCDS) and the 1970 British Cohort Study (BCS70)

	NCDS, age 7	BCS70, age 5	NCDS, age 11	BCS70, age 10	NCDS, age 16	BCS70, age 16	NCDS, age 33	BCS70, at 30
Risk								
Risk→Parental social class	.80	.80	.78	.76	.74	.76	—	—
Risk→Material deprivation	.41	.41	.53	.50	.53	.45	—	—
Academic adjustment (ACA)								
ACA→Copy-a-Design	.48	.62	—	—	—	—	—	—
ACA→Human Figure Drawing	.50	.34	—	—	—	—	—	—
ACA→Reading	.80	.55	.85	.83	—	—	—	—
ACA→Math	.66	—	.88	.83	—	—	—	—
ACA→Exam score	—	—	—	—	.69	.87	—	—
ACA→Highest Qualification at age 16	—	—	—	—	.61	.63	—	—
Social status in adulthood								
Social status→Registrar General's measure of social class	—	—	—	—	—	—	-.88	-.74
Social status→Cambridge Score	—	—	—	—	—	—	.95	.65

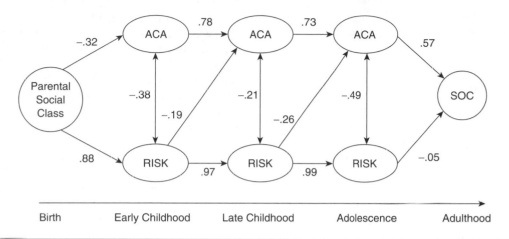

Figure 3.2 The National Child Development Study: Developmental-contextual model of accumulating risk effects from birth to adulthood. ACA = academic adjustment; Risk = socioeconomic risk; SOC = social position in adulthood. See text for further details.

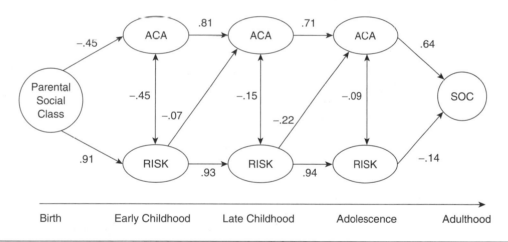

Figure 3.3 The British Cohort Study: Developmental-contextual model of accumulating risk effects from birth to adulthood. ACA = academic adjustment; Risk = socioeconomic risk; SOC = social position in adulthood. See text for further details.

forward in time. In both cohorts these time-lagged risk effects were greatest at the transition from late childhood to adolescence.

The best predictor of attained social status in early adulthood was academic attainment at age 16, which confirmed the crucial role of education in determining adult outcomes. In both cohorts, the direct influence of social risk experienced at age 16 on adult social status was only small, yet in comparison with the NCDS the effect size had nearly trebled in the BCS70. It is important to remember that the experience of social risk does have additional indirect effects on social status operating through the child's academic adjustment. For the NCDS cohort, the combined effect of the variables in the model explained 37% of the variation in adult social status; and for the BCS70 cohort, the model explained 54% of the variation.

Discussion

In the study of human development, laboratories are rare. The closest one can get to them is when the opportunity arises to compare and contrast experiences in different societies or in different sociohistorical contexts. The present study used data collected for two national birth cohort studies born 12 years apart. On comparison of the prevalence of risk indicators that were assessed at roughly the same time (e.g., parental social class or housing tenure experienced by 16-year-olds born in 1958 and 5-year-olds born in 1970, assessed in 1974 and 1975, respectively), it appears that the samples represented well the state of affairs over the historical period covered.

The data suggest that there was a real-time secular shift in material resources. For cohort members born in 1970, the indicator variables point to improved material circumstances for the cohort as a whole. Furthermore, the parents of cohort members born in 1970 experienced upward social mobility while bringing up their children. Those cohort members born in 1970 who suffered deprivation, however, appear to have been more disadvantaged relative to other children in the same cohort than similarly affected children born earlier, in 1958. A strong continuity of social risk effects was observed, which was of similar strength for both cohorts. The strength of the association can be explained by the fact that in addition to indicators of material disadvantage, indicators of SES, which denote relative position in society, were also used. However, despite improved material conditions, and the experience of upward social mobility among parents of the BCS70 cohort, the relative social position remained remarkably stable. Furthermore, the influence of parental social class at birth on academic adjustment was greater for cohort members born in 1970 than for those born in 1958, and the direct influence of social risk experienced in adolescence on adult attainment was only small, but nearly trebled for the later-born BCS70 cohort. These findings suggest that for cohort members born in 1970, contextual factors, to some extent, became more important than for cohort members born in 1958 in shaping the development of academic adjustment, and in influencing attainments in adulthood. Material conditions improved, yet socioeconomic disadvantage continued to be a barrier for individual achievements.

It has been argued that SES at the time of a child's birth is an indicator of the social context, but also reflects hereditary influences, which are assumed to have some role in determining the level of academic functioning (Plomin & Bergeman, 1991; Plomin & McClearn, 1993; Scarr, 1992). The present study's data show that the influence of social class at birth on academic adjustment was of moderate size, and differed slightly for the two cohorts. Socioeconomic disadvantage experienced consequently during childhood had an additional detrimental influence on the level of academic adjustment, suggesting that contextual factors have a role in shaping the level and maintenance of academic adjustment throughout childhood and adolescence. Furthermore, there were smalltime-lagged effects of earlier risk on later academic achievement, indicating that social risk does not always have an immediate impact, and that vulnerabilities may emerge only later in life. On the other hand a considerable stability of individual adjustment was also seen. These results suggest that adaptation is a product of both developmental history and current circumstances (Clarke & Clarke, 1981, 2000; Sroufe, Egeland, & Kreuzer, 1990), shaped by the interactions between individual and context (Bronfenbrenner & Ceci, 1994).

Generally, the findings of this study concur with a large body of previous research, which has reported consistent correlations between measures of social disadvantage and measures of individual academic achievement and occupational attainment (Blau & Duncan, 1967; Bolger et al., 1995; Bynner, Joshi, & Tsatsas, 2000; Campbell & Ramey, 1994; Duncan et al., 1994;

Felner et al., 1995; Pungello et al., 1996; Ramey & Ramey, 1990; Rutter & Madge, 1976; Sewell et al., 1970; Walker et al., 1994). The approach adopted in the present study begins to provide an understanding of the ways in which constellations of social risk and individual adjustment emerge early in the life course, and how they interrelate over time. The findings suggest that pervasive social inequalities exist that influence academic attainment during childhood, and which are consequently reflected in adult achievements. Risk experiences are not randomly distributed in a population, and being born into a relatively disadvantaged family increases the probability of accumulating risks associated with that disadvantage, setting a child onto a risk trajectory (Rutter, 1990). On the other hand, great stability in individual adjustment is also seen, and academic attainment at one time point is a strong predictor of academic attainment at a later time point.

The best predictor of adult social status was academic attainment, which confirmed the crucial role of educational achievement in determining adult outcomes. This is not to deny the influence of social risk on individual development. Experience of early social risk influences the level of academic adjustment, which in turn influences adult attainment. Despite the importance of early childhood, the data did not conclusively support the assumption that parental social class at birth has a strong influence on an individual's adult social status independent of intervening experiences. The early family environment is important in shaping subsequent development, yet intervening processes also have to be considered to obtain a better understanding of adult outcomes. The whole life course is important, not just the early years. The findings of this study lend support to the proposition made by Bronfenbrenner and Ceci (1994) that individual adaptation across the life span is a joint function of the characteristics of the developing person and the context—both proximal and more remote—in which development takes place. The experience of early disadvantage weakens individual adjustment, and this

detrimental effect is then carried forward into the future. Subsequent experiences of adversity add to the deterioration of already reduced adjustment. A general premise of life-course studies postulates that adaptations to change are influenced by what people bring to the new situation. If individual adjustment is already weakened at a very early age, it becomes increasingly difficult to fully develop one's potential. This negative chain effect undermines the academic adjustment of the young person, and ultimately the individual attainments in adulthood. Generally the results imply that cumulative adversity has effects beyond those associated with current or early adversity (Ackerman et al., 1999; Bolger et al., 1995; Duncan et al., 1994; Pungello et al., 1996). As suggested by Sroufe et al. (1990), adjustment problems possibly do not lie with the individual per se but in the persistent adjustment of the individual to adverse conditions over time. Children growing up in households in which they have no room of their own, or possibly even a desk or table at which to complete their homework, are less likely than their more privileged peers to do well in school.

The data further suggest differences in the timing of risk effects. Among cohort members born in 1958 (NCDS), the influence of concurrent social risk was greatest during early childhood, at age 7, and during adolescence, at age 16, when important decisions about future careers are made. Among cohort members born in 1970 (BCS70), the greatest effect of concurrent risk on individual adjustment was found at age 5, whereas at later ages the cohort members appeared to be comparatively unaffected by current socioeconomic family circumstances over and above those already accounted for by previous experiences of socioeconomic adversity. These differences in timing of risk effects might be explained by changes in the sociohistorical context. Cohort members turned 16 in 1974 and 1986, respectively. In consequence to the virtual disappearance of the youth labor market that occurred between 1979 and 1986, the later-born cohort encountered more complex and varied education, training, and employment choices. Although in the 1970s the predominant pattern was to leave school at the minimum age and move directly into a job, by the 1990s most young people continued in full-time education after the age of 16 (Bynner et al., 1999; Bynner, Joshi, & Tsatsas, 2000). Cohort members born in 1970 were under increasing pressure to acquire formal qualifications, whereas most young people born in 1958 could expect to obtain employment regardless of their educational attainment (Bynner et al., 2000). Thus, parents of cohort members born in 1958, especially less privileged parents, might not have pushed their children to obtain good grades, and rather might have encouraged their children to leave school early to earn a wage. Parents in the later-born BCS70 cohort, in contrast, might have generally put more emphasis on achieving good examination results, whatever their socioeconomic circumstances. It could also be that in the later-born BCS70 cohort, other factors—such as support from the school environment or contact with peers—which were not captured in the model, might have played a more important role in influencing academic achievement than in the earlier-born NCDS cohort.

In interpreting the findings, some limitations of the study should be noted. This work involved a cross-cohort comparison of the constellations between adversities and adjustment of individuals growing up 12 years apart. A latent-variable modeling approach was used to convey our theoretical framework for assessing the impact of contextual risk on individual development from birth to early adulthood. The emphasis was on investigating relations between latent variables in the two cohorts, rather than on the relations between observed variables. Great care was taken to measure the latent variables in as similar a way as possible in the two cohorts. As with all research using cohort studies, this work was constrained by data collected up to 40 years ago in light of research practice prevalent at that time. There are always limitations placed on comparative analysis across cohort studies that were not designed to measure the same variables, and stronger associations might have been obtained by using different indicator variables. It may also be that missing data at the individual level and at the variable level affected the validity of the results. Response bias at the individual level would tend to underestimate the magnitude of the effects of social disadvantage on individual adjustment, because sample attrition is greatest among individuals in more deprived circumstances. The results may thus provide a conservative estimate of social inequalities experienced in childhood. Missing data at the variable level may also be nonrandom. The FIML approach has been adopted as a "best effort" technique for dealing with these problems, but bias in the model estimates may still be present. Nonetheless, the data offers a unique opportunity to investigate the processes that link the experience of early socioeconomic disadvantage, academic achievement, and adult occupational attainment in two cohorts growing up in a changing sociohistorical context. Comparisons with other studies on the long-term effects of socioeconomic risk are compromised by the lack of consistency in the measures of social risk and individual adjustment across the life course. This study was designed to measure the extent to which ill effects of social disadvantage persist over time, and the way in which the constellations of social risk and academic adjustment emerge in a changing sociohistorical context. Future research should explore in more detail the factors and processes that modify the constellations between risk and adjustment (e.g., individual temperament or personality characteristics, parenting styles, or characteristics of the school environment) that can act as protective factors by impeding or halting the negative chain process, and enabling the child to move into positive directions (Masten et al., 1990; Rutter, 1990; Schoon & Parsons, 2002b; Werner & Smith, 1992). The present study has shown that the constellations of social risk and academic adjustment vary by age, context, and duration of the experiences, suggesting that different factors and processes might be important at different developmental stages, indifferent contexts, and for different developmental outcomes.

It can be concluded that the contextual perspective within life-course research offers a useful framework that contributes to a fuller understanding of the processes that link social disadvantage to individual development. The impact of risk factors depends on characteristics of the individual, but also on the context, including the proximal family environment as well as the wider sociohistorical context that dictates opportunities and possibilities. The effects of socioeconomic disadvantage are cumulative. Both the timing and duration of risk experiences play a role in shaping individual adjustment, and for a better understanding of successful adaptation it is necessary to consider the dynamic interaction between a changing individual and a changing context. The whole life path is important in shaping individual development, not just the early years. This study has confirmed the vital role of contextual experiences on individual adjustment, and thus underlines the importance of an ecological approach within developmental psychology.

Acknowledgments

This work was funded by the U.K. Economic and Social Research Council (Grant No. R000238051). Previous versions of this article were presented at the XXVII International Congress of Psychology in Stockholm (July 2000), the 42nd Congress of the German Psychological Society in Jena (September 2000), and the London Conference of the British Psychological Society (December 2000). Thanks are due to the anonymous reviewers of an earlier draft of this paper for their helpful and constructive comments.

Addresses and Affiliations

Corresponding author: Ingrid Schoon, Department of Psychology, City University, London, Northampton Square, London EC1V OHB, U.K.; e-mail: i.schoon@city.ac.uk. John Bynner, Heather Joshi, and Samantha Parsons are at The Institute of Education, London; Richard D. Wiggins is also at the City University, London; and Amanda Sacker is at Royal Free and University College Medical School, London.

References

Ackerman, B. P., Schoff, K., Levinson, K., Youngstrom, E., & Izard, C. E. (1999). The relations between cluster indexes of risk and promotion and the problem behaviours of 6- and 7-year-old children from economically disadvantaged families. *Developmental Psychology, 6,* 1355–1366.

Arbuckle, J. C. (1996). Full information estimation in the presence of incomplete data. In G. A. Marcoulides & R. E. Schumacker (Eds.), *Advanced structural equation modelling techniques.* Mahwah, NJ: Erlbaum.

Arbuckle, J. C. (1999). *AMOS for Windows. Analysis of moment structures. Version 4.01 [Computer software].* Chicago: SmallWaters.

Axinn, W., Duncan, G. J., & Thornton, A. (1997). The effects of parents' income, wealth, and attitudes on children's completed schooling and self-esteem. In G. J. Duncan & J. Brooks-Gunn (Eds.), *Consequences of growing up poor* (pp. 518–540). New York: Russell Sage Foundation.

Baltes, P. B. (1987). Theoretical propositions of life-span developmental psychology: On the dynamics between growth and decline. *Developmental Psychology, 23,* 611–626.

Banks, M., Bates, I., Breakwell, G., Bynner, J., Emler, N., Jamieson, L., & Roberts, K. (1992). *Careers and identities.* Milton Keynes, UK: Open University Press.

Baumrind, D. (1993). The average expectable environment is not good enough. A response to Scarr. *Child Development, 64,* 1299–1317.

Bentler, P. M. (1990). Comparative fit indices in structural models. *Psychological Bulletin, 107,* 238–246.

Birch, H. G., & Gussow, J. D. (1970). *Disadvantaged children: Health, nutrition and school failure.* New York: Grune & Stratton.

Blau, P. M., & Duncan, O. D. (1967). *The American occupational structure.* New York: Wiley.

Bolger, K. E., Patterson, C. J., & Thompson, W. W. (1995). Psychosocial adjustment among children experiencing persistent and intermittent family economic hardship. *Child Development, 66,* 1107–1129.

Bollen, K. A. (1989). *Structural equations with latent variables.* New York: Wiley.

Bollen, K. A., & Long, J. S. (Eds.). (1993). *Testing structural equation models.* Newbury Park, CA: Sage.

Bozdogan, H. (1987). Model section and Akaike's Information Criteria (AIC): The general theory and its analytical extensions. *Psychometrika, 52,* 345–370.

Brimer, M. A., & Dunn, L. M. (1962). *English Picture Vocabulary Test.* Bristol, UK: Education Evaluation Enterprises.

Bronfenbrenner, U. (1979). *The ecology of human development: Experiments by nature and design.* Cambridge, MA: Harvard University Press.

Bronfenbrenner, U., & Ceci, S. J. (1994). Nature-nurture re-conceptualized in developmental perspective: A bioecological model. *Psychological Review, 101,* 568–586.

Butler, N., Despotidou, S., & Shepherd, P. (1997). *1970 British Cohort Study (BCS70) ten-year follow-up: A guide to the BCS70 10-year data available at the Economic and Social Research Unit data archive.* London: City University, Social Statistics Research Unit.

Bynner, J., Elias, P., McKnight, A., & Pan, H. (1999). *The changing nature of the youth labour market in Great Britain* (Report to the Rowntree Foundation). York, UK: Joseph Rowntree Foundation.

Bynner, J., Ferri, E., & Shepherd, P. (Eds.). (1997). *Getting on, getting by, getting nowhere. Twenty-something in the 1990's.* Aldershot, UK: Ashgate.

Bynner, J., Ferri, E., Shepherd, P., & Smith, K. (2000). *The 1999–2000 surveys of the National Child Development Study and the 1970 British Cohort Study* (Working paper No. 1). London: Centre for Longitudinal Studies.

Bynner, J., Joshi, H., & Tsatsas, M. (2000). *Obstacles and opportunities on the route to adulthood.* London: Smith Institute.

Caprara, G. V., & Rutter, M. (1995). Individual development and social change. In M. Rutter & D. J. Smith (Eds.), *Psychosocial disorders in young people* (pp. 35–66). Chichester, UK: Wiley.

Campbell, F. A., & Ramey, C. T. (1994). Effects of early intervention on intellectual and academic achievement. A follow-up study of children from low-income families. *Child Development, 65,* 684–698.

Campbell, S. B., Pierce, E. W., Moore, G., Marakovitz, S., & Newby, K. (1996). Boys' externalizing problems at elementary school age: Pathways from early behavioural problems, maternal control, and family stress. *Development and Psychopathology, 8,* 701–719.

Caspi, A., Wright, B. R. E., Moffitt, T. E., & Silva, P. A. (1998). Early failure in the labor market: Childhood and adolescent predictors of unemployment in the transition to adulthood. *American Sociological Review, 63,* 424–451.

Cicchetti, D., & Garmezy, N. (Eds.). (1993). Milestones in the development of resilience. *Development and Psychopathology, 5,* 497–774.

Cicchetti, D., & Tucker, D. (1994). Development and self-regulatory structures of the mind. *Development and Psychopathology, 6,* 533–549.

Clarke, A. D. B., & Clarke, A. M. (1981). Sleeper effects in development: Fact or artefact. *Developmental Review, 1,* 344–360.

Clarke, A. D. B., & Clarke, A. M. (2000). *Early experience and the life path.* London: Jessica Kingsley.

Cohen, J. (1992). A power primer. *Psychological Bulletin, 112,* 155–159.

Conger, R. D., Conger, K. J., Elder, G. H., Lorenz, F. O., Simons, R. L., & Whitbeck, L. B. (1993). Family economic stress and adjustment of early adolescent girls. *Developmental Psychology, 29,* 206–219.

Davie, R., Butler, H., & Goldstein, H. (1972). *From birth to seven: The second report of the National Child Development Study (1958 Cohort).* London: Longman.

Deater-Deckard, K., Dodge, K. A., Bates, J. E., & Pettit, G. S. (1998). Multiple risk factors in the development of externalising behavior problems: Group and individual differences. *Development and Psychopathology, 10,* 469–494.

Duncan, G. J., & Brooks-Gunn, J. (Eds.). (1997). *Consequences of growing up poor.* New York: Russell Sage Foundation.

Duncan, G. J., Brooks-Gunn, J., & Klebanov, P. K. (1994). Economic deprivation and early childhood development. *Child Development, 65,* 296–318.

Duncan, G. J., & Rodgers, W. L. (1988). Longitudinal aspects of poverty. *Journal of Marriage and the Family, 50,* 1007–1021.

Duncan, G. J., Yeung, W. J., Brooks-Gunn, J., & Smith, J. R. (1998). How much does childhood poverty affect the life chances of children? *American Sociological Review, 63,* 406–423.

Ekinsmyth, C., Bynner, J., Montgomery, S., & Shepherd, P. (1992). *An integrated approach to* the design and analysis of the 1970 British Cohort Study (BCS70) and the National Child Development Study (NCDS) (Working paper No. 1). London: City University, Social Statistics Research Unit Cohort Studies.

Elder, G. H., Jr. (Ed.). (1985). *Life course dynamics.* Ithaca, NY: Cornell University Press.

Elder, G. H., Jr. (1999). *Children of the Great Depression. Social change in life experience* (25th anniversary ed.). Boulder, CO: Westview Press.

Elder, G. H., Pavalko, E. K., & Hastings, T. H. (1991). Talent, history and the fulfillment of promise. *Psychiatry, 54,* 251–267.

Featherman, D. L., & Lerner, R. M. (1985). Ontogenesis and sociogenesis. Problematics for theory about development across the life-span. *American Sociological Review, 50,* 659–676.

Feiring, C., & Lewis, M. (1996). Finality in the eye of the beholder: Multiple sources, multiple time points, multiple paths. *Development and Psychopathology, 8,* 721–733.

Felner, R. D., Brand, S., DuBois, D. L., Adan, A., Mulhall, P. F., & Evans, E. G. (1995). Socioeconomic disadvantage, proximal environmental experiences, and socioemotional and academic adjustment in early adolescence: Investigation of a mediated effects model. *Child Development, 66,* 774–792.

Fergusson, D. M., Horwood, L. J., & Lawton, J. M. (1990). Vulnerability to childhood problems and family social background. *Journal of Child Psychology and Psychiatry, 31,* 1145–1160.

Fergusson, D. M., Horwood, L. J., & Lynskey, M. T. (1994). The childhoods of multiple problem adolescents: A 15-year longitudinal study. *Journal of Child Psychology and Psychiatry, 35,* 1123–1140.

Fitzgerald, H. E., Lester, B. M., & Zuckerman, B. S. (1995). *Children of poverty: Research, health, and policy issues.* New York: Garland.

Fogelman, K. (Ed.). (1983). *Growing up in Great Britain. Papers from the National Child Development Study.* London: Macmillan (for the National Children's Bureau).

Garmezy, N. (1985). Stress-resistant children: The search for protective factors. In A. Davids (Ed.), *Recent research in developmental psychopathology* (pp. 213–233). Elmsford, NY: Pergamon.

Garmezy, N. (1991). Resilience and vulnerability to adverse developmental outcomes associated with poverty. *American Behavioural Scientist, 34,* 416–430.

Godfrey Thompson Unit, University of Edinburgh. (1978). *Edinburgh Reading Test.* Sevenoaks, UK: Hodder and Stoughton.

Goldstein, H. (1979). Some models for analyzing longitudinal data on educational attainment. *Journal of the Royal Statistical Society (Series A), 142,* 407–442.

Gottlieb, G., Wahlsten, D., & Lickliter, R. (1998). The significance of biology for human development: A developmental psychobiological systems view. In R. M. Lerner (Ed.), W. Damon (Series Ed.), *Handbook of child psychology: Vol. 1. Theoretical models of human development* (5th ed., pp. 233–274). New York: Wiley.

Goodenough, F. (1926). *Measurement of intelligence by drawings.* New York: Harcourt, Brace & World.

Greenberg, M. T., Lengua, L. J., Coie, J. D., & Pinderhughes, E. E. (1999). Predicting developmental outcomes at school entry using a multiple-risk model: Four American communities. *Developmental Psychology, 35,* 403–417.

Hammen, C. (1992). Cognitive, life stress, and interpersonal approaches to a developmental psychopathological model of depression. *Development and Psychopathology, 4,* 189–206.

Harris, D. B. (1963). *Children's drawings as measures of intellectual maturity.* New York: Harcourt, Brace & World.

Haveman, R., & Wolfe, B. (1994). *Succeeding generations: On the effects of investments in children.* New York: Russell Sage Foundation.

Hoffman, L. W. (1994). A proof and a disproof questioned. *Social Development, 3,* 60–63.

Horowitz, F. D. (2000). Child development and the PITS: Simple questions, complex answers, and developmental theory. *Child Development, 71,* 1–10.

Huston, A. C., McLoyd, V. C., & Coll, C. G. (1994). Children and poverty: Issues in contemporary research. *Child Development, 65,* 275–282.

Jackson, J. F. (1993). Human behavioral genetics. Scarr's theory and her views on interventions: A critical review and comments on their implications for American children. *Child Development, 63,* 1318–1332.

Koppitz, E. M. (1968). *Psychological evaluation of children's human figure drawings.* New York: Grune & Stratton.

Krieger, N., & Williams, D. R. (1997). Measuring social class in US public health research: Concepts, methodologies and guidelines. *Annual Review of Public Health, 18,* 341–378.

Leete, R., & Fox, J. (1977). Registrar General's social classes: Origins and users. *Population Trends, 8,* 1–7.

Lerner, R. M. (1984). *On the nature of human plasticity.* New York: Cambridge University Press.

Lerner, R. M. (1996). Relative plasticity, integration, temporality, and diversity in human development: A developmental contextual perspective about theory, process, and method. *Developmental Psychology, 32,* 781–786.

Lerner, R. M., & von Eye, A. (1992). Sociobiology and human development: Arguments and evidence. *Human Development, 35,* 12–33.

Luthar, S. S., Cicchetti, D., & Becker, B. (2000). The construct of resilience. A critical evaluation and guidelines for future work. *Child Development, 71,* 543–562.

Marsh, C. (1986). Social class and occupation. In R. Burgess (Ed.), *Key variables in social investigation* (pp. 123–152). London: Routledge.

Masten, A. S., Best, K. M., & Garmezy, N. (1990). Resilience and development: Contributions from the study of children who overcome adversity. *Development and Psychopathology, 2,* 425–444.

McLoyd, V. C. (1990). The impact of economic hardships on black families and children: Psychological distress, parenting, and socioemotional development. *Child Development, 61,* 311–346.

OPCS (Office of Population Censuses and Surveys) and Employment Department Group. (1980). *Standard Classification of Occupations (SOC).* London: Her Majesty's Stationery Office.

OPCS (Office of Population Censuses and Surveys) and Employment Department Group. (1990). *Standard Classification of Occupations (SOC).* London: Her Majesty's Stationery Office.

Osborn, A. F., Butler, N. R., & Morris, A. C. (1984). *The social life of Britain's five-year-olds.* London: Routledge.

Pilling, D. (1990). *Escape from disadvantage.* London: Palmer Press.

Plomin, R., & Bergeman, C. S. (1991). The nature of nurture: Genetic influence on "environmental" measures. *Behavioral and Brain Sciences, 14,* 373–427.

Plomin, R., & Daniels, D. (1987). Why are children in the same family so different from one another? *Behavioral and Brain Sciences, 10,* 1–16.

Plomin, R., & McClearn, G. E. (Eds.). (1993). *Nature, nurture and psychology* Washington, DC: American Psychological Association.

Prandy, K. (1990). The revised Cambridge Scale of occupations. *Sociology, 24,* 629–655.

Pringle, M. L. K., Butler, N. R., & Davie, R. (1966). *11,000 seven year olds.* London: Longman.

Pungello, E. P., Kupersmidt, J. B., Burchinal, M. R., & Patterson, C. J. (1996). Environmental risk factors and children's achievement from middle childhood to early adolescence. *Developmental Psychology, 32,* 755–767.

Ramey, C. T., & Ramey, S. L. (1990). Intensive education intervention for children of poverty. *Intelligence, 14,* 1–9.

Robins, L. N., & Rutter, M. (Eds.). (1990). *Straight and devious pathways from childhood to adulthood.* Cambridge, UK: Cambridge University Press.

Rutter, M. (1979). Protective factors in children's responses to stress and disadvantage. In M. W. Kent & J. E. Rolf (Eds.), *Primary prevention in psychopathology* (Vol. 3, pp. 49–74). Hanover, NH: University Press of New England.

Rutter, M. (1990). Psychosocial resilience and protective mechanisms. In J. Rolf, A. S. Masten, D. Chicchetti, K. H. Nuechterlin, & S. Weintraub (Eds.), *Risk and protective factors in the development of psychopathology* (pp. 181–214). New York: Cambridge University Press.

Rutter, M., & Madge, N. (1976). *Cycles of disadvantage: A review of research.* London: Heinemann Educational Books.

Rutter, M., Maughan, B., Mortimore, P., & Ouston, J. (1979). *Fifteen thousand hours. Secondary schools and their effects on children.* London: Open Books.

Sameroff, A. J. (1983). Developmental systems: Contexts and evolution. In W. Kessen (Ed.), P. H. Mussen (Series Ed.). *Handbook of child psychology: Vol. 1. History, theory and methods* (pp. 237–294). New York: Wiley.

Sameroff, A. J., Seifer, R., Baldwin, A., & Baldwin, C. (1993). Stability of intelligence from preschool to adolescence: The influence of social and family risk factors. *Child Development, 64,* 80–97.

Scarr, S. (1992). Developmental theories for the 1990s: Development and individual differences. *Child Development, 63,* 1–19.

Schoon, I., McCulloch, A., Joshi, H., Wiggins, R. D., & Bynner, J. (2001). Transitions from school to work in a changing social context. *Young, 9,* 4–23.

Schoon, I., & Parsons, S. (2002a). Teenage aspirations for future careers and occupational outcomes. *Journal of Vocational Behavior, 60,* 262–288.

Schoon, I., & Parsons, S. (2002b). Competence in the face of adversity: The impact of early family environment and long-term consequences. *Children & Society, 16,* 260–272.

Schulenberg, J., Vondracek, F. W., & Crouter, A. C. (1984). The influence of the family on vocational development. *Journal of Marriage and the Family, 10,* 129–143.

Scott, L. H. (1981). Measuring intelligence with the Good-enough-Harris drawing test. *Psychological Bulletin, 89,* 483–505.

Sewell, W. H., Hailer, A. O., & Ohlendorf, G. W. (1970). The educational and early occupational status attainment process: Replication and revision. *American Sociological Review, 35,* 1014–1027.

Shepherd, P. (1993). Analysis of response bias. In E. Ferri (Ed.), *Life at 33. The fifth follow-up of the National Child Development Study* (pp. 184–188). London: National Children's Bureau and City University.

Shepherd, P. (1995). *The National Child Development Study. An introduction, its origins and the methods of data collection* (Working paper No. 1). London: City University, Social Statistics Research Unit.

Shepherd, P. (1997). Survey and response. In J. Bynner, E. Ferri, & P. Shepherd (Eds.), *Getting on, getting by, getting nowhere. Twenty-something in the 1990's* (pp. 129–136). Aldershot, UK: Ashgate.

Southgate, V. (1962). *Southgate Reading Tests: Manual of instructions.* London: University of London Press.

Sroufe, L. A., Egeland, B., & Kreuzer, T. (1990). The fate of early experience following developmental change: Longitudinal approaches to individual adaptation in childhood. *Child Development, 61,* 1363–1373.

Steiger, J. H. (1990). Structural model evaluation and modification: An internal estimation approach. *Multivariate Behavioural Research, 25,* 173–180.

Szatmari, P., Shannon, H. S., & Offord, D. R. (1994). Models of multiple risk: Psychiatric disorder and poor school performance. *International Journal of Methods in Psychiatric Research, 4,* 231–240.

Tizard, J. (1976). Psychology and social policy. *British Psychological Society Bulletin, 29,* 225–234.

Walker, D., Greenwood, C., Hart, B., & Carta, J. (1994). Prediction of school outcomes based on early language production and socio-economic factors. *Child Development, 65,* 606–621.

Werner, E. E., & Smith, R. S. (1992). *Overcoming the odds: High risk children from birth to adulthood.* Ithaca, NY: Cornell University Press.

APPENDIX A

Bivariate Correlations, Means, SDs, and Sample Sizes for the Variables in the 1958 National Child Development Dataset, Including the Full Information Maximum Likelihood (FIML) Estimates from the AMOS Modeling

	1	2	3	4	5	6	7	8	9	10	11	12	13	14	15	16	17
1. Parental RGSC birth																	
2. Own RGSC at age 33	-.21																
3. Own CS at age 33	-.23	.81															
4. Exam score at age 16	-.26	.26	.28														
5. Highest qualifications at age 16	-.22	.22	.24	.77													
6. Parental RGSC at age 16	.49	-.21	-.23	-.26	-.23												
7. Material conditions at age 16	.35	-.15	-.16	-.18	-.16	.32											
8. Math test at age 11	-.30	.32	.35	.44	.37	-.30	-.21										
9. Reading test at age 11	-.29	.31	.34	.41	.35	-.29	-.20	.72									
10. Parental RGSC at age 11	.56	-.23	-.25	-.28	-.24	.63	.35	-.34	-.33								
11. Material conditions at age 11	.37	-.15	-.16	-.18	-.16	.32	.62	-.23	-.22	.37							
12. Arithmetic test at age 7	-.18	.21	.23	.27	.23	-.18	-.13	.53	.45	-.21	-.14						
13. Reading test at age 7	-.21	.25	.27	.33	.28	-.22	-.16	.56	.58	-.25	-.17	.51					
14. Drawing test at age 7	-.13	.15	.17	.20	.17	-.19	-.10	.35	.33	-.15	-.10	.31	.34				
15. Copy test at age 7	-.13	.15	.16	.19	.17	-.13	-.10	.33	.32	-.15	-.10	.30	.32	.36			
16. Parental RGSC at age 7	.59	-.23	-.25	-.28	-.24	.58	.34	-.34	-.33	.69	.37	-.22	-.27	-.16	-.16		
17. Material conditions at age 7	.30	-.12	-.13	-.14	-.12	.25	.39	-.18	-.17	.28	.48	-.11	-.14	-.08	-.08	.30	
Observed variables																	
M	3.83	3.34	34.98	17.78	1.17	3.62	.86	16.74	16.06	3.68	3.69	5.13	23.40	23.83	7.02	3.77	.85
SD	1.23	1.33	19.11	18.14	.83	1.27	.96	10.29	6.21	1.27	1.28	2.48	7.10	7.07	2.07	1.24	.89
N	10,693	10,838	9,114	9,114	10,320	10,665	13,125	13,129	12,605	12,790	14,065	14,098	13,839	14,056	13,749	13,756	16,994
FIML estimates																	
M	3.83	3.34	33.86	16.74	1.13	3.62	.87	16.65	16.00	3.68	3.69	5.13	23.38	23.81	7.02	3.77	.85
SD	1.23	1.33	19.26	18.22	.84	1.28	.97	10.35	6.25	1.27	1.28	2.48	7.11	7.07	2.01	1.24	.89
N	16,994	16,994	16,994	16,994	16,994	16,994	16,994	16,994	16,994	16,994	16,994	16,994	16,994	16,994	16,994	16,994	16,994

NOTE: RGSC = Registrar General Social Class; CS = Cambridge Score.

APPENDIX B

Bivariate Correlations, Means, SDs, and Sample Sizes for the Variables in the 1970 British Birth Cohort Dataset, Including the Full Information Maximum Likelihood (FIML) Estimates from the AMOS Modeling

	1	2	3	4	5	6	7	8	9	10	11	12	13	14	15	16
1. Parental RGSC birth																
2. Own RGSC at age 30	-.22															
3. Own CS at age 30	-.13	.30														
4. Exam score at age 16	-.28	.20	.18													
5. Highest qualifications at age 16	-.20	.21	.13	.53												
6. Parental RGSC at age 16	.44	-.19	-.11	-.25	-.18											
7. Material conditions at age 16	.27	-.11	-.07	-.15	-.10	.24										
8. Math test at age 10	-.28	.27	.16	.41	.29	-.24	-.15									
9. Reading test at age 10	-.29	.27	.16	.41	.30	-.24	-.15	.75								
10. Parental RGSC at age 10	.55	-.22	-.13	-.28	-.20	.56	.27	-.30	-.30							
11. Material conditions at age 10	.33	-.13	-.08	-.17	-.12	.26	.44	-.18	-.18	.33						
12. Reading test at age 5	-.19	.15	.09	.20	.16	-.15	-.10	.31	.33	-.19	-.11					
13. Drawing test at age 5	-.23	.18	.11	.27	.19	-.19	-.11	.39	.38	-.23	-.14	.30				
14. Copy test at age 5	-.12	.10	.06	.15	.10	-.10	-.06	.20	.24	-.13	-.08	.21	.36			
15. Parental RGSC at age 5	.60	-.23	-.14	-.29	-.20	.52	.25	-.31	-.31	.66	.32	-.21	-.26	-.14		
16. Material conditions at age 5	.30	-.11	-.07	-.14	-.10	.21	.32	-.15	-.16	.26	.42	-.11	-.13	-.07	.30	
Observed variables																
M	3.78	2.97	49.44	21.94	1.40	3.25	.76	43.98	40.25	3.48	.86	32.78	11.34	4.73	3.55	.65
SD	1.20	1.20	16.12	16.65	.69	1.26	1.06	12.33	12.64	1.26	1.05	9.76	3.28	1.97	1.27	.92
N	14,229	8,002	5,183	5,603	6,457	6,590	9,032	11,251	11,258	12,730	10,051	9,805	12,177	12,355	11,929	12,056
FIML estimates																
M	3.77	2.98	48.41	18.00	1.32	3.48	.79	43.91	40.17	3.50	.87	33.18	11.29	4.70	3.58	.66
SD	1.20	1.25	17.13	16.28	.70	1.26	1.08	12.40	12.71	1.27	1.05	9.83	3.29	1.98	1.28	.92
N	14,229	14,229	14,229	14,229	14,229	14,229	14,229	14,229	14,229	14,229	14,229	14,229	14,229	14,229	14,229	14,229

NOTE: RGSC = Registrar General Social Class; CS = Cambridge Score.

Marital Status Continuity and Change Among Young and Midlife Adults: Longitudinal Effects on Psychological Well-Being

Nadine F. Marks and James David Lambert

Abstract

Using a life course theoretical framework, this study examined longitudinal effects of continuity and transitions in marital status on multiple dimensions of psychological well-being. Data came from National Survey of Families and Households 1987–1993 respondents ages 19 to 65 (N = 6,948). Differences between men and women as well as between young and midlife adults were investigated. Multivariate analyses revealed a complex pattern of effects depending on the contrast and the outcome examined. Although marriage continued to promote well-being for both men and women, in some cases—for example, autonomy, personal growth—the single fared better than the married. The effects of continuity in single status were not very different for women in contrast to men. The transition to divorce or widowhood was associated with somewhat more negative effects for women. Midlife adults evidenced more psychological resilience than young adults did in facing the challenges of a marital transition or remaining single over time.

The social institution of marriage and its influence on adult well-being remains an enduring interest of family researchers. Historically, marriage has been quite consistently associated with better psychological well-being than being single, particularly among men (e.g., Gove, Hughes, & Style, 1983; Gove & Shin, 1989; Gove, Style, & Hughes, 1990; Lee, Seccombe, & Shehan, 1991; Ross, Mirowsky, & Goldsteen, 1990). However, there continues to be an ongoing reassessment of the role marriage plays in determining well-being as dramatic changes in the norms, meaning, and dynamics of marriage and marital stability have swept across America during the past several decades. Now that about one in every two new marriages ends in divorce (Castro-Martin & Bumpass, 1989)—sexuality and even parenthood are increasingly less tied to marriage (Bumpass, 1990); gendered aspects of marital, parenting, and employment roles have come under increased scrutiny and influence in marital choice and satisfaction (Goldscheider & Waite, 1991); and the prevalence of single adults and the proportion of the adult lifetime spent single has increased to make it a statistically less deviant adult social status (Schoen & Weinick, 1993; Schoen, Urton, Woodrow, & Baj, 1985)—it might be hypothesized that the importance of marriage for contemporary adults' psychological well-being is changing (Glenn & Weaver, 1988).

The life course and life span developmental perspectives (Baltes, 1987; Elder, 1992; Featherman,

1983) suggest that human development is lifelong and that it is important to examine the sequelae of continuities and changes in adulthood as well as childhood. Child developmentalists track the importance of continuity and change (e.g., loss) in the primary attachment tie with a parent (usually the mother) for a child's well-being (Bowlby, 1969, 1973, 1980; Bretherton, 1992). During adulthood, continuity and change in the primary attachment with a marital partner might also be expected to have important consequences for adult well-being.

Although marriage has been generally associated with better mental health, most of the evidence for the positive effects of marriage on psychological well-being is based on cross-sectional evidence, samples with limited generalizability, or both. A few longitudinal studies of marriage have been used to confirm that the transition to divorced status has negative effects on well being (e.g., Booth & Amato, 1991; Doherty, Su, & Needle, 1989; Mastekaasa, 1995; Menaghan & Lieberman, 1986). Similarly, the psychological distress accompanying the adjustment to widowhood has been confirmed longitudinally (Stroebe & Stroebe, 1987; Wortman, Silver, & Kessler, 1993; see Kitson, Babri, Roach, & Placidi, 1989, for a review). However, no large-scale national longitudinal analysis has simultaneously examined the effects of continuity in varying marital statuses and varying types of marital status change on well-being. Specifically, longitudinal population analyses comparing the well-being effects of the transition from being never married to first married, formerly married to remarried, and married to widowed with being continuously married do not exist. A systematic examination of gender differences in the effects of these different marital statuses and transitions has never been undertaken. In addition, multiple well-being contrasts among persons remaining continuously in a marital status or making a marital transition in young adulthood, in contrast to middle adulthood, have never been carefully examined, even though a considerable number of marital transitions occur during both periods (Uhlenberg, Cooney, & Boyd, 1990). Taking a life course or life span

developmental perspective, we might expect that differential timing of a transition would make a difference in its effect on well-being (Hagestad, 1990; Hagestad & Smyer, 1982; Neugarten, 1979).

Limited outcome measures of psychological well-being plague most studies of gender, marital status, and psychological well-being. Depression, life satisfaction, and global happiness are the most common outcomes examined. However, the multiple dimensions of psychological well-being are becoming increasingly well mapped and well measured (Bryant & Veroff, 1982; Ryff, 1989, 1995; Ryff & Essex, 1991; Ryff & Keyes, 1995). For a more differentiated and comprehensive understanding of the contemporary effects of the marital role on well-being, it is desirable to consider several dimensions of psychological well-being, because marriage may be associated with well-being constraints as well as well-being enhancement.

The focus of this research was to use recent longitudinal national survey data, which included measurement across a wide range of positive and negative psychological well-being dimensions, to examine the effects of marital status continuity and marital status transitions (change) on psychological well-being, and to examine gender differences and age (young adult vs. midlife adult) differences in these effects.

Theoretical and Empirical Background

Continuity and Change in Life Course and Life Span Development

The life course and life span developmental perspectives suggest that adult development is characterized by a complex interplay of continuity and change no less than child development (Baltes, 1987; Elder, 1992; Featherman, 1983). Family life transitions as well as family life continuity are important components of the process that helps constitute adult development and adult well-being (Bengtson & Allen, 1993; Elder, 1991). Social context and how it changes over time (Riley, Foner, & Waring, 1988) also help determine the social meanings, rewards, and sanctions for family life continuities and changes, which are critical for determining the developmental impact of continuity and transitions in family roles.

In addition, the life course and life span perspectives suggest that social clocks help determine an expectable normative sequencing of events for the life course (Bengtson & Allen, 1993). Transitions that are socially normative and "on time" are expected to be more easily incorporated into one's identity and more supported by social institutions, therefore yielding more beneficial effects on well-being than transitions that are non-normative or "off time" (Hagestad, 1990; Hagestad & Smyer, 1982; Neugarten, 1979). The social script for young adulthood in most societies, including 20th-century America, has included entry into marriage. Becoming married as a young adult would be expected to have beneficial effects due to its fulfillment of normative expectations and its societal support.

Continuity, too, can have significant developmental effects. For example, in a social context where remaining never married is considered deviant, remaining a never-married person beyond the socially normative and statistically normative age of first marriage (early to mid-20s in the contemporary United States) (Schoen & Weinick, 1993) might be expected to cause a decline in well-being and development. However, as a larger proportion of young adults are remaining single longer (Schoen & Weinick, 1993) and the modern social order provides them with more opportunities and encouragement to live autonomously (Goldscheider, Thornton, & Young-DeMarco, 1993), remaining never married may no longer carry such social stigma and negative effects.

Dissolution of marriage by divorce has, at least until recently, been viewed as an unanticipated and non-normative transition in the adult life course. The economic and social strains associated with divorce (McLanahan & Sandefur, 1994; Pearlin & Johnson, 1977), coupled with its being viewed as non-normative, might well lead

to the expectation that both the transition to divorce and continuity over time in this status would lead to poorer well-being and development. Yet again, as the texture of social life changes and as more adults have become divorced and have remained divorced longer (Schoen & Weinick, 1993), the social stigma once associated with divorce that helped lead to a decline in well-being among previous divorce cohorts may have diminished for contemporary divorce cohorts.

Widowhood can be anticipated in older age, but given current life expectancy and cumulative survival rates (Schoen & Weinick, 1993), contemporary adults view widowhood in young or middle age to be a non-normative transition and a non-normative status, and therefore we would expect continuity in this marital status or a transition to this marital status to be deleterious to well-being. However, given the relative absence of stigma and generally better social welfare (e.g., Social Security) associated with being a widow in contrast to being divorced, we might expect that widows would do less poorly than divorcées.

Entry into first marriage for an American adult might be expected to lead to an increase in well-being, because it fulfills one social expectation for the adult life course and tends to be associated with economic and social support advantages (Ross et al., 1990). Entry into remarriage, although now relatively common, remains "incompletely institutionalized" (Cherlin, 1978) and may therefore be less beneficial for well-being than entry into first marriage. The life course of the person entering remarriage has included a history of loss or disappointment to some extent, and remarriage often includes a complex reordering of relationships with children and other kin (Pasley & Ihinger-Tallman, 1987).

Another way in which timing of continuity or a transition might be considered important from a life course or life span perspective concerns the developmental readiness and resources a person has to deal with a transition or time spent in a status. For example, the transition to fatherhood after age 30 in contrast to earlier in adulthood has been found to be associated with greater confidence in the paternal role (Nydegger, 1986), more positive paternal affect (Cooney, Pederson, Indelicato, & Palkovitz, 1993), more paternal involvement (Cooney et al., 1993; Daniels & Weingarten, 1982; Heath, 1994), and a more effective balancing of work and family demands (Coltrane, 1990; Frankel & Wise, 1982). These differences have been hypothesized to be the result of greater psychological maturity, self-knowledge, and life-management skills possessed by midlife fathers in contrast to young adult fathers.

Differences in the effects of marital status continuity and transitions at different developmental periods during adulthood have not been carefully studied previously. Age is most often included as a control variable but is not considered a potential moderator of effects. Although a prototypical version of "normative" family development (e.g., Duvall, 1957) might lead us to expect that transitions into marriage occur in young adulthood, transitions out of marriage (through death) occur in later adulthood, and middle adulthood is characterized by marital continuity for the vast majority of persons, the complexity of the modern marital career for a sizable number of contemporary adults now includes transitions both into and out of marriage in middle adulthood (Bumpass, 1990; Bumpass, Sweet, & Martin, 1989; Uhlenberg et al., 1990).

Marital status continuity or change might have a different impact in middle adulthood in contrast to younger adulthood for a variety of reasons. One reason is the relative age normativeness of the transition or marital status as noted above. Another reason is the relative resources each age period provides for adaptation. Young adults might have a well-being advantage in the face of marital loss due to their better prospects of remarriage (Bumpass et al., 1989). On the other hand, differences in psychological maturity and pragmatic life expertise accrued over time (Baltes, 1987; Baltes & Staudinger, 1993; Brim, 1992) might make it easier for midlife adults than for younger adults

to handle the changes associated with, for example, the loss of a spouse due to divorce or death.

The Multiple Dimensions of Psychological Health

Bradburn's (1969) analyses of positive and negative affect provided some of the first empirical evidence that positive and negative well-being were related, yet distinct, components of psychological well-being. Empirical evidence for the legitimacy of differentiating positive aspects of psychological well-being and psychological distress was further supported by factor analytic work done pooling national survey items by Bryant and Veroff (1982). The results of their analysis led them to conclude that psychological well-being, as measured in the national surveys of previous decades, included three distinct components: positive affect, psychological distress, and self-evaluation.

Ryff (1989, 1995), a life span developmentalist, questioned the adequacy of traditional positive measures of psychological well-being (e.g., one-item assessments of happiness and life satisfaction), which have little developmental or theoretical basis, to cover the range of positive mental health and wellness. Drawing from several human development theories, Ryff (1989) generated and provided evidence of discriminant validity (in relation to each other as well as in comparison to prior measures of well-being) of six new measures of distinct dimensions of psychological wellness: positive evaluation of oneself and one's past life (self-acceptance), a sense of continued growth and development as a person (personal growth), the belief that one's life is purposeful and meaningful (purpose in life), the possession of quality relations with others (positive relations with others), the capacity to manage effectively one's life and surrounding world (environmental mastery), and a sense of self-determination (autonomy). Further confirmatory factor analyses undertaken by Ryff and Keyes (1995), using national data, provided additional evidence that these six components of well-being are more appropriately considered different dimensions of wellness than subscales of a single wellness factor; they found that a model positing six separate factors fit better than a model positing one global latent factor.

Examining more complete measurements of psychological wellness, as well as psychological distress, offers the potential to reveal a more comprehensive understanding of the complex psychological effects stemming from involvement in significant and often conflictual social roles, including marriage and parenting (see Umberson & Gove, 1989, for an illustration of this point in relation to parenthood status). Therefore, Ryff's (1989) six dimensions of psychological well-being were examined in this analysis along with the more familiar dimensions of positive affect (global happiness), self-adequacy (self-esteem [distinct from self-acceptance, see Ryff, 1989]), personal mastery (distinct from environmental mastery, see Ryff, 1989), and psychological distress (depression, hostility).

Marital Status Continuity and Psychological Well-Being

Most studies examining marital status and psychological distress have concluded that married men and women have a mental health advantage in contrast to their unmarried peers (Gore & Mangione, 1983; Gove et al., 1983, 1990; Mirowsky & Ross, 1989; Pearlin & Johnson, 1977). Single, formerly married persons—divorced and widowed—typically report poorer well-being and give evidence of more distress than never-married persons (Gove & Shin, 1989; Pearlin & Johnson, 1977).

Research examining whether the psychological benefits of marriage are greater for men or women has yielded mixed results. Gove and Tudor (1973) found that marriage protected the mental health of men more than women. Yet Fox (1980), using data from three national surveys from 1960, 1970, and 1973, did not find strong support for a gender by marital status interaction effect. A recent analysis by Ross (1995) found no gender differences.

However, all of these investigations examined psychological distress or other psychological dysfunction as outcomes. There is less evidence about potential gender differences in positive psychological well-being associated with marriage.

The one positive psychological well-being outcome that has been extensively studied in relation to the marital role and across both men and women is global happiness. Being married has been consistently associated with more global happiness (Glenn, 1975; Glenn & Weaver, 1979, 1988; Lee et al., 1991). However, national trend data from the General Social Survey (GSS) spanning the 1970s and the 1980s examined by Glenn and Weaver (1988) revealed a "narrowing of the happiness gap" between the married and the never-married during these years. This trend was noted particularly for men and for younger adults (ages 25 to 39). The proportion of never-married men indicating they were "very happy" increased between 1972 and 1982, whereas the proportion of younger married women indicating such high levels of positive well-being decreased (Glenn & Weaver, 1988). Lee et al. (1991) extended the analysis of the GSS to 1989 and found that the gap increased somewhat during 1987 and 1988 but then diminished again in 1989. As before, the changes found in happiness by marital status were most pronounced among young adults; specifically, younger never-married men and women reported more happiness in the 1980s than in the 1970s, and younger married women reported less happiness in the 1980s than in the 1970s. Anderson and Stewart (1994) and Gordon (1994) have also reported evidence from their recent qualitative studies that single women report advantages to single status over marriage in terms of personal autonomy and growth.

In their meta-analysis of studies of marital status and well-being, Harding-Hidore, Stock, Okun, and Witter (1985) found evidence of only a small positive association between marriage and subjective well-being. The effects of marriage were smaller for older persons, and they were also smaller for younger cohorts. The results of this meta-analysis suggest that it is important to examine age differences in the importance of marriage and marital transitions and to continue to periodically evaluate associations between marital status and well-being at different points in time.

Marital Status Transitions and Well-Being

A few longitudinal population-based studies on the mental health effects of the transition from marriage to divorce have been conducted. Menaghan and Lieberman (1986) used a probability sample of more than 1,000 adults from the Chicago area followed over 4 years (1972 to 1976) to examine the impact of divorce on change in depressive affect. These researchers found that, in fact, divorce led to an increase in depressive affect; greater economic problems, unavailability of confidants, and a reduction in living standards accounted for a substantial amount of the decline in well-being. No difference in change was found for men in contrast to women. A major strength of this study was its prospective design. However, it was limited to an examination of one measure of psychological well-being (depressive affect), it investigated only one type of marital transition, and it is now a story two decades old.

Doherty et al. (1989) conducted a 5-year (1982 to 1987) longitudinal study of 402 predominantly White, middle-class, middle-aged couples with teenage children randomly selected from the enrollment of a Minnesota health maintenance organization in 1982. They found that women who were separated or divorced during the study period experienced a decline in psychological mood and an increase in substance abuse. The transition to dissolution did not result in declines in well-being for men (although men who separated or divorced rated lower than continuously married men on psychological mood, self-esteem, mastery, and substance abuse both before and after dissolution).

Booth and Amato (1991) analyzed data from a U.S. national sample of more than 2,000 married people ages 55 and younger in 1980 who were followed up longitudinally in 1983 and 1988.

Their analysis of patterns from three time periods led them to conclude that divorce was associated with a short-term (i.e., less than 2 years postevent), but not long-term (i.e., more than 2 years postevent), increase in psychological distress and unhappiness (each outcome measured with a single-item indicator) and that these patterns were similar for men and women.

Mastekaasa (1995) recently examined national Norwegian data for 930 persons married in 1980 or 1983 who were also reinterviewed at least twice subsequent to their initial interview. He found that persons who separated or divorced over the longitudinal follow-up period experienced a significant increase in psychological distress (measured with two items), both short-term (less than 4 years postevent) and long-term (4 to 8 years postevent)

The transition to remarriage has received less attention. Cross-sectional evidence suggests that remarried men may be somewhat happier than once-married men, but remarried women are less happy than once-married women (White, 1979). Spanier and Furstenberg (1982) examined the transition to remarriage longitudinally (1977 to 1979) for their sample of 180 Pennsylvania respondents. They found that remarriage alone did not account for well-being differences between the group that remarried in contrast to the group that remained divorced during the period they studied.

The first few months after the death of a spouse have been consistently associated with higher levels of depressive symptomology (Harlow, Goldberg, & Comstock, 1991; Stroebe & Stroebe, 1987; Wortman, Silver, & Kessler, 1993). Although not totally consistent, current evidence suggests that widowhood may be more psychologically problematic for men than for women (e.g., Gove, 1972; Siegel & Kuykendall, 1990; Stroebe & Stroebe, 1987, 1993) and for younger widows in contrast to older widows (e.g., Ball, 1977; Sanders, 1981). Longitudinal evidence indicates that postbereavement depression effects may be short-lived (1 to 2 years) and that long-term differences in depression between widows and married persons may be minimal

(Harlow et al., 1991; McCrae & Costa, 1993; Sanders, 1981).

However, most research on widowhood has been limited by the use of convenience samples or longitudinal studies begun after the transition to widowhood, by the use of limited measures of well-being (e.g., depression only), by a limited age range (e.g., only the elderly), or by limitation only to women—making gender comparisons impossible (Kitson et al., 1989). This research project sought to add to the literature on the effects of widowhood by (a) using a national sample, (b) investigating the transition to widowhood prospectively, (c) analyzing the effects of widowhood on multiple dimensions of well-being, (d) exploring gender differences in the effects of widowhood, and (e) considering a young adult versus midlife adult contrast for women (in much of the existing literature, "young" widows are actually midlife women).

Research Hypotheses and Questions

In sum, based on life course and life span developmental theory and previous research, this study was designed to examine two hypotheses.

Because marriage is a socially normative life course role for young and midlife adults: (a) Young and midlife men and women continuously unmarried (separated/divorced, widowed, or never married) over a 5-year period will evidence a decline in well-being in contrast to men and women continuously married; and (b) transitions out of marriage will lead to a decline in well-being in contrast to remaining continuously married.

Because research evidence is limited regarding the well-being effects of the transition into first marriage and remarriage (in contrast to remaining continuously married), inconsistent regarding gender by marital status interaction effects, and scant regarding age by marital status interaction effects, we also explored three research questions: (a) Is the transition into first marriage and remarriage associated with increased well-being in contrast to remaining continuously married? (b) Are there gender differences in the psychological well-being effects of marital status continuity or change? and (c) Are there adult age (i.e., young adult vs. midlife adult) differences in the psychological well-being effects of marital status continuity or change?

Methods

Data

The data for these analyses came from the first and second waves of the National Survey of Families and Households (NSFH), which includes information from personal interviews conducted in 1987–1988 (Time 1) and in 1992–1993 (Time 2; 5 years later), with a nationally representative sample of 13,008 noninstitutionalized American adults, 19 years old and older. This survey included a main sample of 9,643 respondents, with an additional over sample of 3,374 African Americans, Mexican Americans, Puerto Ricans, single parents, stepparents, cohabitors, and recently married persons. The response rate at Time 1 (1987–1988) was about 75%. The response rate at Time 2 was about 82% of first wave respondents. This yielded national population coverage at a rate of about 62% for data from both waves. Sampling weights correcting for selection probabilities and nonresponse allow this sample to match the composition of the U.S. population on age, sex, and race (see Sweet, Bumpass, & Call, 1988, for more design details). The analytic sample for this study consisted of NSFH primary respondents ages 19 to 34 or 40 to 60 in 1987–1988, who also responded in 1992–1993, and who had complete and consistent marital status information for the period between the two waves of the survey ($N = 6,948$; 138 cases—2% of Time 2 respondents were excluded due to incomplete information). Respondents ages 35 to 39 in 1987–1988 were excluded from these longitudinal analyses so that we could make a clear differentiation in the age group contrast analyses between persons experiencing marital status continuity and change prior to age 40 and after age 40. (The group ages 35 to 39 between 1987–1988 and 1992–1993 would overlap into their 40s during the 5-year period investigated; thus, we felt including them in the analyses would make this distinction less clear.)

Measures

Outcome measures included a 12-item modified version of the Center for Epidemiological Studies-Depression (CES-D) index (Radloff, 1977) (alpha = .93), a 3-item measure of hostility/irritability (alpha = .85), a standard 1-item measure of global happiness, a 3-item version of Rosenberg's (1965) self-esteem index (alpha = .65), a 5-item personal mastery index consisting of 4 items from the Pearlin Mastery Scale (Pearlin, Lieberman, Menaghan, & Mullan, 1981) along with a single item of control-mastery also used in Wave 1 of the NSFH (alpha = .66), and 3-item versions of Ryff's (1989; Ryff & Keyes, 1995) six psychological well-being scales: Autonomy (alpha = .45), Personal Growth (alpha = .54), Positive Relations With Others (alpha = .53), Purpose in Life (alpha = .37), Self-Acceptance (alpha = .54), and Environmental Mastery (alpha = .56). The relatively lower internal consistency of items used for these scales reflects an a priori decision by Ryff to create short scales that represent the multi-factorial structure of the original scales (which consisted of 20 items) rather than to maximize internal consistency. These dramatically shortened scales have been found to correlate from .70 to .89 with the original highly reliable scales (Ryff & Keyes, 1995).

For three measures—the CES-D, global happiness, and self-esteem—Time 1 assessment of the measures were available and were controlled in the respective analyses. For the Personal Mastery Scale, responses to one item measuring personal mastery that was included at Time 1 of the NSFH was included as a Time 1 control (the correlation of this one item at Time 2 with the other four items of the scale at Time 2 is .57). The hostility index and the six Ryff measures were not included at Time 1, so the CES-D assessment from Time 1 was entered as a control for group selection on well-being in all analyses

of these measures to better estimate the likely longitudinal change in well-being over time due to marital status continuity or transition. (See Appendix A at the end of this reading for descriptives for all variables used in the analysis; see Appendix B at the end of this reading for a list of scale items.)

Marital status contrasts were classified into 10 mutually exclusive and exhaustive categories depending on respondent reports of their marital history over the 5-year period between Time 1 and Time 2 of the NSFH (see Table 3.5). Respondents who were continuously married during this period were classified as married and used as the contrast category in all analyses; respondents who were continuously separated, divorced, or both, were classified as separated-divorced; respondents who were continuously widowed were classified as widowed; respondents who were continuously never married were classified as never married; respondents who were married at Time 1 and separated or divorced at Time 2 were classified as married→separated-divorced; respondents who were married at Time 1 and widowed at Time 2 were classified as married→widowed; respondents who were separated, divorced, or widowed at Time 1 and married at Time 2 were classified as remarried; respondents who were never married at Time 1 and married at Time 2 were classified as first married; respondents who were married at Time 1 and who experienced both a dissolution of that marriage and a remarriage by Time 2 were classified as married→unmarried→remarried; and respondents who were never married, separated, divorced, or widowed at Time 1 and who experienced both a marriage and a dissolution by Time 2 were classified as unmarried→married→unmarried.

Respondents were also classified into two age status categories: young adults—respondents who were ages 19–34 at Time 1, and midlife adults—respondents ages 40–60 at Time 1. Several additional demographic statuses—race or ethnicity, education, household income, parental status, and employment status—were controlled in all analyses because they are

Table 3.5 Weighted Percentage Distribution (unweighted *n*) of 5-Year Marital Status Continuity and Change, National Survey of Families and Households 1987–1993, Primary Respondents, Ages 19–64 (N = 6,948)

	Total Sample		Women		Men	
Marital Status	Unweighted n	Weighted Percentage	Unweighted n	Weighted Percentage	Unweighted n	Weighted Percentage
Continuity						
Married	3,219	51.0	1,822	50.4	1,397	51.6
Separated/Divorced	867	7.2	647	9.5	220	4.8
Widowed	184	1.8	166	3.1	18	0.4
Widowed	1,019	17.0	552	14.3	467	19.9
Change						
Married→Separated/ Divorced	430	5.8	240	5.9	190	5.6
Married→Widowed	92	1.6	82	2.7	10	0.4
Never married→ First married	515	9.2	264	7.6	251	10.9
Separated/Divorced/ Widowed→Remarried	386	3.3	242	3.3	144	3.4
Married→Separated/ Divorced/Widowed →Remarried	121	1.7	74	1.9	47	1.5
Unmarried→Married→ Separated/Divorced/ Widowed	115	1.3	77	1.3	38	1.3
Valid cases	6,948	100.0	4,166	100.0	2,782	100.0

NOTE: Percentage columns do not always total 100.0 due to rounding errors.

associated with both marital status and psychological well-being and might have confounded our results (Menaghan & Parcel, 1990; Ross et al., 1990; Voydanoff, 1990). The following variable coding was used: race-ethnicity (dichotomously coded 1 = African American vs. 0 = all others), education (in years), household income (continuous measure totaled across all types of earned and unearned income for all household members at Time 1), missing on household income at Time 1 (dichotomous flag variable to include all respondents missing on income in the regression analyses), having a child age 18 or younger in the household at Time 2 (dichotomous, 1 = has child vs. 0 = no child), and employment status at Time 2 (dichotomous, 1 = employed vs. 0 = not employed). Ordinary least squares regression models were estimated throughout using SPSS.

Results

Table 3.6 reports the results of models that estimated the effects of multiple marital status contrasts and Gender x Marital Status interactions on well-being. Because there was at least one significant Gender x Marital Status interaction effect in each of the combined gender models estimated (at least at the trend level), it was deemed appropriate to examine separate models for men and women to confirm the gender differences in marital status effects. In addition, for these models, to answer the third research question—Does age status (that is young adult vs. midlife adult) make a difference in the effects of marital status continuity and change on well-being?—we included Age 40+ x Marital Status interaction variables for each marital status contrast where there were enough cases to examine contrasts across age groups. Tables 3.7 and 3.8 provide estimates for models that examined both genders separately for each well-being outcome and also added Age x Marital Status interactions.

We did not create age interactions (a) for continuity in widowhood status, because there were so few continuously widowed men and women under age 40; (b) for the transition from never

married to first married for men or women, because so few cases of this transition were reported for persons aged 40 and older; (c) for the transition from married to widowed for men, because so few cases of this transition were reported by persons under age 40; and (d) for the multiple marriage transitions—unmarried→ married→unmarried and married→unmarried→ married, because so few of these cases occurred at older ages.

Effects of Marital Status Continuity on Well-Being

The results reported in Table 3.6 suggest that there are several significant well-being differences between adults who experienced 5-year continuity as singles in contrast to adults who experienced continuity as marrieds. The continuously separated or divorced evidenced a decline in well-being in comparison to continuously married adults in terms of depression (at a trend level), global happiness, personal mastery, positive relations with others, purpose in life, self-acceptance, and environmental mastery. These patterns did not appear to be significantly different for women in contrast to men.

Being continuously widowed over a 5-year period (almost all respondents in this category were ages 40 to 59) was associated with an increase in depression over time in comparison to being married, but there were no other well-being differences for this group. No gender differences in the effect of being continuously widowed were found for women in contrast to men.

The never married became more depressed and less happy over time; however, a significant gender interaction effect (confirmed by subsequent results provided in Table 3.7) indicated that never-married status led to less unhappiness for women than for men. Never-married respondents also reported more hostility, less positive relations with others, and less self-acceptance than their continuously married counterparts. A significant gender interaction effect indicated that never-married women reported even less self-acceptance than never-married men.

(Text continued on page 82)

Table 3.6 Unstandardized Regression Coefficients for the Effects of Marital Status Continuity and Change on Psychological Well-Being

Predictors	Depression	Hostility	Global Happiness	Self-Esteem	Personal Mastery	Autonomy	Personal Growth	Positive Relations	Purpose in Life	Self-Acceptance	Environmental Mastery
Female	.14***	-.05	-.06	-.08***	-.39***	-.12	.44***	1.04***	.27***	.38***	-.04
Age ≥ 40	-.08*	-.35**	.00	-.04*	-.46***	.29**	-.58***	.03	-.51***	-.19*	.07
Marital Status											
Continuity											
Married	—	—	—	—	—	—	—	—	—	—	—
Separated/Divorced	.15†	.48	-.50***	-.01	-1.00***	.30	-.08	-1.12***	-.96***	-.97***	-.47*
Widowed	.62*	.83	-.24	-.20	-.27	.79	-.39	-.92	-.95	-.19	-.37
Never Married	.19***	.55*	-.40***	.03	-.25	.47***	.57***	-.69***	-.22	-.32*	-.08
Female × Separated/Divorced	.13	.29	.19	-.02	.47	-.01	-.02	-.16	.31	-.29	.27
Female × Widowed	-.53	-1.06	.02	.25	-.38	-.88	-.04	-.02	-.02	-.56	.42
Female × Never married	-.06	.08	.26**	-.00	.33	-.27	-.27†	-.00	.24	-3.6*	.17
Change											
Married→Separated/Divorced	.29***	.23	-0.51***	-.01	-.76**	-.17	.25	-1.04***	-3.9†	-.91***	-.18
Married→Widowed	.21	-2.38*	-.54	.22	-2.108	-.81	-.18	.16	-2.49***	-.04	-.38
Never married→First married	-.25***	-.03	.21*	.11**	.06	.51**	.69***	.52**	.80**	.56***	.63***
Separated/Divorced/Widowed→Remarried	-.16	.59	.21	.11**	.06	.51**	.69***	.52**	.80**	.56***	.64***
Married→Separated/Divorced/Widowed→Remarried	-.28†	-.23	-.01	-.13	-.23	-.30	.31	-.16	.31	-.918	-.07
Unmarried→Married→Separated/Divorced/Widowed	.43*	2.23***	-.49*	-.27**	-1.73**	-.43	-.62	-1.98***	-1.87***	-1.91***	-1.01*
Female × Married→Separated/Divorced	.25*	1.58***	-.01	-.16**	-.37	-.45	-.46†	-.28	-.21	-.83*8	-.72**

78

Predictors	Depression	Hostility	Global Happiness	Self-Esteem	Personal Mastery	Autonomy	Personal Growth	Positive Relations	Purpose in Life	Self-Acceptance	Environmental Mastery
Female × Married→Widowed	.48†	2.91**	−.19	−.42*	1.33	1.10	.48	−.61	2.49***	−.44	.16
Female × Never married→First married	.13	−.23	.11	.05	.77**	−.00	−.18	.05	−.40†	.07	.34
Female × Separated/Divorced/Widowed→Remarried	.24†	−.72	−.03	−.05	.53	−.06	.25	−.25	−.28	−.05	.02
Female × Married→Separated/Divorced/Widowed→Remarried	.51**	.38	.30	.19†	.32	.80†	.24	.24	−.10	.57	.50
Female × Unmarried→Married→Separated/Divorced/Widowed	−.20	−.55	.34	.44***	1.76**	.84	.84	1.22†	1.92**	1.00†	1.58**
Time 1 Well-Being											
Depression	.35***	.91***				−.27***	−.22***	−.41***	−.23***	−.52***	−.50***
Global happiness			.23***								
Self-esteem				.37***							
Personal mastery					.83***						
Constant	1.47***	2.04***	4.30***	2.26***	12.74***	14.46***	12.86***	12.76***	10.92***	13.37***	13.57***
R²	.20	.10	.09	.18	.14	.03	.10	.09	.13	.12	.09

SOURCE: National Survey of Families and Households (1987–1993), primary respondents ($N = 6,948$).

NOTE: All models also included controls for race/ethnicity, employment status, years of education, household income, and presence of a child ≤ age 18 in household.

†$p ≤ .10$. *$p ≤ .05$. **$p ≤ .01$. ***$p ≤ .001$ (two-tailed test).

79

Table 3.7 Unstandardized Regression Coefficients for the Effects of Marital Status Continuity and Change on Psychological Well-Being by Gender

Predictors	Depression		Hostility		Global Happiness		Self-Esteem		Personal Mastery	
	Women	Men	Women	Men	Women	Men	Women	Men	Women	Men
Age ≥ 40 (Time 1)	−.03	−.08	−.14	−.29	−.06	.06	−.01	−.06†	−.95***	−.14
Marital Status										
Continuity										
Married (omitted)	—	—	—	—	—	—	—	—	—	—
Separated/Divorced	.21*	.57***	1.08**	1.59**	−.29*	−.56*	.04	−.09	−.69*	−1.48**
Widowed	.03	.62†	−.39	.76	−.18	−.25	.05	−.20	−.46	−.35
Never married	.12†	.28***	.51†	1.02***	−.14	−.44***	.07†	−.02	−.15	−.25
Age ≥ 40 × Separated/Divorced	.04	−.55**	−.72	−1.41†	.02	.03	−.07	.10	.40	.63
Age ≥ 40 × Never married	−.24	.10	−.05	−1.05	.26	−.04	−.01	−.00	1.16**	−.57
Change										
Married→Separated/Divorced	.63***	.26*	2.19***	−.04	−.54***	−.45**	−.16***	−.05	−1.52***	−.63†
Married→Widowed	.71*	.21	.29	−2.40*	.23	−.62	−.19	.22	−2.73**	−2.24*
Never married→First married	−.14*	−.16†	−.35	.37	.32**	.18†	.19***	.07	.69**	−.01
Separated/Divorced/Widowed→Remarried	.20†	−.01	.03	.98	.05	.16	.03	.09	.50	.19
Married→Separated/Divorced/Widowed→Remarried	.22†	−.24	.12	−.08	.27†	−.01	.07	−.15	.02	−.21
Never married→Married→Separated/Divorced/Widowed	.20	.54**	1.52**	2.68***	−.12	−.55	.20*	−.32**	−.02	.81**
Age ≥ 40 × Married→Separated/Divorced	−.42*	.16	−1.75**	2.68***	−.12	−.55*	.20*	−.32**	−.02	−.81**
Age ≥ 40 × Married→Widowed	−.07	—	.14	—	−1.04*	—	−.00	—	2.39*	—

Predictors	Depression		Hostility		Global Happiness		Self-Esteem		Personal Mastery	
	Women	Men	Women	Men	Women	Men	Women	Men	Women	Men
Age ≥ 40 × Separated/Divorced/ Widowed→Remarried	-.44*	-.18	-.77	-.36	.37	.03	.14	.00	.32	-.28
Time 1 Well-Being										
Depression	.39***	.31***	1.05***	.76***						
Global happiness					.24***	.21***				
Self-esteem							.39***	.34***		
Personal mastery									.83***	83***
Constant	1.51***	1.59***	1.40***	2.56***	4.30***	4.18***	2.03***	2.39***	12.35***	12.69***
R²	.20	.17	.11	.10	.10	.10	.18	.17	.15	.13

SOURCE: National Survey of Families and Households (1987–1993), primary respondents (*N* = 6,548).

NOTE: All models also include controls for race/ethnicity, employment status, years of education, household income, and presence of a child ≤ 18 in household.

†*p* ≤ .10. **p* ≤ .05. ***p* ≤ .01 ***p ≤ .001 (two-tailed test).

Although these results support, overall, our first hypothesis regarding the well-being benefits of marriage, an examination of additional seldom-included other well-being outcomes suggests that the story is more complex. The continuously never-married men and women concurrently rated themselves as more autonomous and as experiencing more personal growth than their married peers.

Overall, we found few gender differences in the effects of continuity in marital status (in partial answer to Research Question 2). A trend level gender interaction effect (also confirmed by subsequent analyses reported in Table 3.7) indicated that never-married women rate themselves lower on personal growth than never-married men (but still not significantly lower on personal growth than the continuously married). These contrasting results confirm that taking a multidimensional approach to well-being is important inaccurately understanding the determinants of psychological well-being, and as life span developmental theory (Baltes, 1987) and structural analyses of well-being have suggested (Bradbum, 1969; Bryant & Veroff, 1982; Ryff & Keyes, 1995), that multidirectional effects for different well-being dimensions can occur simultaneously (Baltes, 1987).

Age Differences in
Marital Status Continuity Effects

A number of interesting age differences in the effects of marital status continuity emerged from these analyses (see Tables 3.7 and 3.8). Midlife men evidenced significantly less of an increase in depression and less hostility (at a trend level) over a 5-year period of remaining separated or divorced than did younger men. Continuously separated or divorced midlife men also reported significantly more self-acceptance than younger men in this marital category. However, these same separated or divorced midlife men also reported significantly less personal growth than did younger separated or divorced men.

Continuously separated or divorced as well as continuously never-married midlife women reported significantly more positive relations with others, and continuously separated or divorced midlife women reported more autonomy than did younger women of the same marital status. Never-married midlife women also rated their personal mastery higher than younger never-married women. Continuously never-married midlife men, however, reported significantly less self-acceptance than never-married younger men. This latter case was the only one where age differences in the effects of remaining single favored young adults; in general, where age differences occurred, they suggested that single midlife adults fare better than single young adults (in response to Research Question 3).

Effects of Marital
Status Change on Well-Being

Several significant well-being differences between the continuously married and those undergoing marital status transitions were also evident (see Table 3.6). The transition from marriage to separation or divorce was associated with an increase in depression and a decline in reported happiness in comparison to remaining married. Those who separated or divorced also reported less personal mastery, less positive relations with others, less purpose in life (at a trend level of significance), and less self-acceptance. Women who experienced marital dissolution reported significantly more of an increase in depression, more hostility, more of a decline in self-esteem, less personal growth (at a trend level), less self-acceptance, and less environmental mastery than men experiencing marital dissolution (all but the personal growth trend were further confirmed in subsequent analyses shown in Table 3.7).

The transition to widowhood in this sample was associated with lower ratings of hostility, personal mastery, and purpose in life. Gender interactions indicated that becoming widowed was associated with significantly more depression (trend level effect), more hostility, less self-esteem, and more purpose in life for women than for men. Subsequent analyses reported in Table 3.7 confirm that women, but not men, who were

Table 3.8   Unstandardized Regression Coefficients for the Effects of Marital Status Continuity and Change on Psychological Well-Being (Ryff scales) by Gender

Predictors	Positive Relations		Purpose in Life		Self-Acceptance		Environmental Mastery		Autonomy		Personal Growth	
	Women	Men	Women	Men	Women	Men	Women	Men	Women	Men	Women	Men
Age ≥ 40 (Time 1)	−.09	−.20	−.57***	−.53***	−.15	−.23†	.09	.08	.28*	.16	−.56***	−.55***
Marital Status												
Continuity												
Married (omitted)	—	—	—	—	—	—	—	—	—	—		
Separated/Divorced	−1.86***	−1.73***	−.62*	−.61*	−1.15***	−1.85***	−.15	−.84†	−.09	−.33	.08	.74†
Widowed	−.68*	−1.08	−.85***	−1.02	−.61*	−.30	.12	−.43	−.07	.84	−.43†	−.41
Never married	−.74***	−.87***	−.01	−.31	−.53**	−.53**	.14	−.18	.19	.33†	.25	.65***
Age ≥ 40 × Separated/Divorced	1.12***	.71	.10	−.60	−.03	1.06*	.01	.46	.62*	−.05	−.25	−1.15*
Age ≥ 40 × Never married	1.06*	−.82	.72†	−.02	.32	−1.07*	.40	−.33	.22	−.17	.56†	−.51
Change												
Married→Separated/Divorced	−1.74***	−1.40***	−.49*	−.75*	−1.77***	−1.45***	−.86***	−.03	−.59**	−.42	−.13	.11
Married→Widowed	−1.87*	.02	−1.90	−2.58***	−.97	−.10	−.01	−.42	−.30	−.73	−.75	−.25
Never married→First married	.54**	.34	.39*	.75***	.73***	.35†	1.07***	.51**	.55***	.33†	.53***	.69***
Separated/Divorced/Widowed→Remarried	−.27	−.03	.30	.30	−.06	−.20	.52†	.55	.49†	.52	.65*	.58
Married→Separated/Divorced/Widowed→Remarried	.07	−.23	.41	.29	−.34	−.98*	.46	−.08	.53†	.36	.57*	.32
Unmarried→Married→Separated/Divorced/Widowed	−.71	−2.22***	−.11	−1.97***	−.79	−2.19**	.63	−1.12*	.42	−.58	.25	−.60
Age ≥ 40 × Married→Separated/Divorced	1.62***	.56	−.43	.80	.16	1.13*	−.18	−.42	−.14	.53	−.17	.46
Age ≥ 40 × Married→Widowed	1.80†	—	2.23**	—	.66	—	−.21	—	.70	—	1.18	—
Age ≥ 40 × Separated/Divorced/Widowed→Remarried	.77	.35	−.01	.41	.03	.15	.26	−.07	.48	.18	.39	−.12
Time 1 Well-Being												
Depression	−.36***	−.46***	−.22***	−.23***	−.51***	−.52***	−.47***	−.54***	−.30***	−.24***	−.21***	−.24***
Constant	12.77***	13.87***	10.90***	11.11***	13.39***	13.67***	3.09***	13.90***	14.41***	14.47***	12.78***	13.25***
R²	.11	.07	.14	.13	.14	.11	.09	.09	.04	.03	.12	.10

SOURCE: National Survey of Families and Households (1987–1993), primary respondents ($N = 6,948$).

NOTE: All models also include controls for race or ethnicity, employment status, years of education household income, and presence of a child ≤ 18 in household.
†$p ≤ .10$. *$p ≤ .05$. **$p ≤ .01$. ***$p ≤ .001$ (two-tailed test).

widowed within the last 5 years report more depression. Men, but not women, who were recently widowed report significantly less hostility than continuously married men (see Table 3.7). Self-esteem differences between the recently widowed and the continuously married do not reach significance for men or women in separate analyses by gender. Lower reports of purpose in life are in evidence for both men and women in comparison to the continuously married, but for midlife women purpose in life does not appear to be as compromised as it is for younger women or men. These results provide partial support for our second hypothesis regarding the decline in well-being associated with transitions out of marriage.

Results reported in Table 3.5 indicate that becoming married for the first time within the last 5 years led to more of an increase in well-being than remaining continuously married on all outcomes except hostility and personal mastery for men (a significant gender interaction confirmed by subsequent results shown in Table 3.7 indicates that personal mastery was also increased by first marriage for women). These consistent beneficial effects among the newly first married suggest that the answer to the first part of Research Question 1—Is the transition into first marriage associated with increased well-being in contrast to remaining continuously married?—is an emphatic yes.

Becoming remarried, however, led to fewer positive effects (similar to the pattern reported by Spanier & Furstenberg, 1982), yet remarriage was also associated with higher reports of autonomy, personal growth, and purpose in life than those reported by the continuously married (a more limited affirmative answer to the second part of Research Question 1). This transition did not appear to have different effects for men in contrast to women.

Respondents who experienced both a dissolution or loss of spouse and a remarriage during this 5-year period were not ultimately very different in well-being from the continuously married, except they did report lower self-acceptance. Respondents who went from single to married

and back to single again across this 5-year period showed clear evidence of poorer well-being in all dimensions other than autonomy and personal growth when contrasted with the continuously married. Several significant gender interaction effects for this group, however, suggest that women actually experienced less negative impact from making these multiple transitions than did men.

Age Differences in the Effects of Marital Transitions

Tables 3.7 and 3.8 provide evidence that age does have a moderating influence on the well-being effects of marital status transitions. Midlife women report less increase in depression and lower levels of hostility after a marital separation or divorce than younger women do. Women ages 40 and over who experienced marital separation or divorce also reported significantly better relations with others and more personal mastery than younger women. Midlife men experiencing a separation or divorce reported significantly more self-acceptance than younger men did.

A trend level effect indicates that midlife women who experience a transition to widowhood may experience more of a decline in global happiness than younger women. However, midlife women who were widowed, as noted previously, reported significantly more purpose in life, more personal mastery, and more positive relations with others (at a trend level of significance) than younger recent widows. In addition, the transition to remarriage was associated with significantly less depression for midlife women than younger women. Overall, in response to Research Question 3, we found that a transition out of marriage had less negative impact on the psychological well-being of midlife adults in contrast to young adults.

Discussion and Conclusions

These results from longitudinal data provide considerable support for the continuing importance of marital status for well-being. In support of our first hypothesis regarding the beneficial effects of marriage, we found numerous cases where a significant negative change in psychological well-being occurred as a result of remaining in a particular single status over a period of 5 years in contrast to remaining married over the same period. We note also that across-sectional analysis of marital status differences would have clustered the newly married together with the continuously married. Our results revealing the considerable well-being boost that comes with becoming married for the first time suggest that the newly married are making a significant contribution to inflating the mean for psychological well-being among the married category in most cross-sectional studies. By distinguishing between the newly married and the continuously married, this study actually yields an even more conservative examination of marital status differences than is typical (e.g., using the GSS), because only veterans of marriage (with somewhat lower psychological well-being) were included in the continuously married comparison group.

The evidence from contrasts between those who experienced a marital transition out of marriage and those who remained continuously married also provides considerable support for our second hypothesis. We found the transition to separation, divorce, or widowhood to be associated with negative effects across several components of psychological well-being.

However, if marriage was always a positive robust influence on all dimensions of well-being, we would not expect to find any instance where the well-being of the married and the unmarried was the same, or where the unmarried evidenced better well-being than the married. Yet, our analysis of multiple dimensions of well-being in many cases does provide evidence of no difference between the continuously married and those who are unmarried or transitioning out of marriage. Indeed, in a few cases, contrary to our first and second hypotheses, the unmarried report better well-being than the married, for example, in their ratings of autonomy and personal growth. These inconsistencies in patterns across outcomes suggest that marriage is not a universal beneficial determinant of all dimensions of psychological well-being. It appears wise, therefore, to continue evaluating the effects of marriage on well-being with a multidimensional lens whenever possible, so that we can obtain a more precise understanding of how and when marriage is important for mental health.

Likewise, this complex analysis does not yield a clear and simple answer to our second research question regarding gender differences in the effects of marriage on psychological well-being. The effects of continuity in single status are not very different for women in contrast to men. Yet, in evaluating the effects of recent marital transitions to single status (i.e., married to separated, divorced, or widowed) we found that women are somewhat more negatively affected by such transitions than men (except in the infrequent case of unmarried to married to unmarried in 5 years). It may be that women experience the transition to single status with more difficulty due to a greater decline in income, a greater share of responsibility for child rearing, and poorer prospects for remarriage.

Regarding Research Question 3, our analyses reveal a number of interesting differences in the effects of marriage on well-being for midlife adults in contrast to younger adults. In most cases (the two robust exceptions being personal growth for separated-divorced men and self-acceptance for never-married men), age group differences suggest greater adaptability (evidenced by higher psychological well-being) among mid-lifers facing singleness or transitions to single status—that is, separation, divorce, or widowhood. This is a noteworthy developmental finding, because marital transitions after age 40 are less statistically normative (Uhlenberg et al., 1990), and usually non-normativeness is hypothesized to be associated with greater stress (Neugarten, 1979). In the case of marital status, however, it may be that a certain degree of expertise in handling life problems and self-management (i.e., wisdom?; see Baltes & Staudinger, 1993; Brim, 1992) has developed by midlife, allowing for significantly greater maintenance of psychological well-being while remaining single or adapting to a transition to single status.

We acknowledge several limitations to this analysis. We have examined a large array of psychological well-being outcomes here, yet we have still omitted other outcomes that might have been additionally informative in terms of psychological maladjustment or distress for men, for example, drinking, drug use, social isolation, and aggressive behavior (Aneshensel, Rutter, & Lachenbruch, 1991). Thus, the gender differences that we found due to transitions out of marriage (e.g., to divorce or widowhood) may have underestimated the impact of these changes on men due to our particular selection of psychological well-being outcomes.

Although we have described more marital status contrasts than any previous study, we still have been forced to omit additional contrasts that might have been further enlightening, for example, cohabitor status and additional duration in status measures. These differentiations are surely important (e.g., Mastekaasa, 1994) and would better describe the continuum of attachment that we agree characterizes contemporary marriage in the United States (Ross, 1995). To add these contrasts to our already lengthy list, we believed would overtax the analysis. A finer-tuned examination of select differences, looking more closely at duration and other potential mediating and moderating factors using the richness of the NSFH data is certainly now in order. For example, there is always heterogeneity in marital quality among the married; we might expect that for some persons in our analysis, ending a marriage may have led to less decline in well-being than remaining in a problematic marriage (Wheaton, 1990). Marital quality distinctions, therefore, might be usefully explored in future work.

This unique prospective study of the transition into first marriage, with its unusual and informative contrast to the continuously married, provided us with an opportunity to address the question (Research Question 1) of well-being differences between those continuously married and those transitioning into marriage. Our analyses yielded interestingly strong evidence that getting married for the first time leads to a considerable elevation in well-being. By comparison, remarriage did not provide nearly so much psychological benefit. What is tempering the "rush" here? These intriguing results also deserve further investigation by subsequent study.

We found it valuable to make distinctions between the life course transition to first marriage and transition to remarriage, as well as among the separated or divorced, widowed, and never-married adults, and we encourage the retention of similar distinctions to future researchers in this area. We also recommend continued attention to examining life span developmental (age) differences and both positive and negative dimensions of psychological well-being, to further a more complete understanding of the ways in which marital status continuity and change influences adult development and mental health.

Note

Support for this research was provided by the John D. and Catherine T. MacArthur Foundation Research Network on Successful Midlife Development and a FIRST Grant Award to the first author from the National Institute on Aging (AG12731). The National Survey of Families and Households (NSFH) was funded by CPR-NICHHD Grant No. HD21009. The NSFH was designed and carried out at the Center for Demography and Ecology at the University of Wisconsin–Madison under the direction of Larry Bumpass and James Sweet. We gratefully acknowledge Larry Bumpass' helpful input to this study. Address correspondence to Nadine F. Marks, Child and Family Studies, University of Wisconsin–Madison, 1430 Linden Drive, Madison, WI 53706–1575; e-mail: marks@sc.wisc.edu

References

Anderson, C. M., & Stewart, S. (1994). *Flying solo: Single women in midlife.* New York: Norton.

Aneshensel, C. S., Rutter, C. M., & Lachenbruch, P. A. (1991). Social structure, stress, and mental health: Competing conceptual and analytic models. *American Sociological Review, 56,* 166–178.

Ball, J. F. (1977). Widow's grief: The impact of age and mode of death. *Omega, 7,* 307–333.

Baltes, P. (1987). Theoretical propositions of life-span developmental psychology: On the dynamics between growth and decline. *Developmental Psychology, 23,* 611–626.

Baltes, P. B., & Staudinger, U. M. (1993). The search for a psychology of wisdom. *Current Directions in Psychological Science, 1,* 75–80.

Bengtson, V. L., & Allen, K. R. (1993). The life course perspective applied to families overtime. In P. O. Boss, W. J. Doherty, R. LaRossa, W. R. Schumm, & S. K. Steinmetz (Eds.), *Sourcebook of family theories and methods: A contextual approach* (pp. 469–499). New York: Plenum.

Booth, A., & Amato, P. (1991). Divorce and psychological stress. *Journal of Health and Social Behavior, 32,* 396–407.

Bowlby, J. (1969). *Attachment and loss. Vol. 1: Attachment* (2nd rev. ed., 1982). New York: Basic Books.

Bowlby, J. (1973). *Attachment and loss. Vol. 2: Separation.* New York: Basic Books.

Bowlby, J. (1980). *Attachment and loss. Vol. 3: Loss, sadness, and depression.* New York: Basic Books.

Bradburn, N. (1969). *The structure of psychological well-being.* Chicago: Aldine.

Bretherton, I. (1992). Attachment and bonding. In V. B. Van Hasselt & M. Hersen (Eds.), *Handbook of social development: A lifespan approach* (pp. 133–155). New York: Plenum.

Brim, O. G. (1992). *Ambition.* New York: Basic Books.

Bryant, F. B., & Veroff, J. (1982). The structure of psychological well-being: Sociohistorical analysis. *Journal of Personality and Social Psychology, 43,* 653–673.

Bumpass, L. L. (1990). What's happening to the family? Interactions between demographic and institutional change. *Demography, 27,* 483–498.

Bumpass, L., Sweet, J., & Martin, T. C. (1989). Changing patterns of remarriage. *Journal of Marriage and the Family, 52,* 747–756.

Castro-Martin, T., & Bumpass, L. L. (1989). Recent trends and differentials in marital disruption. *Demography, 26,* 37–51.

Cherlin, A. (1978). Remarriage as an incomplete institution. *American Journal of Sociology, 84,* 634–650.

Coltrane, S. (1990). Birth timing and the division of labor in dual-earner families. *Journal of Family Issues, 11,* 157–181.

Cooney, T. M., Pederson, F. A., Indelicato, S., & Palkovitz, R. (1993). Timing of fatherhood: Is "on-time" optimal? *Journal of Marriage and the Family, 55,* 205–215.

Daniels, P., & Weingarten, K. (1982). *Sooner or later: The timing of parenthood in adult lives.* New York: Norton.

Doherty, W. J., Su, S., & Needle, R. (1989). Marital disruption and psychological well-being. *Journal of Family Issues, 10,* 72–85.

Duvall, E. M. (1957). *Family development.* Philadelphia: J. B. Lippincott.

Elder, G. H., Jr. (1991). Family transition, cycles, and social change. In P. A. Cowan & M. Hetherington (Eds.), *Family transitions* (pp. 31–57). Hillsdale, NJ: Lawrence Erlbaum.

Elder, G. (1992). The lifecourse. In E. Borgatta & M. Borgatta (Eds.), *Encyclopedia of sociology* (pp. 281–311). New York: Macmillan.

Featherman, D. L. (1983). Life-span perspectives in social science research. In P. B. Baltes & O. G. Brim, Jr. (Eds.), *Life span behavior and development* (Vol. 5, pp. 1–57). New York: Academic Press.

Fox, J. W. (1980). Gove's specific sex-role theory of mental illness: A research note. *Journal of Health and Social Behavior, 21,* 260–267.

Frankel, S. A., & Wise, M. J. (1982). A view of delayed parenting: Some implications of a new trend. *Psychiatry, 45,* 220–225.

Glenn, N. D. (1975). The contribution of marriage to the psychological well-being of males and females. *Journal of Marriage and the Family, 37,* 594–600.

Glenn, N. D., & Weaver, C. N. (1979). A note on family situation and global happiness. *Social Forces, 57,* 960–967.

Glenn, N. D., & Weaver, C. N. (1988). The changing relationship of marital status to reported happiness. *Journal of Marriage and the Family, 50,* 317–324.

Goldscheider, F., Thornton, A., & Young-DeMarco, L. (1993). A portrait of the nest-leaving process in early adulthood. *Demography, 30,* 683–699.

Goldscheider, F. K., & Waite, L. J. (1991). *New families, no families?* Berkeley: University of California Press.

Gordon, T. (1994). *Single women: On the margins?* New York: New York University Press.

Gore, S., & Mangione, T. W. (1983). Social roles, sex roles and psychological distress: Additive and interactive models of sex differences. *Journal of Health and Social Behavior, 24,* 300–312.

Gove, W. (1972). The relationship between sex roles, marital status, and mental illness. *Social Forces, 51,* 34–44.

Gove, W. R., Hughes, M., & Style, C. B. (1983). Does marriage have positive effects on the psychological well-being of the individual? *Journal of Health and Social Behavior, 24,* 122–131.

Gove, W. R., & Shin, H. (1989). The psychological well-being of divorced and widowed men and women: An empirical analysis. *Journal of Family Issues, 10,* 122–144.

Gove, W. R., Style, C. B., & Hughes, M. (1990). The effect of marriage on the well-being of adults. *Journal of Family Issues, 11,* 4–35.

Gove, W., & Tudor, J. (1973). Adult sex roles and mental illness. *American Journal of Sociology, 78,* 812–835.

Hagestad, G. O. (1990). Social perspectives on the life course. In R. H. Binstock & L. K. George, *Handbook of aging and the social sciences* (3rd ed., pp. 151–168). New York: Academic Press.

Hagestad, G. O., & Smyer, M. A. (1982). Dissolving long-term relationships: Patterns of divorcing in middle age. In S. Duck (Ed.), *Personal relationships, Vol. 4: Dissolving personal relationships* (pp. 155–188). New York: Academic Press.

Harding-Hidore, M., Stock, W. A., Okun, M. A., & Witter, R. A. (1985). Marital status and subjective well-being: A research synthesis. *Journal of Marriage and the Family, 47,* 947–953.

Harlow, S. D., Goldberg, E. L., & Comstock, G. W. (1991). A longitudinal study of the prevalence of depressive symptomology in elderly widowed and married women. *Archives of General Psychiatry, 48,* 1065–1068.

Heath, D. H. (1994). The impact of delayed fatherhood on the father-child relationship. *Journal of Genetic Psychology, 155,* 511–530.

Kitson, G. C., Babri, K. B., Roach, M. J., & Placidi, K. S. (1989). Adjustment to widowhood and divorce. *Journal of Family Issues, 10,* 5–32.

Lee, G., Seccombe, K., & Shehan, C. (1991). Marital status and personal happiness: An analysis of trend data. *Journal of Marriage and the Family, 53,* 839–844.

Mastekaasa, A. (1994). Psychological well-being and marital dissolution: Selection effects? *Journal of Family Issues, 15,* 208–228.

Mastekaasa, A. (1995). Marital dissolution and subjective distress: Panel evidence. *European Sociological Review, 11,* 173–185.

McCrae, R. R., & Costa, P. T., Jr. (1993). Psychological resilience among widowed men and women: A 10-year follow-up of a national sample. In M. S. Stroebe, W. Stroebe, & R. O. Hansson (Eds.), *Handbook of bereavement* (pp. 196–207). Cambridge, UK: Cambridge University Press.

McLanahan, S. S., & Sandefur, G. D. (1994). *Growing up with a single parent: What hurts and what helps.* Cambridge, MA: Harvard University Press.

Menaghan, E. G., & Lieberman, M. A. (1986). Changes in depression following divorce: A panel study. *Journal of Marriage and the Family, 48,* 319–328.

Menaghan, E. G., & Parcel, T. L. (1990). Parental employment and family life. *Journal of Marriage and the Family, 52,* 1079–1098.

Mirowsky, J., & Ross, C. E. (1989). *Social causes of psychological distress.* New York: Aldine.

Neugarten, B. L. (1979). Time, age and the life cycle. *American Journal of Psychiatry, 136,* 887–894.

Nydegger, C. N. (1986). Timetables and implicit theory. *American Behavioral Scientist, 29,* 710–729.

Pasley, K., & Ihinger-Tallman, M. (Eds.). (1987). *Remarriage and stepparenting.* New York: Guilford.

Pearlin, L. I., & Johnson, J. S. (1977). Marital status, life-strains and depression. *American Sociological Review, 42,* 704–715.

Pearlin, L., Lieberman, M., Menaghan, E., & Mullan, J. (1981). The stress process. *Journal of Health and Social Behavior, 22,* 337–356.

Radloff, L. (1977). The CES-D Scale: A self-report depression scale for research in the general population. *Applied Psychological Measurement, 1,* 385–401.

Riley, M., Foner, A., & Waring, J. (1988). Sociology of age. In N. J. Smelser (Ed.), *Handbook of sociology* (pp. 243–290). Newbury Park, CA: Sage.

Rosenberg, M. (1965). *Society and the adolescent self-image.* Princeton, NJ: Princeton University Press.

Ross, C. E. (1995). Reconceptualizing marital status as a continuum of social attachment. *Journal of Marriage and the Family, 57,* 129–140.

Ross, C. E., Mirowsky, J., & Goldsteen, K. (1990). The impact of the family on health: The decade in review. *Journal of Marriage and the Family, 52,* 1059–1078.

Ryff, C. (1989). Happiness is everything, or is it? *Journal of Personality and Social Psychology, 6,* 1069–1081.

Ryff, C. (1995). Psychological well-being in adult life. *Current Directions in Psychological Science, 4,* 99–104.

Ryff, C. D., & Essex, M. J. (1991). Psychological well-being in adulthood and old age: Descriptive markers and explanatory processes. In K. Warner Schaie & M. Powell Lawton (Eds.), *Annual review of gerontology and geriatrics* (Vol. 11, pp. 144–171). New York: Springer.

Ryff, C. D., & Keyes, C. L. M. (1995). The structure of psychological well-being revisited. *Journal of Personality and Social Psychology, 69,* 719–727.

Sanders, C. M. (1981). Comparison of younger and older spouses in bereavement outcome. *Omega, 11,* 227–232.

Schoen, R., Urton, W., Woodrow, K., & Baj, J. (1985). Marriage and divorce in twentieth century American cohorts. *Demography, 22,* 101–114.

Schoen, R., & Weinick, R. M. (1993). The slowing metabolism of marriage: Figures from 1988 U.S. marital status life tables. *Demography, 30,* 737–746.

Siegel, J. M., & Kuykendall, D. H. (1990). Loss, widowhood, and psychological distress among the elderly. *Journal of Consulting and Clinical Psychology, 58,* 519–524.

Spanier, G. B., & Furstenberg, F. F., Jr. (1982). Remarriage after divorce: A longitudinal analysis of well-being. *Journal of Marriage and the Family, 44,* 709–720.

Stroebe, M. S., & Stroebe, W. (1993). Determinants of adjustment to bereavement in younger widows and widowers. In M. S. Stroebe, W. Stroebe, & R. O. Hansson (Eds.), *Handbook of bereavement* (pp. 208–239). Cambridge, UK: Cambridge University Press.

Stroebe, W., & Stroebe, M. S. (1987). *Bereavement and health: The psychological and physical consequences of partner loss.* Cambridge, UK: Cambridge University Press.

Sweet, J. A., Bumpass, L. L., & Call, V. (1988). *The design and content of the National Survey of Families and Households NSFH Working Paper No. 1.* Madison: University of Wisconsin–Madison, Center for Demography and Ecology.

Uhlenberg, P., Cooney, T., & Boyd, R. (1990). Divorce for women after midlife. *Journal of Gerontology: Social Sciences, 45,* S3–S11.

Umberson, D., & Gove, W. R. (1989). Parenthood and psychological well-being: Theory, measurement, and stage in the family life course. *Journal of Family Issues, 10,* 440–462.

Voydanoff, P. (1990). Economic distress and family relations: A review of the eighties. *Journal of Marriage and the Family, 52,* 1099–1115.

Wheaton, B. (1990). Life transitions, role histories, and mental health. *American Sociological Review, 55,* 209–223.

White, L. K. (1979). Sex differentials in the effect of remarriage on global happiness. *Journal of Marriage and the Family, 41,* 869–876.

Wortman, C. B., Silver, R. C., & Kessler, R. C. (1993). The meaning of loss and adjustment to bereavement. In M. S. Stroebe, W. Stroebe, & R. O. Hansson (Eds.), *Handbook of bereavement* (pp. 349–366). Cambridge, UK: Cambridge University Press.

APPENDIX A

Descriptive Statistics for Analysis Variables

	Total Sample Mean (SD) N = 6,948	Women Mean (SD) n = 4,166	Men Mean (SD) n = 2,782
Demographic Characteristics			
Female	.52		
Age ≥ 40 (Time l)	.43	.44	.42
Black	.11	.12	.10
Employed	.73	.64	.82
Years of education	13.03 (2.78)	12.81 (2.64)	13.27 (2.90)
Household income (in thousands)	33.37 (41.52)	32.39 (39.58)	39.17 (44.52)
Missing on income data	.32	.30	.33
Child ≥ 18 in household	.42	.45	.39
Psychological Well-Being			
Depression	2.18 (1.16)	2.32 (1.11)	2.04 (1.19)
Depression (Time 2)	2.12 (1.13)	2.28 (1.11)	1.95 (1.12)
Global happiness	5.41 (1.32)	5.39 (1.36)	5.44 (1.28)
Global happiness (Time 2)	5.36 (1.31)	5.33 (1.35)	5.39 (1.26)
Self-esteem	4.12 (.59)	4.12 (.60)	4.12 (.58)
Self-esteem (Time 2)	4.10 (.63)	4.04 (.67)	4.16 (.59)
Personal mastery (1 item)	3.60 (.96)	3.56 (.98)	3.65 (.94)
Personal mastery (Time 2)	18.16 (3.4)	17.87 (3.48)	18.46 (3.28)
Hostility	3.22 (4.21)	3.42 (4.41)	3.01 (3.97)
Autonomy	14.48 (2.50)	14.36 (2.56)	14.61 (2.43)
Environmental mastery	13.79 (2.74)	13.64 (2.81)	13.94 (2.65)
Personal growth	15.13 (2.45)	15.16 (2.48)	15.10 (2.42)
Positive relations	13.70 (3.11)	14.02 (3.11)	13.35 (3.07)
Purpose in life	13.74 (2.87)	13.68 (2.89)	13.82 (2.84)
Self-acceptance	13.84 (2.74)	13.78 (2.78)	13.90 (2.70)
Marital Status			
Continuity			
Separated/Divorced	.07	.10	.05
Widowed	.02	.03	.004
Never married	.17	.14	.20
Age ≥ 40 × Separated/Divorced	.05	.06	.03
Age ≥ 40 × Never married	.02	.02	.02
Female × Separated/Divorced	.05		
Female × Widowed	.02		
Female × Never married	.07		

	Total Sample Mean (SD) N = 6,948	Women Mean (SD) n = 4,166	Men Mean (SD) n = 2,782
Change			
Married→Separated/Divorced	.06	.06	.06
Married→Widowed	.02	.03	.004
Never married→First married	.09	.08	.11
Separated/Divorced/ Widowed→Remarried	.03	.03	.03
Married→Separated/Divorced/ Widowed→Remarried	.02	.02	.02
Never married→Married→Separated/ Divorced/Widowed	.01	.01	.01
Age ≥ 40 × Married→Separated/Divorced	.02	.02	.02
Age ≥ 40 × Married→Widowed	.01	.02	—
Age ≥ 40 × Separated/Divorced/ Widowed→Remarried	.01	.01	.02
Female × Married→Separated/Divorced	.03		
Female × Married→Widowed	.01		
Female × Never married→First married	.04		
Female × Separated/Divorced/ Widowed→Remarried	.02		
Female × Married →Separated/ Divorced/Widowed→Remarried	.01		
Female × Unmarried→Married→ Separated/Divorced/Widowed	.01		

SOURCE: National Survey of Families and Households (1987–1993).

NOTE: Descriptive statistics calculated using weighted data. Dichotomous variable means are proportions.

APPENDIX B

Index Items

I. Ryff Psychological Well-Being Scales (rated on a 6-point scale: strongly disagree to strongly agree)

Autonomy

I tend to be influenced by people with strong opinions.[a]

I have confidence in my opinions, even if they are different from the way most other people think.

I judge myself by what I think is important, not by the values of what others think is important.

Positive Relations With Others

Maintaining close relationships has been difficult and frustrating for me.[a]

I have not experienced many warm and trusting relationships with others.[a]

People would describe me as a giving person, willing to share my time with others.

Purpose in Life

I live life one day at a time and don't really think about the future.[a]

Some people wander aimlessly through life, but I am not one of them.

I sometimes feel as if I've done all there is to do in life.[a]

Self-Acceptance

I like most parts of my personality.

When I look at the story of my life, I am pleased how things have turned out.

In many ways, I feel disappointed about my achievements in life.[a]

Environmental Mastery

The demands of everyday life often get me down.[a]

In general, I feel I am in charge of the situation in which I live.

I am quite good at managing the many responsibilities of my daily life.

Personal Growth

I gave up trying to make big improvements or changes in my life a long time ago.[a]

I think it is important to have new experiences that challenge how you think about yourself and the world.

For me, life has been a continuous process of learning, changing, and growth.

II. Self-Esteem Scale

Please indicate how much you agree or disagree with the following statements:

On the whole I am satisfied with myself.

I am able to do things as well as other people.

I feel that I'm a person of worth, at least on an equal plane with others.

III. Personal Mastery Scale

Please indicate how much you agree or disagree with the following statements:

I can do just about anything I really set my mind to.

Sometimes I feel that I'm being pushed around in life.[a]

There is really no way I can solve some of the problems I have.[a]

I have little control over things that happen to me.[a]

I have always felt pretty sure my life would work out the way I wanted it to.

---

a. Item reverse coded.

IV. Center for Epidemiological Studies Depression Scale (CES-D)

On how many days during the past week did you . . .

Feel you could not shake off the blues even with help from your family and friends?

Feel bothered by things that usually don't bother you?

Feel lonely?

Feel sad?

Feel depressed?

Have trouble keeping your mind on what you were doing?

Not feel like eating, your appetite was poor?

Feel everything you did was an effort?

Feel fearful?

Sleep restlessly?

Talk less than usual?

Feel you could not "get going"?

V. Hostility Scale

On how many days during the past week did you . . .

Feel irritable, or likely to fight or argue?

Feel like telling someone off?

Feel angry or hostile for several hours at a time?

4

SOCIAL LEARNING THEORY

I t seems fair to say that of all the theoretical approaches presented and discussed in this book, social learning theory is the most familiar to the most people, researchers and laypersons alike. This is not to say, of course, that everybody gets it right— for example, one of us doubts that one of his brothers-in-law understands the nuances associated with different schedules of reinforcement! But, terms and ideas like *reinforcement, punishment, conditioning, Pavlovian conditioning, imitation,* and others, unlike much of the terminology of scientific research, are widely understood (at least in a general way). No doubt, some of this familiarity can be attributed to the long history of this theory; it can be traced to the English philosopher, John Locke, and even further back. However, longevity is not a sufficient explanation for general familiarity with the theory because most of the other theories we have discussed also have deep historical roots.

We believe that the general appeal and awareness of the basics of social learning theory and its precursor, learning theory, are attributable to several factors. First, throughout the 1900s there was extensive research on various particular branches of the learning theory tree (broadly, *classical conditioning,* first systematically articulated by the Russian, Pavlov, and then by an American, Watson, and *instrumental* or *operant*

or *Skinnerian conditioning,* developed by B. F. Skinner). Second, from its inception, this research and the learning theory supporting it have been linked very directly to practical applications of individual and family life, such as how children develop skills and competencies, how parents become "good" or "bad" parents, and how people develop fears and phobias. We hypothesize that another reason for the general familiarity with this theory in America is that its basic tenet, that people can change and that there are specific mechanisms that can be identified and implemented to effect that change, is ingrained in the American system of values.

As you already know from whatever basic course you may have had in psychology or human development or, indeed, from your general attentiveness to life, according to learning theory, stated in its simplest form, individuals choose or increase behaviors that are likely to have positive consequences and avoid those that are likely to have negative consequences. Essentially, rewards shape and increase behaviors, and punishments decrease behaviors— although this does not happen automatically. Obviously, there are all kinds of issues that make the matter not so straightforward. For example, the timing of rewards and punishments in relation to the behavior(s) in question influences how well and for how long they work; the individual's prior life history makes some things rewarding that may not be rewarding for others; the context in which the behaviors, rewards, and punishments occur is influential; and, perhaps most important, the things that are called rewards and punishments serve *informative* and *motivational* functions for the person. That is, people observe their own behavior and its consequences and they notice the impact their behavior has on others (the informative function). As Bandura notes, this guides future action. In addition, because of their cognitive (thinking) capacities, people can anticipate future consequences of behavior (the motivational function). The research literature on learning research and theory is as extensive as that for any of the other theories in this book.

Since learning theory is a general theory, many of the same basic principles apply to animals as they do to humans. "However, the cognitive capacities of humans enable them to profit more extensively from experience than if they were unthinking organisms" (Bandura, 1977, p. 17). In addition, this allows people to learn vicariously to a highly refined and significant extent (but don't give your fellow humans too much credit; lion cubs learn vicariously too!). This vicarious, or observational, learning is the bridge to social learning theory: It is learning that occurs from observing the behavior of others and then reproducing that behavior. It is important to note that the reproduction of the observed behavior may or may not be seen immediately (see the Mihalic and Elliott reading in this chapter), and that the imitation of what has been observed can be practiced by thinking about it as well as by doing it.

Bandura (1977, p. 23) provided a schematic representation of the key features of observational learning. We highlight the major element here.

The event or behavior to be modeled (say, the way a father expresses affection) leads to *imitation, or "matching performances."* (Did you ever "practice" something you saw your mom, dad, or a teacher do?) But what things must occur for the observer to successfully and accurately replicate (imitate) or reproduce what has been observed? It is not automatic (as in general learning theory,

learning is not automatic). Here are some of the necessary *intervening variables* that must occur if the observed (modeled) behavior is to be reproduced:

1. *Attentional Processes:* Essentially, the observer must be tuned in to the model and the model must be distinctive and of some relevance to the observer.

2. *Retention Processes:* The observer must be capable of symbolically encoding information, reproducing the information, and practicing it mentally and motorically.

3. *Physical or Motor Reproduction Processes:* The observer must have the physical abilities, the ability to self-observe and self-evaluate attempts to imitate or reproduce, and the availability of component elements needed to reproduce the behavior.

4. *Motivational Processes:* Reinforcement of several types—self, vicarious, and external—must be present to facilitate the observer's interest in paying attention to and reproducing the behavior.

We hope that the above brief summary of the observational learning process makes it clearer that many things happen between the observation and the reproduction of a given behavior. The intervening variables are all required to one degree or another for observational learning to occur. However, you should not construe that our presentation of the social learning model indicates that all research issues and implications of this perspective are settled (but, of course, you know from Chapter 1 of this book that that is impossible—right?). Indeed, there have been literally thousands of studies on all aspects of the social learning model, and this work continues across many areas of importance for children and for families.

As alluded to earlier, the perspective expounded by social learning theory is virtually commonplace in discussions of parenting, child development, family interactions, intergenerational family functioning, and numerous other areas of individual development and family life. For example, how many times have you heard parents say they do things as parents that their own parents did with them? Why do parents not want to smoke or curse in front of young children? What does it mean when your mother says, "Wait until you have kids; you'll see how easy it is!"? Take a look at the two readings in this chapter that address similar questions.

THE READINGS

The readings in this chapter use social learning theory to guide their focuses on the issue of marital violence (Mihalic & Elliot, 1997) and on the intergenerational transmission of constructive parenting (Chen & Kaplan, 2001). The latter article integrates social learning theory with several other perspectives including symbolic interaction theory (Chapter 8), attachment theory, and social participation concepts to explain the consistent research finding that parents tend to use the same kinds of parenting practices that they experienced from their own parents. Chen and Kaplan addressed some of the problems inherent in retrospective studies by employing a research design that used longitudinal data over a period of two decades. In addition, important social learning concepts concerning the ability to retain what is observed for long periods of time and then to imitate those stored memories in a "mechanized" manner received empirical support in this study. Mihalic and Elliott (1997) show directly why a chapter on social learning theory deserves a place in a book of theories that focuses on family and individual development. Their focus is on family violence. Although they clearly acknowledge that their study tests a simplistic model of the relationship between exposure to family violence and the subsequent production of violence, their study does show that social learning theory provides a generally good explanation for some family violence. In one sense, Mihalic and Elliott's work is an extension of Crosbie-Burnett and Lewis's (1993) excellent discussion on social and cognitive-behavioral contributions to understanding families. These authors make a pretty clear case that the basic concepts of social learning theory—modeling, imitation, ability to delay reproduction of observed behaviors, and so forth—which are so widely applicable to individual development, present a powerful tool for family researchers to enhance their understanding of a variety of family issues.

ISSUES FOR YOUR CONSIDERATION

1. What are some family development issues that might be particularly well-suited to study from a social learning perspective?

2. After reading the following articles and Chapter 5 on social exchange theory, discuss how to integrate ideas from social learning theory with ideas from social exchange theory to explain some aspect of child development or some aspect of multigenerational family life. What are some of the similarities and differences between social exchange theory and social learning theory?

3. What other theories in this book might be productively used to investigate the issues that Chen and Kaplan pursued?

FURTHER READING

Akers (1996), Bandura (1977), Bandura (1986), Crosbie-Burnett and Lewis (1993).

A SOCIAL LEARNING THEORY MODEL OF MARITAL VIOLENCE

SHARON WOFFORD MIHALIC AND DELBERT ELLIOTT

Abstract

A social learning theory model of minor and severe marital violence offending and victimization among males and females was tested. Results support social learning as an important perspective in marital violence. However, males and females are impacted differently by their experiences with violence in childhood and adolescence. Prior experiences with violence have a more dramatic impact in the lives of females than males, both during adolescence and adulthood.

Introduction

Social learning theory is one of the most popular explanatory perspectives in the marital violence literature. When applied to the family, social learning theory states that we model behavior that we have been exposed to as children. Violence is learned, through role models provided by the family (parents, siblings, relatives, and boyfriends/girlfriends), either directly or indirectly, and reinforced in childhood and continued in adulthood as a coping response to stress or a method of conflict resolution (Bandura, 1973).

During childhood and adolescence, observations of how parents and significant others behave in intimate relationships provide an initial learning of behavioral alternatives which are "appropriate" for these relationships. If the family of origin handled stresses and frustrations with anger and aggression, the child who has grown up in such an environment is at greater risk for exhibiting those same behaviors witnessed or experienced, as an adult. Gelles (1972) states, "not only does the family expose individuals to violence and techniques of violence, the family teaches approval for the use of violence." Witnessing and experiencing violence may increase one's tolerance for violence. Finkelhor et al. (1988) suggest that those who are abused suffer from a sense of powerlessness, stigma, and inability to trust others which impairs the development of normal coping mechanisms, leading to violence as the ultimate resource.

Numerous studies have found evidence for the intergenerational "cycle of violence" hypothesis which suggests that violent and abusive adults learned this behavior as a result of being the victims of or witnesses of aggressive and abusive behavior as children (Browne, 1980; Burgess et al., 1987; Fagan et al., 1983; Gelles, 1972; McCord, 1988; Roy, 1982; Steinmetz, 1977; Straus et al., 1980; Walker, 1984). A major limitation of all these studies is their retrospective nature, relying on long recall periods, with the possibility of selective recall biases and memory reconstruction problems (Weis, 1989). Another serious complication arises because most of these samples are clinical samples rather than general population samples. This limits generalizability, and appropriate control group

98

comparisons are often missing. Effects of the intergenerational transmission of violence have generally been assessed only for male perpetrators and female victims. Little information is known about the effects of childhood violence on female perpetration and male victimization.

This study tests a predictive model of minor and severe marital violence offending and victimization, among both males and females, based upon a social learning theory of violence. We examine both male offending and victimization as well as female offending and victimization. By using longitudinal data, we avoid the problems inherent in retrospective data. We use path analyses to determine whether violence observed and/or experienced in childhood and adolescence has an impact on marital violence as an adult.

We acknowledge that our path models portray a fairly simplistic representation of social learning theory. They reflect only the linkages between observations of violence and direct experiences with violence during childhood and later behavioral outcomes in adulthood. This study, as well as most others in the family violence literature that have sought to find a direct link between childhood exposure to violence and later marital aggression, has not incorporated the intervening variables which may be ultimately responsible for determining whether a person will perform a learned behavior. According to Bandura (1969), exposure to violence does not ensure observational learning. A comprehensive theory of observational learning includes four component processes that influence the nature and degree of observational teaming: attentional processes, retention processes, motor production processes, and incentive and motivational processes. Some people fail to learn the essential features of the model's behavior, memories may be lost or altered with the passage of time, physical capabilities may restrict performance of a learned observation, and a learned behavior may not be expressed if it holds no functional value for the person or if the behavior is not reinforced. Breakdowns in any of the above processes may result in a failure to translate observational learning to behavior.

Review of the Literature

Intergenerational Transmission of Violence

The strongest support for the theory that being a victim of violence is related to engaging in violence oneself comes from the National Family Violence Surveys (Straus, 1990a; Straus et al., 1980). Straus found that males and females who endured more physical punishment as children had higher rates of marital violence as adults, both ordinary and severe violence. He also found that they reported higher rates of ordinary physical punishment and child abuse towards their own children. He found that men and women who had witnessed parents who hit each other were three times more likely than those who had not to abuse their own partners. Respondents with the experience of being both abused as a child and witnessing parental violence, the "double whammy," had a one in three chance of encountering marital violence in the study year, double the overall rate for annual marital violence (16% for the sample).

A review of findings from six studies indicates that 23 to 40% of battered women witnessed violence between their parents, while in four studies 10 to 33% of battered women were also abused as children (Okun, 1986).

Hotaling and Sugarman (1986), in their review of 52 case comparison studies of marital violence, indicate that witnessing violence between parents was a consistent risk marker for spouse abuse among both males and females. Although not a consistent risk marker, the majority of studies also found an association between being a victim of childhood violence and spouse abuse.

In a study of men in treatment for alcoholism and spouse abuse (Stith and Farley, 1993), support was demonstrated for an indirect path between observing violence as a child and later severe marital violence via sex-role egalitarianism and approval of marital violence, both of which directly influenced the use of severe violence. As egalitarianism decreased and approval of marital violence increased, level of severe violence increased. Observation of parental violence was also related to decreased self-esteem, which increased the level of alcoholism and marital stress, both of which had an effect on the approval of marital violence. The variables in this study were not measured in temporal sequence, hence no conclusions regarding causality can be made.

Intergenerational Transmission by Sex

Rosenbaum and O'Leary (1981) found that the effects of witnessing violence as children on later violent behavior were especially strong for males. Women who were victims of physical marital violence were no more likely than women in two control groups (composed of women who had suffered no physical abuse; one group claimed to have satisfactory marriages and the other group discordant marriages) to have witnessed spouse abuse between their parents. However, abusive husbands were much more likely to have come from families characterized by marital violence than husbands in the two control groups. These researchers also found that nearly 82% of husbands who witnessed marital violence as children were also victims of child abuse by their parents. Such findings support the intergenerational transmission theory only for males. Methodologically, there are several factors that may have contributed to the failure to find between-group differences among females. The cell N's were very small; the sample was comprised of only 92 women. Hotaling and Sugarman also suggest that multiple comparison group designs are unable to discriminate wife abuse victims from nonvictims when the nonvictims are comprised of women in distressed relationships.

In contrast, results of standardized self-report measures of aggression, depression, and anxiety administered to male and female college students showed greater anxiety, depression, and aggressiveness in women who had witnessed parental violence than in control groups of nonviolent discordant families and satisfactorily married families, suggesting that the effects of witnessing parental violence were more profound for women than men (Forsstrom and Rosenbaum, 1985). A

limitation of this study is the nonrepresentativeness of the student sample. Families with children in college may be better functioning than the general population resulting in underestimates of problem behaviors.

A major limitation of many of the studies of intergenerational transmission of violence is that they fail to separate witnessing violence from experiencing violence. These two types of exposure to violence may differentially affect the learning of marital violence. Kalmuss (1984) explored the relationship between childhood family aggression (by those children who directly experienced violence and those who only witnessed it in their families) and severe marital aggression in the next generation, using data from a nationally representative sample of 2,143 adults. In this retrospective study, she found that severe marital aggression was more likely when respondents, males and females, observed hitting between their parents than when they were hit as teens by their parents, although both forms of first generation violence resulted in increased levels of second generation marital aggression. Exposure to both types of childhood aggression led to a dramatic increase in the probability of marital aggression. Additionally, modeling of marital aggression was not found to be sex specific. Females who had observed fathers hitting mothers were just as likely to be the perpetrators of violence as the victims, just as males were as likely to be the victims as well as perpetrators of marital violence. Kalmuss concluded that the intergenerational transmission of aggression involves both generalizable and specific models. Generalized models increase the likelihood of any form of family aggression in the next generation, and specific models increase the likelihood of particular types of family aggression (e.g., children who observe aggressive acts between their parents are more likely to model aggressive behavior in their own marriages). (See also Seltzer and Kalmuss, 1988.) Although she claimed greater relevance for the specific model, she did not test the hypothesis that children who are hit by their parents are more likely to model this behavior as adults and hit their own children. Her tests were limited to marital aggression as an adult.

Mediating Factors Between Childhood Violence and Adult Violence

A large problem with the intergenerational violence studies is that often too much emphasis is given to an association found, and people assume that everyone who had a violent childhood will be violent to their own spouse and children. Kaufman and Zigler (1987) reviewed the literature cited to support the intergenerational theory of violence and postulated that the best estimate of the rate of intergenerational transmission appeared to be 30%, plus or minus 5%. Thus, while approximately one third of those who have suffered physical or sexual abuse or neglect as a child will subject their own children to some form of abuse, two thirds will not. They suggested a careful examination of the mediating factors that diminish the likelihood of abuse being transmitted across generations. Their literature review suggests the cycle is less likely to repeat itself if as a child s/he had the love and support of one parent; a loving, supportive relationship as an adult; fewer stressful events in life; and acknowledgement of the childhood abuse and determination not to repeat it.

Herrenkohl et al. (1983) reported that past or current life stresses or supports are influential in determining whether or not the cycle of violence is repeated. Respondents who were not abused as children but abused their own children reported more neglect, more stresses, and less nurturance in the family of origin than those who did not abuse their own children. Abused respondents who did not abuse their children reported fewer stresses on their family of origin than those abused respondents who had abused their own children.

A British study of working class women with children in the community of Islington revealed that neither the direct experience of violence as a child nor witnessing violence were associated with later violence (Andrews and Brown, 1988). Instead, they found violence to be associated with childhood neglect, irrespective of whether

they had been physically abused in childhood. Premarital pregnancy and teenage marriage were also associated with violence and appeared to provide a link between early neglect and marital violence.

Generalizability of Violence

A key element of social learning theory concerns its generalizability. Is the learning of aggressive behaviors restricted to particular contexts and targets? The Kalmuss study (1984, cited above) found evidence to support both generalizability and role-specificity. Others have investigated this issue and found that learning and modeling violence is generalizable across settings and targets.

Hotaling et al. (1988, 1990), using data from two nationally representative samples and a college student sample, found that both offenders and victims of family assault had higher rates of violent and non-violent crime outside the family. The relationship existed even with controls for socioeconomic class, gender, and severity of violence, although the relationship was, in general, stronger for mates and blue-collar families. Furthermore, children who were assaulted by parents were more violent toward siblings, parents, and persons outside the family. They were also more likely to be involved in property crimes and involved with the police. These authors suggest that it is not just the direct experience of being assaulted that leads to violence, but the experience of living in a multiassaultive family. The highest rates of outside family violence were reported by those respondents who were from families where they witnessed violence between their parents and were directly assaulted by a parent. These findings suggest that there are common links in all types of violence.

Straus (1990a) also discovered common links in several types of domestic violence. He found that the same factors that were associated with child abuse and wife-beating were also associated with the use of ordinary physical punishment and minor violence between spouses.

Widom (1989), in a prospective study of intergenerational transmission of violence, utilized a matched control group for her sample of abused and neglected children who came to the attention of juvenile court. She found that early child abuse and neglect placed one at risk for official recorded delinquency, adult criminality, and violent criminal behavior, even though a larger portion never engaged in adolescent and adult criminality (26% of child abuse and neglect victims had juvenile offenses, and 11% had an arrest for a violent criminal act).

Sex-Role Theory

A subtype of social learning, sex-role theory suggests that early sex-role socialization teaches boys to be the dominant partner, the major wage earner, the head of the household, and to maintain power and control, if necessary, by the use of force. Women are socialized to accept male dominant relationships and taught to meet the needs of others through their main roles as wives and mothers. These roles may leave males and females vulnerable to becoming offenders and victims of marital violence.

Most empirical studies have failed to validate a sex-role interpretation of marital violence (Hotaling and Sugarman, 1986). Walker (1984), contrary to her original supposition, found no evidence in her clinical sample that battered women had traditional sex-role attitudes. Instead, they perceived themselves as more liberal; however, they perceived their mates as traditional. Her research suggested that the discordance in perceived sex roles might lead to conflict within the marriage and hence to marital violence.

This hypothesis was tested by Coleman and Straus (1986), who found that equalitarian couples had the lowest rates of conflict and violence, while male or female dominant couples had the highest rates. Consensus about the legitimacy of the power structure reduced the rate of conflict and violence in male or female dominated families, but when conflict did occur in these families, it was associated with a much higher risk of violence than that of equalitarian families encountering the same level of conflict.

Summary

The research reviewed above supports the proposition that violence is transmitted intergenerationally. Exposure to violence during childhood and adolescence appears to be associated with higher rates of marital violence as an adult. There have been mixed results regarding the differential transmission of violence by sex. Violence has not been found to be transmitted by sex-specific models (Kalmuss, 1984). Males and females who witnessed parental violence were as likely to be the perpetrators as they were to be the victims of marital aggression.

Different forms of violence have also been found to have common links. Ordinary violence and abuse have been found to have a common etiology (Straus, 1990), and marital violence has been found to be associated with violence outside the family (Hotaling et al., 1990).

Studies that have examined mediating factors in the intergenerational transmission of violence suggest that the cycle of violence is less likely to repeat itself if the child had the nurturance, love and support of at least one parent; a loving, supportive relationship as an adult; fewer past and current life stresses; and recognition of the childhood abuse and determination not to repeat it.

Sex-role inequality interpretations of marital violence have not been fruitful. Hotaling and Sugarman (1986) suggest that sex-role inequality may be so pervasive in American society that it functions more as a constant than a variable. The most conclusive evidence (Coleman and Straus, 1986) suggests that disagreement over sex-role orientations may be a bigger factor in marital aggression than the actual orientations held.

The studies cited provide a strong theoretical basis for the social learning perspective of marital violence. We hope to extend this body of knowledge by testing a multivariate causal model of marital violence in a population sample with longitudinal data which includes social learning theory variables generally considered important in family violence research (e.g., witnessing parental violence, child abuse, and adolescent victimization). Although testing a simplified social learning theory model for marital violence is the focus in this paper, our data enables us to address two research questions which have not been commonly explored in the family violence literature: (1) is violence learned in one context generalizable to other contexts; and (2) does the intergenerational transmission of violence differ for male and female offenders and victims of marital violence?

Methods

Subjects

The data for this study were taken from the National Youth Survey (NYS), a multicohort panel design with a national probability sample of 1,725 respondents. The NYS respondents, aged 11 to 17 in 1976 (Wave 1), were interviewed in face-to-face interviews each year through 1980 (Wave 5), and thereafter at 3-year intervals, 1983 through 1992 (Wave 6 through Wave 9).

The sample for the present analysis was limited to married or cohabiting respondents. In the NYS, each married or cohabiting respondent reports on both his/her violence toward their spouse and their spouse's violence toward them. Only one member of each couple is reporting on the behavior of both partners. Hence, the NYS provides information on both male and female offending; and on both male and female victimization.

Subjects were included in the present study based upon a capture-recapture selection model. Subjects could enter the sample if they answered the battery of marital violence questions in 1983; if they were not included in the sample during this first time period (either because of not being married or lack of data for that survey year), they could enter the sample in 1986, and likewise in 1989 (if there was no information for 1983 and 1986). By including three survey years, we were able to increase the number of respondents reporting on marital violence. In most cases,

those added to the sample after 1983 were added because they became married during the intervals between data collection waves.

This sample of respondents who reported on marital violence were then examined with regard to their prior (during childhood and adolescence) exposure to violence: witnessing parental violence, child and adolescent abuse and victimization, and involvement in violence during adolescence. The prior experiences with violence were measures taken from the 1976 through 1980 surveys. Parent to child violence diminishes as children grow older. Straus (1990a) found age 13 to be the point at which many parents stopped using physical punishment, although half of the parents continued using physical punishment at age 13. For this reason, we limited our sample to respondents who were ages 11 to 15 in 1976. Hence, the oldest cohort was 19 years of age in 1980 and, in all likelihood, making the transition to independent living. At the time the marital violence was measured, 1983–1989, respondents were 18 to 28 years of age. After our restrictions, the sample included 797 male and female respondents reporting on marital violence, 374 males and 423 females. The path analyses, with 12 variables in the models covering a time range from 1976 to 1989, restricted the sample further to 360 females and 290 males with complete data.

Measures

Marital Violence

Our measure of marital violence included the eight Conflict Tactics Scale (CTS) items which measure physical violence. The reliability and validity of this scale has been well established (Straus, 1990b). The CTS queries male and female respondents about the means used to resolve conflicts with their spouses by asking respondents to think of situations in the past year when they had a disagreement or were angry with their partner and to indicate if they had engaged in or been a victim of any of the acts included in the CTS.

The eight CTS physical violence items were subclassified into two categories indicating the level of severty of violence: Minor and Severe. Minor violence included the following acts: throwing something, pushing, grabbing, or shoving; and slapping. Serious violence was comprised of kicked, bit or hit; hit with something; beat up; threatened with knife or gun; and used knife or gun. Item frequencies were summed to create the scales. The scale thus reflects the number of these acts committed by the respondent or her or his spouse during the past year. It is a count of violent acts, not of fights or conflicts.

Exogenous Variables

Two exogenous demographic variables were included in our path models. ETHNICITY was a measure of white and non-white (including Black, Hispanic, Indian, and Oriental) respondents. CLASS was a measure of parental class in 1976 (Wave 1) and was measured by Hollingshead's Two-Factor Index of social position (i.e., a combination of educational and occupational attainment). Scores ranged from 11 to 77 (high to low class).

WITNESS PARENTAL VIOLENCE was based on a retrospective question in which respondents at Wave 8 (1989), who were then 24–28 years old, were asked to recall if they had ever witnessed their parents physically hurt each other as a result of an argument or disagreement. We placed this variable exogenously, since we did not know the exact point in time that witnessing parental violence occurred and because observing violence in the family of origin is usually a child's first exposure to violence.

Endogenous Variables

The NYS enables us to examine the history of each respondent prospectively and thus examine prior victimization and assaultive behavior in adolescence and beyond on the part of those engaging in and victimized by marital violence as an adult. These data avoid most of the recall problems associated with long retrospective recall periods. Scales for CHILD ABUSE,

PRIOR VICTIM, MINOR assault, FELONY assault, and PROBLEM ALCOHOL use were created. These scales were composed of items (see Appendix at the end of this reading) from Waves 1 through 5 (1976–1980). With the exception of PROBLEM ALCOHOL use which utilized a five-point scale (described below), all items in these scales were composed of frequencies which were summed over the five-year period. Test-retest reliabilities were previously obtained for MINOR and FELONY assault and are within acceptable ranges, .59 and .67, respectively (Huizinga and Elliott, 1986). A log transform was used for MINOR and FELONY assault to correct for the skewness of these data.

Many studies have found an association between alcohol use and violence. In most of these studies, it is impossible to determine the temporal ordering (i.e., does alcohol use result in higher levels of marital violence, or does marital violence result in higher levels of alcohol use) since alcohol use is examined concurrently to marital violence. We chose to examine problem alcohol use during adolescence rather than concurrently with marital violence because it is clearly prior to marital violence and maintains a correct temporal order. We believe that early problem use is related to later problem use and will result in higher levels of stress and marital dissatisfaction, as well as marital violence. PROBLEM ALCOHOL use involved seven potential problem areas (e.g., problems with partner, friends, family, police, physical health, physical fights, and driving), each of which was scored on a 5-point scale ranging from "never" having this problem to having this problem "more than six times" during the past year. Each item was recoded to obtain a prevalence score (0 = no alcohol use or no problems, 1 = any problems), and then all seven items were summed to obtain a problem use score (0 to 7) for each of the 4 years (W2 to W5). The scores for each year were then summed (0 to 28) over the 5-year period.

A scale for SEXROLE attitude (see Appendix at the end of this reading) was also created. This scale was taken from the Wave 5 (1980) items, since these items were not asked again until 1992. High scores on this scale indicate a traditional or conventional sex-role attitude (Ageton, 1983).

It is believed that the above learning theory variables *will* operate through MARITAL SATISFACTION and STRESS, which were measured co-temporaneously with marital violence. Each of the items in these scales involved a five-point response scale, with higher scores indicating greater partner satisfaction and stress (see Appendix at the end of this reading).

Hypotheses

Exogenous Variables

Prior research reveals that although marital violence occurs in all strata of society, it is more common in the lower classes and among non-whites (Straus et al., 1980). It is our belief that class and ethnicity are proxies for a whole set of experiences and resources, and that the primary paths will be mediated by social learning variables, hence the primary effects of class and ethnicity will be indirect.

Observing parental violence has been found to be associated with marital violence in nearly all studies. Observation of violence in the home is one of the first ways in which we learn about violence, and hence begin to model violence. We propose that the observation of violence in the family of origin will lead to higher rates of adolescent violence (MINOR and FELONY assault) and victimization (CHILD ABUSE and PRIOR VICTIM) as well as PROBLEM ALCOHOL use.

Endogenous Variables

It is hypothesized that the five learning theory variables used in our model—CHILD ABUSE, PRIOR VICTIM, MINOR and FELONY assault, and PROBLEM ALCOHOL use—will be mediated by MARITAL SATISFACTION and STRESS. Learning theory suggests that oftentimes, in the presence of dissatisfaction, conflict or stress, the violence learned in childhood and adolescence will manifest itself in adult forms of violence (e.g., marital violence).

It is believed that sex-role attitudes are learned in early childhood and adolescence. Although studies have suggested that traditional attitudes are conducive to marital violence offending among males and victimization among females, there is little empirical evidence to support this notion. Instead, empirical studies have suggested that the impact of sex-role attitudes on conflict and marital violence is mediated by the degree of consensus in the relationship (Coleman and Straus, 1986). Since dissatisfaction and conflict may create conditions where differences in sex-role expectations lead to violence, we predict indirect paths between SEXROLE and marital violence through MARITAL SATISFACTION and STRESS. We acknowledge that in the literature sex-role attitude has been proposed as a direct causal path, so we utilize this strict interpretation of sex-role theory and also propose a direct path to marital violence (i.e., males with a traditional sex-role attitude will have higher rates of marital offending, and females will be at risk for marital victimization).

Findings

Frequency and Prevalence of Marital Violence

Table 4.1 shows the mean frequency of minor and serious marital violence offending and victimization among males and females for categories of each of the social learning theory model predictors. Table 4.2 shows the prevalence (proportion) engaging in marital violence for categories of each of the predictors.

At the bivariate level, these tables provide strong support for all of the social learning theory variables. Demographic variables indicate that non-whites had a higher frequency and prevalence of marital violence offending and victimization than whites. This was especially true among males, where a statistically significant relationship was found among all forms of marital violence. Among male and female respondents who witnessed parental violence, were abused or victimized during adolescence,

Table 4.1 Mean Frequency of Marital Violence Offending and Victimization

| | Offending | | | | Victimization | | | |
| | Minor | | Serious | | Minor | | Serious | |
	Male	Female	Male	Female	Male	Female	Male	Female
Ethnicity								
White	.89[a]	1.40[a]	.16[a]	.45[a]	1.63[a]	1.25	.79[a]	.52
Non-white	1.36	2.09	.52	1.24	2.61	1.43	1.96	.76
Class								
Middle	.65	1.11	.03	.36	1.24	.92	.45	.29
Working	.97	1.68	.23	.54	2.18	1.26	131	.51
Lower	1.10	1.55	.31	.68	1.84	1.48	1.09	.73
Witness parents								
No	.90	1.35[a]	.20	.50	1.71	1.09[a]	.96	.47
Yes	1.24	2.51	.37	1.04	2.68	2.40	1.66	1.19
Child abuse								
No	.91[a]	1.17[a]	.22	.39[a]	1.77	.88[a]	.98	.34[a]
Yes	1.78	3.80	.53	1.84	2.72	3.46	1.88	1.82
Victim								
No	.52[a]	.97[a]	.07[a]	.31[a]	1.12[a]	.72[a]	.60[a]	.36
Yes	1.16	2.20	.31	.91	2.11	1.84	1.22	.72
Minor								
No	.59	.89[a]	.09[a]	.17[a]	.59[a]	.62[a]	.33[a]	.24[a]
Yes	1.04	1.93	.27	.85	2.02	1.61	1.15	.72
Felony								
No	.72[a]	1.15[a]	.19	.36[a]	1.44[a]	.96[a]	.81[a]	.39
Yes	1.26	2.72	.30	1.30	2.27	2.04	1.31	.99
Problem alcohol								
No	.66[a]	1.10[a]	.19	.33[a]	1.41[a]	.96[a]	.76[a]	.43
Yes	1.27	2.01	.30	.89	2.18	1.51	1.28	.65
Sexrole								
Least traditional	1.16	1.43	.28	.58	1.86	1.09	1.05	.48
Avg. traditional	.91	1.74	.26	.62	1.57	1.56	.78	.70
Most traditional	1.05	1.29	.23	.48	2.12	.95	1.32	.40
Marital satisfaction								
Least satisfied	1.27[a]	2.16[a]	.30	.87[a]	2.43[a]	2.03[a]	1.46[a]	1.01[a]
Most satisfied	.68	.92	.16	.30	1.23	.57	.61	.14
Stress								
Low	.87	1.23	.19	.32	1.64	1.20	1.18	.44
Medium	.79	1.34	.19	.57	1.55	1.03	.68	.54
High	1.47	2.01	.39	.78	2.58	1.73	1.58	.69

a. Significance of t-test at $p < .05$. (Statistical Significance of Class, Sexrole, and Stress not determined.)

engaged in minor or felony assault, and who had problems with alcohol use during adolescence, the frequency and prevalence of marital violence offending and victimization was higher than for those respondents who reported "no" for each of the acts. Many of these relationships were statistically significant, more so for females than for males. Respondents who were least satisfied

Table 4.2   Mean Prevalence of Marital Violence Offending and Victimization

| | *Offending* | | | | *Victimization* | | | |
| | *Minor* | | *Serious* | | *Minor* | | *Serious* | |
	Male	*Female*	*Male*	*Female*	*Male*	*Female*	*Male*	*Female*
Ethnicity								
White	.30[a]	.43[a]	.07[a]	.17[a]	38[a]	.32	.22[a]	.10
Non-white	.48	.56	.19	.32	.66	.37	.51	.16
Class								
Middle	.24	.38	.03	.16	.32	.24	.18	.07
Working	.31	.52	.10	.18	.48	.36	.32	.11
Lower	.38	.43	.11	.21	.44	.34	.28	.13
Witness parents								
No	.34	.44	.08	.17[a]	.43	.29[a]	.27	.10
Yes	.34	.54	.15	.32	.49	.51	.37	.19
Child abuse								
No	.33	.41[a]	.09	.14[a]	.43	.28[a]	.26	.08
Yes	.44	.74	.22	.52	.50	.54	.41	.30
Victim								
No	.21[a]	.37[a]	.06	.13[a]	.33[a]	.23[a]	.19[a]	.06[a]
Yes	.39	.55	.11	.26	.48	.43	.31	.16
Minor								
No	.24	.33[a]	.07	.09[a]	.24[a]	.20[a]	.13[a]	.05[a]
Yes	.35	.53	.10	.26	.47	.40	.30	.14
Felony								
No	.27[a]	.39[a]	.07	.13[a]	.36[a]	.28[a]	.24	.08[a]
Yes	.41	.63	.12	.37	.52	.44	.31	.17
Problem alcohol								
No	.25[a]	39[a]	.08	.12[a]	.33[a]	.27[a]	.23	.09
Yes	.42	.52	.11	.27	.53	.37	.32	.12
Sexrole								
Least traditional	.37	.42	.14	.22	.39	.34	.32	.09
Avg. traditional	.30	.46	.08	.16	.41	.28	.24	.13
Most traditional	.38	.48	.10	.16	.49	.33	.30	.10
Marital satisfaction								
Least satisfied	.42[a]	.57[a]	.11	.26[a]	.53[a]	.45[a]	.38[a]	.20[a]
Most satisfied	.25	.35	.07	.13	.35	.21	.18	.03
Stress								
Low	.37[a]	.39	.09[a]	.15	.44	.27[a]	.33[a]	.13
Medium	.27	.44	.06	.19	.40	.28	.22	.09
High	.44	.52	.16	.24	.52	.43	.35	.15

a. Significance of t-test at $p < .05$. (Significance of Class, Sexrole, and Stress indicated by chi-square, $p < .05$.)

with their marriages and under the most stress had higher rates of marital violence offending and victimization than their counterparts. The relationship for marital satisfaction was statistically significant for all forms of female marital violence.

Path Analyses

The paths among the exogenous and endogenous variables are identical in the four male models, as they are in the four female models. The paths differ only for the outcome measures of marital violence. The reason for this is that the respondents in the sample of male offenders and victims, as well as female offenders and victims, are the same, since each respondent in the sample answered questions about his/her own violence as well as their partners' violence against them. Hence, these endogenous paths will only be discussed once.

Marital Violence Offending

Among males (Figure 4.1), minor marital violence offending was predicted directly by ETHNICITY, PRIOR VICTIM, STRESS, and MARITAL SATISFACTION. These paths were in the expected directions.

Only three variables predicted serious marital offending among males: ETHNICITY, CLASS, and SEXROLE. Non-whites and lower class males had a higher frequency of serious marital offending. In all the models, CLASS had a direct path to SEXROLE, with lower class respondents reporting more traditional sex-role attitudes. Only in the model for male serious offending was there a direct path to marital violence from SEXROLE. However, contrary to sex-role theory, males with a more traditional sex-role attitude had a lower frequency of serious marital violence offending. There were no indirect paths in either of these male models.

Among females (Figure 4.2), WITNESS PARENTAL VIOLENCE drives much of the model, with direct paths to five of the eight endogenous variables. Females who had witnessed violence among their parents experienced more CHILD ABUSE, victimization (PRIOR VICTIM), MINOR assault, STRESS, and less MARITAL SATISFACTION. The only direct paths to minor marital violence were from MARITAL SATISFACTION and FELONY. The greater the satisfaction in the marital relationship, the less marital violence; and females who

had committed felony assaults in adolescence had more minor marital offending. The indirect paths (e.g., WITNESS PARENTAL VIOLENCE and PRIOR VICTIM) were mediated primarily by MARITAL SATISFACTION.

In the serious marital violence model for females, the direct paths to marital violence were also from FELONY and MARITAL SATISFACTION, as well as ETHNICITY. Non-white females were more likely to engage in serious marital violence offending.

Among male victims of minor and serious marital violence victimization (Figure 4.3), the paths were fairly similar. ETHNICITY, PRIOR VICTIM, and MARITAL SATISFACTION had direct paths to minor and serious marital violence victimization, and in the model for minor marital violence, STRESS also had a direct path. The male models included no indirect paths.

Among females (Figure 4.4), the most important predictor of minor and serious marital violence victimization was MARITAL SATISFACTION, with less satisfied females more likely to be victimized. In the serious victimization model, CLASS also had a direct path, with lower class respondents at greater risk of victimization. As in the female offending models, the indirect paths (e.g., WITNESS PARENTAL VIOLENCE and PRIOR VICTIM) were mediated primarily by MARITAL SATISFACTION.

The variances explained in the male and female models for offending and victimization ranged from 9 to 30%. The social learning model worked better for females than males. With one exception (serious male victimization), the learning model predicted minor marital violence better than serious marital violence.

Discussion

Social learning theory focuses upon the indirect and direct experiences with violence in childhood as factors leading to experiences with violence as an adult. We tested a social learning model and found support for this explanation of adult violence. Although we found strong and consistent support for all the social learning

(Text continued on page 113)

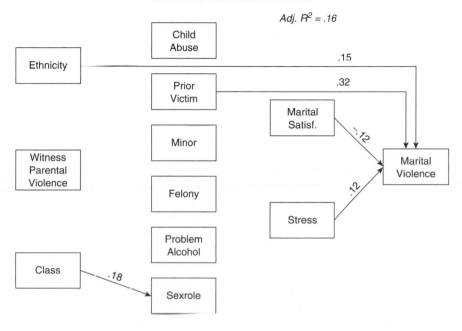

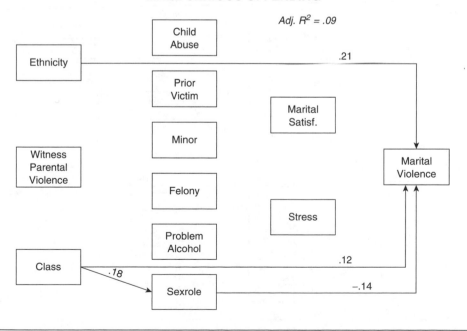

Figure 4.1

FEMALE MINOR OFFENDING

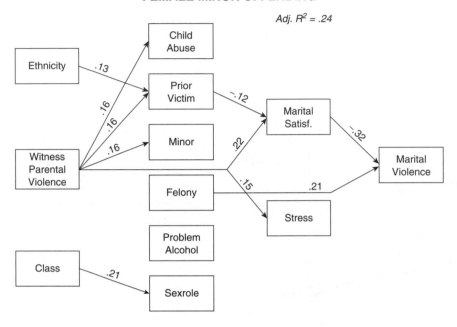

FEMALE SERIOUS OFFENDING

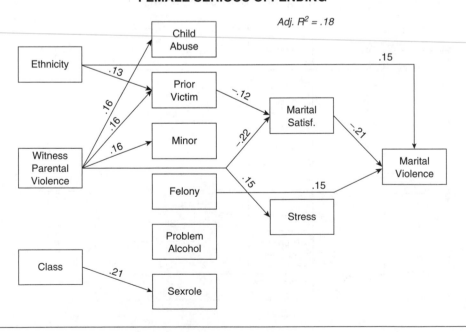

Figure 4.2

MALE MINOR VICTIMIZATION

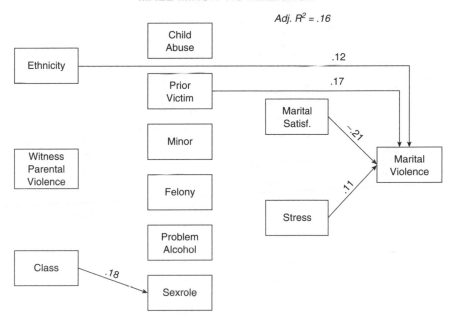

MALE SERIOUS VICTIMIZATION

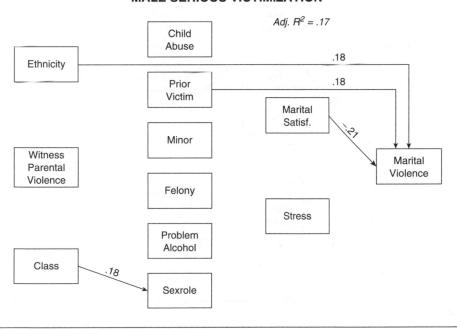

Figure 4.3

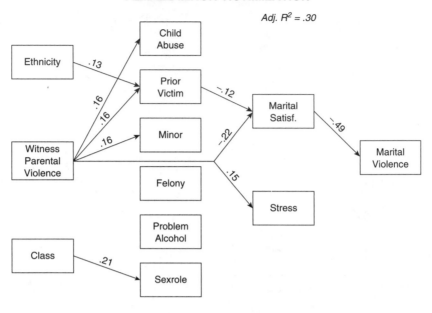

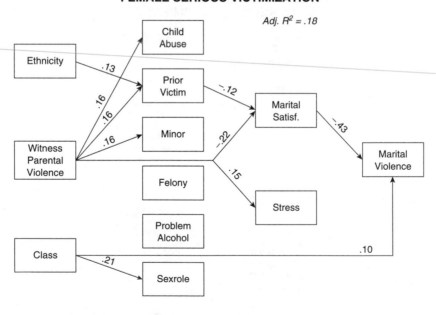

Figure 4.4

theory variables we examined at a bivariate level (except for sex-role attitudes), at a multivariate level several of these variables had no independent effect on marital violence. Most importantly, the impact of the early experiences with violence differed for males and females.

Witnessing violence in the family of origin provided the background for learning violence in the female models. Witnessing violence was associated with higher rates of child abuse, adolescent victimization, and minor assault as an adolescent. It resulted in greater stress and less marital satisfaction as an adult. Although there was no direct path from witnessing violence to marital violence, there were indirect paths through several variables, including marital satisfaction. In every female model, less marital satisfaction was associated with greater marital violence offending and victimization. Another important variable predicting female marital violence offending was committing felony assaults as an adolescent. Presence of felony assault in the female offending models indicates that, for many females, direct participation in violence began in adolescence and continued into adulthood. These findings suggest that violence is generalizable across contexts as suggested by Hotaling et al. (1988, 1990) and Straus (1990a).

Prior victimization was an important learning mechanism among males, with direct paths to marital violence offending and victimization (however, it had no significant impact upon serious offending). It is interesting that victimization often leads to aggression. Straus (1985) suggested that victims of violence may lose faith in the fairness of the world, thus feeling freer to engage in non-conforming behaviors. Hotaling et al. (1990) offer the suggestion that victims of violence see firsthand that violence may be an effective means of achieving one's ends. Important as this variable is in the male models, in the female models the effect of prior victimization was always mediated by marital satisfaction (i.e., females who had been victimized in adolescence were less happily married which was associated with higher rates of marital violence). Ethnicity was the most consistent

predictor of male offending and victimization, with non-whites having higher rates of marital violence. Marital satisfaction and stress were also important correlates of marital violence in several of the male models. (We use the term correlate when we discuss marital satisfaction and stress because these two measures are cotemporaneous with marital violence; this precludes us from ascertaining the temporal order of the variables.) [A 3-year lagged correlation analysis of respondents in a stable marital relationship showed no significant correlation between Marital Satisfaction in 1983 (Wave 6) and Minor and Serious Marital Violence Offending and Victimization in 1986 (Wave 7). This suggests that the effect of Marital Satisfaction is cotemporaneous with Marital Violence.]

The most noteworthy absent paths in the models were those involving child abuse. This variable, so common in the literature, had no impact on marital violence offending or victimization for either sex. Nor did sex-role orientation play a role in either minor or serious offending, or victimization, except in one model. That exception involved serious male offending, and the impact was reverse of that predicted by sex-role theory. Males with the most traditional attitudes had less serious marital violence. Various studies have failed to find a connection between traditional attitudes and marital violence (Hotaling and Sugarman, 1986; Walker, 1984).

Overall, these findings suggest that social learning of violence in childhood and adolescence has a stronger effect upon females than males. Witnessing parental violence and prior victimization, mediated by marital satisfaction (together with felony assault), are the strongest predictors of later violence among females. Among females, these early experiences with violence seem to impact other domains of life (e.g., adolescent violence and victimization, and greater stress and less marital satisfaction as an adult). For males, experiences with prior violence have no apparent impact on stress or marital satisfaction. Additionally, witnessing parental violence has no apparent effect upon either adolescent or adult violence among males. Males appear to be more affected by circumstances occurring concurrently with the marital violence (e.g., higher levels of stress and less marital satisfaction are often associated with marital violence).

Straus (1990a) argues that the training ground for violence begins in the early family experiences of children and that physical punishment is a major mechanism for learning violence. We found that observing parental violence had an effect only on females, and that severe physical punishment had no impact on adult violence for either sex. Kalmuss (1984) also found witnessing parental violence to be a more salient factor in severe marital aggression than being hit as a teen by parents. It is interesting that females were more affected by violence within the family of origin than males. Forsstrom and Rosenbaum (1985) also found the effects of witnessing parental violence to be more substantial among females. Females, with their more nurturing personalities, may have stronger emotional reactions to parental violence, thus impacting their fives to a more significant degree. It is also possible that parental violence may be more visible to females, since they often spend more time at home than males, especially at younger ages. Males are often given greater independence at earlier ages and may be better able to avoid episodes of violence within the home by physical withdrawal.

Social learning remains a viable explanation of marital violence. Our findings suggest that early exposure to violence may be interpreted differently by the sexes and do not have the same impact in either adolescence or adulthood. This suggests the need to examine males and females separately when testing a social learning model. We found evidence of both role specificity (females who witnessed parental violence had higher rates of marital violence, while being beaten by one's parents had no impact) and generalizability (females who witnessed parental violence had higher rates of minor adolescent violence, and adolescent felony assault was a predictor of adult marital violence). While seemingly contradictory, it is plausible that both

conditions exist, although the magnitude of these effects is different. Bandura (1971, 1973) presented experimental evidence that aggressive models transmitted specific as well as general lessons which went well beyond the specific modeled examples.

The generalizability of violence is a largely unexplored domain, and social learning theory provides an excellent starting point for study. Although our research was not focused around the issue of generalizability, this study supports the notion that violence is generalizable across contexts. Our major contribution has been to test a simplified social learning model using longitudinal data from a general population sample. Our finding that the intergenerational transmission of violence is stronger for females (both offenders and victims of violence) and that violence is generalizable provides an impetus for future research.

One final comment needs to be articulated. The above test included a relatively simplistic learning model which looked at the relationship between exposure to violence in various forms (i.e., modeling) and the performance of violent behavior. Formal learning theories (i.e., Bandura's observational learning theory model) specify a set of intervening processes which have not been examined in this paper.

References

Ageton, S. (1983). *Sexual assault among adolescents.* Lexington, MA: Lexington Books.

Andrews, B., & Brown, G. W. (1988). Marital violence in the community. A biographical approach. *Br. J. Psychiatry, 153,* 305–312.

Bandura, A. (1969). *Principles of behavior modification.* New York: Holt, Rinehart, and Winston.

Bandura, A. (1971). *Psychological modeling.* Chicago: Aldine-Atherton.

Bandura, A. (1973). *Aggression: A social learning analysis.* Englewood Cliffs, NJ: Prentice Hall.

Browne, S. F. (1980). Analysis of a battered women population. Denver Anti-Crime Council, 1445 Cleveland 1, Rm. 200, Denver, CO 80202.

Burgess, A. W., Hartman, C. R., & McCormack, A. (1987). Abused to abuser: Antecedents of socially deviant behaviors. *Am J. Psychiatry, 144*(11), 1431–1436.

Coleman, D. H., & Straus, M. A. (1986). Marital power, conflict, and violence in a nationally representative sample of American couples. *Viol. Vict., 1*(2), 141–156.

Fagan, J. A., Stewart, D. K., & Hansen, K. V. (1983). Violent men or violent husbands? Background factors and situational correlates. In D. Finkelhor, R. J. Gelles, G. T. Hotaling, & M. A. Straus (Eds.), *The dark side of families.* Beverly Hills, CA: Sage.

Finkelhor, D., Hotaling, G. T., & Yllo, K. (1988). *Stopping family violence: Research priorities for the coming decade.* Newbury Park, CA: Sage.

Forsstrom, B., & Rosenbaum, A. (1985). The effects of parental marital violence on young adults: An exploratory investigation. *J. Marr. Fam., 47*(2), 467–480.

Gelles, R. (1972). *The violent home: A study of physical aggression between husbands and wives.* Newbury Park, CA: Sage.

Herrenkohl, E. C., Herrenkohl, R. C., & Toedter, L. J. (1983). Perspectives on the intergenerational transmission of abuse. In D. Finkelhor, R. J. Gelles, G. T. Hotaling, & M. A. Straus (Eds.), *The dark side of families.* Beverly Hills, CA: Sage.

Hotaling, G. T., Straus, M. A., & Lincoln, A. J. (1988). Violence and other crime outside the family. In M. Tonry & L. Ohlin (Eds.), *Crime and justice. An annual review of research.* Chicago: University of Chicago Press.

Hotaling, G. T., Straus, M. A., & Lincoln, A. J. (1990). Intrafamily violence and crime and violence outside the family. In M. A. Straus & R. J. Gelles (Eds.), *Physical violence in American families. Risk factors and adaptations to violence in 8,145 families.* New Brunswick, NJ: Transaction Publishers.

Hotaling, G. T., & Sugarman, D. (1986). An analysis of risk markers in husband to wife violence: The current state of knowledge. *Viol. Vict., 1*(2), 101–124.

Huizinga, D., & Elliott, D. (1986). Reassessing the reliability and validity of self-report delinquency measures. *J. Quant. Criminol., 2,* 293–327.

Kalmuss, D. (1984). The intergenerational transmission of marital aggression. *J. Marr. Fam., 2,* 11–19.

Kaufman, J., & Zigler, E. (1987). Do abused children become abusive parents? *Am. J. Orthopsychiatry, 57*(2), 186–192.

McCord, J. (1988). Parental behavior in the cycle of aggression. *Psychiatry, 51*(1), 14–23.

Okun, L. (1986). *Woman abuse: Facts replacing myths.* Albany: State University of New York Press.

Rosenbaum, A., & O'Leary, Y. D. (1981). Children: The unintended victims of marital violence. *Am. J. Orthopsychiatry, 51*(4), 692–699.

Roy, M. (1982). *Battered women: A psychosociological study of domestic violence.* New York: Van Nostrand Reinhold.

Seltzer, J. A, & Kalmuss, D. (1998). Socialization and stress explanations for spouse abuse. *Social Forces, 67*(2), 473–491.

Steinmetz, S. K. (1977). *The cycle of violence. Assertive, aggressive, and abusive family interaction.* New York: Praeger.

Stith, S. M., & Farley, S. C. (1993). A predictive model of male spousal violence. *J. Fam. Viol., 8*(2), 183–201.

Straus, M. (1990a). Ordinary violence, child abuse, and wife beating: What do they have in common? In M. A. Straus & R. J. Gelles (Eds.), *Physical violence in American families. Risk factors and adaptations to violence in 8,145 families.* New Brunswick, NJ: Transaction Publishers.

Straus, M. (1990b). The conflict tactics scales and its critics: An evaluation and new data on validity and reliability. In M. A. Straus & R. J. Gelles (Eds.), *Physical violence in American families. Risk factors and adaptations to violence in 8,145 families.* New Brunswick, NJ: Transaction Publishers.

Straus, M., Gelles, R. J., & Steinmetz, S. K. (1980). *Behind closed doors: Violence in the American family.* Garden City, NY: Anchor Press/Doubleday.

Walker, L. R. (1984). *The battered woman syndrome.* New York: Springer.

Weis, J. G. (1989). Issues in the measurement of criminal careers. In A. Blumstein, J. Cohen, J. A. Roth, & C. A. Visher (Eds.), *Criminal Careers and "Career Criminals," Volume II.* Washington, DC: National Academy Press.

Widom, C. W. (1989, April). The cycle of violence. *Science, 244,* 160–244.

APPENDIX

Scales

A frequency count for each item from W1 to W5 (1976–1980).

Prior minor assault

Hit teacher

Hit parent

Hit student

Prior felony assault

Aggravated assault

Sexual assault

Gang fights

Prior abuse by parents (child abuse)

Beaten by parents

Prior victimization

Beaten by others

Attacked with a weapon

Sexually attacked

Problem alcohol use

Cronbach's Alpha Wave 6 = .61; Wave 7 = .61

A 5-point scale designed to measure problems associated with alcohol recoded for prevalence (0 = never and 1 = 1 or more times). Scores were summed over the 4-year period, W2 to W5 (1977–1980). High scores indicate problems with drinking.

Times in trouble with partner

Times in trouble with friends

Times in trouble with family

Times gotten into physical fights

Times had problems with physical health

Times gotten into trouble with police or been arrested

Times had accidents while driving

Sex-role attitude

Cronbach's Alpha Wave 5 = .84

A 9-item scale with response categories ranging from Strongly Agree to Strongly Disagree, with high scores indicating traditional sex-role attitudes.

Father should have greater authority

Women are able to do most jobs

Men are more reliable

Women are too emotional

Men shouldn't cry

Women's responsibility to care for children

Men's responsibility to earn money

Women are physically weaker

Forceful women are unfeminine

Marital satisfaction

Cronbach's Alpha Wave 6 = .88; Wave 7 = .89; Wave 8 = .74

A scale consisting of nine items, each with five response categories, with high scores indicating greater satisfaction with partner.

Share same interests with partner

Importance of things done with partner

Satisfied with relationship

Warmth and affection received from partner

Satisfied with sexual relations

Support and encouragement from partner

Loyalty for one another

Stress or pressure in relationship

Partner influenced what you've thought and done

Stress

Cronbach's Alpha Wave 6 = .48; Wave 7 = .54; Wave 8 = .55

Each item is measured by a 5-point scale, ranging from "Very Little" to "A Great Deal" of stress. The eight stress domains are summed to obtain a final stress score, with high scores indicating greater stress.

Stress/pressure in relationship with friends

If no friends, stress from not having friends

Stress/pressure from being in school/college

If not in school, stress from significant others about lack of education

Stress/pressure at work

If not working, stress from significant others to get a job

Stress/pressure in relationship with partner

Stress/pressure in relationship with parents

Stress/pressure in relationship with partner's parents

Stress/pressure in relationship with children (coded 0 if no children)

Stress/pressure in sex life

Intergenerational Transmission of Constructive Parenting

Zeng-Yin Chen and Howard B. Kaplan

Abstract

Past research on the intergenerational transmission of parenting concentrates on the continuity of harsh or abusive parenting, for the most part relying on retrospective reports of early upbringing. This study investigates the intergenerational transmission of constructive parenting using a 3-wave longitudinal data set that has spanned 2 decades, obtaining the respondents' contemporaneous reports in early adolescence, early adulthood, and middle adulthood respectively (N = 2,338). The results support the hypotheses that interpersonal relations, social participation, and role-specific modeling explain the intergenerational continuity of constructive parenting.

Parenting has increasingly been recognized as an important predictor for the outcomes of the offspring. Warm and supportive parenting was repeatedly credited for its association with children's higher educational achievement, better psychosocial development, and a lower rate of deviant behaviors (Baumrind, 1991; Dornbusch, Ritter, Leiderman, Roberts, & Fraleigh, 1987; Maccoby & Martin, 1983). For the most part, attention in these studies was focused on the consequences of parenting. Parenting tended to be treated as an independent variable, the variation of which was taken for granted. Since the 1980s, an increased interest in the antecedents of parenting has been observed. Various factors that might be influential in parental behavior

were proposed and tested. These included early developmental history, personality, psychological state, marital satisfaction, social network support, economic hardship, parenting beliefs, and perception of the child, to name a few (see Belsky, 1984; Conger, McCarthy, Young, Lahey, & Kropp, 1984; Erel & Burman, 1995; Orvaschel, Weissman, & Kidd, 1980; Simons, Beaman, Conger, & Chao, 1993). This study is informed by a consistent empirical finding from the literature regarding the intergenerational continuity of abusive or harsh parenting (Belsky, 1993; Egeland, Jacobvitz, & Papatola, 1987; Putallaz, Constanzo, Grimes, & Sherman, 1998; Simons, Whitbeck, Conger, & Wu, 1991; Straus, Gelles, & Steinmetz, 1980) insofar as we investigate the complementary phenomenon of the intergenerational continuity of constructive parenting.

Numerous research has documented the intergenerational continuity of parenting, demonstrating that present-day parents tend to use similar parenting strategies or practices that they themselves received in their childhood (see reviews by Putallaz et al., 1998, and van Ijzendoorn, 1992). A noticeable trend from this literature was its predominant attention to the intergenerational continuity of abusive or harsh parenting. Belsky (1984) pointed out that it was research inquiry into dysfunctional parenting, specifically, research on child abuse, that shed light on the intergenerational transmission of parenting for the general population. Empirical studies from the child abuse literature reported the association between the early experience of parental abuse and individuals' later abusive treatment of their own children (Belsky; Egeland et al., 1987; Straus et al., 1980). This relationship did not disappear even after controlling for socioeconomic status, personality, psychological well-being, and parenting beliefs (Simons, Whitbeck, et al., 1991; Simons, Beaman, et al., 1993). Steinmetz (1987) concluded that early exposure to harsh or abusive parenting was probably the most consistent predictor of the subsequent adoption of coercive parenting practices toward one's own children. The processes observed for extreme cases of child abuse can also be found in the normal range of parenting practices (Belsky).

The findings on the intergenerational transmission of supportive parenting mostly came from the studies of parent-infant relations. It was reported that the pregnant women who recalled their own parents as being supportive, less intrusive, and more sensitive during their early years were assessed as having better adaptation in their interaction with their infants later (Cox et al., 1985). Mothers' responsiveness toward their infants was inversely associated with their recalled conflict in their original family (Heinicke, Diskin, Ramsey-Klee, & Given, 1983). Similar results were reported more frequently in the attachment literature, which has shown that the present-day parents who recalled more warmth and acceptance from their own parents tended to demonstrate more responsiveness to their infants (Main, Kaplan, & Cassidy, 1985; Ricks, 1985; van Ijzendoorn, 1992).

Very few studies have investigated the intergenerational transmission of supportive parenting toward older children. The study by Simons and his associates (1993) confirmed the intergenerational continuity of supportive parenting by using recall data on the respondents' early upbringing, with their own parenting behavior reported by their adolescent children and household observations. Chassin, Presson, Todd, Rose, and Sherman (1998) tested the continuity of parenting across generations in their study on the intergenerational transmission of smoking, with mothers' early parental upbringing assessed in adolescence and mothers' own parenting behavior assessed in adulthood. Although the continuity of parental support was observed from mothers' self-report, the result was not reproduced by their children's perception of maternal support (Chassin et al., 1998).

Some researchers have initiated investigations of the mediating mechanisms linking childhood experiences of parenting to later utilization of similar parenting strategies. Some mediating mechanisms were identified, such as early modeling, depression, parenting beliefs, satisfaction with the child, development of the antisocial behavior trait, negative affects, and the quality of relationships, especially the marital relationship (Meyer, 1988; Putallaz et al., 1998; Simons et al., 1993; Simons, Wu, Johnson, & Conger, 1995).

Limitation of Previous Studies

The methodology of those early investigations on the intergenerational transmission of child maltreatment was considered to have a limitation of "looking backward," or retrospective design (i.e., those parents who maltreated their children were first identified, and then the researchers traced back the cause of child maltreatment to their early inadequate upbringing; Fontana, 1968; Melnick & Hurley, 1969). Using dysfunctional people as a base point was criticized as "leading to biased overgeneralizations of continuity accompanied by an inability to track mediating processes in development unconfounded by the retrospective accounting of early development" (Garmezy, 1988, p. 32).

Good prospective studies on intergenerational continuity of child maltreatment (e.g., Altemeier, O'Connor, Vietze, Sandler, & Sherrod, 1984; Egeland et al., 1987) typically started collecting data from parents (to be) at the time of pregnancy or the birth of a child. Researchers followed over time those subjects who had been identified as being at high risk for child maltreatment. These prospective studies had the advantage of starting to measure parental behavior before any child maltreatment began. A limitation of this kind of longitudinal prospective study was an exclusive reliance on retrospective reports from the present-day parents of their early upbringing experiences. Although the subjective interpretation of early experience in retrospective data should be acknowledged for its merit because of its conceivable influence on the respondents' later behavior, Yarrow, Campbell, and Burton (1970) pointed out that the value of the recollections would be greatly decreased if the objective was to obtain reports about the early upbringing that were uninfluenced by later perceptions, emotional states, and behaviors. The recollections of early experiences tended to be bent to be consistent to current perceptions (Yarrow et al.). Longitudinal studies following the respondents from childhood to parenthood are quite rare. The studies that came to our attention that tested the intergenerational transmission of parenting using the contemporaneous report of the early upbringing (i.e. the grandparents' parenting) were carried out by Elder, Caspi, and Downey (1986), Snarey (1993), Wadsworth (1985), and Chassin and associates (1998).

Although the mediating mechanisms of the intergenerational transmission of harsh or abusive parenting have received considerable attention, very little work has been done on the continuity of authoritative or constructive parenting toward older children across generations. Constructive parenting is not simply the other side of the coin of harsh or abusive parenting. Nonharsh or nonabusive parenting is not necessarily constructive because an absence of coercive or harsh parental behavior could be found among neglectful parents as well. Authoritative parenting has been identified by abundant studies as a powerful predictor for healthy development of the offspring (Baumrind, 1991; Dornbusch et al., 1987; Maccoby & Martin, 1983). Therefore, the determinant of authoritative or constructive parenting is entitled to be explored for its own sake. The study by Simons and his associates (1993) did explore the mediating mechanisms that transmitted both supportive parenting and harsh parenting across generations. There were some limitations in their study imposed by their data set, such as using

retrospective reports for the measure of early parental upbringing, cross-sectional data for the intervening and dependent variables, and a narrowly selected sample of rural, White, and two-parent families. In contrast, our study was based on a three-wave longitudinal data set that obtained the respondents' contemporaneous reports on early upbringing during adolescence, intervening mechanisms in their 20s, and their own parenting practices in the fourth decade of life. Thus, the possibility of retrospective distortion was obviated, and the causal directions were more credible. Further, the sample was diverse in ethnicity, family structure, and socioeconomic status, which contributes to the generalizability of the results.

Theoretical Model

Based on the findings on the existence of the intergenerational continuity of supportive parenting (Simons et al., 1993) and in an attempt to integrate previous theoretical and empirical studies, many of which were concerned with dysfunctional parenting, we estimated a model that specified hypothetical intervening processes in the intergenerational transmission of constructive parenting. Four mechanisms were proposed: psychological state, interpersonal relations, social participation, and role-specific modeling.

Psychological State

A healthy psychological state was hypothesized to mediate the intergenerational transmission of constructive parenting. Under the assumption that the environment continuously makes various demands on individuals and that stress is taken for granted, the concept of resilience has received increased attention (Garmezy, 1993; Kaplan, 1999). Early parental acceptance has been argued to be a protective factor relating to lower vulnerability and higher resilience in adverse situations (Greenbaum & Auerbach, 1992). Adolescents with parents who demonstrated authoritative parenting styles have lower stress levels and are more resilient, mature, and optimistic (Baumrind, 1991).

Retrospective studies on depression among clinical populations have shown that patients with depression tend to report experiences of parental rejection or lack of parental affection in their early childhood (Coyne & Downey, 1991; Crook, Raskin, & Eliot, 1981). A similar pattern was observed in the normal population. Early experiences of parental rejection lead to the development of depressive affect, which in turn contributes to subsequent rejecting parental behavior toward one's own children (Whitbeck et al., 1992).

Symbolic interactionism views a self-concept as based on the principle of "reflected appraisals," or the "looking glass self," that is, an individual sees oneself by taking the role of others (Cooley, 1902; Mead, 1934). Family constitutes an essential part of the "other" for children. Empirical literature provided evidence that parental affection, acceptance, respect, and authoritativeness are positively related to self-esteem (Buri, 1989; Coppersmith, 1967; Macobby & Martin, 1983). Perceptions of a lack of parental support and understanding, as well as parental devaluation and affectionless control, are associated with lower self-esteem or self-rejection (Chen & Dornbusch, 1998; Gecas & Schwalbe, 1986; Kaplan, 1980).

Psychological states have been found to be an important predictor of parenting behavior. Mothers' psychological health is positively related to their adaptation in the interaction with their infants (Cox et al., 1985; Heinicke et al., 1983). Psychological disturbance is negatively associated with supportive parenting (Simons et al., 1993). Depression and anxiety have been documented to relate to child maltreatment (Lahey, Conger, Atkeson, & Treiber, 1984; Whipple & Webster-Stratton, 1991). Depressed mothers tend to display more negative affect in the interaction with their children and thus make the family environment more disturbing, rejecting, and hostile (Orvaschel et al., 1980). Low self-esteem of the parents, as many studies have found, is related to child maltreatment (Belsky, 1993; Culp, Culp, Soulis, & Letts, 1989; Oates & Forrest, 1985).

Hypothesis 1: The experience of good parenting in early adolescence will have an indirect effect on an individual's own constructive parenting via its relationship to lower levels of psychological disturbance in the parent-to-be.

Interpersonal Relations

Early experiences in the parental home may affect one's own parenting behavior later through the engendering of general interaction styles in interpersonal relations. Attachment theory posits that the early relations with attachment figures and caregivers lead to a construction of an internal working model or representation about attachment, which is used to guide behavior in future relations (Bowlby, 1973, 1980, 1982). Although the internal working model in attachment theory is originally based on the parent-infant relationship, Main et al. (1985) extended the concept to attachment patterns of older children and adults, which has been followed by a growing adult attachment literature (Feeney & Noller, 1996; Hazan & Shaver, 1987). Some attachment styles depicted among adults are suggested to be phenotypically similar to those identified among infants (Simpson, Rholes, & Nelligan, 1992). For example, adults who are rated as secure tend to recall warm relations with their parents in their early life and rate themselves as easier to get to know and to be liked; they also are found to have fewer self-doubts and trust others to be generally well-intentioned and good-hearted (Hazan & Shaver). The adult attachment paradigm has contributed to the understanding of the intergenerational transmission of parenting through the mechanism of internal representation of attachment. Early upbringing might lead to the construction of an internal working model regarding attachment, which in turn translates into similar parenting styles later on (Main et al., 1985; van Ijzendoorn, 1992). A strong attachment in an individual's early years should lead to a development of a more positive working model regarding attachment that would be manifested in other relationships before being embodied in the parental role and then would be generalized to the parental role.

Although attachment styles across the life course tend to show continuity, they may be altered by subsequent relationships (Feeney & Noller, 1996). Thus the relationship patterns at any stage of life, including parent-child relations beyond early infancy and childhood, could have an impact on attachment styles. Emotional detachment from parents as measured during adolescence was related to perceived parental rejection and felt insecurity (Ryan & Lynch, 1989), higher psychological distress and lower self-esteem (Chen & Dornbusch, 1998). Therefore, parental behavior reported by adolescents should be no less important in predicting later attachment patterns.

The more recent brain research sheds a fresh light on the transmission of personal qualities from a neurodevelopment perspective (Perry, 1997). Researchers in this field has argued that childhood experiences affect the development of the brain, which in turn influences emotional, behavioral, and cognitive development. The development of the brain is highly use-dependent. Growing up in a violent or neglectful family environment tends to impair the development of the higher and more complex part of the brain, which controls primitive impulses and promotes capabilities of empathy and attachment, while facilitating the development of the lower and simpler portion of the brain, which prompts adaptive survival functions, such as a "fight or flight" state. Conversely, early experiences of good parenting that assist the development of the higher portion of the brain should promote empathetic capabilities for better interpersonal relations. Although brain research focuses on the impact of early experiences, assuming continuity of human behavior, parental behavior assessed during adolescence should in part reflect substantial early experiences.

The personality traits people form in early years and the interaction styles they acquire in the parental home in early childhood are likely to be carried out in their interaction with other people even before parenthood and thus affect their interpersonal relations. When they become parents, the habitual interaction styles they have used in their interaction with other people extend to their children. Belsky's review (1984) on the determinants of parenting summarized the available research to support his process model: Early supportive family environment contributes to the development of a healthy personality, which in turn influences parenting behavior via its influence on the social context surrounding parent-child relations such as marital relations, social networks, and work experience. The early experience of ineffective parenting can lead to the development of antisocial traits and coercive behavior in dealing with other people (Patterson, 1982; Simons et al., 1995). Elder and his colleagues (1986) demonstrated that the early experience of hostile and unaffectionate parental care contributes to the development of unstable personality in adulthood, which in turn predicts marital tension and dysfunctional parenting behavior. Individuals who maltreat their children are reported to be generally lacking impulse control and empathy (Friederich & Wheeler, 1982), more socially isolated from relatives and friends (Kotelchuck, 1982; Polansky, Chalmers, Buttenwieser, & Williams, 1981; Starr, 1982), and less likely to discuss their problems with others (Oates & Forrest, 1985). By the same token, good experiences of early parental upbringing should lead to a development of healthy interpersonal styles, which tends to be carried over later in the form of constructive parenting practices toward their own children. Further, facilitative interpersonal relations should enable one to interact freely and therefore to learn informally from other people's experiences of what constitutes acceptable parental behavior, whereas poor interpersonal relations deprives one such an opportunity.

Hypothesis 2: The experience of good parenting in early adolescence will have an indirect effect on an individual's own constructive parenting via positive interpersonal relations.

Social Participation

An early favorable experience in upbringing is said to affect later constructive parenting via the extent one becomes part of the conventional social order as manifested in continuing participation in schooling and other conventional institutions, such as political activities and voluntary associations (net of their relationship to socioeconomic status). The bulk of research on the effects of parenting demonstrates the relationship between parenting styles and educational achievement of the offspring. Authoritative (as opposed to authoritarian, permissive, or neglectful) parenting style has long been documented to predict better academic achievement of adolescents (Baumrind, 1991; Dornbusch et al., 1987). In turn, education is positively related to the effort to improve one's own parenting, for example, as manifested in the positive relationship between an individual's educational status and the likelihood of participation in childrearing educational programs (Harman & Brim, 1980). Higher parental education is found to be positively associated with authoritative or supportive parenting (Dornbusch et al.; Serbin et al., 1998).

Positive experiences in the family of socialization should be associated with a willingness to participate in social or political activities. Active social participation would make an individual more likely to be part of a conventional order, which functions as a social control to promote conventional parental behavior and constrains deviant parental behavior. Constructive parenting is also a result of a well-developed and well-informed life experience. Through participation in social life, one receives a perspective on how to be a good parent. In fact, parents who maltreat their children are reportedly less likely to be involved in formal organizational membership and informal socializing activities (Polansky et al., 1981). Neglectful parents are reported to participate less in community and church-related activities (Giovannoni & Billingsley, 1970; Polansky, Gaudin, Ammons, & Davis, 1985).

Hypothesis 3: The experience of good parenting in early adolescence will have an indirect effect on an individual's own constructive parenting via active social participation.

Role-specific Modeling

Previous theoretically proposed mechanisms that account for the intergenerational transmission of harsh parenting frequently focused on social learning theory-related mechanisms of observing, modeling, and reinforcement (Burgess & Youngblade, 1988; Simons et al., 1991; Straus et al., 1980). Bandura's (1977) learning theory posits that people are able to retain early images in memory for later modeling. Furthermore, modeling can occur in a mechanical way with little awareness after the learned behavior becomes routinized (Bandura) Crittenden (1984) proposed that learning can occur as a result of observing parents' interaction with other children, the child's own past interaction with parents, and being coached by parents in his or her interaction with another child. Simons and his associates (1991) distinguished various learning processes that might have transmitted harsh parenting across generations, such as direct learning that resulted in a mechanical way, forming a parenting philosophy on the desirability of strict discipline, and developing a hostile personality to act aggressively toward other people including one's own children.

Social learning involves a wide range of behaviors, both negative and positive. Although the social learning process was highlighted by the research on the intergenerational transmission of abusive or harsh parenting, the process should also take place in the intergenerational transmission of constructive parenting.

Hypothesis 4: The experience of good parenting in early adolescence will have a direct positive effect on an individual's own constructive parenting.

If this hypothesis is well grounded, the direct effect from the early positive experience with parents to the later adoption of constructive parenting should remain significant after other intervening processes were taken into account. Unlike the instances of the first three hypotheses, no variables were available that might reflect intervening social learning mechanisms. Hence, we inferred such processes from any observed direct residual effect, as Simons and his colleagues did in their studies (Simons et al., 1991, 1993).

Background Factors

Existing literature has documented the effect of socioeconomic status, gender, and family structure on parenting practices (Dornbusch et al., 1987; Elder et al., 1986; Simons et al., 1991; Wille, 1995). Therefore, these variables were controlled as background variables in the model to eliminate possibly spurious conclusions regarding causal effects of earlier parenting experiences in the family of socialization on parenting practices when the adolescent adopts the parental role in adulthood.

Method

Sample

The present study used three waves of a longitudinal data set to test the hypotheses. The first wave of data was obtained from self-administered questionnaires responded to by the students in the seventh grade (modal age = 13 years) in a random 50% of the 36 high schools in Houston Independent School District in 1971 (Kaplan, 1980). The response rate was 81.6% with 7,618 students turning in usable questionnaires (Time 1). The respondents were followed up by household interviews between 1980 and 1988 when the subjects were in their 20s (Time 2) and between 1993 and 1997 when they were in mid- to late-30s (Time 3). Because our study was concerned with the intergenerational transmission of parenting, the final sample selected only included those respondents who had at least one child aged 6 to 18 years in the third wave to be eligible to answer the parenting questions. Listwise deletion of cases with missing data

resulted in a sample of 2,338 for the estimation of the structural equation models.

Because this longitudinal study covered an interval of over 20 years, an important concern was possible bias introduced by sample attrition. We compared the means and standard deviations of the sociodemographic variables and other variables relevant to this study measured at Time 1 for those who were present for all three waves of survey (4,594) with those who were not present for all three waves (3,024). Compared with the latter, the former reported a somewhat higher percentage of women and Whites, a lower percentage of Mexican Americans, a higher level of parental education, a higher percentage of intact families, a lower percentage of families in poverty, higher scores on experiencing good parenting at home, higher grades, and lower scores on depression and self-rejection. Because of concern that social advantages associated with remaining in the sample might influence the hypothesized relations among the study variables, we proceeded to check the possible moderating effect of being socially advantaged or disadvantaged on the proposed relations in the remaining sample. We created an index of risk factors, which included being a non-White individual in poverty from a nonintact family and having lower parental education (the mean of the two parents' educational level lower than finishing high school) for Time 1 background variables. We tested the proposed full model separately for those who had at most one risk factor (1,574) and those who had two or more risk factors (754) in the remaining sample. All the hypotheses tested received support from both groups, with only one difference in the magnitude of a mediating pathway that was statistically significant: Social participation had a stronger positive effect on later constructive parenting among those who had two or more risk factors than among those who had at most one risk factor (.09 vs. .05, unstandardized coefficients). We concluded that the current sample would not greatly bias the hypothesized relations regarding the intergenerational transmission of parenting. Nevertheless, readers are advised to be cautious in interpreting the results beyond the current sample.

Measures

Control variables. A number of background variables that could conceivably affect the proposed causal relationships among the independent, mediating, and dependent variables are modeled as exogenous control variables, including gender, parental education, family poverty, and family structure, all measured at Time 1. For those who did not provide the information for parental education at Time 1, the values for the same variable at Time 2 are substituted. Parental education averaged the highest level of schooling reported by the two parents (mother or stepmother and father or stepfather). If only one parent was available, the measure reflects the value for that parent. Family poverty was a dichotomized variable, "My family was poor" *(1 = yes, 0 = no,* reverse coded). Family structure was also a dichotomized variable, whether the respondent was currently living with his or her "two real parents." The control variables were modeled as having direct or indirect influence on the independent, mediating, and dependent variables.

The major independent variable, perception of experiencing good parenting, was measured at Time 1 when the respondents were in the seventh grade. The variable was modeled as a latent construct reflected in three additive indexes: (a) two items reflecting whether the respondent was happy at home (alpha = .58), such as "At home I have been more unhappy than happy" (reverse coded); (b) six items describing the perception of receiving good parenting at home (alpha = .52), such as "Sometimes my parents will punish me for doing something that at another time they didn't mind me doing" (reverse coded); and (c) three items indicating the perceived parental acceptance and love (alpha = .60), such as "My parents do not like me very much" (reverse coded). We tested the construct validity of the perception of experiencing good parenting by correlating each of the three indicators with the contemporaneous self-report of school

performance (coefficients ranging from .21 to .23) and deviant behaviors (coefficients ranging from −.26 to −.30). All coefficients were consistent with theoretical expectations and statistically significant (p < .001).

The intervening variables were measured at Time 2 when the respondents were in their 20s. Psychological state, or more precisely, psychological disturbance, was treated as a latent construct reflected in three additive indexes: (a) seven items indicating symptoms of depressive affect (alpha = .67), such as "Do you often feel downcast and dejected"; (b) five items describing symptoms of anxiety (alpha = .58), such as "Are you often bothered by nervousness"; and (c) eight items reflecting self-rejection (alpha = .73), such as "At times I think I am no good at all." The three indicators were adapted from the scales used by previous research that supported the construct validity (Johnson & Kaplan, 1990; Kaplan, Johnson, & Bailey, 1986).

Interpersonal relations constituted a latent construct reflected in two additive indexes: (a) five items describing feelings about relations with relatives (alpha = .74) such as how often, when thinking about their relationship with their relatives, they had feelings of being "ashamed," "bored," "uncomfortable," "unsure" of themselves, "unwanted" or "worried" respectively; and (b) the same five items in describing feelings about relations with friends (alpha = .73).

Social participation was treated as a latent construct reflected in three indicators: (a) educational attainment, the report of years of formal schooling; (b) four items reporting organizational membership in "professional," "civic," "religious," or "social" organizations respectively (alpha = .46); and (c) three items regarding political participation (alpha = .42), such as "Within the last year, did you vote in a public election." Previous work supported the reliability and validity of organizational and political participation (Kaplan, Liu, & Kaplan, 1997).

The dependent variable, constructive parenting, was measured at Time 3 when the respondents were in their mid- to late-30s. This latent construct was reflected in five additive indexes:

(a) four items about monitoring children (alpha = .54), such as "How often would you say you know where they are and who they are with when they are away"; (b) two items relating to communication (alpha = .66), such as "How often would you say children discuss things that happened at school with you"; (c) six items describing their involvement in children's education (alpha = .73), such as "How often would you say you help these children with school work"; (d) two items regarding how often they and children show affection to each other (alpha = .69); and (e) four items relating to discipline, such as how often they talk to children when they did something wrong and praise them when they were good (alpha = .56).

We initially created the five indexes of constructive parenting on the basis of content validity to reflect the dimensions of responsiveness and demandingness (Maccoby & Martin, 1983). We further tested the construct validity of each index by correlating it with the respondents' own report of their children's school performance (coefficients ranging from .12 to .17) and deviant behaviors (coefficients ranging from −.09 to −.20). All coefficients were consistent with theoretical expectations and statistically significant (p < .001).

All indexes in the model were formed by taking the mean of the component items only if at least two thirds of these items had valid values for that case. The index was treated as system missing for any case that had missing data in more than one third of the items.

Analyses

LISREL 8 (Joreskog & Sorbom, 1993) was used to estimate the measurement models and the structural models simultaneously using maximum likelihood estimates. A baseline model was first estimated in which the sociodemographic variables predicted the adolescent perception of experiencing good parenting at Time 1, which in turn predicted later constructive parenting in middle adulthood at Time 3. Next a full model was estimated in which the intervening

constructs of psychological state, interpersonal relations, and social participation measured at Time 2 were specified. The variances of the background variables were allowed to be correlated. The correlations among the disturbance terms for the equations of the three intervening constructs were also relaxed.

Results

Table 4.3 provides the correlation matrix among the 20 variables included in the structural equation model. The estimation of the measurement models and the structural models was based on the covariance matrix of the 20 observed variables.

Figure 4.5 and Figure 4.6 present the results for the baseline model and the full model respectively. For visual clarity, the correlations among the disturbance terms for the intervening constructs and the paths from the sociodemographic variables are omitted from the figures, with these effects reported in Table 4.4 and Table 4.5 respectively. Figure 4.5 presents the baseline model in which the sociodemographic variables predicted the perception of experiencing good parenting in early adolescence at Time 1, which in turn predicted later constructive parenting in middle adulthood at Time 3. After the effect of the sociodemographic variables were taken into account, the adolescent perception of experiencing good parenting had significant positive effect on their own constructive parenting in middle adulthood, with a standardized coefficient of .17.

Figure 4.6 presents the full model in which the intervening variables of psychological state, interpersonal relations, and social participation measured at Time 2 were entered, with the remaining direct effect from the perception of receiving good parenting in early adolescence to later constructive parenting interpreted in terms of role-specific modeling processes. The result showed that the adolescent perception of good parental upbringing predicted less psychological disturbance, better interpersonal relations, and more active social participation in early adulthood. Interpersonal relations and social

Table 4.3 Means, Standard Deviations, and Correlation Coefficients Among 20 Observed Variables Included in the Structural Equation Models

	v1	v2	v3	v4	v5	v6	v7	v8	v9	v10	v11	v12	v13	v14	v15	v16	v17	v18	v19	v20
v1																				
v2	-.01																			
v3	.01	-.10*																		
v4	-.04	.08*	-.10*																	
v5	-.09*	.04	-.19*	.13*																
v6	-.00	.10*	-.16*	.10*	.47*															
v7	.02	.07*	-.19*	.09*	.49*	.42*														
v8	.15*	-.09*	.05*	-.04*	-.15*	-.14*	-.13*													
v9	.15*	-.10*	.03	-.05*	-.17*	-.15*	-.11*	.52*												
v10	.12*	-.06*	.07*	-.05*	-.13*	-.13*	-.15*	.54*	.41*											
v11	-.05*	.05*	-.03	.07*	.11*	.08*	.09*	-.30*	.20*	.31*										
v12	-.03	.06*	-.06*	.05*	.08*	.07*	.09*	-.34*	.29*	.41*	.36*									
v13	-.04	.33*	-.09*	.13*	.13*	.15*	.12*	-.19*	-.20*	.17*	.10*	.11*								
v14	-.00	.15*	-.06*	.06*	.05*	.09*	.05*	-.13*	-.10*	-.15*	.00	.08*	.30*							
v15	-.01	.15*	-.05*	.06*	.05*	.07*	.08*	-.11*	-.09*	-.13*	.04	.10*	.26*	.31*						
v16	.18*	.13*	-.06*	.07*	.07*	.08*	.12*	-.12*	-.09*	-.12*	.05*	.14*	.16*	.12*	.12*					
v17	.21*	.07*	-.03	.01	.06*	.06*	.07*	-.07*	-.03	-.07*	.05*	.12*	.10*	.09*	.07*	.37*				
v18	.29*	.11*	-.03	.06*	.08*	.08*	.09*	-.09*	-.06*	-.08*	.05*	.10*	.20*	.17*	.15*	.46*	.43*			
v19	.11*	.08*	-.04	.04*	.09*	.08*	.07*	-.09*	-.07*	-.11*	.08*	.13*	.13*	.09*	.06*	.37*	.46*	.42*		
v20	.19*	.07*	-.06*	.03	.07*	.07*	.08*	-.07*	.00	-.07*	.04*	.10*	.06*	.08*	.06*	.35*	.42*	.41*	.56*	
M	.63	3.04	.08	.72	.80	.64	.90	.13	.14	.14	2.50	2.79	7.63	.22	.26	2.76	2.59	2.50	2.84	2.90
SD	.48	.81	.26	.45	.34	.27	.22	.20	.21	.20	.39	.29	1.34	.25	.27	.31	.49	.41	.34	.22

v1 = female; v2 = parent education; v3 = poverty; v4 = intact; v5 = happy; v6 = good parenting; v7 = parental acceptance; v8 = depression; v9 = anxiety; v10 = self-rejection; v11 = relatives; v12 = friends; v13 = education; v14 = member of an organization; v15 = political participation; v16 = monitoring; v17 = communication; v18 = affection; v19 = involvement; v20 = discipline. N = 2,338, *p < .05 (two-tailed tests).

127

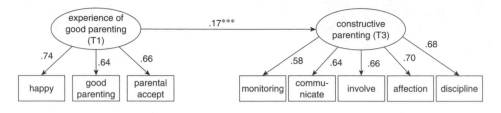

Figure 4.5   Baseline Model—Intergenerational Transmission of Constructive Parenting

NOTE: Exogenous variables = female respondent, parent education, poverty. intact. $N = 2,338$. ***$p < .001$ (two-tailed tests).

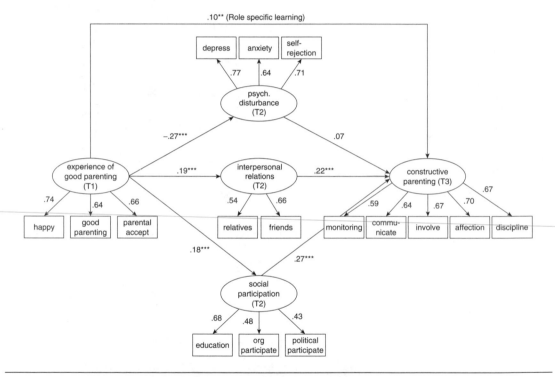

Figure 4.6   Full Model—Intergenerational Transmission of Constructive Parenting

NOTE: Exogenous variables: female respondent, parent education, poverty, intact. $N = 2,338$. **$p < .001$ (two-tailed tests).

participation in early adulthood in turn predicted a higher score in constructive parenting in middle adulthood. Psychological disturbance in early adulthood, however, did not have a significant effect on constructive parenting in middle adulthood net of the effects of the other two mediating constructs.

The intervening mechanisms were not mutually exclusive. Table 4.4 presented the standardized coefficients for the covariance matrix among the disturbance terms for the three equations on psychological disturbance, interpersonal relations, and social participation. Both Table 4.3 and Table 4.4 indicate that these three

Table 4.4   Standardized Coefficients of Covariances Among the Disturbance Terms for the Equations on the Intervening Constructs

	Psychological Disturbance	*Interpersonal Relations*	*Social Participation*
Psychological disturbance			
Interpersonal relations	−.67***	.15***	
Social participation	−.27***		

NOTE: $N = 2,338$.

*$p < .05$. **$p < .01$, ***$p < .001$ (two-tailed tests).

intervening constructs were strongly correlated with each other, with the correlations between psychological states and interpersonal relations having the strongest magnitude. The effect from psychological disturbance on later constructive parenting could be indirect, via its contemporaneous associations with interpersonal relations and social participation.

After the mediating processes of psychological state, interpersonal relations, and social participation were taken into account, the direct effect from the adolescents' perception of experiencing good parenting on their own constructive parenting in middle adulthood persisted, with a standardized coefficient of .10. This direct effect is consistent with the reasoning underlying Hypothesis 4 on role-specific modeling, which functioned side by side with other mediating processes in transmitting parenting practices across generations.

Table 4.5 presents the complete report of the path coefficients for the baseline model and the full model. In the baseline model, parental education and growing up in an intact family predicted higher scores of adolescent perception of receiving good parenting, whereas family poverty predicted lower scores. The variables of female respondent and parental education predicted higher scores of constructive parenting in middle adulthood. In the full model, the predictions from the control variables on later constructive parenting in middle adulthood were very similar to that in the baseline model, with the exception that parental education was no

longer significant in predicting the respondents' own constructive parenting after the intervening variables were entered into the model. In predicting the intervening variables, being a female respondent predicted higher scores of psychological disturbance. Parental education predicted lower scores of psychological disturbance, better interpersonal relations, and more active social participation. Growing up in an intact family also predicted better interpersonal relations and more active social participation.

Discussion

Research on the intergenerational transmission of harsh or abusive parenting is abundant in the literature. This study contributes to the body of research on a parallel phenomenon, the continuity of constructive parenting across generations. Most research on the intergenerational transmission of parenting patterns relies on the retrospective reports of early parental upbringing. Unfortunately, recollections tend to be subject to distortion by current perceptions, emotional states, or behaviors (Yarrow et al., 1970). Our study uses a three-wave longitudinal data set that obtained the respondents' contemporaneous reports on the perception of the parenting received in early adolescence, the mediating processes in early adulthood, and their own parenting behavior in middle adulthood, respectively. The results confirm the existence of modest intergenerational continuity of constructive parenting and support the hypotheses that

Table 4.5 Standardized Path Coefficients for the Structural Equation Models Predicting Constructive Parenting

	Model 1		Model 2				
	Experience Good Parenting (T1)	Constructive Parenting (T3)	Experience Good Parenting (T1)	Psychological Disturbance (T2)	Interpersonal Relations (T2)	Social Participation (T2)	Constructive Parenting (T3)
Female (T1)	-.03	.30***	-.03	.18***	-.05	-.03	.31***
Parental education (T1)	.06**	.12***	.06**	-.09***	.08**	.40***	.00
Poverty (T1)	-.24***	-.01	-.24***	-.02	-.01	-.03	.00
Intact (T1)	.13***	.04	.13***	-.01	.06*	.11***	.00
Experience good parenting (T1)	—	.17***	—	-.27***	.19***	.18***	.10**
Psychological disturbance (T2)	—	—	—	—	—	—	.07
Interpersonal relations (T2)	—	—	—	—	—	—	.22***
Social participation (T2)	—	—	—	—	—	—	.27***
Chi-square	299.80 with 43 df			623.41 with 138 df			
GFI	.98			.97			
AGFI	.96			.96			
RMSEA	.05			.04			

NOTE: $N = 2,338$. T1 = Time 1; T2 = Time 2; T3 = Time 3.

$*p < .05.$ $**p < .01.$ $***p < .001$ (two-tailed tests).

interpersonal relations, social participation, and role-specific modeling explain such continuity of constructive parenting across generations.

The hypothesized intervening process of psychological state was found to be affected by the adolescent perception of parental upbringing but to have no effect on the subsequent report of their own constructive parenting practices in middle adulthood. The mechanisms of psychological state, interpersonal relations, and social participation proposed in this study were not mutually exclusive and were found to be correlated. The effect from the proposed intervening process of psychological state to constructive parenting might have been attenuated because of its contemporaneous association with interpersonal relations and social participation. People with negative psychological states should be less likely to maintain good quality of interpersonal relations and less likely to be active in social participation. Because these intervening variables were measured cross-sectionally, we did not propose the causal directions among them. Nonetheless, we speculate that psychological disturbance may have decreased later constructive parental behavior indirectly via its contemporaneous associations with poorer interpersonal relations and less active social participation.

The remaining direct effect from the early experience of good parenting to later constructive parenting practices after considering the three mediating mechanisms is interpreted as reflecting the underlying process of role-specific modeling. This result is consistent with the finding of Simons and his associates (1993) regarding the persistence of the direct effect from the early experience of supportive parenting to later adoption of similar parenting strategies. Furthermore, the magnitude of the remaining direct effect was still more than half of the total effect after the other three intervening mechanisms were taken into account, indicating the specific role modeling may be the strongest process implicated in the intergenerational transmission of constructive parenting. This finding is consistent with many investigations that report the social learning process as a primary mechanism

(see the review by Putallaz et al., 1998). Nonetheless, it is also possible that other factors not included in the study might have mediated the intergenerational transmission of parenting. For example, the direct effect may also implicate heritability factors and contextual continuity, such as sharing the same physical and social circumstances (van Ijzendoorn, 1992), for which we are not able to test adequately with our data set.

Our findings also indicated a lack of support for the direct effects on later constructive parenting from early family status variables, such as parental education of the respondents, family poverty, and family structure. Although the measurement of family poverty was admittedly inadequate, other less problematic variables such as parental education and growing up in a two-parent household also failed to predict the respondents' own parenting in middle adulthood directly. Apparently, childrearing practices were not affected by these status variables per se, but rather by an earlier upbringing that had been influenced by these status variables. This result is consistent with the view that called for attention to family processes in addition to family statuses (Bronfenbrenner, 1986).

The size of the total effect of the intergenerational transmission of constructive parenting measured in this study is at best moderate. There has been an interval of more than 2 decades between the measurements of the adolescent perception of parental upbringing and their later parenting practices, during which many events in the life course could have possibly altered the impact of the perceived experiences measured during early adolescence. This result is in agreement with the implication from attachment theory on the possibility of restructuring the internal working model formed in early years through other attachment-related experiences, and the topic of the intergenerational discontinuity of parenting deserves no less attention than that of the continuity (Ricks, 1985; Rutter, 1989). Nonetheless, the observation of a significant effect on the continuity after such a long time interval is noteworthy.

Past research has explored gender-specific effect in the intergenerational transmission of behavior (Serbin et al., 1998; Simons et al., 1993). A thorough examination of the gender effect in the intergenerational continuity of parenting in our study was precluded because information about the gender of grandparents to which respondents referred was not always available (i.e., it was unknown to which parent respondents referred when they mentioned early (dis)satisfaction). We did, however. use the available information to perform further analyses using gender as a moderating variable. We found that the pattern and the magnitude of the intergenerational transmission of parenting for men and women were generally similar. This finding may be interpreted as parallel to the results of Cohen, Kasen, Brook, and Hartmark (1998), which showed that the intergenerational continuity of some higher order childhood behavioral dimensions did not vary by gender. Nonetheless, gender differences in the intergenerational transmission of parenting might be more observable with the availability of the grandparents' gender when the two generations could be paired by the same-gender or opposite-gender dyads.

Ideally, the items to measure the early experience of parenting should match that of later parenting practices. This match was not possible in this study because the items about constructive parenting were not available in the first wave. We have attempted to approximate the adolescent perception of parental upbringing using the items available and at the same time acknowledge the shortcoming of that measurement. Furthermore, in the absence of observational measures, there could be a discrepancy between the actual parenting and the adolescent perception of parenting experienced. In addition, the reliance on a single source of self-report for all variables may have artificially inflated associations among all the variables. Future research needs to incorporate multiple sources of data to check the reliability of the measures and to strengthen problematic measures of key variables in these analyses such as family economic situation and interpersonal relations. Another limitation of the study is the absence of data on differential parenting strategies in dealing with different age groups of their children at Time 3. Adolescence is a special period in which parent-child relationship undergoes considerable adjustment. Parenting practices directed toward adolescent children should be conceivably different from those directed toward younger children. Future design should make an effort to differentiate the parenting styles toward different age groups of children.

This study contributes to an increasingly abundant literature that specifies the mechanisms through which early experiences with parents influence one's own parenting practices at a later time. In estimating such models, we tested the credibility of the theoretical premises that guide our analyses.

Note

This research was supported by Grants ROI DA 02497 and R01 DA 10016 and Research Scientist Award K05 DA 00136 to the second author from the National Institute on Drug Abuse.

References

Altemeier, W. A., O'Connor, S., Vietze, P., Sandler, H., & Sherrod, K. (1984). Prediction of child abuse: A prospective study of feasibility. *Child Abuse and Neglect, 8,* 393–400.

Bandura, A. (1977). *Social learning theory.* Englewood Cliffs, NJ: Prentice-Hall.

Baumrind, D. (1991). The influence of parenting style on adolescent competence and substance use. *Journal of Early Adolescence, 11,* 56–95.

Belsky, J. (1984). The determinants of parenting: A process model. *Child Development, 55,* 83–96.

Belsky, J. (1993). Etiology of child maltreatment: A developmental-ecological analysis. *Psychological Bulletin, 114,* 413–434.

Bowlby, J. (1973). *Attachment and loss. Vol. 2: Separation.* New York: Basic Books.

Bowlby, J. (1980). *Attachment and loss. Vol. 3: Loss, sadness, and depression.* New York: Basic Books.

Bowlby, J. (1982). *Attachment and loss. Vol. 1: Attachment* (2nd ed.). New York: Basic Books.

Bronfenbrenner, U. (1986). Ecology of the family as a context for human development. *Developmental Psychology, 22,* 723–742.

Burgess, R. L., & Youngblade, L. M. (1988). Social incompetence and the intergenerational transmission of abusive parental practices. In G. T. Hotaling, D. Finkelhor, J. I. Kirkpatrick, & M. A. Straus (Eds.), *Family abuse and its consequences: New directions in research* (pp. 38–60). Newbury Park, CA: Sage.

Buri, J. R. (1989). Self-esteem and appraisals of parental behavior. *Journal of Adolescent Research, 4,* 33–49.

Chassin, L., Presson, C. C., Todd, M., Rose, J. S., & Sherman, S. J. (1998). Maternal socialization of adolescent smoking—the intergenerational transmission of parenting and smoking. *Developmental Psychology, 34,* 1189–1201.

Chen, Z., & Dornbusch, S. M. (1998). Relating aspects of adolescent emotional autonomy to academic achievement and deviant behavior. *Journal of Adolescent Research, 13,* 293–319.

Cohen, P, Kasen, S., Brook, J. S., & Hartmark, C. (1998). Behavior patterns of young children and their offspring: A two-generation study. *Developmental Psychology, 34,* 1202–1208.

Conger, R. D., McCarthy, J. A., Young, R. K., Lahcy, B. B., & Kropp, J. P. (1984). Perception of child, child-rearing values, and emotional distress as mediating links between environmental stressors and observed maternal behavior. *Child Development, 55,* 2234–2247.

Cooley, C. H. (1902). *Human nature and the social order.* New York: Scribner.

Coppersmith, S. (1967). *The antecedents of self-esteem.* San Francisco: W. H. Freeman.

Cox, M. J., Owen, M. I., Lewis, J. M., Riedel, C., Scalf-Michler, L., & Suster, A. (1985). Intergenerational influences on the parent-infant relationship in the transition to parenthood. *Journal of Family Issues, 6,* 543–564.

Coyne, J. C., & Downey, G. (1991). Social factors and psychopathology: Stress, social support, and coping processes. *Annual Review of Psychology, 42,* 401–425.

Crittenden, P. M. (1984). Sibling interaction: Evidence of a generational effect in maltreating infants. *Child Abuse & Neglect, 8,* 433–438.

Crook, T., Raskin, A., & Eliot, J. (1981). Parent-child relationships and adult depression. *Child Development, 52,* 950–957.

Culp, R. E., Culp, A. M., Soulis, J., & Letts, D. (1989). Self-esteem and depression in abusive, neglecting, and nonmaltreating mothers. *Infant Mental Health Journal, 10,* 243–251.

Dornbusch, S. M., Ritter, R. L., Leiderman, P. H., Roberts, D. E., & Fraleigh, M. J. (1987). The relation of parenting style to adolescent performance. *Child Development, 58,* 1244–1257.

Egeland, B., Jacobvitz D., & Papatola, K. (1987). Intergenerational continuity of abuse. In R. J. Gelles & J. B. Lancaster (Eds.), *Child abuse and neglect: Biosocial dimensions* (pp. 255–276). New York: Aldine de Gruyter.

Elder, G. H., Jr., Caspi, A., & Downey, G. (1986). Problem behavior and family relationships: Life-course and intergenerational themes. In A. M. Sorenses, E. E. Weiner, & L. R. Sherrod (Eds.), *Human development and the* life *course: Multidisciplinary perspectives* (pp. 293–342). Hillsdale, NJ: Erlbaum.

Erel, O., & Burman, B. (1995). Interrelatedness of marital relations and parent-child relations: A meta-analytic review. *Psychological Bulletin, 118,* 108–132.

Feeney, J., & Noller, P. (1996). *Adult attachment.* Thousand Oaks, CA: Sage.

Fontana, V. (1968). Further reflections on the maltreatment of children. *New York State Journal of Medicine, 68,* 2214–2215.

Friedrich, W. N., & Wheeler, K. K. (1982). The abusing parent revisited: A decade of psychological research. *Journal of Nervous and Mental Disease, 170,* 577–587.

Garmezy, N. (1988). Longitudinal strategies, causal reasoning and risk research: A commentary. In M. Rutter (Ed.), *Studies of psychosocial risk: The power of longitudinal data* (pp. 29–44). Cambridge, UK: Cambridge University Press.

Garmezy, N. (1993). Vulnerability and resilience. In D. C. Funder, R. D. Parke, C. Tomlinson-Keasey, & K. Widaman (Eds.), *Studying lives through time* (pp. 377–397). Washington, DC: American Psychological Association.

Gecas, V., & Schwalbe, M. L. (1986). Parental behavior and adolescent self-esteem. *Journal of Marriage and the Family, 48,* 37–46.

Giovannoni, J. M., & Billingsley, A. (1970). Child neglect among the poor: A study of parental adequacy in families of three ethnic groups. *Child Welfare, 84,* 196–214.

Greenbaum, C. W., & Auerbach, J. G. (1992). The conceptualization of risk, vulnerability, and resilience in psychological development. In C. W. Greenbaum & J. G. Auerbach (Eds.), *Longitudinal studies of children at psychological risk: Cross-national perspective* (pp. 9–28). Norwood, NJ: Ablex.

Harman, D., & Brim, O. G. (1980). *Learning to be parents*. Beverly Hills, CA: Sage.

Hazan, C., & Shaver, R. (1987). Romantic love conceptualized as an attachment process. *Journal of Personality and Social Psychology, 52,* 511–524.

Heinicke, C., Diskin, S., Ramsey-Klee, D., & Given, K. (1983). Prebirth parent characteristics and family development in the first year of life. *Child Development, 54,* 194–208.

Johnson, R. J., & Kaplan, H. B. (1990). Stability of psychological symptoms: Drug use consequences and intervening processes. *Journal of Health & Social Behavior, 3,* 277–291.

Joreskog, K. G., & Sorbom, D. (1993). *LISREL 8 user's reference guide*. Chicago: Scientific Software International.

Kaplan, D. S., Liu, X., & Kaplan, H. B. (1997). A longitudinal study of the relationship between adolescent academic achievement and adult community participation. *Applied Behavioral Science Review, 5,* 185–198.

Kaplan, H. B. (1980). *Deviant behavior in defense of self*. New York: Academic Press.

Kaplan, H. B. (1999). Toward an understanding of resilience: A critical review of definitions and models. In M. D. Glantz, J. Johnson, & L. Huffman (Eds.), *Resiliency and development: Positive life adaptations* (pp. 17–83). New York: Plenum Press.

Kaplan, H. B., Johnson, R. J., & Bailey, C. A. (1986). Self-rejection and the explanation of deviance: Refinement and elaboration of a latent structure. *Social Psychology Quarterly, 49,* 110–128.

Kotelchuck, M. (1982). Child abuse and neglect: Prediction and misclassification. In R. H. Starr, Jr. (Ed.), *Child abuse prediction: Policy implications* (pp. 67–104). Cambridge, MA: Ballinger.

Lahey, B. B., Conger, R. D., Atkeson, B. M., & Treiber, F. A. (1984). Parenting behavior and emotional status of physically abusive mothers. *Journal of Consulting and Clinical Psychology, 52,* 1062–1071.

Maccoby, E. E., & Martin, J. (1983). Socialization in the context of the family: Parental-child interaction. In P. H. Mussen (Ed.), *Handbook of Child Psychology* (pp. 1–101). New York: Wiley.

Main, M., Kaplan, N., & Cassidy, J. (1985). Security in infancy, childhood, and adulthood: A move to the level of representation. In I. Bretherton & E. Waters (Eds.), Growing points of attachment theory and research. *Monographs of the Society for Research in Child Development, 50*(1–2), 66–104 (Serial No. 209).

Mead, G. H. (1934). *Mind, self and society*. Chicago: University of Chicago Press.

Melnick, B., & Hurley, J. R. (1969). Distinctive personality attributes of child abusing mothers. *Journal of Consulting and Clinical Psychology, 33,* 746–749.

Meyer, H. J. (1988). Marital and mother-child relationships: Developmental history, parental personality, and child difficultness. In R. A. Hinde & J. Stevenson-Hinde (Eds.), *Relationships within families: Mutual influences* (pp. 119–139). Oxford, UK: Clarendon Press.

Oates, R. K., & Forrest, D. (1985). Self-esteem and early background of abusive mothers. *Child Abuse and Neglect, 9,* 89–93.

Orvaschel, H., Weissman, M. M., & Kidd, K. K. (1980). Children and depression: The children of depressed parents: The childhood of depressed patients; depression in children. *Journal of Affective Disorders, 2,* 116.

Patterson, G. R. (1982). *A social learning approach. Vol. 3: Coercive family process*. Eugene, OR: Castalia.

Perry, B. D. (1997). Incubated in terror: Neurodevelopmental factors in the "cycle of violence." In J. D. Osofsky (Ed.), *Children in a violent society* (pp. 124–149). New York: Guilford Press.

Polansky, N. A., Chalmers, M. A., Buttenwieser, E., & Williams. D. P. (1981). *Damaged parents: An anatomy of child neglect*. Chicago: University of Chicago Press.

Polansky, N. A., Gaudin, J. M., Ammons, R. W., & Davis. K. B. (1985). The psychological ecology of the neglectful mother. *Child Abuse & Neglect, 9,* 265–275.

Putallaz, M., Costanzo, P. R., Grimes, C. L., Sherman, D. M. (1998). Intergenerational continuities and their influences on children's social development, *Social Development, 7,* 389–427.

Ricks, M. (1985). The social transmission of parental behavior: Attachment across generations. In I. Bretherton & E. Waters (Eds.), Growing points of attachment theory and research. *Monographs of the Society for Research in Child Development, 50*(1–2), 211–227 (Serial No. 209).

Rutter, M. (1989). Intergenerational continuities and discontinuities in serious parenting. In D. Cicchetti & V. Carlson (Eds.), *Child maltreatment: Theory and research on the causes and consequences of child abuse and neglect* (pp. 317–348*)*. New York: Cambridge University Press.

Ryan, R. M., & Lynch, J. H. (1989). Emotional autonomy versus detachment: Revisiting the vicissitudes of adolescence and young adulthood. *Child Development, 60,* 340–356.

Serbin, L. A., Cooperman, J. M., Peters, P. L., Lehoux, P. M., Stack, D. M., & Schwartzman, A. E. (1998). Intergenerational transfer of psychosocial risk in women with childhood histories of aggression, withdrawal, or aggression and withdrawal. *Developmental Psychology, 34,* 1246–1262.

Simons, R. L., Beaman, J., Conger, R. D., & Chao, W. (1993). Childhood experience, conceptions of parenting, and attitudes of spouse as determinants of parental behavior. *Journal of Marriage and the Family, 55,* 91–106.

Simons, R. L., Whitbeck, L. B., Conger, R. D., & Wu, C. (1991). Intergenerational transmission of harsh parenting. *Developmental Psychology, 27,* 159–171.

Simons, R. L., Wu, C., Johnson, C., & Conger, R. D. (1995). A test of various perspectives on the intergenerational transmission of domestic violence. *Criminology, 33,* 141–172.

Simpson, J. A., Rholes, W. S., & Nelligan, J. S. (1992). Support seeking and support giving within couples in an anxiety-provoking situation: The role of attachment styles. *Journal of Personality and Social Psychology, 62,* 434–446.

Snarey, S. (1993). *How fathers care for the next generation: A four decade study.* Cambridge, MA: Harvard University Press.

Starr, R. H., Jr. (1982). A research-based approach to the prediction of child abuse. In R. H. Starr, Jr. (Ed.), *Child abuse prediction: Policy implications* (pp. 105–134). Cambridge, MA: Ballinger.

Steinmetz, S. K. (1987). Family violence. In M. B. Sussman & S. K. Steinmetz (Eds.), *Handbook of marriage and the family* (pp. 725–765). New York: Plenum Press.

Straus, M. A., Gelles, R. J., & Steinmetz, S. K. (1980). *Behind closed doors: Violence in the American family.* Beverly Hills, CA: Sage.

van Ijzendoorn, M. H. (1992). Intergenerational transmission of parenting: A review of studies in nonclinical populations. *Developmental Review, 12,* 76–99.

Wadsworth, M. E. (1985). Parenting skills and their transmission through generations. *Adoption & Fostering, 9,* 28–32.

Whipple, E. E., & Webster-Stratton, C. (1991). The role of parental stress in physically abusive families. *Child Abuse and Neglect, 15,* 279–291.

Whitbeck, L. B., Hoyt, D. R., Simons, R. L., Conger, R. D., Elder, G. H., Jr., Lorenz, F. O., & Huck, S. (1992). Intergenerational continuity of parental rejection and depressed affect. *Journal of Personality and Social Psychology, 63,* 1036–1045.

Wille, D. E. (1995). The 1990s: Gender differences in parenting roles. *Sex Roles, 33,* 803–817.

Yarrow, M. R., Campbell, J. D., & Burton, R. V. (1970). Recollections of childhood: A study of the retrospective method. *Monographs of the Society for Research in Child Development, 35,* 1–83.

5

SOCIAL EXCHANGE THEORY

Social exchange theory emerged within family sciences in the latter part of the twentieth century, first being considered in a meaningful way in the early 1960s. It arose out of the philosophical traditions of utilitarianism, behaviorism, and neoclassical economics. Early social exchange theory applications in family science arose out of the work of sociologists (Blau, 1964; Homans, 1961; Thibaut & Kelley, 1959) who focused on the rational assessment of self-interest in human social relationships. At its most basic, social exchange theory may be viewed as providing an economic metaphor to social relationships. The theory's fundamental principle is that humans in social situations choose behaviors that maximize their likelihood of meeting self-interests in those situations.

In taking such a view of human social interactions, social exchange theory includes a number of key assumptions. First, social exchange theory operates on the assumption that individuals are generally rational and engage in calculations of costs and benefits in social exchanges. In this respect, they exist as both rational actors and reactors in social exchanges. This assumption reflects the perspective that social exchange theory largely attends to issues of decision making.

Second, social exchange theory builds on the assumption that those engaged in interactions are rationally seeking to maximize the profits or benefits to be gained from those situations, especially in terms of meeting basic individual needs. In this respect, social exchange theory assumes social exchanges between or among two or more individuals are efforts by participants to fulfill basic needs.

Third, exchange processes that produce payoffs or rewards for individuals lead to patterning of social interactions. These patterns of social interaction not only serve individuals' needs but also constrain individuals in how they may ultimately seek to meet those needs. Individuals may seek relationships and interactions that promote their needs but are also the recipients of behaviors from others that are motivated by *their* desires to meet their own needs.

Social exchange theory further assumes that individuals are goal-oriented in a freely competitive social system. Because of the competitive nature of social systems, exchange processes lead to differentiation of power and privilege in social groups. As in any competitive situation, power in social exchanges lies with those individuals who possess greater resources that provide an advantage in the social exchange. As a result, exchange processes lead to differentiation of power and privilege in social groups. Those with more resources hold more power and, ultimately, are in a better position to benefit from the exchange.

Tied into this concept of power in a social exchange is the principle of least interest. Those with less to gain in terms of meeting their basic needs through a social exchange tend to hold more power in that exchange. In other words, power comes from less basic dependence on a social exchange. This can be seen in patterns of power that exist within family relationships. For example, in terms of basic structural benefits, a young child has more to gain from a parent-child relationship than a parent. The young child relies on the parent for provision of resources to meet her or his basic needs. Because relatively few of the parent's basic needs are met by the child, the parent has less personal interest in the relationship and, consequently, holds more power than the child in the relationship. As the child ages and eventually develops the capacity to meet his or her own basic needs, the power differential that exists in the parent-child relationship weakens. Parent and child now have similar personal interest in the relationship.

From a social exchange perspective, then, human behavior may be viewed as motivated by desire to seek rewards and avoid potential costs in social situations. Humans are viewed as rationally choosing more beneficial social behaviors as a result of rational reviews of all available information. Because all behavior is costly in that it requires an expenditure of energy on the part of the actor, only those behaviors that are rewarded or that produce the least cost tend to be repeated. Thus, social exchanges take on an air of consistency in that patterns of rewards often remain stable in social relationships.

At the heart of social exchange theory are the concepts of equity and reciprocity. Homans (1961) originally introduced the notion that individuals are most comfortable when they perceive they are receiving benefits from a relationship approximately equal to what they are putting into the relationship. The reality, though, is that family life is replete with relationships that promote perceptions of inequality. Relationships between siblings of different ages, parent and child relationships, and spouse relationships are seldom truly equal in all situations. No doubt

you can think back to your own childhood and remember times when you felt you were being treated unfairly. In all likelihood, this belief arose out of your own assessment that you were being asked to do more than others in the relationship (what child hasn't complained about doing household chores?), that you were being unfairly punished, or that you were not receiving a fair benefit or reward for something you had done for someone else in the family.

Social exchanges characterized by perceptions of equality imply the presence of reciprocity. Indeed, all social life requires a degree of reciprocity on the part of actors in social situations. Thus, when individuals perceive relatively balanced levels of reciprocity in a social exchange, they are more likely to be satisfied in that exchange. Social exchange theory suggests that individuals who perceive the presence of reciprocity in their social relationships are more likely to feel satisfied with and maintain those relationships.

Social exchange theory also includes other key concepts that serve to describe the character of social interactions. At the heart of its view of individuals as rational decision makers are the concepts of rewards and costs. Rewards are described as any benefits exchanged in personal relationships. They may be concrete or symbolic and particular to one individual or more universal. In all cases, though, the status of something as a reward is being perceived as rewarding by an individual in a social exchange. For example, receiving praise from a spouse may be a strong reward for one individual although it might mean relatively little to another individual. For the first person, the possibility of receiving praise from his or her spouse may be motivation to behave in a certain way, whereas, for the second person, the possibility of such praise would not significantly alter how he or she chooses to behave.

Generally speaking, social exchange theory proposes that individuals are motivated to gain rewards in social exchanges. In the absence of apparent rewards, individuals in social exchanges may be primarily motivated to avoid costs in those exchanges. Costs are either punishments or forfeited rewards that result from social exchanges. Generally speaking, social exchanges carry three potential costs. Investment costs represent the energy and personal cognitive or emotional investment put into an exchange by the actors involved. Direct costs include time, financial resources, or other structural resources that are dedicated to the exchange. Finally, opportunity costs represent possible rewards that may be lost as a result of the relationship or social exchange. For example, a parent sacrifices considerable possible rewards or benefits in order to responsibly raise children.

To understand a person's behavior in social exchanges, it is important to understand the *comparison level* the person brings to the exchange. The comparison level is the threshold at which an outcome seems attractive to a person. For example, you might refuse to take a job that pays $6.00 per hour but would be willing to accept that same job if it pays $9.00 per hour. In this case, $9.00 would be the threshold at which you would be willing to accept the job.

Evaluations of social exchanges also include a comparison level of alternatives. It is proposed that individuals assess the outcomes of their social exchanges in relation to other possible relationships or exchanges. As outcomes of relationships fall below the level of perceived outcomes from other relationship alternatives, individuals may choose to leave present relationships or social exchanges. For example, a wife may seek to end her marriage if she perceives being divorced from her husband as more advantageous than remaining married.

In families, a social exchange perspective argues that family relationships become interdependent, or interactional. In this respect, power becomes characteristic of the relationship dyad and understanding family relationships includes assessing the power that is held among the actors in those relationships. Family research from a social exchange perspective attends to norms of fairness and reciprocity, dynamics of attraction and dependence in relationships, distribution of power within families, and definitions of the rewards and costs associated with social exchanges in families.

The Readings

Two examples of research from a social exchange perspective are included here. Nomaguchi and Milkie (2003) explore the pattern of costs and rewards associated with becoming a parent for the first time. This research includes a comparison of new parents with those who remain childless and also explores the complex relationship between becoming a parent and a number of other factors in one's life.

Sprecher (2001) applies social exchange concepts to an exploration of satisfaction, commitment, and stability in dating relationships. This article explicitly attends to the issue of perceptions of equity in dating relationships and weighs the importance of equity to other social exchange variables. Sprecher, then, not only offers an example of research informed by social exchange theory, but also tests the relative predictive strength of a number of variables described within the theoretical perspective.

Issues for Your Consideration

1. Are costs and rewards associated with the relationships being examined and identified by each author? If so, what are they?

2. To what degree are family members portrayed as making rational assessments of costs and benefits of behaviors?

3. Is there evidence in either of these articles that those in dating relationships or who are new parents are motivated by a desire to achieve rewards or avoid costs in those relationships?

Further Reading

Blau (1964), Homans (1974), LaValle (1994), Lewis and Spanier (1982), Makoba (1993).

Costs and Rewards of Children: The Effects of Becoming a Parent on Adults' Lives

Kei M. Nomaguchi and Melissa A. Milkie

Abstract

How do new parents differ from their childless counterparts in social and psychological resources, daily strains, and psychological well-being? Using a nationally representative panel of 1,933 adults who were childless at the first interview, we compare 6 indicators of adults' lives for those who became parents and those remaining childless several years later, controlling for earlier states. Becoming a parent is both detrimental and rewarding. With the exception of social integration, which is greater for all groups of new parents compared with their childless counterparts, the effects of parental status on adults' lives vary markedly by gender and marital status. Unmarried parents report lower self-efficacy and higher depression than their childless counterparts. Married mothers' lives are marked by more housework and more marital conflict but less depression than their childless counterparts. Parental status has little influence on the lives of married men.

Two convincing pictures of how children affect adults' lives can be painted: one with bright textures of joy, personal growth, and social benefits that children provide, and one with dark strokes that represent costs and problems they create (Bird, 1997; Umberson & Gove, 1989). Empirical studies have produced inconsistent findings. Some find that parents are less happy or satisfied with their lives and more distressed and angry than nonparents (Barnett & Baruch, 1985; Glenn & McLanahan, 1982; Ross & Van Willigen, 1996), some find that there are no effects of children on adults' psychological distress (Baruch, Barnett, & Rivers, 1983; Cleary & Mechanic, 1983; Gore & Mangione, 1983; Wethington & Kessler, 1989), and others argue that under some conditions, parents may be better off than nonparents in terms of mental health (Bird, 1997; Kandel, Davis, & Raceis, 1985; Ross & Huber, 1985).

Despite mixed evidence, reviews of studies on the effect of children on adults' lives tend to conclude rather bleakly that having children is more costly than rewarding for adults in terms of daily strains, social relationships, and psychological well-being, especially for women and the unmarried, even though authors themselves suggest that there are not necessarily clear-cut findings in the empirical studies (e.g., see McLanahan & Adams, 1987; Ross, Mirowsky, & Goldsteen, 1990; Umberson & Williams, 1999). This is for good reason: There has been little explicit theoretical or empirical analysis of how having children may enhance adults' lives.

This study addresses three challenges in the literature on the effects of parenting on adults' lives. First, we argue that a heavy emphasis on the costs experienced by parents obscures the benefits children may produce. Benefits that may balance parents' lives have strong roots in theoretical work, yet are relatively ignored (but see Bird, 1997; Umberson & Gove, 1989; Voydanoff & Donnelly, 1989). Thus, this study examines indicators that may capture the possible costs *and* rewards of parenting. These include social resources (e.g., social integration), psychological resources (e.g., self-concept), daily strains (e.g., housework, disagreements with one's spouse), and psychological well-being (e.g., depression).

Second, although there have been many studies on the effects of children on adults' lives, few have analyzed longitudinal data using a nationally representative sample. Furthermore, studies have not typically employed comparison groups of nonparents in the same life stage (but see Kurdek, 1993; MacDermid, Huston, & McHale, 1990). It is difficult, however, to assess how parenting affects adults' lives without controlling for earlier states and without explicit recognition of those remaining childless. In this study, using a nationally representative sample of U.S. adults in their childbearing years, we compare social and psychological resources, daily strains, and psychological well-being of those who became parents and those who remained childless after 5 to 7 years, controlling for earlier states of these indicators.

Finally, we argue that how children affect adults' lives may be so dependent on the gender and marital status of those adults that it may not be meaningful to discuss *parents* as a social category (Umberson & Williams, 1999). Therefore, we pay explicit attention to how costs and rewards of becoming a parent are moderated by gender and marital status.

Previous Research: Three Challenges

The Effects of Becoming a Parent on Adults' Lives: The Costs and the Benefits

Research on the effects of parenthood on adults' lives has emphasized the costs of parenting and largely ignored positive aspects of parenting. In the literature, structural role strain

perspectives (Pearlin, 1989) have provided a rich array of approaches to examine how the parent role is related to an amplification of stressors in adults' daily lives such as overload and marital conflict. We argue, however, that the overemphasis on costs of parenting does not give us the whole picture of the effects of children on adults' lives. Becoming a parent fundamentally changes one's life, making it more complex—not only through increasing demands, conflict, and frustrations, but also by deepening joys, activating social ties, and enriching parents self-concepts. Although virtually all young adults have some family members such as spouses, siblings, or parents with whom they maintain contact, the birth or adoption of a first child creates a *new* family. The relationship with their child may increase adults' commitment to affection and enjoyable activities with the child and other family members (Hoffman & Manis, 1982). Moreover, having a child fulfills an expected adult role, one that fits with American cultural ideals that place a premium on having children. Thus, in addition to obligations, the new role contains rights and privileges and carries a sense of legitimacy (Sieber, 1974).

In this article, we examine indicators that capture both costs and rewards of childrearing when adults become parents. They include *social resources,* such as social integration; *psychological resources,* such as self-concept; *daily strains,* such as housework and disagreements with one's spouse; and *psychological well-being,* such as depression.

Social resources. Umberson and Gove (1989) called attention to the importance of social integration as a benefit that children create for adults, emphasizing parenting as a profound relationship that ties adults to others. Social integration refers to the existence or quantity of social ties or relationships (House, Umberson, & Landis, 1988). Whereas many studies emphasize that children constrain adults from social activities (Fischer & Oliker, 1983; Munch, McPherson, & Smith-Lovin, 1997), others find that children strengthen or broaden parents' social networks to a wide range of relatives and neighbors (Gallagher & Gerstel, 2001; Ishii-Kuntz & Seccombe, 1989). Children may give adults opportunities to interact with other people, including relatives, neighbors, friends, and those in community institutions such as schools and religious organizations. Although some may perceive ties to others as burdensome (e.g., see Gerstel & Gallagher, 1993; Lynch, 1998), given the theoretical emphasis and empirical evidence in the mental health literature that social relationships have a positive impact on mental health (House et al., 1988), we assume that greater levels of social integration are a benefit.

Psychological resources. Becoming a parent is a major life transition for adults in which former identities such as worker, student, or spouse shift in salience and are modified to make psychic room for this new commitment in one's life (Cowan & Cowan, 1992). Caring for others is a primary way in which adults grow psychologically or enhance their self-concept. In recent research on fatherhood, the concept of generativity—a commitment to guiding or nurturing others, especially those in the next generation (Erikson, 1950)—has gained attention as key to understanding the importance of caring for others for adult development (McKeering & Pakenham, 2000). The growth of self-esteem and self-efficacy may be a way in which the successful nurturance of others and other problem-solving roles enrich the self (Bandura, 1997; Hoffman & Manis, 1982).

Daily strains. Children create substantial new daily demands on parents' time, physical energy, and emotional energy. New parents spend much time taking care of children, which decreases leisure and downtime (LaRossa & LaRossa, 1981). Parents experience overload from combining family work with employment (Goldsteen & Ross, 1989; Kandel, Davis, & Raceis, 1985; Rosenfield, 1989), or face difficulty arranging child care (Ross & Mirowsky, 1988). One particularly important demand that children create, especially for women, is housework. The chores that children necessitate, such as cleaning,

laundry, and cooking (Sanchez & Thomson, 1997), are arguably repetitive and often onerous and tend to be related to higher levels of distress (Glass & Fujimoto, 1994).

A large literature focuses on increased strains in marital relationships among new parents. A traditional view is that becoming parents is a crisis for married couples, because the marital relationship faces tremendous changes when the first child arrives (LeMasters, 1957; for a review see Demo & Cox, 2000). LaRossa and LaRossa's qualitative study (1981) shows that during this period, husbands and wives tend to experience a lack of couple leisure activities as well as conflict with each other over the division of housework and child care. A more recent qualitative study of couples making the transition to parenthood, however, showed that they had many new strains in their lives, but that couples not making the transition were just as likely to break up and showed the same overall levels of distress (Cowan & Cowan, 1992). Indeed, quantitative studies have found inconsistent results about the effects of becoming a parent on marital relationships (Belsky, Lang, & Huston, 1986; Crohan, 1996; Kurdek, 1993; LaVee, Sharlin, & Katz, 1996; MacDermid, Huston, & McHale, 1990).

Psychological well-being. Reviews of research on the relationship between parental status and psychological well-being during the past few decades have emphasized that parents, especially those with young children, tend to report lower levels of mental health than nonparents (McLanahan & Adams, 1987; Ross, Mirowsky, & Goldsteen, 1990; Umberson & Williams, 1999). Empirical studies, however, have suggested inconsistent results (Barnett & Baruch, 1985; Bird, 1997; Gore & Mangione, 1983; Kandel et al., 1985; Wethington & Kessler, 1989). Stress researchers have provided a well-studied theoretical perspective, the stress process model (Aneshensel, 1992; Pearlin, Menaghan, Lieberman, & Mullan, 1981), which suggests that parenting per se may not relate to increased distress, but contextual factors associated with parenting such as an overload of demands from child care and housework, economic hardship (Bird, 1997; Ross & Huber, 1985), and difficulty arranging child care (Ross & Mirowsky, 1988) may create distress. The stress process perspective also suggests that the link between parenthood and mental health may be modified by social relationships and psychological resources (Bird, 1997; Thompson, 1986).

In this study, we do not examine the *process* in which adults may be exposed to and buffered from stressors related to parental roles. We reexamine, instead, a more basic question regarding the link between parental status and various aspects of adult lives, including depression, while addressing a key methodological issue: the lack of adequate comparison groups.

Methodological Issues: Longitudinal Data and Comparison Groups

A second difficulty in knowing how children affect adult lives is that prior studies have not typically employed longitudinal data nor used key comparison groups for parents. On one hand, most sociological quantitative studies on the costs and rewards of parenting use national, cross-sectional surveys. In those studies, parents, usually considered those who have children under 18 in their households, are sometimes compared with *nonparents,* including both older parents (even beyond age 60) who have already launched children and those who have remained childless into later life (see McLanahan & Adams, 1987, for a review). When parents with young children are compared with (usually older) nonparents, some of the "effects" thought to be from children might instead be a matter of life stage, because higher levels of distress are more common among younger adults (Kessler & Zhao, 1999).

On the other hand, psychologists and family studies researchers have conducted longitudinal studies using small samples of newly married couples, focusing on the effect of the arrival of a child on the marital relationship. Yet most studies only look at couples making the transition to parenthood and not other couples, making it difficult to untangle the "natural" development of marital strain over a period of time from children's independent effects. There have been a few small-scale longitudinal studies of changes in marital relations among newlyweds, comparing parents with those who remain childless (e.g., see Kurdek, 1993; MacDermid et al., 1990). Few researchers have used nationally representative panel data, however.

Gender and Marital Status Differences

The last issue we address in this article is the different life contexts in which people become parents. In particular, research suggests that the effect of children on adults' social and psychological resources, daily strains, and psychological well-being may be vastly different depending on whether they are women or men, married or unmarried (Umberson & Williams, 1999).

Gender. Many scholars argue that women may experience more costs by having children than men: Mothers may be exposed to more daily strains, may face more constraints in broadening social resources, and may experience more distress than fathers. Some emphasize structural explanations or social role perspectives, arguing that women are more likely than men to be exposed to demands from the parental role because they are primary caretakers in childrearing (Aneshensel, Frerichs, & Clark, 1981; Gove & Geerken, 1977; Ross & Van Willigen, 1996). Others emphasize that the salience of the parental role is stronger for women than for men, and thus women are more sensitive to both the strains and rewards of parenting (Mulford & Salisbury, 1964). Although many studies have indicated that after controlling for social position, mothers are still more likely than fathers to report strains from parenting (Scott & Alwin, 1989; Simon, 1992), whether the parental role experience is more strongly related to mental health for women than for men is not clear. Cleary and Mechanic (1983) found that parental satisfaction is related to lower levels of distress among mothers. Simon found, however, that whereas mothers are more likely to experience parental strains, if fathers have high levels of parental strains, they are more vulnerable in terms of psychological distress than mothers.

Despite the differences in emphasis, both structural and role salience explanations share a common assumption: Men and women experience the transition to parenthood and childrearing in different ways (Cowan et al., 1985; LaRossa & LaRossa, 1981). In most studies, fathers are compared with mothers. We argue, however, that comparisons with childless men and childless women, respectively, can be especially informative about how children affect women's versus men's lives.

Married versus unmarried. Many scholars agree that the stress of parenting depends on whether parents are married (Simon, 1998; Umberson & Williams, 1999). A common argument is that single mothers are more likely to report higher levels of distress than married mothers, because, given their disadvantaged social position, they have a greater chance of experiencing strains and have fewer coping resources (Avison, 1995; Pearlin & Johnson, 1977). Others emphasize selection processes, that is, single mothers are more likely than married mothers to have experienced a greater number of depressive episodes during childhood and adolescence, which is significantly related to their current higher levels of distress (Davies, Avison, & McAlpine, 1997).

Currently, it is difficult to disentangle the effects of parental status from that of marital status because in many studies single parents are the focus of study and are compared with married parents, but not with those who are single and remain childless. Additionally, there is little research for some groups, particularly never-married men. Furthermore, many individuals may experience changes in marital status around the period when they become parents. Changes in marital status, both getting married and ending a marriage, are important factors for understanding adult well-being (Marks & Lambert, 1998).

Research Questions and Hypotheses

In this study, we reexamine the costs and rewards of parenting, focusing on two questions: (a) How do parents differ from nonparents in social and psychological resources, daily strains, and psychological well-being? and (b) How do the effects of parental status on social and psychological resources, daily strains, and psychological well-being vary across gender and marital status groups? We focus on the parents of young children, comparing them with adults also in their childbearing years but who remained childless.

We hypothesize that parents' lives become structurally and emotionally complex as they move into a demanding but enriching new role. Thus, we expect that becoming a parent will be associated with both greater benefits in terms of social and psychological resources (i.e., more social integration, self-esteem, and self-efficacy) and greater costs in terms of daily strains and psychological well-being (i.e., more housework, increased marital conflict, and higher levels of depression).

We expect that the differences between nonparents and new parents, including costs *and* benefits, are greater among women than among men. We also expect that costs of becoming a parent are greater for unmarried men and women than for their married counterparts, and the rewards of having a child are fewer. We control for age, race, levels of education, employment status, household income, duration of marriage at Time 1, whether respondents were previously married at Time 1, and dependent measures at Time 1.

Method

Data

Data are drawn primarily from the second wave (1992–1994) of the National Survey of Families and Households (NSFH; Sweet & Bumpass, 1996). We also use a number of measures from the first wave (1987–1988) as controls for earlier states. The original sample in the first survey (Time 1) is a U.S. national probability sample of 13,008 respondents with over samples of minorities and of nonmarried or recently married persons. Among them, 10,008 respondents were reinterviewed in the second survey (Time 2). Although the NSFH includes information from the spouse of the main respondents, information about social integration, self-esteem, self-efficacy, and depression at Time 1 is available only from the main respondent. Thus, we include only main respondents in our analysis. From reinterviewed respondents, we selected first those who were aged 18–44 at Time 1 ($n = 6,370$). Of these respondents, only those who had never had a child by the first survey were selected ($n = 2,165$). Fifteen respondents were excluded because they did not have information about changes in marital status between the two surveys or marital status at Time 2, and 99 respondents were excluded who changed their marital status more than once between the surveys because it is beyond the scope of this study to consider the effects of multiple marital status transitions and parental status on well-being. We also excluded the 107 respondents whose spouse had ever had a child at Time 1 ($n = 1,944$). Finally, we excluded those who have missing data on any control variables except income (see below), and thus $N = 1,933$.

Eligible respondents who dropped out of the Time 2 interview were more likely to be single, younger, non-White, less educated, and not employed, compared with those who remained in the sample used for this study. Differences on the outcome measures between the dropouts and those who remained in the study were minimal, however.

Measures

Dependent variables. Our analyses include six indicators of costs and rewards of parenting: social integration, self-esteem, self-efficacy, hours of housework, marital conflict (for the respondents continuously married from Time 1 to Time 2 only), and depression. For each variable, information at both Time 1 and Time 2 is available. These measures do not directly assess

parenting, because such questions would be meaningless to adults remaining childless (see Umberson & Gove, 1989).

Social integration is a sum of three items: "About how often do you get together socially with (a) relatives, (b) a neighbor, or (c) friends who live outside your neighborhood?" Each ranges from 0 = *never* to 4 = *several times a week*. This measure is similar to those used by Umberson and her colleagues (Umberson, Chen, House, Hopkins, & Slaten, 1996), called informal social integration, and those used by Ishii-Kuntz and Seccombe (1989). Cronbach's alpha is .43 at Time 1 and .41 at Time 2.

Self-esteem is a summed measure of the following three questions available in both waves: (a) "On the whole, I am satisfied with myself," (b) "I am able to do things as well as other people," and (c) "I feel that I'm a person of worth, at least on an equal plane with others" (Rosenberg, 1986). Answers to each item range from 1 (*strongly agree*) to 5 (*strongly disagree*). The index is reversed and thus a higher value indicates a higher level of self-esteem (range 3 to 15). Cronbach's alpha is .63 at Time 1 and .66 at Time 2.

Self-efficacy is measured by the statement, "I have always felt pretty sure my life would work out the way I wanted it to," with responses ranging from 1 (*strongly agree*) to 5 (*strongly disagree*). This item is from an efficacy scale used in previous studies (Downey & Moen, 1987). A reversed code is used.

Hours of housework is a sum of hours spent on nine housework tasks per week. Respondents were asked to indicate "the approximate number of hours per week you normally spend doing the following things": (a) preparing meals; (b) washing dishes and cleaning up after meals; (c) cleaning house; (d) outdoor and other household maintenance tasks (lawn and yard work, household repair, painting, etc.); (e) shopping for groceries and other household goods; (f) washing, ironing, mending; (g) paying bills and keeping financial records; (h) automobile maintenance and repair; and (i) driving other household members to work, school, or other activities. Respondents who answered *inapplicable* to an item were given a score of 0 and those who answered with extreme values were recoded to the 95th percentile by gender to avoid distortion caused by outliers. Because 27.3% of respondents failed to answer at least one housework item in either or both interviews, we tried two kinds of imputation methods. In the first method, respondents who answered six or fewer of the items are dropped from the analysis; those who answered seven or eight items are assigned the mean by gender for the missing item(s) (see South & Spitze, 1994). In the second method, we used a predicted value based on a regression using age, gender, marital status, education, race, and hours of paid work. Because the results were similar regardless of whether the missing data were imputed and regardless of which imputation method was used, we present the results using the first imputation method.

Frequency of disagreements with spouse (for the continuously married only) is measured as "How often, if at all, in the last year have you had open disagreements about each of the following?" with respondents reporting about disagreements on household tasks, money, spending time together, and sex. The four items, ranging from 1 (*never*) to 6 (*almost every day*), were made into an index (range 4 to 24). Cronbach's alpha is .76 at Time 1 and .74 at Time 2.

Depression is measured by the 12-item version of the Center for Epidemiological Studies Depression scale (CES-D; Radloff, 1977). Respondents were asked how many days in the previous week they (a) felt bothered by things that usually do not bother them, (b) did not feel like eating, (c) felt that they could not shake off the blues even with help from their family or friends, (d) had trouble keeping their mind on what they were doing, (e) felt depressed, (f) felt that everything they did was effort, (g) felt fearful, (h) slept restlessly, (i) talked less than usual, (j) felt lonely, (k) felt sad, and (l) felt not able to get going. Each item ranges from 0 to 7 days. The 12 items were averaged. Cronbach's alpha is .93 at Time 1 and .92 at Time 2.

Independent variables. Parental status is a dichotomous variable; those who became a

parent over the 5- to 7-year interval are assigned a 1. We examined the effect of the number of children in the household in the model instead of the dichotomous variable of parental status. The results were similar and thus we chose to use the measure of *parental status* rather than the number of children because using the dichotomous variable makes our analysis of variations by gender and marital status groups easier to interpret. *Gender* is a dichotomous variable, with women coded as 1. *Marital status* is coded as a series of dummy variables for the following four groups: (a) continuously married from Time 1 to Time 2 (18.4%), (b) newly married between Time 1 and Time 2 (29.2%), (c) continuously unmarried from Time 1 to Time 2 (49.0%), and (d) newly unmarried between Time 1 and Time 2 (3.4%, including those who became separated, divorced, and widowed). Table 5.1 presents percentage distributions of marital status by gender and parental status, for all respondents, women, and men.

Control variables. We include several control variables in the models based on their associations with our outcome measures assessing adults' lives. Basic demographic characteristics, such as age and race, and socioeconomic status, such as education, employment status, and household income, tend to be related to social integration, self-concept, and depression (see Aneshensel, 1992, for a review), and hours of housework (see Shelton & John, 1996, for a review). *Age* of respondents is coded in years. *Race* is a dichotomous variable in which 1 indicates *non-White*. *Education* is years of school completed. Respondents who have completed a high school diploma, an associate degree, a bachelor's degree, or a higher degree are, however, assigned 12, 14, 16, and 20, respectively, even if reporting fewer or more years. *Employment status* is measured as 1 = *nonemployed*, 2 = *employed part time* (1–34 hours per week), 3 = *employed full-time* (35 or more hours per week). *Household income* is household income in the previous 12 months. Those who have missing income data were assigned a predicted value based on a regression using age,

Table 5.1 Weighted Percentage Distribution (Unweighted *N*s) of Marital Status at Time 2 by Parental Status at Time 2 for All Respondents, for Women, and for Men

Marital Status	Total Sample			Women			Men		
	Total (N)	New Parents	Remain Childless	Total (N)	New Parents	Remain Childless	Total (N)	New Parents	Remain Childless
Married Time 2									
Continuously married	18.4 (510)	36.7 (319)	10.6 (191)	20.6 (261)	38.0 (152)	12.4 (99)	16.9 (249)	35.6 (157)	9.5 (92)
Newly married[a]	29.2 (508)	43.1 (242)	23.3 (266)	28.0 (365)	39.2 (108)	22.7 (115)	30.1 (285)	46.3 (134)	23.7 (151)
Unmarried Time 2									
Newly unmarried[b]	3.4 (86)	4.4 (33)	3.0 (53)	4.4 (48)	5.0 (17)	4.1 (31)	2.7 (38)	3.9 (16)	2.2 (22)
Continuously unmarried	49.0 (829)	15.8 (94)	63.1 (735)	47.0 (223)	17.9 (51)	60.8 (314)	50.3 (464)	14.2 (43)	64.6 (421)
Total	100.0%	100.0%	100.0%	100.0%	100.0%	100.0%	100.0%	100.0%	100.0%
n	1,933	688	1,245	897	333	559	1,036	350	686
	(100.0%)	(35.6%)	(64.4%)	(100.0%)	(37.7%)	(62.3%)	(100.0%)	(33.8%)	(66.2%)

a. Unmarried at Time 1 and married by Time 2.

b. Married at Time 1 but separated, divorced, or widowed by Time 2.

gender, education, race, and hours of paid work, by marital status. To avoid distortion caused by extreme outliers, income is measured as the log of household income. *Missing income* is a dichotomous variable indicating household income is imputed.

Because recently married respondents were oversampled, we include *duration of marriage at Time 1*, measured as years of current marriage at Time 1 (0 = *not married at T1,* 1 = *married 12 months or less,* 2 = *13–24 months,* 3 = *25–36 months,* 4 = *37–48 months,* 5 = *49–60 months,* 6 = *61–120 months,* 7 = *over 120 months*). A dichotomous variable indicating if respondents had been *previously married at T1* (coded as 1) was included (see Marks & Lambert, 1998).

To diminish selection effects, we included Time 1 states as controls. Thus, in the regression analyses, each model includes the respondent's dependent measure 5 to 7 years earlier. Descriptive statistics for the variables used in the analysis are reported in Table 5.2.

Results

New Parents Versus Those Who Remain Childless

We first assess the relationship of becoming a parent with each outcome measure for all adults, conducting ordinary least squares regressions to examine the main effects of parental status (Model 1 of Table 5.3). The number of cases varies slightly across analyses because of missing data on the dependent variable.

For the first three indicators in Table 5.3 (integration, self-esteem, and self-efficacy) higher levels indicate positive states, and we expected these positive states to be higher for new parents compared with nonparents. New parents do show a higher level of social integration with relatives, friends, and neighbors ($p < .001$), controlling for social integration at Time 1. There are no differences between new parents and those who remain childless on self-esteem. Unexpectedly, new parents show a lower level of efficacy than nonparents ($p < .001$), controlling for earlier efficacy. Although we expected that the new role of parent might provide adults with opportunities to grow psychologically from the experience of nurturing others, our findings appear to support the alternative argument that young children interfere with adults' freedom, which may decrease their sense of power to achieve their own goals.

For the last three indicators in Table 5.3 (housework, disagreements with one's spouse, and depression), higher levels indicate negative states, and we expected these negative states to be higher for new parents compared with nonparents. New parents report more hours of housework than those who remain childless, controlling for earlier hours of housework ($p < .001$). Among continuously married people, new parents show no statistically significant difference in strain in their marital relationship compared with nonparents, controlling for marital strain at Time 1. This finding is in line with studies using small-scale longitudinal data of newlywed couples showing that the marital satisfaction of both parents and nonparents declined overtime (Kurdek, 1993; MacDermid et al., 1990). Finally, contrary to the argument commonly cited, there are no differences between new parents and nonparents in depression, controlling for earlier depression.

In sum, we found a significant effect of becoming a parent on three aspects of adults' lives: social integration, self-efficacy, and hours of housework. Which of these aspects of adults' lives are most strongly affected by becoming a parent? To compare the size of the effect of parental status on these three outcome variables, we calculated partial correlation coefficients between parental status and social integration, self-efficacy, and hours of housework, that is, the correlation coefficients between parental status and each variable controlling for other variables in the model (see Neter, Kutner, Nachtscheim, & Wasserman, 1996, pp. 274–276). The partial correlation coefficients between parental status and social integration, self-efficacy, and hours of housework are $r = .09, .08,$ and .14, respectively. This suggests that increased strains of housework may be the arena where new

(Text continued on page 157)

Table 5.2 Means (*SE*) for All Variables by Parental Status at Time 2

	Total Sample				Women				Men			
	Total	N	New Parents (35.6%)	Remain Childless (64.4%)	Total	N	New Parents (35.6%)	Remain Childless (64.4%)	Total	N	New Parents (33.8%)	Remain Childless (66.2%)
Dependent Variables												
Social and Psychological Resources												
Social integration Time 2	6.03 (2.07)	1,701	6.36 (1.97)		6.06 (1.89)	788	6.45 (1.89)	5.88 (1.86)	6.01 (2.21)	913	6.29 (2.05)	5.89 (2.28)
Social integration Time 1	5.75 (2.38)	1,701	6.01 (2.23)		5.79 (2.15)	788	6.11 (2.13)	5.64 (2.15)	5.71 (2.56)	913	5.92 (2.33)	5.63 (2.66)
Self-esteem Time 2	12.64 (1.71)	1,805	12.56 (1.50)		12.57 (1.66)	850	12.43 (1.46)	12.63 (1.77)	12.70 (1.75)	955	12.68 (1.53)	12.70 (1.86)
Self-esteem Time 1	12.46 (1.75)	1,805	12.40 (11.53)		12.61 (1.60)	850	12.51 (1.39)	12.66 (1.72)	12.34 (1.87)	955	12.30 (1.66)	12.36 (1.97)
Self-efficacy Time 2	3.68 (0.96)	1,834	3.66 (0.86)		3.69 (0.95)	866	3.65 (0.86)	3.70 (0.99)	3.68 (0.97)	968	3.66 (0.86)	3.69 (1.03)
Self-efficacy Time 1	3.61 (0.96)	1,834	3.68 (0.81)		3.60 (0.94)	865	3.68 (0.77)	3.56 (1.02)	3.62 (0.97)	968	3.68 (0.85)	3.60 (1.03)
Daily Strains												
Hours of housework Time 2	21.45 (13.20)	1,654	26.27 (14.27)	19.43 (12.00)	25.03 (14.63)	795	34.68 (15.13)	20.87 (12.27)	18.73 (10.93)	859	19.62 (9.39)	18.37 (11.63)
Hours of housework Time 1	19.43 (13.14)	1,654	21.30 (12.97)	18.65 (13.16)	22.71 (14.57)	795	26.52 (14.61)	21.07 (14.26)	16.95 (11.00)	859	17.18 (9.43)	16.86 (11.74)
Disagreements Time 2	8.24 (2.58)	456	8.64 (2.42)	7.67 (2.76)	8.40 (2.59)	232	9.05 (2.34)	7.44 (2.78)	8.11 (2.58)	224	8.28 (2.47)	7.86 (2.75)
Disagreements Time 1	9.14 (2.57)	456	9.36 (2.46)	8.81 (2.73)	9.01 (2.541)	232	9.16 (2.39)	8.77 (2.77)	9.25 (2.61)	224	9.54 (2.53)	8.84 (2.70)
Psychological Well-Being												
Depression (0–7) Time 2	1.02 (1.10)	1,802	1.04 (1.04)	1.01 (1.13)	1.17 (1.13)	847	1.08 (1.00)	1.21 (1.20)	0.92 (1.05)	955	1.00 (1.08)	0.88 (1.04)
Depression (0–7) Time 1	1.27 (1.34)	1802	1.28 (1.22)	1.26 (1.39)	1.35 (1.27)	847	1.43 (1.22)	1.31 (1.30)	1.21 (1.39)	955	1.15 (1.22)	1.24 (1.47)

(Continued)

Table 5.2 (Continued)

	Total Sample				Women				Men			
	Total	N	New Parents (35.6%)	Remain Childless (64.4%)	Total	N	New Parents (35.6%)	Remain Childless (64.4%)	Total	N	New Parents (33.8%)	Remain Childless (66.2%)
Control Variables												
Age	31.56	1,933	30.70	31.92	31.44	897	29.99	32.13	31.64	1,036	31.27	31.79
	(6.11)		(4.36)	(6.86)	(6.01)		(3.94)	(6.87)	(6.20)		(4.67)	(6.85)
Race (1 = non-White)	0.21	1,933	0.23	0.20	0.20	897	0.24	0.19	0.21	1,036	0.23	0.21
	(0.41)		(0.39)	(0.42)	(0.38)		(0.37)	(0.38)	(0.43)		(0.41)	(0.44)
Education	13.90	1,933	13.46	14.09	14.13	897	13.37	14.49	13.74	1,036	13.53	13.82
	(2.50)		(2.24)	(2.61)	(2.33)		(2.08)	(2.39)	(2.64)		(2.39)	(2.75)
Employment Status												
Not employed	0.14	1,933	0.20	0.12	0.19	897	0.35	0.12	0.11	1,036	0.08	0.12
	(0.35)		(0.37)	(0.34)	(0.37)		(0.42)	(0.32)	(0.32)		(0.26)	(0.35)
Part time	0.11	1,933	0.09	0.12	0.17	897	0.17	0.16	0.07	1,036	0.02	0.09
	(0.31)		(0.26)	(0.34)	(0.35)		(0.33)	(0.36)	(0.27)		(0.13)	(0.31)
Full time	0.75	1,933	0.72	0.76	0.64	897	0.48	0.72	0.82	1,036	0.91	0.79
	(0.43)		(0.41)	(0.45)	(0.45)		(0.44)	(0.44)	(0.40)		(0.28)	(0.44)
Household income (logged)	10.33	1,933	10.42	10.30	10.33	897	10.31	10.34	10.34	1,036	10.51	10.27
	(1.18)		(1.05)	(1.25)	(1.14)		(1.16)	(1.13)	(1.22)		(0.93)	(1.34)
Missing income (1 = *missing*)	0.18	1,933	0.07	0.24	0.15	897	0.06	0.20	0.21	1,036	0.07	0.26
	(0.39)		(0.23)	(0.44)	(0.34)		(0.21)	(0.39)	(0.42)		(0.25)	(0.48)
Duration of marriage Time 1	0.82	1,933	1.27	0.63	0.93	897	1.28	0.76	0.74	1,036	1.26	0.54
	(1.86)		(1.78)	(1.87)	(1.84)		(1.65)	(1.92)	(1.87)		(1.89)	(1.81)
Previously married Time 1	0.03	1,933	0.03	0.03	0.03	897	0.03	0.04	0.02	1,036	0.02	0.02
	(0.16)		(0.14)	(0.16)	(0.17)		(0.15)	(0.18)	(0.14)		(0.14)	(0.15)

NOTE: Means are weighted; *N*s are not weighted.

Table 5.3 Regression Coefficients and Standard Errors for the Effects of Parental Status on Social Integration, Self-Esteem, Self-Efficacy, Hours of Housework, Disagreement With Spouse, and Depression ($N = 1{,}933$)

	Social and Psychological Resources											
	Social Integration						Self-Esteem					
	Model 1			Model 2			Model 1			Model 2		
	b	SE	β	b	SE	β	b	SE	β	b	SE	β
New Parents	0.46***	0.12	0.10	0.30	0.26	0.07	−0.12	0.10	−0.03	0.03	0.21	0.01
Parents × women				0.25	0.24	0.04				0.05	0.19	0.01
Parents × marital status												
Continuously married × new parents (reference)				—	—	—				—	—	—
Newly married[a] × new parents				0.10	0.30	0.02				−0.29	0.23	−0.06
Newly married[b] × new parents				0.32	0.59	0.02				−0.74	0.45	0.05
Continuously unmarried × new				−0.11	0.34	−0.01				−0.08	0.27	−0.01
Gender × marital status												
Continuously married × women (reference)				—	—	—						
Newly married[a] × women				−0.02	0.29	−0.003				0.33	0.22	0.06
Newly married[b] × women				−0.64	0.59	−0.04				−0.02	0.45	−0.001
Continuously unmarried × women				0.38	0.29	0.07				0.36	0.22	0.08
Women	0.03	0.10	0.01	0.20	0.26	−0.05	0.23**	0.08	−0.07	−0.52*	0.20	−0.15

(Continued)

151

Table 5.3 (Continued)

	Social and Psychological Resources												
	Social Integration						Self-Esteem						
	Model 1			Model 2			Model 1			Model 2			
	b	SE	β	b	SE	β	b	SE	β	b	SE	β
Marital status												
Continuously married (reference)	—	—	—	—	—	—	—	—	—	—	—	—
Newly married[a]	0.10	0.24	0.02	0.03	0.34	0.01	0.36†	0.19	0.10	0.40	11.27	0.11
Newly unmarried[b]	0.71*	0.29	0.06	0.96t	0.53	0.08	-0.20	0.23	-0.02	0.17	0.39	0.02
Continuously unmarried	0.25	0.25	0.06	0.06	0.33	0.01	0.09	0.20	0.03	0.06	0.26	0.02
Age	-0.01	0.01	-0.03	-0.01	0.01	-0.03	-0.03***	0.01	-0.12	-0.03***	0.01	-0.12
Non-White	-0.56***	0.12	-0.11	-0.55***	0.12	-0.11	0.03	0.10	0.01	0.02	0.10	0.01
Education	-0.03	0.02	-0.04	-0.03	0.02	-0.04	0.09***	0.02	0.13	0.09***	0.02	0.12
Employment status												
Not employed (reference)	—	—	—	—	—	—	—	—	—	—	—	—
Part time	-0.24	0.20	-0.04	0.24	0.20	-0.04	0.01	0.15	0.002	0.02	0.15	0.004
Full time	-0.15	0.15	-0.03	-0.15	0.15	-0.03	0.14	0.12	0.04	0.13	0.12	0.03
Household income (log)	0.06	0.04	0.03	0.06	0.04	0.04	0.03	0.04	0.02	0.03	0.04	0.02
Missing income	0.14	0.15	0.03	0.15	0.15	0.03	-0.06	0.11	-0.01	-0.05	0.11	-0.01
Duration of marriage Time 1	-0.004	0.005	-0.004	-0.01	0.05	-0.01	0.06	0.04	0.06	0.07t	0.04	0.07
Previously married Time 1	-0.23	0.34	-0.02	-0.20	0.35	-0.01	0.22	0.25	0.02	0.21	0.25	0.02
Time 1 state	0.24***	0.02	0.28	0.24***	0.02	0.28	0.31***	0.02	0.32	0.31***	0.02	0.32
Intercept	4.65***	0.63	0	4.80***	0.66	0	8.14***	0.53	0	8.12***	0.56	0
Adjusted R^2	0.106***			0.106***			0.151***			0.151***			
n				1,701						1,805			

	Social and Psychological Resources (continued)						Daily Strains					
	Self-Efficacy						Hours of Housework					
	Model 1			Model 2			Model 1			Model 2		
	b	SE	β	b	SE	β	b	SE	β	b	SE	β
New Parents	-0.19***	0.05	0.09	0.13	0.12	0.06	4.20***	0.75	0.14	1.55	1.57	0.05
Parents × women				-0.02	0.11	-0.01				8.03**	1.42	0.20
Parents × marital status												
Continuously married × new parents (reference)				—	—	—				—	—	—
Newly married[a] × new parents				-0.34*	0.13	-0.12				-1.22	1.79	-0.03
Newly married[b] × new parents				-0.25	0.26	-0.04				-0.71	3.45	-0.01
Continuously unmarried × new				-0.56***	0.15	-0.12				-0.12	2.02	-0.002
Gender × marital status												
Continuously married × women (reference)				—	—	—				—	—	—
Newly married[a] × women				0.10	0.13	0.03				-0.29	1.72	-0.01
Newly married[b] × women				-0.25	0.26	-0.03				-7.60*	3.34	-0.08
Continuously unmarried × women				-0.07	0.13	-0.03				-4.43**	1.71	-0.13
Women	0.01	0.04	0.01	0.04	0.12	0.02	4.25***	0.61	0.16	4.71**	1.59	0.17

(Continued)

153

Table 5.3 (Continued)

	Social and Psychological Resources (continued)						Daily Strains					
	Self-Efficacy						Hours of Housework					
	Model 1			Model 2			Model 1			Model 2		
	b	*SE*	*β*	*b*	*SE*	*β*	*b*	*SE*	*β*	*b*	*SE*	*β*
Marital status												
Continuously married (reference)	—	—	—	—	—	—	—	—	—	—	—	—
Newly married[a]	-0.05	0.11	-0.03	0.19	0.15	0.09				-0.16	2.07	-0.01
Newly unmarried[b]	-0.48***	0.13	-0.09	-0.16	0.22	-0.03				4.99†	2.83	0.07
Continuously unmarried	-0.27*	0.11	-0.14	0.05	0.15	0.02	0.13*	0.05	0.06	-0.47	2.02	-0.02
Age	-0.02***	0.004	-0.10	-0.01***	0.004	-0.09				0.17*	0.05	0.08
Non-White	-0.01	0.05	-0.004	0.01	0.05	0.002				1.48*	0.75	0.04
Education	0.03***	0.01	0.08	0.03**	0.01	0.07				-0.64***	0.12	-0.12
Employment status												
Not employed (reference)	—	—	—	—	—	—	—	—	—	—	—	—
Part time	-0.05	0.09	-0.02	-0.05	0.09	-0.02	-5.54***	1.17	-0.13	-4.86***	1.15	-0.12
Full time	0.05	0.07	0.02	0.07	0.07	0.03	-5.29***	0.91	-0.17	-3.80***	0.91	-0.12
Household income (log)	-0.003	0.02	0.004	-0.01	0.02	-0.01	-0.21	0.27	-0.02	-0.27	0.26	-0.02
Missing income	-0.04	0.06	-0.02	-0.05	0.06	-0.02	0.98	0.88	-0.03	-0.76	0.86	-0.02
Duration of marriage Time 1	0.01	0.02	0.01	0.03	0.02	0.05	-0.34	0.30	-0.05	-0.32	0.31	-0.04
Previously married Time 1	0.19	0.14	0.03	0.22	0.14	0.04	1.17	1.91	-0.01	-1.92	1.90	-0.02
Time 1 state	0.29***	0.02	0.29	0.29***	0.02	0.29	0.29***	0.02	0.29	0.28***	0.02	0.28
Intercept	2.89***	0.28		2.66***	0.30		26.89***	3.65		23.9***	3.79	0
Adjusted R^2	0.1231***			0.129***			0.244***			0.274***		
n	1,834						1,654					

154

	Daily Strains (continued)						Psychological Well-Being					
	Disagree With Spouse						Depression					
	Model 1			Model 2			Model 1			Model		
	b	SE	β	b	SE	β	b	SE	β	b	SE	β
New parents	0.31	0.30	0.05	−0.22	0.37	−0.04	0.10	0.06	0.04	0.04	0.13	0.02
Parents × women				1.27*	0.53	0.18				−0.52***	0.12	−0.16
Parents × marital status										—	—	—
Continuously married × new parents (reference)												
Newly married[a] × new parents				n/a	n/a	n/a						
Newly unmarried[b] × new parents				n/a	n/a	n/a						
Continuously unmarried × new parents				n/a	n/a	n/a						
Gender × marital status												
Continuously married × women (reference)				n/a	n/a	n/a						
Newly married[a] × women				n/a	n/a	n/a						
Newly unmarried[b] × women				n/a	n/a	n/a						
Continuously unmarried × women				n/a	n/a	n/a						
Women	0.39	0.29	0.06	−0.29	0.41	−0.05	0.19***	0.05	0.09	0.39**	0.13	0.18

(Continued)

155

Table 5.3 (Continued)

	Daily Strains (continued)						Psychological Well-Being					
	Disagree With Spouse						Depression					
	Model 1			Model 2			Model 1			Model		
	b	SE	β	b	SE	β	b	SE	β	b	SE	β
Marital status												
Continuously married (reference)	n/a	n/a	n/a	n/a	n/a	n/a						
Newly married[a]	n/a	n/a	n/a	n/a	n/a	n/a	-0.08	0.12	-0.03	-0.33†	0.17	-0.14
Newly unmarried[b]	n/a	n/a	n/a	n/a	n/a	n/a	0.28*	0.14	0.05	0.11	0.25	0.02
Continuously unmarried	n/a	n/a	n/a	n/a	n/a	n/a	0.21	0.13	0.10	0.02	0.17	0.01
Age	-0.02	0.03	-0.04	-0.01	0.03	-0.02	0.01*	0.01	0.05	0.01†	0.01	0.05
Non-White	-0.04	0.39	0.004	-0.02	0.38	-0.002	0.28***	0.06	0.10	0.24*5*	0.06	0.09
Education	0.02	0.05	0.01	0.02	0.05	0.02	-0.03**	0.01	-0.06	-0.02*	0.01	-0.06
Employment status												
Not employed (reference)												
Part time	0.45	0.49	0.05	0.50	0.49	0.06	-0.11	0.10	-0.03	-0.12	0.10	-0.03
Full time	0.14	0.41	0.02	0.32	0.41	0.05	-0.19**	0.08	-0.08	-0.26***	0.10	-0.10
Household income (log)	-0.14	0.13	-0.05	-0.14	0.13	-0.05	-0.03	0.02	-0.03	-0.02	0.02	-0.03
Missing income	-0.77	1.23	-0.03	-0.68	1.22	-0.02	0.02	0.07	0.01	0.01	0.07	0.004
Duration of marriage Time 1	-0.14†	0.08	-0.10	-0.16	0.08	-0.11	0.01	0.02	-0.01	-0.03	0.03	-0.05
Previously married Time 1	-0.91†	0.51	-0.08	-0.87†	0.50	-0.08	0.07	0.16	0.01	0.02	0.16	0.002
Time 1 state	0.45***	0.04	0.45	0.45***	0.04	0.45	0.25***	0.02	0.30	0.25***	0.02	0.30
Intercept	6.22***	1.74	0	6.04***	1.73	0	0.98***	0.30	0	1.20***	0.32	
Adjusted R^2	0.236***			0.244***			0.157***			0.171***		
n			456							1,802		

a. Unmarried at time 1 and married by Time 2.

b. Married at Time 1 but separated, divorced, or widowed by Time 2.

156

parents likely differ from their childless counterparts the most. Next we assess whether the effects of becoming a parent on adult lives are the same for men and women, for married and unmarried adults.

Variations by Gender and Marital Status in Costs and Benefits of Children

The second question, whether the effect of parental status on adults' lives varies by gender and marital status, is examined in Model 2 of Table 5.3. We evaluated the following two-way interactions: parental status × gender, parental status × marital status, and gender × marital status. We added these interaction terms to the main-effects models shown in Model 1.

The first two outcomes, social integration and self-esteem, are not moderated by gender or marital status. The effect of parental status on self-efficacy, however, depends on marital status. Although Model 1 showed that new parents report lower levels of self-efficacy than those who remained childless, Model 2 shows that there is a significant interaction effect between parental status and marital status. The coefficients for newly married × new parents, newly unmarried × new parents, and continuously unmarried × new parents, are −0.34 ($p < .05$), −0.30 (*ns*), and −0.56 ($p < .001$), respectively, suggesting that those who are newly married and those who are unmarried are disadvantaged relative to those who are continuously married in terms of the effects of parental status on self-efficacy. The results of these interaction effects are shown in Figure 5.1, which presents differences in adjusted means for self-efficacy between new parents and nonparents by marital status (new parents' scores minus nonparents'). Those who have been continuously unmarried are most disadvantaged in terms of the effects of parental status on self-efficacy. Interestingly, the newly married, that is, those who got married and became parents during a relatively short period, are disadvantaged as well compared with those who have been continuously married in terms of the effects of parental status on self-efficacy.

The effect of parental status on hours of housework depends on gender. In Model 2, the coefficient for new parent × women is significant and positive (8.03, $p < .001$). Using the coefficients from the regression analysis, we calculated adjusted means of housework for men and women by parental status. New mothers do 9.07 hours per week more housework than those who remain childless (31.1 hours per week for new mothers vs. 22.0 hours per week for women who remained childless). New fathers, however, spend only 1.04 hours per week more than nonfathers (21.0 hours per week for new fathers vs. 20.4 hours per week for men who remained childless), and the difference is not significant. This result is consistent with Sanchez and Thomson (1997).

The effect of parental status on marital strain also depends on gender. Although Model 1 shows that there was little effect of becoming a parent on marital disagreement, Model 2 shows that the coefficient for new parents × women is significant and positive (1.27, $p < .05$). This suggests that new mothers report more disagreements with their spouse compared with their childless counterparts, whereas this is not the case for new fathers.

Finally, although Model 1 showed that there was little difference between new parents and nonparents in levels of depression, the effect depends on both gender and marital status. For gender, the coefficient for the interaction for new parents × women is −0.52 ($p < .001$), suggesting that there are gender differences in the relationship of parental status to depression. Contrary to arguments commonly cited, however, the negative sign indicates that new mothers are *less* vulnerable to depression than new fathers. For marital status, the coefficients for new parents × continuously unmarried is 0.72 ($p < .001$), suggesting that continuously unmarried people who become parents are more depressed than continuously married adults who do so. The results of these interaction effects are presented in Figure 5.2. It appears that new parenthood is related to higher levels of depression, especially for continuously unmarried (i.e., never married) men.

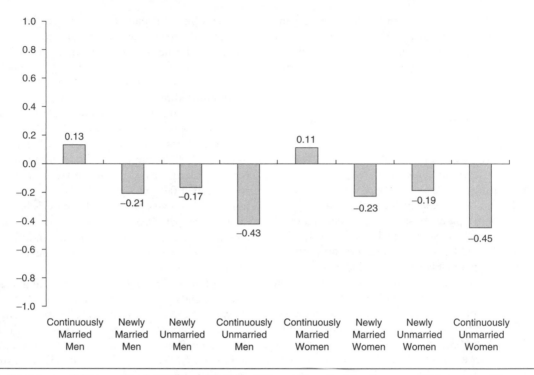

Figure 5.1   Differences in Self-Efficacy (Adjusted Means) Between New Parents and Nonparents (New Parents' Scores Minus Nonparents')

NOTE: Adjusted means were calculated by using unstandardized coefficients from the regression Model 2 of Table 5.3, which controls for age, race, education, employment status, household income, missing income, duration of marriage at Time 1, previously married at Time 1, and self-efficiency at Time 1.

Figure 5.2 also shows that among continuously married women, parents show lower levels of depression than nonparents. We examined separate regressions for subgroups by gender and marital status and found that the negative effect of parental status on depression for never-married men and the positive effect of parental status on married women were statistically significant (data not shown).

Summary

We found that the effect of becoming a parent on adults' lives is multifaceted, with effects dependent on other statuses such as gender and marital status. New parents, regardless of gender and marital status, report higher levels of social integration compared with their childless counterparts and show no differences in self-esteem. For other indicators, the effects of becoming a parent vary by gender and marital status subgroups. Becoming a mother (not a father) means more hours of housework and more disagreements with spouses compared with their counterparts who remained childless. Upon becoming a parent, never-married men and women tend to experience lower self-efficacy. Upon the arrival of children, never-married men are the most disadvantaged in terms of depression; continuously married women are the most advantaged compared with their childless counterparts.

Table 5.4 presents a summary of our findings for the four marital status subgroups. Becoming a parent seems to affect married women by providing benefits (noted by a plus sign indicating

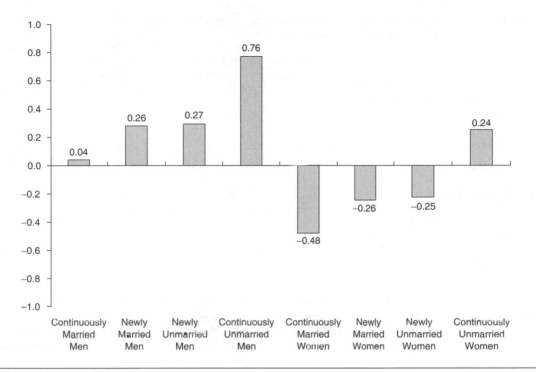

Figure 5.2   Differences in Depression (Adjusted Means) between New Parents and Nonparents (New
Parents' Scores Minus Nonparents')

NOTE: Adjusted means were calculated by using unstandardized coefficients from the regression Model 2 of Table 5.3, which
controls for age, race, education, employment status, household income, missing income, duration of marriage at Time 1, previously married at Time 1, and self-efficiency at Time 1

more of a positive state) and costs (noted by a
minus sign indicating less of a positive state).
Married women enjoy greater social integration
and lower levels of depression but do more
housework and have more disagreements with
their spouse. The smallest effect of becoming a
parent on well-being among the four subgroups
occurs for married men; the only effect was that
these new fathers report expanded contact with
relatives, friends, and neighbors. For unmarried
men and women, becoming a parent may bring
more costs than benefits to their lives. Upon
becoming parents, unmarried women show an
increase in social integration but a decrease in
self-efficacy and an increase in housework.
Unmarried men also show an increase in social
integration but have decreased self-efficacy and
increased depression.

Discussion

The effect of parenthood on adults' lives has
been of great interest among researchers. Whereas
many studies have focused on costs of parenting,
we have argued that being a parent with young
children may provide benefits as well as costs
to adults, including opportunities to broaden and
activate social networks and to develop psychological resources such as self-esteem and self-efficacy.
We have suggested that the strong focus on strains
of childrearing might result in misleading interpretations of the effect of children on adults' lives.
This is not to say, of course, that research on
parental strains is unwarranted—indeed, it is
important and necessary to uncover parental strain
processes and the ways in which social policies
can alleviate parents' burdens (Glass, 2000).

Table 5.4 Summary of Findings on the Effects of Becoming a Parent on Adults' Lives by Marital Status at Time 2 and Gender of Respondents

	Married Women	Married Men	Unmarried Women	Unmarried Men
Social and psychological resources				
Social integration	+	+	+	+
Self-esteem				
Self-efficacy			—	—
Daily strains				
Housework	—	—	—	
Disagreements with spouse	—		n/a	n/a
Psychological well-being				
Depression	+			—

NOTE: + = better states; — = worse states; n/a = not applicable.

Using longitudinal data gathered from a national representative sample, and comparison groups carefully chosen in terms of parents' and nonparents' stage in the life course, this study suggests that some rethinking is needed about conclusions that overall, the effect of children on adults lives is detrimental. The findings generally show that becoming a parent can entail both greater costs and higher levels of benefits compared with those who remain childless, depending on the adult's social position.

We find that the costs and rewards of becoming a parent vary greatly by marital status and gender subgroups. Our findings suggest that if researchers continue to examine the lives of parents without considering differences among fathers and mothers, or among married and unmarried parents, they will fail to capture the complex nature of the parental role and its effect on adults' lives. Our findings indicate that for married women, although becoming a mother is associated with greater costs in terms of more housework and more disagreements with spouse, it is also associated with better mental health in terms of depression. Married men who become fathers show few changes in terms of costs and benefits. Our findings also indicate that generally, costs of becoming a parent accrue to those who have never been married, especially to

never-married men. Even after selection effects are minimized, among the four subgroups, unmarried men are the most vulnerable to distress when they become parents. Unmarried fathers (particularly the never married) have received little attention in parental research. Although the predominant image of unmarried fathers may be that they are "bad dads"—irresponsible, absent fathers who do not fulfill their child support obligations (Furstenberg, 1988), they may be as vulnerable as unmarried mothers to hardships in their parental roles (for example, see Simon, 1998; Umberson & Williams, 1993). The majority of the continuously unmarried fathers in this study probably never shared a coresidential relationship with their child. Nonetheless, they are more depressed than their married counterparts after becoming a parent and may feel a strong psychological loss, perhaps by not having much contact with their new offspring. Further research on this group is warranted.

The choice of indicators to assess the effect of parenthood on adults' lives is challenging. Because our dependent variables do not include indicators that directly assess parental experiences, such as hours of child care, disagreements with spouse about the child, and joys and satisfaction with and concerns about childrearing, our results may underestimate both the positive and negative effects of parental status on adults' lives. For example, the increase in housework hours for women who become mothers is probably an underestimate because we do not have a measure of child-care hours, which is likely fairly high for mothers compared with nonmothers. Child care itself, moreover, is both rewarding and frustrating, exemplifying the increase in both joys and burdens accruing to adults who become parents.

We are cautious about our findings because of potential problems regarding sample attrition that may have affected our results. For example, our findings on the effect of becoming a parent on self-efficacy or depression may be underestimated if those who became parents after the first interview and who were highly distressed by having a child were more likely to drop out of the sample. Another possible bias is that although we use marital status as one of our primary independent variables, changes in marital status between the two interviews may not be independent from the presence of children. It is possible that those who experienced greater marital conflict upon becoming parents may have split up before the second interview. The question on the effect of the presence of children on marital dissolution is still debatable (e.g., see Ono, 1998; Sayer & Bianchi, 2000; South & Spitze, 1986) and is beyond the scope of this paper.

Whereas our analysis showed statistically significant effects of parental status on adults' lives, the explained variance of the models is relatively small, and the mean differences between new parents and those remaining childless are minimal. This is surprising, given that reviews of previous studies and some qualitative research emphasize costs and struggles during the transition to parenthood. On one hand, the small effects may be because of limitations of our outcome measures. One of the outcome measures, self-efficacy, was a one-item assessment rather than an index, making it less reliable and perhaps more difficult to discern the effects of parental status. Also, as we discussed earlier, we do not examine outcome variables directly related to

parental roles such as child care. On the other hand, our findings of the small effect of parental status on six indicators of adults' lives are similar to findings from other quantitative studies.

Future research should consider how the types and degree of costs and benefits of parenting change as children grow. In data not shown, we examined the effects of the duration of parenthood rather than parental status on each indicator of adults' lives assessed in this study. The results were similar; however, the data provide insight into only a relatively small window of parenting through the preschool years. One avenue for future research that seems warranted, then, is to compare parents of older children with nonparents at a similar life stage (perhaps middle age). For parents with preschool children, strains may include demands of daily care of the children, but for parents of older children, trouble in the parent-child relationship may constitute a burden of parenting (Umberson, 1989; Umberson et al., 1996). Benefits may change as well: Those with older children, for example, are shown to be even more integrated than those with younger or no children (Gallagher & Gerstel, 2001).

In conclusion, from the day children are born, they become a source of joy and a source of burden for their parents. Men and women becoming parents take on a profound status for the rest of their lives. Explicit examination of the processes through which costs and benefits ebb and flow in parents' and nonparents' lives, and perhaps lead to different levels of well-being, will provide us with a deeper understanding of how parenting does—and does not—affect adults.

Note

We wish to thank Suzanne Bianchi and Steven Martin for helpful comments on earlier drafts of this article.

References

Aneshensel, C. S. (1992). Social stress: Theory and research. *Annual Review of Sociology, 18,* 15–38.

Aneshensel, C. S., Frerichs, R. R., & Clark, V. A. (1981). Family roles and sex differences in depression. *Journal of Health and Social Behavior, 22,* 379–393.

Avison, W. R. (1995). Roles and resources: The effects of family structure and employment on women's psychological resources and psychological distress. *Research in Community and Mental Health, 8,* 233–256.

Bandura, A. (1997). *Self-efficacy: The exercise of control.* New York: Freeman.

Barnett, R. C., & Baruch, G. K. (1985). Women's involvement in multiple roles and psychological distress. *Journal of Personality and Social Psychology, 49,* 135–145.

Baruch, G., Barnett, R., & Rivers, C. (1983). *Lifeprints: New patterns of love and work for today's women.* New York: New American Library.

Belsky, J., Lang, M., & Huston, T. L. (1986). Sex typing and division of labor as determinants of marital change across the transition to parenthood. *Journal of Personality and Social Psychology, 50,* 517–522.

Bird, C. E. (1997). Gender differences in the social and economic burdens of parenting and psychological distress. *Journal of Marriage and the Family, 59,* 809–823.

Cleary, P. D., & Mechanic, D. (1983). Sex differences in psychological distress among married people. *Journal of Health and Social Behavior, 24,* 111–121.

Cowan, C. P., & Cowan, P. A. (1992). *When partners become parents: The big life change for couples.* New York: Basic Books.

Cowan, C. P., Cowan, P. A., Heming, G., Garrett, F., Coysh, W. S., Curtis-Boles, S. H., & Boles, A. J., III. (1985). Transitions to parenthood: His, hers, and theirs. *Journal of Family Issues, 6,* 451–481.

Crohan, S. (1996). Marital quality and conflict across the transition to parenthood in African American and White couples. *Journal of Marriage and the Family, 52,* 475–486.

Davies, L., Avison, W. R., & McAlpine, D. D. (1997). Significant life experiences and depression among single and married mothers. *Journal of Marriage and the Family, 59,* 294–308.

Demo, D. H., & Cox, M. J. (2000). Families with young children: A review of research in the 1990s. *Journal of Marriage and the Family, 62,* 876–895.

Downey, G., & Moen, P. (1987). Personal efficacy, income, and family transitions: A longitudinal study of women heading households. *Journal of Health and Social Behavior, 28,* 320–333.

Erikson, E. (1950). *Childhood and society.* New York: Norton.

Fischer, C., & Oliker, S. (1983). A research note on friendship, gender, and the life cycle. *Social Forces, 62,* 124–132.

Furstenberg, F. F. (1988). Good dads—bad dads: Two faces of fatherhood. In A. J. Cherlin (Ed.), *The changing American family and public policy* (pp. 193–218). Washington, DC: Urban Institute Press.

Gallagher, S. K., & Gerstel, N. (2001). Connections and constraints: The effects of children on care giving. *Journal of Marriage and the Family, 63,* 265–275.

Gerstel, N., & Gallager, S. K. (1993). Kinkeeping and distress: Gender, recipients of care, and work-family conflict. *Journal of Marriage and the Family, 55,* 598–607.

Glass, J. (2000). Envisioning the integration of family and work: Toward a kinder, gentler workplace. *Contemporary Sociology, 29,* 129–143.

Glass, J., & Fujimoto, T. (1994). Housework, paid work, and depression among husbands and wives. *Journal of Health and Social Behavior, 35,* 179–191.

Glenn, N. D., & McLanahan, S. (1982). Children and marital happiness: A further specification of the relationship. *Journal of Marriage and the Family, 44,* 63–72.

Goldsteen, K., & Ross, C. E. (1989). The perceived burden of children. *Journal of Family Issues, 10,* 504–526.

Gore, S., & Mangione, T. W. (1983). Social roles, sex roles, and psychological distress: Additive and interactive models of sex differences. *Journal of Health and Social Behavior, 24,* 300–312.

Gove, W. R., & Geerken, M. R. (1977). The effect of children and employment on the mental health of married men and women. *Social Forces, 56,* 66–76.

Hoffman, L. W., & Manis, J. D. (1982). The value of children in the United States. In F. I. Nye (Ed.), *Family relationships: Rewards and costs* (pp. 143–170). Beverly Hills, CA: Sage.

House, J. S., Umberson, D., & Landis, K. R. (1988). Structure and processes of social support. *Annual Review of Sociology, 14,* 293–318.

Ishii-Kuntz, M., & Seccombe, K. (1989). The impact of children upon social support networks throughout the life course. *Journal of Marriage and the Family, 51,* 777–790.

Kandel, D., Davis, M., & Raccis, V. (1985). The stressfulness of daily social roles for women: Marital, occupational, and household roles. *Journal of Health and Social Behavior, 26,* 67–78.

Kessler, R., & Zhao, S. (1999). Overview of descriptive epidemiology of mental disorders. In C. S. Aneshensel & J. C. Phelan (Eds.), *Handbook of the sociology of mental health* (pp. 127–150). New York: Plenum.

Kurdek, L. A. (1993). Nature and prediction of changes in marital quality for first-time parent and non-parent husbands and wives. *Journal of Family Psychology, 6,* 255–265.

LaRossa, R., & LaRossa, M. M. (1981). *Transition to parenthood: How infants change families.* Beverly Hills, CA: Sage.

LaVee, Y., Sharlin, S., & Katz, R. (1996). The effect of parenting stress on marital quality: An integrated mother-father model. *Journal of Family Issues, 17,* 114–135.

LeMasters, E. F. (1957). Parenthood as crisis. *Marriage and Family Living, 19,* 352–355.

Lynch, S. (1998). Who supports whom? How age and gender affect the perceived quality of support from family and friends. *The Gerontologist, 38,* 231–238.

MacDermid, S. M., Huston, T. L., & McHale, S. M. (1990). Changes in marriage associated with the transition to parenthood: Individual differences as a function of sex-role attitudes and changes in the division of household labor. *Journal of Marriage and the Family, 52,* 475–486.

Marks, N. F., & Lambert, J. D. (1998). Marital status continuity and change among young and midlife adults: Longitudinal effects on psychological well-being. *Journal of Family Issues, 19,* 652–686.

McKeering, H., & Pakenham, K. I. (2000). Gender and generativity issues in parenting: Do fathers benefit more than mothers from involvement in child care activities? *Sex Roles, 43,* 459–480.

McLanahan, S., & Adams, J. (1987). Parenthood and psychological well-being. *Annual Review of Sociology, 13,* 237–257.

Mulford, H. A., & Salisbury, W. W. (1964). Self-conceptions in a general population. *Sociological Quarterly, 5,* 35–46.

Munch, A., McPherson, J. M., & Smith-Lovin, L. (1997). Gender, children, and social contact: The effects of childrearing for men and women. *American Sociological Review, 62,* 509–520.

Neter, J., Kutner, M. H., Nachtsheim, C. J., & Wasserman, W. (1996). *Applied linear statistical models* (4th ed.). New York: WCB McGraw-Hill.

Ono, H. (1998). Husbands' and wives' resources and marital dissolution. *Journal of Marriage and the Family, 60,* 674–689.

Pearlin, L. (1989). The sociological study of stress. *Journal of Health and Social Behavior, 30,* 241–256.

Pearlin, L. I., & Johnson, J. S. (1977). Marital status, life-strains and depression. *American Sociological Review, 42,* 704–715.

Pearlin, L. I., Menaghan, E. G., Lieberman, M. A., & Mullan, J. T. (1981). The stress process. *Journal of Health and Social Behavior, 22,* 337–356.

Radloff, L. S. (1977). The CES-D scale: A self-report depression scale for research in the general population. *Applied Psychological Measurement, 1,* 385–401.

Rosenberg, M. (1986). *Conceiving the self.* Malabar, FL: Krieger.

Rosenfield, S. (1989). The effects of women's employment: Personal control and sex differences in mental health. *Journal of Health and Social Behavior, 30,* 77–91.

Ross, C. F., & Huber, J. (1985). Hardship and depression. *Journal of Health and Social Behavior, 26,* 312–327.

Ross, C. F., & Mirowsky, J. (1988). Child care and emotional adjustment to wives' employment. *Journal of Health and Social Behavior, 29,* 127–138.

Ross, C. F., Mirowsky, J., & Goldsteen, K. (1990). The impact of the family on health: The decade in review. *Journal of Marriage and the Family, 52,* 1059–1078.

Ross, C. F., & Van Willigen, M. (1996). Gender, parenthood, and anger. *Journal of Marriage and the Family, 58,* 572–584.

Sanchez, L., & Thomson, F. (1997). Becoming mothers and fathers: Parenthood, gender, and the division of labor. *Gender & Society, 11,* 747–772.

Sayer, L., & Bianchi, S. (2000). Women's economic independence and the probability of divorce. *Journal of Family Issues, 21,* 906–943.

Scott, J., & Alwin, D. F. (1989). Gender differences in parental strain: Parental role or gender role? *Journal of Family Issues, 10,* 482–503.

Shelton, B. A., & John, D. (1996). The division of household labor. *Annual Review of Sociology, 22,* 299–322.

Sieber, S. D. (1974). Toward a theory of role accumulation. *American Sociological Review, 39,* 567–578.

Simon, R. W. (1992). Parental role strains, salience of parental role identity and gender differences in psychological distress. *Journal of Health and Social Behavior, 33,* 25–35.

Simon, R. W. (1998). Assessing sex differences in vulnerability among employed parents: The importance of marital status. *Journal of Health and Social Behavior, 39,* 38–54.

South, S. J., & Spitze, G. (1986). Determinants of divorce over the marital life course. *American Sociological Review, 51,* 583–590.

South, S. J., & Spitze, G. (1994). Housework in marital and nonmarital households. *American Sociological Review. 59,* 327–347.

Sweet, J. A., & Bumpass, L. L. (1996). *The National Survey of Families and Households—Waves 1 and 2: Data Description and Documentation.* Center for Demography and Ecology, University of Wisconsin–Madison. Retrieved January 10, 2003, from http://www.ssc.wisc.edu/nsfh/home

Thompson, M. S. (1986). The influence of supportive relations on the psychological well-being of teenage mothers. *Social Forces, 64,* 1006–1024.

Umberson, D. (1989). Relationships with children: Explaining parents' psychological well-being. *Journal of Marriage and the Family, 51,* 999–1012.

Umberson, D., Chen, M. D., House, J. S., Hopkins, K., & Slaten, F. (1996). The effect of social relationships on psychological well-being: Are men and women really so different? *American Sociological Review, 61,* 837–857.

Umberson, D., & Gove, W. (1989). Parenthood and psychological well-being: Theory, measurement, and stage in the family life course. *Journal of Family Issues, 10,* 440–462.

Umberson, D., & Williams, C. L. (1993). Divorced fathers: Parental role strain and psychological distress. *Journal of Family Issues, 14,* 378–400.

Umberson, D., & Williams, K. (1999). Family status and mental health. In C. S. Aneshensel & J. C. Phelan (Eds.), *Handbook of the Sociology of Mental Health* (pp. 225–253). New York: Kluwer Academic/Plenum.

Voydanoff, P., & Donnelly, B. W. (1989). Work and family roles and psychological distress. *Journal of Marriage and the Family, 51,* 923–932.

Wethington, E., & Kessler, R. D. (1989). Employment, parental responsibility, and psychological distress: A longitudinal study of married women. *Journal of Family Issues, 10,* 527–546.

Equity and Social Exchange in Dating Couples: Associations With Satisfaction, Commitment, and Stability

Susan Sprecher

Abstract

A longitudinal study with romantic couples was conducted to examine the importance of equity relative to other social exchange variables (i.e., rewards, investments, and alternatives) in predicting relationship satisfaction, commitment, and stability. Underbenefiting inequity (but not overbenefiting inequity) was associated with a lower level of satisfaction and commitment and a greater likelihood of breakup. However, little evidence was found that equity at one time predicted change in satisfaction and commitment. Slightly more evidence was found for a reverse causal direction: Satisfaction and commitment contributed to a decrease in under benefiting inequity, although these results were not consistent across time. Women's commitment was the strongest predictor of relationship stability. In addition, women's under benefiting inequity and alternatives and men's alternatives were associated with breakups in some of the analyses, and women's rewards and satisfaction and men's satisfaction were associated with relationship stability in some of the analyses. Because of the multiple waves and the extended length of the longitudinal study, the findings make a unique contribution to the literature on equity and exchange.

Some relationships develop, are maintained, and last a lifetime. Other relationships become dissatisfying to one or both partners and are terminated. Considerable prior research has focused on identifying the factors associated with relationship satisfaction and success. Among the factors considered have been social exchange elements of the relationship, which include two categories of theoretical variables. One set of variables refers to the distributive justice norms, particularly equity (e.g., Walster [Hatfield], Walster, & Berscheid, 1978). The second set derives from Thibaut and Kelley's interdependence theory (Kelley & Thibaut, 1978; Thibaut & Kelley, 1959) and more recently has been represented in Rusbult's (1980, 1983) investment model. The central focus of the present research is on the importance of equity in predicting relationship satisfaction, commitment, and stability, but its importance is assessed relative to other social exchange variables (rewards, investments, and comparison level for alternatives). These associations are examined with a longitudinal sample of couples, all of whom were dating at the first wave of the study.

Theoretical Background

Equity refers to the perceived balance in the partner's contributions and outcomes. An individual is underbenefited in a relationship if he or she contributes more but receives less than his or her partner. The state of overbenefit occurs when one is contributing less but receiving more than one's partner. (The two partners may not agree in their perceptions of equity.) Equity theorists (e.g., Hatfield, Utne, & Traupmann, 1979; Walster et al., 1978) predict that both underbenefiting inequity and overbenefiting inequity cause distress, but that underbenefiting inequity is more distressing. The theory further predicts that the distress is likely to strain the relationship and decrease overall satisfaction and commitment. This distress leads an individual to seek to restore equity by either changing his or her own contributions, convincing the partner to change his or hers, or convincing him or herself that the inequity does not exist (i.e., change perceptions and expectations of each partner's contributions and outcomes). If these attempts fail, the relationship is likely to end.

The variables included in investment theory (e.g., Rusbult, 1980, 1983; Rusbult & Buunk, 1993; Rusbult, Drigotas, & Verette, 1994) are rewards, costs, comparison level (general expectations of what one deserves), comparison level for alternatives (expectations of rewards one could obtain elsewhere), and investments (what one gives to the relationship that cannot be retrieved if the relationship were to end). This framework distinguishes between predictors of satisfaction or positive affect experienced in the relationship and commitment, or the intent to maintain and feel psychologically attached to the relationship. The investment model predicts that satisfaction will be greater the higher the rewards and the lower the costs, both as compared to the individual's comparison level. A person's commitment to the relationship is predicted to be affected positively by satisfaction (which is further predicted by the positive difference between rewards and costs) and investments, and negatively by desirable alternatives. Stability of the relationship is expected to be affected directly by commitment and thus indirectly by the other social exchange variables.

Both equity theory and the investment model purport to predict relationship outcomes such as satisfaction, commitment, and stability, although there have been few attempts to compare the relative explanatory power of equity and investment model variables. The general goal of this investigation is to extend the integration of the two social exchange theories by examining the contribution of equity, relative to several investment model variables, in predicting relationship satisfaction, commitment, and stability. Relationship and family researchers, theoreticians, and practitioners have long been interested in identifying the factors that contribute to relationship happiness and success, and this investigation contributes to this body of literature.

Representative Research on Equity

Early research that examined equity in intimate relationships found that individuals who reported underbenefit in their relationships experienced the most distress, those who reported equity experienced the least distress, and those who were overbenefited were intermediate between these two groups (for a review, see Hatfield et al., 1979). Research also has provided support for the prediction that distress experienced as a result of inequity strains the overall relationship and is associated with lower satisfaction and commitment (e.g., Davidson, 1984; Sabatelli & Cecil-Pigo, 1985; Sprecher, 1988; Traupmann, Hatfield, & Wexler, 1983; Traupmann, Peterson, Utne, & Hatfield, 1981; Utne, Hatfield, Traupmann, & Greenberger, 1984).

Other research focused on comparing equity with reward level or equality (another justice norm) in predicting relationship quality. These studies found equity to be less important than rewards as a predictor of relationship quality (Cate, Lloyd, & Henton, 1985; Cate, Lloyd, Henton, & Larson, 1982; Cate, Lloyd, & Long,

1988; Desmarais & Lerner, 1989; Martin, 1985; Michaels, Acock, & Edwards, 1986; Michaels, Edwards, & Acock, 1984). Sprecher (1988) compared equity with several investment variables—satisfaction, investments, and alternatives (as well as with the degree of social network support)—in predicting relationship commitment. She found comparison level for alternatives to be the strongest predictor of commitment but also found that equity, satisfaction, and network support explained unique variance in commitment (investments did not explain any additional variance in commitment when the other variables were included in the model). Floyd and Wasner (1994) found equity to be correlated with commitment in bivariate analyses but unrelated to commitment when satisfaction and desirable alternatives also were included in multivariate analyses.

Although equity appears to be at least modestly associated with satisfaction and commitment in concurrent analyses, it appears to do less well in forecasting later relationship stability (see Berg & McQuinn, 1986; Felmlee, Sprecher, & Bassin, 1990; Lujansky & Mikula, 1983). In addition, very little evidence has been found that equity at one time contributes to a change in relationship quality over time (see Cate et al., 1988; Lujansky & Mikula, 1983). However, VanYperen and Buunk (1990), with a Dutch sample of men and women most of whom were married, found that the more equity that wives perceived at Time 1, the smaller the decrease (or the greater the increase) in their satisfaction a year later. In addition, Grote and Clark (2001), in a longitudinal study of husbands and wives making the transition to parenthood, found that inequity in division of labor at one time contributed to an increase in conflict and a decrease in satisfaction 6 to 8 months later, although for wives only.

Although equity appears not to be a strong predictor of change in relationship quality, what about the reverse causal direction? Is there evidence that dissatisfaction in a relationship leads people to perceive or create inequities? Some exchange theorists (e.g., Grote & Clark, 2001) have argued that this causal direction is also likely to occur in part because dissatisfaction, as a negative emotion, can trigger people to become more focused on what is going on in their relationship and possibly lead to biased retrieval of information on who is contributing what. In support of this prediction, Grote and Clark (2001) found that conflict and dissatisfaction measured at one time (for both husbands and wives) predicted greater inequity in household tasks several months later.

A Brief Overview of Research on the Investment Model

Rusbult and her students have provided several tests of the predictions derived from the investment model (e.g., Duffy & Rusbult, 1986; Rusbult, 1980, 1983; Rusbult, Johnson, & Morrow, 1986; Rusbult & Martz, 1995; Rusbult, Martz, & Agnew, 1998). In addition, others have tested some of the associations predicted from the theory (e.g., Bui, Peplau, & Hill, 1996; Felmlee et al., 1990; Floyd & Wasner, 1994; Kurdek, 1992; Sacher & Fine, 1996; Simpson, 1987). This previous research has found satisfaction to be generally predicted by rewards but less affected by costs. In a majority of the studies, commitment has been found to be associated positively with investments and rewards and associated negatively with comparison level for alternatives. However, and as noted earlier, very little research has examined investment model variables along with justice norms (e.g., equity). In addition, very little of the research has been longitudinal, particularly of the type that includes measures of the theoretical variables at later time points (see, however, Rusbult, 1983).

Purposes of This Investigation

The first purpose of this study is to examine the unique association of equity with commitment and satisfaction, relative to rewards, investments, and comparison level for alternatives, with all variables measured concurrently. I hypothesize that inequity (particularly underbenefiting inequity) and alternatives will be associated negatively with commitment and satisfaction, and that rewards and investments will be associated positively with commitment and satisfaction. Although prior research (e.g., Cate et al., 1988; Martin, 1985) suggests that rewards will be a more important predictor of satisfaction and commitment than equity, little prior research has compared equity with other investment model variables, and thus the importance of equity relative to the other variables will be explored.

The second purpose is to examine whether equity predicts change in satisfaction and commitment over time. As noted previously, most of the research demonstrating links between equity and relationship outcomes has been based on cross-sectional data. Only VanYperen and Buunk (1990) and Grote and Clark (2001) found any evidence that equity may contribute to a change in satisfaction, and for women only. In the present study, panel analyses examine how equity measured at Time n predicted satisfaction (and commitment) at Time n + 1 controlling for satisfaction (commitment) at Time n. As a comparison, similar analyses are conducted with the other social exchange variables.

The third purpose is to test the reverse causal direction between equity and relationship quality—does inequity arise out of relationship unhappiness? Individuals may perceive preexisting inequities or create new ones only if a relationship dips below a certain threshold of relationship quality. Panel analyses examine how satisfaction (and commitment) measured at Time n predicts inequity at Time n + 1 controlling for inequity at Time n. As a comparison, similar analyses are conducted with the other social exchange variables.

The final purpose of this study is to examine the degree to which equity predicts the stability of the relationship, also in comparison with other social exchange variables. Although inequity should have a negative effect on the entire relationship and lead to dissolution, previous research (e.g., Berg & McQuinn, 1986; Felmlee et al., 1990; Lujansky & Mikula, 1983) has found almost no support for the theory that equity predicts which couples break up and

which remain together over time. Investment model variables (e.g., comparison level for alternatives) have done better in forecasting the final status of the relationship (e.g., Berg & McQuinn, 1986; Bui et al., 1996; Rusbult et al., 1998), although most previous longitudinal studies have followed couples over a limited period of time or at only one follow-up (the Bui et al. study is an exception).

In sum, through both concurrent and longitudinal analyses, equity is compared to other social exchange variables in predicting satisfaction and commitment (including change in satisfaction and commitment) and relationship stability with a sample of romantic couples. In addition, the longitudinal data allow for the examination of the degree to which change in equity (and the other exchange variables) is affected by satisfaction and commitment.

Method

Overview of the Data

The data are from a longitudinal study conducted at a Midwestern university with a volunteer sample of romantic couples. The original sample consisted of both partners of 101 dating couples who completed a self-administered questionnaire in fall 1988. The first follow-up was conducted 6 months later (spring, 1989), and then three additional follow-ups were conducted approximately annually (spring-summer of 1990, 1991, and 1992).

Most of the participants were university undergraduate students when they first participated at Time 1. They were recruited primarily through advertisements in the student newspaper and posters placed around campus. The mean age of the participants at Time 1 was approximately 20 years (by Time 5, the participants were, on the average, 24–25 years of age). Most of the sample was White (97.5%) and of the middle or upper-middle class (86.6%). The mean number of months the couples had been dating was 18.7.

All of the participants at Time 1 and some of the participants at the follow-ups completed the questionnaire in a university office. In the follow-ups, the couples were initially contacted over the phone to determine the current status of their relationships. Participants who had moved away were mailed the questionnaire, with a stamped, self-addressed return envelope. Generally, there was very little refusal to participate, particularly among couples whose relationships remained intact. Of the 41 couples who remained together over the study, 38 of the women and 36 of the men participated at all five waves of the study. (Six participants from five different relationships did not participate in one of the waves, and one couple [two participants] were missing at two waves.) A higher rate of non-response occurred in the final contact (the breakup questionnaire) for the subsample of couples who broke up, although the response rate was still high (86%).

Measurement

Social Exchange Measures. At each wave of the study, equity, rewards, and investments were assessed by both a detailed measure and a global item. The detailed measure for each exchange variable was based on the six resources included in Foa and Foa's (1974) classification of resources—love (affection, warmth); status (prestige, esteem); money (cash, credit, earning potential, paying on dates); material goods (gifts, sharing possessions); services (favors, comfort); and information (knowledge, common sense); it also included the resource sex (meeting needs and preferences) (see also Cate et al., 1988; Michaels et al., 1984). The exchange variables were assessed in the following order:

Rewards. Participants were first asked to indicate how rewarding their partner's contributions have been in each of the seven resource areas. A 1 (*very unrewarding*) to 7 (*very rewarding*) response scale followed each resource. The mean of these seven items represents the participant's score on the rewards scale. Cronbach's alpha ranged from .70 to .93 for men and women across the five waves of the study. Participants

also were asked the global item: "When you think about everything that your partner has to offer to you and the relationship (in the areas above as well as in other areas), how unrewarding or rewarding are his/her contributions?" This was followed by a 1 (*very unrewarding*) to 7 (*very rewarding*) response scale. Because the scores on the rewards scale and the global reward item were highly correlated (*r* ranged from .60 to .82 for men and women across the waves), they were averaged for a total rewards score.

Investments. Participants were then asked to indicate how much they had invested of each of the resources listed. An investment was defined as "something you put into the relationship that cannot easily be taken back if the relationship were to end." The same list of seven resources was provided, with each item followed by a 1 (*very little invested*) to 7 (*a great deal invested*) response scale. Cronbach's alpha ranged from .63 to .75. The global item of investments was: "Overall, how much have you invested into the relationship?" (options ranged from 1 = *very little invested* to 7 = *a great deal invested*). The mean score to the investment scale and the global item were correlated (*r* from .48 to .75) and were averaged for a total investments score.

Equity. Participants were then asked to indicate the degree to which the exchange in each resource area was fair or unfair. Participants responded to each resource on a 7-point scale, where 1 = *very unfair; I'm getting the worse deal;* 4 = *fair;* and 7 = *very unfair; I'm getting the better deal.* A total score on the equity scale was represented by the mean of the seven items. Cronbach's alpha ranged from .48 to .72. A global equity measure was represented by the Hatfield Global Equity Measure (described in Hatfield et al., 1979), which asks participants to indicate who is getting a better deal in the relationship (options ranged from 1 = *I am getting a much better deal than my partner* to 7 = *My partner is getting a much better deal than I am;* 4 was the equitable response). This item was recoded so that the lower scores (1–3) represented an underbenefiting response, and the higher scores (5–7) represented an overbenefiting response. Scores on the equity scale and the global item were correlated (*r* ranged from .43 to .73) and were averaged for a total equity score.

Equity, as measured in this study, differs from the other social exchange variables because it is curvilinear (the midpoint represents equity, and low and high scores represent two types of inequity). Various analytic approaches have been used in prior research to deal with equity in combination with linear variables (for a review of these strategies, see Sprecher & Schwartz, 1994). The approach used here was to develop underbenefiting and overbenefiting indices created from the mean of the equity scale and the Hatfield global item (also see Sprecher, 1986). The analysis is similar to dummy variable regression in that there are two variables that represent the three possible categories of equity. If a participant had an equity score of 4 or higher, his or her score on the underbenefiting index was 0; otherwise the score on the underbenefiting index was the absolute value away from the midpoint of the equity score. A participant's score on the overbenefiting index was 0 if he or she had a score of 4 or lower on the equity score; otherwise the score was the absolute value away from the midpoint of the equity score. For example, a mean equity score of 3.79 resulted in a score of .21 on the underbenefiting index and a score of 0 on the overbenefiting index. A mean score of 4.14 resulted in a score of .14 on the overbenefiting index and a score of 0 on the underbenefiting index.

Comparison level for alternatives. Later in the questionnaire, five items were included to measure the quality and likelihood of alternative situations in comparison to continuing the relationship. These were: "Considering what you have to offer, how difficult/easy would it be to find a new partner?" (1 = *very difficult;* 7 = *very easy);* "Considering the number of 'eligibles' you are aware of, how difficult/easy would it be to find a new partner?" (1 = *very difficult* to

7 = *very easy*); "Considering what you have to offer and the number of 'eligibles' you are aware of, how do you think you would fare in finding a new partner? That is, how would the new partner compare to your present partner?" (1 = *far worse than present partner* to 7 = *far better than present partner);* "Think about the alternative of being unattached (not dating anyone for a while). Right now, how desirable is this alternative compared to your current situation?" (1 = *far worse than current situation* to 7 = *far better than current situation*); and "Consider your alternatives to the relationship. These alternatives could include beginning a relationship with another person, begin seeing several people, or spending time alone. All things considered, how do your alternatives compare with your relationship with your partner?" (1 = *relationship with partner is much worse than alternatives* to 7 = *relationship with partner is much better than alternatives*). Comparison level for alternatives was represented by the mean of these five items, after the last item was reverse scored. The higher the score, the better and more likely are the alternatives. Cronbach's alpha ranged from .54 to .81.

Relationship Quality Measures. There are two major subcategories measuring relationship quality:

• *Satisfaction.* The Hendrick (1988) Relationship Assessment Scale was used to measure general satisfaction in the relationship. Example items of this seven-item scale include, "In general, how satisfied are you with your relationship?" and "To what extent has your relationship met your original expectations?" A 5-point response scale was provided for each item. The mean of the seven items represents the total score. Cronbach's alpha ranged from .65 to .87.

• *Commitment.* Five items were included to measure relationship commitment. Four of these items were from the commitment scale developed by Lund (1985) and include "How likely is it that your relationship will be permanent?" and "How likely are you to pursue another relationship or single life in the future?" The final item was the direct question, "How committed are you to your partner?" Each item was followed by a 7-point response scale. The mean of the five items represents the total score. Cronbach's alpha ranged from .52 to .97.

Results

The analyses presented are based on the participants' data from Time 1 and from each of the follow-ups at which their relationship was intact.

Preliminary Analyses

At each wave of the study, men and women described their relationship as generally equitable, the rewards they received to be high, their investments to be considerable, and alternatives to be only slightly desirable and available. A table of means and standard deviations for the exchange variables is available by writing the author. The participants also reported high levels of satisfaction and commitment (see Sprecher, 1999).

As part of preliminary analyses, I also examined the intercorrelations among the exchange variables at each wave of the study (for each gender separately). Scores on the underbenefiting and overbenefiting indices at each wave of the study were moderately and negatively correlated ($-.16$ to $-.34$, mean $r = -.26$). Underbenefiting inequity was correlated negatively with rewards ($-.19$ to $-.66$, mean $r = -.46$), generally unrelated to investments ($-.16$ to $.10$, mean $r = -.01$), and generally positively related to perceptions of alternatives ($.02$ to $.49$, mean $r = .25$). Overbenefiting inequity was generally unrelated to the other exchange variables, with the exception of a significant ($p < .01$) negative correlation with investments at Time 3 for men ($-.35$) and women ($-.46$) and at Time 4 for men ($-.39$), and a positive correlation ($.26$, $p < .01$) with rewards at Time 1 for women. Rewards and investments were positively correlated ($.43$ to $.81$, mean $r = .63$). Finally, alternatives were negatively correlated with rewards ($-.13$ to $-.68$,

mean $r = -.43$) and with investments, although less so ($-.09$ to $-.46$, mean $r = -.24$). In general, then, with the exception of a few high correlations between rewards and investments (particularly at later waves of the study), multicollinearity among the independent variables was not a problem. For a table of the specific correlations, write to the author.

The Association Between Exchange Variables and Satisfaction and Commitment. The first major purpose of this study was to examine how equity and the other exchange variables were related to satisfaction and commitment, all measured concurrently. Table 5.5 presents these correlations for each wave of the study. Because of the number of correlations considered in these analyses, statistical significance was set to $p < .01$ (rather than the standard $p < .05$) in order to reduce the likelihood of a Type I error.

The first two columns of Table 5.5 present the correlations between the exchange variables and satisfaction and commitment, all measured at Time 1 for the full sample. These correlations generally support the first set of predictions. For both men and women, satisfaction and commitment were associated negatively with underbenefiting inequity (although the correlation with commitment did not reach significance for men) and alternatives and were associated positively with rewards and investments. Overbenefiting inequity, however, was not significantly associated with either satisfaction or commitment.

Multiple regressions also were conducted with the full sample at Time 1 in order to examine the unique contribution of equity, relative to the other social exchange variables, in predicting satisfaction and commitment. These results are presented in Table 5.6. As a set, the exchange variables accounted for a significant amount of variance in both satisfaction ($R^2 = .60$ for men and .56 for women) and commitment ($R^2 = .59$ for men and .57 for women). For men, satisfaction was uniquely predicted by underbenefiting inequity, rewards, and alternatives (in that order). For women, satisfaction was uniquely predicted by rewards and also by alternatives, although less

Table 5.5   Correlations of Exchange Variables With Satisfaction and Commitment at Five Waves

	Time 1		Time 2		Time 3		Time 4		Time 5	
Variable	*M (100)*	*W (101)*	*M (80)*	*W (79)*	*M[a]*	*W (62)*	*M (46)*	*W (48)*	*M (37)*	*W (39)*
Satisfaction										
Underbenefiting inequity	-.56***	-.41***	-.51***	-.38**	-.45***	.00	-.61***	-.36	-.10	-.11
Overbenefiting inequity	.08	.21	.15	.11	-.08	-.27	.04	-.03	-.14	-.05
Rewards	.67***	.73***	.74***	.78***	.71***	.63***	.72***	.71**	.73***	.43**
Investments	.34**	.41***	.52***	.48***	.48***	.56***	.30	.69***	.53**	.43**
Alternatives	-.51***	-.37***	-.67***	-.46***	-.64***	-.48***	-.57***	-.46***	-.62***	-.17
Commitment										
Underbenefiting inequity	-.24	-.37***	-.34**	-.37**	-.06	.03	-.39**	-.46**	-.01	.01
Overbenefiting inequity	.00	.11	.01	.11	-.03	-.38**	-.09	-.04	-.19	.07
Rewards	.55***	.56***	.68***	.60***	.64***	.60***	.67***	59***	.67***	.36
Investments	.46***	.49***	.57***	.34***	.34**	.56***	.40**	.55***	.42**	.35
Alternatives	-.69***	-.57***	-.73***	-.61***	-.72***	-.65***	-.75***	-.76***	-.75***	-.34

NOTE: M = men; W = women.

a. n = for satisfaction = 57; n for commitment = 59.

**$p < .01$. ***$p < .001$.

172

| Table 5.6 | Multiple Regression of Satisfaction and Commitment on Social Exchange Variables at Time 1 |

Variable	β	
	Men	Women
Satisfaction		
Underbenefiting inequity	−.35***	−.05
Overbenefiting inequity	−.04	.04
Rewards	.34***	.60***
Investments	.15	.10
Alternatives	−.25**	−.16*
R^2	.60***	.56***
Commitment		
Underbenefiting inequity	.05	−.22*
Overbenefiting inequity	.00	.00
Rewards	.30**	.14
Investments	.20*	.37***
Alternatives	−.54***	−.59***
R^2	.59***	.57***

*$p < .05$. **$p < .01$. ***$p < .001$.

so. Commitment was uniquely predicted by alternatives, rewards, and investments (in that order) for men and by alternatives, investments, and underbenefiting inequity (in that order) for women.

Multiple regressions were not conducted with the follow-up data, because the results could be misleading with the smaller *n* sizes in combination with the number of independent variables. However, the correlations conducted at the follow-ups, which are presented in Table 5.5, indicate that the positive associations of rewards and investments with satisfaction and commitment and the negative associations of alternatives with satisfaction and commitment were generally found (with a few exceptions that did not reach significance) in each wave's subsample. However, the correlations of inequity with satisfaction and commitment were somewhat less consistent across the panels of the study. Generally, underbenefiting inequity was associated negatively with satisfaction, although this association was not found in the Time 3 and Time 4 subsamples for women and was also not found for either

gender in the Time 5 subsample. Similarly, underbenefiting inequity was unrelated to commitment for both genders in the Times 3 and 5 subsamples. Overbenefiting inequity was generally unrelated to satisfaction and commitment but was associated negatively with commitment for women in the Time 3 subsample. It must be noted that the correlations in Table 5.5 cannot be compared for drawing conclusions about how the associations change over time because the subsamples of participants differed (declined) across waves of the study.

Equity and Social Exchange as Predictors of Change in Satisfaction and Commitment

The second purpose of this investigation was to examine whether equity contributes to a *change* in satisfaction and commitment. This was first examined by regressing the Time 2 score of satisfaction (commitment) on the Time 1 score of underbenefiting inequity, controlling for the Time 1 score on satisfaction (commitment). Similar analyses were conducted with overbenefiting inequity. A significant beta for the predictor variable (e.g., underbenefiting inequity) would indicate that it is significantly associated with change in the dependent variable (e.g., satisfaction) over time. In these results, satisfaction at Time 1 was a significant predictor of satisfaction at Time 2 (6 months later), and furthermore, commitment at Time 1 was a significant predictor of commitment at Time 2 (betas ranged from .43 to .65, $p < .001$). However, underbenefiting inequity at Time 1 did not predict satisfaction and commitment at Time 2, controlling for satisfaction and commitment at Time 1 (betas ranged from −16 to .05). Thus, no evidence was found that equity contributes to a change in satisfaction and commitment over time.

I also conducted similar regressions for underbenefiting inequity only (with satisfaction and commitment) for Times 2 and 3, Times 3 and 4, and Times 4 and 5. In the analyses for consecutive later waves, some evidence was found that Time n underbenefiting inequity predicted Time n + 1 satisfaction or commitment, although only for men. For men, Time 4 satisfaction was predicted by Time 3 underbenefiting inequity (beta = −.37, $p < .01$), controlling for Time 3 satisfaction. Furthermore, men's Time 4 commitment was predicted by their Time 3 underbenefiting inequity (beta = −.24, $p < .05$), controlling for their Time 3 commitment. Thus, men experienced greater increases in their satisfaction and commitment between Times 3 and 4 the lower their underbenefiting inequity score at Time 3 (i.e., the more equity they perceived).

A similar set of over-time regressions was conducted for rewards, investments, and alternatives with Times 1 and 2 data only. Some evidence was found that women's perceptions of rewards at Time 1 predicted an increase in their satisfaction and commitment 6 months later. The beta for Time 1 rewards as a predictor of Time 2 satisfaction was .21 ($p < .05$), controlling for Time 1 satisfaction. In addition, for women, the beta for Time 1 rewards as a predictor of Time 2 commitment was .21 (marginally significant at $p = .055$), controlling for Time 1 commitment. Women's investments at Time 1 also contributed to a change in commitment 6 months later. The beta for Time 1 investments as a predictor of Time 2 commitment, controlling for Time 1 commitment, was .24 ($p < .05$).

Satisfaction and Commitment as a Predictor of Changes in Equity and Social Exchange

The third purpose of this research was to examine the reverse causal direction. Does satisfaction or commitment measured early in the relationship contribute to a later change in equity? To examine this, Time 2 underbenefiting inequity was regressed on Time 1 satisfaction and commitment (one at a time), controlling for Time 1 underbenefiting inequity. For men, Time 2 underbenefiting inequity was not predicted by either Time 1 satisfaction or Time 1 commitment, controlling for Time 1 underbenefiting inequity. However for women, Time 2 underbenefiting inequity was predicted by Time 1

satisfaction (beta = −.28, $p < .01$), controlling for Time 1 underbenefiting inequity. Time 1 commitment also had a near significant effect (beta = −.19, $p = .06$) on Time 2 underbenefiting inequity, controlling for Time 1 underbenefiting inequity. These results indicate that women experienced a greater increase in underbenefiting inequity between Time 1 and Time 2 the lower their satisfaction and commitment at Time 1. No evidence was found that satisfaction and commitment contributed to a change in overbenefiting inequity by Time 2 for either men or women.

Evidence of a reverse causal direction was also found at the later follow-ups. Men experienced a decrease in their underbenefiting inequity between Times 2 and 3, the greater their satisfaction at Time 2 (beta = −.26, $p < .05$). In addition, there was a near significant effect (beta = −.27, $p = .053$) of women's commitment at Time 3 as a predictor of their underbenefiting inequity at Time 4, controlling for Time 3 underbenefiting inequity.

Such a reverse causal direction also was examined for the other exchange variables in a set of regressions conducted with the Times 1 and 2 data. Evidence was found that Time 2 rewards were predicted by Time 1 satisfaction, controlling for Time 1 rewards for women (beta = .29, $p < .01$). Furthermore, for women, Time 2 rewards were predicted by Time 1 commitment (beta = .21, $p < .01$), controlling for Time 1 rewards. These results indicate, then, that for women only, greater satisfaction and commitment at Time 1 were associated with an increase in rewards by Time 2. However, no evidence was found that Time 2 investments or alternatives were predicted by Time 1 satisfaction or commitment, for either gender.

Predicting Stability of the Relationship

The final purpose of this study was to examine how equity and the other social exchange variables, as well as satisfaction and commitment, were associated with the likelihood of relationship dissolution. Spearman correlations were first used to examine these associations. The analyses conducted were the following: (a) correlations between the exchange variables measured at Time 1 and the likelihood of breakup by Time 2 (1 = intact; 2 = broken up); (b) correlations between the exchange variables measured at Time 1 and the likelihood of breakup at any time during the study (1 = intact; 2 = broken up); and (c) correlations between the exchange variables measured at Time 1 and the timing of the breakup, operationalized as: 1 = not broken up yet; 2 = broken up between Times 4 and 5; 3 = broken up between Times 3 and 4; 4 = broken up between Times 2 and 3; and 5 = broken up between Times 1 and 2; thus, the higher the score, the earlier the breakup. These correlations are presented in Table 5.7.

The strongest and most consistent predictor of the likelihood of a breakup was the woman's commitment (significant in all three correlations). Women's perception of alternatives also was a consistent predictor of breakups, as indicated by the correlations. Variables associated significantly with two (out of three) operationalizations of breakup were men's commitment, women's underbenefiting inequity, women's rewards, and women's satisfaction. The significant effects found were in the directions predicted. Commitment, satisfaction, and rewards were associated negatively with the likelihood of breakup, and underbenefiting inequity and alternatives were associated positively with the likelihood of breakup. (Women's overbenefiting inequity score was actually associated with the lesser likelihood of a breakup by Time 2.) Investments were not associated with breakups, regardless of how breakup was operationalized.

Second, regressions were conducted with all of the predictors included, with each operationalization of breakup as the dependent variable one at a time. In predicting the likelihood of breakup at Time 2 and in predicting the likelihood of breakup ever in the study (dichotomous

Table 5.7 Spearman Correlations of Equity, Other Exchange Variables, Satisfaction, and Commitment with Likelihood of Breaking Up

	Broken Up by Time 2/Time 1 Predictors	Broken Up by Time 5/Time 1 Predictors	How Soon Broken Up/Time 1 Predictors
Men's scores			
Underbenefiting inequity	−.02	.03	.06
Overbenefiting inequity	.13	−.08	−.04
Rewards	−.10	−.13	−.18
Investments	−.05	−.11	−.16
Alternatives	.20*	.09	.16
Satisfaction	−.13	−.17	−.23
Commitment	−.26**	−.17	−.25*
Women's scores			
Underbenefiting inequity	.38***	.12	.25*
Overbenefiting inequity	−.22*	−.04	−.14
Rewards	−.28**	−.15	−.22*
Investments	−.14	−.11	−.15
Alternatives	.35***	.25*	.32**
Satisfaction	−.31**	−.18	−.25*
Commitment	−.46***	−.42***	−.52***

*p .05. **p < .01. ***p < .001

dependent variables), logistic regression was used. In the logistic regression for relationship status at Time 2, none of the Time 1 predictors reached significance for either men or women. (However, in analyses that included only the Time 1 exchange variables as predictors, without also satisfaction and commitment, underbenefiting inequity and alternatives were significant [$p < .05$] and positive, unique predictors for women.) In the logistic regression for relationship status at the end of the study, no Time 1 predictor was significant for men. However, for women, commitment was a unique, significant ($p < .001$) predictor of breakups. In predicting the timing of the breakups, linear regression was used. Once again, women's commitment was a significant ($p < .001$) unique predictor of the likelihood (and timing) of breakups. In a regression equation that included only the Time 1 exchange variables (without satisfaction and commitment), underbenefiting inequity and alternatives were significant ($p < .05$) unique predictors of breakups for women.

Discussion

This study makes an important contribution to the equity and social exchange literatures because contemporaneous effects of equity and exchange were examined at multiple times, effects of equity and exchange on changes in relationship quality across time points were examined, and reverse causal directions (relationship quality leading to changes in equity and exchange) were explored. Furthermore, this study extended prior investigations on determinants of breakups by monitoring the status of the relationships over an extended period of time (almost 5 years), including data from both partners of the couple, and comparing predictors from two theoretical frameworks on social exchange (equity and interdependence-investment). However, because of the number of ways that the theoretical associations could be tested with multiwave data, interpretations can be problematic, particularly because findings are not always consistent across times, as will be discussed in the following.

Equity as a Predictor of Relationship Satisfaction and Commitment

The prediction from equity theory that the distress associated with inequity is likely to strain the overall relationship and decrease satisfaction and commitment in the relationship received some support in the concurrent analyses, although only for underbenefiting inequity. In bivariate correlational results, underbenefiting inequity was found to be associated negatively with both satisfaction and commitment, for both genders, although not at all five waves. For example, in the Time 5 subsample, underbenefiting inequity was not associated significantly with satisfaction or commitment for either gender. A selection effect may explain the decreasing association between underbenefiting inequity and relationship quality. For example, the couples who survived to Time 5 are a select group of couples whose satisfaction with the relationship may have been generally unaffected by fairness concerns. Further analyses (not presented in the paper but available by writing the author) were conducted to examine how the correlations changed over time specifically for the subsample of respondents who remained in their relationship and participated at all waves of the study. For the men in this subsample, the negative association of underbenefiting inequity with satisfaction and commitment was reduced to nonsignificance by Time 5. For women in this select group, the association of underbenefiting inequity with satisfaction and commitment was weak at all waves of the study. These are happy and committed couples at one of the most exciting stages of their relationship (most were approaching marriage or going through the honeymoon phase). Any inequities experienced during this stage may be perceived positively— as signs of one's own or one's partner's willingness to sacrifice. Thus, there may be a window of time in the progression of heterosexual romantic relationships, shortly before and after marriage, during which perceived inequities are less consequential for the quality of the relationship. The relatively small sample by

Time 5 (< 40 couples), however, reduces the generalizability of these results.

The Importance of Equity Relative to Other Social Exchange Variables

The present study generally indicated that underbenefiting inequity was a unique predictor, distinct from rewards and other exchange variables, of relationship quality. For example, in the multiple regression results conducted at Time 1, underbenefiting inequity (controlling for the other social exchange variables) explained unique variance in satisfaction for men and unique variance in commitment for women. Nonetheless, and consistent with the previous studies (e.g., Cate et al., 1982; Cate et al., 1988; Desmarais & Lerner, 1989; Martin, 1985; Michaels et al., 1986; Michaels et al., 1984), there was some evidence that rewards were more important than equity in predicting relationship quality. For example, the correlational results conducted at each wave indicated that rewards were consistently associated with satisfaction and commitment, whereas underbenefiting inequity was not (as noted earlier). Rewards were particularly important as a predictor of satisfaction, especially for women.

In support of the investment model, investments were generally correlated significantly and positively with commitment (as well as satisfaction) for both genders at each wave of the study. In addition, investments were a significant predictor of commitment for both men and women in the multiple regression analyses. Contrary to the results of the present study, an earlier study (Sprecher, 1988) found that investments did not explain any unique variance in commitment, once equity and other investment model variables were controlled. However, there are at least two differences between the studies that may explain the stronger effect of investments in the present study. Sprecher (1988) included among the predictor variables social approval from networks of family and friends, which was found to be a positive predictor of commitment. Embeddedness in a larger network of supportive family and friends may be an important component of feeling invested in the relationship, and thus the variance left to be accounted for by general investments may have been reduced. The other difference is that investments were measured by only one item in the Sprecher (1988) study. The limited variance of a one-item measure may have reduced the amount of unique variance that can be explained. In contrast, investments were operationalized in this study by a combination of detailed measures and a global item.

Of all the variables considered in this study, comparison level for alternatives was most highly associated with commitment in the multiple regression analyses. Alternatives also were found to be a significant and unique predictor of satisfaction. Furthermore, the correlational results conducted at each wave of the study indicated that alternatives were consistently and negatively correlated with both commitment and satisfaction for both genders. Several other previous studies also found comparison level for alternatives to be an important predictor of a relationship outcome variable (e.g., Michaels et al., 1986; Rusbult, 1983; Sprecher, 1988). The strength of alternatives in the contemporaneous results is not surprising. Those who lack alternatives are likely to remain committed (and satisfied), but also those who are satisfied and committed to the relationship are likely to devaluate alternatives (e.g., Johnson & Rusbult, 1989).

In sum, underbenefiting inequity was a unique predictor of satisfaction (for men) and commitment (for women) at Time 1, controlling for the other social exchange variables, but was less consistently correlated with satisfaction and commitment over time than were the other exchange variables.

Equity and Social Exchange as Predictors of Change in Satisfaction and Commitment

Very little evidence was found in this study that inequity in a relationship at one time can erode the relationship and decrease satisfaction and commitment at a later time. For example, no evidence was found that underbenefiting inequity at Time 1 contributed to a change in satisfaction or commitment by Time 2 for either men or women. However, the more underbenefited men perceived themselves to be at Time 3, the more their satisfaction and commitment decreased by Time 4. There are many possible explanations for the general failure of equity to contribute unique variance in satisfaction and commitment at a later date (controlling for earlier equity). First, the participants' satisfaction and commitment scores were already quite high early in the study, and thus ceiling effects may have been reached, preventing further increases. Second, the relationships tended to remain generally equitable over time, and furthermore, the types of inequities that may have been experienced were probably not severe enough to set in motion a chain of events that would decrease satisfaction or commitment 6 months to 1 year later. Finally, it may be that those couples who were most susceptible to having a decrease in satisfaction or commitment at a later time because of an earlier equity broke up and thus were removed from the sample.

Equity was not unique in its weak over-time effects. The other exchange variables also did not evidence strong links with later increases or decreases in satisfaction and commitment. However, there was some evidence that rewards and investments measured at Time 1 were associated with an increase in relationship quality by Time 2, but for women only.

Satisfaction and Commitment as Predictors of Change in Equity and Social Exchange

Critics of equity theory have argued that people may not perceive inequities or become upset about inequities until the relationship becomes dissatisfying. For example, Duck (1982) suggested that evaluations of equity and exchange do not occur in earnest until initial stages of the breakup process. Equity theory predictions are not necessarily incompatible with the prediction that a decreased level of satisfaction and commitment is likely to lead to inequity. Both processes could operate, possibly at different times in the relationship.

As discussed previously, there was only a small amount of evidence that equity measured at one time led to changes in satisfaction and commitment at a later date. Only slightly stronger support was found for the opposite causal direction. High scores on satisfaction and commitment at Time 1 were associated with decreases in underbenefiting inequity by Time 2 for women. Furthermore, high satisfaction at Time 2 was related to a decrease in underbenefiting inequity by Time 3 for men. There was also slight evidence that other social exchange variables (e.g., rewards) change as functions of earlier satisfaction and commitment. However, in general, the evidence for the reverse causal direction (relationship quality leading to changes in social exchange) was no more consistent across times and genders than was evidence for the causal directions predicted by the social exchange theories. Nonetheless, the significant results that were found point to the importance of examining social exchange variables not only as predictors of relationship quality but also as consequences. When relationships experience a downturn, for whatever internal or external reason, a process may be set in motion in which the partners are particularly sensitive to equity and exchange issues.

These findings also highlight the importance more generally of studying consequences of change in relationship satisfaction and commitment. In most research, relationship quality is the dependent variable rather than the independent variable (see Glenn, 1990). However, relationship quality variables (e.g., commitment) are likely to affect several interactional, behavioral, cognitive, and affective phenomena in relationships, including those experienced by the partner.

Equity and Social Exchange as Predictors of Relationship Stability Versus Dissolution

The degree to which equity and the other exchange variables, as well as satisfaction and commitment, were associated with later stability (vs. breakup) of the relationship also was examined. Through both bivariate and multivariate analyses, the associations of the predictor variables measured at Time 1 were examined with all of the following: (a) likelihood of breakup by Time 2, which was 6 months later; (b) likelihood of breakup at any time during the study; and (c) timing of breakup (i.e., how soon the relationship ended). In both the correlational and the regression results, the strongest predictor of stability was women's commitment. The more committed women were, the more likely the couple was to be together 6 months to several years later (men's commitment also was important but was less consistently associated with stability). In addition, in at least some of the analyses, satisfaction and rewards were associated negatively and underbenefiting inequity and alternatives were associated positively with breakups. Thus, the associations that were found were consistent with predictions from equity and exchange theories, although the effects were not as strong as might be expected. Surprisingly, investments were not a significant predictor of breakups in any of the analyses. The finding that women's commitment was most highly associated with breakups suggests that women can better forecast the outcome of the relationship or can determine whether the relationship lasts, which is consistent with some prior research (e.g., Rubin, Peplau, & Hill, 1981). More generally, these results also suggest that women may be more sensitive than men to the quality of the exchange, in part because of their greater relationship focus (e.g., Acitelli & Holmberg, 1993).

Limitations

Although this study has the strengths of multiple-wave longitudinal data and data collected from both partners, there are limitations. One primary limitation is the sample. The sample consisted of heterosexual, romantic couples who were initially dating. Whether similar findings would be obtained for other types of relationships (e.g., homosexual, friendship) or for other stages of heterosexual romantic relationships (e.g., long-term marriage) needs to be

investigated in future research. Furthermore, the sample was rather homogeneous on background and demographic characteristics (most were White, middle class, and in college, and all were from the United States). A second potential limitation of the study was the long intervals between measurement. The longitudinal design was based on data collected approximately once a year. Such data may mask fluctuations in equity and relationship quality that occur within that period of time.

Conclusions

The results of this study, as well as the results of several other studies conducted in the past two decades (for a review, see Sprecher & Schwartz, 1994), suggest that equity may not be as important as suggested by early theoretical statements (e.g., Walster [Hatfield] et al., 1978) and by the early research testing equity theory, which was characterized primarily by cross-sectional data and the omission of other exchange variables. Nonetheless, judgments about equity, particularly underbenefiting inequity, may play a role in affecting relationship outcomes, although it may be only one link in a larger chain of processes that occur as relationships grow, change, and deteriorate. Perceptions of equity may sometimes contribute to feelings of satisfaction and commitment and may sometimes be influenced by changes in satisfaction and commitment. The exact association between equity (inequity) and the quality of the relationship may depend on the overall state and stage of the relationship. As two people become acquainted, equity issues are likely to be salient and affect whether a relationship is even established. If they are grossly mismatched, they are likely to discover this in the get-acquainted stage. Once a relationship enters a stage of long-term commitment, equity issues may no longer be as salient, and if perceived, they may not be that harmful for the relationship. Most of the relationships represented in this study, particularly those that remained intact, were of this nature. Such couples probably have strong optimism as they approach marriage. Later in most long-term relationships, however, couples face changes, transitions (including parenthood), and stressors, and dissatisfaction may arise because of both internal and external factors, which can lead the partners to perceive inequities. In a study of the association of equity and relationship quality for married couples during the transition to parenthood, Grote and Clark (2001) proposed a process model, which states that the perception of inequity may initially arise out of feelings of distress, but that the perceived inequity may then escalate the distress (in accord with equity theory). A challenge for future research is to determine what other factors are associated with perceptions of equity becoming salient and having detrimental effects on relationships. One possible such factor is the awareness that in comparison to others in similar roles, one is less well off, which has been referred to as *referential comparisons* (e.g., VanYperen & Buunk, 1994).

Note

The data collection for this longitudinal study was funded by several small grants from Illinois State University Graduate School, and the paper was written during a research sabbatical granted the author from Illinois State University. Portions of the paper were presented at the 1999 American Sociological Association Meetings, Chicago, Illinois. The author would like to thank Diane Felmlee and Daniel Perlman for comments on an earlier draft of this paper.

References

Acitelli, L. K., & Holmberg, D. (1993). Reflecting on relationships. The role of thoughts and memories. In D. Penman & W. H. Jones (Eds.), *Personal relationships* (Vol. 4, pp. 71–100). London: Kingsley.

Berg, J. H., & McQuinn, R. D. (1986). Attraction and exchange in continuing and noncontinuing dating relationships. *Journal of Personality and Social Psychology, 50,* 942–952.

Bui, K. T., Peplau, L. A., & Hill, C. T. (1996). Testing the Rusbult model of relationship commitment and stability in a 15-year study of heterosexual couples. *Personality and Social Psychology Bulletin, 22,* 1244–1257.

Cate, R. M., Lloyd, S. A., & Henton, J. M. (1985). The effect of equity, equality, and reward level on the stability of students' premarital relationships. *The Journal of Social Psychology, 6,* 715–721.

Cate, R. M., Lloyd, S. A., Henton, J. M., & Larson, J. H. (1982). Fairness and reward level as predictors of relationship satisfaction. *Social Psychology Quarterly, 45,* 177–181.

Cate, R. M., Lloyd, S. A., & Long, E. (1988). The role of rewards and fairness in developing premarital relationships. *Journal of Marriage and the Family, 50,* 443–452.

Davidson, B. (1984). A test of equity theory for marital adjustment. *Social Psychology Quarterly, 47,* 36–42.

Desmarais, S., & Lerner, M. J. (1989). A new look at equity and outcomes as determinants of satisfaction in close personal relationships. *Social Justice Research, 3,* 105–119.

Duck, S. (1982). A topography of relationship disengagement and dissolution. In S. W. Duck (Ed.), *Personal relationships: Vol. 4. Dissolving personal relationships* (pp. 1–30). New York: Academic Press.

Duffy, S. M., & Rusbult, C. E. (1986). Satisfaction and commitment in homosexual and heterosexual relationships. *Journal of Homosexuality, 12,* 1–23.

Felmlee, D., Sprecher, S., & Bassin, B. (1990). The dissolution of intimate relationships: A hazard model. *Social Psychology Quarterly, 53,* 13–30.

Floyd, F. J., & Wasner, G. H. (1994). Social exchange, equity, and commitment: Structural equation modeling of dating relationships. *Journal of Family Psychology, 8,* 55–73.

Foa, U. O., & Foa, E. B. (1974). *Societal structures of the mind.* Springfield, IL: Charles C. Thomas.

Glenn, N. D. (1990). Quantitative research on marital quality in the 1980s: A critical review. *Journal of Marriage and the Family, 52,* 818–831.

Grote, N. K., & Clark, M. S. (2001). Perceiving unfairness in the family: Cause or consequence of marital distress? *Journal on Perspectives in Social Psychology, 80,* 281–293.

Hatfield, E., Utne, M. K., & Traupmann, J. (1979). Equity theory and intimate relationships. In R. L. Burgess & T. L. Huston (Eds.), *Social exchange in developing relationships* (pp. 99–133). New York: Academic Press.

Hendrick, S. S. (1988). A generic measure of relationship satisfaction. *Journal of Marriage and the Family, 50,* 93–98.

Johnson, D. J., & Rusbult, C. B. (1989). Resisting temptation: Devaluation of alternative partners as a means of maintaining commitment in close relationships. *Journal of Personality and Social Psychology, 57,* 967–980.

Kelley, H. H., & Thibaut, J. F. (1978). *Interpersonal relations: A theory of interdependence.* New York: Wiley.

Kurdek, L. A. (1992). Relationship status and relationship satisfaction in cohabiting gay and lesbian couples: A prospective longitudinal test of the contextual and interdependence models. *Journal of Social and Personal Relationships, 9,* 125–142.

Lujansky, H., & Mikula, G. (1983). Can equity theory explain the quality and the stability of romantic relationships? *Journal of Social Psychology, 22,* 101–112.

Lund, M. (1985). The development of investment and commitment scales for predicting continuity of personal relationships. *Journal of Social and Personal Relationships, 2,* 3–23.

Martin, M. W. (1985). Satisfaction with intimate exchange: Gender-role differences and the impact of equity, equality, and rewards. *Sex Roles, 13,* 597–605.

Michaels, J. W., Acock, A. C., & Edwards, J. N. (1986). Social exchange and equity determinants of relationship commitment. *Journal of Social and Personal Relationships, 3,* 161–175.

Michaels, J. W., Edwards, J. N., & Acock, A. C. (1984). Satisfaction in intimate relationships as a function of inequality, inequity, and outcomes. *Social Psychology Quarterly, 47,* 347–357.

Rubin, Z., Peplau, L. A., & Hill, C. T. (1981). Loving and leaving: Sex differences in romantic attachments. *Sex Roles, 7,* 821–835.

Rusbult, C. E. (1980). Commitment and satisfaction in romantic associations: A test of the investment model. *Journal of Experimental Social Psychology, 16,* 172–186.

Rusbult, C. E. (1983). A longitudinal test of the investment model: The development (and deterioration) of satisfaction and commitment in heterosexual involvements. *Journal of Personality and Social Psychology, 45,* 101–117.

Rusbult, C. E., & Buunk, B. R. (1993). Commitment processes in close relationships: An interdependence analysis. *Journal of Social and Personal Relationships, 10,* 175–204.

Rusbult, C. E., Drigotas, S. M., & Verette, J. (1994). The investment model: An interdependence analysis

of commitment processes and relationship maintenance phenomena. In D. Canary & L. Stafford (Eds.), *Communication and relational maintenance* (pp. 115-139). San Diego, CA: Academic.

Rusbult, C. E., Johnson, D. J., & Morrow, G. D. (1986). Predicting satisfaction and commitment in adult romantic involvements: An assessment of the generalizability of the investment model. *Social Psychology Quarterly, 49,* 81–89.

Rusbult, C. E., & Martz, J. M. (1995). Remaining in an abusive relationship: An investment model analysis of nonvoluntary dependence. *Personality and Social Psychology Bulletin, 21,* 558–571.

Rusbult, C. E., Martz, J. M., & Agnew, C. R. (1998). The investment model scale: Measuring commitment level, satisfaction level, quality of alternatives, and investment size. *Personal Relationships, 5,* 357–391.

Sabatelli, R. M., & Cecil-Pigo, E. F. (1985). Relational interdependence and commitment in marriage. *Journal of Marriage and the Family, 47,* 931–937.

Sacher, J. A., & Fine, M. A. (1996). Predicting relationship status and satisfaction after six months among dating couples. *Journal of Marriage and the Family, 58,* 21–32.

Simpson, J. A. (1987). The dissolution of romantic relationships: Factors involved in relationship stability and emotional distress. *Journal of Personality and Social Psychology, 53,* 683–692.

Sprecher, S. (1986). The relationship between inequity and emotions in close relationships. *Social Psychology Quarterly, 49,* 309–321.

Sprecher, S. (1988). Investment model, equity, and social support determinants of relationship commitment. *Social Psychology Quarterly, 51,* 318–328.

Sprecher, S. (1999). "I love you more today than yesterday": Romantic partners' perceptions of changes in love and related affect over time. *Journal of Personality and Social Psychology, 76,* 46–53.

Sprecher, S., & Schwartz, P. (1994). Equity and balance in the exchange of contributions in close relationships. In M. J. Lerner & G. Mikula (Eds.), *Entitlement and the affectional bond* (pp. 11–41). New York: Plenum.

Thibaut, J. W., & Kelley, H. H. (1959). *The social psychology of groups.* New York: Wiley.

Traupmann, J., Hatfield, E., & Wexler, P. (1983). Equity and sexual satisfaction in dating couples. *British Journal of Social Psychology, 22,* 33–40.

Traupmann, J., Peterson, R., Utne, M., & Hatfield, E. (1981). Measuring equity in intimate relationships. *Applied Psychological Measurement, 5,* 467–480.

Utne, M. K., Hatfield, E., Traupmann, J., & Greenberger, D. (1984). Equity, marital satisfaction, and stability. *Journal of Social and Personal Relationships, 1,* 323–332.

VanYperen, N. W., & Buunk, B. P. (1990). A longitudinal study of equity and satisfaction in intimate relationships. *European Journal of Social Psychology, 20,* 287–309.

VanYperen, N. W., & Buunk, B. P. (1994). Social comparison and social exchange in marital relationships. In M. J. Lerner & G. Mikula (Eds.), *Entitlement and the affectional bond: Justice in close relationships* (pp. 89–115). New York: Plenum.

Walster (Hatfield), E., Walster, G. W., & Berscheid, E. (1978). *Equity: Theory and research.* Boston: Allyn and Bacon.

6

SOCIAL CONFLICT THEORY

Social conflict theory reflects sociological attention to competition between or among social classes and patterns of competition in society for scarce resources. In such competition, the groups that hold more power typically gain access to more resources. At the same time, access to greater resources provides a group with more power. Because social classes often have competing interests, conflicts develop among class groups. At times of such conflict, the power differential among competing groups is particularly salient.

The philosophy of Karl Marx is generally viewed as the foundation for social conflict theory. Marx's attention to social and economic change through patterns of conflict has informed later considerations of patterns and influence of conflict in social life. Sociologists such as Max Weber and George Simmel later applied Marxian concepts to interpersonal interactions. As a social institution, the family is viewed as an extension of these basic patterns of social conflict. Over the past 30 years, social conflict theory concepts have been applied to a variety of family issues.

A social conflict perspective views self-interest as a basic human motivation. Conflict between individuals and groups arises out of competing interests. Social conflict theory,

however, challenges the notion that conflict is problematic. Instead, it is argued that social change occurs as a result of such conflict. This perspective suggests that conflict is necessary and often desirable. Without conflict to stimulate change, a status quo that is essentially unfair to those individuals and groups who lack power in social settings will be maintained.

In attending to patterns of conflict in social settings, social conflict theory builds on various assumptions. The first of these is that conflict is a basic element of human life. Because self-interest is viewed as a basic human drive, conflicting self-interests are present in all social interaction. Rather than viewing conflict as inherently problematic, a social conflict perspective suggests that conflict must be accepted and understood as a basic element of human interaction.

As mentioned above, social conflict theory assumes that humans are motivated primarily by self-interest. While some may suggest this motivation by self-interest can be compared to the motivating value of benefits or rewards in social exchange theory, the two concepts are different. Whereas benefits or rewards are assessed rationally, self-interest as described in social conflict theory is a more primitive drive. It arises out of a basic will to survive and reflects a strong desire to fulfill needs and desires in life.

Social conflict theory further assumes that conflict between or among social groups is inevitable. This inevitability is tied to the belief that individuals and groups compete for scarce resources. Whether it be financial resources, prestige, status, power, authority, or any other desirable commodity, individuals and groups compete to gain as much as they can inasmuch as there is not enough to go around. Further, because conflict is viewed as inevitable, it is considered normal for individual and group social interactions to be characterized by conflict. Living in harmony is not viewed as a natural state. While it is common to desire harmony in family relationships, social conflict theory suggests that it is unrealistic to expect that conflict will not be present in those relationships.

Because conflict is assumed to be an inherent aspect of families as social systems, families are characterized as power systems built on gender and age stratification. Social conflict theory argues that power is unequally distributed in families, with young children typically holding less power than adults and women typically holding less power than men. From this perspective, then, it is argued that the self-interests of females and children are typically subjugated to adults and males in families. It is argued that these essential power differences are reflected in such issues as differential participation in household labor, patterns of abuse and neglect, and influence and participation in decision making, among others. These essential patterns of inequality are assumed to exist at all levels of society. Social conflict theory assumes that the family, as a social institution, reflects the inherent inequalities that exist in all social institutions and within society as a whole.

Because of these patterns of inequality and conflict in social situations, social conflict theory is primarily concerned with strategies families use to manage conflict. This is of special interest because members of families interact differently than actors in other social groups. As such, members within family situations experience and respond to conflict differently than members of other social groups.

A number of concepts are at the heart of social conflict theory. One of these, competition,

Sprey (1979) defines as a state of negative interdependence between individuals in social situations. Because competition is inherent in social relationships, it is argued that there are no relationships in which all actors come out as winners. Rather, all social relationships involve "win-lose" relationships in which one individual or group benefits to the detriment of other individuals or groups in those settings. Family life is, therefore, a series of outcomes of situations in which someone ultimately benefits while someone else suffers. Such competition exists among individuals in families but also exists among family groups.

The prevalence of competition in social settings contributes to the presence of conflict in families and other social groups. Conflict arises out of competition among family members over scarce resources, controversy regarding the means to achieve goals, and/or incompatible goals. Such conflict implies and requires consensus among family members over definitions of what is valuable.

Because competition is at the center of family relationships, social conflict theory attends to the concept of power in families. Power in families is reflected in patterns of authority that exist within family units. Typically, those family members who hold greater authority also hold greater power to influence other members of the family. Of particular interest from a social conflict perspective is the way that those who hold power in families may use it to either positively or negatively influence others.

A social conflict perspective suggests that issues of competing self-interest are resolved through negotiation and bargaining. Both of these may be viewed as processes of exchange between and among family members. In the case of negotiation, the focus is on arriving at resolutions that reflect collective agreement. While this may not include consensus over the resolution of an issue, it does reflect at least a basic acceptance of resolution by all concerned. Bargaining, on the other hand, reflects an exchange process wherein each actor is focused on achieving a resolution that best meets his or her own self-interests. The focus here is on achieving what is best for oneself, to the detriment of other family members involved in the issue. Simply put, bargaining is a process through which individual family members seek situations or outcomes that maximize their own self-interests, whereas negotiation is a process through which the best possible resolution is sought for all involved in the negotiation.

A further result of the conflict and competition that exists within families is the presence of assertive or aggressive behaviors. These are behaviors directed by a family member toward others in an attempt to influence them to meet the family member's needs. Patterns of assertiveness are evident in family members choosing to exert or reinforce their rights, while aggression typically involves a forceful attempt to address one's needs at the expense of other family members.

Finally, social conflict theory focuses on the messages family members who hold power use to try to ensure compliance of other family members in meeting their interests. Threats are messages that convey the threat of punishment for noncompliance on the part of other family members. Promises, on the other hand, are messages that convey the possibility of reward for compliance on the part of other family members. While promises may be viewed as more positive than threats, they share the goal of attempting to influence family members in situations in which self-interests compete.

THE READINGS

The following two articles provide examples of social conflict perspectives on family issues. In the first, Witt (1989) provides an example of the application of social conflict theory concepts to the issue of family violence, suggesting a theoretical model of family violence informed by conflict theory. Social conflict perspectives have been applied to issues of family violence perhaps more than any other area of family life. Because physical abuse is perhaps the most overt instance of conflict in families, social conflict theory lends itself well to considerations of family abuse and factors contributing to it. Witt offers a

theoretical consideration that has informed research in the years since it was first published.

The second reading provides an example of research directly informed by aspects of social conflict theory. Tichenor (1999) explores status and income as potential sources of marital power in couples in which wives hold more of each than their husbands. In focusing on structural factors often attributed as influencing marital power, this article represents a direct test of the influence of those factors over other aspects of gender in marital relationships. From a social conflict perspective, this issue of marital power is a critical one. While it is generally acknowledged that husbands typically hold greater levels of marital power than their wives, there are numerous perspectives on the sources of this differential. Tichenor's consideration of structural factors contributing to power differentials in marriage offers a perspective grounded in concepts drawn from social conflict theory.

ISSUES FOR YOUR CONSIDERATION

1. To what degree does each article portray conflict as inevitable in the family relationships being described?

2. Is conflict between or among family members viewed as problematic in these articles? What problems arise from conflict within the relationships described?

3. Does each article acknowledge and attend to power differentials in family relationships? Who is viewed as holding power in these relationships?

4. Do the articles focus on family members' strategies for influencing other family members? What strategies are used?

FURTHER READING

Coser (1956), Simmel (1956), Sprey (1969), Sprey (1979).

A Conflict Theory of Family Violence

David D. Witt

Abstract

This paper makes a theoretical accounting of family violence in terms of the antagonistic elements in our culture and society that serve to irritate family relationships. Using conflict theory as the interpretive tool, the existence of family violence is explained as a direct effect of the economic values of the culture. To further strengthen this theoretical position, portions of other theories are included, such as some of the feminist arguments dealing with the historical development of patriarchy and a symbolic interaction perspective on the process of socialization for the use of violence in stressful situations.

Introduction

Ideally, we define the family as the social group to nurture us, instruct us in social and moral values, and protect us from harm. This is the case in virtually every postindustrial society where people from "relatively isolated and autonomous small family unit(s)" tend to depend emotionally on their immediate family (Williams, 1970, p. 91). The statistical reality is that the American family stands an estimated 20% chance of becoming the stage for violence (Gelles & Straus, 1980). In fact, family violence researchers assert that the family is the most violent social grouping in the country, with individuals being more likely to be harmed by an angry family member than by anyone else (Gelles & Straus, 1979; Witt, 1980).

Theoreticians attempting to explain violence in the family are legion, despite a paucity of confirming empirical research. Gelles and Straus (1979), in a comprehensive review of family violence theory, count 15 separate models from the disciplines of psychology, social psychology, and sociology. This paper is an attempt to narrow the field. To do so requires an integration of three theories. The "culture of violence" theory lays the groundwork for the incidence of violence in the family. Symbolic interaction theory explains our socialized ability for violent behavior. The conflict feminist approach offers the influence of economic and historical development of society as potentially resulting in violence within family relationships.

The Groundwork for Theory

Culture of violence maintains that violence is unevenly distributed in our society (Coser, 1967; Wolfgang & Ferracuti, 1967). One is led to envision pockets of hostility and conflict, scattered throughout certain racial, ethnic, and social class strata that reside alongside subcultures of nonviolence. Violence is characterized as a learned response directly attributable to membership in a particular group. Thus, when looking for family violence, one might expect to find higher rates of spouse battering and child abuse in lower classes and among ghetto dwelling ethnic families. This expectation has been only marginally realized in hypothesis testing (Gelles, 1979; Straus et al., 1980). Violence exhibited toward children and spouses declines only slightly among the highest income groups (Gelles & Straus, 1979). While no comparative studies have been done, intrafamily violence does not seem to vary from one ethnic group to another. Rather, it seems to be present in families regardless of their socioeconomic status or ethnic group membership.

However, by shifting our focus from subculture to culture in general, the idea of an entire culture predisposed to violent behaviors begins to inform the issue of family violence. What more probable source of a nasty sneer or hurtful remark is there than from a disappointed wife, husband, or child. Family members are likely to remind each other of his or her shortcomings. Blame for material inadequacies can easily escalate into violent episodes. From the old broken down car in the driveway to an inability to afford good schools for the children, blame is attributed by family members to "his" lack of ambition or "her" failure to be supportive in times of stress. Further, violence in the family is normative in nature. We feel guilty, out of place, or ashamed when we behave in socially unacceptable ways. On the surface, we view the abusive behavior of parents and spouses as abnormal; however, when taken in the broadest context, the American family is subject to norms that often suggest various forms of violence as necessary, correct, and "good for" family members. It is this intent of the parent or spouse which distinguishes intrafamilial violence from street violence.

When we think of violence or abuse in the family, images of bleeding and broken children or husbands who beat up their wives for no particular reason are immediately brought to mind. Yet, this type of overt behavior is only part of the range of abusive behaviors that may occur in the family. Most of the time, violence never reaches public consciousness since it is "normal violence"—that is, it follows the implicit rules of our culture (Gelles & Straus, 1979).

Such phrases as "this will hurt me more than it will hurt you," "beat some sense into you," and "teach you a lesson you won't forget" are part of the language of discipline and subordination. Whether or not the words are followed by an act of violence is almost irrelevant. The violent

expressive character of these rather common threats illustrates the necessary cultural precedent for violence (Garbarino, 1977).

Also implicit in our culture is the idea of ownership of spouses and children. This notion often precludes any respect for individual rights. Norms defining people as property operate to permit the use of corporal punishment within one's family, while disallowing such violence toward persons outside one's family.

Finally, cultural norms which define the family as a private grouping tend to encourage family violence indirectly. Behavior occurring "behind the closed doors" of the household is not to be discussed with outsiders (Pizzey, 1974; Straus et al., 1980). Women in abusive marital relationships have reported that neither do they know of a safe haven for escape, nor do they confide their victimization to others. To do so would constitute "telling family business" (Witt, 1980). The family is popularly conceptualized as a sovereign entity wherein the head of the household is, in many cases, absolute monarch (e.g., "a man's home is his castle").

The notion of the home as an especially private place is shared and acknowledged by other social institutions. The courts are hesitant to intervene in family matters because of their commission to preserve the boundaries of the family against the rights of the individual. The police are limited to taking action only (and not simply the residual bruises or bleeding), or when the victim officially complains.

Thus, it becomes clear that ours is indeed a culture that often points us to violence as one response to stressful family situations. One of the shortcomings of the culture argument is that it fails to explain the origins of these cultural elements. The task is later met conceptually with conflict theory. Another shortcoming is met by using the symbolic interaction approach to socialization into violence.

Socialization and the Cycle of Violence

One of the main assumptions of students of family violence is that violent behavior is a learned response (Gelles & Straus, 1979; Steinmetz, 1977). Social learning theory suggests that continuous reciprocal interaction between the individual and the environment (i.e., children and parents, children and the media, children and schoolmates) provides the basis by which the consequences of behavior are learned, and thus, the behavior is performed (Bandura, 1972). Similarly, research findings generally reflect a fairly consistent relationship between exposure to violence or violent attitudes in childhood and manifestation of those same attitudes and behaviors in adulthood (Gelles, 1980; Gelles & Straus, 1979; Lewis, 1965). Children who have witnessed conjugal violence or have been victims of child abuse are more likely to engage in family violence later on in their lives. The statement that "violence begets violence" is encompassed by social learning theory.

Two fundamental concepts of personality development address the perpetuation of violence in the family. First, there is the process of the "looking glass self," whereby individuals come to evaluate themselves and alter their behavior in terms of the reactions of others (Cooley, 1964). Second, there is the developmental construction of the "generalized other" (Mead, 1934). One learns to anticipate the expectations of others by imitating at first, and later perceiving others' evaluation of one's behavior through others' "eyes." Expected behavior is learned by steadily increasing the number of other roles through play until a generalized set of expectations is internalized. After countless repetitions of Mead's "I-me" dialectic, the values and norms of a culture can be fully internalized (Coser, 1971). In violent families, this process of development is evident. Unless alternative modeling replaces the imitation of parents as they fight their way through a marriage, spousal, and parental role sets containing punitive and possessive elements will continue to be transmitted to the oncoming generation.

One of the consequences of sex role socialization, from a conflict perspective, is the social manufacture of stereotypical sets of expectations concerning the behavior of boys and girls. For example, there is the social production of women who are dependent on males for material and emotional welfare as argued by Chapman (1978). It can almost be asserted that the same relationship between employers and employees—that employee's labor is the property of "benevolent" bosses (Ollman, 1971), can be found in husband/wife relations (Becker & Abel, 1978). This is a major point in that males, when defined by the culture as the only responsible provider for their families, will tend to concentrate their labors on the accomplishment of that provider role. Of course, this arrangement benefits the cause of the economy, as long as there is an opportunity for the provider role to be performed.

In times when portions of the work force must be placed in reserve (e.g., during economic depressions or recessions), the provider role becomes increasingly more difficult to realize. Children internalize the conservation of violence for "emergency use only," such as the times in adulthood when the availability of work and money becomes scarce. Perhaps we tend to direct our anger toward those who remind us of our "failures," and not the real source of difficulty. Since quality role behavior needs practice, research shows that rehearsals for these situations do occur prior to marriage. In addition to corporal punishment of children (Steinmetz, 1977), which is the introductory course for many of tomorrow's abusers, siblings practice their techniques on each other (Gully et al., 1981), as do dating couples (Cate et al., 1981; Makepeace, 1981), and persons cohabiting (Yllo & Straus, 1981).

Reasons for violence given by the dating college student sample fall right in line with the conservation argument (Cate et al., 1981). Of the sample of 355 college students, 22.3% reported dating violence. Of that number, 73% interpreted their own or their partner's aggressive behavior a response to anger, and almost half pointed to "confusion," with 80% responding out of "love." Thus, whether or not conflict theory is ecologically valid, there is support for the proposition that children are viewing violence as the appropriate response to thwarted expectations and disappointment.

The ill effects of internalizing the norms of a violent culture extend beyond the production of physically violent citizens. As Liazos (1972) points out:

> In violence, a person is violated—there is harm done to his person, his psyche, his body, his dignity his ability to govern himself ... Seen this way a person can be violated ... by a system that denies him a decent job, or consigns him to a slum, or causes him brain damage by near-starvation during childhood, or manipulates him through the mass media, and so on endlessly. (Liazos, 1972, p. 112)

By inadvertently offering "violent" examples as models used to prepare children for adult relationships, we are in fact violating future generations.

> It is the family, of course, which is a major mission belt for the diffusion of cultural standards to the oncoming generation. But what has until lately been overlooked is that the family largely transmits that portion of the culture accessible to the social stratum and groups in which the parents find themselves. It is, therefore, a mechanism for disciplining the child in terms of the cultural goals and mores. The child is exposed to social prototypes in the witnessed daily behavior and causal conversations of parents. (Merton, 1968, p. 212)

Thus far, the discussion has dealt with tendencies for action and socialization practices that are contained in a larger code of conduct—the culture. In the conflict model of society this configuration of ideals is termed the "superstructure," having an "infrastructure" consisting of economic relations (Ruis, 1973). Therefore, family violence exists to some extent because it is functional to the economy.

The Conflict Approach to Family Violence

A brief sketch of the structural determinants of culture and ideology in conflict theory illustrates the theory's explanation of family violence. This tradition views the "superstructure" as containing all religious, moral, legal, and familial values which are created, implemented, and modified in accordance with the vested interests of those in control of the economy. These are social norms. Accordingly, behavior that violates these rules—crimes against person and property—constitutes punishable deviant behavior.

In addition to these legal proscriptions, there are other implicit norms, the violation of which places the perpetrator within the definition of deviant (e.g., the economic failure of the head of a household, the failure of marital relationships ending in separation and divorce, the presence of economic and social stresses, and unhealthy family life). In a patriarchy, like that of most of western culture, the inability of the male head of household to control the actions, and even the thoughts, of his spouse and offspring is tantamount to making a contribution to the weakening of the ship of state. Of course, this is due to the appealing populist political argument that the "chain of command" for the nation begins with top quality family relationships. Thus, according to the conflict perspective, family heads of households are required to perform impossible tasks.

The request for a return to the "traditional" family seems to have its genesis in politically conservative factions who see changes in male/female relationships of the past 20 years as the source of current family problems. Even though feminists have revealed the "traditional" family form to be a cultural myth (Thorne, 1982), these ideas run contrary to the evidence for four additional reasons. First, consensus has it that for most "working" women who have families (well over 60% of the national work force), domestic chores are still a large part of their work load in addition to job or career demands. Employment outside the home does not necessarily negate a woman's commitment to family members. Second, while most women work for pay, they work because their family needs the income, and not necessarily for the fulfillment of a career. Third, the focus on the stability of the family as the first cause of a healthy national character results in conservative policies that may have an undermining effect on the actual material welfare of families. For example, one of the needs of working parents, particularly working mothers, is some type of modestly priced child care. Lack of such facilities is precisely the device that keeps battered wives financially dependent on abusive mates (Gelles, 1980; Witt, 1980). The conservative bias against the economic independence of women and toward mythical traditions was summed up in the remarks of President Nixon on his veto of a national child care bill.

> Good public policy requires that we enhance rather than diminish both parental authority and parental involvement with children—particularly in those decisive years when social attitudes and a conscience are formed and religious and moral principles are first inculcated. (Feeley, 1972, p. 75)

The spirit of these words reflects the ideology of industrialization. In order to foster a deep commitment to traditional families, women necessarily must remain full-time mothers. Feminist arguments consistent with a conflict approach assert that the economy still relies on the traditional structure of monogamy and the nuclear family to realize economic growth. This structure determines that males perform the paid work, while females serve nurturant functions for the production of future generations of participants in the economy (Rowbotham, 1973).

Ultimately, the perpetuation of rigid financial self-reliance of the traditional nuclear family places a potential for emotional and economic stress on each family member. Conflict theorists maintain that a capitalistic economy makes each family responsible for providing for its own members "from the care of the young to the welfare of the old" (Feeley, 1972, p. 73). Research has shown that the levels and intensities of family violence are directly associated with social stress (Gelles, 1980). Parents, particularly mothers, are many times locked into social roles having obligations that were largely unforeseen at the time of marriage—obligations that often cannot be met. Viewing the inability to remain economically solvent while providing for

the emotional needs of children and other family members is stressful; one can begin to interpret the results of past research in terms of a dialectic. Stressful conditions of unemployment and financial distress have been related to family violence (Gil, 1970; Prescott & Letko, 1977; Straus et al., 1980). One hardly needs to point out the direct influence of political and economic policy decisions on the employment status of many Americans. However, the message often transmitted is that everything will be stable if we have strong, wholesome families. By propagating an ideology that "hard work always leads to success," those in control of the economy set up double-bind expectations that become increasingly more difficult to either meet or escape. Without accompanying opportunity to improve the substance of family life, the symbolism is pointless and empty. Living under conditions whereby the feeble security of the family could be totally destroyed by any one of several sources of economic distress, family members become alienated from each other in a culture already primed for violent reactions. Instead of facilitating caring and concern, it appears that we encourage intrafamily conflict. Family members, as participants in the economy, are lulled into a kind of false consciousness as they attempt to enact traditional family roles. Then, as failures to realize the traditional ideal begin to mount, at least one option for relief from the emotional alienation of such an existence is to strike out at the nearest perceived source of discomfort.

Given conflict theorists' tendency to emphasize economic differences between social classes (to the exclusion of other unjust distributions of power, such as gender differences), a conflict theory interpretation of spouse abuse may seem to violate some assumptions. The additional consensus among researchers that spousal violence is not strongly related to social class makes the case for a conflict approach to family violence seemingly more difficult. However, taking the feminist view that male dominance, while historically adaptive, has been the constant factor in the ageless subjugation and harsh treatment of women, a class distinction emerges within the two conflict classifications—management and labor—and that is men and women.

From national sample data, the incidence of husband to wife violence (12.1 incidences per 100 husbands) is not much different from the incidence of wife to husband violence (11.6 incidences) (Straus, 1980). Among roughly half of the respondents sampled, reciprocal violent acts had been committed by both spouses at least once during the survey year. Further, among violent spouses only, the average number of violent acts from husbands (7.1) was different from the average number from wives (6.8) by only 0.3 acts of violence. And yet, almost all of the literature dealing with spousal violence attributes the genesis of violence to the male.

To be fair, students of spousal violence argue that women are violent out of one of two social norms: either self-defense or reciprocity. Further, because of average differences in physical size, women are not as capable as men of inflicting equally destructive force in a single blow, and are more likely to use "equalizers" or weapons to balance this disparity (Witt, 1980). This evidence is interpreted to suggest that women are indeed more prone to greater victimization from men; and that wives, by virtue of their participation in reciprocal family violence, increase their losses and the likelihood of further victimization (Straus, 1980).

The conflict/feminist argument might be that it makes no difference to theory that males and females are equally violent, or that family violence probably varies little between social classes. Both men and women of all social classes are subject to the normal codes of conduct contained in the culture's superstructure. For example, the overwhelming tendency for corporal punishment as the chastisement of choice by parents (Steinmetz, 1978) indicates homogeneous levels of violence across class and gender categories, reflecting the perceived instrumentality of violence in the culture. Correlates of family violence such as unemployment, social stress, and inadequate income are sufficient to facilitate violence in the family, even though research biases tend to hide its prevalence among the upper classes (Steinmetz, 1977). Conflict theory derives most of its explanatory power from the dynamics of capitalist economy.

In order for conflict theory to inform family violence, there must necessarily be some degree of change in either the use or the interpretation of violence in relationships that corresponds to the pulse of economic transformations of society. Demos (1979), using historical documents, detailed the concomitant changes in the family that followed changes in the economy.

Beginning around 1820, prior to industrialization and massive urbanization, Demos characterized the family as a community in which family boundaries were almost completely confounded with community boundaries. The family of industrialized society, termed a refuge from the dangerous and grueling world of factory production, adapted to a "natural division of labor" in which the female population was relegated to domestic chores and child rearing. The needs of industrialization had demanded more control of the population in order to maintain a ready pool of labor.

As a refuge, the family of this period served as the domain of the subordinated male worker, a place where he could command respect not received on the job. Conflict theorists maintain that this configuration of family relationships served the important function of defusing worker anger and contempt by supplying him with a group to rule and transforming his responsibility to the family into a harness that "conservatized" his frustration. Here, the male worker would have to compromise family responsibilities in order to make a living. Violence could be used here to ensure the domesticity of the family, much discordance being his only source of pleasure.

Demos sees the postindustrial family as an encounter group. During industrialization, many of the functions of the family were stripped away to ensure the presence of workers. By 1950, the need for ironfisted control of family members by the father was beginning to be replaced by compulsory education, pervasive medical care, stylized religion, and social service agencies.

Emotional expressivity was the last remaining family function. Work was much less physically demanding and much more monotonous. The several functions of the family have been reduced to only a few. Where the family was the unit of production, it now serves mainly as a place for the satisfaction of emotional needs of its members. The economy now needs contented workers and fewer of them. To combat frustrations on the job such as boredom, the worker is still allowed to vent his anger in the family. Only the reasons for violence had changed.

Summary

This paper began with the premise that family violence could be explained using widely accepted theories from social science. Elements of theory were integrated, to various degrees of argument, as follows: (1) There exists a culture predisposed to the advocacy of the use of "pragmatic" violence, which serves as an interpretive "umbrella" for members of society. (2) The norms of this culture are transmitted through socialization practices largely within the family. (3) This tendency to use violence "as necessary" is embodied in an ideology kept salient by the relationship between economic classes. (4) The economy finds the "threat of violence" beneficial to the social system's goals. (5) Women in this system have been uniformly subordinate to their husbands, creating a class of potential victims.

It follows from this conflict approach that producing change in the levels of family violence involves radical change in several aspects of the culture. The goal is to reduce the amount of social stress produced by economic flux and to devalue violence as an appropriate response to stress in other aspects of social life. Women have approached parity with men in their participation in the economy. Continued efforts toward equal participation should reduce violence of the dominant/submissive variety. However, as long as the culture rewards male aggression on the playground, it will continue to produce young men who perceive threat in every social situation and are capable of expressing ritual violence on the spur of the moment.

References

Bandura, A. (1972). *A social learning analysis.* Englewood Cliffs, NJ: Prentice Hall.

Becker, J. V., & Abel, G. G. (1978). Men and the victimization of women. In J. R. Chapman & M. Gates (Eds.), *The victimization of women,* Sage Yearbooks in Women's Policy Studies, Vol. 3. Beverly Hills, CA: Sage.

Cate, R. M., Henton, J. M., Koval, J., Christopher, F. S., & Lloyd, S. (1981). Premarital abuse: A social psychological perspective. *J. Fam. Issues, 3,* 79–90.

Chapman, J. R. (1978). The economics of women's victimization. In J. R. Chapman & M. Gates (Eds.), *The victimization of women,* Sage Yearbooks in Women's Policy Studies, Vol. 3. Beverly Hills, CA: Sage.

Cooley, C. H. (1964). *Human nature and the social order.* New York: Schocken.

Coser, L. A. (1967). *Continuities in the study of social conflict.* New York: Free Press.

Coser, L. A. (1971). *Masters of sociological thought: Ideas in historical and social context.* New York: Harcourt Brace Jovanovich.

Demos, J. (1979). Images of the American family, then and now. In V. Tufte & B. Myerhoff (Eds.), *Changing images of the family.* New Haven, CT: Yale University Press.

Feeley, D. (1972). The family. In L. Jenness (Ed.), *Feminism and socialism.* New York: Pathfinder Press.

Garbarino, J. (1977). The human ecology of child maltreatment: a conceptual model for research. *J. Marriage Fam., 39,* 721–730.

Gelles, R. J. (1979). *Family violence.* Beverly Hills, CA: Sage.

Gelles, R. J. (1980). Violence in the family: A review of research in the seventies. *J. Marriage Fam., 42,* 873–884.

Gelles, R. J., & Straus, M. (1979). Determinants of violence in the family: Toward a theoretical integration. In W. R. Burr, R. Hill, F. I. Nye, & I. L. Reiss (Eds.), *Contemporary theories about the family.* New York: Free Press.

Gelles, R. J., & Straus, M. (1980). Violence in the American family. *J. Social Issues, 35,* 15–37.

Gil, D. (1970). Violence against children. *J. Marriage Fam., 33,* 637–657.

Gully, K. J., Dengerink, H. A., Pepping, M., Bergstrom, D. (1981). Research note: Sibling contribution to violent behavior. *J. Marriage Fam., 43,* 333–337.

Lasch, C. (1978). *The culture of narcissism: American life in an age of diminishing expectations.* New York: Norton.

Lewis, O. (1965). *La vida.* New York: Random House.

Liazos, A. (1972). The poverty of the sociology of deviance. Nuts, sluts, and perverts. *Social Problems, 20,* 103–120.

Makepeace, J. M. (1981). Courtship violence among college students. *Fam. Relat., 30,* 97–102.

Mead, G. H. (1934). *Mind, self and society.* Chicago: University of Chicago Press.

Merton, R. K. (1968). *Social theory and social structure.* New York: Free Press.

Ollman, B. (1971). *Alienation.* Cambridge, UK: Cambridge University Press.

Pizzey, E. (1974). *Scream quietly or the neighbors will hear.* Baltimore: Penguin.

Prescott, S., & Letko, C. (1977). Battered women: A social psychological perspective. In Roy, M. (Ed.), *Battered women: A psychosocial strategy of domestic violence.* New York: Van Nostrand and Reinhold.

Rowbotham, S. (1973). *Woman's consciousness, man's world.* Baltimore: Penguin.

Ruis. (1973). *Marx for beginners.* New York: Pantheon.

Steinmetz, S. K. (1977). *The cycle of violence: Assertive, aggressive and abusive family interaction.* New York: Praeger Press.

Steinmetz, S. K. (1978). Violence between family members. *Marriage Fam. Rev., 1,* 1–16.

Straus, M. (1980). Victims and aggressors in marital violence. *Am. Behav. Sci., 23,* 681–704.

Straus, M., Gelles, R. J., & Steinmetz, S. K. (1980). *Behind closed doors.* Garden City, NY: Doubleday.

Thorne, B. (1982). Feminist of the family: An overview. In B. Thorne, & K. Yalom (Eds.), *Rethinking the family: Some feminist questions.* New York: Longman.

Williams, R. (1970). *American society: A sociological interpretation.* New York: Alfred Knopf.

Witt, D. D. (1980). Domestic in Amarillo: Estimated prevalence and assessment of needs. A research report published by The Junior League of Amarillo.

Wolfgang, M., & Ferracuti, F. (1967). *The subculture of violence.* New York: Barnes and Noble.

Yllo, K., & Straus, M. (1981). Interpersonal violence among married and cohabitating couples. *Fam. Relat., 30,* 339–347.

Status and Income as Gendered Resources: The Case of Marital Power

Veronica Jaris Tichenor

Abstract

This article examines marital power dynamics in couples in which wives earn more than their husbands, work in higher status occupations, or both to determine if wives with resource advantages are able to exercise greater power in their relationships than wives in more conventional marriages. The results do not bear out this hypothesis. This article argues that the logic of resource and exchange theories breaks down when women bring more money and status to the marital relationship. This suggests that the balance of marital power is more closely related to gender than to income or status. This article examines what Komter (1989) calls the hidden power in marriage and highlights how these couples do gender in ways that reinforce the husband's power.

Traditionally, husbands have exercised greater control in marriage, and this power has been linked with the income and status that men have provided as the breadwinner. Women have moved into the paid labor force, but their contributions to income and status have not increased their power proportionately. This article examines marital power dynamics in couples in which wives exceed their husbands' income, occupational status, or both. These couples are referred to as status-reversal couples because the relative contribution of the resources of status and income by spouses is the reverse of what has been typical in two-earner couples. A few conventional status couples are used as a comparison group. In these cases, husbands equal or exceed their wives' income and occupational status. By examining these two types of couples, I explore whether wives can use greater income and status to negotiate more egalitarian power relationships with their husbands or whether these resources are gendered sufficiently so that they are less important, less powerful when contributed by wives.

Insights From Past Research

Efforts to examine the link between women's employment and their power in marriage have been driven by the assumptions of resource and exchange theories, which reflect the idealized notion of separate spheres—breadwinning for men, domestic labor for women (Coltrane, 1996; Ferree, 1990). Men's greater power in marriage is explained by their contributing the "more important" monetary resource. As more women have moved into paid labor, research on marital power has demonstrated that these economic resources have a relatively minimal impact on women's power in terms of control over money, decision making, and the division of domestic labor (Berk, 1985; Blood & Wolfe, 1960; Blumberg, 1984; Blumstein & Schwartz, 1983; Hochschild, 1989; Pleck, 1985; Safilios-Rothschild, 1967;

Scanzoni, 1978; Whyte, 1990). The failure of resource and exchange perspectives to explain marital power dynamics in two-earner couples has led researchers to investigate alternative explanations, such as relative time demands on each spouse and stated gender attitudes or ideology. These have similarly proved to be inadequate indicators of the balance of power in two-earner marriages (Hochschild, 1989; Huber & Spitze, 1983). However, these studies examine conventional couples, in which husbands' income and status exceed that of wives. It is possible that these variables will demonstrate different effects in status-reversal couples.

Recent research on marital power has examined couples who seem to have succeeded in negotiating more egalitarian relationships. Couples studied by Risman and Johnson-Sumerford (1998) and Blaisure and Allen (1995) achieved more equitable relationships because of the spouses' determination to subvert traditionally gendered divisions of labor and power. Couples studied by Schwartz (1994) developed more egalitarian relationships, not as a goal, but as part of their efforts to create more companionate, collaborative marriages. These studies emphasize somewhat different dynamics in these egalitarian relationships, but the findings are strikingly similar on one key point: Spouses in more equitable marriages see the wife's paid work as at least as important as the husband's. In fact, Risman and Johnson-Sumerford see the valuing of women's paid work as a necessary condition to achieving a more equitable relationship. How spouses view each other's work is an important question in this study as well.

One final consideration is the quality of the marital relationship. Given a cultural prescription for a husband's income and occupational status to exceed his wife's, an unconventional marriage may be uncomfortable for spouses, and some research reports that such couples are dissatisfied with their relationships (Burr, 1973; Collins, 1991; Hornung & McCullough, 1981). Marital satisfaction may not be clearly linked to socioeconomic variables but may be more directly related to the congruence between role expectations and performances of spouses or perceived threats to the gender role identities of spouses (Lewis & Spanier, 1979; Vannoy-Hiller & Philliber, 1989). These possibilities are explored here.

Analytic Framework

In order to analyze the marital power dynamics of status-reversal couples, as well as spouses' perceptions of these dynamics, I use two alternative approaches to the study of marital power. The first is Aafke Komter's (1989, 1991) conceptualization of the hidden or ideologically based power that exists in a marriage. The second is West and Zimmerman's (1987) conceptualization of doing gender, in which through everyday interaction, men and women recreate the gender structure that accords men more power than women on all levels.

Komter (1989) attempts to expand our understanding of marital power dynamics by analyzing the meanings behind reported behavior or what she calls the "hidden power" in marriage. Hidden power is shaped by gender ideology and can be exercised in marriage, even in the absence of overt or latent conflict between spouses. Komter (1991) argues that hidden power can be uncovered by examining "regularities in the inconsistencies and contradictions in the common-sense thought and daily experiences of married men and women" (p. 60). For example, Komter (1989) reports that couples use ideological justifications of presumed gender differences to reinforce a traditional and unequal division of domestic labor in their households. There is no conflict over this issue because gender ideology has sufficiently shaped the expectations and experiences of these spouses (e.g., she enjoys it more, or he's not as good at it). Spouses see inequalities in the division of domestic labor as equitable and acceptable. I use Komter's insights by exploring how status-reversal couples make practices that may look inequitable to the outside observer feel equitable or acceptable to them.

Similarly, West and Zimmerman's (1987) approach illuminates the subtleties of marital interaction and "doing gender." When asked to describe how they reach decisions or work out conflicts, spouses often demonstrate a joint effort to ensure that these unconventional marriages do not feel too unconventional to the spouses involved. For example, wives with more resources do not use these resources to make claims to greater power but rather the reverse. They often defer to their husbands in order to demonstrate that they are not making claims to power. Through this kind of interaction, this doing of gender, spouses preserve the husband's power in the relationship, despite the potential power advantage of the wife's greater resources.

The results are presented by theme, and three essential themes guide the analyses. The first takes up the issue of the division of domestic labor. The central questions are: Who bears the burden of household chores and childrearing tasks (and why), under what circumstances do wives get the greatest contribution to domestic labor from their husbands, who is responsible for making sure things get done in each household, and do spouses perceive the division of domestic labor as fair? The issue of fairness is important because some research suggests that perceptions of equity or the meanings that spouses attach to the division of domestic labor may be more important than the actual or objective division of labor itself (Hochschild, 1989; Perry-Jenkins & Folk, 1994). More to the point, Fenstermaker, West, and Zimmerman (1991) claim that "the persistence both of an unequal distribution of household labor and the belief that the distribution of those tasks is fair and equitable suggests that, in doing housework, both men and women also do gender" (p. 303). All of these issues are important in the analysis of the division of labor in status-reversal couples.

The second theme revolves around money management and decision making. The central questions are: Who takes care of the bills, is any power or control exercised in performing this task, who has control over discretionary income, who seems to have more say in household decisions and under what circumstances, and do spouses see a link between money and power in their relationships? This analysis is concerned with power as a process, i.e., how do couples arrive at decisions, and how do spouses conceptualize their role in the decision making process? Answers to these questions help illuminate the hidden power in these relationships.

The final theme revolves around the issue of marital satisfaction. The central questions are: Do spouses seem to be satisfied with the wife's higher income and status, is this arrangement stressful or uncomfortable for spouses in any way, and if so, how do they manage their dissatisfaction or tension? The section on marital satisfaction specifically highlights how spouses react to the cultural expectation that the husband's income and occupational status exceed his wife's.

Research Design

Data Collection and Analyses

This study attempts to separate income, status, and gender (though they are clearly linked in practice) by recruiting specific types of couples: status-reversal couples in which wives' income, occupational status, or both are higher than that of their husbands (22 of the couples fit this description), and conventional couples in which husbands' income and occupational status are higher than their wives' or in which spouses are relatively equal on both variables (eight couples). The data reported here are the results of in-depth interviews with these 30 couples. The couples were living in a major metropolitan area in the Eastern United States. Couples were recruited primarily through ads placed in a local newspaper that was delivered free to all households in the surrounding communities once a week. The ad asked for volunteers for a study on work, marriage, and family life and stated that "especially needed are couples in which the wife's income and/or occupational status is higher than the husband's." I also received several referrals from acquaintances. Respondents were screened during the initial phone contact to determine their eligibility and to inform them that participation required filling out a questionnaire and completing an interview. Six couples who initially agreed to participate failed to return the questionnaires. Another couple declined to be interviewed after returning the questionnaires. Recruitment efforts ceased after 30 couples had completed the entire data collection process.

Respondents were first sent individual but identical questionnaires. The questionnaires included fixed-choice items about household decision making and the division of domestic labor. Items were taken directly from Blood and Wolfe's (1960) research. The questionnaire also asked for standard information about respondent's income, education, occupation, class background, and current marriage. The small, nonrandom nature of the sample meant that I could not analyze these data using standard statistical techniques. However, the questionnaires did yield background information about the respondents and illuminated areas of disagreement between spouses. This information was helpful in the interviews. Once the questionnaires were returned, respondents were contacted to schedule face-to-face interviews. Spouses were interviewed individually, usually consecutively, in their homes. The interviews were structured around a detailed interview schedule, but most questions were designed to be open ended. The interview topics included personal background (including information about family of origin), current work and work history, the history of the couple's relationship, the division of domestic labor and childrearing, money handling and decision-making practices, and conflict resolution strategies. In general, the questions were designed to assess the contributions of each spouse, both domestic and occupational, as well as the value that each individual placed on their own contributions and those of their spouse, and to assess how these contributions may or may not be linked to the balance of power in the relationship. In order to gauge the link between these contributions and marital power, at the end of the interview, I asked each respondent to reflect on issues of status and power in his or her marital relationship.

Interviews were conducted, taped, and transcribed by the author. I used a constant comparative method (Glaser & Strauss, 1967) and analytic induction as tools for analysis. Interviews were first coded using descriptive codes derived from the interview questions, and comparisons were made between spouses to look for discrepancies in perceptions and reports of behavior. I then coded interviews by pattern or theme as part of the movement from data description to conceptual clarification and theorizing. Here, comparisons were made between wives and husbands as groups. Also at this stage, comparisons were made between status-reversal and conventional groups. Husbands and wives then were matched again in an effort to explain why some couples seemed to fit the pattern or theme under examination and others did not. Therefore, in some parts of the analyses, status-reversal wives are compared with their husbands. In other parts they are compared with other status-reversal wives, and at other points, their experiences are contrasted with those of conventional wives— all in an effort to tease out the relative effects of gender, income, and status on the balance of marital power in these couples. Data analyses are based on reports by both husband and wife from both the questionnaire and the interview. Spouses did not always agree in their reports of who does what and how often. Typically, respondents gave themselves more credit than they gave their spouses. On occasion, what respondents reported on their questionnaire differed from the picture they painted in the interview. All of this makes it difficult to arrive at precise numbers of hours or percentages of time spent by each spouse on domestic labor and childrearing, for example. Therefore, I report differences in rough proportions in order to assess the equity of the arrangements, given the assumptions of exchange and resource theory. In cases in which spouses disagreed greatly over the division of domestic labor, I gave more weight to the wives' responses because husbands have been found to overreport their participation in domestic labor at a greater rate than their wives (Press & Townsley, 1998; Wright, Shire, Hwang, Dolan, & Baxter, 1992).

Sample Characteristics

This sample is composed primarily of wives whose income and occupational status are greater than those of their husbands. Defining what constitutes a great disparity is a rather arbitrary decision. Previous work on wives with higher incomes has used income differences as small as a few thousand dollars per year (McRae, 1986), but I wanted to examine larger differences—ones that would be difficult to ignore. Therefore, I defined a wife as higher on income when she earned at least 50% more per year than her husband (e.g., a woman making $45,000 per year married to a man making $30,000). Status differences were defined by a combination of factors: established occupational rankings, such as Duncan's Socioeconomic Index, education required for the job, and position in the bureaucratic hierarchy. In practice, I relied largely on the last two factors. For example, a mid-level bank manager was judged to be higher in status than her husband who worked as a welding technician. All couples were two-income couples with at least one child at home, and all wives were employed full-time. However, five husbands spent most of their time in the home (earning, at most, $3,000 per year) and were classified by their part-time occupations. Note that, although the status-reversal group includes men whose primary job is househusband, there are no housewives in the conventional group. I was most interested in contrasting the effects of wives' employment with the effects of wives having a higher income and occupational status.

The two groups were well matched on key demographic variables. On average husbands were only slightly older than their wives (37 years vs. 36 years for status-reversal couples, 35 years vs. 34 years for conventional couples). Status-reversal couples had been married about 8 years, with an average of 1.75 children; conventional couples, for 10 years with 2.0 children. There were also no gross discrepancies between the two groups in terms of class background, ethnicity, or religiosity. However, as expected, the groups vary more widely on income. Status-reversal husbands

made $22,000 to their wives' $47,000 in the year prior to their interviews. Conventional husbands made $45,000 to their wives' $33,000.

This sample is distinctive because it is racially homogeneous. The sample included only two Asian Americans, two African Americans, one Latino, and one émigré from the Middle East. All remaining respondents were White. The sample is also highly educated. Over two thirds of the respondents had bachelor's degrees, and most had at least some graduate training. In over a third of the status-reversal couples, the wives have had more education than their husbands. This gap generally reflects the fact that a wife has a master's degree and her husband does not. (In two cases, the education of the status-reversal husband exceeded his wife's for the same reason.) Among the conventional couples, the husband's education equaled or exceeded his wife's in all but one case. In short, status-reversal couples are similar to conventional couples on key variables, with the exception that status-reversal wives were more likely to possess more advanced degrees than their husbands and to out-earn them by a considerable margin.

The Division of Domestic Labor

Who Bears the Burden?

Status-reversal wives tend to receive more help from their husbands than conventional wives. The five wives whose husbands are home full-time get substantial relief from domestic labor. Their husbands perform more than half of the household and child-care chores. In all five cases the couples sat down and made a conscious decision that one parent would be home with the children, and because the wife in each of these families had greater economic potential than the husband, the husband stayed home. Of the 17 remaining status-reversal couples, 41% of the husbands perform from one third to one half (in one case) of the domestic labor. Only 25% of the conventional husbands contribute at this level. All remaining husbands in both groups contribute less than one third of the domestic labor. This speaks for the ability of status-reversal wives to "buy" some relief from household labor, but the picture should not be painted too optimistically. These are women who earn a great deal more than their husbands and are substantially higher in status as well. Yet they are not able to trade these resources for a similarly substantial reduction in their burden of domestic labor. Surprisingly, few couples employed outside help with household chores. Only three status-reversal couples and two conventional couples used paid housecleaners on a regular basis, and in all five cases, the wives performed the majority of the remaining household chores.

Wives in both groups also maintained responsibility for running the household and making sure things got done. (The exceptions were four out of the five status-reversal wives who had husbands who were primarily at home.) Half of the status-reversal wives and three quarters of the conventional wives experienced this responsibility as an additional burden. One status-reversal wife explained that although

the father may have significant participation in doing any family tasks, the planning, etc. is frequently all a mother's work. You don't highlight who calls the YWCA for the program schedule, who makes sure there is change each day for lunch money, who decides it is time for a dental checkup, who realizes that last year's snow boots won't fit before this year's first snow, . . . who sees that young children use the toilet before a trip in the car, who sets up the car pool for church school, soccer, scouts. . . . All this, or most of this, is constant, continual planning. The actual execution is a cakewalk by comparison!

Important Work

There is a great deal of variability in the sharing of domestic labor by status-reversal couples that was not explained by status and income differences. Stated gender attitudes, such as egalitarian attitudes about women's paid employment and men's domestic labor, also did not match actual sharing behavior in any systematic way.

Similarly, relative time demands, reflected in the number of hours spent working, commuting, working overtime, and traveling, did not seem to drive the division of domestic labor. I then tried to assess whether one job had priority over the other by examining the opportunities for advancement for each spouse, including the possibility of relocating for those opportunities, whether one spouse's work tended to define the family's daily schedule, whether spouses discussed each other's work, and how much respect each spouse seemed to have for the other's work. This line of inquiry seemed a more fruitful way to explain variations in patterns because most couples seem to have a sense that one spouse's job was more important than the other spouse's job. The spouse doing the important work was allowed to contribute less at home. In some cases, the status-reversal wives were seen as having more important jobs, and they performed less domestic labor. For example, Chris, a status-reversal husband, said: "[H]er job is more important. My job is basically money . . . and because of that, I assumed the roles of the one who will pick up the kids and will take them in the morning . . . take 'em to the doctor and so on." In other cases, the husband's job was seen as more important, despite the disparity in income, and he did less at home. For example, Joyce said that it was important that she remain in a high-paying job "because Evan's more important job, in terms of subject matter and impact on life, pays government rates." Her husband contributes little to domestic labor and child care, and she vents about the load she carries at home and its disproportionate impact on her work responsibilities and those of her husband:

I get completely frustrated by it. It is unrelenting; it is never-ending. . . . So I am resentful of the fact that, starting about 2 or 3 weeks ago, in the back of my mind, if I end up going on the trip to Florida next week, I have to do this and this and this and this and this. Whereas Evan has, on numerous occasions, blown out of the country on a business trip, on minimal notice, and the most he's had to do is remember to pack his socks. I will vent these frustrations to Evan, and he will continue to read his book, and he isn't really listening to me. He just waits for me to finish.

In the two cases where conventional couples did not accord extra importance to either spouse's work, domestic labor was also divided more equally. Amanda and Joe are such a couple. Amanda considers Joe to be "the wife" in their household because of all the house work and child care he performs. She says that they work together to meet the demands of work and family: "We're equals. We basically bring home the same thing, and we both bust our butt for it. We respect each other for it."

Despite the fact that performing important work helped some wives achieve a more equitable division of labor at home, no husband (employed full-time) took on more than 50% of the domestic labor, no matter how much money his wife made or how important her job was. The most that status-reversal wives received from a husband was a one-third to one-half (in one case) contribution.

Perceptions of Equity

Despite the economic and domestic contributions that status-reversal wives make to their families, many of these women feel they don't contribute enough. Half of the status-reversal wives feel they should do more housework and child care, and a significant proportion already carries most of the household burden. Two of these women couldn't think of anything specific when asked "what more do you think you should be doing?" This is an expectation they have of themselves because their husbands think these wives do "plenty." Even more striking is the fact that some of these women generate all or most of the family's income. They seem to feel that supporting the family does not compensate for the household labor that their husbands perform. One wife, a critical care nurse whose husband is primarily at home, listed her household contributions and then said, "What kind of mother am I? I do very little around here!" Another wife, a physician who is married to a part-time high

school coach, worries that she's not home enough to "take care" of her family: "I have a paycheck, which is probably only incidental. . . . I can't say I'm the strong point in the whole family, except for that paycheck, because I'm just not here often enough." And Bonnie, a lawyer who makes $114,000 and whose husband, Wayne, is home with their son, states:

> You know, it's funny. I sort of feel like I don't contribute enough. Because he's so [pause], it sounds like he does so much. I mean, he does lots of things. I think, because if you try to list things at the end of the day, there's really only a number of things I do because a large category of what I do is just work, office work. And right from the morning, he'll get up, get [our son] fed and off to school, though usually I do that, then Wayne takes him to school, and then he'll go for a run, and come back and pay bills or balance the checkbook, and then he'll go to a meeting of the church finance board, and then he'll have lunch or . . . go to school and help out during recess, and then he'll come home for an hour, and then he might take a nap, but then he'll go pick up [our son]. Then he'll spend the rest of the day with him. And in the meantime, he's done three loads of wash, scrubbed down the patio chairs, vacuumed, washed the car. I don't know. There's tons of things to manage on the home front.

No conventional husband spoke about his wife's domestic contributions with such awe or admiration, nor did they downplay their own economic contributions to their families. These status-reversal women seem to place a greater value on their gender-appropriate contributions to the household. Their paychecks are only incidental. Some of them have a hard time listing what they think they contribute to the household because they aren't contributing in conventionally feminine ways. By contrast, only one conventional wife, Amanda, felt that she should be doing more. She and Joe have relatively equal incomes and status, and make relatively equal contributions to domestic labor, but this is not comfortable for her. She feels that she should do more, so he can do less, and she can be the wife.

Money Management and Decision Making

Control over Money: Paying the Bills Versus Discretionary Spending

Making more money does not directly translate into more power for the women in the sample. It does not give them more decision-making power, nor do they adopt an "I-make-more-I'll-decide how-it's-spent" attitude. For most couples, the power dynamics are driven by the way their money is organized and managed. Women tend to manage the checkbook (77% of status reversal-wives and 63% of conventional wives did), regardless of the number or kinds of accounts a couple had, but these percentages are an inadequate measure of money control. A better measure is to examine the couples in which wives control the checkbook and money is only pooled. Forty-one percent of status-reversal couples and 25% of conventional couples fit this description. These wives had many opportunities to exercise control. One status-reversal wife, Jean, when asked if she feels like she has enough control over how the money is spent, said, "Oh yeah, you bet. It spends most of its time in my wallet, so. . . . He who has the cash has the last word." These wives often act as gatekeepers of the family's money. Because they know the monthly financial arrangements and obligations, they are in a position to determine whether and when the family can afford a particular purchase.

This kind of control seems to work for men as well. In 23% of status-reversal couples and 38% of conventional couples, money is only pooled, and husbands pay the bills. One status-reversal husband, Wayne, explained:

> A recent example would be [that] I spent a thousand bucks on an electronic air cleaner for our house. . . . [F]irst I discussed it with her, and she thought it was too much money, and then I just went and did it, and uh, you know, she kind of winced a little bit. But you know, I paid the bill, and she didn't have to see it or think about it, so it just kind of went through the system.

For some couples, the money is organized by one spouse to give themselves a financial advantage. For example, one third of all the men in the study (32% of status-reversal husbands and 38% of conventional husbands) have money set aside. For two of them, it is a leftover from their single days—an account they never closed into which they put a few dollars every payday. The rest opened accounts specifically to have money deposited into them before contributing to the common pot. One status-reversal husband, Evan, describes why he felt justified in setting up a separate account for himself.

> When I did my own accounting, I would tend to allocate. Even in a single checking account, I would have in my mind so much set aside for this and so much set aside for that. Here it just goes into this gaping maw and never gets reallocated for anything. So I've dealt with that in a, I think, modest and pernicious way.

His wife, Joyce, seems unaware of his actions. She maintains that they have no separate accounts: "We've never had separate accounts. I'm amused by friends who have all kinds of accounts. Life's too short. Besides, it would just be another account for me to balance." They both claim that there's not a lot of money left over and that they run the checking account down to zero each month.

In a few couples in which money is substantially pooled, wives also have separate accounts. This was true for 14% of status-reversal wives and 13% of conventional wives. These separate accounts are maintained for tax or business purposes only. Another 14% of status-reversal wives have separate accounts because the bills are divided in their household, and each spouse pays certain bills each month. None of these women describes these accounts as providing them with extra spending money the way the men do.

Another 18% (four) of status-reversal couples have unique systems of money management. In two of the couples, the wives, with husbands who were primarily at home, had accounts in their names only. All their money went into these accounts, and whatever money their husbands earned would be turned over to their wives. Both couples reported that they arranged the finances in this manner because the men are irresponsible, can't be trusted with money, and the families are in difficult financial straits. On the face of it, this would give the wives a great deal of control, but the husbands work around these constraints. They take money from their wives' wallets or add money to the check they write for groceries and pocket the cash. In the other two cases, having a separate account does work in the wives' favor. Both spouses have individual checking and savings accounts from their single days, as well as joint checking and savings accounts. Each payday they contribute equally to the joint account to cover joint bills, and the rest of the money is used to pay individual bills (e.g., student loans or credit cards) or for discretionary spending. Because they contribute equally to joint bills, the wives are left with a substantial surplus to spend as they see fit—even purchasing things for the home that their husbands don't think the family can afford. Ironically, their commitment to equality on joint bills sets up substantial inequality in favor of these two wives.

The Gendered Link
Between Money and Power

I asked several questions designed to encourage couples to reflect on the possible link between money and power in their relationship. Most spouses, especially husbands, completely dismissed the idea that such a link exists for them. Status-reversal wives seemed to be the most uncomfortable with the idea. One example is June, a military officer who makes more than twice what her enlisted husband makes:

> Gosh, see, I'm afraid Adam's gonna say, "Yeah, yeah, she's got all the power 'cause she's got all the money," and I don't see it that way. . . . I don't see myself as being "in control." In fact, most of the time I feel out of control.

She's afraid that her husband sees her as powerful. This fear is played out in her reluctance to exercise control over money management and decision making. Her husband senses that there is something odd about the way they make decisions. He says:

> If it's a thing we both agree upon that we wanna do, she'll say, "Okay, do it if you think it's okay." And I'll go ahead and do it. If it's something that she agrees on, that I'm just making the phone calls for, and I tell her what the phone call said, she goes, "Well, what do ya think?" [I laugh at his tone.] "I don't care, Honey, it's up to you." "Well, what do you wanna do?" And finally I'll just say, "Okay, fine," and we'll go for it. It's weird, too, because I feel like I'm making all the decisions even though I'm not making all the decisions, and she's the one that carries the wallet in the family.

June is not the only status-reversal wife who seems to feel uncomfortable forging a link between money and power in her relationship. No status-reversal wife demands extra authority over how the money is spent. No status-reversal wife says, "I make more money; I'll decide where it goes" (though several conventional status husbands made such statements). The women who bring home more money (some of them are nearly sole providers) are careful to say that all their marital assets are joint. They can share what they have, but they eschew any attempt to paint themselves as superior to their husbands, as staking some claim to an extra measure of control over money or decision making. Some of them even realize that, if they were in the same position, their husbands would have that kind of control automatically, and this doesn't seem to be a problem for them. At least they describe it in a matter-of-fact way. For example, Bonnie, a lawyer who earns $114,000, whose husband is at home with their son, explains:

> I think there is a link [between money and power] but only the other way. If Wayne were making all the money, I'd be resentful because I'd feel less [pause], I'd feel as if I had less of a say in how it was spent, regardless of what he thought. But if I'm the only one making the money, we've tried all along to make sure that all the money and assets that we have are clearly joint, regardless of where

it all came from. . . . I mean, he's out there buying all these toys, these treadmills and vacuum cleaners, whereas I think if I were, if the situation were reversed, and I was at home, I mean, I'd be even more of a penny pincher.

Jill, a midlevel bank manager married to a former car salesman who is trying to start his own business, says:

I've brought in more money, and I don't feel like I had more power because I'm not ever supposed to mention, [pause] I try not to mention the fact that I make more money, because that's just a taboo thing. It would send him through the roof. . . . I think in his mind money is power, and he thinks he'll be a much better husband the more money he makes.

Jill also reported that she backed away from exercising control over decision making to avoid being labeled a "bitch" by her husband and his friends.

Decision Making

Decision-making patterns among status-reversal couples do not seem to be related to income and status variables. Wives with higher incomes and occupational status do not make automatic claims to a greater say in household decisions. But as with financial matters, they are often in a better position to shape household decisions. This happens largely through their role as organizers of the household. Many wives argue that being responsible for the household and planning for the future means that they can direct discussions and shape final outcomes. One status-reversal wife, Sandy, spoke convincingly about the potential power of being the family organizer. Sandy also controls the checkbook and says her husband has to go through her to get something he wants. She feels that her organizing responsibilities give her an edge when they disagree. She tries to reason things out with him from her side:

We can't afford it, or we can't do it because of this. And that, perhaps unfortunately, can be real effective when I have that resource at my disposal. I know the details of what we've got

planned when, and where our money is. It's a lot easier for me to control the discussion.

At the end of the interview, I asked if she thought either of them had more power or influence in the relationship. She responded:

I would say I do because of thinking of it ahead of time and being prepared, spending more time thinking about the options and doing that. So if I've made a choice in my own mind, it's easy. If the only case on the table is what I'm going to put out, it will happen.

Her husband agrees that he has a "diminished" role in decision making because Sandy is the planner and financial manager.

Nearly half of all women interviewed (all but two from status-reversal families) perceive that their role as household organizers allows them to exercise some control over decision making. Though most of the literature on marital decision making has not viewed these typically feminine responsibilities as powerful, these women sometimes do. But there is a potential check on this power in the form of the husband's veto. Husbands reported going along with their wives on most issues, but 25% of both status-reversal and conventional husbands reserved the fight to "put their feet down" over something they just couldn't live with. These husbands also exerted their will over decisions when they felt they had more expertise, for example, when purchasing homes or cars.

Some women are able to exert influence in specific spheres of their expertise. For example, women with CPAs or MBAs are experts in financial matters. Other women have influence in the area of interpersonal relationships in the family, due to training in early childhood development or the therapeutic process. What is striking about their expertise is that these women do not have the same kind of veto power that the men seem to have. Even when husbands acknowledge this expertise, the wives still must make their case, and the husbands often seem unwilling to back down without an argument. For example, Don and Cindy have frequent disagreements over childrearing and discipline. Don says:

Well, you know, Cindy's got a master's degree in early childhood and special education, and stuff so, you know. She doesn't tell me how to fix a car, so. . . . We have arguments about it, but in the long run I figure she's probably right and she knows what she's talking about.

There is an asymmetry in the influence that spouses are able to exert. Logic and persuasion are how women win their points because husbands eventually can be moved by argument without loss of face. Ultimatums and vetoes do not allow this and are, therefore, not part of the woman's arsenal. For these couples, veto power seems to have little to do with income, status, or even expertise. It has everything to do with gender. Jim, a physician who is married to a senior corporate vice-president, says it best:

I've never felt it's really important for me to exert my power as the husband because the fact of the matter is that we are fairly equal in terms of our earnings and in terms of our responsibilities, in our own way. And I like that. I think Maggie is, in every sense of the word, a partner in this relationship.

Whether this "power as the husband" refers to veto power or something more far-reaching is unclear. It is clear, however, that Jim, like many of the other men interviewed, senses that being a husband affords him at least the opportunity for greater control.

Managing the Tensions Created by Income and Status Differences

Marital Satisfaction

More than half (64%) of the status-reversal couples are dissatisfied with their relationships on some level. The corresponding figure for the conventional group is 13%. Satisfaction among status-reversal couples is largely determined by how the spouses got to this point or the "path" to the status-reversal marriage. The three possible paths are: differences in income and status at the time of marriage, greater upward mobility for the wife, downward mobility or occupational stagnation

for the husband. The element of choice seems key in assessing how satisfied status-reversal spouses are with their relationships. All of the status-reversal husbands except one have specific plans for moving up in their field by going back to school, changing jobs, or moving into paid employment. This is probably because status reversal, in this sample, is most typically due to occupational stagnation for the husband, often coupled with the more rapid upward mobility of the wife. The spouses do not feel they have chosen this arrangement, which may help to explain the general dissatisfaction with the experience. Focusing on future plans is the most common way husbands attempted to manage their dissatisfactions.

The chief complaint of status-reversal wives is that their husbands aren't living up to their potential. For some wives, that means that their husbands are doing work that is beneath them. For other wives, their dissatisfaction centers around the fact that they want their husbands to bring home more money. In over one third of the cases, the wives' dissatisfaction seems to be linked to their desire for a more conventional relationship. These women seem to be dissatisfied with their husbands' inability to support the family. This lack of achievement on the part of their husbands keeps the wives from living more firmly in the domestic realm. One wife says:

[S]ometimes I feel resentful that I make more. Like I wish it was the other way around. Because I feel like the responsibility, like [pause] it's just like I can't go part-time, you know? It's like I would like to go part-time and stay home with [my daughter] and do more house things and have less stress. But I feel like I can't because I am the one that makes more.

For both husbands and wives, the tension revolves around the fact that husbands are not meeting their traditional obligations of status and income. Only two status-reversal husbands complained that their wives' work interferes with family obligations. The fact that status-reversal wives meet their traditional obligations by carrying most of the burden of domestic labor, as well as responsibility for the household, may mean that there is less reason for these husbands to complain.

Hiding and Avoiding
Income and Status Differences

Spouses seem to do their best to ignore or minimize their income and status differences. Most commonly, respondents simply deny that differences exist or admit differences only reluctantly. When asked if she sees a status difference between their jobs, one midlevel manager married to a computer technician says: "A little bit. I really don't think of it that much, to tell the truth. You're asking, so I say, 'Okay, I do have a better job than he does.'" A few couples go beyond protestations. They seem to have organized their lives in ways that minimize their income or status differences. Two couples have elaborate systems of individual and joint bank accounts and are committed to contributing equally to joint expenses. This tends to leave the wives with more discretionary money because they came substantially more, but the husbands are insulated from this fact because they don't face the actual numbers every month. This allows them to feel like equal contributors. Three other couples have separate accounts, and each spouse pays certain bills each month. In these cases, the women take on more bills than their husbands because they make more and think it is only fair. In fact, they have taken on so many bills that in two of the three cases the wives barely scrape by each month although their husbands have some discretionary income at their disposal. This arrangement insulates the husbands from the fact that their wives make more. Husbands do not have to face the reality of their wives' greater income each month, and the wives use up whatever surplus or advantage there might be in bringing home substantially more money.

Two other couples work hard to avoid the status differences between them. Cindy is a special education teacher with a master's degree. She is married to Don, a mechanical technician. She describes their situation this way:

Well, sometimes it's hard with a relationship. Like Don doesn't read. He doesn't read the newspaper; he looks at the ads. He doesn't read books. I think he had learning disabilities . . . that were never really looked at. When he writes, I can tell. But I think sometimes the fact that he's not as educated as I frustrates me, and I wonder if I had not been in a situation where I was 19 and my parents were separating, if I had maybe dated more guys, then I would know for sure. Right now, I just don't know.

These spouses live in separate worlds generated by their separate statuses. They socialize individually, rather than jointly. They seem to use this strategy to maintain their life together. They avoid the distance between them by spending their time with people who are like them. Another couple, a military officer married to an enlisted man (June and Adam), has even greater difficulties with the status difference between them. The military is deliberate about its rank structure, and the gulf between an officer and an enlisted soldier is enormous. Because they cannot separate their statuses the way Don and Cindy do, they have chosen to live in the lower-status world of the husband. They socialize only with his friends—other enlisted people. He says simply: "I don't change. I'm the same person. If she can deal with my lifestyle and enjoy my friends, it'll work." Conventional couples, by contrast, tend to socialize with friends from church or the neighborhood. In couples in which social connections are made through work, the relationships with the husband's (higher status) work seem to be the most important.

Redefining the Provider Role

Couples find other, less drastic, ways to manage or reduce the status and income differences between the spouses. When asked if they see either spouse as the provider, many reply that provider is no longer a useful term. Most commonly, status-reversal wives reinforce the position of their husbands by expanding the notion of providing. For them, providing is not just about money. Lily, a nurse, speaks for many when she says both she and her husband, a maintenance worker, provide for the family:

> There are more ways than just financial. I mean, when you talk about being a provider, I think that just maybe it's too broad a thing—emotional, physical, financial. . . . Just because my actual paycheck may be larger, that doesn't mean a darn thing. I think it means as a person you provide for your family in more ways than just money.

Even wives who earn nearly all the family's income are reluctant to identify themselves as providers. Bonnie, a lawyer, whose husband, Wayne is at home says:

> I guess [I am], but I don't think of it in those terms. I don't think about that at all. I sort of see our family as being the "cause," and Wayne and I are doing our parts to advance our family's interests. So I guess we're both providers.

Similarly, husbands find ways to see themselves as providers. Several husbands point to their investments as ways that they contribute money to the family. One husband lost a lucrative job that allowed him to provide all of the family's income, but he sees himself as providing opportunities and new experiences for his family by living and working in this metropolitan area. This reworking of what it means to be a provider is unique to status-reversal couples. For conventional couples with a small gap in earnings, spouses see themselves as coproviders. As the gap increases, the husband is identified as the main provider or breadwinner.

Discussions and Conclusions

The assumptions of resource and exchange theory, as they relate to marital power, continue to be challenged by the findings presented here. Variations in occupational status and income appear to have relatively little impact on marital power. In fact, these couples often organize their lives in ways that ignore or hide variations. The assumptions of resource and exchange theory are challenged most directly by the division of domestic labor in these families. Status-reversal wives are bearing the larger burden of domestic labor and contributing the lion's share of the family's income and status. They do not, as a group, see this as unfair because they tend to judge their success as wives and mothers by how much they do around the house, rather than how much they bring home.

In terms of financial management, wives often exercise a great deal of influence when they control the checkbook and when money is only pooled. Husbands exercise similar influence when money is only pooled and when they control the checkbook, though this is less common. The issue of separate money and what it means is also key to understanding power dynamics in these couples. Although a few women have separate money because of how the finances are arranged, no woman in this sample talked about being entitled to spending money off the top or to setting up separate accounts specifically for that purpose, the way some of their husbands did. This does not mean that wives have no opportunities for discretionary spending, but the fact that they use joint funds for their purchases means that their discretionary spending is public. A husband with money set aside has the ability to make purchases more privately. Wives' discretionary spending also was tempered by the budgetary needs of the household. This is in contrast to husbands who paid themselves first. (See Blumberg, 1991, for similar results.) This practice of husbands helps to subvert the link between earning money and having money power in status-reversal relationships.

Wives tend to organize the household. This means that they often shape the couple's decision-making process, but the results also illuminate some limits on wives' power. Opportunities to exercise control can be cut short by the husband's power to veto his wife's decisions. Wives may be reluctant to exercise control out of fear of appearing to be powerful or even a "bitch." A bitch is not a wife—she is domineering, uncaring, and unlovable. Being a wife demands, if not a certain amount of submission, certainly no claim to superiority over a husband.

As Connell (1987) has said, "dominance over the other sex is absent from the social construction of femininity" (p. 187). Therefore, many of these status-reversal wives back away from whatever power they might derive from their income and status. They either give up control or adopt strategies that make it appear that their husbands are in control. (See Blumberg, 1991; Stamp, 1985, for similar results.) Doing gender in this way reaffirms them as "women" and reinforces their position as "wives" in the marital relationship, thereby reproducing the gendered relations of power in their marriages.

The majority of status-reversal couples find that income and status differences between spouses are problematic. They attempt to hide or ignore differences with a variety of strategies. The most common is the joint effort to redefine what it means to be a provider. Stay-at-home fathers and husbands who contribute a smaller proportion of the family income are accorded provider status that is unthinkable for women in similar circumstances. A housewife may be seen as contributing vitally to the family through her efforts at home and in the community, and these contributions may be highly valued by both spouses, but she is unlikely to be called a provider. Similarly, women who earn significantly less than their husbands are unlikely to be called providers. They are more likely to be viewed as helpers. This, in fact, is the pattern for conventional couples. Broadening the notion of providing is unique to status-reversal couples and seems to be part of an overall effort to construct a relationship that conforms to the conventional marital contract.

Perhaps most significant is the finding that women who perform important work outside the home enjoy a more equitable division of labor in the home. These results add to the growing body of literature that suggests that without a high level of respect for the wife's work, a more egalitarian relationship is unlikely (Blaisure & Allen, 1995; Risman & Johnson-Sumerford, 1998; Schwartz, 1994). What is perhaps missing from these status-reversal relationships, compared with Risman and Johnson-Sumerford's

postgender couples, is the deep commitment to equality or to feminist ideals. Without a concerted effort to subvert traditionally gendered behaviors and meanings, status-reversal couples rework those meanings to make their relationships look and feel more conventional and comfortable. Ironically, their discomfort and dissatisfaction are still palpable.

Clearly, there is a material component to equality in marriage, but it is not income nor status that translates into power. It is the meaning attached to these contributions that seems to be primary. In the absence of a firm commitment to egalitarian or feminist ideology as a tool for transforming marriage, the institution of marriage itself, coupled with and shaped by hegemonic gender, structures and organizes the experience of these status-reversal couples. Above all, the results presented here further document the range of challenges facing couples who attempt to alter the conventional marriage contract.

Note

I thank Marty Whyte, Pepper Schwartz, Julia McQuillan, and anonymous reviewers for helpful comments on earlier drafts of this article.

References

Berk, S. F. (1985). *The gender factory: The apportionment of work in American households.* New York: Plenum Press.

Blaisure, K., & Allen, K. (1995). Feminists and the ideology and practice of marital equality. *Journal of Marriage and the Family, 57,* 5–19.

Blood, R., & Wolfe, D. (1960). *Husbands and wives: The dynamics of married living.* New York: Free Press.

Blumberg, R. L. (1984). A general theory of gender stratification. In R. Collins (Ed.), *Sociological theory 1984* (pp. 23–101). San Francisco: Jossey-Bass.

Blumberg, R. L. (Ed.). (1991). *Gender, family, and economy: The triple overlap.* Beverly Hills, CA: Sage.

Blumstein, P., & Schwartz, P. (1983). *American couples: Money, work, sex.* New York: William Morrow.

Burr, W. (1973). *Theory construction and the sociology of the family*. New York: Wiley.

Collins, R. (1991). Women and men in the class structure. In R. L. Blumberg (Ed.), *Gender, family, and economy: The triple overlap* (pp. 52–73). Beverly Hills, CA: Sage.

Coltrane, S. (1996). *Family man: Fatherhood, housework and gender equity*. New York: Oxford University Press.

Connell, R. W. (1987). *Gender and power: Society, the person and sexual politics*. Stanford, CA: Stanford University Press.

Fenstermaker, S., West, C., & Zimmerman, D. (1991). Gender inequality: New conceptual terrain. In R. L. Blumberg (Ed.), *Gender, family, and economy: The triple overlap* (pp. 289–307). Beverly Hills, CA: Sage.

Ferree, M. (1990). Beyond separate spheres: Feminism and family research. *Journal of Marriage and the Family, 52*, 866–884.

Glaser, B., & Strauss, A. (1967). *The discovery of grounded theory: Strategies for qualitative research*. New York: Aldine de Gruyter.

Hochschild, A. (1989). *The second shift*. New York: Viking.

Hornung, C., & McCullough, C. (1981). Status relationships in dual-employment marriages: Consequences for psychological well-being. *Journal of Marriage and the Family, 43*, 125–141.

Huber, J., & Spitze, G. (1983). *Sex stratification: Children, housework, and jobs*. New York: Academic Press.

Komter, A. (1989). Hidden power in marriage. *Gender and Society, 3*, 187–216.

Komter, A. (1991). Gender, power and feminist theory. In K. Davis (Ed.), *The gender of power* (pp. 42–62). Newbury Park, CA: Sage.

Lewis, R., & Spanier, G. (1979). Theorizing about the quality and stability of marriage. In W. Burr, R. Hill, F. I. Nye, & I. Reiss (Eds.), *Contemporary theories about the family* (pp. 268–294). New York: The Free Press.

McRae, S. (1986). *Cross class families: A study of wives' occupational superiority*. Oxford, UK: Clarendon Press.

Perry-Jenkins, M., & Folk, K. (1994). Class, couples, and conflict: Effects of the division of labor on assessments of marriage in dual-earner families. *Journal of Marriage and the Family, 56*, 165–180.

Pleck, R. (1985). *Working wives, working husbands*. Beverly Hills, CA: Sage.

Press, J., & Townsley, E. (1998). Wives' and husbands' housework reporting: Gender, class and social desirability. *Gender and Society, 12*, 188–218.

Risman, B., & Johnson-Sumerford, D. (1998). Doing it fairly: A study of post-gender marriages. *Journal of Marriage and the Family, 60*, 23–40.

Safilios-Rothschild, C. (1967). A comparison of power structure and marital satisfaction in urban Greek and French families. *Journal of Marriage and the Family, 29*, 345–352.

Scanzoni, J. (1978). Social processes and power in families. In W. Burr, R. Hill, F. I. Nye, & I. Reiss (Eds.), *Contemporary theories about families* (pp. 295–316). New York: The Free Press.

Schwartz, P. (1994). *Love between equals: How peer marriage really works*. New York: The Free Press.

Stamp, P. (1985). Research note: Balance of financial power in marriage: An exploratory study of breadwinning wives. *Sociological Review, 33*, 546–557.

Vannoy-Hiller, D., & Philliber, W. (1989). *Equal partners: Successful women in marriage*. Newbury Park, CA: Sage.

West, C., & Zimmerman, D. (1987). Doing gender. *Gender and Society, 1*, 125–151.

Whyte, M. (1990). *Dating, mating, and marriage*. New York: Aldine de Gruyter.

Wright, E. O., Shire, K., Hwang, S., Dolan, M., & Baxter, J. (1992). The non-effects of class on the gender division of labor in the home: A comparative study of Sweden and the U.S. *Gender and Society, 6*, 252–281.

7

FEMINIST THEORY

The focus of feminist theory is generally on examinations of how gender is perceived, patterns of gendered behaviors, and inequalities associated with gender. Gender is viewed as a salient feature of family life and a source of subjugation or oppression within families. Feminist theory in family science arose out of the feminist movement of the 1960s and 1970s and reflects the various perspectives and agendas of that movement. Over the past 30 years, however, feminist theory has continued to evolve and presently includes a variety of theoretical perspectives.

The basic goal of feminist theory is to inform and encourage change in social structures that will ultimately empower women. Feminist theory is focused on empowering women and other disenfranchised groups. The focus then, goes beyond understanding gender differences and biases to actively seeking to change social conditions under which women and disenfranchised groups exist. Feminist theory is essentially focused on changing the social experiences and understandings of women. Therefore, the emphasis of feminist theory is on women and their experiences. Feminist theory argues that, under present social arrangements, social institutions such as families are essentially patriarchal and contribute to patterns of subordination and repression for women who exist within them. Feminist theorists are committed to ending such subordination.

Feminist theory argues that gender and gender relations are fundamental to all social life. Just as social conflict theory argues that conflict is a basic aspect of social situations, feminist theory argues that gender holds such an integral place in social situations. From a feminist perspective, it is impossible to understand social environments without considering the presence of gender and gendered patterns within those environments. In particular, to understand families as social units, one must understand women's experiences in families.

From a feminist perspective, gender is viewed as a social construction. While there are biological differences between males and females, these are not the source of our understanding of gender. Rather, gender arises out of societal beliefs concerning males and females and differing expectations for their behaviors, values, and attitudes. As a social construction, gender legitimizes power differences in family relationships. This social construction is reflected in women's and men's different participation in employment and household labor, in different patterns of socialization of boys and girls, and even in the labels applied to males and females and their characteristics in our language. All of these reflect different societal values ascribed to males and females.

Because gender is a social construct, social and historical contexts are important in understanding women's experiences. This results in attention to social forces that contribute to shaping women's experiences in families and historical changes in women's experiences as a result of those social forces. From a feminist perspective, it is argued that women are negatively impacted by broad social forces in a variety of ways. Because women exist within family domains, these negative impacts ultimately affect families.

Feminist theory also suggests there is no one typical family form and that it is a failure to suggest that a particular family form is ideal, especially when that family form is built on a patriarchal family model. Rather, feminist theory suggests that a diversity of family forms must be recognized and that the strengths and weaknesses of each must be considered. Indeed, some feminists argue that the notion of family, itself, is a myth.

Finally, feminist theory embraces the use of research methodologies that are value committed. In other words, from a feminist perspective, research must acknowledge the values and biases that exist among researchers and all members of society. To this end, feminist theory suggests that researchers must acknowledge and attend to the social constructions that guide their work. It is impossible to study families or other social settings with the objectivity that is typically the claim of social scientists.

Further, unlike a family systems perspective, feminist theory suggests that families should not be studied as whole units. This focused attention at the family level results in those who lack power in families being overlooked or subjugated by the voices and perspectives of those who hold power. Rather, research should focus on the specific experience within families of each member of those families. Only through attention to the individual experience of all family members can we truly come to understand patterns of subjugation and oppression that exist in families.

A variety of theoretical perspectives have developed within the feminist theoretical tradition. These reflect different political orientations that exist within the feminist community. *Liberal feminism* focuses on equality of rights and strategies for challenging the various social factors that contribute to subjugation and oppression of women. *Radical feminism* is focused on obliterating patriarchy in families and other social institutions. This perspective argues that oppression of women is fundamental in a patriarchal society and reflects the absolute power and authority men hold over women in such a society. Radical feminism argues that families, as a primary social institution, contribute directly to oppression of women and, as such, should be abandoned. *Socialist feminism* argues that class and gender must be considered together in that both class oppression and gender oppression are strong social forces in our society. *Interpretive feminism* is focused on demystifying the "naturalness" of women's subordination, suggesting that there are male and female realities that do not arise out of biological differences between the sexes. Finally, *postmodern feminism* focuses on deconstructing those ideologies and practices that are oppressive. The focus here is on better understanding the nature of the oppressive forces themselves and the nature of their contribution to oppression and subjugation.

Building on these assumptions, feminist theory includes a number of key concepts. Sex and gender are at the heart of feminist perspectives. Sex is defined as the genetic status of being male or female while gender reflects the social meanings, expectations, and realities tied to one's sex. From a feminist perspective, sex is genetically determined while gender is learned. Part of learning gender is the process of categorization, or the process of applying labels and symbolic meanings to behaviors and roles associated with each sex. For example, a baby dressed in blue is typically assumed to be a boy whereas a baby dressed in pink is assumed to be a girl.

Feminist theory is concerned with patterns of stratification tied to gender characteristics. The issue here is the degree to which characteristics labeled as typically male come to be valued over characteristics labeled as typically female. Out of this stratification come patterns of privilege in which those who possess typically male-labeled characteristics come to hold more power and value in society. Because males typically hold more of the characteristics that have come to be valued in society, they assume positions of privilege in social institutions, leaving women oppressed and subjugated.

Feminist theory is concerned with social deconstructions or attempts to understand the processes through which society has come to assign both male and female characteristics and differential values to those characteristics. Out of these social deconstructions, substantial discourse on gender in society may develop. Only through truly open discourse can oppression and subjugation be addressed.

THE READINGS

Two articles are included here that provide perspectives on and are informed by feminist theory. In the first, Allen (2001) discusses family patterns from a variety of feminist theoretical perspectives. She attends, in particular, to a number of feminist ideas and concepts that have influenced the experiences of women in families. Consistent with a feminist approach, Allen then goes on to apply a number of these ideas to her own experience. This selection offers the reader an opportunity to consider concepts central to feminist thought as well as a comparison of various perspectives within feminist theory.

While Allen offers a thoughtful consideration of feminist theory as it relates to family patterns, Kaufman (2000) offers an example of research grounded in aspects of feminist theory. This research considers the influence of gender on patterns of family formation and dissolution. Kaufman specifically compares the influence of gender role attitudes among men who hold more egalitarian gender attitudes to women and men who hold more traditionally patriarchal gender role attitudes.

ISSUES FOR YOUR CONSIDERATION

1. Which feminist theoretical perspectives are reflected in each of these articles? How would you label the authors in terms of the various feminist perspectives?

2. To what degree do these authors argue for the subjugating influence of gender on women in families? What examples are provided of that influence?

3. To what degree does each author show a willingness to consider factors other than gender that might influence women's experiences in families?

4. To what degree does each of the authors acknowledge her own values and the roles they play in her work?

5. Are there inconsistencies between some of the assumptions of feminist theory and the concepts we conveyed in Chapter 1? What do you think Dr. S. Canon might say about these?

FURTHER READING

Andersen (1991), Baber and Allen (1992), Chodorow (1995), Litton Fox and Murray (2000), Nelson (1997), Stacey (1996).

Feminist Visions for Transforming Families: Desire and Equality Then and Now

Katherine R. Allen

Abstract

Using a social-historical perspective, the author provides a synthesis of key feminist ideas that have been influential in the lives of women and their families. The author addresses a variety of feminist theories and strategies for knowledge production. These ideas are illustrated with examples from her own life course as a way to demonstrate the transformative value of feminist insights for family studies.

Feminist visions for transforming families must be placed in social historical context, consciously referencing the past, grounded in the present, and envisioning the future. In this article, I address topics that often run counter to prevailing assumptions about family development and change. The method I use to construct my argument is to rely on my own structural and processual connections to the ideologies and activism I describe. I weave in stories from my private life to illustrate a key principle of feminism, that the personal is political. What occurs in private life is a reflection of power relations in society. The analytic strategy I employ in this article is to reveal the connection between the personal and political by using my own life as a bridge for the transfer of feminist insights into family studies. My aim is to invite others into the conscious, reflexive practice of applying feminist knowledge to one's own life and scholarship.

In reading these ideas, saturated with personal and political implications, I trust others will take the risk to incorporate their own resonances about private life and power relations. By inviting others into their own feminist journey from "silence to language to action" (Collins, 1990, p. 112), I show one way that we as a community of scholars can produce more realistic perspectives about the families we study (Allen, 2000).

Defining Feminism

Like building a sandcastle on the beach, my working definition of *feminism* reflects the historical moment in which it is posed. In sharing this definition, I am aware of the elements that attempt to knock down my metaphoric sandcastle-to whisk it away with the daily flow of the tides or to flagrantly step on it as a mischievous child might do when no one is looking. Whatever the tide or the children do not level, the cleaning machines that rumble down the beach after dark surely will. Like sand fashioned into temporary figures, feminism can never be encapsulated in a singular treatise, and neither can it remain static after being printed on the page. In proposing a working definition of *feminism,* I take the risk of representing and misrepresenting in unique ways the ideas that fascinate me.

With these caveats in mind, I work toward an understanding of feminism that holds such constraints lightly and still has the courage to be stated. It is dangerous to speak seriously as a feminist scholar in a field in which feminist ideas continue to be marginalized (Thompson & Walker, 1995). Human perceptions and relationships are so fragile and tentative that the opportunities for misunderstanding are vast. The potential for connecting around the politicized inquiry associated with feminist family scholarship requires an inclusive, open mind and a patient, loving heart (Allen, 2000). The rewards for looking at family life through a feminist lens include a deepening connection between how we live and what we study. Feminism is against the status quo. It is an activist endeavor with the goal of social change.

Feminism is a way of being in the world (ontology), a way of investigating and analyzing the world (methodology), and a theory or model of how we know what we know about the world (epistemology) (for variations on these analytic categories, see Cook & Fonow, 1986; Harding, 1987; Hawkesworth, 1989; Riger, 1998). Feminism is not just an idea or a theory; it is also a praxis, the term that Marx used to "distinguish between what one does and what one thinks and to distinguish revolutionary practice from other types of activity" (Nielsen, 1990, p. 34). Praxis is "that continuous reflexive integration of thought, desire, and action" (Simon, 1992, p. 49). Nielsen (1990) further explained that praxis, originating with critical theory, is the active, reflective process that allows us to demystify and expose the real nature of the power relations that drive human interactions and transactions and motivate the desire for social change. Feminist praxis is a conscious, inclusive, and impassioned way of thinking about and operating in the world (Allen, 2000).

Feminism is a liberationist project emerging most recently from the civil rights movement for American Blacks in the 1950s and 1960s and spawning the gay liberation movement in the 1970s. The women's liberation movement, or second-wave feminism, was ignited in the mid-1960s as more and more women started to speak about what they were enduring under capitalist patriarchy, topics that until the publication of Friedan's (1963) *The Feminine Mystique* were still taboo to either name or discuss (Brownmiller, 1999). The grassroots attempt to emancipate women from oppression, starting in consciousness-raising (CR) groups, grew into a multitude of liberationist efforts (Christensen, 1997). In its current manifestations, feminism is joined with other ideologies and practices embraced by those on the margins to seek justice for all people exploited by global patriarchal capitalism (see Agger, 1998; Alexander & Mohanty, 1997; Ebert, 1996; White, 1991). Combining theory and praxis, then, feminism is a conscious action with the goal of unsettling the normativity (e.g., status quo) that gives unearned privileges to an elite few and exploits the labor, life, and desire of multiple others (Collins, 1990; Lorde, 1984; McIntosh, 1995). This exploitation occurs in systematic ways through the structural and ideological mechanisms of racism, sexism, heterosexism, classism, ethnocentrism, ageism, ablebodyism, and colonialism.

Feminism shares with other critical theories and practices a challenge to the oppressive conditions that contribute to the individual's alienation from self, other, and society by unfairly harming some and irrationally privileging others (Agger, 1998). There are countless varieties of feminism and, as in any liberationist movement, many internal and external debates. For example, Brownmiller (1999) chronicled the birth, growth, and transformation of the women's movement, addressing key feminist issues for the 30 years following 1968, including abortion, rape, heterosexuality and lesbianism, racial injustice, sexual harassment, and pornography. Also, in a recent exchange in the premier journal for feminist scholarship, *Signs: Journal of Women in Culture and Society,* Walby (2001a, 2001b), Harding (2001), and Sprague (2001) debated current ideas about the role of science in feminist scholarship. Each day, each conversation, each published work brings a new way to pose a feminist perspective of knowing, being, and acting in the world.

There are many feminist theories (for various accounts, see Ebert, 1996; Herrmann & Stewart,

1994; Jaggar & Rothenberg, 1984; Rosser, 1992; Spender, 1983), including some of the following. Feminism has a liberal slant, wanting to secure equal rights and help women get their fair share of the economic and legal pie. Feminism has a radical slant, characterized by the admonition to "get your laws and your hands off my body." Feminism has a lesbian slant, in which women choose a woman-centered private life in congruence with their politics as well as their desire (Rich, 1980). Feminism has a cultural slant of valorizing and celebrating women's unique and, to some, superior ways of being in the world, as in "men have had the power for so long, and look at what a mess they've made of things." Feminism has a multicultural slant, decentering what Morrison (1992) called *white things* as the unquestioned authority on agency and free space for all people, including people of color. Feminism has a critical slant, aimed at redistributing the means and ends of production so that "the hand that picks the grapes also gets to drink the wine."

Locating Myself in Feminism

The feminisms from which I draw traverse all of these categories. As an educated, middle-class, White woman who came of age and into a radical consciousness in the second wave of feminist activity in the United States, I have certain unearned privileges that to an extent tolerate and even indulge my challenge of male dominance. When I am seeking equity in work, pay, and legal rights, I am aligned with liberal feminism (Rosser, 1992). When I came to realize that the feelings I had for another woman were passionate love—what women in the 19th century called "the love that dared not speak its name" (Faderman, 1991)—I claimed a lesbian life, aligning myself with lesbian feminism. The merger of lesbianism and feminism is a cohort phenomenon initiated by women who came of age in the late 1960s and early 1970s (Faderman, 1991). I am a lesbian feminist, then, in the sense that I found in feminism congruence between my lived reality of desiring an end to embodied

oppression and my liberationist epistemology. I abandoned heterosexual privilege and let my career slow down to pursue this love that would change my standpoint or the way I looked at the world. When I am critical of feminist ideologies and practices in and of themselves or questioning of my own lesbian standpoint, I am a postmodern feminist (Elam & Wiegman, 1995; Gagnier, 1990).

I am also a critical antiracist White feminist (Frankenberg, 1993), which brings me to the work that ignites my passion now, interrogating my own race and class privilege, opening myself to a feminist politics in which I seek to understand how my identity as a middle-class White woman is complicit in the oppression of others (Allen, 2000). Antiracist feminism, with ties to radical-critical theory (Osmond, 1987), gives me the tools to deconstruct the ways that I am marked by the privilege and power of White patriarchal wealth (Alexander & Mohanty, 1997; Collins, 1990; Ellsworth, 1997; McIntosh, 1995). My praxis is to uncover how I manipulate and employ privilege for my own gain so that I can consciously oppose any participation in racist, classist, or sexist action. I wish to use my knowledge of how unearned privilege wounds those without it to challenge and redirect my impulse to reach for the choicest piece of pie.

Looking through the lens of diverse feminist perspectives on methodology (Harding, 1998), when conducting research in family gerontology, I am a feminist empiricist (Allen, Blieszner, Roberto, Farnsworth, & Wilcox, 1999). When combining my identity politics as an antiracist lesbian feminist, I am drawing from feminist standpoint theory (e.g., Allen, 2000). When applying postmodern theory to feminist family science as a reconstructionist of women's experiences in families (Baber & Allen, 1992), I am a feminist postmodernist. Feminists both critique and may incorporate any or all of the following perspectives on science: empiricist, standpoint, and postmodern (Harding, 1987; Hawkesworth, 1989; Riger, 1998; Rosser, 1992).

Feminism is a worldview, but it is also a home base. Feminism is a way of living in which I can struggle free from the alienating bonds of patriarchal expectations for a truncated life and envision and then become an authentic self even as I know that authenticity can never be fully realized (Sawhney, 1995). Feminism gives me a position from which to tell the truth, particularly to myself, even if it means speaking bitterness from my raised consciousness. Feminism gives me the courage to love those I desire with passion and without shame. Feminism is the place where my deepest connections are found. With an active feminist awareness, I can name my fears about the future, face my demons from the past, handle the assaults of an unforgiving world, and find joy in living through the process of becoming as fully conscious as my mind, heart, spirit, and body allow (see Krieger, 1996, for an elegant evocation of such a synthesis). This process, of course, has been called many things, from *conscientization* (Freire, 1970/1997), to *enlightenment* (Wilber, 1998), and even *salvation* or *serenity*. Feminists did not make it up, but at the same time, feminist scholars and activists have generated innovative ways to pursue the conscious desire for truth, justice, equality, integrity, and freedom in terms of exploring sexism (Morgan, 1970), materialism (Ebert, 1996), and racism (Christensen, 1997; Collins, 1990), among other manifestations of oppression. With this as background, I now illustrate feminist desire and equality in the past and present, constructing a sense of feminist history and its influence on family change.

Love As Equals in the 19th Century

Consider the following passage describing "the beautiful friendship of two ladies" and the time frame in which it was written:

> In their youthful days, they took each other as companions for life, and this union, no less sacred to them than the tie of marriage, has subsisted, in uninterrupted harmony, for 40 years, during which they have shared each other's occupations and pleasures and works of charity while in health, and watched over each other tenderly in sickness. . . . They slept on the same pillow and had a common purse, and adopted each other's relations, and . . . I would tell you of their dwelling, encircled with roses . . . and I would speak of the friendly attentions which their neighbors, people of kind hearts and simple manners, seem to take pleasure in bestowing upon them. (Faderman, 1991, p. 1)

This passage was published in an American newspaper in 1843 by William Cullen Bryant, describing a trip to Vermont, where he met these unmarried women (e.g., "maiden ladies") who lived together. In the 19th century, female same-sex love, or *romantic friendship,* was a respected social institution in America. At the height of the Industrial Revolution, the worlds of White middle-class men and women were highly segregated. It was during this time that contemporary gender roles took root. Men worked outside the home in the business world, and women of means withdrew from the world of commerce to the female world of love and ritual (Smith-Rosenberg, 1975).

Gender-segregated marriage was a radical departure from the corporate family unit common in Colonial America over the previous two centuries, where the homestead was the center of life and survival (Hareven, 1991). In the 19th century, women were not yet full citizens. The U.S. Constitution enfranchised only one third of the population: White, landowning men. Women, native people, and people of color were excluded. Black males, in principle, gained the right to vote with the passage of the 15th Amendment in 1870, but in practice, the Black Codes and Jim Crow laws, particularly in the South, severely restricted full citizenship for those of African descent whose ancestors had been brought to this country by force (Bell, 1992; D'Emilio & Freedman, 1997). Women derived their rights through men; a woman had no sovereignty over her own body, children, or livelihood.

Perhaps because women were second-class citizens, their love for each other did not threaten the establishment. Women who loved other women were invisible (Faderman, 1981). There was no such thing as a lesbian until the late

19th century because women were not believed to be sexual. By the time the emerging discipline of modern sexology came into being, women who loved each other passionately were now considered deviant and labeled as *female sexual inverts* (D'Emilio & Freedman, 1997; Gagnon & Parker, 1995).

By the 20th century, women who realized they were lesbian had little chance to lead an authentic life (Faderman, 1991). They were forced to deny, repress, or hide their feelings because being out had serious consequences. Some women did sacrifice what little freedom they had throughout the past century. Despite being labeled as *other,* they carved out a life economically, socially, and sexually independent of men, creating a lesbian subculture, most notably among working-class butch or femme women, that never existed before love between women was defined as abnormal and unusual (Davis & Kennedy, 1986; Faderman, 1991). Their legacy for 21st-century women is that now some women find a lesbian identity viable, appropriate, and healthy (Baber & Allen, 1992). For some, it is a consciously chosen way of life.

In the 19th century, women of color experienced double and triple jeopardy in their struggle for full citizenship (Dill, 1988). The Chinese Exclusion Act of 1882 prohibited entry of Chinese women except as prostitutes or wives of merchants, teachers, and students. The bulk of Chinese immigrants were laborers, and their wives and daughters were not allowed to immigrate (Chow, 1998). By 1890, females comprised about 3% of the Chinese population in the United States. Most of these women had been sold to men in Hong Kong who later forced them into prostitution. Chinese women were not permitted to enter this country until 1943 when the Chinese Exclusion Act of 1882 was repealed (Chow, 1998). Consider, as well, the following quote from an older Black woman that reveals a profound understanding of female oppression in the context of race difference: "The black woman is the white man's mule and the white woman is his dog" (Collins, 1990, p. 106). One was forced to work much harder than the other, but both women were still the personal property of the master. Feminist historians have uncovered the reality of the constraints placed on women, retelling history from perspectives other than military and political events. They have uncovered ways that women of all backgrounds resisted and created their own lives in spite of the severe restrictions carved into law and everyday practice (Kerber & DeHart-Mathews, 1987).

Feminist Experiments for Radical Change in the 20th Century

After a 70-year struggle of organized activism on many fronts, women earned the right to vote in 1920 with the passage of the 19th Amendment. The next major historic milestone did not occur until half a century later when another significant female cultural revolution was ignited. Feminist essayist Robin Morgan, editor of the classic 1970 text *Sisterhood Is Powerful,* called the New Left and its student members "the little boys movement" because its leaders were White, middle-class young men who were challenging the hegemonic, militaristic, and capitalist values of their fathers. Yet few acknowledged their debts to the Black civil rights movement. Fewer recognized how they were repeating the very patriarchal privilege of the establishment males that they were rebelling against by using women only as sex partners and servants. Second-wave feminism arose out of women's dissatisfaction that they were often the invisible laborers in all the liberation movements in which they were involved. Male leaders and partners were not taking their quest for or right to emancipation seriously.

Women started rap groups, or CR groups, anywhere and everywhere—suburban kitchens, urban mental health centers, and church basements. I attended my first "speak out" in 1972 when I was a freshman at San Diego State University. I was alarmed by observing women who were speaking and acting with anger. I felt like I was witnessing something taboo, obscene, foreign, and wrong when I heard women speak their bitterness by naming and challenging the patriarchy that severely restricted their opportunities in life.

A year later, I transferred to the University of Connecticut and joined my first CR group. We were a collection of undergraduate and graduate students, faculty wives, women exploring their feelings for other women, and young mothers in turmoil over their seemingly isolated inability to be satisfied with the domestic monotony of their lives. I still have the mimeographed sheets of questions that were distributed in the CR group, which I reread periodically to remind myself that dialogue has always been a revolutionary self-help activity (Freire, 1970/1997). This early process of interrogating the social construction of gender steered me toward the qualitative methodologies I employ as a social scientist today.

We explored messages and expectations from childhood, puberty, and young adulthood. We addressed sex roles and perceptions of masculinity/femininity. We discussed what virginity meant to us and whether any of us still had it. We spent a lot of time discussing our bodies and self-image. We talked about sex, men, and men's bodies—our desire for them but our disappointment that men did not respond to us in the physical and emotional ways we wanted. We called ourselves *emotional lesbians* and wore buttons announcing "Together Women Together." Acknowledging that we felt more comfortable in female space but being too afraid to cross some imaginary line into an authentically embodied space, most of us were unable to transcend the rigid boundaries that heterosexism enforced on all of us from birth. We fought and challenged each other. It was in that context that I began to consciously practice the self-interrogation and rhetorical skills that I incorporate into my scholarship and teaching today.

As embarrassing as it is to tell, I take the risk to share the following story because only in our most vulnerable disclosures can we reveal the truth of how inauthenticity is internalized. Krieger (1991, 1996) explained that such theorized self-disclosure, in which one tells on oneself, is a particular window into the general phenomenon of structural oppression. One Tuesday night in 1975, I was in the midst of describing to my CR sisters how I no longer wanted to go out with a guy I was seeing because he was too nice. My friends pressed me for further information. Baffled by my own untheorized analysis of what was wrong with my partner, I mumbled something about his penis being too small. One of the older participants in the group—a woman in her late 40s who had raised five children and whose husband, a psychology professor, had a reputation for sleeping with students—challenged the absurdity of what I was saying: "What do you mean, 'too nice'?" "What do you mean, 'too small'?" She attacked these parroted gendered messages that I had internalized—messages that I needed a real man who was rough around the edges and well endowed underneath his clothes—to make me a woman. I broke into tears, I felt hatred for her, I shot back with something like, "You are a pathetic wife who puts up with your husband's infidelity in the name of love," but the truth is, she got to me. She broke through my denial, the distorted sexual script that had been spoon-fed to me by my sexist culture. She held up a mirror so that I could confront the convoluted fundamentals of heterosexuality that were motivating my behavior and poisoning any potential partnership with a man.

That CR group endured for the 3 years I spent as an undergraduate at Connecticut. In all its messy confusion and gut-wrenching challenges, it got me through young adulthood and paved the way for deepening my feminist consciousness through reading political texts—a process that taught me how to theorize my experience. Faderman (1991) explained that out of this CR context, a new vision of equality emerged. In its purest form, it became the lesbian feminism of the 1970s and 1980s, before AIDS devastated the gay male community in the 1980s (Gagnon & Parker, 1995) and before the lesbian baby boom in the 1980s and 1990s (Patterson, 1994). Similar to the anomalous decade of the 1950s, with the majority of women staying at home, men in the workforce, and the baby boom in full force (Coontz, 1992), lesbian feminism as a political ideal is historically situated—a product of the late 20th-century liberation movements.

Lesbian feminism began with a radical separatist impulse. Women who loved women defined themselves in opposition to patriarchy and in opposition to the reformers in the National Organization for Women who wanted lesbians purged from the White middle-class women's movement (Brownmiller, 1999). But separatism is a project that is doomed to failure, at least on a large scale, as many of the alternative communities (e.g., Shakers, Oneidans, and Free Lovers) of the 1800s showed (D'Emilio & Freedman, 1997). Formed in reaction to male-dominated culture, separatism is fueled by negative energy to not do things, such as vote, interact with males, or support the patriarchy (Johnson, 1989). An us-versus-them mentality is responsible for the demise of many liberation movements and ideological feuds, such as the capitalists versus the communists, the men versus the women, the straight women versus the lesbians, the Blacks versus the Whites, the structural functionalists versus the symbolic interactionists, and the Hatfields versus the McCoys. These binary oppositions make neat boxes to dump our confusing thoughts into, but all they produce are scapegoats, heartache, and further oppression (Lorde, 1984). The challenge is to be for something without necessarily being against some arbitrary other.

Today, feminist desires for equality no longer freeze on gender as the only category. Black women, Latina women, Asian American women, working-class women, lesbians, old women, and men who love women, among others, have demonstrated that an analysis of gender alone is not sufficient to resist and transform oppressive social structures and processes. We must interrogate the intersections among gender, race, class, and sexual orientation by examining issues in all of their complexity. Bernice Johnson Reagon, a scholar, performer, and activist who organized the African American women's vocal ensemble *Sweet Honey in the Rock,* is unapologetic about the need for all of us, regardless of race, class, gender, ethnicity, or sexual orientation, to acknowledge our debt to the Blacks who started and sustained the civil rights movement and to

correct our reluctance to recognize more than one form of oppression as primary (Christensen, 1997). Reagon (1983) uses her standpoint as a Black woman from which to begin any project and as grounds for reforming and redefining political expression:

> Black folks started it, Black folks did it, so everything you've done politically rests on the efforts of my people—that's my arrogance! Yes, and it's the truth; it's my truth. You can take it or leave it, but that's the way I see it. So once we did what we did, then you've got women, you've got Chicanos, you've got the Native Americans, and you've got homosexuals, and you got all of these people who also got sick of somebody being on their neck. And maybe if they come together, they can do something about it. And I claim all of you as coming from something that made me who I am. You can't tell me that you ain't in the Civil Rights movement. You are in the Civil Rights movement that we created that just rolled up to your door. But it could not stay the same, because if it was gonna stay the same it wouldn't have done you no good. (p. 362)

Feminist Visions for Now and Into the Future

World Traveling

Feminist scholars have demonstrated how inaccurate it is to treat gender as a separate and singular analytic category (Christensen, 1997; Hawkesworth, 1997). Yet in the discipline of family studies, even talking about gender is a taboo subject in many quarters (see the critique by Thompson & Walker, 1995). The dominant discourse about gender roles is still protected and rarely questioned (for an elaboration of how privilege and oppression operate in the theory and science of family studies, see recent analyses by Allen, 2000; Marks, 2000; Walker, 2000). But there is a progressive energy in family studies to acknowledge how the world is changing. Underscoring this energy is the spiritual ability to hold oneself responsible as a positive force for change (Allen, 2000). I desire social justice not just for myself and those I love but for anyone who is at risk. As we enter the 21st century, feminist theory is incorporating a renewed critique of the "exploitive relations of production and the unequal divisions of labor, property, power, and privilege these produce" (Ebert, 1996, p. xi) into the current postmodern trend in which a "localist genre of descriptive and immanent writing" (Ebert, 1996, p. xii) prevails. Both social critique and cultural analysis are needed to enable a transformative feminism "of transnational equality for all people of the world" (Ebert, 1996, p. xiii).

Feminist practice in family studies is active and ongoing, but still much more work needs to be done. We cannot just talk about how oppression has affected and made us into the women and men we are today. Feminist praxis is revolutionary. Thompson and Walker (1995) concluded that feminism has had a far greater effect on family pedagogy than on family research. Indeed, activist feminist teaching continues to inspire the discipline (for recent examples, see Allen, Floyd-Thomas, & Gillman, 2001; Baber & Murray, 2001; Fletcher & Russell, 2001). We can make greater progress in terms of how we envision and study families by incorporating feminist lessons into our work. Lugones (1990) proposed the metaphor of world traveling to apply the principle of the personal is political to our practice in coming to value and respect the humanity of others. She described how we can bridge the span between our own experiences and those of others, thereby challenging traditional assumptions about individuals, families, and societies:

> There are worlds we enter at our own risk, worlds that have agon, conquest, and arrogance as the main ingredients in their ethos. These are worlds that we enter out of necessity and which would be foolish to enter playfully. But there are worlds that we can travel to lovingly and traveling to them is part of loving at least some of their inhabitants. The reason why I think that traveling to someone's world is a way of identifying with them is because by traveling to their world we can understand what it is to be them and what it is to be ourselves in their eyes. Only when we have traveled to each other's worlds are we fully subjects to each other. (p. 401)

Building on Lugones's (1990) suggestion, we can adopt an attitude of careful curiosity toward the experiences of others (Thompson, 1995). What does it mean to travel to someone else's world? What can we gain by becoming "fully subjects to each other"? I offer a glimpse of this process in a story from my own life. I hope, like Hansel and Gretel in one of Grimm's fairy tales (Lang, 1969), that by leaving these stones, others can retrace their steps out of the forest of denial and into a place of renewed commitment to uncovering the realities of family life from the perspectives of those who live it.

Traveling to My Son's World

My son, at 14, has just experienced his mother's second divorce. The first one occurred when his father and I parted company after a long and difficult decision-making process, concluding that our marriage was never going to work out as planned. Matt was 2 at the time, and although I retained physical custody, his father has remained an active part of his life. After this divorce, I entered a lesbian partnership with another woman, who assumed most of the primary caregiving for our chosen family. Eventually, we had a second child (born to her), whose father was my brother's life partner. Our family seemed complete, and we proudly professed to the world how well our chosen family was working. Open in our community, we enjoyed the lesbian poster-family status we achieved, feeling protected and secure in how we presented ourselves to the world.

Then, the unfathomable happened, at least from my perspective. My former partner and I had just gotten a civil union in the state of Vermont, the first state in the United States to offer marriage-like benefits to gay and lesbian partners. We had also completed the legal work to add her last name onto Matt's name and to give me joint custody of our second child. It seemed that after 12 years in a committed partnership, we now had as many legal safeguards in place as possible. Yet soon after the civil union in Vermont, my partner found herself falling in love with another woman in our community, a divorced, heterosexual mother of two whose children also attended our children's school. In a matter of weeks, my partner confessed her newfound love and left our home and family to be with this woman and her children. She took our second child with her, leaving Matt and me behind.

Like most people who are left in marriage or other domestic partnerships, I experienced the abrupt ending of this relationship as a painful surprise (Chodron, 1997; Fisher & Alberti, 2000; Kingma, 2000; Murray, 1994). After all, we had just repeated our vows to love and care for each other for the rest of our lives. I was not prepared for her seemingly sudden change of heart, but after several months of denial, I had to admit to myself that she was gone. Almost overnight, the old definition of our family as headed by two lesbian mothers raising two young sons with several fathers in the picture was also over. I have had to play catch-up to my former partner in terms of coming to terms with the fact that the family I had staked my identity on no longer existed. What's worse, we were unable to negotiate a new family relationship. The odd branches we had sprouted on the family tree (Stacey, 2000), of which I had once been so proud, had been chopped off, and my ex-partner no longer resembled the person I once cherished.

As self-absorption with my own pain subsided, I started to notice my son's reactions to this ordeal. He seemed happier now that it was only the two of us. I was unprepared for his point of view on the family breakup: Now he finally had me, his mom, all to himself. He said that although he felt abandoned by my ex-partner, our home was much more relaxed without her rules and without having to share me with his sibling.

It has taken me a while to face up to the fact that my son's definition of our family was not the same as mine. My writings about chosen family ties and the careful construction of a lesbian family disintegrated under his scrutiny. As I experienced this unitarily constructed definition of my family crumble, like those grains of sand in my metaphoric sandcastle, I learned some painful lessons that are already in the family studies literature but were not yet real to me. I had not yet lived through the crucible in which I felt the heat of their truth. My son was a major teacher of these lessons.

He was taking the breakup of my partnership and our chosen family in stride. He was sorry that I was so sad to be left by someone I trusted and loved, but from his point of view, life was far easier with only one doting parent in his home. Having had two mothers was fine, he said, when he was little, but now that he was about to enter high school, he asked me, with a slight smile, if I would start dating guys until he graduated. The things that mattered to him were not really what I thought would matter. He wanted to be reassured that his standard of living would not decrease, that I would get the emotional support I needed from friends and therapy to still be a strong person, that I would have more time to spend with him in the ways he wanted me available (e.g., at home but not scrutinizing his activities too closely), and that I would continue to have my own life and not meddle in his. I thought he would be devastated by the loss of his other mother and his sibling, but to the contrary, he expressed relief.

In these conversations with and observations of my son, I saw that the person I was raising was thinking very differently than I. I saw that one loving and relatively well-functioning parent was enough for him to feel safe and secure. I witnessed something I had given lip service for years—that children need somebody to be intensely connected to them (Bronfenbrenner & Weiss, 1983). I saw that I needed to be as strong and healthy as I could and not give into my grief over being left because my primary responsibility was to raise this boy to adulthood. I saw that grief takes the course that all the self-help books say it does: at least 1 year to recover from the catastrophic exit of a life partner. I saw that despite the two divorces to which I had subjected my son, he was wise beyond his years and more loving toward me than I thought I deserved. Contrary to being the failure I felt I was in my own eyes, I was a capable and successful adult in his. He wanted me to know that nothing could take away his love for me, and I did not need a second adult in the home to cushion his transition to adulthood.

This experience has taught me the importance of social support, adequate economic resources, sobriety in thought and deed, and a deepening appreciation for a spiritual power beyond my own control. At midlife, I learned that although life can deal some devastating blows, it is possible to renew and rebuild. I could not have gained this perspective without traveling to my son's world or without the incredible support I received from friends in my private life and teachers in the books I read. A feminist vision for transforming families is one in which clear-sighted honesty for what is really going on takes precedence over the myths we tell ourselves of how things should function (Ruddick, 1989).

Traveling to Others' Worlds

In this article, I have activated my own experience to illustrate how feminist ideas can inform family scholarship because I am committed to the revolutionary project of social change. I want to see families taken seriously at all levels. To do that, we need clear-sighted vision, not cockeyed optimism or gloomy denial found in traditional family social science. Real life is the greatest teacher, and it is not surprising that some of the most profound and lasting insights have come from lived experience, as evident in the process by which Piaget's observations of his three children metamorphosed into an intellectual industry in the behavioral and social sciences.

To initiate one's own journey for a deeper consciousness about the families we study, I offer the following reflective inventory of questions. These questions are guides for making the personal-to-political connection, thereby facilitating the journey of discovering how what goes on in private life reflects what goes on in the world.

1. What is it about my personal experience that is unresolved? What do I not yet understand about myself? In what areas of my experience do I feel negative emotions (e.g., shame, doubt, guilt, and remorse)? In what areas of my experience do I feel positive emotions (peace, acceptance, joy, and happiness)? How are these emotions connected to my thoughts about families?

2. What are my motivations for doing this work? Who am I trying to impress? What would I rather be doing than working on this project? What do I hope to contribute to my own life and to family scholarship by pursuing this work?

3. What is my responsibility to the people whose lives I am studying? What do I owe them for giving me the opportunity to get inside their lives? What do I want to give back? What do I now understand about human existence (my own included) as a result of conducting this work? How can this work benefit the well-being of others?

By answering these questions, it will become clear that the process of reflecting on one's life and writing down the responses without self-censorship can be the kind of liberatory experience feminism promises. By freeing the writer within (Goldberg, 1986), we can replace our distanced stance from the subjects of our study with a critical eye toward the private-public connection. Taking these steps brings us closer to the revolutionary feminist praxis I have described in this article. In these ways, we can travel from silence to language to action (Collins, 1990), learning to theorize private experience in the service of creating a more just world.

References

Agger, B. (1998). *Critical social theories.* Boulder, CO: Westview.

Alexander, M. J., & Mohanty, C. T. (1997). Introduction: Genealogies, legacies, movements. In M. J. Alexander & C. T. Mohanty (Eds.), *Feminist genealogies, colonial legacies, democratic futures* (pp. xii–xiii). New York: Routledge.

Allen, K. R. (2000). A conscious and inclusive family studies. *Journal of Marriage and the Family, 62,* 4–17.

Allen, K. R., Blieszner, R., Roberto, K. A., Farnsworth, E. B., & Wilcox, K. L. (1999). Older adults and their children: Family patterns of structural diversity. *Family Relations, 48,* 151–157.

Allen, K. R., Floyd-Thomas, S. M., & Gillman, L. (2001). Teaching to transform: From volatility to solidarity in an interdisciplinary family studies classroom. *Family Relations, 50,* 317–325.

Baber, K. M., & Allen, K. R. (1992). *Women and families: Feminist reconstructions.* New York: Guilford.

Baber, K. M., & Murray, C. I. (2001). A postmodern feminist approach to teaching human sexuality. *Family Relations, 50,* 23–33.

Bell, D. (1992). *Faces at the bottom of the well: The permanence of racism.* New York: Basic Books.

Bronfenbrenner, U., & Weiss, H. B. (1983). Beyond policies without people: An ecological perspective on child and family policy. In E. E. Zigler, S. L. Kagan, & E. Klugman (Eds.), *Children, families and government: Perspectives on American social policy* (pp. 393–414). Cambridge, UK: Cambridge University Press.

Brownmiller, S. (1999). *In our time: Memoir of a revolution.* New York: Delta.

Chodron, P. (1997). *When things fall apart: Heart advice for difficult times.* Boston: Shambhala.

Chow, E. N-L. (1998). Family, economy, and the state: A legacy of struggle for Chinese American women. In S. J. Ferguson (Ed.), *Shifting the center. Understanding contemporary families* (pp. 93–114). Mountain View, CA: Mayfield.

Christensen, K. (1997). "With whom do you believe your lot is cast?" White feminists and racism. *Signs: Journal of Women in Culture and Society, 22,* 617–648.

Collins, P. H. (1990). *Black feminist thought: Knowledge, consciousness, and the politics of empowerment.* Winchester, MA: Unwin Hyman.

Cook, J. A., & Fonow, M. M. (1986). Knowledge and women's interests: Issues of epistemology and methodology in feminist sociological research. *Sociological Inquiry, 56,* 2–29.

Coontz, S. (1992). *The way we never were: American families and the nostalgia trap.* New York: Basic Books.

Davis, M., & Kennedy, E. L. (1986). Oral history and the study of sexuality in the lesbian community: Buffalo, New York, 1940–1960. *Feminist Studies, 12,* 7–26.

D'Emilio, J., & Freedman. E. B. (1997). *Intimate matters: A history of sexuality in America* (2nd ed.). Chicago: University of Chicago Press.

Dill, B. T. (1988). Our mothers' grief. Racial ethnic women and the maintenance of families. *Journal of Family History, 13,* 415–431.

Ebert, T. L. (1996). *Ludic feminism and after: Postmodernism, desire, and labor in late capitalism.* Ann Arbor: University of Michigan Press.

Elam, D., & Wiegman, R. (Eds.). (1995). *Feminism beside itself.* New York: Routledge.

Ellsworth, E. (1997). Double binds of whiteness. In M. Fine, L. Weis, L. C. Powell, & L. M. Wong (Eds.), *Off white: Readings on race, power and society* (pp. 259–269). New York: Routledge.

Faderman, L. (1981). *Surpassing the love of men: Romantic friendship and love between women from the Renaissance to the present.* New York: William Morrow.

Faderman, L. (1991). *Odd girls and twilight lovers: A history of lesbian life in twentieth century America.* New York: Penguin.

Fisher, B., & Alberti, R. (2000). *Rebuilding when your relationship ends* (3rd ed.). Atascadero, CA: Impact.

Fletcher, A. C., & Russell, S. T. (2001). Incorporating issues of sexual orientation in the classroom: Challenges and solutions. *Family Relations, 50,* 34–40.

Frankenberg, R. (1993). *White women, race matters: The social construction of whiteness.* Minneapolis: University of Minnesota Press.

Freire, P. (1997). *Pedagogy of the oppressed* (M. B. Ramos, Trans., New rev. ed.). New York: Continuum. (Original work published 1970)

Friedan, B. (1963). *The feminine mystique.* New York: Norton.

Gagnier, R. (1990). Feminist postmodernism: The end of feminism or the end of theory? In D. L. Rhode (Ed.), *Theoretical perspectives on sexual difference* (pp. 21–30). New Haven, CT: Yale University Press.

Gagnon, J. H., & Parker, R. G. (1995). Conceiving sexuality. In R. G. Parker & J. H. Gagnon (Eds.), *Conceiving sexuality: Approaches to sex research in a postmodern world* (pp. 3–16). New York: Routledge.

Goldberg, N. (1986). *Writing down the bones: Freeing the writer within.* Boston: Shambhala.

Harding, S. (1987). Introduction: Is there a feminist method? In S. Harding (Ed.), *Feminism and methodology* (pp. 1–14). Bloomington: Indiana University Press.

Harding, S. (1998). Subjectivity, experience, and knowledge: An epistemology from/for rainbow coalition politics. In M. F. Rogers (Ed.), *Contemporary feminist theory* (pp. 97–108). New York: McGraw-Hill.

Harding, S. (2001). Comment on Walby's "Against epistemological chasms: The science question in feminism revisited": Can democratic values and interests ever play a rationally justifiable role in the evaluation of scientific work? *Signs: Journal of Women in Culture and Society, 26,* 511–525.

Hareven, T. K. (1991). The history of the family and the complexity of social change. *American Historical Review, 96,* 95–124.

Hawkesworth, M. (1997). Confounding gender. *Signs: Journal of Women in Culture and Society, 22,* 649–695.

Hawkesworth, M. E. (1989). Knowers, knowing, known: Feminist theory and claims of truth. *Signs: Journal of Women in Culture and Society, 14,* 533–557.

Herrmann, A. C., & Stewart, A. J. (Eds.). (1994). *Theorizing feminism: Parallel trends in the humanities and social sciences.* Boulder, CO: Westview.

Jaggar, A. M., & Rothenberg, P. S. (1984). *Feminist frameworks: Alternative theoretical accounts of the relations between women and men* (2nd ed.). New York: McGraw-Hill.

Johnson, S. (1989). *Wildfire: Igniting the she/volution.* Albuquerque, NM: Wildfire.

Kerber, L. K., & DeHart-Mathews, J. (Eds.). (1987). *Women's America: Refocusing the past* (2nd ed.). New York: Oxford University Press.

Kingma, D. R. (2000). *Coming apart: Why relationships end and how to live through the ending of yours.* Berkeley, CA: Conari Press.

Krieger, S. (1991). *Social science and the self: Personal essays on an art form.* New Brunswick, NJ: Rutgers University Press.

Krieger, S. (1996). *The family silver. Essays on relationships among women.* Berkeley: University of California Press.

Lang, A. (Ed.). (1969). *The blue fairy book.* New York: Airmont.

Lorde, A. (1984). *Sister outsider. Essays and speeches.* Freedom, CA: Crossing Press.

Lugones, M. (1990). Playfulness, "world"-traveling, and loving perception. In G. Anzaldua (Ed.), *Making face, making soul: Haciendo caras: Creative and critical perspectives by feminists of color* (pp. 390–402). San Francisco: Aunt Lute Books.

Marks, S. R. (2000). Teasing out the lessons of the 1960s: Family diversity and family privilege. *Journal of Marriage and the Family, 62,* 609–622.

McIntosh, P. (1995). White privilege and male privilege: A personal account of coming to see correspondences through work in women's studies. In M. L. Andersen & P. H. Collins (Eds.), *Race, class, and gender: An anthology* (2nd ed., pp. 76–87). Belmont, CA: Wadsworth.

Morgan, R. (Ed.). (1970). *Sisterhood is powerful.* New York: Random House.

Morrison, T. (1992). *Playing in the dark: Whiteness and the literary imagination.* New York: Vintage.

Murray, N. P. (1994). *Living beyond your losses: The healing journey through grief.* Ridgefield, CT: Morehouse.

Nielsen, J. M. (1990). Introduction. In J. M. Nielsen (Ed.), *Feminist research methods* (pp. 1–37). Boulder, CO: Westview.

Osmond, M. W. (1987). Radical-critical theories. In M. B. Sussman & S. K. Steinmetz (Eds.), *Handbook of marriage and the family* (pp. 103–124). New York: Plenum.

Patterson, C. J. (1994). Children of the lesbian baby boom: Behavioral adjustment, self-concepts, and sex-role identity. In B. Greene & G. Herek (Eds.), *Contemporary perspectives on lesbian and gay psychology: Theory, research and application* (pp. 156–175). Thousand Oaks, CA: Sage.

Reagon, B. J. (1983). Coalition politics: Turning the century. In B. Smith (Ed.), *Home girls: A Black feminist anthology* (pp. 356–368). New York: Kitchen Table Press.

Rich, A. (1980). Compulsory heterosexuality and lesbian existence. *Signs: Journal of Women in Culture and Society, 5,* 631–660.

Riger, S. (1998). Epistemological debates, feminist voices: Science, social values, and the study of women. In D. L. Anselmi & A. L. Law (Eds.), *Questions of gender: Perspectives and paradoxes* (pp. 61–75). New York: McGraw-Hill.

Rosser, S. V. (1992). Are there feminist methodologies appropriate for the natural sciences and do they make a difference? *Women's Studies International Forum, 15,* 535–550.

Ruddick, S. (1989). *Maternal thinking: Toward a politics of peace.* Boston: Beacon.

Sawhney, S. (1995). Authenticity is such a drag! In D. Elam & R. Wiegman (Eds.), *Feminism beside itself* (pp. 197–215). New York: Routledge.

Simon, R. I. (1992). *Teaching against the grain: Texts for a pedagogy of possibility.* New York: Bergin & Garvey.

Smith-Rosenberg, C. (1975). The female world of love and ritual. *Signs: Journal of Women in Culture and Society, 1,* 1–29.

Spender, D. (Ed.). (1983). *Feminist theories: Three centuries of key women thinkers.* New York: Pantheon.

Sprague, J. (2001). Comment on Walby's "Against epistemological chasms: The science question in feminism revisited": Structured knowledge and strategic methodology. *Signs: Journal of Women in Culture and Society, 26,* 527–536.

Stacey, J. (2000). The handbook's tail: Toward revels or a requiem for family diversity. In D. H. Demo, K. R. Allen, & M. A. Fine (Eds.), *Handbook of family diversity* (pp. 424–439). New York: Oxford University Press.

Thompson, L. (1995). Teaching about ethnic minority families using a pedagogy of care. *Family Relations, 44,* 129–135.

Thompson, L., & Walker, A. J. (1995). The place of feminism in family studies. *Journal of Marriage and the Family, 57,* 847–865.

Walby, S. (2001a). Against epistemological chasms: The science question in feminism revisited. *Signs: Journal of Women in Culture and Society, 26,* 485–509.

Walby, S. (2001b). Reply to Harding and Sprague. *Signs: Journal of Women in Culture and Society, 26,* 537–540.

Walker, A. J. (2000). Refracted knowledge: Viewing families through the prism of social science. *Journal of Marriage and the Family, 62,* 595–608.

White, S. (1991). *Political theory and postmodernism.* Cambridge, UK: Cambridge University Press.

Wilber, K. (1998). *The marriage of sense and soul: Integrating science and religion.* New York: Broadway.

Do Gender Role Attitudes Matter? Family Formation and Dissolution Among Traditional and Egalitarian Men and Women

Gayle Kaufman

Abstract

The effect of gender role attitudes on family formation and dissolution is analyzed using data from the 1987/1988 and 1992/1994 waves of the National Survey of Families and Households. Results indicate that egalitarian women are less likely to intend to have a child and actually to have a child than traditional women. Unlike women, egalitarian men are more likely to intend to have a child and less likely to divorce than traditional men. Single men with egalitarian attitudes are more likely to cohabit than their traditional counterparts. The gap between traditional women and traditional men in divorce, fertility intentions, and fertility outcomes is significant.

This study focuses on the effect of gender role attitudes on family formation and dissolution, including those relevant to home and work roles. We use longitudinal data from the National Survey of Families and Households to examine the effect of attitudes measured at one point on changes in union status and parenthood in the following 5 years. We work from a theoretical perspective that takes into account the various roles men and women play within families and how these roles make marriage and childbearing more or less attractive to each. Fenstermaker, West, and Zimmerman (1991) argue

that men and women "do gender" daily through their productive activities. However, different situations produce variations in normative gender behavior; Shelton and John (1993) argue that this variation is because of the production of "particular gendered roles." Specifically, they suggest that wives and husbands share more gendered roles than unwed couples. In this study, the question is whether those who emphasize more gendered roles respond differently from those who emphasize them less to the opportunity to produce or reproduce gender through marriage and childbearing. Do those who prefer less gendered roles opt out of marriage and family, instead choosing to cohabit? Does the situation vary for men and women? We compare the family formation and dissolution behavior of traditional and egalitarian men and women, examining women and men separately to see how the effects of attitudes are mediated by gender.

Recent decades have seen marked changes in gender role attitudes (Davis, 1984; Thornton, Alwin, & Camburn, 1983). Men and women are increasingly apt to approve of wives and mothers working and to think that men should help with housework (Thornton, 1989). Changes in beliefs about appropriate behavior for women and men at work and home are bound to affect family dynamics. Attitudes matter because they signify the internalization of role responsibility, which goes beyond acting out a role (Perry-Jenkins & Crouter, 1990).

Previous research suggests that, at least for wives, traditional views are more conducive to a stable marriage and family life. Yet, complementary roles in marriage continue to decline as parallel roles emerge (Ross, Mirowsky, & Huber, 1983). This may bode ill for the family (Popenoe, 1993), as nontraditional women do not need marriage and family for success or rewards (Ross & Sawhill, 1975). The feminist movement encouraged women's liberation from restrictive roles by rejecting motherhood's centrality (Hewlett, 1986; Nock, 1987). However, these changes may benefit the family because egalitarian roles and perceptions of a fair division of household labor are important for marital happiness (Gerson, 1993; Hochschild, 1989; Suitor, 1991). Egalitarian husbands do more housework (Ferree, 1991), support their wives more (Vannoy-Hiller & Philliber, 1989), practice more equitable decision making (Scanzoni & Szinovacz, 1980), and are more involved with their children (Gerson, 1993). Blaisure and Allen (1995) argue that improving marriage for women requires men to believe in equality, as well as to actively support and practice equality.

Disentangling the effects of attitudes on behavior is important because behavior may also influence attitudes. For instance, divorced women have more nontraditional attitudes than married women (Finley, Starnes, & Alvarez, 1985), but these attitudes may have become less traditional following divorce (Ambert, 1985). Likewise, Morgan and Waite (1987) find that parenthood can change one's attitudes. Therefore, longitudinal data are necessary to determine how much attitudes matter. In addition, family formation behavior may be affected in significantly different ways by men and women's gender role attitudes, so we need to test the effects of gender role attitudes separately for each group.

Understanding Gender Roles and Family Processes

Few studies address whether gender role attitudes affect union formation, yet because marriage is a traditional institution, one might expect gender role attitudes to influence the probability of marrying. Becker (1991) suggests that traditional roles encourage marriage. He argues that spouses who trade services by implementing a traditional division of labor benefit most from marriage. On the other hand, men and women who are oriented toward a less specialized division of labor or one in which gender roles are reversed benefit less from marriage. These women and men also find it more difficult to find a compatible partner, and so most either do not wed or they marry and divorce. Indeed, Goldscheider and Goldscheider (1992) find young egalitarian women less likely to leave home to marry than traditional women. However, the limited evidence about men suggests that egalitarian men are more likely to expect to wed and to leave home to marry than traditional ones (Affleck, Morgan, & Hayes, 1989; Goldscheider & Goldscheider, 1992). Goldscheider and Goldscheider (1992) suggest that egalitarian responses to questions about the household division of labor may mean something qualitatively different for young men and women. Whereas egalitarian women might see their responses as indicating a desire to reduce their responsibility for home and family tasks, egalitarian men appear willing to share in activities centered on children and family—thus, egalitarian attitudes can be seen as pro-family views for them. Unlike marriage, cohabitation is not considered a traditional institution but a more contemporary living arrangement, so we might not expect those with traditional attitudes to cohabit. One study finds egalitarian men and women more likely to enter a cohabiting union than traditional men and women (Clarkberg, Stolzenberg, & Waite, 1995).

Do gender role attitudes affect union dissolution for those in unions? Becker argues that specialization, or trading of services, within marriage is necessary for marital stability. A traditional gender-based division of labor contributes to marital stability because each partner contributes something to the marriage that the other spouse relies on (Becker, 1991). Changing the traditional balance of activities may thus disturb spouses' mutual dependence on one another and their need to exchange services within marriage. Lueptow, Guss, and Hyden (1989), for example, find that women with traditional views are less apt to divorce or separate, whereas nontraditional attitudes may create stress in a marriage (Finley et al., 1985), pushing egalitarian women to consider or anticipate divorce (Huber & Spitze, 1980; Lye & Biblarz, 1993).

But Oppenheimer (1994; Oppenheimer & Lew, 1995) argues that specialization in marriage may actually be a disadvantage as it puts family welfare at risk and places burdens to provide on the husband. Instead, a more collaborative marriage with similar roles and activities may better sustain companionate marriages. Under these conditions, the greater flexibility of egalitarian couples may ease adjustments to disruptions affecting the family. Although studies of wives often find a negative relationship between egalitarian gender role views and marital stability, studies of men often find that husbands' gender role attitudes are important in determining marital stability and that traditional rather than egalitarian attitudes in men are more harmful for marital relationships (Gerson, 1993; Perry-Jenkins & Crouter, 1990). Perry-Jenkins and Crouter (1990) find that traditional husbands of working wives report less marital satisfaction. Traditional men may feel competition with successful wives, which can strain marital relationships and lead to divorce (Gerson, 1993). By contrast, egalitarian men have higher marital satisfaction, less marital conflict, and are happier in marriage (Lye & Biblarz, 1993).

Two studies that examined both wives and husbands provide further evidence of a differential effect of men's and women's gender role attitudes on marital stability. Blair (1993) finds that husbands with egalitarian views about family roles are more apt to report very low chances of divorce and very high levels of marital happiness than traditional husbands, whereas wives with egalitarian attitudes report more open disagreements than traditional wives. Amato and Booth (1995) find that husbands whose attitudes became more egalitarian reported increased marital happiness and interaction and decreased marital problems and disagreements, but wives whose attitudes became more egalitarian experienced the reverse.

When it comes to having children, Becker (1991) argues that a less specialized division of labor reduces women's desire for children. Nock (1987) suggests that childbearing is a "core symbolic experience" with different meanings for egalitarian versus traditional women. To him, fertility decisions "reflect a woman's views about the role of women in society" (p. 384). Traditional women see motherhood as central to their lives and identity. Egalitarian women's decisions about having children are based on their own needs or desires—motherhood is only one part of their lives and identity. Men, too, shape their ideas about parenthood based on their gender role orientations (Rindfuss, Morgan, & Swicegood, 1988). Traditional men lump the goals of a successful career, marriage, and children together, and having wives who care for their children makes parenthood easier and establishes and confirms their masculine identity (Gerson, 1993; Marsiglio, 1993).

The literature has much evidence that traditional men and women are more likely to have children. Young women and couples who have children are more traditional than those who do not and these differences precede the first birth (Morgan & Waite, 1987; Waite, Haggstrom, & Kanouse, 1986). Traditional couples are more likely to plan for and have a child soon after marriage (Goldscheider & Waite, 1991; Rindfuss et al., 1988; White & Kim, 1987). By contrast, egalitarian wives and married couples have lower fertility intentions than their traditional counterparts (Chapman, 1989; Scanzoni, 1976).

Scanzoni (1976) finds there is a system of inverse rewards and costs for having children:

> The more strongly the couple prefers the *rewards* inherent in greater marital egalitarianism, the less they prefer the *rewards* [italics in original] that accompany additional children. By the same token, willingness to bear or "accept" the particular costs of egalitarianism varies inversely with willingness to accept the costs of additional children. (p. 687)

However, Scanzoni considers husbands and wives together, when each may have a different outlook on rewards. The rewards of egalitarianism and the rewards of having children need not always be inversely related if these rewards differ by gender. For example, men may see rewards of egalitarianism and of children as similar, whereas women may see them as different. If egalitarianism offers men the opportunity to be involved in raising their children, then the rewards of egalitarianism will increase the rewards of having children. Extending Oppenheimer's arguments to childbearing, we may argue that a traditional division of labor causes undue stress for women and excludes men from full participation in childrearing. A more traditional view is apt to reserve most of the hardships and joys of raising children for women. Conversely, a more equal division of labor may reduce stress on women and increase men's enjoyment in their children's lives. In fact, one study finds liberal male students are more likely to expect to have children (Affleck et al., 1989).

The theoretical explanations above leave us with questions of whether traditionalists really are more likely to get married, stay married, and have children. Furthermore, given the more rapid change in women's work roles than in men's domestic roles, we may ask whether men and women are influenced similarly by their gender role attitudes. We expect that each will react differently. Specifically, we anticipate that women who believe in traditional gender roles will be more likely to marry and have children and less likely to divorce. Egalitarian women may have different desires or face more obstacles en route to marriage and family life. It is harder to predict the influence of attitudes on men's behavior. The gendered roles marriage and children offer may be more appealing to traditional men. If this is so, traditional men, like their female counterparts, should be more likely to marry and have children and less likely to divorce. Conversely, egalitarian men may indeed be seeking more involvement in family life—if so, egalitarian rather than traditional men should be the ones more apt to marry and have children and less apt to divorce.

Data and Variables

Data for this analysis come from the 1987/1988 and 1992/1994 waves of the National Survey of Families and Households (NSFH1 and NSFH2, respectively). The survey is nationally representative of the U.S. population age 19 years and older. The same respondents were interviewed about 5 years later, with a response rate of 77%. For this study, the sample is limited to single men younger than 45 years old and married or cohabiting men whose partners are younger than 40 during NSFH1. The sample of women consists of those younger than age 40 at NSFH1. Questions about fertility intentions and behavior are limited to the age group above. The sample is also limited to those who have no children at NSFH1. This limitation takes into account two considerations. First, it lets us focus on the transition to parenthood rather than any fertility decision. Second, decisions about marriage, cohabitation, and divorce are likely to be different for those with children, who may face a different marriage market. This leaves us with 2,621 childless men and women in their childbearing years.

Changes in relationship status. These variables measure change in relationship status in the 5-year period following NSFH1. Those who were not married and not cohabiting at NSFH1 could either marry, cohabit, or remain single. About 29% married and an additional 15% entered a cohabiting union. Those who were cohabiting at NSFH1 could either marry their partner, separate from their partner, or remain in the cohabiting union. These cohabiting unions were fairly unstable, consistent with Thornton (1988). For women, equal numbers married and separated (42% each), whereas for men, more than one half married and another one third separated. Finally, those who were married at NSFH1 could either separate/divorce or remain married. Widowhood was not a factor for this sample of young married people. Only three men and four women who were married at NSFH1 were widowed by NSFH2. Fully one fifth of married men and women divorced in the 5-year

Table 7.1 Descriptive Statistics for Union Variables, Fertility Variables, and Gender Role Attitudes (in Percentages)

Time 1[a]	Time 2[b]	All	Men	Women
Union variables				
Single, noncohabiting	Married	29.4	28.6	30.6
	Cohabiting	15.0	15.4	14.4
	Still single	55.6	56.0	55.0
Cohabiting	Married	47.9	42.4	53.9
	Separated	37.9	41.6	33.9
	Still cohabiting	14.2	16.0	12.2
Married	Divorced or separated	20.7	20.6	20.8
	Still married	79.3	79.4	79.2
Fertility variables				
Intend to have a child		81.6	82.7	80.1
	Fathered/gave birth to child or pregnant/ partner pregnant**	29.6	27.8	31.8
Gender role attitudes				
Traditional**		11.4	13.3	9.0
Neutral**		19.7	23.7	14.5
Egalitarian**		68.9	63.0	76.4

a. These are data from the National Survey of Families and Households in 1987/1988.

b. These are data from the National Survey of Families and Households in 1992/1994.

**Difference between men and women significant at .05 level.

interval. Table 7.1 presents descriptive statistics for the union variables, fertility variables, and gender role attitudes.

Fertility intentions. Fertility intentions are measured at NSFH1 by the question, "Do you intend to have (a/another) child some time?" This variable is dichotomous for *intend to have a child* versus *do not intend to have a child.* Although most men and women intend to have a child (82%), a substantial proportion plan on remaining childless.

Fertility outcome. Actual fertility is measured at NSFH2 with questions about whether respondents had fathered or given birth to a child since NSFH1. Because of the short period of 5 years between waves, we also include those who were pregnant or whose partner was pregnant at NSFH2 in the fertility measure. Not surprisingly,

a large proportion of this childless sample had a child in the 5 years between waves. About 32% of women gave birth or were pregnant, and 28% of men fathered a child or had a pregnant partner. This difference is significant at the .05 level, mainly due to differences in reporting among single men and women.

Gender role attitudes. This variable is measured by combining two questions. Respondents were asked to indicate agreement-disagreement with the following statements: "It is much better for everyone if the man earns the main living and the woman takes care of the home and family" and "If a husband and a wife both work full-time, they should share household tasks equally." The first question considers proper work and home roles for men and women. Almost one half of women and one third of men disagreed with this statement. On the other hand, one fifth of women and almost one third of men agreed with this statement, indicating their traditional attitudes. The second question considers the sharing of domestic responsibilities between men and women. Most men and women agreed that husbands and wives should share housework equally when both work. Factor analysis showed that the two variables share one common underlying dimension. Higher values indicate an egalitarian attitude whereas lower values indicate a traditional attitude. Overall, 63% of men and 76% of women held egalitarian views.

Control variables. Controls for age, education, income, occupational prestige, religion, race/ethnicity, and attitudes toward marriage are included in all models. Fertility intention and outcome models also include relationship status. Fertility outcome models include fertility intentions and a dummy for preconception marriage in between waves.

Findings

Table 7.2 shows differences in the dependent variables by gender role attitudes for men and women. Although there is little difference in relationship status at NSFH2 by gender role attitudes for single women, single men who hold more egalitarian attitudes were twice as likely to cohabit as traditional men (19% vs. 9%) and somewhat more likely to marry, 28% compared to 22% of traditional men. These findings indicate that traditional men rather than egalitarian men are more likely to remain single (69% vs. 53%). For those who were cohabiting at NSFH1, there appears to be no pattern between men's gender role attitudes and relationship status at NSFH2. However, women with egalitarian attitudes do seem to be more likely to separate from their partners, 41% compared to 22% of traditional women. Interestingly, men with egalitarian attitudes were less likely to divorce than traditional men, whereas women with egalitarian attitudes were more likely to divorce than their traditional counterparts. Fully one quarter of traditional men divorced within the 5-year

period compared to 16% of egalitarian men. By contrast, one fifth of egalitarian women and 17% of traditional women divorced.

Men and women show opposite patterns for the relationship between attitudes toward gender roles and fertility intentions. Men with egalitarian attitudes were more likely than men with traditional attitudes to intend to have a child. Whereas 84% of men with egalitarian attitudes intended to have a child, 78% of men with traditional attitudes intended to do so. By contrast, women with egalitarian attitudes were less likely than women with traditional attitudes to intend to have a child—79% versus 90%. This results in a significant gap between traditional men and women.

As with fertility intentions, egalitarian women were less likely than traditional ones to have experienced a fertility outcome, although the difference is not as large, 30% versus 35%, respectively. By contrast, egalitarian men were similar to traditional men. The findings above suggest that gender role attitudes may have very different effects on men's and women's family formation and dissolution. Egalitarian men appear to be more likely to enter and less likely to exit unions and more likely to intend to have children. By contrast, egalitarian women appear to be less likely to marry a cohabiting partner, more likely to dissolve a union, and less likely to intend to or actually experience childbirth. Nevertheless, a number of other factors may account for these effects.

Table 7.3 shows the logistic regression results for the relationship between gender role attitudes and union formation and dissolution, fertility intentions, and fertility outcomes. All analyses are done separately for men and women, with pooled models to test for gender differences (models not shown).

Although gender role attitudes appear to have no effect on the decision to marry for single men and women, holding egalitarian attitudes does increase the likelihood of entering a cohabiting union for men (Table 7.3). Attitudes do not have a significant effect on cohabitors' decisions to marry or separate. This may be due to the small sample of cohabitors. What stands out in the

Table 7.2   Differences in Union Status Changes, Fertility Intentions, and Fertility Outcomes by Gender Role Attitudes (in Percentages)

Time 1[a]	Time 2[b]	Men		Women	
		Traditional	*Egalitarian*	*Traditional*	*Egalitarian*
Union variables					
Single, noncohabiting	Married	22.0	28.2*	27.1	30.1
	Cohabiting	9.3	19.1**	16.7	16.4
	Still single	68.6	52.7**	56.3	53.5
Cohabiting	Married	40.0	40.8	55.6	45.1
	Separated	46.7	44.9	22.2	40.9
	Still cohabiting	13.3	14.3	22.2	14.1
Married	Divorced or separated	25.0	15.5	16.7	20.3
	Still married	75.0	84.5	83.3	79.7
Fertility variables					
Intend to have a child		77.9	83.7*	89.7	78.7**
	Fathered/gave birth to child or pregnant/ partner pregnant	26.7	26.2	35.2	30.0

a. These are data from the National Survey of Families and Households in 1987/1988.

b. These are data from the National Survey of Families and Households in 1992/1994.

*Difference between traditional and egalitarian significant at .10 level.

**Difference between traditional and egalitarian significant at .05 level.

relationship status models is that married men who had egalitarian attitudes were significantly less likely to divorce or separate than their traditional counterparts. For each one-point increase in egalitarian attitudes (on a scale of 2–10), there is a 25% decrease in a man's likelihood of divorce. The effect of holding egalitarian attitudes on divorce for women is positive but not significant. However, the difference in the effect of gender role attitudes on divorce for men and women is significant (refer to gender interaction column in Table 7.3), suggesting that men with egalitarian attitudes are less likely to divorce than similar women.

Results for fertility intentions (Table 7.2) indicate that women with egalitarian gender role attitudes were significantly less likely to intend to have a child than women with traditional attitudes. Unlike women, men with egalitarian attitudes, women are 26% less likely to intend to

have a child whereas men are 24% more likely to intend to have a child. Although these results are quite dramatic, they present only a cross-sectional view of the relationship between gender role attitudes and fertility intentions. Therefore, we must look at fertility outcomes within the following 5 years to discern better the effect of attitudes on behavior.

The results for fertility outcomes (Table 7.2) are similar to those for fertility intentions but less striking. Women with egalitarian attitudes were significantly less likely to have had a child than their more traditional counterparts. Men with egalitarian attitudes were more likely to have fathered a child, although this effect does not reach significance. However, as with fertility intentions, the difference between men and women in the effect of gender role attitudes on actual fertility is significant, indicating that egalitarian men were more likely to have a child than

Table 7.3   Logistic Regression Coefficients for the Relationship Between Gender Role Attitudes and Family Formation and Dissolution

Dependent Variable				*Gender*
Time 1[a]	*Time 2[b]*	*Men*	*Women*	*Interaction[c]*
Union formation and dissolution between 1987/1988 and 1992/1994				
Single, noncohabiting	Married vs. still single	.0096	.0232	.0493
	Cohabiting vs. still single	.2709***	.1050	.1906
	Chi square	291.12	210.93	469.21
	N	713	480	1,193
Cohabiting	Married vs. still cohabiting	.1405	−.2620	.2276
	Separated vs. still cohabiting	.3939	−.2639	.2944
	Chi square	62.33	70.59	94.52
	N	110	102	212
Married	Divorced/separated vs. still married	−.2862**	.0363	−.3405**
	Chi square	43.99	24.87	61.23
	N	320	341	661
Fertility intentions in 1987/1988		.2109***	−.2964***	.3664***
	Chi square	220.36	239.40	427.02
	N	1,153	932	2,085
	Fertility outcomes between 1987/1988 and 1992/1994	.0684	−.1735***	.2703***
	Chi square	272.40	275.89	523.13
	N	1,225	999	2,224

NOTE: Controls for age, education, income, occupational prestige, religion, ethnicity, and attitudes toward marriage are included in models. Age at marriage is also included in divorce models, and marital status is included in the fertility models. Fertility intentions and marriage prior to Time 2/conception are also included in the fertility outcome models.

a. These are data from the National Survey of Families and Households in 1987/1988.

b. These are data from the National Survey of Families and Households in 1992/1994.

c. Interaction between gender and gender role attitudes obtained from pooled models.

**p < .05.

***p < .01.

similar women. For each one-point increase in egalitarian attitudes, women are 16% less likely to have had a child whereas men are 7% more likely to have fathered a child. It does appear that egalitarian attitudes act to decrease women's entrance into parenthood at the same time that they act to increase men's entrance into parenthood.

Discussion

The results above provide fairly strong evidence for the existence of differential effects of gender role attitudes on men's and women's family formation and dissolution. As hypothesized, egalitarian women were less likely to intend to have a child and actually to do so than their more traditional counterparts. The story for men is quite different. As might be expected, single men with egalitarian attitudes were more likely to cohabit than their traditional counterparts. Interestingly, egalitarian men were less likely to divorce than traditional men, and this difference between men and women is also significant. Whereas men with egalitarian attitudes were more likely to enter a less stable union—cohabitation—these same attitudes increased the stability of marriage. Furthermore, unlike women, egalitarian men were more likely to intend to have a child and to do so than traditional men. Although the latter effect does not reach significance, egalitarian men were significantly less likely to be dissuaded from having children than egalitarian women. Rather than "doing gender," these men seem to be more interested in "doing family."

There are several possible explanations for these gender differences in the effect of gender role attitudes. The effect on men's entrance into cohabitation may indicate that egalitarian men find cohabitation to be a more acceptable living arrangement than do traditional men. Egalitarian men are more open to alternative living arrangements, which usually involve a more equitable division of labor than marriage. This effect may also be produced by the greater attractiveness of egalitarian men. Consistent with the greater fairness in the division of labor among cohabiting couples, men who are willing to share in household tasks are more likely to cohabit than those unwilling to share. These men are also likely to be less intimidated by their female partner's performance in the labor force.

In addition to being more attractive partners, egalitarian men may be better able to keep their partners attracted to them, as witnessed by their lower likelihood of divorce. This suggests that men who share more equally with their wives (or think that they should) have fewer conflicts with their wives. Egalitarian men are accepting of working wives and of sharing more in household chores. This is likely to alleviate pressure on and reduce conflict with their wives, making for a

happier marital relationship. Men who want to share chores with their wives are not likely to hear objections from their wives. On the other hand, women who want their husbands to share may face resistance and conflict. This is consistent with Bowen and Orthner's (1983) finding that traditional husbands and nontraditional wives have the lowest marital quality. Egalitarian attitudes in women strain marriage because of older norms emphasizing the traditional division of labor between husbands and wives. On the other hand, egalitarian attitudes in men support marital happiness because the wives are likely to have egalitarian attitudes. This points to the importance married women place on men's sharing job and home roles. Most women want men who will share in the responsibilities of the household.

Gender role attitudes also have an important effect on how men and women view parenthood. Although children may continue to be an important part of the traditional family for women, results from this study make it apparent that egalitarian men want children even more than traditional men, and rather than being symbolic, children are very much an interactive part of an egalitarian man's family.

Traditional women, as indicated in the questions, feel that it is their duty to stay home and care for their children while their husbands work. They are likely to feel that children are necessary to fulfill their role as mother and wife. By contrast, egalitarian women want to spend more time on their careers and less time doing housework and child care. The potential costs of children may reduce their desire for children, thus the negative effect on fertility intentions and behavior. In addition, egalitarian women may feel as though they lack support from men. Women who think that tasks should be shared equally may realize that reality does not mirror hope, and if child care is not going to be shared, they may decide not to have a child.

On the other hand, egalitarian men may want children because they want to share with their partners and be involved in caring for their children. They think that raising a child (as opposed to simply supporting a child) is the responsibility of both parents. These are the men who do not wish to pass off on their wives the responsibility of taking care of their children. This is an interesting finding, given that traditional men would be expected to want children more. Traditional men may also want children but for different reasons, such as completing the family. However, they may realize that, because of their role as provider, their participation in child rearing will be minimal. If this is the case, children may be seen as taking attention from wives that would otherwise be bestowed on themselves.

Becker (1991) suggests that traditional roles are conducive to marital stability and childbearing. However, the benefits of a traditional division of labor may only be seen as beneficial by traditional people. Traditional women may still look to marriage and children as their primary source of identity and role structure, but it is no longer clear what other men and women expect from these family institutions.

There seems to be a mismatch in the impact of gender role attitudes on fertility and family formation. Egalitarian men want children, and they stay married. The opposite is true for egalitarian women. This difference may be because of the different ideas men and women hold about what being egalitarian means. Although egalitarianism includes equality at work and home, the focus on personal change may be different. For women, personal change may involve more time working away from home and less time working at home. These women struggle for opportunities and rewards for working outside the home, and they desire less emphasis on family and home roles, hoping that men will take on their fair share. For men, personal change may involve increasing participation at home and making room for women at work. These men are more willing to share domestic responsibilities, including raising their children. It would then seem, as posited by Goldscheider and Goldscheider (1992) that egalitarian men are pro-family. However, egalitarian women want more out of life than domestic responsibility, and they seem to have low expectations of receiving help from men. By contrast, egalitarian men may expect that their involvement with their children and with household tasks will be supported by women. For change to occur, egalitarian women need the support of egalitarian men. Egalitarian women might be more likely to want children and might be more content in their relationships if they received more support from men.

This study is limited by the constrained measurement of gender role attitudes. Although our measure includes an indicator about employment and an indicator about household labor, it is not clear what roles and role changes are being emphasized by men compared to women. Another limitation is the translation of attitudes into behavior. The egalitarian men in this study think they should share domestic responsibilities, and this seems to help their marriages. However, whether these men actually share equally and what consequences sharing has for marriage and parenthood in the long term are further questions.

A study based on interviews of egalitarian men and women might increase our understanding of how these people view their roles and how this might affect their union and fertility decisions. Future studies could focus on particular aspects of men's and women's role attitudes that lead them to embrace marriage and children. In addition, a distinction between ideology and behavior and its impact may be made.

Note

Marital satisfaction is important for marital stability although there is some evidence that traditional couples are less likely to divorce even with lower relationship satisfaction (Fowers, Montel, & Olson, 1996).

References

Affleck, M., Morgan, C. S., & Hayes, M. P. (1989). The influence of gender role attitudes on life expectations of college students. *Youth & Society, 20,* 307–319.

Amato, P. R., & Booth, A. (1995). Changes in gender role attitudes and perceived marital quality. *American Sociological Review, 60,* 58–66.

Ambert, A. M. (1985). The effect of divorce on women's attitudes toward feminism. *Sociological Focus, 18,* 265–272.

Becker, G. S. (1991). *A treatise on the family.* Cambridge, MA: Harvard University Press.

Blair, S. L. (1993). Employment, family, and perceptions of marital quality among husbands and wives. *Journal of Family Issues, 14,* 189–212.

Blaisure, K. R., & Allen, K. R. (1995). Feminists and the ideology and practice of marital equality. *Journal of Marriage and the Family, 57,* 5–19.

Bowen, G. L., & Orthner, D. K. (1983). Sex-role congruency and marital quality. *Journal of Marriage and the Family, 45,* 223–230.

Chapman, B. E. (1989). Egalitarian sex roles and fertility in Canada. In J. Legate, T. R. Balakrishnan, & R. P. Beaujot (Eds.), *The family in crisis: A population crisis?* (pp. 121–139). Ottawa: Royal Society of Canada.

Clarkberg, M., Stolzenberg, R. M., & Waite, L. J. (1995). Attitudes, values, and entrance into cohabitational versus marital unions. *Social Forces, 74,* 609–632.

Davis, K. (1984). Wives and work: The sex role revolution and its consequences. *Population and Development Review, 10,* 397–417.

Fenstermaker, S., West, C., & Zimmerman, D. H. (1991). Gender inequality: New conceptual terrain. In R. L. Blumberg (Ed.), *Gender, family, and economy: The triple overlap* (pp. 289–307). Newbury Park, CA: Sage.

Ferree, M. M. (1991). The gender division of labor in two-earner marriages: Dimensions of variability and change. *Journal of Family Issues. 12,* 158–180.

Finley, B., Starnes, C. E., & Alvarez, F. B. (1985). Recent changes in sex-role ideology among divorced men and women: Some possible causes and implications. *Sex Roles, 12,* 637–653.

Fowers, B. J., Montel, K. H., & Olson, D. H. (1996). Predicting marital success for premarital couple types based on PREPARE. *Journal of Marital and Family Therapy, 22,* 103–119.

Gerson, K. (1993). *No man's land: Men's changing commitments to family and work.* New York: Basic Books.

Goldscheider, F. K., & Goldscheider, C. (1992). Gender roles, marriage, and residential independence. *Sociological Forum, 7,* 679–696.

Goldscheider, F. K., & Waite, L. J. (1991). *New families, no families? The transformation of the American home.* Berkeley: University of California Press.

Hewlett, S. A. (1986). *A lesser life: The myth of women's liberation in America.* New York: William Morrow.

Hochschild, A. (with Machung, A.) (1989). *The second shift: Working parents and the revolution at home.* New York: Viking.

Huber, J., & Spitze, G. (1980). Considering divorce: An expansion of Becker's theory of marital instability. *American Journal of Sociology, 86,* 75–89.

Lueptow, L. B., Guss, M. B., & Hyden, C. (1989). Sex role ideology, marital status, and happiness. *Journal of Family Issues, 10,* 383–400.

Lye, D. N., & Biblarz, T. J. (1993). The effects of attitudes toward family life and gender roles on marital satisfaction. *Journal of Family Issues, 14,* 157–188.

Marsiglio, W. (1993). Adolescent males' orientation toward paternity and contraception. *Family Planning Perspectives, 25,* 22–31.

Morgan, S. P., & Waite, L. J. (1987). Parenthood and the attitudes of young adults. *American Sociological Review, 52,* 541-547.

Nock, S. L. (1987). The symbolic meaning of childbearing. *Journal of Family Issues, 8,* 373–393.

Oppenheimer, V. K. (1994). Women's rising employment and the future of the family in industrial societies. *Population and Development Review, 20,* 293–342.

Oppenheimer, V. K., & Lew, V. (1995). American marriage formation in the 1980s: How important was women's economic independence? In K. O. Mason & A. M. Jensen (Eds.), *Gender and family change in industrialized countries* (pp. 105–138). Oxford, UK: Clarendon.

Perry-Jenkins, M., & Crouter, A. C. (1990). Men's provider-role attitudes: Implications for household work and marital satisfaction. *Journal of Family Issues, 11,* 136–156.

Popenoe, D. (1993). American family decline, 1960–1990: A review and appraisal. *Journal of Marriage and the Family, 55,* 527–542.

Rindfuss, R. R., Morgan, S. P., & Swicegood, G. (1988). *First births in America: Changes in the timing of parenthood.* Berkeley: University of California Press.

Ross, C. E., Mirowsky, J., & Huber, J. (1983). Dividing work, sharing work, and in-between:

Marriage patterns and depression. *American Sociological Review, 48*, 809–823.

Ross, H. L., & Sawhill, L V. (with MacIntosh, A. R.). (1975). *Time of transition: The growth of families headed by women.* Washington, DC: Urban Institute.

Scanzoni, J. (1976). Gender roles and the process of fertility control. *Journal of Marriage and the Family, 38*, 677–691.

Scanzoni, J., & Szinovacz, M. (1980). *Family decision-making: A developmental sex role model.* Beverly Hills, CA: Sage.

Shelton, B. A., & John, D. (1993). Does marital status make a difference? Housework among married and cohabiting men and women. *Journal of Family Issues, 14*, 401–420.

Suitor, J. J. (1991). Marital quality and satisfaction with the division of household labor across the family life cycle. *Journal of Marriage and the Family, 53*, 221–230.

Thornton, A. (1988). Cohabitation and marriage in the 1980s. *Demography, 25,* 497–508.

Thornton, A. (1989). Changing attitudes toward family issues in the United States. *Journal of Marriage and the Family, 51,* 873–893.

Thornton, A., Alwin, D. F., & Camburn, D. (1983). Causes and consequences of sex-role attitudes and attitude change. *American Sociological Review, 48*, 211–227.

Vannoy-Hiller, D., & Philliber, W. W. (1989). *Equal partners: Successful women in marriage.* Newbury Park, CA: Sage.

Waite, L. J., Haggstrom, G. W., & Kanouse, D. (1986). The effects of parenthood on the career orientation and job characteristics of young adults. *Social Forces, 65,* 43–73.

White, L. K., & Kim H. (1987). The family-building process: Childbearing choices by parity. *Journal of Marriage and the Family, 49,* 271–279.

8

SYMBOLIC INTERACTIONISM

More than a single theoretical perspective, symbolic interactionism reflects a diverse family of theories. Arising out of the work of philosophers and social scientists such as Charles Darwin, William James, and John Dewey and the work of early sociologists such as George Herbert Mead and Charles Cooley, symbolic interactionism focuses on patterns of interpretation and "meaning making" in social settings. Central to a symbolic interactionist perspective is the notion that humans share a set of commonly understood symbols (signs, language, etc.), and the acquisition and generation of meaning is at the heart of human social interactions.

This view builds on a number of assumptions. First, it is assumed that behavior can only be understood in terms of the meanings the actor attributes to it. That is, the reasons or meanings that underlie the behavior are more important to understanding than the behavior itself. Symbolic interactionism, then, focuses on the meanings that exist in social life. It is more important to understand the meanings and definitions actors assign to a situation than to understand dimensions of the situation itself.

It is further assumed that the meanings we hold develop through interactions with others. Meanings, then, are learned in social settings. Without social interactions, an individual will not develop an understanding of the meanings attached to symbols and behaviors in a society. This suggests a circular process. Individuals come to understand meanings through social interactions, and their understanding of meanings and ascription of meanings to behaviors then influence their participation in social interactions.

Symbolic interactionism, then, assumes that humans are born with no social dimension. Over time, the asocial infant is exposed to and internalizes a wide variety of socializing messages that contribute to meaning making and social understandings in that child. Ultimately, all behavior must be understood as socially learned. This arises out of the complex social environments within which humans live. These environments include complex sets of symbols about which individuals make evaluative distinctions. In other words, symbols come to hold different values and meanings for each individual.

This suggests that individuals are profoundly influenced by society. Societal norms, values, expectations, and patterns of behavior and interaction all contribute to the meanings one comes to understand. It is through everyday interaction with society that one comes to understand society. This understanding contributes to the meanings that guide human behavior.

Beyond society, though, symbolic interactionism also focuses on an individual's sense of self. In fact, symbolic interactionism is the only commonly used theory in family science that focuses on this construct. From this perspective, one's sense of self arises out of social interactions as well. It reflects our experience of social interactions and our interpretation of how we are perceived by others through those interactions. This suggests that behaviors reflect not only an individual's values and attitudes but also that individual's interpretation of how behaviors are perceived by others. (You might wish to compare some of these ideas with those we highlighted in Chapter 4 when we discussed social learning theory.) No doubt you can think of times when you may have done something (or not done something) merely because you believed it would be hurtful or disappointing to someone else. This implies that individuals develop awareness of and sensitivity to the perceptions of those around us. This awareness and sensitivity is tied into an individual sense of personal qualities and characteristics. At the heart of this are individuals' perceptions of how they are perceived by others. This socially constructed sense of self, then, provides a motive for behavior.

Reflected in all of this is the symbolic interactionism viewpoint that humans maintain a complex relationship with society (or any social group in their environment). It is assumed that individuals are influenced by larger groups and processes and, through such influences, behaviors are somewhat constrained by the norms and values of those groups. The details of social structure are worked out through the social interactions and everyday situations that individuals encounter. Through these interactions and situations, individuals and society mutually impact one another.

Even with this assumption of mutual impact, symbolic interactionism assumes that society precedes individuals. Individual minds are the result of society but society is not the result of individual minds. This implies that society includes powerful social forces that are not significantly altered by individual interpretation of those forces.

These assumptions are reflected in a number of key concepts within symbolic interactionism. The first of these is the concept of identities, or self-meanings, that individuals associate with their participation in a social role. These identities, or self-meanings, become hierarchically organized by the level of salience they hold for an individual. More salient roles are more often invoked by individuals and may come to indicate a stronger commitment on the part of the individual toward that particular role.

Roles are defined as shared norms applied to occupants of social positions. These shared norms become systems of meanings that allow individuals to anticipate how those in social roles will act and react. These norms also contribute to definitions of how people should behave in social roles. For example, think about motherhood as a social role. If you were asked to define a "good mother," you would, in all probability, list a set of characteristics that are surprisingly similar to those that others would list. (You might want to try this out on a group of your fellow students.) The fact that there are somewhat universal understandings of appropriate behavior in various social roles suggests that individuals in those roles may use those understandings to guide their own behaviors.

Symbolic interactionism also attends to the concept of interaction. From this perspective, interaction is not the content of social encounters but, rather, the levels of meaning that exist in those social encounters. For example, a married couple may have a habit of saying "I love you" to one another whenever they finish a telephone conversation. For one spouse, this may be a highly important part of the conversation that reflects deep meaning. For the other, it may merely be something that is done as rote repetition, perhaps repeated mostly to make the other spouse happy. In this case, while both spouses engage in the same behavior, it would be difficult to argue that it holds the same meaning for each. This is another example of how symbolic interactionism attends to interaction in terms of the meaning that underlies behavior.

A final key concept within this perspective is the concept of self. The self may be viewed as a process of behavior in which individuals come to determine and control their own conduct. It involves an individual building a set of roles for herself or himself and coming to value certain roles over others. For one person, the parent role may be central to self-definition; that is, it carries a lot of weight in determining how he or she sees himself or herself as a person. Another person in the parent role may see it as clearly secondary to other roles. It might be anticipated that these two individuals would participate in parenting activities differently.

The self develops out of interactions between individuals and their environments, with each contributing to determinations of where attention and effort should be directed. It requires understanding of language and other symbols of society as well as exposure to socialization processes throughout life. The self involves elements of both role taking (developing a perspective on how to behave in the social roles one assumes) and role making (actual patterns of behaviors in those social roles). As mentioned earlier, in many ways one's sense of self becomes a motivator in and of itself in that it contributes to the meanings assigned to various situations and behaviors.

The Readings

The two readings that follow incorporate elements of symbolic interactionism into examinations of specific family issues. Hopper (2001) takes a symbolic interactionist approach to divorce in exploring the symbolic origins of conflict in divorce. While there has been substantial research on structural factors associated with divorce, far less attention has been directed to the symbolic meanings that underlie these structural

relationships. This article is one example of such attention.

Seccombe, James, and Walters (1998) examine societal conceptions and definitions of welfare mothers. These authors attend to ways in which women's own definitions of themselves as welfare recipients differ from societal definitions. These differences play out in a number of meaningful ways in both welfare policy and practices associated with enactment of welfare reform. This article provides an excellent example of how meanings and definitions can profoundly impact both social policy and those who are affected by it.

Issues for Your Consideration

1. What patterns of meaning making are evident in these two articles? How do those experiencing divorce and/or welfare status assign meaning to their experiences?

2. To what degree do symbols contribute to an understanding of the issues addressed in each of these articles? How, specifically, would you describe these relationships?

3. Was there evidence of an influential sense of self in the perceptions of the subjects of these two studies? Can you provide specific examples of this influence?

4. To what degree do you feel social policy is influenced by the meanings and definitions of policymakers? To what degree would you argue this is a problem?

Further Reading

Blumer (1969), Cade (1986), Harter (1999), Marks and MacDermid (1996), Reiss (1981).

THE SYMBOLIC ORIGINS OF CONFLICT IN DIVORCE

JOSEPH HOPPER

Abstract

Divorce often constitutes a dramatic transformation of a close, personal, and usually harmonious relationship into one that is deeply antagonistic and bitter. Explanations among family researchers typically focus on opposing material interests, the adversarial nature of the legal system, latent or manifest conflict in marriage, or psychological reactions to the pain of divorce. A broadly designed fieldwork investigation of divorce suggests an important dimension largely ignored by these explanations, the symbolic or cultural. This article describes the process by which a sample of divorcing subjects confronted and solved major interpretive dilemmas posed by virtue of the shared meaning they and those around them had of marriage. It shows that the ways in which they solved such dilemmas created an oppositional structure by which they subsequently affected divorce.

Fieldwork and clinical studies suggest that a large majority of divorces, even those that are settled out of court, are characterized by high levels of conflict (Ahrons, 1981; Erlanger, Chambliss, & Melli, 1987; Johnston & Campbell, 1988, 1993; Kressel, Jaffee, Tuchman, Watson, & Deutsch, 1980; Weiss, 1975). Divorces may be characterized by any number of battles, including property disputes, verbal fights, custody battles, kidnappings, noncooperation with court orders, burglaries, physical threats and violence, property destruction, name calling, harassment, and stalking; a substantial portion (estimated at one third) of divorced couples continue in prolonged and bitter disputes for many years after their divorces (Ahrons, 1981; Arendell, 1986; Dillon & Emery, 1996; Johnston & Campbell, 1993). Not all divorces are highly conflictual, and a number of studies have begun to explore the varieties of process and outcome (Ahrons, 1981, 1994; Ahrons & Rodgers, 1987; Goldsmith, 1980; Isaacs & Leon, 1988; Masheter, 1997). But even researchers who have focused on the possibility of "good divorces" report that couples who manage to negotiate workable and friendly postmarital relations generally must overcome an initially hostile and oppositional dynamic (Ahrons, 1994); indeed, a "smooth" divorce, as Kressel et al. report, is still likely to be infused with hostility, anger, and hatred (see also Erlanger et al., 1987).

Previous research has suggested at least four explanations for this conflict. First, conflict may stem from resource or power differentials. Conflict is frequently a product of each side trying to maximize his or her take of money, property, and scarce resources (including children) in a situation where much is at stake and outcomes potentially lopsided (Weitzman, 1985). Gender may play an important role to the extent that women are disadvantaged in terms of money and power and must fight hard for an equitable outcome. Second, conflict in divorce maybe generated by the adversarial nature of our legal system

240

and by the procedures and practices of attorneys who serve as its functionaries. Researchers have cited the accusatory nature of motions, the requirements of generating evidence and filing briefs with the court, and the definition of interests as separate rather than joint; because nearly all divorces must be processed through this legal system, such practices may create enemies out of spouses who were otherwise getting along (Johnston & Campbell, 1988; Knox, 1990; Sprey, 1979; Felstiner, Abel, & Sarat, 1981). Third, conflict may originate out of psychological responses to being hurt, shamed, or humiliated by divorce. Considering the way in which marriage encompasses one's total personality, divorce cuts to the core of one's sense of self and dignity (Johnston & Campbell, 1988; Simmel, 1908/1955). Individual psychopathologies also may play a role, such that aspects of the divorce begin to "resonate with long-standing vulnerabilities" (Johnston & Campbell, p. 76). Divorce may additionally pose a problem of "individuation," a kind of internal identity struggle that often manifests itself in conflict with significant others (Kerr, 1988; Wallace, & Fogelson, 1965), or it may generate significant distress from attachment loss (Bowlby, 1969, 1973) and provoke conflict as a way of maintaining at least some form of significant relating. Fourth, conflict may emerge as an expression of prior and deeply rooted differences in marriage (Goode, 1956; Vaughan, 1986). In other words, conflict may exist in relationships before divorce, and this conflict, often itself a cause of divorce, then continues during and afterward.

What none of these explanations address, however, are the intensely moral concerns that seem to characterize most divorce conflict, and to the extent that morality is about groups bestowing (and enforcing) meaning upon objects and ideas (Durkheim, 1915/1965), there may be an important symbolic source of conflict in addition to the four outlined above. By "moral" concerns, I mean not only religious matters, but more generally the everyday proprieties manifest when divorcing people talk in terms of betrayal, abuse, blame, embarrassment, and stigma (Gerstel, 1987;

Hagestad & Smyer, 1982; Johnston & Campbell, 1988; Kitson, 1992). There are also the ways in which divorcing people redefine themselves as appropriately single rather than coupled, thereby accruing new social rights and obligations (Bohannan, 1971; Vaughan, 1986; Weiss, 1975); and even more broadly, there are the ways in which divorcing people construct rhetorics that help "motivate" their divorces in socially legitimate ways, imposing order onto otherwise chaotic processes of dissolution (Hopper, 1993a, 1993b; Riessman, 1990). These aspects of divorce are prominent not only in and of themselves, but they permeate the other dimensions of conflict as well. In terms of material factors, for example, partners may fight over property, money, and custody "on principle" and for revenge; in terms of legal institutions, maneuvers by lawyers and courts are seen not merely as procedural, but as imbued with the significance of justice or injustice; psychological processes matter, in part, because partners must save face against the ignominy of divorce.

With data from a qualitative fieldwork study of divorce, I propose an additional explanation rooted in the symbolic dimension of family life that helps account for the origins of conflict and for its moralistic nature. This symbolic dimension consists of the larger structure of meanings that define marriage in our culture along with the interpretive logic that people then use to make sense of their own experiences. I hope to show that this dimension, in and of itself, may shape how divorces unfold, giving the process an oppositional dynamic with a force quite its own. The explanation, in brief, is as follows: The profound value attached to marriage engenders an important problem of meaning when couples go through divorce. Namely, because most people get married with the belief that marriage is forever, they face a difficult interpretive problem in explaining why theirs are ending. To resolve the problem, they undo the previous meanings of their marriages: initiators of divorce come to see their marriages as having been not true marriages from the start, so efforts to preserve their marriages seem absurd; noninitiating partners come to see their spouses as having deceived them, so efforts to negotiate a divorce seem rife with lies. In short, the solutions thus formulated effectively resolve the interpretive problems posed, but they put partners dramatically at odds with each other.

I lay out the argument and the evidence for it in four stages. First, I examine the meaning of marriage in terms of its being a sacred institution; second, I describe the dilemma of "dissolving the sacred" thus posed; third, I show how many initiators solve the dilemma via a conception of "the marriage that never was"; and fourth, I describe how many noninitiating partners thereby derive the notion that their marriages were lies. Before proceeding, however, I describe the research from which this emphasis on the symbolic aspects of divorce evolved.

The Research

My emphasis on the symbolic dimension of divorce emerged out of an extensive and detailed fieldwork and interview study conducted over the course of 4 years. The study began in 1991 as a broadly defined fieldwork effort to understand the experiences of divorcing people, and 2 years later it was expanded to include the family, friends, attorneys, counselors, and ministers of divorcing people. I involved myself as a participant observer in multiple settings relevant to divorce: (a) I attended workshops and seminars given by local service agencies; (b) I took part in a 10-week group seminar program in which 30 divorcing women and men talked about their experiences and situations; (c) I attended a single father's support group over the course of 6 weeks; (d) I attended a 2-month advanced lawyer-development program in which two experienced attorneys taught a large group of attorneys how to manage divorce cases. I maintained an overt research role in each of these settings, explaining to facilitators and participants that my involvement and research were motivated in part by an effort to understand my parents' divorce. I conducted semistructured interviews with select and willing participants from each setting, and I supplemented these with

several interviews solicited from fliers and contacts at agencies. I additionally sought interviews with the family members and friends of divorcing people already interviewed. In all, I formally interviewed 99 people: 40 divorcing people (12 of whom had participated in the divorce group seminar), 4 married people who were trying to avoid divorce, 23 professionals, 16 family members, and 16 friends and neighbors. Data for this report come primarily from the 40 interviews with divorcing people.

Subjects for interviews were selected according to relevant theoretical concerns that emerged during the fieldwork itself—a process termed "theoretical sampling" by Glaser and Strauss (1967). This is a procedure in which data are gathered, coded, and analyzed during the fieldwork process, and subjects are selected with an eye toward emerging categories and conceptual trends. As I became interested in the dynamics between initiators and noninitiators, for example, I sought good representation of both, I sought subjects who did not conform to the emerging patterns being discerned, and I sought subjects who described their divorces as having been decided mutually. This process allowed the expanding sample to generate data that continually introduced variation, and that refined, displaced, and eventually sustained the conceptual categories being used to understand the phenomenon. As with most fieldwork of this nature, the extent to which these subjects represent a larger population is difficult to assess. They were, however, demographically diverse: They included both younger and older people; people in lower, middle, and upper income brackets; people who had been married a few months as well as many years; people in both first and second marriages; and people with and without children.

Analysis proceeded according to the grounded theory approach, which involved a continual process of transcribing field notes and interviews into files, reading and rereading transcripts for common themes, and then tabulating and clustering field observations and interview quotes around those themes until categories became "saturated," substantiated, or rejected (Glaser &

Strauss, 1967). Specific questions about conflict were not formulated before beginning the research. My questions were general ones about the process of getting divorced, the kinds of interpretive practices that divorcing people engage in, and the ways of making sense amidst the difficulty of dissolving marriage. The problem of conflict emerged as the research was underway and was sharpened only later during the analysis phase. This limits the analytic possibilities but also serves as a strength in qualitative research. The disadvantage is that the study provides only suggestive answers, and much of my effort brings general data to bear upon a set of specific questions. The advantage, however, is that interviews were not steered in ways that might provide one-sided evidence with regard to the specific questions I now ask. One important component of the analysis in this article revolves around the distinction between initiators and noninitiators in divorce. Braver, Whitley, and Ng (1993) have noted at least four ways to define the two positions, depending on whether we focus on who first suggested divorce, who is most to blame, who decided in the end, or who filed. For purposes here, I adopt the third definition, that is, the initiator is the one who ultimately declared the marriage over. Qualitative studies of divorce (Hopper, 1993a, 1993b; Nevaldine, 1978; Vaughan, 1986; Weiss, 1975) have found that this definition most closely aligns with divorcing partners' own sense of who left whom. Research also suggests that the distinction thus defined is relatively unambiguous, is typically agreed on by divorcing partners, and is stable over time (Braver et al.; Gray & Silver, 1990; Hopper, 1993; Nevaldine). Accordingly, I classified 12 divorcing people in my sample as initiators, 21 as noninitiating partners, and 7 as people who decided mutually with their partners to divorce.

All excerpts presented represent themes found in a majority of cases unless otherwise noted. Also, the empirical generalizations I make are nearly always consistent with other descriptions of divorce (Harvey, Wells, & Alvarez, 1978; Riessman, 1990; Vaughan, 1986; Weiss, 1975), lending confidence to the data's reliability, to the methods used, and to the wider applicability of the findings.

The Meaning of Marriage

Divorce being the dissolution of marriage may seem a trivial point to the extent that one is defined in terms of the other, but I hope to show that among the people I interviewed, there was an important, socially meaningful way in which divorce was literally and substantially an *undoing* of marriage. In other words, it was not merely a transition from one kind of relationship to another or the end of one phase and the beginning of another; it was far more than the separation of two intimately related people. It was a retroactive nullification—a substantive and thoroughgoing reinterpretation—of what once existed. I begin, then, by examining marriage and how people conceived of marriage, for it is this that got "undone" and this that set up the interpretive difficulties that divorce entailed.

For purposes here, I begin with a narrow premise that encompasses one aspect of what it meant to be married: For most, marriage was considered a sacred bond that was presumed to last forever. This was evident among the vast majority of people interviewed. "Marriage is supposed to be something that is forever. And it's traditional. And you take those vows and there's something that is sacred," I was told in one interview. Another said:

> I went into marriage fully committed, fully focused on making it last forever. I didn't go into it thinking it was a fairy tale. I went into it knowing that it was going to be hard, and there was going to be ups and downs, but that the marriage was going to make it. That it was sacred, if you want to put it that way.

For many this sacredness was literal: Marriage was an inviolable union consecrated through and before God. In this respect, the people in my study were like most Americans, among whom an estimated 80% of marriages are presided over by a member of the clergy (Whyte, 1990). But even among those for whom religion played no part, there was a more general, sociological sense in which their marriages were sacred. As Durkheim (1915/1965, p. 52) reminds us:

> By sacred things one must not understand simply those personal beings which are called gods or spirits; a rock, a tree, a spring, a pebble, a piece of wood, a house, in a word, anything can be sacred. A rite can have this character; in fact, the rite does not exist which does not have it to a certain degree.

And as he remarks with regard to the development of marriage specifically (Durkheim, 1892/1978, p. 237):

> It has completely ceased to be a personal contract and become a public act. A [magistrate] presides over the contracting of the marriage. Not only does the ceremony have this public character, but if the constituent formalities are not accurately fulfilled, the marriage is not valid. And we know that no legal act assumes solemn forms unless it assumes great importance.

Marriages were sacred in the general sense, then, that the social collectivity brought them into being; they represented and embodied the power, sentiments, and beliefs of our society. They were socially "inviolable" (*Oxford English Dictionary,* 2nd ed., s.v. "sacred"). It was in this broader sense that nearly every divorced person with whom I spoke evidenced some conviction in the sacredness of marriage, a sacredness or inviolability that set marriage apart from other kinds of relationships. If they did not talk literally in such terms, they nearly always talked of having believed that their marriages were permanent and forever. "I know at the time I thought we'd stay together forever," one woman told me; and another said, "I really got married with the attitude that I was to be married forever." In one sense these were vague hopes and dreams, but in another sense the ideal of marriage pervaded the reality of their daily lives; they knew divorce was common, but most said they had eliminated

thoughts of divorce as a well-defined possibility for themselves. I challenged one woman who was leaving her marriage after 24 years: "So you weren't even saying, 'Maybe this will last 10 years or 20 years, a lot of people get divorced.' You said, 'This is for life'?" To which she responded: "Yeah, I was naive." Another explained:

> I had promised this person that I would be with them forever. So I thought, "Oh god, that means forever; I'm in this forever." I didn't even think I could really get out of it. That just didn't seem like an option for me.

Second marriages seemed no different from first marriages in this regard. One woman who had married and divorced the same man twice said, "Really, when we married, even the second time, I figured it would be for the rest of my life." Even when marriages suffered from moments of serious marital difficulties, such marriages were considered permanent:

> Maybe that was partly naive on my part. But even after he had had an affair with another person, I didn't have the same amount of trust, but I still had this feeling that this was forever.

Another explained:

> There was never any question—if we went for joint counseling—there was never any question in either of our minds that our marriage was in danger or anything. It was just taken for granted that we'd made this commitment, and that was there, and that we were committed to this relationship. I never ever, while I was doing counseling, considered questioning the fact that my marriage was going to hold up through all this. Just that I had these discontents and unhappiness and things that I had to work on. Obviously I didn't like his drinking and I didn't like the way he treated me, but we sort of approached it by, "Can I get him to change some of that, can I get him to understand why it bothers me, and can I change what I'm doing so that I have more of a life of my own?" I was spending all my time with the kids at that point, going through all those crises. And neither of us really ever questioned that the marriage was going to be still there.

The point in emphasizing the sacred nature of marriage, as manifest in the pronounced belief that marriages are forever is that dissolving such marriages—even "bad" marriages—thus subsequently involved substantial symbolic work. Dissolving marriage meant profaning the sacred, ending that which was presumed to be forever, the consequences of which will become clear in the sections that follow. Is the premise of marriage being sacred too strong, however? The divorce rate is high, marriage and divorce laws increasingly depart from religious precepts, the stigma associated with divorce is waning (Gerstel, 1987), and couples obviously view divorce as a way out of unsatisfactory marriages. Clearly, the inviolability of marriage is no longer absolute. Nonetheless, marriage still has its rituals, legitimating agencies, privileged status, and rights of passage associated with it. It still consists of explicit rules and implicit assumptions—sexual exclusivity, loyalty, a division of labor, priority, reciprocity, and so on—the infringement of which provokes sanction and rebuke. People still talk of marriage as being sacred. A few even talked in ways reminiscent of Durkheim's sharp distinction between the sacred and the profane, describing marriage in terms of it being an all-or-nothing proposition: "I was brought up to think you are with somebody for your whole life, or you're not. It's one or the other, and you're not sort of doing what I'm doing." Another said, "The term 'divorcing' just kind of throws me off a little bit because I don't believe in divorce. To me, either a marriage is or it isn't." Moreover, such beliefs are not unique to my sample. In the period between 1992 and 1994, 76% of respondents to the National Survey of Families and Households (NSFH) believed that "marriage is a lifetime relationship and should never be ended except under extreme circumstances" (Center for Demography and Ecology, University of Wisconsin, 1997). Furthermore, research continues to show that most Americans view marriage as a central and defining institution in their lives, and that, in fact, its importance may be increasing (Blumstein & Schwartz, 1983; Glenn, 1996; Hopper, 1998). Patterns of marriage and divorce may be changing, but evidence suggests that many of our attitudes and beliefs about marriage have changed little over the recent past (Whyte, 1990).

Thus, although a characterization of marriage as sacred does not fully capture the depth and variability of meanings that people embraced in their marriages, there was clearly a "taken-for-granted image of marriage" that most shared (Berger & Kellner, 1964), and this was an image relatively "fixed, bounded, and deeply felt" (Sewell, 1996). Furthermore, it seemed to be an image put into practice, one that guided how they conceptualized their relationships and how they interacted with one another and with those around them.

Dissolving the Sacred

Beyond the practical difficulties of separating two closely intertwined lives, then, divorce involved an important symbolic dimension because it involved profaning the sacred. More particularly, because their marriages were defined as being permanent, divorce involved confronting and resolving the contradiction posed by the relationships being dissolved. This, however, was no easy task, and for two reasons. First, most upheld the notion of marriage being forever even as they were getting divorced. Only two of the divorcing people I interviewed began to disavow the sacred ideal of marriage. Most therefore had to work with the other side of the contradiction, reconfiguring the meanings of their particular marriages and finding fault in their own instantiations of the ideal. But second, marriage being sacred meant that there was a strong presumption that nearly any event, problem, or difficulty could and should be overcome in their particular marriages. Their marriages were, as we say, "for better, for worse, for richer, for poorer, in sickness and in health." Thus, something much stronger than a casual account of what went wrong was required. Something had to nullify the presumption that the particular relation was inviolable. In Durkheim's words, dissolving the sacred required a transformation *"totius substantiae—of* the whole being" such that the old object "cease[d] to exist, and . . . another [was] instantly substituted for it" (1915/1965, p. 54).

Indeed, against the backdrop of marriage being sacred, the "accounts" tradition of divorce research seems only to have scratched the surface of what divorcing people are doing when they attempt to explain their situations. Such research has effectively documented the "complaint themes" that emerge when divorcing people are asked about their situations and about the reasons for divorce—alcoholism, poor communication, infidelity, emotional cruelty, and so on—and it has examined how these themes vary historically and how they differ for women and men (Goode, 1956; Kitson & Raschke, 1981; Kitson, 1992; Kurz, 1995; Raschke, 1987; Riessman, 1990). It has suggested that the accounts divorcing people generate serve important purposes in that they facilitate coping (Weiss, 1975), provide a sense of closure (Duck, 1982), and shore up personal identities in the process (La Gaipa, 1982; McCall, 1982). But it has not elaborated how such accounts function vis-à-vis the sacred coming undone; it has not shown how such accounts actually affect the kind of transformation that Durkheim describes.

To dissolve the sacred, an account must penetrate to the very foundation of what defined the marriage and made the relation what it was. Whatever the particular contents of that account, it must have an "essentialist" character that penetrates to a definitional core the relationship. In what follows, I focus precisely on this, for the divorcing people I interviewed were indeed constructing deeply rooted and fundamental reinterpretations of their marriages that went to the core of what had constituted those marriages. At one level they were proffering accounts for what went wrong in their marriages, but more profoundly, they were redefining the nature of their marriages so as to resolve the contradiction posed by those marriages ending. In the next two sections, I consider first how initiators of divorce did this and then how noninitiating partners did this. As other studies have

shown, the initiator and noninitiator identities emerge as central constructs around which important aspects of divorce get defined and played out (Hopper, 1993a, 1993b; Vaughan, 1986; Weiss, 1975). Here the distinction was important because even though each side had to explain the same circumstance of marriage being dissolved, the interpretive burden was shaped differently depending on whether one had to justify the decision or respond to it; and this, together with the foundational, essentialist nature of the accounts that emerged, set the stage for the intense conflict that followed.

The Marriage That Never Was

For initiators, undoing the sacred required an explanation that did two things: first, it had to cut to the definitional core of one's marriage; second, it had to neutralize one's own culpability for the violation, for it was initiators who were ostensibly responsible for the sacred coming undone. Of the 12 initiators I interviewed, 11 did this by reconstruing their marriages into "marriages that never were," in effect symbolically disassembling their marriages back to first principles. They argued that their marriages were not "true" marriages in the first place, negating, undoing, nullifying, and annulling them. They effected a transformation in meaning that was, to borrow Garfinkel's words (1956, p. 421), "the destruction of one social object and the constitution of another. . . . It is not that the old object has been overhauled; rather it is replaced by another. One declares, '*Now,* it was otherwise in the first place.'"

There were generally four successive aspects to this redefinition: First, they began seeing their marriages in negative terms; second, they began seeing their marriages as bad from the start; third, they linked this view to an emerging sense that their marriages were fundamentally and irrevocably flawed; fourth, they subsequently conceived of their marriages as having been "false," only now revealed for what they truly were. The first three aspects have been noted as well by Vaughan (1986) in an earlier study of divorce, and so I touch on them only briefly here; the fourth is an as-yet unelaborated consequence of the first three, and importantly shows how the emerging reinterpretation helped solve the problem of the sacred coming undone.

To begin, initiators described marriages that were unhappy and of poor quality. They focused on complaints and problems, old and new, reported long-standing irritations and failures, and lent considerable weight to the negative side of the intense ambivalence they had felt preceding their decisions to divorce (see also Davis, 1973; Vaughan, 1986; Weber, 1992). Moreover, most initiators came to see their marriages as having suffered from the start rather than souring over time. As such, their negative accounts began to reach all the way back to the beginning—back to "day one" as one initiator told me. One woman projected back 25 years to the time of courtship: "I can see patterns that were there even while we were dating, that were still there all the way through the marriage." Another initially explained that she and her husband simply grew apart after 22 years of marriage, but when I asked whether things were basically good until then, she retreated: "Not really. I don't think so. From the very beginning there was a real big gap."

With a negative chronology that went back to the beginnings of their marriages, most initiators subsequently argued that there was something fundamentally wrong with their marriages, something irrevocably flawed. It was not merely that problems were never addressed or that spouses failed to communicate effectively. Rarely did I hear someone explain a divorce solely in terms of an affair, for example, or a job change, or in terms of newly emerging problems such as illness. Instead, they came to see their difficulties as being deeply rooted and their relationships as suffering from "structural flaws," as one man put it. Specific problems were thus cast as symptomatic of something deeper, and catalyst events were separated conceptually from the "ultimate reasons for divorce. A number of initiators pointed in particular to what they regarded as insuperable personality differences. They saw

themselves as having gotten "mismatched" with their spouses, an idea that again reinforced claims that their relationships had not turned bad, but had been as such all along. I asked one woman, for example, who told me that living with her husband had become unbearable, whether her husband had changed since she married him, and she puzzled, "I don't see him as having changed at all. It's funny, isn't it?"

Finally, with such negative and essentialist redefinitions of their marriages taking shape, initiators began to assert that their marriages had, in fact, not been "real" marriages at all. They asserted this in not just a superficial way of arguing that real marriages are good marriages and thus theirs was not much of a marriage, but in a substantive, ontological way. They were suggesting that their relationships had been phony likenesses of marriages, hollow shells that looked like marriages but really were not. In so many words, they began telling of having lived false marriages and of having lived a lie. An initiator remarked, for example:

I came to realize after all this time that there had been a very long time when we really had no life together. We just sort of shared a house, and sort of took care of the kids together. But mostly I did that with the kids and he went and did his thing, and we were sort of this phony family for friends and neighbors and the relatives.

Another argued that his marriage was insincere, and that "really" he knew this all along. He described his marriage as being "just sort of a form" that he went through:

I was 25 when I got married. And I would say we sort of went through the motions of getting married and taking the vows and everything, but I don't think I actually believed that it would last.

I asked him whether he thought, at least at the time, that he was entering into a lifetime commitment, and he answered:

Well, I think in my heart I wasn't. I don't think I ever would have said those words then. To anyone who asked, I would have said, "Yes, I am." But my sense of it now is that I never was, really.

Another told me about her real life beginning only once her marriage was over:

It's sort of like it happened, and then I got on with my real life. [Interviewer: Do you feel like it wasn't a real life before that?] Yeah. Really I do. I never felt married when I was married. I never felt like a wife. So I kind of felt like I was living a lie. So when I got divorced, it was like now I can be me, and really be myself.

Beneath the phoniness, too, was the "real" reality that had somehow been concealed. As one initiator told me, "It was just this little game that we played," underneath which "we were all miserable." Another described having been "divorced" even while being married, telling me: "I was truly in a divorced state for so long, even though I wasn't divorced." Many, indeed, puzzled over how they had lived for so long unaware of or unmotivated by the reality of their relationships. One initiator said, "The question is not why I got divorced, the question is truly why I remained married so long." Some talked in psychological terms about denial and self-deception; others talked about having been blinded by beliefs, hopes, and dreams. One said, "I guess sometimes you get into such a rut that you don't look at it objectively. You don't stand back and look at the situation." Another reflected, "Part of me is scared [about ever getting married again] because I see how a relationship I think is one way could really be another way."

In short, initiators produced what were, in effect, annulments of their marriages. They engaged in an interpretive process by which the bonds of marriage were not merely dissolved, *they were replaced with the notion that such bonds never existed.* Their reinterpretations were radical ones that went back to first principles, and their marriages became untrue originally and all along. This solved the interpretive problem they faced: The sacred was not really violated, for there was nothing sacred to begin with.

Indeed some, for whom the interpretation was most thoroughgoing, described literal "blank spots" in their memories, or inabilities to think much about their years of marriage; several talked with regret about time being "wasted" or lost. Many talked about needing to "start from scratch" with new lives once their divorces were final. One person I interviewed provided an apt analogy when she likened divorce to the process of gay men and lesbians "coming out." Coming out in our culture is a process of admitting to oneself and revealing to others the truth of one's real sexual identity. Announcing and explaining divorce, for these initiators, was likewise a process of coming to know and share with others the "truth" of what one's marriage had been all along.

Of course initiators engaged in this process to different degrees, and I do not mean to suggest that they had unambiguous and unchanging points of view. What I have described was, for most, one dimension of a complex and often unstable effort to make sense of marital dissolution. Many shifted among different kinds of accounts, moving, for example, between explanations that they simply grew apart to explanations that they were never really together in the first place. Some said they were in love when they got married, but then qualified it by saying that it was not a "real" or mature love. Some vehemently maintained that their marriages were obvious nightmares, whereas others engaged in a quieter and more subtle reconstruction that nevertheless ended in a belief that their marriages were flawed from the beginning. The people I interviewed were also in various phases of coming to terms with the failure of their marriages. Many would struggle, revisit the past, reconstruct what had happened and why; they would do this throughout their divorces and even afterward, at different times and under different circumstances. There were, indeed, elements of time and circumstance involved; as one initiator related, "It took me a while to really figure it out, too. Not that I've finished figuring it out. I was surprised as I got distance from it to realize how abusive a relationship it was." But elements of the reinterpretation here described were clearly discernable in nearly all cases, and whatever else might be going on, noninitiators discerned this as well.

Two points of variation should be noted as well. First, the one initiator who did not conform to the pattern I have described also managed to resolve the contradictions involved in her marriage dissolving, but she took the other interpretive route. Instead of emphasizing that her marriage was a mistaken instance of a sacred ideal, she questioned the ideal itself, saying, "I just always assumed that when you got married it was forever. And it sort of shattered my image of that, and so I'm having to rework my image of marriage." Second, when alcoholism figured prominently in an account, reinterpretations of the marriage were often more equivocal in the sense that initiators often believed that good marriages would have and could have been possible. This is consistent with the general claim that initiators tend to resolve the interpretive dilemma they face by seizing on explanations that are "foundational" with regard to the marriage. Because alcoholism in our society is conceptualized largely in medical and biological terms, it may well provide alternative grounds that explain a marriage's failure.

The Other as Crazy

One can imagine that the emerging interpretations of their marriages as false were not happily received by the noninitiating spouses to whom these were announced. Even if accounts were tactfully worded, and even if noninitiators had been struggling with such decisions themselves, the sudden revelation that their marriages were shams and that their spouses had been merely "playing along" came as a painful shock to noninitiators. For reasons to be elaborated in the next section, noninitiators did not share this newly articulated interpretation, and most responded by opposing initiators' claims and efforts. I anticipate this response here to complete a description of the typical initiator's stance. The idea that one's marriage was false was important in

provoking conflict not only because it presented a harsh new sense of reality to which the other had to respond, but also because it made any ensuing opposition look crazy and vengeful.

With a focus on the negative and an emerging sense that their marriages were flawed and phony, initiators understandably saw divorce as inevitable. Divorce became the obvious, natural, fated, and logical outcome of the past; there was, in the words of one man, a "natural law, like gravity almost" at work in bringing such relationships to an end. Indeed, most saw themselves as merely recognizing situations over which neither they nor their partners had any control:

> It's something that had to happen, and it wasn't something that either one of us really controlled. It was just an awful situation that we had to get out of, and I recognized it and he didn't.

Any proposals for marital counseling or for efforts to work things out thus became futile. "I don't think there was anything there to work with," one initiator explained. A few admitted to having not worked hard to save their marriages, but they felt that the hollowness of their marriages would have made such efforts useless:

> I had wanted that forever—the white picket fence and the whole dream. But it didn't come true. But I was at least smart enough to realize it wasn't happening and no matter what I did, it wasn't going to.

The Marriage That Never Was thus emerged as far more than a possible, alternative way of seeing one's relationship; it became *the* way of seeing the relationship. It became reality. And to the extent that divorce was a decision at all, it was something that could be announced and explained, but not negotiated. A woman I interviewed about her parents' situation described it thus:

> He was done. He was all finished. She again said she didn't want to end the relationship. He said he was sure that there was no reason to continue it. He couldn't imagine what she wanted to hold on to. What was there? To him, it's over and done with, over and closed, the end.

With divorce as a "fait accompli," as one man put it, initiators in most cases pushed hard for their divorces, moving quickly to accomplish physical separation and usually moving quickly to accomplish a legal split as well. Many wanted to proceed without attorneys, hoping to avoid the cost and potential animosity of litigation. Most told me that they would give and do almost anything to be out of their relationships quickly and painlessly. Nor did the emerging interpretation of the falseness of one's marriage preclude the possibility of being friendly with their spouses, for although divorce was difficult and regrettable, it was merely the correction of a mistake.

The consequence was that initiators were disappointed, even baffled, when noninitiators did not agree with their assessment and, in fact, opposed their efforts. Opposition made no sense; it was "bizarre," in the words of one initiator. Their partners seemed not to see what, to them at least, was obvious. The informant previously quoted described this phenomenon as she continued with the story of her parents:

He says, "The year [of being separated] is over. You're right, we need to move forward. I want a divorce." And she's saying, "What?!" And his response is, "Why are you surprised?" He was shocked. He was sure that she would want it, too, by that point. He was really surprised when she said, 'Whoa, this is not what I expected."

Some initiators attributed the emerging opposition on behalf of their spouses to a kind of denial or to a stubborn unwillingness on the part of their spouses to face what they perceived as reality. "I think he just wasn't really paying attention to what was happening in the relationship," one initiator explained to me. Another said, "I think he was [feeling like the relationship was falling apart], but he didn't want to admit it to himself." A third explained:

It's one of those situations where it's because I was the one who had the nerve to do it. And I always wind up saying, "Well, it doesn't mean it was my fault." He tried to turn it into, "It's your fault, you wouldn't try." And I don't buy into that.

[Interviewer: That's interesting that you said it was because you're the one who had the nerve to do it. What does that mean?] I think he knew something was wrong, too. He just wouldn't deal with it. He still won't.

Others attributed their spouses' opposition to psychological disorders or to vengeance. Their spouses, they concluded, were "out of touch." One woman described in disbelief letters from her husband that ignored what she saw as the basic facts of what happened. Another said, "I just look at him and think, 'What world do you live in? Do you have any connection to what's going on around you?'" A third initiator puzzled:

I think he probably wants this. I think he probably wants it as much as I do. I don't think he really knows what he wants, to tell you the truth. I mean, I can't imagine him saying anything to Bobby about maybe he'd get back with me. He must be just a little bit loony or something.

In the eyes of many initiators, then, their spouses had become crazy. Preposterous behavior and seemingly absurd beliefs became indicative of serious maladjustments, perceptions that were only intensified by the desperate, sometimes violent, ways in which noninitiators responded:

Talk to him and he'll say, "Oh, well *she's* crazy." But he truly is not okay. He's done many things. . . . One was ramming my car on the street a dozen times. And luckily he was seen by a neighbor, and he subsequently was charged with it. Very violent acts. When I say he's not okay, I mean he's really not okay.

Johnston and Campbell (1988) report on this phenomenon as well, noting the extreme degree to which spouses in divorce frequently come to believe that the other is truly malicious, dangerous, crazy, neglectful, or mentally ill. These researchers do not, however, give much emphasis to the two positions in divorce nor do they delineate the ways in which such attributes are linked to the specific interpretive problems faced by each side. Presumed "craziness," was not evenly distributed; it was instead attributed by initiators to noninitiators. The reason, I argue, was that only initiators seized upon a reinterpretation that undid their marriages in the way described above, and only from this frame of reference did subsequent behaviors seem out of touch with reality. Malevolent attributions of the other did, however, go both ways, for the essentialized reconstructions wound up making initiators look deceitful and disingenuous. This, together with the new emphasis on negative aspects of the marriage, provoked a set of counter claims and a moral indignation such that noninitiators put up forceful and bitter opposition. It is to this side of the emerging conflict that I now turn.

The Big Lie

Whatever the circumstances and whatever moves and countermoves had been going on during the time leading up to divorce, the partner who actually announced and carried through with a decision to divorce was pressed immediately to justify it. An interpretation that remade particular marriages into flawed, untrue, hollow, and essentially bad marriages from the beginning emerged for these initiators because it was an effective and persuasive way to nullify marriage and warrant divorce, and it did so while still upholding the sacredness of marriage in general. Noninitiating partners also faced the problem of explaining why their marriages were dissolving, and as with initiators, there were two possibilities: They could impugn the notion of marriage as a cultural ideal, or they could impugn their particular instantiation of that ideal. Only one noninitiator with whom I spoke disavowed the idea that marriage is sacred and forever, thus seeing her divorce simply as a transition to a new form of relating. As for the rest, they had to find fault in their own situations.

Now one way of doing this would be to see their marriages as having been mistaken instances of the ideal, as initiators typically did. Not many (only 4 of the 21 noninitiators interviewed) did so. The explanation that most seized

upon instead was this: Their spouses must have been disingenuous participants in their marriages. Their spouses, they argued, had said they were committed when they were not, had led them along in what were now claimed to be "false" marriages, and had sabotaged what could have been successful relationships. In this section I describe this solution to the problem of explaining divorce, a solution that had significant consequences for how most divorces subsequently progressed.

Before elaborating, however, it is worth considering why so few would resolve the interpretive problem they faced in terms of "the marriage that never was." Most noninitiators had complaints about their marriages; many were ambivalent, unhappy, and contemplating divorce; and some admitted that even with more time and effort, their marriages might fail. In this, they were much like initiators (Hopper, 1993a, 1993b). Three factors, however, help explain why most did not similarly begin to conceptualize their marriages as mistakes. First, they were not pushed toward a negative reconstruction of marriage, as were initiators, because they did not decide on their divorces and were thereby not pressed to justify them in the same way. The possibility of a good marriage remained "at least open to question," as one noninitiator put it. And although noninitiators still had to explain what was happening, they now found themselves with an opportunity to seize the moral high ground, which many of them did by emphasizing the sanctity of marriage in general and the positive aspects of their own (see also Vaughan, 1986). Second, with initiators articulating interpretations that made divorces seem like foregone conclusions, noninitiating partners faced the question as to why, if indeed their marriages were bad enough to warrant divorce, did they themselves not initiate them? Although one woman admitted feeling embarrassed for having "no spine" in her relationship as evidenced by not having left it herself, most answered the question by simply denying such interpretations. Third, an emerging focus on positive aspects of their relationships, in many cases, seemed to be part of a counterbalancing mechanism that family systems theory has described (Bowen, 1978; see also Kerr, 1988). Because family members are defined and self-identified in terms of each other and in terms of the whole, they frequently manifest complementary traits and sentiments. In this case, one member of a couple strongly emphasizing the negative might generate a counterbalancing effort by the other, and this was clearly happening in many situations. One woman, for example, who had been getting ready to leave her marriage described "falling apart" and begging for another chance when her husband announced it first. Another said: "I realized [then] that I didn't want it to end. I mean, I didn't even know that that's what I was thinking at first." Weber (1992), too, provides similar examples from her study of relationship loss. In short, in the initial stages of divorce, a generally more positive and protective view of their marriages—a view which precluded seeing those marriages as mistakes—helped answer the question as to why, despite their own ambivalence, they were not the ones leaving.

Of course, the fact that noninitiating partners did not conceptualize their marriages as irretrievably and fundamentally bad only exacerbated the interpretive difficulty they faced. But another solution presented itself: They and their marriages were evidently victims of initiators' deceit, a solution not all that surprising, given that initiators themselves were supplying the information used to formulate it. Initiators argued, for example, that their decisions were not sudden and impulsive and that they had always been discontent. They argued that their marriages had "really" been over for quite some time, even that their marriages were not real marriages in the first place. Noninitiators were now hearing more than that their spouses were unhappy (which in many cases they had known). They were, in fact, being told that their marriages were phony, pretend, and untrue. One noninitiator thus surmised that his wife had been "playing games" and that she had "an agenda in her mind to not make this work." Another said that his wife's emotional investment in the marriage

"wasn't genuine," though he did not realize it at the time. "I look at it now," said another, "and think she was just using me." I asked one woman to characterize her relationship overall and she responded: "It was dishonest." Elsewhere in the interview she remarked: "Nothing on the outside's what it is truly. I think it's really hard when you're a dumpee to understand that." Thus noninitiators described not knowing then, but realizing now, that their spouses had fooled them, had led them along, had put on an act.

Most painfully, many recounted ways in which their spouses informed them that they, the partners, had never been loved: "He told me that he didn't love me and that he never had." Another explained, "What she told me was that she married me without being in love with me." A third related this story:

> He claims that he never loved me like I loved him. He suggested in all this that I was the one that pursued him. And that he wasn't quite sure what to do with my love. And suggested, in fact, that I go back and read the love letters he wrote to me when we were dating. And I did it, and I wrote him my angry letter. I said, "You suggested I go back and read the love letters that you wrote to me, and I did, and I got about half way through and I stopped on the one where you were arguing with me that you loved me more than I loved you. It must be very convenient for you, and an insult, for you to say now you didn't love me. Or love me like I loved you." But I understand that this is a fairly common pattern. That men will say now, "Oh, I didn't love you like you loved me." Apparently this is not real unusual.

In and of themselves, "I never loved you" were exceptionally harsh words to hear. What made it worse was the deceit implied. Initiators intimated that they had lied about wanting to be married from the beginning and had led their spouses on for years. By their own admission, initiators seemed to have decided to leave quite some time ago and simply kept it secret. As one partner explained, "She told me that she had wanted to divorce just a few months after we were married." And as they heard this, noninitiators surmised (and their spouses often confirmed) that initiators emotionally and psychologically had "left" their marriages weeks, months, even years before. They had disinvested in the marriage long ago and only now decided to disclose it. One woman explained, "It came as a surprise that he had made that decision and yet hadn't shared it." Another described this in terms of the initiator being on a "different train" and never bothering to say so. Even if a decision was reached in the process of marital counseling, noninitiators described feelings that their relationships were ending in duplicity.

With their marriages and what was going on in them seen in this new light, there emerged the sense that initiators themselves were essentially duplicitous people, and this was the source of the trouble according to noninitiating partners. There was, in Johnston and Campbell's (1988, p. 14) words, "a sense of discovery as to who the ex-spouse *really* was—that is, she or he was in fact . . . fundamentally untrustworthy." As one noninitiator said, "I don't know anything about her. I thought I did." Some noninitiators came to believe that their partners were out and out liars. "He's kind of a pathological liar," one told me. Another remarked, realizing that the lies may even have been unintentional: "You know, the most dangerous people in the world are liars that don't know that they're liars." Others used less harsh terms, sometimes referring to initiators as cunning and masterful salesmen, or as good actors who were expert at giving false impressions: "Milt is very good at giving people impressions. And unless you're a lawyer and ask real specific things, you will walk away thinking he said or meant something that he didn't at all." Most frequently I heard the word *manipulative* being used to describe initiating spouses. Among noninitiators, 8 of 21 used it to refer to their spouses. None of the 12 initiators used it to describe noninitiators, but interestingly, two of them used it to describe themselves. None of the people involved in mutual divorces used the word at all. "She's a real pouty, manipulative person. She had me wrapped the whole time," one man described. A noninitiating wife said, "He does exactly what he wants. You know what I mean?

He's real manipulative that way. He certainly does what he wants when he wants. And a lot of it I see now." When I asked one partner whether she had any indications that her husband was serious about leaving, she answered:

No. No. Although it's always real hard to tell with Saul. He's very manipulative. And for me it was real hard because for a long time I didn't even know that it was happening. And then finally somebody pointed it out to me.

Even ostensibly good things, such as satisfying sexual relations in one man's case, were interpreted as having been "manipulative and calculating." In his words: "While she had these strengths [providing good sex], at times it appeared to me that she used them mostly to achieve some part of her agenda, rather than being genuine." An interview with a financial planner who works primarily with divorcing women helped corroborate this impression:

When they come in as a couple, before they come in, the wife [who is being left] has told me how manipulative he is and how he's going to just draw me into it. But they're never that way when they come in. The men are always matter of fact, quiet, seemingly interested in looking at the numbers, seemingly interested in making it work out. So it's an interesting dynamic and I'm not sure why that is. Because the women are always concerned and always afraid that the men are going to walk all over me. But it's never happened.

Not surprisingly, affairs came to figure prominently in the stories that noninitiators told, for affairs became emblematic of the secrecy and deception that noninitiators now saw. Some initiators did, in fact, have affairs, but so did some noninitiators. Some affairs sounded dubious, but with noninitiators now focused on ways in which duplicity and betrayal penetrated the whole of their marriages, the veracity of particular events mattered little, as this woman noted:

He still never admitted that he was seeing her, that he planned to leave with her, anything. . . . He said they hadn't been seeing each other until June, 6 months after we separated. I never believed that. Maybe they weren't sleeping together, I don't know. But it didn't matter. It was clear to me that I'd never know the truth.

In some cases sexual liaisons had been open and agreed upon, but noninitiators angrily looked back on them as having been dishonest.

Of course there was an important emotional component to all of this as well. As they talked about being lied to, noninitiators described with remarkable vividness what it felt like to have one's sense of reality suddenly transformed: "You absolutely feel like you're floundering. And that the ground that you were on has been literally pulled out from under your feet." Another described a "deep down pain" that was a "knot of fear and doubt and being lied to all the time so that I didn't believe in anything anymore."

The result of all this was "a really deep-seated bitterness that I've never felt for anyone in my life," one noninitiator told me. Some declared that they wanted vengeance, some wanted to see the initiator suffer. Others, even if they did not feel personally vengeful, argued that friendliness was precluded simply because a trust had been violated: "I don't make friends with people I can't trust," explained one noninitiator. Another said: "There's too much of a feeling of betrayal. He has betrayed a trust that he was given." One woman who was embroiled in a conflict over her child thus saw the matter in purely practical terms: "I'm dealing with this person who can drop out, or lies, or is not trustworthy. He's young and irresponsible. And that's part of his charm, but that's not a great dad." Later in the interview she continued:

> He screamed at me one night, "You used to trust me. You trusted me enough to have a child with me. How can you not trust me now to be good to her and take care of her?" So in the letter I wrote something about trust. How many times is he going to show me this trust is ill-founded? And it is.

The Big Lie, then, emerged as the interpretive counterpart to The Marriage That Never Was, and together these two interpretive stances put divorcing spouses directly at odds. Initiators saw their marriages as irrevocably, even originally, broken, a frame of reference that made noninitiators' reluctance to agree seem crazy and vengeful. Noninitiators reasserted a frame in which marriage was sacred and in which initiators' ending them seemed to be yet another maneuver in a now-obvious pattern of deceit. Some noninitiators reacted with threats, violence, or suicide attempts. This, of course, only confirmed the idea that they were dangerous and crazy. Sometimes initiators, who saw their marriages as effectively over, became sexually active with new or old friends, and this confirmed suspicions of adultery. The new interpretive stances of each shaped the reality according to which each now acted and reacted, and each was thus "compelled to fight consciously and righteously to protect" themselves from "what they believed to be the dangerous and pernicious influence of the other" (Johnston & Campbell, 1988, pp. 14–15, 66). As one noninitiator assured me, "I think sometimes she believes I'm fighting for vindictiveness, and I'm not."

Thus, initial hypotheses conjured to resolve certain dilemmas became self-fulfilling prophecies, and new problems and realities emerged that took situations on unforeseen paths. Each partner provoked the other and confirmed negative images of themselves; a cycle of preemptory and protective moves—a dynamic of conflict through which most divorces subsequently unfolded—was begun.

Conclusion

As the divorcing persons I interviewed attempted to define and redefine their relationships and as they worked to shape the content of their experiences into meaningful and consistent wholes, they faced a difficult interpretive dilemma. Marriage in our society, despite the prevalence of divorce, is believed to be both sacred and forever, and most marriages I learned about were unequivocally conceived of in terms of that ideal. When divorce began, however, and for whatever reasons it began, divorcing people found themselves in the midst of the sacred coming undone. They usually resolved the dilemma in one of two ways that preserved the meaning of marriage while explaining the failure of their own, with initiators seeing their particular marriages as false and noninitiators seeing their spouses as duplicitous. Certain problems of symbolic congruency were posed, and certain solutions presented themselves, such that partners began seeing each other in the worst of ways. Paradoxically, it was their mutual conformity to a world of shared meaning that ultimately generated a rather intense form of conflict between them.

Of course any analysis in terms of a single dimension necessarily simplifies and distorts. Among the people I interviewed, conflict played out through the legal system, too, and surely the high stakes involved when it came to property and children made material factors an essential contributing factor. Power differentials associated with gender were sometimes critical sources of conflict as well, particularly if men used violence in efforts to intimidate or control (Arendell, 1995; Kurz, 1995). Moreover, friends and family formed alliances (Johnston & Campbell, 1988), advocating on behalf of each side, distorting perceptions, often begetting a "spiral of conflict" (Heirich, 1968) where the conflict itself and how it was waged caused shifts in structures, resources, meanings, and perceptions that confirmed suspicions and brought about new grounds of contention.

The analysis is partial in two other respects as well. First, I did not elaborate fully on variations of the interpretive processes described here, and second, such interpretations were clearly not the only and final ones that divorcing people constructed. The malleable nature of symbols and meanings leaves room for nonconformity, resistance, improvisation, and change. People may import alternate meanings from other realms of the social world to shift what marriage means,

and then—either knowingly or not—the process of divorce. Some of the people I interviewed did, in fact, disavow the sacred nature of marriage; some resisted having their divorces defined and structured around the initiator and noninitiator identities. Meanings were apt to shift in different spheres of activity around divorce, and certain kinds of accounts became important or not depending on whether persons were among family, in a courtroom, or recounting their histories to me in an interview. Furthermore, divorcing people not only reconstructed their pasts, but, as Stacey (1990) and Johnson (1988) have pointed out, they also fashioned them into new stories and relational structures that built their post divorce families in complex and creative ways.

Nonetheless, the findings in this report suggest a strong role for the symbolic dimension in divorce, and in family life more generally (Gubrium & Holstein, 1990; Holstein & Gubrium, 1994)—indeed, a much stronger role than previous research has recognized. Even studies that have focused on narratives, accounts, and other symbolic resources have tended to treat the symbolic world as merely reflecting the goings-on of family life. Such studies have implied that there is everyday reality, and then there are the stories that we tell ourselves and each other about that reality; symbols are epiphenomenal from this perspective, though they are sometimes important because they affect how people cope with and adjust to reality. Divorce researchers, in particular, have treated opposing narratives in divorce as reflecting deep, long-standing differences in partners' feelings and experiences in marriage (e.g., McCall, 1982; Vaughan, 1986); the implication of which is that conflict in divorce is rooted in the divergent paths taken during marriage (a view that fits under the marital history perspective on conflict outlined earlier), and partners' interpretive stances during divorce come to articulate that. The findings presented here give evidence for a much stronger symbolic thesis, suggesting that symbols often create the goings-on of divorce in the first place. In previous work, I have shown that important aspects of the narratives divorcing people tell are rhetorical constructs (Hopper, 1993b); in this study, I have shown that the symbolic structure and logic of how such narratives get constructed can generate the conflict that typically characterizes divorce. Together, these findings suggest that family researchers ought to be looking closely at the symbolic dimension of family life to understand how interpretive processes may themselves be a source of important phenomena in families.

References

Ahrons, C. R. (1981). The continuing coparental relationship between divorced spouses. *American Journal of Orthopsychiatry, 51,* 415–428.

Ahrons, C. R. (1994). *The good divorce.* New York: Harper Collins.

Ahrons, C. R., & Rodgers, R. H. (1987). *Divorced families: A multidisciplinary developmental view.* New York: Norton.

Arendell, T. (1986). *Mothers and divorce.* Berkeley: University of California Press.

Arendell, T. (1995). *Fathers and divorce.* Thousand Oaks, CA: Sage.

Berger, P., & Kellner, H. (1964). Marriage and the construction of reality: An exercise in the microsociology of knowledge. *Diogenes, 46,* 1–23.

Blumstein, P, & Schwartz, P. (1983). *American couples.* New York: Pocket Books.

Bohannan, P. (1971). The six stations of divorce. In P. Bohannan (Ed.), *Divorce and after* (pp. 33– 62). Garden City, NY: Anchor Books.

Bowen, M. (1978). *Family therapy in clinical practice.* New York: Aronson.

Bowlby, J. (1969). *Attachment and loss. Vol. 1: Attachment.* New York: Basic Books.

Bowlby, J. (1973). *Attachment and loss. Vol. 2: Separation: Anxiety and anger.* New York: Basic Books.

Braver, S. L., Whitley, M., & Ng, C. (1993). Who divorced whom? Methodological and theoretical issues. *Journal of Divorce & Remarriage, 20,* 1–19.

Center for Demography and Ecology, University of Wisconsin. (1997). *National survey of families and households: Wave I, 1987–1988, and wave II, 1992–1994 [MRDF].* Ann Arbor, MI: Inter-University Consortium for Political and Social Research.

Davis, M. S. (1973). *Intimate relations.* New York: Free Press.

Dillon, P. A., & Emery, R. E. (1996). Divorce mediation and resolution of child custody disputes: Long-term effects. *American Journal of Orthopsychiatry, 66,* 131–140.

Duck, S. (1982). A typography of relationship disengagement and dissolution. In S. Duck (Ed.), *Personal relationships: Vol. 4. Dissolving personal relationships* (pp. 1–30). London: Academic Press.

Durkheim, E. (1965). *The elementary forms of the religious life.* New York: Free Press. (Original work published 1915)

Durkheim, E. (1978). The conjugal family. In M. Traugott (Ed.), *Emile Durkheim on institutional analysis* (pp. 229–239). Chicago: University of Chicago Press. (Original work published 1892)

Erlanger, H. S., Chambliss, E., & Melli, M. S. (1987). Participation and flexibility in informal processes: Cautions from the divorce context. *Law and Society Review, 21,* 585–604.

Felstiner, W. L. F., Abel, R. L., & Sarat, A. (1981). The emergence and transformation of disputes: Naming, blaming and claiming. . . . *Law and Society Review, 15,* 631–654.

Garfinkel, H. (1956). Conditions of successful degradation ceremonies. *American Journal of Sociology, 61,* 420–424.

Gerstel, N. (1987). Divorce and stigma. *Social Problems, 43,* 172–186.

Glaser, B. G., & Strauss, A. L. (1967). *The discovery of grounded theory.* Hawthorne, NY: Aldine de Gruyter.

Glenn, N. D. (1996). Values, attitudes, and the state of American marriage. In D. Popenoe, J. B. Elshtain, & D. Blankenhorn (Eds.), *Promises to keep: Decline and renewal of marriage in America* (pp. 15–33). Lanham, MD: Rowman and Littlefield.

Goldsmith, J. (1980). Relationships between former spouses: Descriptive findings. *Journal of Divorce, 2,* 1–20.

Goode, W. J. (1956). *After divorce.* Glencoe, IL: Free Press.

Gray, J. D., & Silver, R. C. (1990). Opposite sides of the same coin: Former spouses' divergent perspectives in coping with their divorce. *Journal of Personality and Social Psychology, 59,* 1180–1191.

Gubrium, J. F., & Holstein, J. A. (1990). *What is family?* Mountain View, CA: Mayfield.

Hagestad, G. O., & Smyer, M. A. (1982). Dissolving long-term relationships: Patterns of divorcing in middle age. In S. Duck (Ed.), *Personal* relationships: *Vol. 4. Dissolving personal relationships* (pp. 155–188). London: Academic Press.

Harvey, J. H., Wells, G. L., & Alvarez, M. D. (1978). Attribution in the context of conflict and separation in close relationships. In J. H. Harvey, W. Ickes, & R. F. Kidd (Eds.), *New directions in attribution research* (Vol. 2, pp. 235–260). Hillsdale, NJ: Erlbaum.

Heirich, M. (1968). *The spiral of conflict.* New York: Columbia University Press.

Holstein, J. A., & Gubrium, J. F. (1994). Constructing family: Descriptive practice and domestic order. In T. R. Sarbin & J. I. Kitsuse (Eds.), *Constructing the social* (pp. 232–249). London: Sage.

Hopper, J. (1993a). Oppositional identities and rhetoric in divorce. *Qualitative Sociology, 16,* 133–156.

Hopper, J. (1993b). The rhetoric of motives in divorce. *Journal of Marriage and the Family, 55,* 801–813.

Hopper, J. (1998, August). *The symbolic origins of conflict in divorce.* Paper presented at the annual meetings of the American Sociological Association, San Francisco, CA.

Isaacs, M. B., & Leon, G. (1988). Divorce, disputations, and discussion: Communicational styles among recently separated spouses. *Journal of Family Psychology, 1,* 298–311.

Johnson, C. L. (1988). *Ex familia.* New Brunswick, NJ: Rutgers University Press.

Johnston, J. R., & Campbell, L. E. G. (1988). *Impasses of divorce.* New York: Free Press.

Johnston, J. R., & Campbell, L. E. G. (1993). Instability in family networks of divorced and disputing parents. In E. J. Lawler & B. Markovsky (Eds.), *Social psychology of groups: A reader* (pp. 197–223). Greenwich, CT: JAI Press.

Kerr, M. E. (1988, September). Chronic Anxiety and defining a self. *Atlantic Monthly,* pp. 35–58.

Kitson, G. C., & Raschke, H. J. (1981). Divorce research: What we know; what we need to know. *Journal of Divorce, 4,* 1–37.

Kitson, G.C., with Holmes, W.M. (1992). *Portrait of divorce.* New York: Guilford Press.

Knox, D. (1990). A sociologist's encounter with divorce lawyers. *Free Inquiry in Creative Sociology, 18,* 197–198.

Kressel, K., Jaffee, N., Tuchman, B., Watson, C., & Deutsch, M. (1980). A typology of divorcing couples: Implications for mediation and the divorce process. *Family Process, 19,* 101–116.

Kurz, D. (1995). *For richer, for poorer.* New York: Routledge.

La Gaipa, J. J. (1982). Rules and rituals in disengaging From relationships. In S. Duck (Ed.), *Personal relationships: Vol. 4. Dissolving personal relationships* (pp. 189–210). London: Academic Press.

Masheter, C. (1997). Former spouses who are friends: Three case studies. *Journal of Social and Personal Relationships, 14,* 207–222.

McCall, G. J. (1982). Becoming unrelated: The management of bond dissolution. In S. Duck (Ed.), *Personal relationships: Vol. 4. Dissolving personal relationships* (pp. 211–231). London: Academic Press.

Nevaldine, A. (1978). *Divorce: The leaver and the left.* Unpublished doctoral dissertation, Minneapolis, University of Minnesota.

Raschke, H. J. (1987). Divorce. In M. B. Sussman & S. K. Steinmetz (Eds.), *Handbook of marriage and the family* (pp. 597–624). New York: Plenum Press

Riessman, C. K. (1990). *Divorce talk: Women and men make sense of personal relationships.* New Brunswick, NJ: Rutgers University Press.

Sewell, W. H., Jr. (1996). *The concept(s) of culture.* Unpublished manuscript, Departments of Political Science and History, University of Chicago.

Simmel, G. (1955). *Conflict.* New York: Free Press. (Original work published 1908)

Sprey, J. (1979). Conflict theory and the study of marriage and the family. In W. R. Burr, R. Hill, F. I. Nye, & I. L. Reiss (Eds.), *Contemporary theories about the family* (Vol. 2, pp. 130–159). New York: Free Press.

Stacey, J. (1990). *Brave new families.* New York: Basic Books.

Vaughan, D. (1986). *Uncoupling.* New York: Oxford University Press.

Wallace, A. F. C., & Fogelson, R. D. (1965). The identity struggle. In I. Boszormenyi-Nagy & J. L. Framo (Eds.), *Intensive family therapy* (pp. 365–406). New York: Harper and Row.

Weber, A. L. (1992). The account-making process: A phenomenological approach. In T. L. Orbuch (Ed.), *Close relationship loss: Theoretical approaches* (pp. 174–191). New York: Springer-Verlag.

Weiss, R. S. (1975). *Marital separation.* New York: Basic Books.

Weitzman, L. J. (1985). *The divorce revolution.* New York: Free Press.

Whyte, M. K. (1990). *Dating, mating, and marriage.* New York: Aldine de Gruyter.

"They Think You Ain't Much of Nothing": Social Construction of the Welfare Mother

Karen Seccombe, Delores James, and Kimberly Baffle Walters

Abstract

Welfare reform is in the forefront of the political and social agenda in the United States. This research examines the ways that women on welfare interpret welfare use. From in-depth interviews with 47 women who received cash assistance in 1995, we examined the theories behind their accounts of the stigmatizing of welfare recipients and why they, and other women, use the welfare system. Although the respondents tended to blame the social structure, the welfare system itself, or fate for their own economic circumstances and welfare use, they invoked popular and mainstream individualist and cultural "victim-blaming" theories to explain other women's reliance on the system. Many women believed popular constructions of the welfare mother as lazy and unmotivated and evaluated their own situation as distinctly different from the norm. The hegemony of the individual perspective is a strong and stubborn barrier to dealing constructively with poverty and welfare reform.

I've had people who didn't know I was receiving assistance, and everything was just fine. But when people find out you're receiving assistance, it's like, why? Why did you get lazy all of the sudden?

Leah, a 24-year-old mother

Approximately 39 million people are poor in the U.S., according to recent data from the U.S. Bureau of the Census (1997a). Within this large segment of the population are the approximately 3.5 million families, mostly mothers and their dependent children who receive cash welfare assistance, which until recently was called Aid to Families with Dependent Children (AFDC). President Bill Clinton signed monumental welfare reform legislation, which became federal law on July 1, 1997. P.L. 104–193 abolished the AFDC program and replaced it with a new program called Temporary Assistance to Needy Families (TANF). Turning many of the details of welfare law over to the states, it sets lifetime welfare payments at a maximum of 5 years, and the majority of adult recipients are required to work after 2 years. Twenty-five percent of recipients in each state must be working by the end of 1997. By the year 2002, 50% must be employed. Other changes under this reform include child-care assistance, at least 1 year of transitional Medicaid, the identification of the children's biological fathers, and the requirement that unmarried recipients who are minors must live at home and stay in school in order to receive benefits.

AFDC and TANF are virtually synonymous with the word "welfare" in the minds of most people. In the larger sense of the word, "welfare" could also encompass schools, parks, police and fire protection, as the term "welfare state," popular in most of Western Europe, implies. However, in the U.S. welfare generally brings to mind the cash assistance programs of AFDC and TANF, and therefore "welfare," "AFDC," and "TANF" are used interchangeably here for ease of discussion. Although welfare was originally created to serve primarily White widows and their children, welfare's recipient base has shifted over the years to mostly divorced and never-married women with children. Many people think that cash programs provide benefits to a large number of never-married, young, African American women and their children, a stereotype that has undoubtedly contributed to the growing sentiment against welfare (Piven & Cloward, 1993; Quadagno, 1994). Yet, African Americans constitute only 36% of recipients (U.S. House of Representatives, Committee on Ways and Means, 1996). AFDC is criticized as an extravagant and costly program that is spiraling out of control and is responsible for a sizable component of our federal deficit, but it approximates only 1% of federal spending (*Congressional Digest*, 1995; U.S. House of Representatives, Committee on Ways and Means, 1996). Although money is often cited as the source of these tensions, American values of financial independence and hard work are usually at the heart of the hostility toward welfare (Meyer, 1994).

Numerous stereotypes of able-bodied persons who receive welfare persist. Women who are without husbands to support them and their children are viewed as suspect and potentially undeserving (Abramovitz, 1996; Gordon, 1994; Miller, 1992). They are "manless women," as Dorothy Miller reveals, a stigmatized group that is "reduced in our minds from a whole and usual person to a tainted, discounted one" (Goffman, 1963, pp. 3–4). Women who receive welfare have been accused of being lazy, unmotivated, of cheating the system or having additional children simply to increase the amount of their benefit check. The underlying belief is that these women are looking for a free ride at the expense of the American taxpayer (Davis & Hagen, 1996). They are criticized for their supposedly long-term

dependency, despite evidence that the median length of a welfare stay is 23 months (U.S. House of Representatives Committee on Ways and Means, 1996). Although some of these women have intermittent spells of employment (Ellwood, 1986; Harrris, 1993, 1996), only 7% of recipients remain continuously on welfare for 8 years or longer (*Congressional Digest*, 1995). Race, class, and gender stereotypes become intertwined. Our society despises poor women, particularly African American poor women, who are seen as rejecting the traditional nuclear family that contains at least one and possibly two breadwinners and, instead, "choosing" to remain dependent on the public dole. This is in sharp contrast to the considerably less-stigmatized images of welfare recipients and public programs in most of Western Europe (Bergmann, 1996; Kamerman & Kahn, 1978).

Conceptual Framework

This research examines the social constructions of welfare mothers that are internalized by the welfare recipients themselves. Based on in-depth interviews with women who receive welfare, this study examines how they interpret the stigma attached to welfare use and the ways in which they construct their identity and rationale for using welfare. Scott and Lyman (1968) refer to these as "accounts—how people explain unanticipated or untoward behavior, both their own and someone else's." The social construction of welfare recipients is largely rooted in the beliefs about the causes of poverty and wealth more generally. These competing perspectives have been commonly summarized as (a) individualism, (b) social structuralism, (c) the culture of poverty, and (d) fatalism (Feagin, 1975; Hunt, 1996; Rank, 1994; Smith & Stone, 1989). Research has documented the persistent popularity of these perspectives within the more affluent population. However, it is not known whether, and to what degree, women on welfare subscribe to these explanations of poverty and welfare use. A review of these perspectives can help us organize and interpret the complexity of the way they account for the use of welfare.

Perspectives on Social Inequality, Poverty, and Welfare Use

Why are people poor, and why are they on welfare? These questions have a multitude of contradictory answers. The perspective of rugged individualism suggests that people, themselves, are primarily responsible for their own economic position in society and that opportunities are available to all who are willing to work hard and who have motivation and initiative. Because virtually everyone has the opportunity to acquire the skills, traits, and human capital needed for upward mobility, those who fail to make it have largely themselves to blame. In this almost social Darwinian view, welfare recipients are a particularly blatant example of those who have failed to make it and, therefore, reside at the bottom of the economic hierarchy. Studies conducted over the past several decades show the persistent popularity of the individual perspective in this country (Feagin, 1972, 1975; Hunt, 1996; Kluegel & Smith, 1982; Smith & Stone, 1989). Respondents in national surveys cite lack of motivation, drive, and thrift as primary reasons for poverty and suggest that hard work, talent, and drive are the leading causes of wealth.

Welfare recipients are perhaps the most stigmatized subset of the poor. Yet a critical social fact is often ignored: The majority of welfare recipients are dependent children and their unmarried mothers. Given day-to-day household and child-care responsibilities and the time constraints resulting from these tasks, single mothers do not have the same opportunities to pull themselves up by their bootstraps as do other adults who are unencumbered with children. To ignore the emotional commitment and the time involved in taking care of dependent children and to fail to recognize how caretaking can inhibit women's ability for social mobility is to ignore the reality of many women's existence.

A social-structural perspective assumes that poverty is a result of economic or social imbalances within our social structure that serve to restrict opportunities for some people. Some suggest that poverty is an inherent feature of capitalism (Marx & Engels, 1968), and the subsequent control over other social structures, such as education and the polity, is designed to serve the interests and maintain the dominance of the wealthy class (Foucault, 1980). Others point to the structural features of a changing economy, such as the growth in low-paying service sector jobs and the erosion of the minimum wage.

Feminist theorists suggest that we expand our concerns to other aspects of the social structure that inhibit women's upward mobility, in particular. This may include the structural features of marriage and family life that affect a woman's ability to transcend economic marginality, such as a father's lack of involvement in child care, the limited availability of day care facilities, or insufficient enforcement of child support polices by the government (Abramovitz, 1996; Miller, 1992).

A corollary of the social-structural perspective, often referred to as "Big Brother" (Rank, 1994; Schiller, 1989), suggests that social programs and welfare policies, themselves, contribute to poverty and exacerbate welfare use by trapping people in poverty and welfare dependency instead of helping them escape. This twist on structuralism is popular with social conservatives (Anderson, 1978; Murray, 1984, 1988) and is cited as evidence to advocate a dismantling of welfare programs. Proponents argue, as did de Tocqueville over 100 years ago, that people are inherently lazy and will lose motivation and incentive if they know that government programs will take care of them. They suggest that people will snub work at low-paying jobs and will rely, instead, on the free money of welfare if given the opportunity. Thus, they argue that eliminating or drastically reducing welfare is the first step to curbing poverty. However, these discussions are problematic because welfare is not a gender-neutral program. Recipients are predominantly women, and the needs and concerns embedded in women's real life experiences as caretakers of dependent children are not contextualized within recommendations to reduce or eliminate welfare. For example, should a woman with young, dependent children who forgoes minimum wage work to remain on welfare always be considered lazy—even if employment means losing crucial health insurance and other benefits and thereby placing her children at risk?

Another perspective, the culture of poverty, is a blend of individualism and social structuralism. It often is associated with African Americans and suggests that a subcultural set of values, traits, and expectations have developed as a direct result of the structural constraints associated with living in isolated pockets of poverty. Although there is a range of opinion about the specific antecedents, features, and consequences of the subculture (Gilder, 1981; Lewis, 1966; Mead, 1992; Moynihan, 1965; Valentine, 1968; Wilson, 1987, 1993), proponents of this point of view voice concern about the transmission of these values from parents to children. The question of whether poverty and welfare use are intergenerational—passed on from parents to their children—is an enduring theme. Some theorists argue that when parents and neighbors rely heavily on welfare and live in poor neighborhoods in relative isolation, the stigma associated with welfare disappears. Wilson (1987) attributes poverty among the African American underclass in inner cities to their social, economic, and geographic isolation. He argues that the loss of well-paying manufacturing jobs from urban areas has increased male unemployment, thereby reducing the pool of men eligible for marriage and increasing the number of children born out of wedlock. Women may develop their own adaptations to poverty and inequality, such as relying on extended families to care for their children or pooling their financial resources (Edin, 1991; Edin & Lein, 1997; Jarrett, 1994, 1996; Seccombe, 1999; Stack, 1974).

Finally, fatalism attributes the causes of wealth and poverty to quirks of birth, chance, luck, human nature, or other forces over which people have no control. Poverty is not viewed as anyone's fault, per se, but rather is a consequence of unplanned, random, or natural human events.

Herrnstein and Murray (1994), for example, suggest that low intelligence is a primary cause of poverty and welfare dependency. Claiming that intelligence is largely genetic, they argue that poor people with low IQs give birth to another cohort with low IQs, and thus the children remain in poverty.

The U.S. population generally does not believe that bad luck is a sufficient reason for poverty. Feagin (1975) found that only 8% of his respondents agreed that bad luck was a very important reason for poverty. More recently, Smith and Stone (1989), with 200 randomly selected respondents, found that only 10% attributed poverty to bad luck. We suggest that these low figures may be due to the fact that the poor are discussed as though they are nameless, faceless, genderless, and generic beings. They are not. The poor are primarily women and children. But when we fail to identify them as such, when we do not specifically refer to the poor as "women" or as "she," the male image emerges. Our tolerance for attributing poverty to bad luck or to fate is likely gendered. Men are expected to be independent and to be able to actively construct their own lives. We do not take kindly to men simply having bad luck and, therefore, falling into poverty and needing assistance. Women, in contrast, traditionally have been socialized to be more dependent on others for their economic and social position. Therefore, they are more vulnerable to fluctuations in their status through no fault of their own. Welfare was originally created to protect women who were single mothers from vulnerabilities beyond their control, such as violence, abuse, or desertion (Abramovitz, 1996; Gordon, 1994; Miller, 1992). Today, however, Americans are less sure of the type of protection women need, and they are less enthusiastic about providing it.

Research Questions

We examine the ways in which women on welfare interpret the public stigmatization of welfare recipients and the perspectives they draw on to account for why they and other women receive AFDC. We anticipate that welfare recipients are aware of the stigma attached to welfare recipients and are cognizant of the basic tenets of these perspectives, including the popularity of individualism. Goodban (1985), for example, found that nearly two thirds of her sample of 100 African American women on AFDC said they experienced some sense of shame for being on welfare. Second, although middle- and upper-class people make judgments from media stereotypes, the poor make judgments not only out of these influences, but also out of their own real experiences with limited opportunities for employment, lack of available child care, and other constraints. Consequently, we anticipate that recipients, themselves, will generally reject the individualist perspective and instead will subscribe to more structural or fatalistic perspectives that blame forces outside of their own control for their economic circumstances. Third, we anticipate that women who receive welfare will see that they have common experiences with other recipients. A sense of group consciousness could emerge if they are cognizant of the negative sentiment toward welfare recipients and if they believe that it is unwarranted and should be changed (Davis & Robinson, 1991; Giddens, 1973). They have considerable contact with other welfare recipients at the welfare office when they go there to pick up their monthly food stamps and for periodic recertification by their caseworkers, and many live in large public housing projects. Through a process of awareness of their own subordinate group status, we anticipate that they will attribute both their own and other women's reliance on welfare to factors embedded in the social structure or to fate. We assume that, rather than accept the popular constructions of welfare mothers as lazy and unmotivated, they will attribute their own failure at making it and the failures of other welfare recipients to larger forces outside their control.

Methods

For this study, we use phenomenology (Van Manen, 1990) and grounded theory (Glaser & Strauss, 1967; Wilson & Hutchinson, 1991). These approaches are drawn from symbolic interactionism and are based on the assumption that people actively construct their own realities from the symbols around them via social interaction (Blumer, 1969). We draw on phenomenology to accurately describe and interpret participants' meanings and practices through detailed narratives, and we use grounded theory to categorize their views of why women receive welfare. Together, phenomenology and grounded theory reveal the uniqueness of shared meanings that can inform the way welfare and welfare recipients are perceived and can offer a conceptual framework for understanding why people may be on welfare.

The data were obtained from in-depth and semistructured interviews in the fall of 1995 with 47 women who were receiving AFDC benefits. They reside in several rural and urban communities in Northern Florida. Because our goal is to discover meaning, rather than measure the distribution of attributes across the population, we utilize a purposive sampling strategy to elucidate particular population types, such as variation in race, age, housing type, community size, and whether they had a telephone.

The initial sample came from volunteers who were waiting in line to pick up their monthly food stamps. Telephone numbers, if available, and addresses were obtained from persons willing to be interviewed later. Several other respondents were friends, relatives, neighbors, or acquaintances of women who were interviewed initially. The authors and two graduate students conducted interviews. All interviewers were women; two were African American, and three were White. Their ages ranged from late 20s to late 40s.

The interviews, conducted in the homes of respondents, ranged from 45 minutes to nearly 3 hours. Each interview was audiotaped with permission and later transcribed verbatim. The data were coded thematically with a provisional start list of descriptive codes, which was later expanded to include unanticipated information (Glaser & Strauss, 1967; Miles & Huberman, 1994; Strauss & Corbin, 1990). We identified common themes, key issues, trends, and conceptual frameworks after substantial immersion in the interview data.

The respondents ranged in age from 19 to 48 years, with a mean age of 29.9 years. Eighteen respondents were White, and 29 were African American. Although this distribution roughly reflects the racial background of recipients in the interview area, it overrepresents the proportion of African Americans on welfare throughout the U.S. Most respondents ($n = 28$) had never been married, and they had a mean of 2.3 children. Only nine of the respondents reported having less than a high school education. Eighteen had completed high school or had received a GED, and 19 had taken some college or vocational courses beyond high school. (Data from one respondent were missing.) At the time of the interview, 19 women reported that they were enrolled in school or job training—working toward their GED, taking community college or university courses, receiving vocational training, or participating in an education and training program sponsored by the district welfare office. As expected, the majority of respondents were not employed outside the home for pay, although some worked in the informal sector by babysitting or hair styling. Seven were employed part-time, and three worked full-time. Among those who were employed, incomes were not sufficient to pull them above the poverty line, and they continued to collect a partial AFDC benefit. The majority of respondents ($n = 29$) lived in subsidized housing, which ranged from large multi-storied projects to single-family dwellings. Unfortunately, data on the length of time on welfare are incomplete.

Results

Awareness of Societal Attitudes Toward Welfare Recipients

We found respondents cognizant of their stigmatized status. When asked if they ever hear negative comments about people on welfare, they overwhelmingly answered, "Yes," and most claimed that criticism has been directed at them personally. Consistent with research that indicates the popularity of individualist explanations of poverty, most welfare recipients interviewed—African American and White, young and old—reported that they hear considerable personal blame and criticism. For example, asked what kinds of things she had heard about welfare recipients, Rhonda, a 28-year-old White woman with a young son, explained:

> I've heard one girl was going to quit working because all the taxes come to us. Plus, you know, they downgrade us in every kind of way there is. They say we look like slobs; we keep our houses this way and that way. And our children, depending on the way they're dressed, we're like bad parents and all sorts of things like that.

The theme of laziness, an image embodied in the individualist perspective, emerged with relative consistency. Lonnie, an African American mother of five who has been on and off of welfare several times and has most recently received benefits for 2 years reported:

> They say you lazy. They say you lazy and don't want to work. You want people to take care of you. You want to sit home and watch stories all day, which I don't. And they say that it's a handout. I stood in the welfare line, and I heard what they called me. And I've went in the grocery store, and when you get ready to buy your groceries, people have made nasty little remarks about the groceries you're buying. They'll go, "We're paying for that." Once there was some university students, and I guess they felt like that. They had a small amount in their buggy, and I had large amounts. He started talking, so his girlfriend kept trying to get him to be quiet. And he kept talking and talking. And then he said, "That's why the President is trying to cut off welfare, because of people like that!" I turned to him, and I say, I say, "Well, you know something? I have worked in my time, too. And I will work again. It's not like I'm asking you for anything. And I hope you don't come and ask me for anything 'cause with me and my five kids I couldn't give you none anyway!" And he stomped out of there when I told him that. But I was being honest

with him. I have worked. I felt real bad that day, I really did.

Racist overtones are evident, as well. One woman heard welfare recipients referred to as "White and Black niggers sucking off the system." One of the many reasons that welfare is stigmatized is because it is incorrectly associated with primarily African Americans (Quadagno, 1994). Whites tend to deny that our social structure limits the opportunities for African Americans (Bobo & Smith, 1994; Kluegel & Smith, 1982; National Opinion Research Center, 1993). They sometimes feel that they, themselves, are victimized by policies of "reverse discrimination" and that African Americans reap employment and social welfare benefits. For example, fewer than 40% of Whites support increased social spending to help African Americans, according to data from the General Social Survey (Bobo & Smith, 1994). This view was epitomized in the comments made by a 27-year-old White woman named Beth when she was asked what kinds of things she had heard people say about welfare recipients:

> Oh, they say silly stuff, prejudiced stuff: "The Black people are getting it, so we might as well— you might as well go ahead and get it too while you can. They're driving Cadillacs," and this and that.

Dee is an African American woman, aged 24 with three children, 4 years old and younger. She attends school full-time and plans to become an accountant. She told us that the most negative comments she has heard come from White males:

> That's mainly who I hear it from. I mean, I hear a couple of things from Black guys, but a lot of Black guys I know grew up on the system. You know, they are trying to get off that system. So you don't really hear it much from them. They have firsthand experience with it. Those who don't have firsthand experience have friends who have. So, the majority of them have come into contact with it sometime in their lifetime. As for the White males, a lot of them grew up in the upper-middle class,

you know, above the poverty line, so they never run across it, unless they had friends who were on the system. But there are as many White people on it as Black people.

The grocery store was one social context where negative comments were reported to occur most often. There, stigma symbols, such as food stamps, are in full view and cannot be hidden (Goffman, 1963). Looking for evidence of fraud, cashiers and others closely scrutinize the food that women purchase. The assumption is made that welfare mothers live high on the hog at taxpayers' expense and must be closely monitored in order to prevent irresponsible behavior and abuse of the system. The public looks for women who buy steak with food stamps and feel vindicated when they find them.

A second context where frequent negative comments were heard was the welfare office itself. Rather then seeing the welfare office as a plan for help, recipients view it with suspicion and distrust. They suggest that the people who run it are self-serving and show contempt for their clients. "They think you ain't much of nothing . . . ," "they try and make you feel bad and say little mean things . . . ," "some of them talk to you like dirt . . ." were frequent comments. Respondents felt that the administrative culture of AFDC is more concerned with enforcement of eligibility and compliance than with actually helping clients. "They act like it's their money they're giving away," one woman told us.

Ten women, African Americans and Whites, said that neither they nor their children have ever experienced stigma or discrimination because of being on welfare, although several followed up this claim with statements such as, "and I don't listen to it anyhow." Three women suggested that people had been especially kind to them when they revealed that they were on welfare. Several other women said that they had not experienced problems because they do not let other people know that they are on welfare: "I tell people I receive aid from the state." I was told that dressing in name-brand clothing and shoes to appear middle class was an important strategy to keep sons away from drug dealers, who offer young children these items as a way to entice them to sell drugs for them. Other respondents said that they try to buck the stereotype and pass as members of the middle class. One young White mother said:

> I think it's all in how you carry yourself. I don't want my children looking any kind of way. I don't want them to think that they're no less, that everybody is better than them, and they're not. So my kids wear name-brand shoes just like anybody else. . . . So I mean, I try not to make them want for nothing.

In sum, it appears that most welfare recipients in our sample are aware of the popular, individualistic stratification beliefs in our society. They know that, as a group, welfare recipients are considered largely responsible for their own economic circumstances and their use of welfare. The majority of the women interviewed said that they, personally, have experienced stigma and discrimination.

Why Are They and Other Women on Welfare?

Given the general cognizance of the stigma attached to welfare use, how do respondents feel about themselves? How do they account for their own use of welfare? How do they regard other welfare recipients? Do they have a sense of class consciousness, and do they recognize their common experiences with other women? Of the four perspectives—individualism, structuralism, culture of poverty, and fatalism—which ones do they use to explain why they and other women receive welfare?

The interviews first and foremost revealed that most respondents believe that there are multiple causes for receiving welfare. Generally, the reasons given for other women's welfare use could not be pigeonholed into one theoretical perspective. Yet, further discussion often revealed that one reason tended to dominate. The individualist perspective emerged most frequently from both African American and White women in their discussions about other women. They attributed other women's use of welfare to their laziness, drug use, lack of human capital, personal choice, or other personal shortcomings or irresponsible behavior. The views of one 19-year-old White woman, Janie, who has a 2-year-old child, characterized the individualist perspective. She has been on welfare for 2 years, ever since bearing a child who was conceived during a gang rape:

> There are some people on welfare who don't need to be on welfare. They can go out and get a job. They have nothing better to do than to live off of welfare and to live off the system. I'm sorry. I have no sympathy. Look at all the signs on the road: "Will work for food." Go down to day labor, for crying out loud. They'll pay you more money than you can make in a regular day. It's by choice. Either (a) they don't want to work, (b) they are being supported by others, or (c) they don't give a damn about themselves.

Another woman, Cassandra, a 27-year-old African American with three children who has been on welfare for 7 years, referred to the idea that people on welfare are lazy. She did not include herself in this category, despite the fact that some people might be concerned about the length of time she has been on welfare.

> I think a lot of them are on it just to be on it. Lazy. Don't want to do nothing. Lot of them on it 'cause a lot of them are on drugs. Keep having kids to get more money, more food stamps. Now that's abusing the system. And a lot of women are abusing the system.

Janie and Cassandra, like other women on welfare, distanced themselves from other respondents, physically, emotionally, or both. Clear distinctions were drawn between "me" and "them." Most women thought that other women did not deserve to receive welfare, were bad mothers who neglected their children, or committed fraud or deliberately abused the system. Several women, both African American and White, admitted that they didn't know anyone who committed fraud or abuse personally but insisted that "there are a lot of people like that out there." They subscribed to the popular stereotypes of welfare mothers, even though these views contradicted their own experience and contradicted the lives of other women they know. Tamara, a 31-year-old African American with three children, expressed this concern:

Tamara: A lot of those mothers on AFDC get food stamps and stuff and take the stamps and sell them. If not, they'll take the money and, you know, buy crack and leave the kids hungry, and they don't have clothes to put on and shoes to wear. Once they're on drugs, they'll do anything to get them.

Interviewer: Do you know of cases where people are actually doing this?

Tamara: I've heard of some people, but, it's happening everywhere.

We found that both African American and White women also frequently invoked the culture of poverty to explain why other women are on welfare. Themes that emerged from the data revolved around (a) women who rely on welfare as a long-term way of life, (b) intergenerational welfare use, (c) unmarried teenagers who have babies and assume that welfare will take care of them, (d) women who have additional children simply to increase the amount of their welfare benefits, and (e) the cultural milieu in the housing projects. Again, recipients distanced themselves from these cultural contexts and, in doing so, voiced that they have little in common with other recipients.

Amy's responses were typical. She is a 23-year-old White mother of one child. She attends a university full-time and plans to go to graduate school. She expressed concern that some people have developed a subculture in which they see welfare as a long-term way of life. She believes her situation is different from the norm, despite the fact that many welfare recipients are obtaining further education or training in order to increase their job prospects.

Well, there are people like me who are using it as a means to make ends meet while they are preparing themselves to support themselves. And I think we are a pretty small number. I think that there are those people for whom welfare and AFDC are a way of life. Their parents were on it, their parents' parents were on it, and this is how they live. I think they are not the majority, but I think they exist.

Many women, both African American and White, were alarmed by intergenerational welfare use. Some claimed to know families in which the mothers and then the daughters received welfare, which they referred to as "a cycle that keeps on going." They suggested that young girls be educated about the difficulties of raising children and that they be told that welfare is likely to be changed in the future and cannot be relied on to help them. In reality, the number of people affected by intergenerational welfare use is small—only one quarter of current welfare recipients also received some assistance when they were children (U.S. House of Representatives, Committee on Ways and Means, 1996). Nonetheless, many welfare recipients exaggerate the frequency of the intergenerational use of welfare.

Respondents expressed concern and anger over unmarried teenage girls who have babies and automatically assume that welfare will support them, although national data indicate that only 6% of AFDC recipients are younger than 20 years old (U.S. House of Representatives, Committee on Ways and Means, 1996). They alluded to a culture of poverty, of sorts. Young girls haven't been taught that reliance on welfare is not a good thing. Older women who, several years earlier, also had babies out of wedlock while they were teenagers, often voiced this concern. For example, Kim, a 29-year-old, never-married African American woman who had her first of three children when she was 17, commented:

These girls are having babies younger and younger, and I say it's more to having a baby than just getting a check and some food stamps. I say they shouldn't even give them a cheek until they graduate. 'Cause a lot of them, that's all they are waiting for, . . . and they just steadily having babies. They having babies at 12 and 13. They aren't even at a legal age to get a job.

A controversial issue, with passionate arguments on both sides, was whether women continue to have children simply to increase the size of their welfare check. This issue is a prominent component of current welfare reform. Some women argued that a $50-a-month increase in benefit level would not be enough to warrant having additional children. "That's ridiculous," we were told repeatedly. Others, however, felt differently and argued that many women do have additional children to increase the size of the check. Kate, a 42-year-old African American mother of two young children, voiced this common sentiment:

Interviewer: I think some lawmakers think that women on AFDC have more children just. . . .

Kate: Just to get more AFDC. I believe that, too. I really believe that, too. But not me. No. Some women are just breeders.

Interviewer: They're just breeders? What does that mean?

Kate: They like to have babies. If they don't go get themselves stopped, they'll just keep having them. If it were me, I wouldn't have no more babies just to get more AFDC. No.

Interviewer: But you do think some people do it?

Kate: Yeah, I do. I really do.

Again, we found that women on welfare distanced themselves from others who received aid. Kim, Kate, and others distinguished between "me" and "them." Other welfare recipients are viewed as having deviant values and engaging in negative behaviors that fuel their dependence on the system.

Finally, the cultural milieu in the housing projects where one quarter of the sample resided was also of considerable concern. These large,

often multilevel structures are home to hundreds of families, all on AFDC. The women who lived there characterized the projects as noisy, lacking in privacy, in disrepair, full of loiterers, and breeding grounds for drug use and other illegal activities. Many respondents dreamed of the day when they would be in a financial position to leave the projects, and they expressed surprise, concern, and contempt that their neighbors often seemed to be satisfied living there. One African American woman, Coreen, who attends community college and intends to be a teacher, described the cultural milieu in the projects. Because she felt that she had little in common with the hundreds of other families in her project, she did not socialize with neighbors, usually kept her curtains closed, and generally did not allow her young daughter to play outside.

I live out here, and this place really puts you down. A lot of people don't realize about living in projects: It puts you down. I mean, because you have no one to encourage you to get out. If you try to accomplish or achieve anything, then you must think you are better than them, and they won't like you. You have people here in the projects who always compete with you about how your house looks, but they won't compete with you about trying to get out of here. You know what I'm saying? Don't compete with me because of my apartment, compete with me with school, compete with me about trying to get out of here. Let's try to race to get out, you know? Some people just don't want to get out.

In sum, the data revealed that explanations of individualism and the culture of poverty are used most frequently to explain other women's use of welfare. Further analyses revealed that these explanations were used by both African American and White women, younger and older women, and women who had few children and those who had many.

These two perspectives, more than the others, lay at least some blame on the recipient. Yet, despite the tendency to blame other women's use of welfare on their inadequacies, their lack of motivation, or their deviant values, respondents rarely blamed their own welfare use on these factors. Instead of relying on theories of individualism or the culture of poverty to explain their own use of welfare, respondents were more likely to invoke structuralist or fatalist perspectives. Respondents generally felt that, unlike other poor women, they were on welfare through no fault of their own.

Concerns with the social structure, when cited, tended to revolve around a lack of jobs that paid a living wage; a lack of good quality and affordable day care; a lack of father involvement and child support enforcement; an inadequate transportation system; broader problems in our social structure, such as racism or sexism; and a welfare system that penalizes women for initiative and eliminates benefits prematurely.

Jackie's case illustrates the structural problems that many single mothers face. She is an African American with three children. Jackie has completed high school and a program at a local community college. She works part-time but continues to receive a partial AFDC check because her income is not sufficient to pull her above the poverty threshold. She has been on and off welfare numerous times for the past 10 years. Why?

> Because most of the jobs I've had—well, the first one I had was permanent, but I had a babysitting problem, so I was there maybe 2 months. So I work a lot on campus but mostly in temporary positions, maybe 2 months, 3 months here, and some weeks there. I'm really trying to get a full-time job somewhere. So mainly it's just problems with jobs being only temporary. And then also transportation, sometimes. See, that's why I want a job early in the morning. I can ride the bus. I have no problem getting up early riding the bus. But basically I need to work in the morning so that I can help my kids with their homework and just be here with them at night.

Many women said that most jobs that they find do not pay enough to support a family or even pull them above the poverty line. At $5.25 an hour, working 40 hours per week yields approximately $840 a month before taxes. Working 52 weeks a year, an employee averages $10,080 a year. For even the smallest families who have only one or two children, living and surviving on these wages pose a serious challenge. Moreover, according to analyses from the National Medical Expenditures Survey, approximately half of low-income jobs fail to offer critical benefits such as health insurance to the employee (Seccombe & Amey, 1995).

Lack of safe and affordable child care also emerged as a common reason why women turn to or remain on welfare. Women often did not feel comfortable leaving their children with nonfamily members. Living in high density, high crime areas, they worried about the safety of their children. Moreover, they worried about the cost of daycare. A recent study that compared child-care costs in six communities around the nation found that average costs for the care of a 2-year-old ranged from $3,100 a year in Birmingham, Alabama, to almost $8,100 a year in Boulder, Colorado (Clark & Long, 1995). The size of an AFDC grant for a mother and one child in the interview region is $241 a month, which obviously makes full-time child care impossibility. As Rhonda pointed out, jobs that welfare recipients take are often in the service sector and require work during evenings and weekends when child care might not be available (Presser & Cox, 1997):

> My hardest problem is (I can find a job) . . . trying to work around my son. On weekends, I ain't got nobody on weekends to watch him. Like my sister, she's busy with her own kids. And that's the only problem I have. It's like they always want nights and weekends. See, I can do days while he's in school, you know.

Fathers' participation in the emotional or financial upbringing of their children was noticeably absent in the majority of cases. Absentee fathers represent a growing and an alarming national trend. Despite the passage of the 1988 Family Support Act, fewer than half of fathers who are court ordered to provide child support pay the full amount regularly (U.S. Bureau of the Census, 1997b). Molly, a White mother of three sons, attends a community college where she is completing the prerequisites needed to enter the university program in nursing. She voiced a commonly expressed sentiment about the lack of father involvement and child support:

> The big thing is the men. They aren't taking care of their responsibilities. We cannot do it alone. I can, once I get an education, but it's hard to try to take care of three kids by yourself. It's the money thing. We have to have money to live. But we have to do everything. I have to be mother and father. I can't just go to the store in the morning. I have to load all the kids up, you know? I think a big problem is that the men are not there. They are not being made to take the responsibility.

Transportation is a major barrier to women getting or keeping jobs. Participants in job-training programs report that the lack of affordable transportation presents a barrier even more serious than lack of child care to securing employment (Kaplan, 1998). Most women cannot afford to buy an automobile. Those who did own cars revealed that their cars were in a constant state of disrepair. Women complained that their car, although a necessity in many respects, also helped keep them poor: "It's either your tires or extra gas or a part tearing up on your car. No, I can never really get ahead."

Although public transportation is available in the largest community in the county where we conducted interviews, women complained that it was expensive ($1.00, plus an additional 25 cents per transfer), unreliable, and inconvenient. Public transportation was not available in some of the smaller communities within the county. Several women explained elaborate transportation logistics that allowed them to work or to go to school. Lynda, a 35-year-old African American, told me of her transportation difficulties and how they impeded her ability to keep her job:

> I just had a job in September, where I worked 6 days. But I had to quit my job because I had to pay transportation. I don't have my own transportation, and transportation was costing me, like $40 a week. Sometimes at night it was difficult because

the shift that I was working was 3 to 12. Three in the afternoon to 12 at night. And a lot of people don't want to get up and come get you. So I had to quit the job because of the transportation costs that I had to pay.

Several women felt that racism or sexism was a significant factor in their lives. It can be blatant or more subtle. A few African American women told us directly that racism had hindered their ability to get or keep a well-paying job, or they knew of close friends, families, and neighbors who had been victims of racial discrimination: "They did her real bad." Stephanie, a White woman in the nursing program at the university, explicitly acknowledged that sexism, as well as racism, likely limited opportunities for social mobility:

> Why are people on welfare? There have to be at least a thousand reasons why people are on welfare. Like I tell my daughter, life isn't fair. Things happen, and you have to do the best you can. There are lots of socioeconomic groups in this country, races, Blacks, Hispanics, women who don't really have the same opportunities that most people consider normal opportunities. I mean, for myself, look who got stuck taking care of the child.

A corollary argument to structuralism, the Big Brother perspective, suggests that the system, itself, is responsible for welfare dependency. A few women did think that the welfare system could make people get lazy, as some welfare critics have argued. However, the majority of women who expressed concerns with the welfare system said it wasn't that it made recipients lazy, but rather that the welfare system had built-in disincentives or penalties for work. Working, especially at minimum-wage jobs that usually lacked health insurance and other benefits, would not achieve their goals of self-sufficiency and, in fact, would jeopardize the health and well-being of their children because they would lose critically needed benefits. Moreover, as good mothers, they said they would never want to jeopardize their children's well-being. It was clear that without continued assistance with health insurance, child care, transportation, food stamps, and subsidized housing, working becomes not only prohibitive but sometimes downright dangerous. Many women claimed that they wanted to work or that they could find a job or even that they had a job previously, but they felt compelled to quit because working and the resulting reduction of their welfare benefits actually lowered their standard of living or jeopardized their children's health. They expressed frustration that the welfare system actually discourages them from working by raising their rent, eliminating Medicaid, and cutting off needed social services before these women have a chance to establish themselves. Jo, a White mother of two young children, claimed:

> I've had a job before, and I know I can get a job. It's just really hard. It's like, I got a job at Hardee's [a fast food franchise], and I had a friend take me back and forth. I was paying her $20 a week for gas. I got off the system. I was honest about it and told them I had a job. They took my assistance away, and they raised my rent $200. And they said they weren't going to give me any Medicaid for my kids either, and I didn't have any health insurance. I had a baby at the time, and she was only a year old. She had to go to the periodic appointments and stuff, and I was like, "Okay, well. I'm going to try to do it." And I had to work there 6 months to a year to get health insurance. I was really scared. Like, what am I going to do? But I'm gonna do it. So I started doing it, and then I started realizing that, you know, that after about 2 months, I was under the welfare level, I mean, by making minimum wage, I couldn't keep my bills up, and I could never afford to take her to the doctor. It wasn't getting me ahead, I was being penalized for trying to get off the system, and it's happened to all my friends that are on welfare. It's like a trap, and they don't help.

Of all the types of benefits received, Medicaid was alluded to frequently as the most important. It is well documented that persons without health insurance or with inadequate insurance use the health-care system less frequently than do others, resulting in a variety of negative health outcomes (Seccombe, 1995; U.S. Congress,

Office of Technology Assessment, 1992). Stephanie expressed a common concern about losing Medicaid:

> We gripe and we gripe about the fact that we are paying all this money for people who don't seem to be doing very much for themselves, but if you looked at the system from an insider's point of view, you would see that there are actually penalties built into the system for a person with initiative, going out to get a job, or doing something to try to better themselves. As soon as you earn a buck, they take it away from you. You are penalized if you have any kind of asset whatsoever. You have to be so damn poor that it's not even funny . . . Next summer in nursing school there are no classes. Yet I can't work, and I will tell you why. I would like to work as a nurse's aide, and that is something I can do with my training that I have had. But I can't afford to lose my benefits, specifically my medical benefits. Because if I went to work, they would cut me off. Even though I would not be making enough to pay my bills, I would be cut off from Medicaid. And I can't afford that, you know? It's part-time, usually a nurse's aide gets $5-$6 an hour, which is not that much above minimum wage, and . . . you work 20 or 30 hours a week. No health benefits; no nothing. So I can't work. It's not that I don't want to work. I'd love to work, but I can't.

Patrice is an African American mother of two who works part-time but continues to receive a partial AFDC benefit. She explained how her benefits were reduced when she began to work:

> The thing that gets me, being a single parent, once my income exceeds a certain amount, I'm in a project, and my rent goes up. It has been like close to $300 for this. [She laughs and sweeps her arms around the room.] And then I have to end up paying expensive child care, and the Medicaid stops for me and my children. You know, most jobs the health insurance is so expensive you can't afford it. Then, you pretty much be where you started from. You end up with nothing.

These data, grounded in the real-world experience of welfare recipients, suggest that the presumed link between social programs and welfare dependency touted by social conservatives is flawed. Yes, on a cursory glance, the welfare system does appear to reduce the incentive to work, but a more thorough examination from an insider's perspective reveals that social programs do not necessarily encourage laziness or dependency. Both White and African American women talked about desperately wanting to work, but they felt that employment reduced their already meager standard of living and often placed their children at risk because it eliminated or reduced their eligibility for medical and social services. They rationally, although grudgingly, acknowledged that in some contexts it may be in their children's best interest to remain on welfare.

Finally, fatalism was also frequently mentioned as a justification of their own use of welfare. Our respondents told us that they turned to welfare because of bad luck or because of a relationship gone awry. They felt that they simply couldn't help it; they were victims of unfortunate and unplanned circumstances. For example, several who were unmarried teenagers when they had their first child told me of their surprise and bad luck at becoming pregnant. Some didn't know that sexual activity caused pregnancy, or they didn't know that they could get pregnant the first time they had sexual intercourse. They were confused and lacked basic knowledge about sex. Many disclosed that they had had intercourse as a way to please a boyfriend. Peer pressure to have sex is powerful and difficult to avoid. One recent study involving 1,000 girls in Atlanta found that 82% said the subject they wanted to learn most about in their sex education class was how to say no without hurting the other person's feelings (Besharov, 1993).

For other women, bad luck translated into health problems that interfered with their ability to look for or keep a job. Nearly one third of the welfare recipients interviewed complained of health problems, consistent with national trends (Loprest & Acs, 1996; Meyers, Lukemeyer, & Smeeding, 1996). Ailments included asthma, depression, high blood pressure, or back pain. In others cases, the children were sickly. Poor children are more likely to suffer an array of ailments, both chronic and acute, than are more affluent children (Children's Defense Fund, 1994). Children in this research suffered from lead paint poisoning, asthma, seizures, or Attention Deficit Disorder. Consequently, their mothers did not feel comfortable leaving them with babysitters. Nor did they feel comfortable accepting employment that would mean that they would lose their medical benefits.

Many women reported that they had bad luck with men. They were involved in detrimental relationships, and receiving welfare was perceived as a method of regaining control over their lives. Some women reported that they were deserted by their partners and left alone to care for their children. They needed welfare, they said, because they could not yet support a family on their own. Although both men and women go through financial adjustments after a divorce or the ending of a relationship, women's incomes decline more dramatically than men's (Peterson, 1996). Dee, with three small children, left the Army to become a housewife at her ex-husband's insistence. Soon afterward, he deserted her. Dee described her situation: "My husband left us with no food. The rent was due. You know, when he left, he just split. It was like he was never there, no clothes, nothing." Dee and more than a dozen other women we interviewed were back in school taking courses so they could find jobs that paid more than minimum wage to support their families.

Two women told us that they bore children as a result of rapes. Although we asked no direct question about violence, many other women volunteered that they were fleeing abusive relationships or had left an abusive relationship in the past. Straus and Gelles (1986) report that during marriage, over one quarter of the relationship contained violent episodes. Molly, a White mother of three young sons, turned to welfare for support after escaping from her husband. They lived in a rural, mountainous area, 30 miles from the nearest town. Her husband deliberately kept her isolated from family and friends and put a block on the telephone. He was abusive to both her and the children:

I left my husband when he was asleep. I stayed in a shelter. I grabbed some clothes for the kids and left. My mom came up and got us. I had no car, no nothing. No furniture. Zero. That was August of '92. So I had to start completely over from scratch. I got a few of my things back, but basically I lost everything that I had.

Fatalism—the belief that poverty and welfare use is something that is beyond their control, something that was put on them—was commonly used to explain their own use of welfare. Because of bad luck, poor health, detrimental relationships, or other personal situations over which they had no control, many felt that they had no other choice than to turn to welfare to help them out of an unplanned but potentially desperate situation. They indicated that they were not to blame, and in fact, for many, welfare was a source of empowerment. It allowed them to be independent of an abusive spouse, to take care of their family when a husband or lover deserted them, and it provided financial assistance while they upgraded their education and job skills. However, as was the case with structural explanations, fatalism was rarely used to account for why other women receive aid.

Discussion

This research examined the perspectives used by welfare recipients to interpret public attitudes toward them and their rationalizations of why they and other women receive welfare. We found that respondents are aware of the stigma associated with welfare and recognize the individualistic perspective commonly used by the general public. Our respondents acknowledged that they were thought of as lazy, unmotivated, lacking in human capital, and suspect mothers.

We anticipated that respondents would reject these impressions. We found that they did attribute their own reliance on welfare to structural factors, to fate, or to the idiosyncrasies of the welfare system itself. However, they attributed welfare use by other women to laziness, personal shortcomings, or other inadequacies.

This was the case for both the African American and White women interviewed. They viewed the stratification system as essentially legitimate. They generally believed the popular constructions of the welfare mother but evaluated their own situation as distinct from the norm. When asked directly how their situation was different from other women, only a few women reported that there were no differences or few differences. The majority claimed that they were different because, unlike other women on welfare, (a) they wanted to make something of themselves, (b) they didn't abuse the system, (c) they made a concerted effort to live within their means, (d) they had health problems or some other serious difficulty that prohibited them from working, and (e) they were on it for their children. Janie, who had been on AFDC since her daughter was born 2 years ago, denied being on welfare altogether:

> I'm not on welfare. I don't even know exactly what welfare is. I'm just receiving AFDC, and that might be considered welfare. I'm not sure. As it stands, most of them get on it because they don't want to work; they don't want to take care of their kids. I've seen more people on welfare lose their kids because of it, rather than to take care of themselves. Why they do that is beyond me.

Our research is not alone in these findings. In a classic study, Briar (1966), using a quota sample from 92 families receiving AFDC with an equally proportioned group of Blacks, Whites, and Mexican Americans, found that the respondents almost never referred to welfare recipients as "we" but instead used the word "they." This estrangement, identified as a coping mechanism for dealing with stigma, was apparent in the tendency to view oneself as an atypical recipient, disassociating oneself from other recipients. More recently, interviewing 16 women in focus groups, Davis and Hagen (1996) also found that welfare recipients viewed themselves as atypical recipients. For example, although they were quick to condemn others for being welfare frauds, they did not see their own actions as fraudulent. Instead, they were merely beating the system by working to get extra money to pay for necessary items that their checks could not pay for.

Given the strong negative messages about welfare and welfare recipients, perhaps it is not surprising that poor White and African American women who receive welfare also subscribe to individual or cultural perspectives of blame. Yet, while blaming other women, they find structural and fatalistic perspectives more compelling to account for their own use of welfare. What may explain this apparent inconsistency? The data suggest that there is little class consciousness among Whites or among African Americans. Why do many women not see the commonalities of their experiences? Why do they accept institutionalized inequality as legitimate for others but not for themselves?

An enduring theme in sociology has been to explain the persistence of social stratification. Sociologists and others from diverse perspectives regard legitimation—justifications that are widely believed and taken for granted—as one of several important mechanisms through which stratification is maintained (e.g., Bourdieu, 1977; Dahrendorf, 1959; Davis & Moore, 1945; Foucault, 1980; Habermas, 1973; Lenski, 1966; Parsons, 1949). A plausible theory of legitimation ultimately must address how justifications for stratification become part of individuals' social consciousness and how they become accepted by welfare recipients (or other subordinate groups), even if it contradicts their own self-interest.

We suggest that, instead of class consciousness, an integration of critical theory (Bourdieu, 1977; Foucault, 1980; Habermas, 1973) with Della Fave's self-evaluation hypothesis (1980) and attribution theory (Kelley, 1973; Ross, 1977) may merit attention. Critical theorists like Foucault suggest that social structures produce cultural ideologies of truth and knowledge that are disadvantageous to the less powerful. These cultural ideologies camouflage the self-serving interests of the powerful by making them appear as though they are natural, normal, and in the interests of everyone. Likewise, Gramsci's (1971) notion of "ideological hegemony" refers to the process by which consensus is obtained between dominant and subordinate groups, such as the rich and the poor. Social arrangements in the best interest of the dominant group are presented as being in everyone's best interests. Subordinates accept these interests as their own, and the contradictions inherent in the interests of the dominant and subordinate groups are ignored. Thus, ideologies reflect the interests and perspectives of the elite. They become "commonsense." Applying critical theory here, we find that our respondents fail to see the shared political nature of their problems and, instead, internalize them. Poverty is relegated to the realm of a personal problem, rather than a social problem (Mills, 1956). Class conflict is averted because they have internalized the commonsense ideology that a need for welfare represents a personal inadequacy, rather than a weakness or contradiction within the social structure.

Della Fave elaborates on these themes in his self-evaluation hypothesis (1980). He suggests that the level of resources viewed as just for oneself is directly proportional to one's level of self-evaluation. Those with more wealth and other critical resources tend to be perceived as having a wider range of positive characteristics than those with fewer resources. Moreover, people believe that those who appear to be superior deserve to be more richly rewarded. This circular reasoning also implies that those lower in the stratification system will attribute to themselves more negative characteristics and, therefore, will believe that they deserve to have fewer resources. A cultural ideology is established. Thus, a given stratification system tends to reproduce itself when self-evaluations reinforce the status quo that generated it initially. This process is maintained in a variety of ways, including within our social institutions, such as schools and the workplace where communication largely takes place within homogeneous groups. Legitimacy occurs when an individual's self-evaluation with respect to society becomes congruent with his or her command of resources. Thus, we see that welfare mothers are evaluated in a negative light, and their minimalist resources are justified. They deserve little, the creed goes, because they are lazy and unmotivated.

However, Della Fave (1980) also suggests that "the more incongruent the distribution of resources and self-evaluation, the more likely is the delegitimation of stratification" (p. 964). Why did our respondents see incongruence between resources and self-evaluation for themselves but see congruence for other welfare recipients? Attribution theory examines how we try to sort out the causes of people's behavior. Does a person's behavior (extended here to include social position and use of welfare) reflect an underlying disposition of that person, or is it primarily a consequence of the structural situation in which the person is placed? Research has concluded that people have a tendency to overestimate the degree to which other people's behavior is caused by their own individual traits or dispositions and to underestimate the degree to which it is caused by structural factors. Even when strong structural constraints are known, one is likely to overestimate the role of personal disposition when explaining the behavior of others. In contrast, although we tend to attribute other people's actions to their own personal traits or dispositions, we are more likely to attribute our own behaviors to the social structure or to situational factors (Jones & Nisbett, 1972).

Applying attribution theory to this study, we asked welfare recipients to explain why they, themselves, and other women are on welfare. This is not perceived as a single question; it is clearly two separate issues. Consistent with attribution theory, our respondents assigned individual traits or dispositions to other women to explain their use of welfare, ones that are legitimized by the media and within the larger cultural milieu. As our data revealed, these traits are well known to welfare recipients. They include laziness, deficiencies in human capital, and little desire to better themselves. Moreover, the culture of poverty surrounding welfare recipients is assumed to encourage teen pregnancy, long-term dependency, and cheating the system. Thus, it appears that welfare recipients, like those who are not on welfare, overestimate the degree to which

individualistic notions of negative personality traits or dispositions shape the use of welfare. Yet, when it comes to explaining their own behavior, they are likely to attribute it to structural or situational causes that are beyond their control. The stratification system is delegitimized. They assess little personal blame; it is simply not their fault: "There are no jobs." "How can I take care of all my kids and work too?" "I would be fine if he would just pay child support." "I was raped." "I was beaten and abused." "He deserted us, and I'm trying to get my feet on the ground." "I'm trying to better myself." "The welfare system penalizes me if I get a job." These were reasons that were frequently voiced. This is also consistent with attribution theory.

Although all of these factors may be justifiable reasons why a woman would turn to welfare, they are reasons that can apply to all women. Indeed, they did apply to the majority of women interviewed. Few women were nonchalant about welfare. Instead, most were embarrassed, pained, appreciative, or resigned. They applied for welfare as a last resort. Most had dreams of getting off welfare. Many had already left welfare for a time. Yet, they turned or returned to welfare because of broken relationships; because of jobs that failed to pay wages that enabled them to support themselves; so that they could go to college or obtain vocational training; because of fathers who refuse to pay child support; because of concern that their children were not being adequately cared for; and in order to receive valuable benefits, such as health insurance, that their jobs did not provide. Moreover, they turned to welfare because they felt tired, weary, and demoralized from the stress of raising children alone, from juggling bills, and from working in boring and low-paying jobs in the service sector. These are not isolated concerns found among a few welfare recipients. They are consistent themes found within the narratives of the 47 women interviewed.

With the passage of welfare reform in Washington and numerous statewide initiatives underway, there is likely to be a crisis looming for many families on welfare. Millions of women and children, in particular, will find strict time limits on their benefits. When the time limits are up, they will be forced to find and survive on minimum-wage employment. The hegemony of the individualist perspective is one of the most stubborn barriers to dealing constructively with poverty and welfare use. These data suggest that this perspective may be broader than previously assumed and may run deep in the psyches of the poor within our nation.

Note

The authors acknowledge Cheryl Amey and Sylvia Ansay for their assistance in the collection of the data, Goldie MacDonald and Janice Weber for their coding contributions, Meg Galletly for her technical assistance, and Katherine Allen, M. Kimberly Beal, Wanda Clarke, Joe Feagin, J. Elizabeth Norrell, Karen D. Pyke, Leslie Richards, and Stephen Roguski for their insightful comments on various stages of this manuscript. Special appreciation goes to the women whose enthusiastic contributions made this study possible. Funding was provided by the American Sociological Association. An earlier version of this article was presented at the annual meetings of the National Council on Family Relations, November, 1996, Kansas City, Missouri.

References

Abramovitz, M. (1996). *Under attack, fighting back: Women and welfare in the United States.* New York: Monthly Review Press.

Anderson, M. (1978). *The political economy of welfare reform in the United States.* Palo Alto, CA: The Hoover Institution.

Bergmann, B. (1996). *Saving our children from poverty: What the United States can learn from France.* New York: Russell Sage Foundation.

Besharov, D. J. (1993). Teen sex. *American Enterprise, 4,* 52–59.

Blumer, H. (1969). *Symbolic interactionism.* Englewood Cliffs, NJ: Prentice Hall.

Bobo, L., & Smith, R. A. (1994). Antipoverty policy, affirmative action, and racial attitudes. In S. H. Danziger, G. D. Sandefur, & D. H. Weinberg (Eds.), *Confronting poverty* (pp. 365–395) Cambridge, MA: Harvard University Press.

Bourdieu, P. (1977). *Outline of a theory of practice.* New York: Cambridge University Press.

Briar, S. (1966). Welfare from below: Recipients' views of the public welfare system. *California Law Review, 54,* 370–385.

Children's Defense Fund. (1994). *Wasting America's future.* Washington, DC: Author.

Clark, A. L., & Long, A. F. (1995). *Child care prices: A profile of six communities final report.* Washington, DC: The Urban Institute.

Congressional Digest. (1995, June-July). Welfare overview (pp. 163–165). Washington, DC: U.S. Government Printing Office.

Dahrendorf, R. (1959). *Class and class conflict in industrial society.* Stanford, CA: Stanford University Press.

Davis, K., & Moore, W. E. (1945). Some principles of social stratification. *American Sociological Review, 10,* 242–249.

Davis, L., & Hagen, J. (1996). Stereotypes and stigma: What's changed for welfare mothers. *Affilia, 11,* 319–337.

Davis, N. J., & Robinson, R. V. (1991). Men and women's consciousness of gender inequality: Austria, West Germany, Great Britain, and the United States. *American Sociological Review, 56,* 72–84.

Della Fave, R. L. (1980). The meek shall not inherit the earth: Self-evaluation and the legitimacy of stratification. *American Sociological Review, 45,* 955–971.

Edin, K. (1991). Surviving the welfare system: How AFDC recipients make ends meet in Chicago. *Social Problems, 38,* 462–474.

Edin, K., & Lein, L. (1997). Work, welfare, and single mothers' economic survival strategies. *American Sociological Review, 61,* 253–266.

Ellwood, D. T. (1986). *Targeting "would be" long-term recipients of AFDC* (Reference No. 7617–953). Princeton, NJ: Mathematica Policy Research.

Feagin, J. R. (1972). God helps those who help themselves. *Psychology Today, 6,* 101–111.

Feagin, J. R. (1975). *Subordinating the poor: Welfare and American beliefs.* Englewood Cliffs, NJ: Prentice Hall.

Foucault, M. (1980). *Power/knowledge: Selected interviews and other writings, 1972–1977.* New York: Pantheon.

Giddens, A. (1973). *The class structure of advanced societies.* New York: Barnes and Noble.

Gilder, G. (1981). *Wealth and poverty.* New York: Basic Books.

Glaser, B. G., & Strauss, A. L. (1967). *The discovery of grounded theory.* New York: Aldine de Gruyter.

Goffman, E. (1963). *Stigma.* Englewood Cliffs, NJ: Prentice Hall.

Goodban, N. (1985). The psychological impact of being on welfare. *Social Service Review, 59,* 403–422.

Gordon, L. (1994). *Pitied but not entitled.* New York: The Free Press.

Gramsci, A. (1971). *Selections from the prison notebooks of Antonio Gramsci* (Q. Hoare & G. N. Smith, Eds. & Trans.). New York: International Publishers.

Habermas, J. (1973). *Legitimation crisis.* Boston: Beacon Press.

Harris, K. M. (1993). Work and welfare among single mothers in poverty. *American Journal of Sociology, 99,* 317–352.

Harris, K. M. (1996). Life after welfare: Women, work, and repeat dependency. *American Sociological Review, 61,* 407–426.

Herrnstein, R., & Murray, C. (1994). *The bell curve: Intelligence and class structure in American life.* New York: Free Press.

Hunt, M. O. (1996). The individual, society, or both? A comparison of Black, Latino, and White beliefs about the causes of poverty. *Social Forces, 75,* 293–322.

Jarrett, R. L. (1994). Living poor: Family life among single-parent, African-American women. *Social Problems, 41,* 30–49.

Jarrett, R. L. (1996). Welfare stigma among low-income African American single mothers. *Family Relations, 45,* 368–374.

Jones, E. E., & Nisbett, R. E. (1972). The actor and the observer: Divergent perceptions of the causes of behavior. In E. F. Jones, D. Kanouse, H. Kelley, S. Valins, & B. Weiner (Eds.), *Attribution: Perceiving the causes of behavior.* New York: General Learning Press.

Kamerman, S., & Kahn, A. (1978). *Family policy government and families in 14 countries.* New York: Columbia University Press.

Kaplan, A. (1998). Transportation and welfare reform [On-line]. Available from http://www.welfareinfo.org/transita.htm

Kelley, H. H. (1973). The process of causal attribution. *American Psychologist, 28,* 107–128.

Kluegel, J. R., & Smith, E. R. (1982). Whites' beliefs about Blacks' opportunity. *American Sociological Review, 47,* 518–532.

Lenski, G. (1966). *Power and privilege.* New York: McGraw-Hill.

Lewis, O. (1966). The culture of poverty. *Scientific American, 215,* 19–25.

Loprest, P., & Acs, G. (1996). *Profile of disability among families on AFDC.* Washington, DC: The Urban Institute.

Marx, K., & Engels, F. (1968). *Selected works.* New York: International Publishers.

Mead, L. M. (1992). *The new politics of poverty: The non-working poor in America.* New York: Basic Books.

Meyer, C. (1994). The latent issues of welfare reform. *Affilia, 9,* 229–231.

Meyers, M. K., Lukemeyer, A., & Smeeding, T. M. (1996). Work, welfare, and the burden of disability: Caring for special needs children in poor families (Income Security Policy Series, Paper No. 12). Syracuse, NY: Center for Policy Research, Maxwell School Citizenship and Public Affairs, Syracuse University.

Miles, M. B., & Huberman, A. M. (1994). *Qualitative data analysis* (2nd ed.). Thousand Oaks, CA: Sage.

Miller, O. C. (1992). *Women and social welfare: A feminist analysis.* New York: Praeger.

Mills, C. W. (1956). *The power elite.* New York: Oxford University Press.

Moynihan, D. P. (1965). *The Negro family.* Washington, DC: U.S. Department of Labor.

Murray, C. (1984). *Losing ground: American social policy 1950–1980.* New York: Basic Books.

Murray, C. (1988). *In pursuit of happiness and good government.* New York: Simon and Schuster.

National Opinion Research Center. (1993). *General social surveys, 1972–1993: Cumulative codebook.* Chicago: J. Davis.

Parsons, T. (1949). An analytical approach to the theory of social stratification. In T. Parsons (Ed.), *Essays in sociological theory* (pp. 69–88). New York: Free Press.

Peterson, R. R. (1996). A re-evaluation of the economic consequences of divorce. *American Sociological Review, 61,* 528–536.

Piven, F. F., & Cloward, R. A. (1993). *Regulating the lives of the poor: The functions of social welfare.* New York: Vintage.

Presser, H. B., & Cox, A. G. (1997, April). The work schedules of low-educated American women and welfare reform. *Monthly Labor Review, 120,* 25–33.

Quadagno, J. (1994). *The color of welfare. How racism undermines the war on poverty.* New York: Oxford Press.

Rank, M. R. (1994). *Living on the edge: The realities of welfare in America.* New York: Columbia University Press.

Ross, L. D. (1977). Problems of interpretation of "self serving" asymmetries in causal attribution. *Sociometry, 40,* 112–114.

Schiller, B. (1989). *The politics of poverty and discrimination.* Englewood Cliffs. NJ: Prentice Hall.

Scott, M. B., & Lyman, S. M. (1968). Accounts. *American Sociological Review, 33,* 46–62.

Seccombe, K. (1995). Health insurance coverage and use of services among low-income elders: Does residence influence the relationship? *The Journal of Rural Health, 11,* 86–97.

Seccombe, K. (1999). *So you think I drive a Cadillac? Welfare recipients' perspectives on the system and its reform.* Needham Heights, MA: Allyn and Bacon.

Seccombe, K., & Amey, C. (1995). Playing by the rules and losing: Health insurance and the working poor. *The Journal of Health and Social Behavior 36,* 168–181.

Smith, K. B., & Stone, L. H. (1989). Rags, riches, and bootstraps: Beliefs about the causes of wealth and poverty. *The Sociological Quarterly, 30,* 93–107.

Stack, C. B. (1974). *All our kin: Strategies for survival in a Black community.* New York: Harper and Row.

Straus, M. A., & Gelles, R. J. (1986). Societal change and change in family violence from 1975 to 1985 as revealed by two national surveys. *Journal of Marriage and the Family, 48,* 465–479.

Strauss, A., & Corbin, J. (1990). *Basics of qualitative research.* Newbury Park, CA: Sage.

U.S. Bureau of the Census. (1996). *Poverty in the United States: 1995* (Current Population Reports, Series P-60, No. 194). Washington, DC: U.S. Government Printing Office.

U.S. Bureau of the Census. (1997a). *Poverty in the United States: 1996* (Current Population Reports, Series P-60, No. 198). Washington, DC: U.S. Government Printing Office.

U.S. Bureau of the Census. (1997b). *Statistical Abstract of the United States* (117th ed.). Washington, DC: U.S. Government Printing Office.

U.S. Congress, Office of Technology Assessment. (1992). Does health insurance make a difference?—background paper (OTA-BP-H-99). Washington, DC: U.S. Government Printing Office.

U.S. House of Representatives, Committee on Ways and Means. (1996). *Green book.* Washington, DC: U.S. Government Printing Office.

Valentine, C. (1968). *Culture and poverty: Critique and counter-proposals.* Chicago: University of Chicago Press.

Van Manen, M. (1990). *Research in lived experience.* London, Ontario: Althouse Press.

Wilson, H. S., & Hutchinson, S. A. (1991). Triangulation of qualitative methods: Heideggerian hermeneutics and grounded theory. *Qualitative Health Research, 1,* 263–276.

Wilson, W. J. (1987). *The truly disadvantaged: The inner city the underclass, and public policy.* Chicago: University of Chicago Press.

Wilson, W. J. (1993). *The new urban poverty and the problem of race (The Tanner Lecture).* Ann Arbor: University of Michigan.

9

FAMILY SYSTEMS THEORY

Family systems theory emerged from general systems theory. While many of the elements that became the foundation of family systems theory emerged as early as the 1920s, the theory as it is commonly understood has existed since the 1960s. Within general systems theory, a system is viewed as a set of interrelated elements surrounded by a boundary and exhibiting common characteristics or traits. A family is viewed as such a system in that family members interact with one another, exhibit coherent behaviors, and share some degree of interdependence. Family systems theory largely attends to two key aspects of families: the elements that comprise them and the processes that exist within families and between families and their environments.

From a family systems theory perspective, then, a family may be viewed much like a machine, as comprising a set of interconnected elements that together make a coherent whole. Further, when these parts interact in a meaningful way, the entire system functions in a way that produces a set of outputs. Much as an engine operates when it receives meaningful inputs and its parts are all appropriately connected, a family functions in ways that reflect both inputs received by the family and patterns of interaction among members of the family.

Family systems theory includes a number of key concepts:

Interdependent Components: Members of the family and the roles they perform are viewed as the components of the family system. The members of the family are held together by degrees of interdependence. This interdependence exists on both emotional and instrumental levels. The interdependence that exists among family members is not only the glue that holds family system together but it also defines the nature of relationships in families. Within a family system, patterns of interdependence result in all members of the family system being impacted by change in one member.

Inputs/Outputs: Inputs reflect information received by the family that may impact family functioning. These inputs may come from outside the family in the form of messages or information to which the family attends or from within the family in terms of members' monitoring of family functioning. Outputs reflect the way a family is received by those outside the family—its public face, so to speak.

Boundaries: A boundary exists around each family system. This boundary is the point of interface between the family and its environment and is defined by those within and outside the family. Boundaries are characterized by degrees of rigidity that influence how much information is allowed into or out of a family system. The presence of very rigid boundaries suggests that a family is less influenced by events and information from its environment and that family members are isolated from the environment.

Hierarchy of Systems: A hierarchy of systems exists within and beyond family systems. A layering of subsystems is found within family systems. Subsystems reflect patterns of relationships among family members. Each subsystem is surrounded by a boundary with degrees of permeability much like the boundary around the family system. From a systems perspective, then, a key issue in families is the location and relative strength of the boundaries within the family system. Further, various subsystems may hold differing levels of power within the family system. Power in family systems is typically held by the members of the subsystem that are higher on the hierarchy of subsystems within the family.

Rules: Rules reflect repeated patterns in family systems. Rules are implicitly understood by family members. They reflect patterns of relationship that serve to prescribe family members' behavior, roles, patterns of authority, expression of emotion, and communication—indeed, all aspects of family member interactions.

Goals: Family systems strive to achieve goals and these goals change over time as family members grow and change. This concept suggests that family interactions and behaviors are goal-oriented and that these goals become interwoven into the rules and boundaries of the family system. It is important to understand that goals, as described here, exist at the family system level and may not always coincide with goals of individual family members.

Feedback Mechanisms: Families reflect endless feedback loops or patterns of monitoring their

status. From a systems perspective, families strive to maintain equilibrium in their functioning and are constantly monitoring the degree to which their functioning is consistent with system goals. When members of the family sense incongruity between system and individual goals, behaviors, or functioning, family members may engage in patterns of change to try to achieve a level of equilibrium.

Nonsummativity: While family systems comprise a set of elements or parts, the system cannot be simplistically viewed as merely the sum of its parts. Within families, patterns of interaction, emotional and instrumental connection, and functioning all contribute to a definition of the family system. Thus, family systems theory addresses both the structure of families and patterns of interaction that exist within families and between families and their environment.

Change: Family systems tend to reorganize themselves and adapt new patterns of interaction in response to information that is received either from outside the family or within the family. Often this need for change is reflected in changing developmental issues or imperatives. Thus, a family system reflects a pattern of morphogenesis, or a tendency to change its basic structure or functioning over time. Processes and patterns of change are critical to understanding a family system.

Equifinality: Equifinality is defined as the ability of a system to achieve a goal through different means or routes. Thus, different family systems may achieve the same outcomes through very different approaches or processes. A family may also use more than one approach to achieving change based on the characteristics of the family system itself.

THE READINGS

Two examples of work utilizing family systems theory are included in this book. These include Mullis, Brailsford, and Mullis's (2003) examination of the relationship between characteristics of family systems and identity formation in young adults. This article not only incorporates a family systems perspective, but also highlights the importance of considering family system variables in understanding individual developmental outcomes. While identity is a concept closely tied to individual development, it is clear from the findings reported by these authors that the family system may profoundly influence the quality of identity formation. The authors of this article specifically consider the influence of two family system–level variables on identity formation: family cohesion and family adaptability.

Also included is Vetere's (2001) application of family systems concepts to a model of family therapy. Because family systems theory is frequently utilized by family therapists, this article represents an example of an important link between family systems theory and an area of practice. Vetere explains and explores structural family therapy, a therapeutic approach that focuses, in particular, on an individual's relationship contexts and the potential generation of distress in those relationships. Structural family therapy explicitly attends to the organizational characteristics of the family, a central focus of family systems theory. Vetere's work, therefore, provides an illustration of both family systems theory concepts and a therapeutic model built on those concepts.

ISSUES FOR YOUR CONSIDERATION

1. To what degree does each article attend to issues of family structure and boundary arrangements within families?

2. Are rules of family interaction described in these articles? If so, what are examples of the rules that guide family interactions?

3. To what degree does each article offer support for a relationship between family system–level variables and individual outcomes?

FURTHER READING

Berrien (1968), Bertalanffy (1951), Broderick (1993), Larsen and Olson (1990), Marks (1989).

Relations Between Identity Formation and Family Characteristics Among Young Adults

Ronald L. Mullis, John C. Brailsford, and Ann K. Mullis

Abstract

Relations between identity formation and family characteristics among young adults were examined. The Family Adaptability and Cohesion Evaluation Scales II and the Ego Process Questionnaire were administered to 57 male and 94 female college students between the ages of 18 and 25. There were 78 Caucasian and 73 African American youth. Significant relations were found between identity exploration and commitment, and family cohesion and adaptability. In addition, moderating effects of race and gender also were found for relations between identity formation and family variables for this sample of young adults. African American participants were found to explore interpersonally more often than Caucasians when family cohesion and family adaptability were low. Family cohesion was positively related to interpersonal and ideological identity commitments for males but only for interpersonal commitment for females. Implications for future research are addressed.

Family influences on identity formation during adolescence and early adulthood have received increasing attention in the literature including the influences of parenting processes (Hauser & Bowles, 1990; Phinney, 2000) and the role of individuality and connectedness in the development of identity (Archer & Waterman, 1994). Erikson (1968) theorized that the task of identity formation among adolescents and young adults is one of making choices by exploring alternatives and committing to roles. According to Erikson, identity formation among adolescents and young adults requires sifting through a range of choices in our lives before we make commitments around key areas of interpersonal relations, work and career choices, and ideology (beliefs and values).

Erikson's (1968) model of identity achievement has been expanded, clarified, and empirically tested in recent years by Marcia (1980, 1994). Marcia (1980) has theorized that individuals begin the identity formation developmental process in a state of diffusion and progress through a process of exploration until they are committed to an option or set of options as an integral part of the self.

Some researchers have challenged and criticized the identity theories of Erikson and Marcia as incomplete because they emphasize individual differences in identity achievement and have overlooked the pattern of developmental change that takes an individual from identity diffusion through identity achievement. Thus, the debate is one of focus on either individual difference outcomes or the developmental processes of internal and external factors that enhance or restrict development of identity achievement.

For example, Oyserman, Gant, and Ager (1995) criticized Erikson and Marcia because they portrayed identity as "an autonomous, bounded, independent entity created by the individual" (p. 1217). According to Oyserman et al., this view of identity formation virtually ignores the social context in which identities are constructed. Thus, identities are negotiated within a framework of one's interpersonal encounters and partly in a wider social context.

Kroger (1999) has observed that few studies of identity have extended beyond the age of 21 despite evidence that adolescents and young adults may take longer in their identity formation. This may be particularly true for college students in comparison with non-college students who are in an environment that asks them to question previously held ideas (Lytle, Bakken, & Romig, 1997). Studies of college students have indicated that progression in identity formation is primarily in the occupational areas and often not in identity formation more generally (Waterman, 1992).

In addition to expanding age considerations in identity formation, gender differences in identity formation add greater complexity to the process. For example, there is evidence that females are more willing than males to postpone career exploration for greater emphasis on interpersonal exploration (Cooper & Grotevant, 1989; Marcia, 1994). Research on the relation between identity and intimacy has often focused on gender differences, with most studies indicating that intimacy issues arise earlier for females than for males, so that females often accomplish intimacy before identity (Grotevant, 1983; Schiedel & Marcia, 1985). Some have argued further that developmental processes of intimacy and identity are integrated for females (Archer & Waterman, 1994) and that, although compelling, gender differences in identity formation may be less evident today than in the past (Archer & Waterman, 1994; Lacombe & Gay, 1998).

In addition to gender differences in identity formation, broader social considerations include race. Cote (1996) noted that it is possible that race is more important for certain dimensions of identity formation than gender, such that depending on their class and age, women of a given race may subjectively experience more in common with men of their own race as they form their sense of identity. One aspect of the growing capacity of self-reflection for adolescents and young adults who are members of ethnic minorities is likely to be a sharpened awareness of what it means for them to be a member of their minority group. For example, there is evidence that identity exploration is higher among ethnic minority young adults than among White American young adults (Phinney & Alipuria, 1990).

The family is likely the most powerful of social systems that adolescents and young adults experience as they go through the process of identity formation (Marcia, 1993). Grotevant and Cooper (1986) observed that parents play an important role in how they help their offspring become either more or less individuated in their relationships. Adolescents and young adults in an individuated relationship with their parents have a clear sense of themselves as distinct from other people yet feel emotionally connected with them. Research on individuation suggests that youth who achieve high levels of individuation can remain close to their parents without a loss of their own distinctiveness and identity (Mazor & Enright, 1988). Some have argued that the difficulties experienced by youth within families in recent years are symptomatic of a generation of youth endeavoring to become more individuated in their struggles for both peer and parental acceptance (Arnett, 2001; Jones, 1992). For example, parents who have a history of accepting their children and positively interacting with them facilitate their children's identity development in different social contexts more than parents who have a history of judging and devaluing their children (Arnett, 2001). Fullwider-Bush and Jacobvitz (1993) found that college-age daughters who were bound to at least one parent (less individuated) had lower scores on measures of identity development and exploration. College women who were more individuated had higher scores on identity development and exploration. Such findings suggest that family interaction styles that consistently give their offspring the right to question and to be different, within the context of mutuality and support, tend to foster more individuated patterns of identity exploration and commitment later in life.

Olson, Russell, and Sprenkle (1983) identified two salient dimensions of processes within the family, cohesion and adaptability, that define family functioning and have a highly profound influence on individual family members. According to Olson, Russell, et al. (1983), balanced levels of family adaptability (flexibility and structure) and cohesion (togetherness and separateness) are essential for positive family functioning, whereas extreme levels of adaptability (rigidity and chaos) are associated with extreme levels of structure or constant change in family functioning. According to Olson (1993), families that reflect balance in structure and flexibility are in a better position to adapt to change over the life cycle.

There is increasing evidence to support a relation between dimensions of family interaction and the identity development of individual family members (Baumeister & Muraven, 1996; Grotevant, 1983; Marcia, 1980). High levels of parental control, a characteristic of rigid families, have been associated with difficulties in identity development among adolescents and young adults (Quintana & Lapsley, 1990). When parents encourage their children to be autonomous while maintaining closeness, they have children who are more likely to engage in identity exploration (Fullwider-Bush & Jacobvitz, 1993). Similarly, individuals who have the ability to express emotions outside the family (appropriate individuation) have more positive identity development (Papini, Sebby, & Clark, 1989). Although these findings are suggestive of relations between family characteristics and identity formation in young adults, specific links between family and individual variables have not been well established (Kroger, 1999).

The purpose of this study was to examine relations between identity formation processes among young adults and characteristics of their families. Specific questions addressed in this study were (a) How do relations between dimensions of identity formation (exploration and commitment) and family cohesion and adaptability differ with respect to ideological and interpersonal domains? and (b) How do relations between identity formation and family cohesion and adaptability differ with respect to gender and race?

Method

Participants

The sample for this study consisted of 151 male and female young adults enrolled in undergraduate courses in a southeastern university; there were 57 males and 94 females between the ages of 18 and 25 (mean age: 20.69). The racial/ethnic makeup by self-report of participants included 73 African Americans and 78 Caucasians (9 Hispanics and 15 "Other" designations were excluded from the sample). Participants categorized their families as intact (69%), blended (10%), divorced (16%), widowed (3%), and in foster care (2%). Most participants described their religious affiliation as Catholic (25%), Protestant (26%), or Other Christian (36%), Muslim, and Agnostic/Atheist made up the remaining categories (13%) of the sample.

Measures

The Ego Identity Process Questionnaire (EIPQ). The EIPQ is a 32-item measure of identity exploration and commitment (Balistreri, Busch-Rossnagel, & Geisinger, 1995). The EIPQ is designed to assess levels of identity exploration and commitment in eight different domains. These domains include politics, religion, occupation, values, friendship, dating, sex role, and family. The first four of these domains are considered to be intrapersonal, or agentic. The last four domains are considered to be interpersonal, or communion oriented. Each domain-specific subscale consists of four items, two measuring exploration and two measuring commitment in that particular domain. Items are randomly ordered across the two dimensions and eight domains.

Of the 32 items on the EIPQ, there are 20 positive-oriented and 12 negative-oriented items. Participants indicated their level of agreement or disagreement with each of these statements using a 6-point Likert-type scale. Total exploration and commitment scores are obtained by summing individual item scores yielding scores that range from 16 to 96.

The internal consistency estimates (alpha coefficients) reported by Balistreri et al. (1995) were .80 (commitment) and .86 (exploration), respectfully. Test-retest reliability coefficients (1 week posttest) were .90 for commitment and .76 for exploration. Correlations between these two dimensions and social desirability were .23 ($p < .05$) for commitment and $-.32$ ($p < .01$) for exploration. A correlation of $-.35$ $p < .05$) was found between the dimensions of exploration and commitment for this study. Internal consistency estimates for the current .sample (alpha coefficients) were .86 (commitment), and .84 (exploration), .79 (ideological commitment), .81 (ideological exploration), .83 (interpersonal commitment), and .85 (interpersonal exploration).

Family Adaptability and Cohesion Evaluation Scales (FACES) II. Family researchers have generally used the FACES II and III to measure the underlying dimensions of the Circumplex Model of Family Systems (CMFS) (Olson, Sprenkle, & Russell, 1979). The most common challenge to the CMFS is associated with the issue of curvilinearity. Studies involving the direct testing of this assumption have generally shown linear relationships between family cohesion and adaptability and healthy family functioning. For purposes of this study, FACES II was used to measure perceived cohesion and adaptability because reliability and validity of this instrument have been demonstrated over the years and because the issue of curvilinearity was not of particular interest in this study.

FACES II is the second in a series of FACES instruments developed to assess the two fundamental dimensions of family functioning, cohesion and adaptability, outlined in the CMFS. Family cohesion is defined as the emotional bonding that family members have toward one another. Other concepts incorporated into this dimension include emotional bonding, boundaries, the use of time, and shared interests. Family adaptability is defined as the ability of a marital or family system to change its power structure, role relationships, and relationship rules in response to situational and developmental stress. Concepts incorporated into this dimension include power, discipline, rules, and negotiation styles.

FACES II consists of 30 items with responses to a 5-point Likert-type scale. There are 16 items related to cohesion and 14 items related to adaptability with a range of possible scores between 16 and 80 for cohesion and 14 and 70 for adaptability. Olson, Portner, and LaVee (1985) reported internal consistency estimates for cohesion and adaptability of .87 and .78, respectively, and test-retest reliability coefficients (4–5 weeks posttest) of 83 for cohesion and .80 for adaptability. Comparing it with the Dallas Self-Report Family Inventory also has tested the concurrent validity of FACES II. High correlations were found between family health and cohesion ($r = .93$) and adaptability ($r = .79$). Despite a relatively high correlation between scores on the two scales ($r = .65$), common variance between scales has not been problematic and unique variance is indicated. Alpha coefficients for the current sample were .90 for the total score of FACES II, .87 (family cohesion) and .78 (family adaptability).

Results

Data Analysis

Preliminary descriptive analyses were performed, including cross-tabulations and tests for homogeneity of variance to identify any irregularities in the overall sample, including outlying scores, missing data, and data clusters. Tests were also conducted to inspect characteristics of the score distributions, including normality, symmetry, and kurtosis. This information was used to determine limitations of making inferences based on sample characteristics and eliminate erroneous or anomalous scores from the data set. Pearson correlation coefficients were conducted to examine relations between all variables. Following these analyses, regressions were performed to assess the combined effects of perceived levels of family cohesion and adaptability, gender, and race on identity formation processes. Race was coded as 1 = Caucasian and 2 = African American.

Table 9.1 presents intercorrelations of major variables of this study. Significant correlations were found between family cohesion and identity commitment ($r = .23$, $p < .01$) and family cohesion and interpersonal commitment ($r = .27$, $p < .001$) for the total sample. Examination of correlations by gender and race revealed that family cohesion was significantly correlated with ideological commitment for males ($r = .27$, $p < .05$) and family cohesion was significantly correlated with interpersonal commitment for females ($r = .30$, $p < .01$). Family cohesion was positively related to ideological exploration ($r = .26$, $p < .05$) and negatively correlated with interpersonal exploration ($r = -.34$, $p < .01$) for African American participants. Both ideological commitment and interpersonal commitment were correlated with family cohesion for Caucasian participants ($r = .27$, $p < .05$; $r = .32$, $p < .01$, respectively). Only one significant correlation was found between family adaptability and identity formation variables—namely, family adaptability was negatively correlated with interpersonal exploration for African American participants ($r = .35$, $p < .01$).

Multiple regression analyses were performed to explore the variables of family cohesion and family adaptability in the prediction of identity exploration and identity commitment among young adult participants. The moderating effects of gender and race also were examined. Table 9.2 shows the regression results for overall identity

exploration and identity commitment. The model for identity commitment was significant ($F = 6.13$, $p < .01$), family cohesion significantly predicted identity commitment ($t = 3.48$, $p < .001$), and family adaptability significantly predicted identity commitment ($t = -1.97$, $p < .05$). The interactions of race with cohesion and race with adaptability also were significant ($t = 2.09$, $p < .05$; $t = 2.43$, $p < .01$, respectively).

Regressions also were run for the subscales of identity exploration and identity commitment and are presented in Tables 9.3 and 9.4. The models for ideological exploration and interpersonal exploration were not significant. However, the models for ideological commitment and interpersonal commitment were significant ($F = 3.01$, $p < .05$; $F = 6.83$, $p < .001$, respectively). Family cohesion predicted ideological commitment ($t = 2.31$, $p < .05$) and family adaptability predicted ideological commitment ($t = -2.13$, $p < .05$). Family cohesion predicted interpersonal commitment ($t = 3.43$, $p < .001$). Race acted as a moderating variable in the relations between family cohesion and ideological commitment ($t = 2.42$, $p < .01$) and between family adaptability and ideological commitment ($t = 2.67$, $p < .01$).

Discussion

Researchers have demonstrated that commitment to a given life course by adolescents is facilitated by close and adaptive family relationships (Arnett, 2001; Protinsky & Shilts, 1990). The results of this study utilizing a sample of young adults partially support these earlier findings. The relation between family cohesion and identity commitment was significant among all White and male participants, with levels of identity commitment being higher in cohesive families. Among female participants, however, the relations between family cohesion and identity commitment were only found for the interpersonal domain of identity formation. Whereas young women in cohesive families were more committed interpersonally, there were no significant effects of family cohesion on the ideological

Table 9.1 Intercorrelations Between Identity Variable and Family Variables

	Family Cohesion					Family Adaptability				
Identity Variable	Total Sample (n = 151)	Males (n = 57)	Females (n = 94)	Caucasian (n = 78)	African American (n = 73)	Total Sample (n = 151)	Males (n = 57)	Females (n = 94)	Caucasian (n = 78)	African American (n = 73)
Exploration	.07	.07	.04	.04	.03	.03	.01	.02	−.05	.04
Commitment	.23**	.27*	.18	.32**	.14	.03		.04		.17
Ideological Exploration	.14	.08	.16	.03	.26*	.12	.08	.14		.17
Interpersonal Exploration		.04	.11	.04	−.34**	−.08	−.07	−.12	−.08	−.35**
Ideological Commitment	.1	.27	−.02	.27*	.25	−.07	−.08	−.06	−.05	−.08
Interpersonal Commitment	.27***	.2	.30**	.32**	.29*	.1	.07	.13	.03	.25

*p < .05. **p < .01. ***p < .001.

287

Table 9.2 Regression Results for Predictors of Overall Identity Exploration and Commitment

Independent Variable	Identity Exploration			Identity Commitment		
	b	β	t	b	β	t
Family Cohesion	.1086	.005	.93	.3564	.3628	3.48***
Family Adaptability	1.642	.0097	2.01*	−.1977	−.2051	−1.97*
Cohesion × Adaptability	1.643	.0097	2.01*	−.4337	.0097	−.54
Gender × Cohesion	.1827	.5386	2.15*	.0276	.5386	.33
Gender × Adaptability	.1860	.5587	2.19*	.0410	.5587	.49
Race × Cohesion	−.0467	.5587	−.56	.1660	.5587	2.09*
Race × Adaptability	−.0352	.5720	−.43	.1891	.5720	2.43**
R^2		.0071			.0766	
Adjusted R^2		−.0067			.0641	
Constant		3.5939			3.6272	
F		.50			6.13**	

*$p < .05$. **$p < .01$. ***$p < .001$.

Table 9.3 Regression Results for Predictors of Ideological and Interpersonal Exploration

Independent Variable	Identity Exploration			Interpersonal Exploration		
	b	β	t	b	β	t
Family Cohesion	.1270	.0968	.91	.0901	.0733	.68
Family Adaptability	.0784	.0609	.57	−.1536	−.1274	−1.18
Cohesion × Adaptability	1.850	.0098	2.28*	.9105	.0098	1.10
Gender × Cohesion	.0332	.5386	.39	.2857	.5386	3.45***
Gender × Adaptability	.0322	.5587	.38	.2925	.5588	3.53***
Race × Cohesion	−.1215	.5587	−1.48	.0476	.5587	.57
Race × Adaptability	−.1135	.5720	−1.40	.0592	.5721	.72
R^2		.0208			.0970	
Adjusted R^2		.0075			−.0040	
Constant		3.039			4.1483	
F		1.57			.70	

*$p < .05$ ***$p < .001$.

commitment of women. It is clear that the inclusion of both male and female participants in this study has resulted in findings that contradict earlier assumptions based on research with predominantly White male samples.

Marcia (1989) suggested that societies and families promote certain individual identity characteristics based on common values and beliefs. These social expectations often differ according to the gender of the individual being influenced.

Whereas the advancement of this explanation for gender differences in identity formation seems to have been at least partially motivated by a lack of appreciation of identity commitment, the current findings are suggestive of a relationship between family cohesion and identity formation that is gender specific.

Although gender differences in the influence of family cohesion on identity commitment may represent efforts of participants' families to

Table 9.4   Regression Results for Predictors of Ideological and Interpersonal Commitment

Independent Variable	Identity Commitment			Interpersonal Commitment		
	b	*β*	*t*	*b*	*β*	*t*
Family Cohesion	.2711	.2459	2.31*	.4459	.3558	3.43***
Family Adaptability	−.2450	−.2265	−2.13*	−.1518	−.1233	−1.18
Cohesion × Adaptability	−.5271	.0098	−.65	−.1813	.0098	−.23
Gender × Cohesion	.0420	.5387	.50	.0096	.5387	.12
Gender × Adaptability	.0063	.5588	.78	.0096	.5588	.12
Race × Cohesion	.1950	.5587	2.42**	.0917	.5587	1.15
Race × Adaptability	.2107	.5720	2.67**	.1144	.5721	1.46
R^2		.03904			.2906	
Adjusted R^2		.0261			.0721	
Constant		3.9110			3.3312	
F		3.01*			6.83***	

*$p < .05$. **$p < .01$. ***$p < .001$.

influence the identity formation process according to the sex of their children, these differences also may represent the influence of gender on the identity formation process itself. Josselson (1996) noted that female perceptions of family cohesion represent their own sense of identity as much as actual levels of family cohesion. In other words, foreclosed women view their families as emotionally close because they are comfortable in their foreclosure, not because their society or family wants them to view their family relationships in a certain way. If women tend to feel comfortable with higher levels of interpersonal commitment, those with higher levels of interpersonal commitment are more likely to view their families as cohesive. Findings from Fullwider-Bush and Jacobvitz (1993) suggesting that college-age females who were less individuated had lower scores on identity exploration would seem to support this view. In a similar way, if men are more comfortable making ideological commitments, those with higher levels of ideological commitment are more likely to view their families as cohesive.

As Josselson (1988) observed, traditional theories of human behavior often are contradicted when women are included in research. Despite a lack of attention to identity formation in women,

Erikson (1968) believed that there are gender differences in the nature and timing of identity formation (Matteson, 1993). Subsequent research has confirmed this assumption (Archer, 1992; Arnett, 2001). Whereas men deal with the ideological dimensions of identity formation prior to dealing with the interpersonal dimensions, women focus on both interpersonal and ideological dimensions at the same time (Bilsker & Marcia, 1988; Shiedel & Marcia, 1985). For men, ideological exploration takes place in the context of relatively distant and undefined relationships. For women, interpersonal exploration and commitments are addressed more fully than other dimensions of identity formation.

Racial differences did emerge in this study. Among White participants, identity commitments were made more readily in cohesive families. The finding is consistent with previous research on the influence of family characteristics on identity formation (Protinsky & Shilts, 1990; West, Hosie, & Matthews, 1989). Not surprisingly, participants in these earlier studies were almost exclusively White.

For African American young adults, negative relations were revealed between family cohesion and ideological and interpersonal exploration, and between family adaptation and interpersonal exploration. No comparable relations were found for Caucasian young adults. Although both racial groups are similar in the relations between family cohesion and identity commitments, they seem to be somewhat different in the relations between identity exploration and family cohesion and family adaptability. These findings are supported by others who have reported a higher incidence of identity foreclosure among members of racial minority groups (Marcia, 1989, 1993). Cote (1996) noted that the variable of race is more important for certain dimensions of identity formation than gender, such that depending on class and age, young adult women of a given race may subjectively experience more in common with men of their own race than with women of another race as they explore their identities. Moreover, African American young adults who perceive their families as cohesive and adaptive just may not feel the need at this point in their lives to engage in interpersonal exploration. The moderating effect of race on relations between family characteristics and identity formation in this study are certainly suggestive of a need for future researchers to examine further the racial differences in identity formation and family characteristics.

The results of this study also indicate that family adaptability is not related to ideological commitment in young adults. It follows that ideological commitment is more likely to occur in families that provide individual family members with structure and guidance. This does not necessarily mean that rigid, controlling families will promote ideological commitment. Although proponents of the CMFS might predict that extremely high levels of family adaptability will be associated with a drop in levels of ideological commitment, this hypothesis cannot be accurately tested because the FACES instruments do not measure family cohesion and adaptability in a curvilinear fashion (Anderson & Gavazzi, 1990).

Implications

Just as the inclusion of women in studies on identity status added important information to the study of the identity formation process, the inclusion of racial and ethnic minorities promises to enhance the quality of such research in the future. Given the lack of racial diversity in past samples, it is impossible to compare the findings regarding race in this study with existing literature.

The findings of this study underscore the importance of examining issues of individual development and family development over time. For example, Combrinck-Graham (1985) has proposed a cyclical model of family development that has implications for individual models as well. She has challenged principles of traditional theories of family development. She questions presumptions of linear, epigenetic development over time and proposes that family development be viewed as a cyclical process of growth and change over the entire life course. Future research of individual identity formation characteristics within the context of family development might be well served by using this kind of a developmental model. Fluctuations in identity status have been found that resemble the developmental fluctuations in families mentioned above, but more needs to be known about the mechanisms of these fluctuations before predictions can be made regarding the identity formation process among youth and young adults over time.

Sample diversity is needed in future research. As mentioned earlier, both CMFS and identity status concepts were developed based on data collected from predominantly White male samples. In Marcia's (1989, 1993) initial research on identity statuses, only male subjects participated. Members of racial minority groups, in particular, have been traditionally underrepresented in these two bodies of literature and deserve more attention by researchers in the future.

References

Anderson, S. A., & Gavazzi, S. M. (1990). A test of the Olson Circumplex Model: Examining its curvilinear assumption and the presence of extreme types. *Family Process, 29,* 309–324.

Archer, S. L. (1992). A feminist's approach to identity research. In G. R. Adams, T. P. Gullotta,

& R. Montemayor (Eds.), *Adolescent identity formation* (pp. 25–49). Newbury Park, CA: Sage.

Archer, S. L., & Waterman, A. S. (1994). Adolescent identity development: Contextual perspectives. In C. B. Fisher & R. M. Lerner (Eds.), *Applied developmental psychology.* New York: McGraw-Hill.

Arnett, J. J. (2001). *Adolescence and emerging adulthood.* Englewood Cliffs, NJ: Prentice Hall.

Balistreri, E., Busch-Rossnagel, N. A., & Geisinger, K. F. (1995). Development and preliminary validation of the Ego Identity Process Questionnaire. *Journal of Adolescence, 18,* 179–192.

Baumeister, R., & Muraven, M. (1996). CH4 identity as adaptation to social, cultural, and historic context. *Journal of Adolescence, 19,* 405–416.

Bilsker, D., & Marcia, J. E. (1988). Sex differences in identity status. *Sex Roles, 18*(3/4), 231–236.

Combrinck-Graham, L. (1985). A developmental model for family systems. *Family Process, 24*(2), 139–150.

Cooper, C., & Grotevant, H. D. (1989, April). *Individuality and connectiveness in the family and adolescents' self and relational competence.* Paper presented at the meeting of the Society for Research in Child Development, Kansas City, MO.

Cote, J. E. (1996). Identity: A multidimensional analysis. In G. R. Adams, R. Montemayor, & T. P. Gullotta (Eds.), *Psychosocial development during adolescence: Progress in developmental contextualism.* Thousand Oaks, CA: Sage.

Erikson, E. (1968). *Identity: Youth and crisis.* New York: Norton.

Fullwider-Bush, N., & Jacobvitz, D. B. (1993). The transition to young adulthood: Generational boundary dissolution and female identity development. *Family Process, 32,* 87–103.

Grotevant, H. D. (1983). The contribution of the family to the facilitation of identity formation in early adolescence. *Journal of Early Adolescence, 3,* 225–237.

Grotevant, H. D., & Cooper, C. (1986). Individuation in family relationships: A perspective on individual differences in the development of identity and role-taking skill in adolescence. *Human Development, 29,* 82–100.

Hauser, S. T., & Bowles, M. K. (1990). Stress, coping, and adaptation. In S. S. Feldman & G. R. Elliott (Eds.), *At the threshold: The developing adolescent* (pp. 135–167). Cambridge, MA: Harvard University Press.

Jones, R. M. (1992). Ego identity and adolescent problem behavior. In G. R. Adams, T. P. Gullotta,

& R. Montemayor (Eds.), *Adolescent identity formation* (pp. 69–107). Newbury Park, CA: Sage.

Josselson, R. (1987). *Finding herself: Pathways to identity development in women.* San Francisco: Jossey-Bass.

Josselson, R. (1988). The embedded self: I and thou revisited. In D. K. Lapsley & F. C. Power (Eds.), *Self ego, and identity: Integrative approaches* (pp. 91–106). New York: Springer-Verlag.

Josselson, R. (1996). *Revising herself: The story of women's identity from college to midlife.* New York: Oxford University Press.

Kroger, J. (1999). *Identity development: Adolescence through adulthood.* London: Sage.

Lacombe, A. C., & Gay, J. (1998). The role of gender in adolescent identity and intimacy decisions. *Journal of Youth and Adolescence, 27,* 795–802.

Lytle, L. J., Bakken, L., & Romig, C. (1997). Adolescent female identity development. *Sex Roles, 37,* 175–185.

Marcia, J. E. (1980). Identity in adolescence. In J. Adelson (Ed.), *Handbook of adolescent psychology* (pp. 159–188). New York: John Wiley.

Marcia, J. E. (1989). Identity and intervention. *Journal of Adolescence, 12,* 401–410.

Marcia, J. E. (1993). Epilogue. In J. E. Marcia, A. S. Waterman, D. R. Matteson, S. L. Archer, & J. L. Orlofsky (Eds.), *Ego identity: A handbook for psychosocial research* (pp. 22–41). New York: Springer-Verlag.

Marcia, J. E. (1994). The empirical study of ego identity. In H. A. Bosma, T. L. G. Graafsma, H. D. Grotevant, & D. J. De Levita (Eds.), *Identity and development.* Thousand Oaks, CA: Sage.

Matteson, D. R. (1993). Differences within and between genders: A challenge to the theory. In J. E. Marcia, A. S. Waterman, D. R. Matteson, S. L. Archer, & J. L. Orlofsky (Eds.), *Ego identity: A handbook for psychosocial research* (pp. 69–110). New York: Springer-Verlag.

Mazor, A., & Enright, R. D. (1988). The development of the individuation process from a social-cognitive perspective. *Journal of Adolescence, 11,* 29–47.

Olson, D. H. (1993). Circumplex model of marital and family systems. Assessing family functioning. In E. Wash (Ed.), *Normal family process* (2nd ed., pp. 104–137). New York: Guilford.

Olson, D. H., Portner, J., & LaVee, Y. (1985). *FACES III.* St. Paul: University of Minnesota.

Olson, D. H., Russell, C. S., & Sprenkle, D. H. (1983). Circumplex model of marital and family systems: VI. Theoretical update. *Family Process, 22,* 69–83.

Olson, D. H., Sprenkle, D. H., & Russell, C. S. (1979). Circumplex model of marital and family systems: I. Cohesion and adaptability dimensions, family types, and clinical applications. *Family Process, 18*, 3–28.

Oyserman, D., Gant, L., & Ager, J. (1995). A socially contextualized model of African American identity: Possible selves and school persistence. *Journal of Personality and Social Psychology, 69*(6), 1216–1232.

Papini, D. R., Sebby, R. A., & Clark, S. (1989). Affective quality of family relations and adolescent identity exploration. *Adolescence, 24*(94), 457–466.

Phinney, J. S. (2000, March). *Identity formation among U.S. ethnic adolescents from collectivist cultures.* Paper presented at the biennial meeting of the Society for Research on Adolescents, Chicago.

Phinney, J. S., & Alipuria, L. L. (1990). Ethnic identity in college students from four ethnic groups. *Journal of Adolescence, 13*, 171–183.

Protinsky, H., & Shilts, L. (1990). Adolescent substance use and family cohesion. *Family Therapy, 17*(2), 173–175.

Quintana, S. M., & Lapsley, D. K. (1990). Rapprochement in late adolescent separation individuation: A structural equations approach. *Journal of Adolescence, 13*, 371–385.

Schiedel, D. G., & Marcia, J. E. (1985). Ego identity, intimacy, sex role orientation, and gender. *Developmental Psychology, 21*(1), 149–160.

Waterman. A. S. (1992). Identity as an aspect of optimal functioning. In G. R. Adams, T. P. Gullotta, & R. Montemayor (Eds.), *Adolescent identity formation.* Newbury Park, CA: Sage.

West, J. D., Hosie, T. W., & Matthews, F. N. (1989). Families of academically gifted children: Adaptability and cohesion. *The School Counselor, 37*, 121–127.

Structural Family Therapy

Arlene Vetere

Abstract

Structural Family Therapy was developed by Salvador Minuchin and colleagues during the 1960s as part of the growing interest in systemic ways of conceptualising human distress and relationship dilemmas, and in working therapeutically with those natural systems and relationships, thought to give rise to distress. Structural family therapy is underpinned by a clearly articulated model of family functioning, and has been developed and used most consistently in services for children and families. A growing body of empirical evidence attests to the efficacy of structural family therapy. As an approach it was extensively critiqued during the 1980s by feminist writers and during the 1990s by those interested in the implications of a social constructionist position. Structural family therapy continues to evolve in response to challenges mounted from within and outwith the systemic field, and as part of integrative practice and multisystemic approaches, with practitioners ever mindful of the need for regular feedback from family members themselves.

Introduction

Structural family therapy is a body of theory and techniques that approaches individuals in their social and relational contexts. It was developed in the context of therapeutic work with families and young people. It is predicated on family systems theory, and brings with it many of the strengths and weaknesses associated with the appropriation of general system theory (von Bertalanffy, 1968) into the realm of social behaviour. This article reflects my interpretation of structural family theory and therapy, modified by my longstanding and continuing use of the ideas and methods. For me, the central creative thesis of structural family therapy is embodied within the paradigm shift of the relational therapies, that distress can be understood not only in the context of the relationships within which it arises and is maintained, but also in seeing the potential for relationships to be the cause of distress. The excitement and challenge of structural family therapy is in the focus on family members' interaction and in the broad definition of communication to be more than what we say and the way in which we say it.

Structural family therapy is an approach mainly identified with the work and writing of Salvador Minuchin, although many other influential thinkers have worked in association with the development of the ideas, such as Jay Haley, Braulio Montalvo, Lynn Hoffman, Marianne Walters, Charles Fishman and George Simon. Many of the concepts are familiar, such as family rules, roles, coalitions, triangulation of conflict subsystems and boundaries, organisation, feedback, stability and change. However, the thinking and practice of a structural family therapist will likely be characterised by formulation of family members' difficulties in terms of family structure and dynamic organisation and a preference for working in the here and now. At this point I wish to note that in my experience in the

UK, few working family therapists adhere rigidly to one school of thought; rather an integrated pragmatic approach to conceptualisation and practice is more likely, with a consideration of the fit between family members' style and preferences, therapist style and the nature of the difficulties driving the dominance of one family therapy model over another. Nor would I want this article to reflect the view that family therapy, of whatever approach, is always the treatment of choice when confronted with human distress. It may be the treatment of choice, or it may be part of an integrated package of care.

Model of Change

The term structure refers to the organisational characteristics of the family at any point in time, the family subsystems, and the overt and covert rules that are said to influence interpersonal choices and behaviours in the family. Thus an aim of this therapy is to alter the organisational patterns, particularly where the modes of communication are thought to be unhelpful and where behaviours are considered to be abusive and neglectful or to have the potential to be so. When the structure of the relational group changes, the positions of members in the group changes. Thus it is said, each individual's experience changes and therein lies the potential to alleviate symptomatic distress. Structural family therapy works with the processes of feedback between circumstances and the people involved, tracking how changes made to our circumstances feedback into choices and decisions about further change.

This is a competence model, encouraging people to explore the edges of their known repertoires of responding, assuming that family members have the ability to innovate and draw on less tapped interpersonal and intrapersonal resources. Enactment as a structural family therapy technique is seen as central to this model of change (Simon, 1995), i.e., encouraging family members to problem solve and generate alternative responses to each other in the relative safety of the therapeutic relationship. Thus intervention is promoted at three levels: challenging symptomatic behaviour, challenging the family structure, and challenging family belief systems. The therapy is based on the tenet of action preceding understanding, and vice versa, with the use of cognitive techniques such as reframing. Family members are encouraged to think beyond symptomatic behaviours and current complaints and see their behaviour and choices in the context of family structures and process and in the relationships between the family group and other societal systems. The structural family therapy model of change does not exclude other models of change and structural therapists can work alongside other therapeutic approaches to change as part of a co-ordinated package of care.

Principal Features of Structural Family Theory

The theory is based on the clinical experience of Minuchin and his associates with families in distress. The development of the theory can be traced through their major publications: *Families of the slums* (1967), which focused on issues of parental authority and leadership in Black American women who headed lone parent families where children were in trouble with the law; *Families and family therapy* (1974), which outlined the key constructs, such as enmeshment and disengagement; *Psychosomatic families* (1978), where conflict, its avoidance and resolution, and styles of parent-child interaction are described; *Family therapy techniques* (1981), which detailed the different techniques of structural family therapy. *Family kaleidoscope* (1984), which brought family systems thinking to a general readership; and *Mastering family therapy* (1996), which provided a revision of some of the earlier principles and methods of the approach.

The key features of the approach can be summarised thus:

- The family is seen as a psychosocial system, embedded within wider social systems, which functions through transactional patterns; these transactions establish patterns of how, when and to whom to relate, and they underpin the system;

- The family tasks are carried out within bounded subsystems;
- Such subsystems are made up of individuals on a temporary or more permanent basis, and members can be part of one or more subsystems, within which their roles will differ;
- Subsystems are organised hierarchically in a way that regulates power within and between subsystems;
- Cohesiveness and adaptability are key characteristics of the family group, within which the balance between emotional connectedness and developing autonomy is seen to change as family members mature and live through life cycle transitions.

Minuchin writes about family structure metaphorically, as a device for describing family interaction in the here and now. His writing is *less* concerned with how family members evolve their interactional style and negotiate their interpersonal tasks and expectations. The boundaries of a subsystem are said to be the rules defining who participates and how. The function of boundaries is to protect the differentiation of the subsystem. Every family subsystem is said to have specific tasks and make specific demands on its members; and the development of interpersonal skills achieved in these subsystems is predicated on the subsystem's freedom from interference by other subsystems, as might be seen with a diffuse subsystem boundary. According to this approach, proper functioning within subsystems implies clear boundaries. Clarity is seen as more important than composition, for example, the responsibility for proper supervision and care of the children needs to be identified with person/s able to sustain and discharge such responsibilities. Family subsystems might include: parental, couple, parent-child, grandparent, male/female, organised by history, power, hobbies, interests and so on. Relationships between and within subsystems can be described as affiliations, coalitions, with patterns of conflict resolution, detouring, enmeshment and disengagement.

The notion of a couple subsystem straddles different modes of family household composition and recognises the needs of adults for affection, confiding relationships, shared decision making and is seen as the primary mediator between the household group and the outside world. The parental or executive subsystem is vested with the authority for the care and safety of the children and fulfils major socialisation requirements within the family. If more than one person is responsible for caring for the children, this approach stresses the importance of teamwork and the ability to negotiate conflicting interests. Adaptability is seen as necessary because of developmental changes in the children and pressures of age related expectations from societal institutions. The parent/child subsystem is the context for affectional bonding, gender identification and modelling, and where children learn to develop a degree of autonomy within unequal power relationships. The sibling subsystem was highlighted as an important social group early in the writings of Minuchin and colleagues, long before it attracted the interest of current researchers (see Brody, 1996). This is seen as the social context within which children learn to co-operate, compete, resolve conflict, cope with jealousy, and prepare for peer related activities and friendships as they mature.

The structural approach assumes families and family members are subject to inner pressures coming from developmental changes in its own members and subsystems, and to outer pressures coming from demands to accommodate to the significant social institutions that have an impact on family members. Inherent in this process of change and continuity are the stresses of accommodating to new situations. The strength of the family system depends on the abilities of family members to mobilise alternative transactional patterns when internal and/or external conditions of the family demand restructuring. A family is said to adapt to stress in a way that maintains family continuity while making restructuring possible. If family members respond to stress with rigidity, for example, by reapplying 'old' solutions, unhelpful transactions may ensue.

Symptomatic behaviour is seen as a maladaptive reaction to changing environmental and developmental requirements, and thus the presence or absence of problems does not define normality.

Thus we can see that the 'as if' notion of structure is helpful in providing a framework for thinking about belonging and loyalty, proximity, exclusion and abandonment, power, aggression (as reflected in subsystem formation), the relative permeability of boundaries, working alliances and coalitions. In the 1996 publication *Mastering family therapy,* Minuchin and colleagues made a commitment to the original formulation of family functioning, with a shift in perspective in the following areas of therapist functioning:

- Modified intensity of therapeutic encounters;
- A more fluid commitment to a key 'alphabet of therapist skills';
- An increased use of the self of the therapist in therapy, with a greater emphasis on feedback to family members of the effects of interaction on the therapist, aimed at offering more information about their interactions with one another;
- An increased interest in supervision, aimed at developing the therapist's under-utilised skills;
- Admission of his own impatience and speed in reading non-verbal cues;
- The recognition of relative perspectives, with the structural frame as an organiser of therapists' perceptions rather than universal truths;
- The role of the therapist in activating the family members' own alternative ways of relating: 'While the therapist has ideas and biases about family norms, and about the best family fit, she can only go in the direction that the family indicates when they enact their drama and show possible alternatives' (Minuchin, Lee, & Simon, 1996).

Assessment for Therapy

Structural therapy posits that for therapy to be effective, the therapist needs to form a new system with the family group (family plus therapist system). In order to do this, the therapist relies on techniques of accommodation and joining. Accommodation is said to be the process of adjustment of the therapist to the family members, which includes: a) planned support for the family structure, i.e., offering support for what is going well, and helping to create changes in structures that will work; b) carefully tracking the content and process of family interaction; and c) accommodating to the family members' style and range of affect through mirroring. Joining refers to those actions of the therapist aimed directly at relating to family members. The therapist must therefore be aware of taking sides, and must offer support at times when being confrontational. This emphasis on the importance of the therapeutic relationship recognises its potential as a vehicle for therapeutic change.

Structural therapists assess and explore the family's structure (for example, subsystems, boundaries, functions, relationships, external relationships and social support) to identify areas of strength and resilience, possible flexibility and change. Assessment includes: a) family members' preferred transactional patterns and available alternatives; b) flexibility and the capacity to change, often based on responses to earlier demands for change within the family group; c) family members' sensitivity to members' needs, behaviours, attitudes, and so on; d) developmental issues, tasks and requirements; e) the meaning and relational significance of symptomatic behaviour; and f) the context of family life, with specific reference to sources of social support and sources of stress. Pitfalls within the assessment process can include: a) ignoring the developmental processes of family members and changing family subsystems; b) ignoring some family subsystems; and c) joining and supporting only one family subsystem.

Therapeutic change is seen to be a delicate process, whereby too little involvement by the therapist will lead to maintenance of the status quo and too much involvement and directiveness might lead to panic and premature ending of therapy by the family members. Change is thought to occur through the trusting relationship with the therapist, within which a context is created to actualise family transactional patterns through enactment and reenactments, to recreate communication channels, to help members manage psychological distance and space, to delineate and reinforce individual and subsystem boundaries, such as helping a lone mother regain her parental authority with her children, to create therapeutic intensity by emphasising differences and exploring conflicts and their resolution, to offer support, education and guidance, and to assign agreed tasks and opportunities to try out new solutions developed within the session between sessions.

Fish and Piercy (1987) used a Delphi procedure to examine the similarities and differences in the theory and practice of structural family therapy and strategic family therapy in the United States with the help of a panel of knowledgeable and well known structural and strategic therapists (which included practitioners of Milan family therapy). Of interest here are the findings that: a) structural panellists endorsed differently those theoretical assumptions that pertain to subsystems, hierarchy, boundaries, and families as organisations; b) structural panellists endorsed different goals of therapy, which included reorganisation of the family structure, the lessening of rules/roles constrained by narrow bounds of transactions, and resolution of the presenting problems through structural reorganisation; c) all panellists endorsed relabeling and reframing as a shared therapeutic technique, whereas structural therapists did not endorse any indirect techniques, only direct methods of working; d) all panellists endorsed a view of therapeutic change occurring when unhelpful sequences of interaction were altered, through a change in both family members' behaviours and perceptions. This study provides an interesting glimpse into the panellists' perceptions of family therapy practice in the mid 1980s, at a time when all schools of family therapy were reorganising to take account of the recent major critiques of thinking and practice.

Challenges to Structural Family Therapy

Like most schools of family therapy, structural therapy was critiqued during the 1980s by feminist commentators (Hare Mustin, 1987), and by those concerned with issues of race and culture (Holland, 1990). The thrust of the feminist informed critiques was that family theorists and therapists had paid attention to issues of power and the effect on relatedness *between* the generations, i.e., the politics of growing up, but had systematically failed to address the issue of power *within* same generational relationships, such as couple relationships. Although it should be said that a power skew in either direction of the couple's relationship was seen as more likely associated with widespread distress and general problems within the family. The gender informed critique coincided with a growing body of demographic data that identified high rates of physical violence from men to their women partners (Straus & Gelles, 1990). This was a serious omission within the field that has been addressed recently. See the work by Goldner (1998) and that of Vetere and Cooper (2000), which privileges the issues of responsibility and safety, when working with abuses of power in family relationships, and seeks to find ways of giving voice to women as they regain their parental authority with their children, and to redress relative power inequalities within couple relationships.

The challenges to structural family therapy have come from different quarters. The approach to assessment has been criticised as located solely within the household family group, ignoring the roles of extended family, neighbourhood and other social institutions and leading to an incomplete picture of the presenting difficulties. The problem here, in my view, lies more in the local application of the ideas, as there is nothing in the theoretical language and model that constrains assessment of wider systemic issues in the therapist's formulation (Vetere, 1992).

The direct and involved therapeutic style of the structural therapist does not find favour within the UK, amidst concerns of therapist burnout. Earlier excesses of enthusiasm around the therapist as leader and director of the therapy have led to moderation in the description and promotion of structural therapist style. Research by Hampson and Beavers (1996) has highlighted the importance of the fit between family members' emotional style and that of the therapist. The influence of constructivism and social constructionism have been profound, in that the focus on issues of therapist reflexivity have led to profound changes in how we think about our own a priori assumptions about families and cultural norms and in our increased search for integration of theory. However, an overemphasis on the value of uncertainty and uniqueness, often associated with postmodern critiques, runs the risk of injustice by assuming that abuse and issues of structural inequality can be seen as one narrative amongst others (Minuchin, 1991).

Arguably, many family therapists are interested in integrative practice, both within the field of family therapy and across the major psychotherapeutic domains (see Larner, 2000). Thus the structural focus on the here and now, in the description and attempted alleviation of symptoms, limits the ability to explain and predict symptomatic behaviour and possibly leads the therapist to search for other models that address these issues. In the absence of well articulated attempts to integrate theory at the conceptual level, this criticism remains a problem of application and practice. Therapists seem more interested in seeking multi-dimensional views of family members' behaviour and general functioning and tailoring their approaches to families rather than slavishly following 'schools.' There is no doubt in my mind that theory can be used narrowly and prescriptively; the challenge lies in using theory in an elaborated and skeptical way, such that we can be held accountable ethically for the connections between our thinking and our practice.

Another set of challenges have revolved around the structural view of problem maintenance and the purported function of symptomatic behaviour. The notion that the system is maintained by the problem has been popular within structural thinking, with a recognition that symptomatic behaviour is often the ironic consequence of attempts to solve problems and adapt. The punctuation of this thinking has been criticised for failing to acknowledge that symptomatic behaviour may take on functional significance within the family group, or that a structural therapist may see dysfunction where none exists, i.e., a family group is temporarily off track, so to speak. The structural focus on competence and strengths within the family is likely to temper this criticism, although Gorell Barnes (1998) highlights that an assumption of resilience may not be born out in practice, particularly with more fragile family forms, such as some newly formed step-family arrangements.

It is of interest to me that Minuchin has always been interested in his writing in the social and economic conditions that support family members' functioning. In particular, his awareness of the unrelenting and numerous external pressures on poor inner city families, that lead to problems in family functioning, and the legal context of the Courts and social policy changes around substitute care that serve to undermine the functioning of/and break up poor families (Minuchin, 1992). Structural therapists have always advocated cultural relativity in their practice, asking, does this family's structure, at this time, in this particular cultural and social grouping, sufficiently meet the needs of family members? However, recent critiques have questioned the extent to which any notion of structure, with its associated implications of norms and normality, can be helpful when addressing issues of cultural diversity.

An Illustration of Structural Family Therapy

The following excerpt is from an early therapy session with a family, self referred over their concern for Caroline's drinking problem. It is preceded by some information about the family to help the reader put the therapy session into context.

The household members are the mother and father and their adult younger daughter, Caroline, 22 years old. Jean, her older sister by two years, moved to live in independent lodgings over a year ago. Jean has a successful career in a software company. Caroline misses her sister. Caroline cannot help but compare herself adversely with her older sister. Caroline struggled with a college course in art and design and, since leaving, has not been able to find employment. Both parents are employed in a professional capacity. Caroline describes her drinking problem as a direct result of believing she has nothing to get up for in the morning.

The family therapy complements Caroline's individual work with her alcohol keyworker. The family work was requested by all family members as they wished to think together about the consequences of Caroline's drinking for family relationships and to understand how best to support her in her recovery. Initially tacitly, and then subsequently, overtly, the parents wished to understand whether their relationships with their daughter had somehow made it more likely she would turn to alcohol for solace in the face of distress and disappointment. The alcohol keyworker made the referral to the family therapy team when Caroline had been abstinent from alcohol for a period of 2 months.

The family therapy team uses an integrative approach; however, this excerpt, which occurred in the third meeting with the family, is chosen to emphasise the structural aspects of the team's thinking and practice. In the early stages of the work, the team focused on family members' roles, relationships and expectations of each other, both in the context of their recent life cycle changes and the iterative, problem maintaining effects of drinking. Early in the third session Caroline said that she did not know how any of her family felt about anything any more, what they felt about their jobs, their lives, about each other, about her. Caroline's mother replied in a hesitant way that talking to her these past few years had been like walking on egg shells, unpredictable, uncertain and never knowing what would upset her, leading her mother to believe it was safest and prudent not to discuss anything of a potentially sensitive nature. Caroline listened to her mother intently, and then expressed deep regret at the loss of contact and personal understanding of each other that seemed to have crept

up on them all. Jean looked at Caroline, seemed to take a deep breath, and said directly and clearly, that she wanted to talk to Caroline, not Caroline plus the bottle. At this point, the therapist asked the two sisters if they wanted to continue this discussion without having to talk over their parents who were seated between them. Jean moved with alacrity to sit next to Caroline, and in what seemed like a gesture of support and intimacy, held each other's arms. They continued to talk further to each other about the importance of their relationship as sisters, their wish to confide in each other, their wish to support each other, thus reclaiming some of their past sense of closeness. In recognising how alcohol had come between them, as Caroline had seemed to form a primary relationship with alcohol, which she now wanted to challenge in her wish to reconnect with her sister, Caroline drew on the support of the therapist and the team as a bridging relationship to her family members.

Further on in this session, the father produced a set of house rules that he and his wife had agreed and then given to Caroline in an attempt to help her maintain her abstinence and to continue to live with them. The therapist asked about the rules, whose ideas were they, and what did Caroline think? Caroline said she had agreed to the list of rules and that she respected them. In our view this seemed to be linked to Caroline's attempt to reclaim her own sense of self-respect and to develop a different voice in her own family. Caroline took the list from her father and read out the first few rules to the therapist. The first one was 'To behave like an adult.' The therapist asked what this meant. Caroline paused and seemed very thoughtful. She raised her head and looked at everyone, 'It means to take more responsibility for my behaviour.' This generated much discussion, and afforded an opportunity for Caroline's father to praise her definition, saying it was much better than his, previously offered one. Caroline thought her father's praise was important, as she had previously described her father to the team as overly critical of her as a growing young woman. This interaction led the team to speculate that perhaps Caroline's father had an uncertain sense of his importance to his developing and now adult daughter. This theme was explored in subsequent meetings where we learned that Caroline's father had been raised as an only child, with an authoritarian father, as he saw it, with whom he had only made a more adult relationship in his mid-thirties. Caroline's father told us he had left home to get married to Caroline's mother. Thus connections between the generations and their remembrance and understanding of developmental transitions and relationship changes formed another bridge between Caroline and her mother and father.

This small excerpt can only offer a flavour of the complexity of the family work. The team's thinking complemented the family's focus on roles, communication and relationships, and how the transition into adulthood for Caroline had challenged family members' expectations of her and each other. Much that was hurtful had been said during periods of intoxication, and communication withdrawal had characterised periods of sobriety, creating an equilibrium within which nothing seemed to change or could seem to change. In our view, Caroline's commitment to working with her keyworker formed the first step in reorienting her to relationships with people, thus paving the way for the family work to create a context for coping and support that facilitated forgiveness, reconciliation and hopefulness for the future.

Applications and Efficacy

A recent survey of family therapists' practice in the UK identified that 21% of respondents identified themselves with structural family therapy (Bor, Mallandain, & Vetere, 1998). Jonathan Dare (1996) lamented what he saw as the decline in structural family therapy practice in the UK and his perception of common misunderstandings about such practice, such as the belief that structural therapists imposed Eurocentric middle class beliefs on everyone else. However, a significant minority of UK family therapists and systemic practitioners identify a primary loyalty to this modality, alongside a growing body of empirical research that attests to the efficacy of

structural and behavioural based approaches to working with families. The field of outcome research does not differentiate between the earlier schools of family therapy, such that reviews include structural, strategic and some Milan based therapies with both families and couples.

According to Bergin and Garfield (1994), the marital and family approaches have been subjected to rigorous research scrutiny, with only a few forms of psychotherapy studied as often. Studies report the use of controlled and uncontrolled group comparison designs, single case designs, and a few studies comparing the relative efficacy of the different family therapy approaches. The overwhelming findings from the research reviews and the meta-analytic studies is that family therapy works compared to untreated control groups, with some demonstrated superiority to standard and individual treatments for certain disorders and populations. Meta-analysis demonstrates moderate, statistically and clinically significant effects (Markus, Lange, & Pettigrew, 1990; Shadish et at., 1995; Goldstein & Miklowitz, 1995). The following list of people and problems is found to benefit both clinically and significantly from the marital and family therapies compared to no psychotherapy: marital/couple distress and conflict; outpatient depressed women in unsatisfactory marriages; adult drinking problems and drug misuse; adolescent drug misuse; adult schizophrenia; adolescent conduct disorder; child conduct disorders; aggression and non-compliance in children with a diagnosis of ADHD; chronic physical illness in children; obesity in children and cardiovascular risk factors in children. Marital and family therapy appears not to be harmful, in that no RCT study has reported poorer outcomes for treated clients than for untreated control family members (Pinsof & Wynne, 1995).

In my view, the structural model is attractive because it is parent-friendly, with its emphasis on team working and practical problem solving. It is a contractual and time limited model, it emphasises the importance of giving clear feedback and responding to the presenting problems, it is a consciousness raising model for families and organisations, and avoids using covert methods of intervention. It meets many of the criteria identified by Reimers and Treacher for 'user friendly approaches' (Reimers & Treacher, 1995). As Minuchin (1998) argues, it focuses on family interaction and multi-channel communication processes and keeps alive the value of family process for therapists in these days of the narrative therapies. Its applications have been wider than its original formulation within the field of child and family mental health, including the services and problems listed above and, in my experience, in services for people with learning disabilities (Vetere, 1993). *Family therapy in the 90s,* edited by John Carpenter and Andy Treacher, identifies further applications of the approach for the interested reader.

Sigurd Reimers, writing in the first number of the 2000 edition of the *Journal of Family Therapy,* comments that practitioners should never forget family therapists' excesses of certainty that preceded the postmodern challenges. In his view, collaboration with family members will be the most treasured contribution offered by recent advances, alongside the more explicit recognition of the 'as if' quality of our ideas about families and family members (Reimers, 2000).

Whilst agreeing with Sigurd Reimers, I would add to his reflections an enduring belief in the helpfulness of the notion of scepticism, born out of my training as a social scientist within the tradition of British empiricism. It seems to me that amongst the clinical competencies we seek in ourselves, and in those whom we train as family therapists, are the abilities to be curious about what we do, to ask questions, to refine those questions in the light of observation and experience, to evaluate and re-evaluate our understandings, constantly checking with all participants as we go along. This list, for me, also describes a structural family therapist.

References

Bergin, A., & Garfield, S. (Eds.). (1994). *Handbook of psychotherapy and behavior change* (4th ed.). New York: Wiley.

Bor, R., Mallandain, I., & Vetere, A. (1998). What we say we do: Clinical practice patterns of UK family therapists. *Journal of Family Therapy, 20,* 334–352.

Brody, G. (Ed.). (1996). *Sibling relationships: Their causes and consequences.* Norwood, NJ: Ablex.

Carpenter, J., & Treacher, A. (Eds.). (1993). *Family therapy in the 90s.* Oxford, UK: Blackwell.

Dare, J. (1996). Ladybird book therapy and the dinosaur. *Context, 26,* 6–10.

Fish, L. S., & Piercy, F. P. (1987). The theory and practice of structural and strategic family therapies: A Delphi study. *Journal of Marital and Family Therapy, 13,* 113–125.

Goldner, V. (1998). The treatment of violence and victimisation in intimate relationships. *Family Process, 37,* 263–286.

Goldstein, M., & Miklowitz, D. (1995). The effectiveness of psychoeducational family therapy in the treatment of schizophrenic disorders. *Journal of Marital and Family Therapy, 21,* 361–376.

Gorell Barnes, G. (1998). *Family therapy in changing times.* London: Macmillan.

Hampson, R., & Beavers, W. (1996). Family therapy and outcome: Relationships between therapist and family styles. *Contemporary Family Therapy, 18,* 345–370.

Hare Mustin, R. (1987). The problem of gender in family therapy theory. *Family Process, 26,* 15–27.

Holland, S. (1990). Psychotherapy, oppression and social action: Gender, race and class in black women's depression. In R. Perelberg & A. Miller (Eds.), *Gender and power in families.* London: Routledge.

Lamer, G. (2000). Towards a common ground in psychoanalysis and family therapy: On knowing not to know. *Journal of Family Therapy, 22,* 61–82.

Markus, E., Lange, A., & Pettigrew, T. (1990). Effectiveness of family therapy: A meta-analysis. *Journal of Family Therapy, 12,* 205–221.

Minuchin, S. (1974). *Families and family therapy.* London: Tavistock.

Minuchin, S. (1984). *Family kaleidoscope.* Cambridge, MA: Harvard University Press.

Minuchin, S. (1991). The seductions of constructivism. *Family Therapy Networker,* September/October, 47–50.

Minuchin, S. (1992). *Family healing.* New York: Macmillan.

Minuchin, S. (1998). Where is the family in narrative family therapy? *Journal of Marital and Family Therapy, 24,* 397–403.

Minuchin, S., & Fishman, C. (1991). *Family therapy techniques.* Cambridge, MA: Harvard University Press.

Minuchin, S., Lee, W. Y., & Simon, G. (1996). *Mastering family therapy: Journeys of growth and transformation.* New York: Wiley.

Minuchin, S., Montalvo, B., Guerney, B., Rosman, B., & Schumer, F. (1967). *Families of the slums: An exploration of their structure and treatment.* New York: Basic Books.

Minuchin, S., Rosman, B., & Baker, L. (1978). *Psychosomatic families: Anorexia nervosa in context.* Cambridge, MA: Harvard University Press.

Pinsof, W. M., & Wynne, L. C. (1995). The efficacy of marital and family therapy: An empirical overview, conclusions, and recommendations. *Journal of Marital and Family Therapy, 21,* 585–613.

Reimers, S. (2000). Therapist reflections: Triple-mindedness. *Journal of Family Therapy, 22,* 24–28.

Reimers, S., & Treacher, A. (1995). *Introducing user-friendly family therapy.* London: Routledge.

Shadish, W., Ragsdale, K., Glaser, R., & Montgomery, L. (1995). The efficacy and effectiveness of marital and family therapy: A perspective from meta-analysis. *Journal of Marital and Family Therapy, 21,* 345–360.

Simon, G. (1995). A revisionist rendering of structural family therapy. *Journal of Marital and Family Therapy, 21,* 1726.

Straus, M. A., & Gelles, R. J. (1990). *Physical violence in American families: Risk factors and adaptations to violence, in 8,145 families.* New Brunswick, NJ: Transaction Publishers.

Vetere, A. (1992). Working with families. In J. M. Ussher & P. Nicolson (Eds.), *Gender issues in clinical psychology.* London: Routledge.

Vetere, A. (1993). Using family therapy in services for people with learning disabilities. In J. Carpenter & A. Treacher (Eds.), *Family therapy in the 90s.* Oxford, UK: Blackwell.

Vetere, A., & Cooper, J. (2000). Working systemically with family violence. In N. Singh, J. Leung, & A. Singh (Eds.), *International perspectives on child* and *adolescent mental health.* New York: Elsevier Science.

von Bertalanffy, L. (1968). *General system theory.* Harmondsworth, UK: Penguin.

10

ECOLOGICAL THEORY

A fundamental assumption of ecological theory is that development and change occurs as a result of interactions between the "thing" developing and the environmental context broadly conceived. We say "thing" because this theoretical perspective applies to the development of individuals as well as to families and other entities (e.g., schools and workplaces). Bubolz and Sontag's (1993) excellent overview of human ecological theory, in fact, mentions the theory as being relevant in sociology, geography, political science, economics, and human-environment relations. The wide array of interrelated disciplines that constitute and came to be known as home economics (also known as, in recent times, human ecology or family and consumer sciences) first applied this perspective to issues of family life in the late 19th century. For our purposes, more recent developments occurred in the 1960s through the 1970s, with further refinements and applications occurring on a regular basis since, that focused on families (Hook & Paolucci, 1970) and on individual development (Bronfenbrenner, 1979).

An essential feature of the basic assumption noted above is the emphasis on interaction. That is, individuals and families are not simply shaped by environmental influences and contexts; they also impact those contexts. For example, first consider the human infant, an individual. A key environmental-contextual variable for the infant is the personality and other characteristics of the mother. Is the mother comfortable with being a mother? Does the mother like to cuddle infants or is she more likely to allow the infant more personal space? What happens if the mother is a cuddler, but the infant's temperament is more difficult? What happens in general with mothers and infants is that there is an ongoing process of mutual adjustment (say, in developing feeding patterns that work for both) that develops over time with each member of the dyad influencing the other. Ecological theory predicts exactly this kind of adjustment process. Similarly, in terms of family development (both in terms of the family as a unit and in terms of individual development of family members), the relevance of contextual issues is ongoing. Consider, for example, the impact of a new individual joining the family (via birth, adoption, or foster care) on the family as well as the reverse. Consider newfound competencies of children as they develop (e.g., walking or driving) that influence the family as a unit as well as changes among other family members (e.g., personal difficulties, illness, or desires to change careers) that influence other family members.

What we have just briefly described is perhaps the most intimate of human contexts—the kinds of things that occur within families. This is, however, but one kind of context that "contains" the individual. The second assumption of

303

ecological theoretical perspectives is that there are several levels of environmental context. In one particular and highly influential incarnation of ecological theory, Bronfenbrenner (1979) and Bronfenbrenner and Morris (1998), for example, describe micro-, meso-, exo-, and macrosystem contexts. These systems, or contexts of influence, refer to, respectively, settings that contain and directly influence the individual (e.g., family and school), the relationship between settings that contain the individual (e.g., neighborhoods and child care), settings that do not contain the individual but have indirect influence (e.g., parental workplaces), and broader societal level values and ideologies that provide a total context for the other systems (e.g., levels of family violence in a society or societal messages about personal support for fellow citizens). Each of these ecological or system levels is presumed to impact the individual either directly or through other systems.

Although Bronfenbrenner focuses on individual development (as distinct from family development), the same kinds of contextual factors apply to families (Ray, 1988). For example, a microsystem for a family, in addition to their own home, is the neighborhood in which they live. A mesosystem for a family includes their church or community center and their relationship to local health care, and an exosystem for a family is the local school board, or the tax base in a community. The family macrosystem includes the same kinds of things as it does for individuals (e.g., television programming, national decisions of war and peace). We have already emphasized that the individual (or the family) is engaged in constant reciprocal interaction at each of the contextual levels—being influenced by and influencing the specific contextual factors within levels. A third assumption of ecological theory takes this a step further and says that the contextual levels also interact with one another on an ongoing basis.

This key assumption, one that derives directly from biological perspectives on the nature of the physical ecosystem, is important to understand. The very important perspective that is gained

from this assumption is that all individuals and all families develop in contexts with contextual characteristics that themselves influence and are influenced by the other contexts. We illustrate with an example: Consider the case of a family decision to allow or not allow (if there is a choice—sadly, sometimes there is not) an 11-year-old child to come home after school without a parent or caregiver being present.

What kinds of things might be evaluated in assessing whether or not this is a good idea? It may be helpful to contrast two scenarios. First, we shall assume that the parents see their child as mature for an 11-year-old (itself a judgment based on a broad range of microsystem-level variables such as direct observation of the child in numerous family and other contexts) and that the child seems comfortable with the idea of spending an hour or so alone after school. We'll further assume that one or both parents or an older sibling who lives nearby would be available by phone, and that the family's local mesosystem is generally supportive (e.g., neighbors talk to one another and there are physical settings with adults around to observe children in the neighborhood). Finally, children in the neighborhood have nice green space in which to play—the direct result of zoning decisions and local support for family-friendly leisure alternatives (exosystem variables).

Compare the above set of interacting contextual factors with a set of factors that are diametrically opposite: the child has special needs, there is high crime in the neighborhood, and neighbors seem to isolate themselves. Although any one of these contextual factors would argue against a decision to leave the child alone after school (again, if there were even a choice), it is the combination that seems especially dangerous. Further, the nature of the particular components that comprise each of the system levels is the result of other system-level influences. We invite you to think of how available neighbors might be, for example, in the context of a community that does not support positive, child-friendly environments for children. Or consider how the level of internal family stress and the quality of intrafamily communication (micro-system variables) might be impacted by restrictions on school funding (an exosystem, and, ultimately, a microsystem and mesosystem variable).

THE READINGS

Three readings are presented in this chapter to illustrate important features of ecological theory. The first (Berry & Rao, 1997) deals with workplace issues and family stress, and the researchers provide a thorough discussion of the practical implications of their research. The authors talk about risks and opportunities associated with each of the ecological system levels and highlight how the different levels work in an interactive matter to influence families. This article also provides a nice conceptual linkage between ecological theory (which has primarily focused on individual development) and systems theory (which has primarily focused on family development). Huston (2000) provides an ecological framework for studying marital relationships (broadly conceived to include unions, mates, and partners) and some of the everyday issues that individuals face in such relationships, such as conflict resolution and sexual activity. An important feature of the Huston piece is that it links the development of an ecological framework to research methodology issues—a key feature of theory development and testing as we indicated in Chapter 1. The final article in this chapter focuses on the study of community collaborations from an ecological perspective (Perkins, Ferrari, Covey, & Keith, 1996). In so doing, it provides several clear schematics of ideas presented in this chapter and draws clear linkages to a wide range of important community issues and activities that relate directly to the support of families through an interlacing system of interacting and influential variables.

ISSUES FOR YOUR CONSIDERATION

1. What do you think are the strongest and weakest features of the ecological perspective on families and individuals?

2. Assuming that you have neither the funds nor the time (a reasonable assumption!) to study *all* aspects of the ecological model at the same time, which system level do you think is most influential in determining child well-being and in influencing the quality of family relationships?

3. If we asked you to develop a community collaboration with researchers that would potentially have a positive impact on reducing family violence, what ecological system variables would you focus on?

FURTHER READING

See Bronfenbrenner (1979), Bubolz and Sontag (1993), and Hook and Paolucci (1970).

Balancing Employment and Fatherhood: A Systems Perspective

Judy O. Berry and Julie Meyer Rao

Abstract

Fathers in dual-earner families (N = 447) participated in three studies. The first two studies were designed to devise a brief measure of stress experienced by employed men in dual-earner families. The resulting Workplace/Family Stress Scale was found to be a reliable and valid measure of this construct. An ecological systems framework was utilized for study design and analyses in the third study. This study explored contributions from various system levels to the work/family stress dynamic. Results indicated that all system levels examined (the individual, the family microsystem, and the workplace microsystem) contributed to experienced stress, with the greatest contribution coming from the family microsystem. Implications of these findings for fathers involved in multiple roles and for their families are discussed.

Fatherhood is receiving increasing attention in venues ranging from the research literature to the popular press. There is interest in the historical perspective of fatherhood as well as in how contemporary fathers manage their day-to-day lives. Much of the focus of this attention is on the changing role of fathers and how this change influences these men as well as the women and children in their lives. An example of this change is provided in the recent passage of the Family and Medical Leave Act (Lechner & Creedon, 1994). Of particular note is that the word *family* (rather than *maternal*) *is* used, which denotes eligibility of men as well as women—fathers as well as mothers. This gender-neutral language can be attributed to the changing roles of both fathers and mothers.

Statistics show that more than two thirds of American mothers are now employed outside the home, including more than half of mothers with children younger than age 3 (Voydanoff, 1993). The "culture of fatherhood" (LaRossa, 1988, p. 451) or society's beliefs and values concerning the role of the male parent is also changing (Gilbert, 1993; Marsiglio, 1993). These changes, however, can lead to so-called equal opportunity stress for both men and women involved in juggling work and family roles, which is supported by findings of 72% of men and 83% of women reporting significant stress and conflict between work and family roles (Rosen, 1991). Voydanoff (1993) contends that "it is not sufficient to view work/family issues as women's issues that affect men only as husbands of working women" (p. 99). She urges focusing on work/family issues from a multiple roles perspective.

Theoretical work by Pleck (1977) postulated that work and family roles of men and women comprise a family/work role system. That is, a man's role in one domain (work or family) reciprocates with his own role in the other domain as well as with his spouse's role in the same domain (e.g., his family role is related to his wife's family role). Recent studies have shown a decrease for wives and an increase for husbands in time spent with housework and child care (Pleck, 1985).

However, mothers still do more housework and child care than fathers (e.g., Hochschild, 1989; Lechner & Creedon, 1994). Increased father involvement has been targeted as a means of reducing stress for working mothers (Scarr, Phillips, & McCartney, 1989).

With certain exceptions (e.g., fathers who are emotionally harsh or punitive), as fathers become more involved in home responsibilities, their wives and children stand to benefit; and this involvement can be rewarding and satisfying for these men. However, there are also potential costs because these home responsibilities intertwine with the workplace. The workplace has traditionally expected fathers to be present and productive, and family needs, such as caring for a sick child, were considered the responsibility of the wife—if they were considered at all. Pleck (1984) stated that "the working mother has been well established as a social issue; the working father has not" (p. 11). He further noted that the reluctance of employers to implement policies supporting employed fathers is derived, at least in part, from the deep-seated societal belief that breadwinning, rather than direct involvement with children, is a father's fundamental parental responsibility. This is supported by Griswold's (1993) historical work on fatherhood in which he framed the issue this way: "How we came to expect more than ever before from fathers without knowing quite what to expect, is the story of fatherhood in the twentieth century" (p. 9).

So how do fathers cope with changing expectations at home and a workplace that may not support changes on the homefront? Most studies to date have addressed the impact on adjustment and relationship quality for mothers and fathers in dual-earner families when fathers share child care and other home responsibilities (e.g., Crouter, Perry-Jenkins, Huston, & McHale, 1987; Kessler & McRae, 1982; Ross & Mirowsky, 1988). However, research typically has not addressed family role demands for fathers as they relate directly to work role demands.

Three recent studies of dual-earner couples have addressed the interface of the parental and workplace roles of fathers. In their study, Baruch and Barnett (1986) found that increased participation in child care by fathers was related to higher self-esteem and to feeling more competent and satisfied in their parental role. However, these fathers also reported having too little time for their careers and feeling that their family responsibilities interfered with their work. Guelzow, Bird, and Koball (1991) found that men with more flexible work schedules had less role strain and lower levels of marital, professional, and parental stress. Barnett, Marshall, and Pleck (1992) examined family role variables for men—specifically, role quality. They reported that parental role quality was a significant predictor of men's psychological distress and that parental role, marital role, and job role quality scores were similar in the strength of their association with distress scores.

These studies suggest a relationship between parental and workplace stress among fathers in dual-earner families. However, this relationship has been assessed only in fairly broad terms. Therefore, there is a need first to better define the kinds of parental responsibilities fathers become involved in that affect their work roles and, second, to determine how stressful these experiences are. The work of Bronfenbrenner (1979) presents a theoretical framework that can be used to explore fathers' multiple roles. Bronfenbrenner views the individual as being in the center of a series of concentric systems. According to Bronfenbrenner, these systems surround the individual "as a set of nested structures, each inside the next, like a set of Russian dolls" (p. 22). He termed these systems in order of increasing distance from the individual: the microsystem, the mesosystem, the exosystem, and the macrosystem.

Microsystems are the individual's most immediate setting or day-to-day reality, such as the family and the workplace. Mesosystems involve the relationships between the various microsystems that the individual occupies. The individual does not participate directly in exosystems, but they do exert power and influence. Finally, the overarching macrosystem represents broad ideological patterns of a particular culture (Garbarino & Abramowitz, 1992).

Mesosystem links for employed fathers involve connections between their workplace and family microsystems. Exosystems include family-related policies of their employer and schedules and policies of their child care provider. Federal policy regarding family leave and the ideology of a father's role provide examples of relevant macrosystem influences. Bronfenbrenner and Crouter (1984) discussed the relevance of the "evolving pattern of ever-more-powerful reciprocal influences between the world of work on the one hand and the family as a context for human development on the other" (p. 40) and the implications of this for public policy.

The purpose of this study was to devise a brief measure of work/family stress experienced by employed men in dual-earner families. A second purpose was to explore contributions from various system levels to this work/family stress dynamic.

Method and Results (Studies 1 and 2)

Two scale development studies were conducted. These preliminary studies focused on (a) identifying the kinds of child-related responsibilities fathers assume that affect their employment roles and (b) determining the levels of stress of these experiences. Results from all three studies are reported on fathers in dual-earner couples, or marriages in which both parents are employed outside the home at least 30 hours per week. In the first study, participants were 77 fathers (in dual-earner couples) with at least one child under 18 years of age living at home (mean child age = 6.4). The mean age for these fathers was 37.4, and more than half (67%) occupied managerial or professional positions. Participants for all three studies were recruited from child care and after-school care programs. Questionnaires were distributed by the directors of these programs. No fathers participated in more than one study.

The fathers in the first study were asked to describe, in writing, any fathering experiences that affected their roles as employed men. A total of 231 experiences were obtained, with a mean of three experiences per respondent. Categories of experiences were determined by a Q-sort performed by three people practicing psychology in family settings. Three classifications emerged: children's needs, work/family conflict, and family discord. Children's needs were the focus of 69% of the total responses. Experiences shared by these fathers included situations in which the child had minor and major illness, school-related situations, such as programs and teacher conferences, and the child's extracurricular activities, such as sports or lessons. Of the responses, 19% were in the category of work/family conflict and included experiences, such as needing to provide care for the child when typical child care arrangements broke down or when the wife's work schedule changed in a way that made the wife unavailable for child care (such as out of town travel) and experiences involving transporting the child to and from care situations. The remaining 12% of the total responses were categorized as family discord. Examples of responses in this category included conflict with spouse or child, telephone calls at work from spouse describing parental stress, and irritability toward family members stemming from work overload.

A 40-item scale was developed for Study 2, using experiences broadly sampled from the three categories of child-related responsibilities emerging from Study 1. This questionnaire was completed by 172 employed fathers (in dual earner couples) who had at least one child under the age of 18 living at home (mean child age = 11.7). The mean age of these fathers was 38.0, and 63% occupied managerial and professional positions. Participants were instructed that questionnaire items reflected experiences that fathers in a previous study had found to contribute to stress in their work role. For each item, participants were asked to state whether this experience had happened to them (occurrence) and then to rate, on a 7-point Likert-type scale (in which 1 = *least stress* and 7 = *most stress*), the level of disturbance or stress (intensity).

With the goal of creating a brief measure, means and standard deviations of the ratings were calculated for each experience. In addition, data were subjected to a principal axis factor analysis with varimax rotation. The criterion for retention of a factor was an eigenvalue of 1.0 or greater. This resulted in three factors, which accounted for 55.1% of the explained variance. Inspection of item content for items loading greater than 0.45 on each factor suggested factor labels that confirmed the Q-sort categories: Factor 1 (45.7% of variance), Child Needs; Factor 2 (5.9% of variance), Family Discord; Factor 3 (3.5% of variance), Work/Family Conflict.

The items selected for the final measure reflected the three categories and represented the full range of means (5.22 to 1.86). An additional criterion for selection was that at least 40% of the fathers surveyed had to have actually experienced the situation. These procedures resulted in the nine-item Workplace/Family Stress Scale (see Table 10.1). Items reflecting the three categories are as follows: Family Discord, Items 1 and 2; Work/Family Conflict, Items 3, 4, 5, and 6; and Children's Needs, Items 7, 8, and 9. The Workplace/Family Stress Scale was found to have adequate reliability. Coefficient alpha for intensity ratings of these nine items with this sample was .88, and the mean interitem correlation was .45. Item whole correlations varied from .42 to .70, with a mean of .62.

Method (Study 3)

A third study was then conducted using the Workplace/Family Stress Scale. Participants in this third study were 198 full-time employed fathers in dual-earner couples with at least one child under the age of 12 living with them. This younger child age was selected because of the higher care and parent involvement needs of younger children. Men in the sample averaged 37.0 years of age, and the number of children ranged from one to five with a median of two. The mean age of the children was 6.5 years. The sample was predominantly White (96.1%) and college educated, and more than half of the participants (67.4%) occupied managerial or professional occupational roles. More than three fourths of the sample reported annual family incomes in excess of $40,000. The mean work hours per week for the men was 47.4 and for their wives was 42.1 hours.

Participants completed the previously described Workplace/Family Stress Scale (items listed on Table 10.1 were placed in random order). They were asked to rate each item on intensity of experienced stress (5-point Likert-type scale ranging from 1, *not stressful,* to 5, *very stressful)* and on likelihood of occurrence (5-point Likert-type scale ranging from 1, *unlikely occurrence,* to 5, *likely occurrence).* Participants also completed the Perceived Stress Scale (S. Cohen, Kamarck, & Mermelstein, 1983). The Perceived Stress Scale is a 14-item measure of life stress with adequate internal (coefficient alpha > .84) and test-retest reliability ($rs = .85$ for 2 days, .55 for 6 weeks).

Additional instruments were selected to examine workplace/family stress from the standpoint of the systems approach delineated by Bronfenbrenner (1979). To assess individual traits, participants completed the agreeableness and conscientiousness subscales of Goldberg's (1992) Big Five personality adjective markers. These scales consist of both positive and negative adjectives that are descriptive of the constructs of agreeableness and conscientiousness (e.g., cold, generous, kind for agreeableness; thorough, organized, negligent for conscientiousness). Reported coefficient alphas for agreeableness (.97) and for conscientiousness (.96) reflect high reliability for these scales. It was felt that these personality traits would be relevant to the status of occupying the multiple roles of employee and father.

To address the parental microsystem, participants completed the Parental Stress Scale (Berry & Jones, 1995), an 18-item measure of the stress arising from the parenting role. This measure has been shown to be highly reliable, both internally and over time (coefficient alpha = .83 and

Table 10.1   Workplace/Family Stress Scale

	Rating	
Experience	Mean	Standard Deviation
I had an argument with my spouse over sharing child care responsibilities	4.99	1.71
I argued with my child over getting ready to go in the morning	4.53	1.84
I needed to work at home but was unable to because of my child	4.16	1.75
I missed part of a day of work because child care was not available	3.63	1.69
I was late to work because of transporting my child to school/daycare	3.31	1.85
I had to change my work schedule in order to take care of my child	2.93	1.70
I missed part of a day of work in order to take my child for a scheduled visit to the doctor	2.28	1.41
I missed work to attend a routine parent-teacher conference	2.18	1.37
I left work to attend a program at my child's school	1.86	1.28

test-retest reliability = .81 for 6 weeks) and to be equally appropriate for mothers and fathers. In addition, participants completed an inventory of general child care activities (e.g., feeding, bathing, reading, playing) rated in terms of frequency of performance.

To address the employment microsystem of these fathers, participants completed a short version of the Workplace Flexibility Scale (Meyer & Berry, 1995). This brief version had five items that were specific to flexibility of the job (e.g., "My job leaves little time for home responsibilities"; "My supervisor is understanding about family needs") and had a coefficient alpha of .72. Participants also reported their work hours.

Results (Study 3)

Initially, psychometric properties of the Workplace/Family Stress Scale were again addressed for the intensity of stress. With this sample of fathers, coefficient alpha was .86, and the mean interitem correlation was .41. Item whole correlations varied from .49 to .67, with a mean of .59 indicating adequate reliability. In addition, the Perceived Stress Scale was significantly correlated with both intensity of stress ($r = .15, p < .05$) and the likelihood of occurrence of the event ($r = .16, p < .05$), supporting validity of the Workplace/Family Stress Scale.

Next, a multiple regression was performed to examine the predictors of work/family stress (intensity) as related to the systems model. The following combination of variables was entered into the regression equation and predicted work/family stress (intensity) ($R = .48. p < .01$): likelihood of occurrence of workplace/family stress events, parental stress, agreeableness, and workplace flexibility. Agreeableness and workplace flexibility had negative relationships with work/family stress (betas = −.17 and −.16, respectively); likelihood of occurrence of workplace/family stress events and parental stress had stronger and positive betas (.29 and .22, respectively). All betas were significant at the .01 level.

Correlations were then computed between the Work/Family Stress Scale (for both intensity and likelihood of occurrence ratings) and the other work and family measures used in this study. Likelihood of occurrence of the workplace/family stress events and the intensity of experienced stress were themselves significantly correlated ($r = .32, p < .01$). Table 10.2 presents additional correlations between work/family stress and individual, family, and work measures.

The total scale is brief, and the authors recommend using the total scale rather than separate categories. However, the reliability for the category of work/family conflict is adequate to use as a subscale for intensity (.80), as is the category

Table 10.2   Correlations Between Work/Family Stress and Related Measures

	Individual Measures		*Family Measures*		*Employment Measures*	
	Agreeableness		*Parental Stress*		*Job*	*Work*
	Conscientiousness		*Child Care Activities*		*Flexibility*	*Hours*
Work/family stress intensity	−.24**	−.04	.29**	−.00	−.18*	.19**
Work/family stress occurrence	−.04	.05	.19**	.24**	.10	.09
Job flexibility	.19**	.05	−.03	.32**	—	.39**
Work hours	−.12	.05	.17*	−.19**	−.39**	—

*$p < .05$

**$p < .01$

of children's needs for intensity (.73) and occurrence (.77). Significant findings from these categories will be presented in the text when there is variation between category findings and overall findings.

Scores indicating intensity of stress experienced (with the full nine-item Workplace/Family Stress Scale) were significantly related to individual (less agreeableness), family (greater parental stress), and employment (less job flexibility, longer work hours) measures. This pattern was also found for the work-family conflict category. Work-family conflict was significantly correlated with agreeableness ($r = −.20, p < .01$); parental stress ($r = 25, p < .01$); job flexibility ($r = −.15, p < .05$); and work hours ($r = .17, p < .05$). For the children's needs category, this pattern continued as follows: agreeableness ($r = −.26, p < .01$); parental stress ($r = .21, p < .01$); job flexibility ($r = −.24, p < .01$); and work hours ($r = .22, p < .01$). An additional significant finding in this category was a relationship reflecting less stress for those fathers who participated more in general child care activities ($r = −.19, p < .01$).

A different pattern emerged with respect to likelihood of occurrence of the workplace/family stress events with significant relationships only involving the family measures. Fathers who experienced these situations more often (occurrence) reported participating more extensively in general child care activities. They also reported experiencing greater parental stress. However,

for the category of children's needs, the relationship with parental stress was not significant ($r = .08, p > .05$). In addition, fathers who reported greater job flexibility worked fewer hours and engaged in more child care activities. Fewer work hours were also associated with more child care activities and less parental stress.

Finally, the stress events were assessed in terms of likelihood of occurrence of these work/family stress events. The three situations rated most likely to occur—all of which involve prescheduled events—were those with the lowest stress ratings: Item 7 (scheduled doctor visit, 38%), Item 8 (parent-teacher conference, 29%) and Item 9 (child's school program, 39%). Situations rated least likely to occur involved child care: Item 3 (unable to work at home because of child, 10%), Item 4 (missed work because child care not available, 8%) and Item 6 (changed work schedule to care for child, 8%). Percentages indicate participant's rating of a 4 or 5 on a 5-point Likert-type scale of the likelihood of occurrence, with 5 being the most likely.

Discussion

Fathers are clearly involved with their children in a variety of ways that have an impact on their work roles and that result in varying levels of stress. Indeed, greater involvement in these situations that interface with the workplace role predicts greater stress. Asking fathers to describe actual child-related experiences and to rate them for stress intensity resulted in the identification of a range of stress levels for these experiences. The resulting Workplace/Family Stress Scale appears to be a useful measure for examining the family/work role system. Future studies need to address expanding the construct validity of the measure.

All levels examined—individual traits, family and employment microsystems, and mesosystem connections—contributed to experienced stress. As fathers engaged in more child-related events that affected their workplace roles, they experienced more stress. Workplace/family stress was associated not only with the occurrence of child-related situations and parental stress (the family microsystem) but also with individual characteristics and the workplace microsystem. However, the regression analysis indicated that the family microsystem contributed more to this experienced stress than either the workplace microsystem or the personality of the individual.

From the perspective of the individual, the personality trait of agreeableness appears to be important in reducing stress and in lessening family discord. This may be because men with higher levels of agreeableness find social network connections easier and are more likely to think well of other people's intentions. It is interesting that fathers higher in agreeableness also reported more job flexibility. Although a conclusion cannot be drawn concerning the cause and effect of this relationship, it might be explained by a more positive perception of the job situation by more agreeable men or that more agreeable men are able to negotiate more workplace flexibility.

In terms of the family microsystem, fathers who experienced more of these stressful events (the occurrence measure of the scale) were more involved in general child care and experienced more parental stress. However, greater participation in general child care was not significantly related to parental stress. It appears to be the role conflict (or the involvement in child-related events that interfere with work responsibilities) that is stressful. This supports previous findings (e.g., Baruch & Barnett, 1986; Guelzow et al., 1991).

Parental stress was related to both workplace/family stress and occurrence of these events overall but not for occurrence in the children's needs category. The intensity of workplace/family stress in this category was also less for fathers who participate more in general child care. These findings are probably explained by the fact that the items from the children's needs category describe prescheduled events that are likely to be considered positive (Item 9) or important (Items 7 and 8). Furthermore, fathers who spend more time caring for their children generally may simply be better prepared to engage in these activities.

Workplace flexibility and work hours were significantly related to workplace/family stress (intensity) for both children's needs (prescheduled events) and work/family conflict (unscheduled events), and fathers who worked more participated less in general child care activities. These findings regarding the workplace microsystem are consistent with previous findings that longer work hours predict less involvement with children (Biernat & Wortman, 1991), which is an availability issue. Also supported were previous findings that less flexible work schedules predicted stress and role strain (Galinsky & Stein, 1990; Guelzow et al., 1991). Lack of flexibility decreases locus of control, which can be stressful in and of itself.

Prescheduled events have been reported as being the arena in which fathers are becoming most involved when work and family overlap are considered (Fernandez, 1986; Hochschild, 1992). They were shown in the second study to produce the least stress and in the third study to be the situations in which fathers were most likely to be engaged. In contrast, situations involving child care, such as Item 4, missing work because child care was not available, had very low levels of father involvement. Furthermore, fathers reporting greater workplace flexibility and shorter work hours found the events from the Workplace/Family Stress Scale less stressful (intensity), but they were not more likely to occur for these fathers than for fathers with less flexible jobs and longer work hours.

So who is taking care of the situations involving child care and emergency care? Numerous studies (e.g., Fernandez, 1990; Galinsky, Bond, & Friedman, 1993; Hochschild, 1989; Leslie, Anderson, & Branson, 1991) would say the answer is mom. This may explain results from the second study that showed the family discord items as being the most stressful. Fathers and mothers are negotiating new roles, for which they probably did not have role models in their own parents, within a workplace exosystem that has typically not been supportive of the needs of working parents of either gender.

Implications

The results of these studies have implications for both the family and the workplace. Results indicate, first, that fathers are involved with their children in ways that affect their workplace roles and may be stressful and, second, that greater involvement in these events is related to greater stress. Yet, fathers are not that involved. That is, the events involving role conflict for fathers do not occur that often. Involvement by fathers was primarily in prescheduled, nonemergency, less stressful events. If the goal is greater and more extensive involvement by fathers in rearing their children, then the advice of Silverstein and Levant (1996, p. 19) should be considered. They suggested redefining mothering and fathering. This redefinition would involve both men and women as coproviders and conurturers. If fathers find limited involvement stressful, then they may resist more extensive involvement. Therefore, an examination of cause and prevention of stress is in order.

Garbarino and Abramowitz (1992), presenting Bronfenbrenner's (1979) framework, wrote of opportunities and risks at each level of the ecological system. Although these three studies were exploratory, there are implications for maximizing opportunity (to become coproviders and conurturers) and minimizing risk (stress) for families, as well as implications for future research, at each of the system levels examined. The following discussion will use the systems model to address these opportunities and risks.

The Individual

The contribution of individual traits to workplace/family stress has received limited empirical attention, but both empirical and anecdotal findings from this study indicate that more attention is warranted. The relationship between the personality trait of agreeableness and stress was intriguing and suggests that individual personality characteristics, self-esteem, and psychological well-being should be considered when addressing stress management, particularly stress stemming from meeting or failing to meet children's needs. For example, one father in the first study wrote that he was in a hurry one morning and failed to give his 3-year-old breakfast. He stated that he felt guilty about it all day. Another noted the stress involved in being separated from his children because of out-of-town travel. However, fathers also felt that the positive aspects of these events may, at times, outweigh the negative features. This was shown by a father who stated, when discussing staying home from work with a sick child, "not every instance was inconvenient or stressful from a job relationship and in some cases was welcomed for the time to be home with my child." This suggests the role of fatherhood in achieving generativity, as was discussed by Hawkins, Christiansen, Sargent, and Hill (1993). In addition, it speaks to the value of intimacy in the father/child relationship. Intimacy is central to positive development for the child (Silverstein & Levant, 1996) and can be the best part of parenting for the father (Adler, 1996).

The Family

The strongest contribution to workplace/family stress came from family role involvement. The work and family mesosystems of both mothers and fathers combine to constitute the family/work role system (Pleck, 1977). Statements from fathers in the first study reflect both cooperation and tension in this role system. For example, some fathers stated that they were more likely than their wives to take on certain responsibilities, such as taking a child to the doctor, because their jobs were more flexible. They also wrote positively about swapping responsibilities and "tag team" scheduling. But other fathers indicated resentment toward their wives because they felt they were doing more than their share. Marital tension may be due to perceptions of fairness by the marital partners (e.g., Benin & Agnostinelli, 1988; Hochschild, 1989), or to being at different developmental places in terms of achievement of generativity (Hawkins et al., 1993), or related to spillover of stress from work to home (Menaghan, 1991). The presence of marital tension noted by these fathers supports an abundance of literature documenting the relationship between parenting and marital stress (e.g., Cowan et al., 1985; Hetherington et al., 1976). Although there is substantial literature on parental stress experienced by mothers, parental stress experienced by fathers has received limited research attention. Most research that has included fathers has focused on families with children who have clinical needs. However, two recent studies addressing stress experienced by both mothers and fathers in nonclinical families found similar levels of parental stress for mothers and fathers (Berry & Jones, 1995; Deater-Deckard & Scarr, 1996). Further study should address the nature of parental stress experienced by fathers and mothers as well as the impact of various levels and types of parent participation on both parental stress and marital satisfaction.

The Workplace

The workplace contribution to work/family stress was seen in findings concerning job flexibility, specifically lack of flexibility. The amount of flexibility available is determined by company policy, or the exosystem, over which families have little control. From the standpoint of corporate America (the exosystem) Rosen (1991) presented this image: "The portrait of the traditional American worker is fading fast, yet the frame still hangs on the walls of American business. It shows a middle-aged, married man with a couple of kids and a wife who doesn't work" (p. 265).

As companies address the reality that approximately 40% of their workforce is composed of dual-earner couples, they run up against a stumbling block—the attitudes of their own upper management (Zedeck & Mosier, 1990). Hochschild's (1992) recent research also shows that management views work/family balance as a so-called women's issue.

Although not examined empirically, macrosystem issues of cultural expectations and federal policy were also concerns of fathers in these studies. Comments of fathers in the first study often pointed to the value placed on "face time" in their work environments. They wrote about taking a day of vacation to stay home with a sick child and about going to a child's school program while out on a sales call so their boss would not know they were engaging in these family tasks. These anecdotes support past findings (e.g., Hall, 1990; Hyde, Essex, & Horton, 1993; Pleck, 1988, 1993) concerning underutilization by fathers of such policies as parental leave. T. F. Cohen's (1993) work stresses the role of the workplace in encouraging or prohibiting family involvement by fathers. He advised as follows: "To maximize what men are available for and encouraged to do as parents will require reducing or restructuring what they are required or expected to do as workers" (p. 20). Future studies are needed to address the availability and utilization of "family friendly" policies and the impact of gender differences on policy utilization.

Workplace attitudes are likely to be contributors to stress for both men and women but perhaps more so for men due to expectations based on the culture of fatherhood. In the first study, a father wrote that he was leaving work at noon to take care of his son who was ill. The response of his boss was, "Why can't your wife do that?" The father stated, "I had to explain to him that it was my turn and that he is my kid, too."

Conclusion

Increased involvement of fathers with their children is changing roles within the family and has potential for workplace change as well. This involvement may change work/family balance from a women's issue to an employee issue; or it may not, if men limit their involvement in family tasks or do not seek and use family benefits.

These studies were limited by the use of self-report measures, from a demographically narrow sample, to briefly survey a number of important constructs. However, they offer empirically based avenues to better understanding and support of families and suggest areas for future exploration.

In conclusion, there are three important points to consider. First, father involvement that intertwines with the workplace role is quite limited, and yet that limited involvement is perceived as stressful. Second, to increase and expand father involvement, empirical evidence of what fathers actually do, and the stress involved, is necessary. Third, studying fathers involved in multiple roles from a systems perspective reveals the importance of considering the family microsystem and family roles as well as characteristics of the individual and workplace policy. Lechner and Creedon (1994) provided a summary statement that is particularly applicable to this study: "Partnerships are needed between men and women, between employees and employers, and between the government and all other bodies in order to provide for two of society's basic tasks—economic production and the care of dependent persons" (p. 28).

Note

A preliminary version of this article was presented at the 101st Convention of the American Psychological Association Convention in Toronto, Ontario, Canada, in August 1993.

References

Adler, J. (1996, June 17). Building a better dad. *Newsweek,* 58–61, 63–64.

Barnett, R. C., Marshall, N. L., & Pleck, J. H. (1992). Men's multiple roles and their relationship to men's psychological distress. *Journal of Marriage and the Family, 54,* 358–367.

Baruch, G. K., & Barnett, R. C. (1986). Consequences of fathers' participation in family work: Parents' role strain and well-being. *Journal of Personality and Social Psychology, 51,* 983–992.

Benin, M. H., & Agnostinelli, J. (1988). Husbands' and wives' satisfaction with the division of labor. *Journal of Marriage and the Family, 50,* 349–361.

Berry, J. O., & Jones, W. H. (1995). The Parental Stress Scale: Initial psychometric evidence. *Journal of Social and Personal Relationships, 12,* 463–472.

Biernat, M., & Wortman, C. B., (1991). Sharing of home responsibilities between professionally employed women and their husbands. *Journal of Personality and Social Psychology, 60,* 844–860.

Bronfenbrenner, U. (1979). *The ecology of human development. Experiments by nature and design.* Cambridge, MA: Harvard University Press.

Bronfenbrenner, U., & Crouter, A. C. (1984). Work and family through time and space. In S. B. Kamerman & C. D. Hayes (Eds.), *Families that work: Children in a changing world* (pp. 39–83). Washington, DC: National Academy Press.

Cohen, S., Kamarck, T., & Mermelstein, R. (1983). A global measure of perceived stress. *Journal of Health and Social Behavior, 24,* 385–396.

Cohen, T. F. (1993). What do fathers provide? Reconsidering the economic and nurturant dimensions of men as parents. In J. Hood (Ed.), *Men, work, and family* (pp. 1–22). Newbury Park, CA: Sage.

Cowan, C. P., Cowan, P. A., Henning, G., Garrett, E., Coysh, W. S., Curtis-Boles, H., & Boles, A. J. (1985). Transitions to parenthood: His, hers, and theirs. *Journal of Family Issues, 6,* 451–481.

Crouter, A. C., Perry-Jenkins, M., Huston, T. L., & McHale, S. M. (1987). Processes underlying father involvement in dual-earner and single-earner families. *Developmental Psychology, 23,* 431–440.

Deater-Deckard, K., & Scarr, S. (1996). Parenting stress among dual-earner mothers and fathers: Are there gender differences? *Journal of Family Psychology, 10,* 45–59.

Fernandez, J. P. (1986). *Child care and corporate productivity: Resolving family/work conflicts.* Lexington, MA: Lexington Books.

Fernandez, J. P. (1990). *The politics and reality of family care in corporate America.* Lexington, MA: Lexington Books.

Galinsky, E., Bond, J. T., & Friedman, D. E. (1993). *Highlights: The national study of the changing workforce.* New York: Families and Work Institute.

Galinsky, E., & Stein, P. J. (1990). The impact of human resource policies on employees. *Journal of Family Issues, 11,* 368–383.

Garbarino, J., & Abramowitz, R. H. (1992). The ecology of human development. In J. Garbarino (Ed.), *Children and families in the social environment* (2nd ed., pp. 11–33). New York: Aldine De Gruyter.

Gilbert, L. A. (1993). *Two careers/one family.* Newbury Park, CA: Sage.

Goldberg, L. R. (1992). The development of markers for the big-five factor structure. *Psychological Assessment, 4,* 26–42.

Griswold, R. L. (1993). *Fatherhood in America: A history.* New York: Basic Books.

Guelzow, M. G., Bird, G. W., & Koball, E. H. (1991). An exploratory path analysis of the stress process for dual-career men and women. *Journal of Marriage and the Family, 53,* 151–164.

Hall, D. T. (1990). Promoting work/family balance: An organizational-change approach. *Organizational Dynamics, 18,* 4–18.

Hawkins, A. J., Christiansen, S. L., Sargent, K. P., & Hill, E. J. (1993). Rethinking fathers' involvement in child care. *Journal of Family Issues, 14,* 531–549.

Hetherington, E. M., Cox, M., & Cox, R. (1976). Divorced fathers. *Family Coordinator, 25,* 417–428.

Hochschild, A. (1989). *The second shift: Inside the two-job marriage.* New York: Viking.

Hochschild, A. (1992, November). *Beyond the second shift: Denying needs at home or contesting rules at work?* Paper presented at the annual conference of the National Council on Family Relations, Orlando, FL.

Hyde, J. S., Essex, M. J., & Horton, F. (1993). Fathers and parental leave: Attitudes and experiences. *Journal of Family Issues, 14,* 616–641.

Kessler, R. C., & McRae, J. A. (1982). The effect of wives' employment on the mental health of married men and women. *American Sociological Review, 47,* 216–226.

LaRossa, R. (1988). Fatherhood and social change. *Family Relations, 37,* 451–457.

Lechner, V. M., & Creedon, M. A. (1994). *Managing work and family life.* New York: Springer.

Leslie, L. A., Anderson, E. A., & Branson, M. P. (1991). Responsibility for children: The role of gender and employment. *Journal of Family Issues, 12,* 197–210.

Marsiglio, W. (1993). Contemporary scholarship on fatherhood: Culture, identity, and conduct. *Journal of Family Issues, 14,* 484–509.

Menaghan, E. (1991). Work experiences and family interaction processes: The long reach of the job? *Annual Review of Sociology, 17,* 419–444.

Meyer, J. A., & Berry, J. O. (1995, May). *Development and validation of a measure of workplace flexibility.* Poster session presented at the annual conference of the Society for Industrial and Organizational Psychology, Orlando, FL.

Pleck, J. H. (1977). The work-family role system. *Social Problems, 24,* 417–427.

Pleck, J. H. (1985). *Working wives, working husbands.* New York: Sage.

Pleck, J. H. (1988). Fathers and infant care leave. In E. F. Zigler & M. Frank (Eds.), *The parental leave crisis* (pp. 177–191). New Haven, CT: Yale University Press.

Pleck, J. H. (1993). Are "family supportive" employer policies relevant to men? In J. Hood (Ed.), *Men, work, and family* (pp. 217–237). Newbury Park, CA: Sage.

Pleck, J. H. (1994, June). The workplace: A new focus for fatherhood activists. *Nurturing News, 2,* 10–11.

Rosen, R. (1991). *The healthy company.* Los Angeles: Jeremy Tarcher.

Ross, C. E., & Mirowsky, J. (1988). Child care and emotional adjustment to wives' employment. *Journal of Health and Social Behavior, 29,* 127–138.

Scarr, S., Phillips, D., & McCartney, K. (1989). Working mothers and their families. *American Psychologist, 44,* 1402–1409.

Silverstein, L. B., & Levant, R. F. (1996, Spring). Children need fathers not patriarchs: An editorial comment. *Family Psychologist,* pp. 18–19.

Voydanoff, P. (1993). Work and family relationships. In T. Brubaker (Ed.), *Family Relations* (pp. 98–111). Newbury Park, CA: Sage.

Zedeck, S., & Mosier, K. L. (1990). Work in the family and employing organization. *American Psychologist, 45,* 240–251.

THE SOCIAL ECOLOGY OF
MARRIAGE AND OTHER INTIMATE UNIONS

TED L. HUSTON

Abstract

This article provides an interdisciplinary framework for studying marital and other intimate relationships. Three levels of analysis are distinguished: (a) the society, characterized in terms of both macrosocietal forces and the ecological niches within which particular spouses and couples function; (b) the individual spouses, including their psychosocial and physical attributes, as well as the attitudes and beliefs they have about each other and their relationship; and (c) the marriage relationship, viewed as a behavioral system embedded within a larger network of close relationships. The discussion focuses primarily on the interplay between the spouses and their marriage, emphasizing the importance of distinguishing, both analytically and operationally, the individual from the dyadic (or group) levels of analysis. It is also argued that in order to appreciate how marriages work, social scientists must understand not only how these 2 levels of analysis interpenetrate each other but also how macrosocietal forces and the ecological niches within which couples live impinge on partners and their marital relationship.

This article sets forth an ecological framework that can be used to examine the marital system, considered as a whole, or to examine any particular marital behavior pattern, such as division of labor, companionship, the expression of affection and hostility, patterns of conflict resolution, and sexual activity. My analysis is intended to apply to any marriage-like union, regardless of its gender composition or whether the partners live under the same roof. The framework could readily be expanded to encompass friendships, or even plural marriages, such as exist among subpopulations of Mormons in Utah who practice polygamy (Altman & Ginat, 1996). My goal is to provide a broad prolegomenon for research, rather than to summarize past research or to show how cultural, interpersonal, and psychological factors combine to create distinctive lifestyles. The terms *marriage* and *union* will be used interchangeably, and *mate, spouse,* and *partner* will be used alternately to designate the individuals who constitute the marital pair.

The historical, multilayered, interdependent causal pathways that produce, maintain, and modify marital behavior create enormous analytic problems that must be overcome by scholars who wish to understand why marriages function the way they do. The present framework distinguishes three broad levels of analysis: (a) the society, characterized in terms of both macrosocietal forces and the ecological niches within which particular spouses and couples function; (b) the individual spouses, including their psychosocial and physical attributes, as well as the attitudes and beliefs they have about each other and their relationship; and (c) the marriage relationship, viewed as a behavioral system embedded within a larger network of close relationships (Bates & Harvey, 1975; Berscheid, 1998; Hinde, 1987;

317

Kelley et al., 1983; Levinger, 1994). These three types of factors—societal, individual, and marital—interpenetrate each other, and they operate together in a complex, interdependent fashion. The framework offered here, much like a framework put forth by Kelley and his colleagues, is intended to provide a conceptual blueprint, one that provides a sense of the types of questions that would be asked about marriage from an ecological perspective. As with the framework of Kelley et al., the approach "transcends any one specific theory, disciplinary approach, and any single relationship phenomenon" (p. 15). Nonetheless, the framework is intended to challenge social scientists to build their research programs during the 21st century with a greater appreciation of four fundamental ideas: (a) that marriages are interpersonal systems (and hence must be studied as small groups), (b) that spouses' psychological and physical qualities shape their individual and collective efforts to maintain a successful union, (c) that both marriage relationships and the partners themselves are dynamic (i.e., they change by context and they evolve over time), and (d) that marital unions are embedded in a social context.

The portraits of marriage that social scientists create often tell us as much about the person behind the camera (i.e., the reporter) as they do about the relationship; many relationship portraits provide such a blurred image that they give us little more than a fuzzy sense of the quality of the marriage, or a general sense of marital behavior patterns. Other portraits, which are taken at close range, are clearly focused; they provide a wonderful, richly drawn view of a specific interactional phenomena—such as how a couple resolves a problem in a particular setting. They usually include little information, however, about the psychological, social, and environmental contexts within which the interaction is embedded. The propensity of researchers to use either an unfocused lens or to zero in on narrow and isolated slices of the larger marital terrain has produced a literature on marriage that provides limited insight into how marriages actually work. Such a state of affairs also has undermined the development of sophisticated theories designed to link the qualities and dispositions of the spouses to features of their marriage relationship and has hindered efforts to examine how the ecological context influences the details of couples' day-to-day married life. The framework outlined below describes the kinds of data needed, maps out the larger terrain of marriage, and draws attention to the kinds of distinctions researchers need to make to conduct sound research. It is offered with the hope that it will provide a set of operating principles that will help improve the quality of research during the first few years of the 21st century.

The conceptualization outlined below is ecological, in the sense that marital behavior patterns are seen as a reflection of the environmental context within which they are embedded, and social psychological, in that the goal is to relate the qualities of the individual spouses to the characteristics of their marriage relationship. Figure 10.1 provides a schematic view of the interplay among the macroenvironmental context (box A), the characteristics of the individuals who constitute the marital pair (box B), and the marital relationship as a behavioral system (box C; cf. Hinde, 1987; Kelley et al., 1983; Levinger, 1994; Robins, 1990). It is important to keep in mind, of course, that the macroenvironment, the individuals who make up the marital system, and spouses' marital behavior influence each other continuously over time.

This article considers three issues that can be illustrated in the boxes of Figure 10.1. First, I focus on conceptual issues associated with describing marital behavior in its context. Second, I take up issues pertaining to the interplay between individuals and the marriage relationships they create (box B → C). Third, I show how the macroenvironment within which marriage relationships are embedded affects the individuals (box A → 4B) and the marital microsystem (box A→ C) and how the decisions that individuals and couples make affect the context of their own marriage and, in aggregate, contribute to stability or change in macrosocietal patterns (both B & C→ A).

Many writings on marriage and other intimate relationships blur the distinction between the individual (Figure 10.1, box B) and the marriage

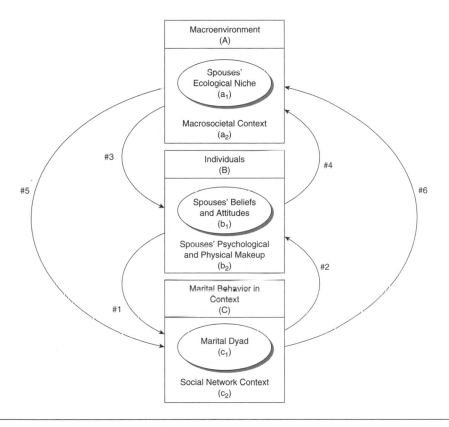

Figure 10.1 A Three-Level Model for Viewing Marriage

relationship (Figure 10.1, box C; cf. Fincham & Bradbury, 1987; Kelley et al., 1983; Thompson & Walker, 1982). The significance of this confusion for research on marriage, however, has not been fully appreciated because if it had been, omnibus measures of marital quality and satisfaction—such as the Locke-Wallace scale (Locke & Wallace, 1959) and the Dyadic Adjustment Scale (Spanier, 1976)—would have fallen out of favor years ago. These omnibus scales combine spouses' general evaluations of their marriage (e.g., whether they are happy-unhappy), their beliefs about how similar they are to each other with regard to various matters (e.g., how they handle such matters as finances or their leisure interests), and their characterizations of marital behavioral patterns (e.g., how affectionate or companionate the spouses are with each other or how well they get along). Researchers need to recognize that how spouses

feel about their marriage—how happy they are, how much they love each other—undoubtedly affects both their characterizations of how similar they are to each other and their beliefs about how well they get along. It is also likely that spouses who believe that they are of like mind or who characterize their marriage as highly affectionate infer from these ratings that they are happy. Suppose we want to use the Locke-Wallace scale to examine connections between marital happiness (an individual-level variable) and how marital couples interact with each other in a laboratory problem-solving situation (i.e., behavioral patterns). This is problematic; given that some items on the Locke-Wallace scale require spouses to characterize how well they get along, what do we conclude, for example, when analyses based on observational data show that couples who are responsive to each other's ideas score higher on the scale? Are they happier with their marriage? Or are they merely able to characterize, in general terms, how well they actually do get along? Thus, because it is important to understand the roots of marital satisfaction, researchers should discard standard measures of satisfaction in favor of measures that are purely evaluative (see Fincham & Bradbury, 1987).

Marriage as a Behavioral Ecosystem

The box at the bottom of Figure 10.1 (box C shows the marital dyad as a sphere (c_1) embedded within a larger box representing the social network (c_2) or the other individuals who constitute the immediate social environment within which marital activities and interactions are embedded. *Marital behavior is* the foundation on which careful descriptions of marriage relationships can be built. Figure 10.1 (box C) points to the idea that marital activities and interactions (c_1) often take place in the presence of other family members and friends (c_2). Usually, however, researchers focusing on the dynamics of marital interaction study couples as two-person units, as if they rarely spent time together as part of a social group (see Gottman & Notarius, 2000, for a review of the marital interaction literature). However, the presence or absence of others can have an important impact on the types of behavior spouses exhibit. Some kinds of marital behavior rarely occur in public settings (e.g., sexual intercourse or physical aggression). Parenthood not only changes the extent and nature of the time spouses spend with each other, it also affects how frequently they pursue activities with friends and kin (Huston & Vangelisti, 1995). Couples who have young children schedule regular "dates," just so they can spend some time periodically doing something fun together as a couple. Moreover, it is important to keep in mind that some features of marriage—such as the propensity of either of the spouses to seek support from friends or kin (Surra & Milardo, 1991), the proclivity of individual partners to form coalitions with their children to influence their mate (Gilbert, Christensen, & Margolin, 1984), or the inclination of spouses to flirt with others in front of their partner—can only be understood when

couples are studied in group settings. Finally, the centrality of the spouses in each other's day-to-day lives, as well as their joint and independent involvement with friends and kin, may reveal much about the nature of the spouses' marital relationship.

Both a wide-angle and a close-up lens must be used to create a rich, comprehensive portrait of a marriage relationship. The use of a wide-angle lens brings macrobehavioral patterns into view and shows how couples spend their time—what they do together and apart. The use of a close-up lens brings into focus microbehavioral patterns—the details of husband-wife interaction. Sociologists (Bernard, 1964; Bott, 1971; Burgess & Locke, 1945) typically write about macrobehavioral patterns (such as division of labor and companionship), whereas psychologists and communications scholars usually study microbehavioral patterns, seeking to understand the interpersonal patterns that lead to distress and divorce (Gottman, 1994; Gottman & Krokoff, 1989; Noller, 1984; Wills, Weiss, & Patterson, 1974).

Taking a Wide-Angle View of Marriage: Describing Molar Behavior Patterns

"Time, like money, is a scarce resource that can be spent in different ways" (Medrich, Roizen, Rubin, & Buckley, 1982, p. 14), and the way spouses use their time reveals much about the nature of their marital relationship. Couples must garner economic resources, maintain a household, care for children (if they become parents), maintain connections with friends and relatives, and manage their joint and individual leisure time. When social scientists write about matters such as the division of labor, marital companionship, and the ties spouses maintain with friends and kin, they often have time use patterns in mind. Marriages thus can be distinguished in terms of what the spouses do with their time, who they do various activities with, and details of the give-and-take that make up the interpersonal dialogues they have with each other.

How might a social scientist, interested in creating an ecologically valid description of marriage as a behavioral system, proceed?

Ideally, one would follow husbands and wives over a representative sample of days, unobtrusively recording details of their activities and interactions. The movement of individual spouses from activity to activity consists of sequences of behavior with beginnings, endings, and transition points. Here is a portrayal in such terms of a day in the life of a married couple, John and Cindy:

John and Cindy rise early Friday morning and *pack lunches* for the family, after which John *prepares breakfast;* meanwhile, Cindy wakes up their daughter, Jessica, and *helps her get dressed* for school. The family *eats breakfast* and *talks* about their plans for the day. Cindy showers and gets dressed for work, while John *puts away the dishes.* John then showers and gets dressed for work while Cindy *drives* Jessica to school. John and Cindy begin *working* at their separate offices around 8 a.m. They *chat* briefly on the telephone and decide to go for a walk in the park during their lunch hour. They enjoy a leisurely *walk* at noon and, as they *eat lunch, discuss* their evening plans. They both return to work, at midafternoon. John leaves to *retrieve Jessica* from school to take her to a piano lesson. After work, Cindy *stops by the bank* and then *goes to the grocery store.* While Cindy and John get ready to go out, Cindy's mother stops by their home to pick up Jessica and *visits* for a few minutes before returning home. John and Cindy meet another couple for *dinner* before going to a *concert.* They drive home, and their evening draws to a close after they *have sex* and drift off to sleep.

The decisions that wives and husbands—like Cindy and John—make as they move from one activity to another and from one day to another cumulate to create macrobehavioral marital patterns (Huston & Rempel, 1989; Levinger & Huston, 1990). If spouses' mundane activities are tracked over a representative sample of days, their marital lifestyle comes into focus. We are then able to map how they divide up household work, how involved they are in child care activities, what leisure activities they do together, and the character of the interpersonal ties they maintain, together and separately, with others (Huston, Robins, Atkinson, & McHale, 1987). These kinds of macrobehavioral activity patterns

have been the staples out of which social scientists have built portraits of marital lifestyles (e.g., Bernard, 1964).

Obtaining diary data. The portrait of John and Cindy's day was intended to foreshadow a telephone diary approach my colleagues and I have developed and refined over many years to obtain reliable and valid data about couples' marital lifestyles (Huston & Rempel, 1989; Huston et al., 1987). We presumed that the characteristics and distinguishing features of couples' marital lifestyles would come into sharp focus if we gathered data about their activities and interactions over a number of days, rather than a single day.

The telephone diary procedure tracks spouses' comings and goings over a representative series of days, yielding a rich multidimensional portrait of the multiple facets of married life. Rather than obtaining open-ended reports of spouses' activities—which we knew would produce data of highly uneven quality—we created a highly structured interview in which we queried each of the spouses about a comprehensive list of the kinds of activities husbands and wives do when they are not at work (Huston et al., 1987). To secure representative information about each couples' day-to-day life together, we telephoned spouses on multiple occasions, spaced over a 2- to 3-week period; during each telephone interview, we obtained from each of the spouses systematic information about their participation in activities and their interactions with each other over the 24-hour period ending at 5 p.m. the day of the call. Spouses reported their own participation in specific activities pertaining to household work, child care, leisure, and conversations—and indicated for each activity whether they did the activity with their spouse or independently. They were also asked to report who, if anyone, other than the spouse was involved with them in the activity. We have recently elaborated the telephone diary procedure to obtain spouses' ratings of how they felt while doing each activity, using a 7-point scale anchored by a frowning and a happy face.

Spouses were asked to indicate the frequency with which their partner enacted several specific positive and negative behaviors during the 24-hour period, as well as the total number of conflicts they had during the period covered by the telephone interview. Finally, at the end of each daily interview, spouses reported how they felt about their marriage that day and how hassled or relaxed the day had been. This telephone procedure for collecting diary data, though labor intensive, produces high-quality data that overcome many of the limitations of self-report data (Huston et al., 1987; see Reis & Gable, 2000, for a broader discussion of diary methods).

Summarizing diary data. Spouses' activities during each day can be summarized by interdigitating the diary data generated from both partners, yielding a record of their day, much like that shown for Cindy and John in Tables 10.3 and 10.4. Table 10.3 provides total counts of some phenomena (e.g., amount of affection), as well as evaluations of the day (e.g., of marital satisfaction). Table 10.4 illustrates the kinds of summary data that can be obtained on a day-to-day basis from participants. The particular information researchers might choose to capture using telephone diary interviews will undoubtedly vary, of course, depending on investigators' ideas and interests. The record of John and Cindy's activities, as portrayed in Table 10.4, thus is intended to be illustrative rather than proscriptive. Each activity is shown as a row; the information that was gathered about each activity is shown in columns. The specific activities in which John and Cindy engaged what they did (the italicized words in the paragraph above—are shaded in Table 10.4. The two columns to the left of the activity show when the activity was done. The column to the

immediate right of the activity shows how the macrobehavior might be categorized more generally (e.g., as a household task, child care activity, or leisure pursuit). The next column shows who participated in the activity: the husband, wife, child, and other members of the family's social network. The coding scheme we use also allows us to make finer distinctions among those others, differentiating, for example, activities done with the husband's relatives from those done with the wife's relatives. The last set of columns provides information about John's and Cindy's reported affect while engaging in each activity. Many aspects of spouses' phenomenological experience could be indexed, such as excited-bored, relaxed-nervous, and cooperative-competitive; we show ratings of the affect they reportedly experienced because writings about marital success emphasize the importance of affective experiences (e.g., Larson & Richards, 1994). Affective experiences, because they are apt to vary depending on the activity and the social context within which they are embedded, may provide insight into spouses' more general feelings about each other and their relationship. Thus, for example, spouses who are high in levels of romantic love, compared with those spouses who are less enamored, may experience elevated levels of positive affect when they do activities together. What we see on the macrobehavioral surface of marriage may reflect the patterns of affect spouses experience when they are together. Thus, if the time spouses spend in leisure activity together is not particularly enjoyable (compared with the time they spend in such pursuits alone or with others), they may begin to spend less time together.

Table 10.3 Summary of Diary Data From a Day in the Life of John and Cindy: Spouses' Day (Overall)

	Total No. of Expressions of Affection (As Reported by Spouse)	*Total No. of Negative Behaviors (As Reported by Spouse)*	*Total No. of Conflicts*	*Daily Marital Satisfaction (1 = dissatisfied, 7 = satisfied)*	*Daily Hassles (1 = relaxed, 7 = hassled)*
John	6	1	1	6	4
Cindy	7	0	1	5	3

Table 10.4 Summary of Diary Data From a Day in the Life of John and Cincy: Chronology of Activities

Beginning Time	Duration (min)	Activity	Type of Activity	Participant(s)				Affect (1 = negative, 7 = positive)	
				Husband	Wife	Child	Others	Husband	Wife
6:45 a.m.	10	Pack lunches	Household	✓	✓	—	—	4	3
6:55 a.m.	15	Prepare breakfast	Household	✓	—	—	—	4	—
7:00 a.m.	10	Help child dress	Child care	—	✓	✓	—	—	4
7:10 a.m.	20	Eat breakfast	Eat, conversation	✓	✓	✓	—	6	6
7:30 a.m.	10	Do dishes	Household	✓	—	—	—	5	—
7:30 a.m.	15	Drop off child	Household	—	✓	✓	—	—	4
8:00 a.m.	240	At work	Paid work	—	✓	—	—	4	4
8:00 a.m.	240	At work	Paid work	✓	—	—	—	5	—
11:00 a.m.	5	Talk on phone	Conversation	✓	✓	—	—	5	5
12:00 p.m.	35	Go for a walk/talk	Leisure, conversation	✓	✓	—	—	7	6
12:35 p.m.	15	Eat lunch	Eat a meal	✓	✓	—	—	3	2
1:00 p.m.	150	At work	Paid work	✓	—	—	—	3	—
1:00 p.m.	240	At work	Paid work	—	✓	—	—	—	4
3:30 p.m.	15	Pick up child	Child care	✓	—	✓	—	4	—
3:45 p.m.	60	Take child to a lesson	Child care	✓	—	✓	—	4	—
5:00 p.m.	10	Go to bank	Household	—	✓	—	—	—	4
5:10 p.m.	20	Pick up groceries	Household	—	✓	—	—	—	4
6:30 p.m.	15	Visit	Leisure	✓	✓	—	Wife's mom	—	5
7:00 p.m.	120	Go to dinner	Leisure, conversation	✓	✓	—	Cpl friends	6	6
9:00 p.m.	180	Go to a concert	Leisure	✓	✓	—	Cpl friends	7	6
12:00 a.m.	45	Sexual intercourse	Leisure, socioemotional behavior	✓	✓	—	—	7	7

NOTE: Personal grooming was omitted from table activities.

Profiling marital lifestyles. Profiles of couples' marriages can be built from telephone diary data when such data are gathered from spouses over several days (see Huston et al., 1987). By aggregating the data over a representative sample of days, it is possible to create summary indices of various aspects of marriage, including (a) marital *role patterns* (as shown by spouses' participation in household and child care activities); (b) marital *companionship* (as reflected in the extent to which spouses talk to each other and spend leisure time together); (c) *socioemotional patterns* (as evident in how affectionate spouses are with each other, how often they express negativity, and the frequency with which they have sexual intercourse); and (d) *spouses' involvement with friends and kin* (as reflected in the amount of time they spend engaging in recreational activities and conversation).

My own program of research illustrates how the diverse and rich data generated by the telephone diary technique make it possible to study a variety of aspects of marriage. We have used such diary data to create typologies of marital lifestyles (Johnson, Huston, Gaines, & Levinger, 1992) and to study a variety of specific aspects of marriage—such as the division of labor (Atkinson & Huston, 1984), the expression of positive and negative feelings in marriage (Huston & Vangelisti, 1991), and factors that predict the amount of time spouses spend with friends and kin (Huston & Geis, 1993). Because we gathered diary data yearly over the early years of marriage, we have been able to track how marital behavior patterns change over time. These data show that marriages typically lose some of their romantic intensity over the first year, evolving away from a romantic, recreational relationship toward more of a working partnership (Huston, McHale, & Crouter, 1986). More specifically, couples show less affection and spend proportionately more of their joint time doing chores (rather than recreational pursuits); their feelings of romantic love also tend to become weaker with time. Because couples differ in whether or not they become parents and, if they do, in how long they wait, we have also

been able to separate analytically normative changes in marriage from changes associated with parenthood (Crawford & Huston, 1993; MacDermid, Huston, & McHale, 1990). When couples become parents, their division of labor becomes more gender differentiated (MacDermid et al., 1990); parenthood also alters the extent to which husbands and wives engage in leisure activities, together and separately, that they enjoy (Crawford & Huston, 1993). Moreover, recently, we obtained long-term follow-up data on couples whom we had studied during their early years of marriage using telephone diary methods. These data indicated, among other things, that couples who subsequently divorced showed sharper declines in their level of affection over the first 2 years compared with couples who stayed married (Huston, Caughlin, Houts, Smith, & George, 2001).

An important strength of diary-type data is that they can be aggregated in a variety of ways, depending on the investigator's purpose (see Herbst, 1965). The basic macrobehavioral unit—an activity—can be characterized in terms of both the social context within which it takes place, as well as in terms of the actor's psychological state (e.g., emotions); thus, it is possible to examine, for instance, the significance of particular types of activities and activity patterns as sources of pleasure and displeasure in a marriage. Because multiple activities take place each day and because those activities differ from day to day, it is possible to identify the kinds of activities and events that covary, for example, with day-to-day fluctuations in marital satisfaction. Moreover, when diary data are gathered from both partners, the importance of each partner's activities for the other spouse can also be assessed.

Additional uses of diary-type data to study marriage. Whereas my colleagues and I have used diary data to create portraits of marriage relationships, others have used diary data to examine how contextual variables affect marital experiences. Because diary procedures are designed to preserve information concerning the context within which activity occurs, they are particularly suitable for studying the interplay between day-to-day events, emotions, and behaviors. Some diary techniques require the spouses to record their behavior at either the first opportunity or at the end of the day (Almeida, Wethington, & Chandler, 1999; Thompson & Bolger, 1999; Wills et al., 1974); others use a beeper technique to obtain reports on what spouses are doing and how they are feeling during randomly selected moments throughout the day (Larson & Richards, 1994). Usually, these strategies yield data that are of insufficient scope to produce multidimensional profiles of marriage. Nonetheless, such diary approaches have yielded interesting findings concerning how spouses experience their day-to-day life. They have been used to examine the interpersonal circumstances that give rise to positive and negative emotions and the conditions under which emotions are transmitted from one spouse to another (Gable & Reis, 1999; Larson & Almeida, 1999). Thompson and Bolger (1999), for example, used diary data gathered from spouses over several days as one of the partners moved closer to taking an important examination (the New York State Bar). Examinees' depressed mood on a given day became less strongly related to their partners' daily feelings about their relationship as the exam day approached, indicating that partners increasingly made allowances for examinees' negative affect. Using the beeper technique, Larson and Richards (1994) showed that the extent to which married partners reported that positive affect was elevated when they were doing things together, compared with their baseline level, depended on their overall level of marital satisfaction.

Strengths of diary data over other techniques. Because gathering diary data is time consuming, why not simply ask spouses to characterize how household work is divided, how companionate they and their partner are, or how their partner reacts on days when they are stressed? Several problems associated with using survey-type questions for obtaining data about these marital patterns are behind the appeal of diary-type data.

First, many factors other than spouses' actual marital patterns or experiences in marriage influence global summary reports; some of these factors also systematically bias such reports (Huston & Robins, 1982; Noller & Guthrie, 1991; Reis & Gable, 2000; Robins, 1990; Schwarz, 1990; Sudman, Bradburn, & Schwartz, 1996). When spouses are asked to provide accurate summary reports of division of labor, for instance, they have to decide what to include in the domain of household labor. Is mowing the lawn or shoveling snow to be included in the equation? Researchers have solved this problem by providing spouses with a list of household activities and asking them to indicate, for each, who takes primary responsibility. Even when this is done, however, and even if we assume that spouses are sufficiently motivated to answer the questions accurately, problems remain. Spouses must have kept track of both their own contribution and that of their mate; they must also be able to retrieve the information from memory when asked; furthermore, they must select a time frame to apply to the task and decide what weight to give the various chores—they could use the amount of time spent, the number of chores done, or any of a number of other criteria; finally, they must calculate how the behavior pattern relates to the options available on the scale. Most spouses, when faced with survey-type questions, no doubt report their general impressions. These impressions may be influenced by relationship schema (e.g., their beliefs about appropriate marital roles), how much in love or how satisfied they are with their marriage, or their sensitivities (e.g., a spouse philosophically committed to equally sharing responsibility for household duties may keep better track of each partner's contributions). Some of the shortcomings of global self-report data can be overcome by creating a latent variable based on the reports of both spouses (and others), but consideration must be given to the possibility that the reports are biased in the same way. Spouses who are both deeply in love, for instance, may characterize their own and each other's behavior in rosy terms.

However, even when participant reports of general patterns are accurate, they are limited because they focus on overall patterns of behavior, rather than on how behavior fluctuates by context and on a day-by-day basis. Diary data can be aggregated in a variety of ways, making it possible, for example, to examine how fluctuations in husbands' and wives' work around the house affects their day-to-day ratings of marital satisfaction; thus, for example, are wives happier on days when their husband performs more household tasks than he usually does? Is marital well-being enhanced the more spouses do household work together, as a team, rather than independently?

In spite of my reservations about questionnaire data, I would argue that social scientists ought to continue obtaining global reports of marital patterns but should also view such reports as reflecting the spouses' beliefs about their marriage (Figure 10.1, box B), rather than as capturing relationship properties (Figure 10.1, box C). Such beliefs may, in turn, affect how they act in marriage or react to their spouses' behavior. Partners who see their mate as more affectionate than diary or interactional data suggest, may perhaps be happier with their marriage than those who seem to have more accurate views of their relationship. The idea that dating couples and newly married spouses idealize each other (Huston et al., 2001), for instance, might be usefully studied by examining how well people are able to sustain a positive image of their partner when it is inconsistent with the day-to-day reality of their experiences in the relationship.

Diary data is most frequently used, however, to depict molar behavior. John and Cindy's day seemed almost choreographed in that family members' movements from one activity to another appear well coordinated. The portrait provides little sense, however, of how John and Cindy interacted with each other when they were together: How responsive were they to each other's ideas during their lunch hour conversation? More generally, how effective are they at solving problems together? How do they respond to each other's criticisms or expressions of anger? Although diary reports can provide

information about macrobehavioral patterns and the overall affective tenor of the day-to-day life of the couple, the give-and-take that makes up episodes of interaction cannot be investigated effectively without using direct observation techniques.

Using a Close-Up Lens: Describing Microbehavioral Marital Behavior

Directly observing spouses as they ruminate together about their day or as they work toward resolving a disagreement provides much richer data about marital interaction than does daily diary data (see Gottman & Notarius, 2000). Microbehaviorally oriented researchers, for instance, have coded face-to-face interaction in terms of the content of what people say, the affect in their voices, their facial expressions while they speak, and the expressions on the faces of the spouses as they listen to each other. The daily diary reports of affect, shown in Table 10.3, associated with each activity suggest that John and Cindy's day went well, except for their lunch together, which both John and Cindy found unpleasant. Suppose, for purposes of illustration, we had tracked that lunch hour conversation between John and Cindy using a coding system like those developed by researchers who have studied the nuances of marital interaction (Markman & Notarius, 1987). We would have seen John attempt to beg off taking Jessica to her piano lesson, citing pressing business matters. Cindy might have responded, perhaps with sarcasm in her voice, that his business concerns seem more important to him on days when he has family responsibilities. As Cindy lodged her accusation, John's face might have become more tense, and his body might have pulled away from Cindy. Observational data, by capturing communication on multiple levels, has been used to identify behavioral causes and manifestations of marital distress (Figure 10.1, link 2; Karney & Bradbury, 1995). Particular interaction styles, for example, defensiveness, stubbornness, high levels of criticism, the tendency to reciprocate negativity, and withdrawal during conflict, have been found both to covary with satisfaction and to predict decreases in satisfaction in marriage (Gottman, 1990, 1994; Gottman & Krokoff, 1989; Markman, 1981; Markman, Floyd, Stanley, & Storaasli, 1988).

Macrobehavioral and microbehavioral patterns are usually examined in isolation from one another. Macrobehavioral activities, however, provide the larger ecological context within which microbehavioral marital behaviors are played out. Thus, microbehavioral activities can be seen as intermittent interpersonal gatherings, punctuating the spouses' day and sometimes redirecting them as they move across their environment, pursuing various activities. Little is known, however, about how patterns of activity affect the details of marital interaction or how the particulars of marital interaction serve to alter the terrain that couples travel. Until the linkages between macro- and microbehavioral patterns are explored, the contributions that either of the two camps make to understanding marriage will be limited.

The Psychological Infrastructure of Marriage

John and Cindy appear to have worked out a generally successful modus vivendi, or what Burgess (1926) might have called a "well-adjusted" marriage, if we can take the day we tracked them as representative of their life together. Their activities are smoothly coordinated (Berscheid, 1985), joint pursuits generally produce positive affect in both of them (Kelley, 1979), and their interactions are peppered primarily by positive rather than negative affect (Karney & Bradbury, 1995). The morning proceeded such that each spouse's activities played smoothly off the other's. Had John, Cindy, or Jessica failed to perform specific activities in a timely fashion, the tuneful harmony of their morning might well have turned dissonant—perhaps creating disappointment, anger, or overt conflict (Berscheid, 1983). The rest of the day also unfolds smoothly, with the exception of their negative exchange at lunch.

Why were John and Cindy able to work out such a successful set of understandings? The portrait of John's and Cindy's day contains no more than clues about John and Cindy's motivations—why they do what they do and why they respond to each other in particular ways. We can sense that they are both close and on common ground because their plans and activities are well articulated. Their marriage also appears to be embedded in a supportive and friendly network of kin and friendship alliances. I now turn to an examination of the psychological infrastructure of marriage—the meshing of the psychological proclivities of the spouses, their feelings about each other, and the understandings they have developed—that might lie beneath the surface of marriages like that of John and Cindy.

Marriage was seen as a "unity of interacting personalities" by Burgess (1926) who, in taking *personality* to mean the spouses' total sense of themselves and their partner in the relationship, placed issues of marital adjustment and adaptation at the very heart of marriage. "A well adjusted marriage," wrote Burgess and Cottrell (1939) 13 years later, may be defined as "a marriage in which the attitudes and actions of each of the partners produce[s] an environment which is highly favorable to the proper functioning of the personality structures of each primary, particularly in the sphere of relationships." The idea that marriage involves a continuing give-and-take between spouses has been noted at periodic intervals by family scientists (e.g., Bernard, 1964; Waller, 1938). Waller, in his usual colorful fashion, suggests (p. 308):

> The social form created by marriage must find its way in a sort of tentative process; it must grow as a grapevine grows, blindly reaching out its tendrils, making many false starts but attaining at last to light and solidity . . . each member must try out many patterns of behavior in the new situation. Some patterns will appear highly successful; these will stabilize in the form of powerful habits. Other patterns of behavior will be penalized by conflict or other forms of failure; it is thus that the limits of interaction are defined.

This section of the article focuses on the two interrelated matters that Burgess (1926), Waller

(1938), and Bernard (1964) took as central to understanding marriage: First, marital adjustment is a process that takes place over time through which spouses seek to adapt to each other. Second, these adaptations, though they continue throughout the course of marriage, vary in their success, thereby producing unions that differ in closeness, satisfactoriness, and stability.

Marital Adjustment as an Adaptation Process

The three-dimensional, layered character of Figure 10.2 is intended to convey the idea that husbands' and wives' psychological proclivities lie beneath the surface of their day-to-day life together (cf. Bradbury & Fincham, 1988; Huston & Robins, 1982; Robins, 1990). Spouses' proclivities shape their activities and anchor their reactions to each other. The two-headed arrows connecting marital interaction and behavior to the spouses is intended to convey the idea that married partners are themselves changed by their experiences in marriage. Marital interaction is shown in the foreground of the figure as a sequence of interwoven subjective events and overt behaviors (see Kelley et al., 1983). Figure 10.2 portrays "states of being" as lying beneath the surface of marital activities and interactions. The embeddedness of each spouse's activities and marital interaction in states of being, as shown in Figure 10.2, is intended to suggest that such states are experienced in context and that they change, both in response to spouses' own behavior and that of others. Such states regulate spouses' movements from one activity to another, as well as direct their functioning during interaction. Marital interaction is intermittent, and thus it punctuates at various intervals each spouse's on going, day-to-day activities. What spouses have been doing, are doing as they interact, or plan to do later often structures their discussions. The figure also points to the idea that spouses influence each other, both directly in terms of the activities they choose to enact when they are together (shown in the foreground as marital interaction) as well as indirectly, as when

one spouse prepares breakfast while the other reads the paper (see Peplau, 1983). Thus, the two-headed arrow that connects husbands' and wives' activities serves to remind us both that what each spouse does, even when the spouses are apart, often matters to the other and that spouses' activities are coordinated (in varying degrees).

The processes depicted in Figure 10.2 stand in front of an implied background consisting of the sociocultural environment and the ecological niches in the society within which particular married couples function. The spouses who constitute the marital pair both live within and have been raised in a specific living environment or, more likely, in a series of such environments (households, neighborhoods, etc.), and their lives span a specific series of historical eras (e.g., the Great Depression, the Vietnam War). These settings and experiences shape individuals' dispositions, values, psychological states, and habits of thought, which are then brought into their marriage (Figure 10.1, link 3). Thus, for example, spouses' prior experiences may lead them to bring patriarchal or egalitarian values to their marriage, to have particular social values, political leanings, and leisure interests, to be invested in varying degrees in the welfare of others in their life (e.g., parents, siblings, friends), or to feel either secure or insecure about their relationships with significant others.

A general model of marital adjustment. The model portrayed in Figure 10.2 can be summarized in terms of ten interrelated axioms. The first axiom, implicit in Waller's (1938) depiction of marital adjustment processes, is that husbands and wives bring stable social, physical, and psychological attributes to marriage that bear upon how they behave and what they seek from each other. A husband who holds patriarchal values, for instance, will behave very differently in marriage compared with one who holds egalitarian attitudes. Some qualities—such as psychological expressiveness—make spouses easy to be around (Huston & Geis, 1993; Lamke, 1989), whereas other qualities—such as moodiness and

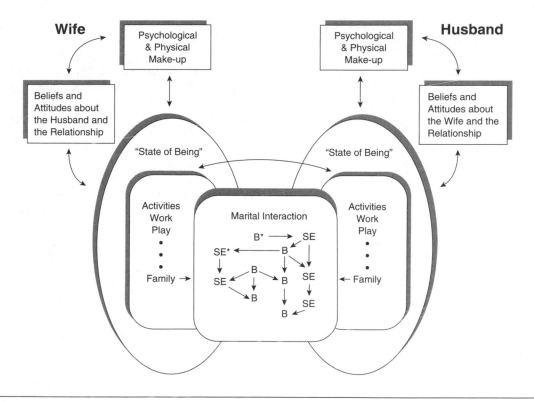

Figure 10.2   The Psychological Infrastructure of Marriage

NOTE: B = Behavior; SE = Subjective Event.

emotional lability—produce conflict and undermine marital satisfaction (Caughlin, Huston, & Houts, 2000).

The second axiom is that these relatively stable, general proclivities are latent until they are activated in situ. Psychological causes always operate locally, even though they may be rooted in the distant past (see Cook & Campbell, 1979). Thus, to account for a spouse's behavior in marriage, researchers need to pay equal attention to his or her general proclivities and to the situations that activate them. A person who is high strung or who is high in trait anxiety might be expected to show more anger and hostility in marriage in general, but his or her propensity toward negativity may increase under stress. Thus, the actual amount of negativity that spouses express toward their mate should be a conjoint function of their trait anxiety and the frequency with which they are confronted with environmental stressors. Figure 10.2 thus shows that a spouse's state of being (i.e., thoughts and emotions at a particular time)—whether it be anger, jealousy, tenderness, obligation, or some other state—results from a confluence of dispositions and circumstances and suggests that states of being are manifest in terms of specific types of activities and behavior.

This brings me to the third axiom, namely that spouses are interdependent, such that what each spouse says and does influences the other, both immediately and over time. This influence process, of course, lies at the heart of theoretical writings about marital adjustment (e.g., Bernard, 1964; Waller, 1938). The reader might recall the conflict over lunch between John and Cindy:

John quickly reversed field when Cindy strongly resisted, and he backed off his proposal that Cindy leave work to take Jessica to her piano lesson. The lunch hour conflict might have gone seriously awry had either spouse been anger-prone or if John had pushed Cindy hard to comply with his request. Even though the conflict appears to have been resolved reasonably amicably, the exchange was seen as unpleasant by both of the spouses (as shown in Table 10.3). The dialogue also affected how John and Cindy spent at least part of their afternoon; also, the feelings and thoughts generated during the exchange may have resurfaced later, perhaps in another context. The placement of spouses' subjective states underneath their activities and interactions in Figure 10.2 is designed to remind us that subjective states not only feed into behavior, as noted earlier, but are also altered as a result. Moreover, depending on the kinds of thoughts and emotions stimulated by an activity or an exchange, spouses may refine their views and evaluations of each other and the marriage.

Thus, the fourth axiom is that on the basis of their experiences in the relationship, spouses refashion the following: (a) their beliefs about each other's personality, values, interests, and attitudes; (b) their schemas and understandings about the nature of their marital relationship; and (c) their evaluations of each other and the marriage. Of course, newlyweds develop ideas about each other and their relationship during courtship, and these ideas reflect, at least to some extent, knowledge of each other's relatively stable psychological attributes. Thus, even though newlyweds continue to chisel out an experientially based understanding of each other, this chiseling is not done in marriage either dispassionately or anew.

The fifth axiom parallels the second one, except the focus shifts to spouses' beliefs and attitudes about their partner and the relationship rather than being on their more general psychological qualities and dispositions. Relationship-specific knowledge structures and dispositions are latent until they are activated in a specific situation. Once they are activated, they affect

spouses' behavior and their reactions to each other's behavior. The phrase "beliefs and attitudes" (shown in Figure 10.2) is intended as a general moniker that includes spouses' working models, their schemas, and their evaluations that are specific to the partner and the relationship. Such relationship-specific cognitions and evaluations are shown in Figure 10.2 as feeding into spouses' states of being, which, in turn, are shown as lying beneath the surface of their overt behavior. Thus, even though Cindy may love John, her love for him may be latent until circumstances actuate her love; when her love is actuated, a collection of thoughts and emotions surfaces (a subjective state), which, in turn, channel her to express her love toward John.

The next axiom, the sixth, is that spouses' stable psychological qualities, as well as their working models, schemas, and evaluations of each other and the relationship, affect how they respond to each other's behavior and to marital patterns of behavior, over time. Cindy's negative reaction to John's proposal that she take Jessica to the piano lesson, for example, may have been rooted in her sense that the proposal was inappropriate, given both her own ideas about gender roles in marriage and her belief that they had an understanding about how to handle this kind of situation.

The seventh axiom is that spouses' behavior reflects, in varying degrees, not only their own dispositional tendencies but also, indirectly, those of their mate. Thus, John's level of participation in household work may be anchored in both his own and Cindy's ideas about gender roles. Similarly, their joint leisure pursuits may reflect an equal compromise between their individual interests, or they may be weighted toward one or the other spouse's interests. The exploration of *partner effects,* or the influence of one partner's dispositions on the other's behavior, is rare in research on marriage, but now that the statistical tools are available, such research will become increasingly common (cf. Kenny & Cook, 1999). Finally, when influence is examined over time, it is possible to ferret out the extent to which each spouse's ideas about such matters as household responsibilities or leisure interests change toward the views of the partner.

The eighth axiom, somewhat implicit in the seventh one, is that marital partners' psychological makeup, as well as their working models and their schemas, fit together in varying degrees. Compatibility theory (Huston & Houts, 1998; Levinger & Rands, 1985) and interdependence theory (Kelley, 1979) both suggest that certain combinations of psychological attributes that combine to promote marital harmony, rather than conflict, are apt to create a sense of marital well-being. Such well-being, in turn, ought to encourage partners to become increasingly invested in each other's well-being. (Harmonious relationships, of course, are not necessarily healthy or close [cf. Berscheid, 1998]. Alcoholics may reinforce each other's drinking, but hasten themselves to premature deaths, and couples who have very traditional ideas about marital roles and few leisure interests in common may spend little time in each other's company.)

This brings me to the ninth and tenth axioms, which I will treat in tandem. Spouses' working models, schemas, and evaluations change as a result of their experiences in the marriage (axiom 9); these changes, in turn, may lead them to alter the physical and social environment (axiom 10). These changes in the individuals and in the context of their marriage (Berscheid & Lopes, 1997; Kelley, 1983) may increase or decrease marital harmony and stability. The focus of research, up to now, has been on interpersonal factors that change spouses' marital satisfaction. The dominance of the social learning tradition in behavioral research on marriage has led most researchers to assume that changes in how spouses feel about their marriage are accretive, reflecting patterns of rewards and costs (see Karney & Bradbury, 1995), and that these changes affect marital interaction. Spouses who are uncertain they can trust their mate may, for instance, try to reduce the opportunities their mate might have to betray their trust. Moreover, some changes in spouses' views of each other may be abrupt rather than accretive; trust may take a dramatic plunge when a spouse feels betrayed by his or her mate's indiscretion. The concentration of research on marital satisfaction leaves us with information about how spouses come to believe their marriage is egalitarian or about how spouses come to see their partner as having moral fiber or as being resilient. Thus, spouses' views of each other's character, and hence their attraction, may depend, in part, on how well they handle crises, on their ability to meet their responsibilities, and on how they interact with children. The roots of these changes that occur in the heads of the spouses, which are rarely studied, may provide the basis for a strengthened alliance or may move the couple toward disenchantment and, perhaps, divorce.

These ten axioms, when considered together, suggest that the individual partners and the marriage relationship affect each other continuously over time. The psychological and physical characteristics spouses bring to their day-to-day life together set the stage for their interpersonal dialogues, but the nature of these dialogues depends partly on particular behaviors (or patterns of behavior) that take place and on the fact that the same behavior can be interpreted and evaluated (or coded) in a variety of ways. Thus, spouses' expressions of anger may be rooted, for example, in their personality traits, situational stress, the behavior of their mate, misunderstandings, a violation of agreed upon relationship norms, their mate's personality, or marital dissatisfaction. Moreover, each spouse's behavior may have either positive or negative consequences for either or both of the partners. These consequences are sometimes anticipated and intended, but spouses do not always think about the consequences of their actions. Finally, the same behavior (or pattern of behavior) may be viewed differently by the spouses, as when they disagree about whether a spouse whose behavior has negative consequences for his or her mate meant to do harm. As noted earlier, the idea that marriage involves a continuing dialogue between the spouses has been noted periodically (e.g., Bernard, 1964; Waller, 1938), but rarely have researchers intensively studied couples from courtship through the early years of marriage, even though it is during this period that marital relationships take on much of their social form (cf. Bradbury, 1998).

Social scientists interested in linking the spouses' psychological qualities to marital behavior patterns have proceeded intuitively rather than systematically. As a consequence, few efforts have been made to distinguish various types of attributes and to specify the psychological and interpersonal mechanisms through which they affect marital adjustment. In the following subsections, I identify key concepts and processes that researchers studying the interplay between spousal qualities and their marital activities and interactions need to think through. In addition to marital satisfaction, researchers need to examine such matters as how spouses come to understand their power in the relationship, how they develop and lose respect for each other, or how they maintain strong feelings of love.

Spouses as architects of their marriage. The movement of spouses from activity to activity through the course of the day is volitional, even though people may not pause to think about what to do. Although spouses' actions—even seemingly spontaneous ones—are rooted in their states of being, they do not always actively contemplate the alternatives before them at each choice point. John and Cindy's choreographed morning script certainly has a routine feel to it. Social psychologists suggest that habits, which are defined as propensities to behave in particular ways given a familiar context, are often embedded in volitional and intentional action systems (see Ouellette & Wood, 1998). Self-consciousness and introspection often betray the conflicting nature of the psychological forces toward and away from engaging in a particular action; similarly, reflection might occur when people are drawn toward doing something that is taboo or when they become aware that pursuing their own interests might undermine the interests of others. People motivated to maintain a balance between their role commitments may often be faced with trying to balance conflicting demands (cf. Marks & MacDermid, 1996).

When we move to marital interaction, behavior that seems spontaneous nonetheless is viewed as reflecting particular actors' subjective states. Gottman (1994), for instance, identifies *criticism* as reflecting disapproval, *complaint* as rooted in aggrievement, *defensiveness* as resulting from an attempt to avoid blame, *contempt* as a manifestation of disdain, and *stonewalling* as reflecting hostile, closed-off feelings. It is easy to imagine that these thoughts and behaviors are more likely to be activated when the actor's immediate goals are frustrated or at times when the actor is under stress. Such behavioral proclivities toward the partner can be stable or transient, and if stable, they can reflect the psychological makeup of the spouse or how they think and feel about their spouse (or others; Gottman, 1994). A sense of self-importance, for example, may cause a husband to show contempt toward his wife, or such contempt may reflect a well-earned lack of respect. Unfortunately, behavioral researchers have rarely attempted to trace the psychological reasons why spouses feel and behave in particular ways toward their partner during interaction. We know little more than that spouses who are distressed about their marriage express negativity more often and show greater reciprocity in negativity than happy couples. But the question of why unhappy spouses feel and show contempt or disapproval or feel potentially blameworthy is largely left unanswered (cf. Karney & Bradbury, 1995).

A particular line of action or way of behaving toward one's mate may be characterized and experienced by actors in a number of ways. The nature of the act, the context within which the act occurs, and the consequences the act has for the actor and for others all play a part in the motives attributed to the spouse who acts. Thus, acts can be seen as reflecting the actor's needs, sense of morality, unconscious drives, goals, or purposes (Wegner & Vallacher, 1986). How acts are characterized, both by the actor and others, serves to define how spouses see each other and their marriage relationship.

Lewin's (1948) analysis of voluntary action, as applied to marriage, suggests that potential activities and behaviors, situated in particular social and environmental contexts, are often evaluated in terms of the relative strength of the valences associated with them (cf. Herbst, 1952, 1953; Levinger & Huston, 1990). The notion that spouses' choices depend on the valences of various lines of activity suggests the importance of identifying factors that affect such valences. It is also important to keep in mind that when the valences associated with a particular line of action are highly and consistently positive, actors will develop particular habits of behavior. Thus, an extrovert may gravitate toward social gatherings, rather than toward solitary pursuits, even though he or she may not identify his actions in terms of this proclivity. It is easier to identify the valences associated with lines of action when actors' alternatives have similar values or when the consequences of the choices for the self and for other people are salient. A wife who is behind in her work at the office may be confronted with a choice between staying late to clean up her desk and returning home for dinner. The decision she reaches is no doubt rooted, at least in part, in her values, attitudes, and the like, as well as in the expectations of her coworkers, superiors, and family.

The valences of alternative activities and behaviors, according to Lewin's (1948) analysis, differ in both quality (positive or negative) and strength. Thus, an actor's ambivalence and uncertainty intensify if the valence changes when the line of action is examined from different perspectives. Although Lewin (1948) did not distinguish between types of factors that might affect valences, Heider (1958) suggested that self-regulated behavior is generally seen as reflecting, in varying degrees, what (a) actors seem to *want, need,* or *desire;* (b) what they feel they *ought* to do; and (c) what they believe they have the *ability* to do. These three types of psychological forces may be internal or general and thus reflect actors' psychological makeup; or, they may be situationally or relationship specific, as when partners negotiate a set of understandings regarding their rights and responsibilities for particular types of situations.

The importance of distinguishing matters such as what people want to do (or desire to do) from what they feel they ought to do and what they feel competent to do has a number of important implications for researchers studying marriage. First, the pertinence of the three facets of spouses' psychological makeup for marriage may depend on the activity or behavior under consideration. Spouses are generally seen to do household work primarily because they feel they ought to do it, whereas they are thought to pursue recreation largely for pleasure. Whether the motives associated with these various types of activities are indeed empirically reducible in these ways should not be assumed. My colleagues and I made this mistake when we failed to inquire about how much spouses would enjoy or dislike doing various household and child care tasks and focused, instead, on their beliefs about which partner ought to do each task and their ideas about how well they each could do the tasks (Atkinson & Huston, 1984; McHale & Huston, 1984).

Second, sociologists have tended to focus on the idea that spouses' behavior in marriage is regulated by their understanding of what they ought to do. This reflects sociologists' longstanding interest in social structure, power, and roles (e.g., Bates & Harvey, 1975). Psychologists, with their interest in the hedonic basis of behavior, turn to actors' basic wants, needs, or desires or to their love and attraction as causes of behavior. Third, what people want to do, feel they ought to do, and believe they have the ability to do are not always aligned within a particular individual. Spouses may restrain themselves from doing something they want to do because they feel it is morally wrong or because they are not sure how to go about doing it (McHale & Huston, 1984). Fourth, the three types of considerations may differ in importance from one person to another. A person who seeks pleasure wherever it can be found, with little internal moral constraint or concern for others, might be characterized as self-absorbed or, perhaps, narcissistic. A person who has a considerable range of competencies and who places only moderate importance on matters of social correctness might be characterized as a competent pragmatist. When marriage partners' actions toward each other and their commentaries about each other's behavior resonate to issues of right and wrong, their relationship may take on the overtones of a morality play.

Figures 10.1 and 10.2 distinguish between what might be thought of as personological factors that affect marital dynamics and the beliefs and attitudes spouses develop about each other and the relationship. The idea that a person's psychological makeup affects marital dynamics has a long history (Auhagen & Hinde, 1997). Terman and his colleagues (1938), for example, suggested the following:

> Whether by nature or nurture, there are persons so lacking in qualities which make for compatibility that they would be incapable of finding happiness in any marriage. There are others, less extreme, who could find it only under the most favorable circumstances; and still others whose dispositions and outlooks upon life would preserve them from acute unhappiness however unfortunately they were mated (p. 110).

Any quality that a mate brings to marriage that might affect how spouses either behave in marriage or react to each other's behavior fits within what I mean when I speak of spouses' psychological makeup and physical makeup. Personality traits, values, interests, social attitudes, and physical qualities exemplify features of spouses' makeup that might affect marital dynamics. These relatively durable qualities also include spouses' core values: their sense of identity, their attitudes (e.g., about politics, hunting, the opera, or the institution of marriage), their stereotypes (e.g., implicit theories about men and women), their intelligence, their skills, their temperament, their passions, and their ideas about what they want in a marriage or in a partner. Spouses may enter marriage with particular ideas or knowledge structures about how relationships work, such as believing that relationships cannot work without love, or that men and women must

equally share household chores (Fletcher & Kinmouth, 1992). To the extent that these preferences precede marriage and endure once couples marry, they may affect how couples structure their marriage and how they come to evaluate each other and their marriage.

Moreover, because these features of a person's psychological makeup are thought to reflect general and stable proclivities, they bear upon how people react to a variety of situations. People who are moody or tense, by nature, may react more strongly to stressors than others. A man with a love of fishing, for instance, relates to the world, in part, through a fisherman's eyes, a man who thinks of himself as the primary breadwinner may be feel threatened when he is out of work, and a woman who thinks of herself as intelligent will likely become angry if she is patronized.

These general, stable attributes and proclivities can be distinguished from those that are specific to the partner or the relationship. Spouses love, admire, and trust one another in varying degrees, and these kinds of attitudes both shape and are shaped by how spouses relate to one another. Other in-the-head phenomena specific to the partner and the marriage include satisfaction with the marriage, the understandings that partners develop about appropriate behavior, beliefs they have about their marriage (e.g., who is dominant, how household work is divided, or the centrality of the marriage in each of the partner's lives), and ideas the spouses have about each other's psychological makeup (e.g., their goals, values, interests, or personality).

These attitudes and beliefs need to be distinguished from spouses' psychological and physical makeup for two primary reasons. First, they develop and change as a consequence of the relationship and thus both shape and are shaped by the marriage relationship. Second, such specific attitudes and evaluations develop out of the interplay between spouses' general dispositions and the history of the spouses in their relationship. A spouse thus may trust his or her mate, at first, because the spouse generally believes people are trustworthy. This initial trust, in turn, may cause the trusting individual to behave in ways that encourage trustworthy behavior. Thus, a generalized trust in others may foreshadow the development of trust in particular relationships. A similar kind of process may link attachment styles, as general dispositions, to how spouses come to feel about a particular intimate partner. Regardless of how much trust or security a person feels initially, such trust or security is apt to give way quickly should it be violated. Thus, it is particularly important when examining emergent, relationship-specific beliefs and evaluations to recognize that they are apt to result from the interplay between psychological and interpersonal forces. Although it makes sense to treat stable personality dispositions as exogenous variables in models of marital adjustment, relationship-specific beliefs and attitudes are more usefully modeled as both causes and consequences of marital activities and behavior.

Affect, cognition, and changes in spouse's beliefs and attitudes about each other. This impact of participation in a marriage on the spouses is shown in Figure 10.2 as the upward element of the arrows emanating from each spouse's state of being. We know very little about how spouses' experiences in the marriage affect their attitudes and beliefs about each other and the relationship or about how these internal changes, in turn, produce changes in marital patterns. A husband who enters marriage with the general idea that women ought to be "put on a pedestal," for instance, may initially be comfortable making decisions for the two of them without seeking his wife's input. This combination of values and behavior may be reinforced or undermined over time, depending on whether his wife wants to be put on a pedestal in such a fashion. If she is uncomfortable with such a role (perhaps because she has different ideas about gender roles or perhaps because he tends to make poor decisions), she may confront him. She may keep her concerns to herself, however, if she believes he will not be open to them. Thus, depending on the spouses' psychological

makeup and how their interactions unfold, spouses may deal with situations in which the husband makes decisions for the couple with any number of thoughts and feelings that, in turn, affect how they see each other and the world within which they function.

Most research on marriage has focused primarily on marital satisfaction. The roots of other attitudes and beliefs, such as how spouses' sense of trust, love, or respect develops in marriage, are poorly understood. We know precious little about the conditions that sustain feelings of love or lead a spouse to admire his or her mate, or about what experiences encourage a spouse to develop a superior attitude. My sense is that the focus of recent research on the affective substrate of marital interaction will prove less useful when researchers shift their attention from studying the antecedents of marital satisfaction to examining the marital patterns that give rise to some of these other beliefs and evaluations. Researchers will no doubt need to know something about the spouses' psychological qualities—their values, role preferences, and the like—as well as something about macrobehavioral activities to account for such matters as whether spouses feel household tasks are divided equitably or whether they feel their partner is worthy of admiration. A wife may come to admire her husband, for example, largely by such matters as his willingness to make time for his mother or his children, by his ability to handle stress, or by his success in the occupational world.

Just as it is important to recognize that particular behaviors can reflect a variety of underlying motives, researchers need to take into account that they may produce varied reactions, depending on how the behavior is interpreted. Behavior that actually reflects an actor's disapproval, for instance, may produce varying degrees of discomfort in its target, depending on whether the disapproval is seen as emanating from the communicant's critical nature, whether the disapproval is seen as reflecting a loss of affection, or whether the target feels the disapproval is well deserved. Spouses thus react not only to each other's behavior in terms of whether it supports their interests but also to the attitudes and beliefs that seem to lie beneath the behavior (cf. Kelley, 1979). Indeed, when partners in intimate relationships are asked to identify specific behaviors they would like their partner to change, they often report, instead, more global complaints that center on their partner's personality, character, or attitudes about the relationship (Kelley, 1979).

Because husbands' and wives' psychological makeup, knowledge structures, and attitudes are reflected in their behavior (as well as in their reactions to each other's behavior), spouses' dispositions play off one another. A wife who is ambivalent about her marriage, for example, may express little or intermittent affection toward her husband, which, in turn, may trigger a strong reaction from him, particularly if he is insecure. Spouses relate to each other's personality as it is manifest in the relationship. A person who is prone to emotional ups and downs, for example, may be harder to live with on a day-to-day basis compared with someone who is even tempered (Caughlin et al., 2000). Selfishness, depression, and aggressiveness no doubt undermine marriage (Kitson, 1992), whereas qualities like warmth and openness appear to enhance marriage relationships (Lamke, 1989). The extent to which married partners' psychological qualities fit together ought to relate to the degree to which the partners are able to establish a harmonious, mutually satisfying marriage bond, according to compatibility theories of marriage (Huston & Houts, 1998). Thus, over time, the images, attitudes, and feelings the spouses develop about each other reflect the psychological qualities that lie beneath the surface of their behavior.

Spouses develop new understandings, their motivations to behave in particular ways become stronger or weaker, and individuals acquire, sharpen, or lose their sense of skill with regard to particular matters. Each spouse provides a context for the other, and both partners are influenced, individually and jointly, by events outside the relationship that impinge on them. Thus, although husbands and wives come to their relationships with beliefs about appropriate ways to behave, inclinations to act in particular ways, and a package of skills, these initial propensities, rooted in their personality and values (or more generally, in their psychological makeup) are often muted or amplified in the context of the marriage relationship. Spouses who have a strong bond with one another may increasingly internalize each other's ideas about appropriate behavior. A husband who is tough-minded, in general, may be tenderhearted when it comes to his wife. Partners' dispositions toward each other in the relationship are themselves causally interdependent (Kelley, 1979, 1983). Thus, for example, the inclination of one partner to show love will be dampened if it is not, over time, reciprocated. Similarly, a competitive spouse who makes choices that preempt the partner may indirectly encourage the partner to seek similar advantage.

A few observations can be made to conclude this section, using Figure 10.2 as a point of reference. If we are to effectively meet Burgess's (1926) challenge of studying marriage as a "unity of interacting personalities," we need to recognize first that spouses' marital behavior, when examined in its totality, is anchored in a mix of the spouses' behavioral dispositions. The amalgam of psychological forces that regulate marital behavior is mediated through the spouses' states of being, which, in turn, are partly anchored both in the spouses' psychological makeup and in their beliefs and attitudes about each other and the marriage. Marital behavior is too often studied as if its significance to the actors can be understood apart from the history of the spouses' relationship with each other; the propensity of researchers to disembody marital behavior from the spouses' psychological characteristics has made it difficult to trace the deeper psychological roots of marital interaction and the roots of distress.

Second, because behavior is the medium through which dispositions are expressed, researchers need to gather data not only about what people do and how they act when they are together but also data that bear on why people do what they do and act as they do. Third, spouses influence each other, and this influence extends over time; thus, longitudinal research carried out with couples that examines how the spouses' ideas about each other and their motives both shape and are shaped by their history together is sorely needed.

Marital Success and Stability

Up to now, my focus has been on marital adjustment as a process. As noted earlier, marital adjustment is also used as a summary evaluation of the quality of the marriage relationship at a particular time in its history. I question two assumptions that appear to underlie the focus on marital satisfaction as the primary cause of marital stability. First, as Karney and Bradbury (1995) recently pointed out, "the magnitude of the linkage [between satisfaction and divorce] has not been large" (p. 25). Second, satisfaction typically has been used as the sole indicant of the extent to which spouses are drawn to each other and, hence, motivated to stay married.

Johnson's (1991, 1999) model of commitment points to the idea that the decisions spouses make to stay married or divorce reflect, in varying degrees, not only the extent to which the spouses want to stay married (what Johnson calls *personal commitment*) but also the extent to which they feel they ought to stay married (Johnson's *moral commitment*) and the degree to which they think they have to stay married (*structural commitment*). The moral obligation that people feel to stay married may reflect, in one degree or another, relatively stable values about the morality of divorce anchored in their upbringing, spouses' concerns about the welfare of their children, understandings spouses have reached with each other about the permanence of their union, and the degree to which they see themselves as steadfast in keeping their commitments. Moral commitment, thus, is rooted partly in a person's values and personality, and partly in the marriage itself. Structural commitment, in contrast to both personal and moral commitment, is experienced as emanating from the outside. People may feel they have to stay in a

relationship because of financial concerns, because they lack the opportunity to form competing relationships, or because they worry about negative social sanctions. The root causes of structural commitment can generally be located in the spouse's social network or ecological niche. Spouses who are very strongly drawn to each other, according to Johnson, may rarely think about moral and structural constraints, but if their personal commitment declines, moral and structural barriers are apt to become more salient.

The reasons why spouses are committed to staying married, according to Johnson (1991, 1999), undoubtedly affects how spouses relate to one another, how much time they spend together, and whether they pursue other relationships that might compete with the marriage. Spouses who no longer want to stay married but do so out of a sense of obligation or external constraint, for example, may show little interest in and affection toward their mate. Research linking configurations of commitment to marital behavior, however, has yet to be undertaken.

The second problem with the focus on marital satisfaction is that it provides only a pale representation of the total constellation of psychological forces that draw spouses toward one another. Love, admiration, a sense of being compatible, and trust are probably just as important, if not more important, than satisfaction in accounting for spouses' desire to stay married (cf. Lamm, Wiesmann, & Keller, 1998). These various assessments also are rooted in a variety of marital experiences and as such, they reinforce the importance of researchers moving beyond focusing on how spouses communicate at a randomly selected time in their relationship. Marital satisfaction clearly resonates to the affective character of marital interaction (see Gottman & Notarius, 2000). Factors that generate and sustain love, admiration, and trust, however, are apt to be anchored in how spouses respond to particular kinds of situations—such as those in which spouses help each other, solve a problem together, overcome a difficulty, or resist temptation—rather than be rooted in the kinds of features of communication styles commonly studied in marital interaction research.

Researchers have just begun to examine changes in spouses' evaluations of their marriage at multiple points in time, beginning with the newlywed years, rather than focusing on single cross-sectional snapshots of couples who have been married varied lengths of time (see Bradbury, 1998). We found in a recent longitudinal study, for instance, that declines in love over the first 2 years of marriage foreshadowed divorce, whereas newlywed differences in love that were stable over the first 2 years of marriage predicted marital satisfaction 13 years into marriage among the couples who stay married (Huston et al., 2001). Thus, if researchers are to study disaffection as a process (Kayser, 1993), they need to obtain evaluations from spouses on multiple occasions.

The Macroenvironmental Context of Marriage

The macrosocietal context (Figure 10.1, box A) includes features of the society, culture, and physical environment within which an aggregate of individuals and couples live. Had I opened this article with a thumbnail sketch of marriage in contemporary Japanese culture, where the divorce rate is less than half that of the United States, I would have described a society in which the macrosocietal sanctions against divorce are so strong as to render the feelings the spouses have toward one another largely irrelevant to marital stability. Although Japanese culture is changing, spouses generally begin marriage with the expectation that marriage requires considerable patience and tolerance. According to a 37-nation survey recently carried out by Japanese researchers (Kristol, 1996), Japanese couples are remarkably incompatible, more so than couples almost anywhere in the world. The patriarchal value system within which marriage relationships in Japan are embedded puts pressure on wives, rather than husbands, to accommodate, and it provides little social support for marriage patterns that deviate from the norm.

This brief characterization points to differences between cultures in the extent to which marital behavior is regulated by factors that arise outside the marriage.

Figure 10.1 schematically shows the linkages between the macroenvironment, the individual spouses, and marital behavior patterns. I subdivide the macroenvironment into the macrosocietal context (a_1) and the spouses' ecological niche (a_2) within the macroenvironment. At the macrocosmic level, nations, subcultures, and neighborhoods can be described in terms of societal conditions, in terms of historical events, and in terms of the belief systems that members of a cultural or subcultural group hold about various matters and the way that particular societal institutions ought to function. When belief systems are widely shared within a society or group, they are often internalized as moral imperatives. Such imperatives are often codified into law, and they affect the way societal institutions function. The opportunities and constraints placed on various categories of people—for example, men and women—affect the kinds of skills they acquire and the extent to which societal institutions provide incentives to encourage or discourage particular types of behavior. Spouses' ideas about marital roles and their understandings of the rules that regulate the behavior of wives and husbands in the culture reflect, at least to some extent, macrosocietal forces. In rural Japan, for instance, couples contemplating divorce would be hard-pressed to find support for taking such an action (Kristol, 1996); such support could be found more readily, however, in major urban centers in Japan. Societies and subcultures differ, of course, in the pluralism of the members' values, as well as in how much contact is encouraged between subgroups holding different values. The pluralistic nature of the macrosociety within which inhabitants of the United States currently live, in contrast to societies that are more homogeneous, makes it possible for couples to fashion a network supportive of a wide range of marital lifestyles or of divorcing for a variety of reasons.

The particular ecological niche, defined as a constellation of behavior settings within which spouses function on a day-to-day basis, affects both the spouses and the marriage relationship. Couples who live in poor, urban neighborhoods must deal with very different issues than those who live in metropolitan suburbs, small towns, or rural areas (Burton & Jarrett, 2000). The behavior settings within which a dual-worker couple with two young children live out their lives are very different from those of a retired elderly couple, whose children were married and moved away years ago.

The behavior settings within which people function also provide the medium through which cultural values are articulated, reinforced, or undermined. The link between societal conditions and the marital relationship (Figure 10.1, link 5) suggests that the embeddedness of the marriage in a macrosocietal milieu can directly affect husband-wife interaction. For example, the economic depression of the 1930s put people out of work and created economically pressed households, often populated by members of a nuclear family, their extended family, and friends.

Macrosocietal changes can affect marital and family dynamics (e.g., Conger & Elder, 1994; Elder, 1964) by altering the ecological niches within which subsets of the population function. What happens in behavior settings outside the home can, and often does, affect the internal dynamics of the marriage relationship. The effects of features of a couple's environmental niche on marital interaction, however, are often mediated through their effects on the husband, the wife, or both partners (in Figure 10.1, link 3, followed by link 1). Work-related stress may be transported by the worker into the home and thereby create conflict in the marital relationship (Bolger, DeLongis, Kessler, & Wethington, 1989; Crouter, Perry-Jenkins, Huston, & Crawford, 1989; Halford, Gravestock, Lowe, & Scheldt, 1992). Economic hardship, for example, tends to produce anxiety and depression (Figure 10.1, link 3), which, in turn, is associated with marital conflict (link 1; Conger, Reuter, & Elder, 1999). Qualities of the husband and wife, however, may also either amplify or diminish (i.e., moderate) the impact of

macroenvironmental conditions. The impact of economic hardship on marital conflict, for example, may be buffered by the amount of social support spouses provide one another (Conger et al., 1999), or may be intensified if either the husband or wife has a psychological propensity toward moodiness or irascibility, or if either spouse is already distressed about the marriage.

Conclusions

The ecological model described in this paper focuses on issues pertaining to causal processes that cut across the three prime units of analysis. Most theories about marriage and other intimate relationships focus attention on only part of the whole causal system. Biologically oriented social scientists ordinarily start with the attributes of husbands and wives—their physical appearance, health status, and temperament—and examine how these qualities are reflected in the spouses' proclivities relevant to marital relationships (Figure 10.1, link 5) or, more rarely, to marital interaction (link 3). Evolutionary theorists take an essentialist view of sex differences, seeking to explain gender differences in intimate relationships in terms of the principles of natural selection (link 1). Sociologists, particularly feminists, take a constructivist view of gender, seeing it as a social category, the significance of which depends on the social and cultural context. Thus, for example, power differences experienced in marriage are traced to patriarchal macrosocietal structures (links 3 and 5). Symbolic interactionists (e.g., McCall & Simmons, 1978) suggest that people are gratified by, and hence become attached to, others who validate their identity (i.e., their general sense of themselves; links 1 and 2). Sociologists and developmental psychologists suggest that the ecological niches within which the spouses were raised affect their marital proclivities (link 3), which, in turn, affect marital patterns (link 1; Tallman, Gray, Kullberg, & Henderson, 1999).

Role theorists (e.g., Bates & Harvey, 1975) invoke "culture" to explain the recurrence of similar patterns of activity by different sets of actors in marriage, as well as the stability of such patterns over time. Once a norm is learned and established, it becomes a part of the personality of the actors in the relationship, serving both as an internal rudder regulating the spouses' behavior and as a basis for sanctioning behavior that deviates from normative prescriptions. Sociologists and family social scientists also have examined the interplay between kin and friendship networks and the marital relationships (within box C of Figure 10.1, the link between c_1 and c_2). Behavioral psychologists often focus on the interplay between marital interaction and marital satisfaction (Figure 10.1, links 1 and 2). Social psychologists often begin with the attributes of the individual spouses (e.g., personality, values, compatibility) and seek to link these to marital behavior and, ultimately, to the attitudes and beliefs spouses develop toward each other (Figure 10.1, links 1 and 2).

The ecological study of marriage also requires researchers to link constructs across the levels—societal, individual, and marital—recognizing that each level provides the context for the others. The macrosocietal context within which marriage relationships are embedded is affected by the mix of decisions individual spouses and married couples make; similarly, individual spouses not only shape the contours of their marriage but are shaped by it, as well. The circular patterns of cause and effect, when examined with the idea that these cause-effect relationships also depend on contextual factors, imply that no single effort to understand the interplay between marriage and context can capture more than a sliver of the dynamic and circular processes involved. New ways of analyzing data that simultaneously take into account individual-, dyadic-, and group-level effects make ecologically sensitive research easier to do than was heretofore possible (see Kashy & Grotevant, 1999). Moreover, if researchers working on subparts of the larger reciprocal causal system are aware of what their colleagues are doing in related disciplines, our collective efforts to understand marriage will show remarkable advances in the 21st century.

Note

The author would like to thank Laura George for her help in thinking through the broad outlines of the ecological model and to thank Gilbert Geis, Sylvia Niehuis, Sharma Smith, Paul Miller, and Christopher Rasmussen for their thoughtful reflections on an earlier draft of this manuscript. Work on this article was supported by grants from the National Science Foundation (SBR9311846) and the National Institute of Mental Health (MH 33938).

References

Almeida, D., Wethington, E., & Chandler, A. L. (1999). Daily transmission of tensions between marital dyads and parent-child dyads. *Journal of Marriage and the Family, 61,* 49–61.

Altman, I., & Ginat, J. (1996). *Polygamous families in contemporary society.* New York: Cambridge University Press.

Atkinson, J., & Huston, T. L. (1984). Sex role orientation and division of labor early in marriage. *Journal of Personality and Social Psychology, 46,* 330–345.

Auhagen, A. E., & Hinde, R. A. (1997). Individual characteristics and personal relationships. *Personal Relationships, 4,* 63–84.

Bates, E. L., & Harvey, C. C. (1975). *The structure of social systems.* New York: Gardner.

Bernard, J. (1964). The adjustment of married mates. In H. T. Christensen (Ed.), *Handbook of marriage and the family* (pp. 675–739). Chicago: Rand McNally.

Berscheid, E. (1983). Emotion. In H. H. Kelley, E. Berscheid, A. Christensen, J. H. Harvey, T. L. Huston, L. A. Peplau, & D. R. Peterson (Eds.), *Close relationships* (pp. 110–168). New York: Freeman.

Berscheid, E. (1985). Compatibility, interdependence, and emotion. In W. Ickes (Ed.), *Compatible and incompatible relationships* (pp. 143–162). New York: Springer-Verlag.

Berscheid, E. (1998). A social psychological view of marital dysfunction and stability. In I. N. Bradbury (Ed.), *The developmental course of marital dysfunction* (pp. 441–459). New York: Cambridge University Press.

Berscheid, E., & Lopes, J. (1997). A temporal model of relationship satisfaction and stability. In

R. J. Sternberg & M. Hojjat (Eds.), *Satisfaction in close relationships* (pp. 129–159). New York: Plenum Press.

Bolger, N., DeLongis, A., Kessler, R. C., & Wethington, E. (1989). The contagion of stress across multiple roles. *Journal of Marriage and the Family, 51,* 175–183.

Bott, E. (1971). *Family and the social network: Roles, norms, and external relationships in ordinary urban families* (2nd ed.). New York: Free Press.

Bradbury, T. N. (Ed.). (1998). *The developmental course of marital dysfunction.* New York: Cambridge University Press.

Bradbury, T. N., & Fincham, F. D. (1988). Individual difference variables in close relationships: A contextual model of marriage as an integrative framework. *Journal of Personality and Social Psychology, 54,* 713–721.

Burgess, E. W. (1926). The family as a system of interacting personalities. *Family, 7,* 3–9.

Burgess, E. W., & Cottrell, L. (1939). *Predicting success or failure in marriage.* Englewood Cliffs, NJ: Prentice-Hall.

Burgess, E. W., & Locke, H. J. (1945). *The family: From institution to companionship.* New York: American Book.

Burton, L., & Jarrett, R. L. (2000). In the mix, yet on the margins: The place of families in urban neighborhood and child development research. *Journal of Marriage and the Family, 62,* 444–465.

Caughlin, J. P., Huston, T. L., & Houts, R. M. (2000). How does personality matter in marriage? An examination of trait anxiety, interpersonal negativity, and marital satisfaction. *Journal of Personality and Social Psychology, 78,* 326–336.

Conger, R., & Elder, G. (1994). *Families in troubled times: Adapting to change in rural America.* New York: Aldine deGruyer.

Conger, R. D., Reuter, M. A., & Elder, G. (1999). Couple resilience to economic pressure. *Journal of Personality and Social Psychology, 76,* 54–71.

Cook, T. D., & Campbell, D. T. (1979). *Quasi-experimentation: Design and analysis issues for field settings.* Chicago: Rand McNally.

Crawford, D. W., & Huston, T. L. (1993). The impact of the transition to parenthood on marital leisure. *Personality and Social Psychology Bulletin, 18,* 39–46.

Crouter, A., Perry-Jenkins, M., Huston, T. L., & Crawford, D. (1989). The influence of work-induced psychological states on behavior at home. *Basic and Applied Social Psychology, 10,* 273–292.

Elder, G. (1964). *Children of the depression.* Berkeley: University of California Press.

Fincham, F. D., & Bradbury, T. N. (1987). The assessment of marital quality: A reevaluation. *Journal of Marriage and the Family, 49,* 797–809.

Fletcher, G. J. O., & Kinmouth, L. (1992). Measuring relationship beliefs: An individual differences measure. *Journal of Research in Personality, 26,* 371–397.

Gable, S. L., & Reis, H. T. (1999). Now and then, them and us, this and that: Studying relationships across time, partner, context, and person. *Personal Relationship, 6,* 415–432.

Gilbert, R., Christensen, A., & Margolin, G. (1984). Patterns of alliances in nondistressed and multiproblem families. *Family Process, 23,* 75–876.

Gottman, J. M. (1990). How marriages change. In G. R. Patterson (Ed.), *Depression and aggression in family interaction* (pp. 75–101). Hillsdale, NJ: Erlbaum.

Gottman, J. M. (1994). *What predicts divorce? The relationship between marital processes and marital outcomes.* Hillsdale, NJ: Erlbaum.

Gottman, J. M., & Krokoff, L. J. (1989). The relationship between marital interaction and marital satisfaction: A longitudinal view. *Journal of Consulting and Clinical Psychology, 57,* 47–52.

Gottman, J., & Notarius, C. I. (2000). Observing marital interaction. *Journal of Marriage and the Family, 62,* 927–947.

Halford, W. K., Gravestock, F. M., Lowe, R., & Scheldt, S. (1992). Toward a behavioral ecology of stressful marital interactions. *Behavioral Assessment, 14,* 199–217.

Heider, F. (1958). *The psychology of interpersonal relations.* New York: Wiley.

Herbst, P. (1952). The measurement of family relationships. *Human Relations, 5,* 3–35.

Herbst, P. (1953). Analysis and measurement of a situation: The child in the family. *Human Relations, 6,* 113–140.

Herbst, P. (1965). Problems of theory and method in the integration of the behavioural sciences. *Human Relations, 18,* 351–359.

Hinde, R. (1987). *Individuals, relationships, and culture.* New York: Cambridge University Press.

Huston, T. L., Caughlin, J. P., Houts, R. M., Smith, S. E., & George, L. (2001). The connubial crucible: Newlywed years as predictors of marital delight, distress, and divorce. *Journal of Personality and Social Psychology, 80,* 237–252.

Huston, T. L., & Geis, G. (1993). In what ways do gender-related attributes and beliefs affect marriage? *Journal of Social Issues, 49,* 87–106.

Huston, T. L., & Houts, R. (1998). The psychological infrastructure of courtship and marriage: The role of personality and compatibility in the evolution of romantic relationships. In T. N. Bradbury (Ed.), *The developmental course of marital dysfunction* (pp. 114–151). New York: Cambridge University Press.

Huston, T. L., McHale, S. M., & Crouter, A. (1986). When the honeymoon's over: Changes in the marriage relationship over the first year. In R. Gilmour & S. Duck (Eds.), *Theoretical frameworks for personal relationships* (pp. 109–132). Hillsdale, NJ: Erlbaum.

Huston, T. L., & Rempel, J. (1989). Interpersonal attitudes, dispositions, and behavior in family and other close relationships. *Journal of Family Psychology, 3,* 177–198.

Huston, T. L., & Robins, E. (1982). Conceptual and methodological issues in studying close relationships. *Journal of Marriage and the Family, 44,* 901–925.

Huston, T. L., Robins, E., Atkinson, J., & McHale, S. (1987). Surveying the landscape of marital behavior: A behavioral self-report approach to studying marriage. In S. Oskamp (Ed.), *Family processes and problems: Social psychological aspects* (pp. 45–71). Beverly Hills, CA: Sage.

Huston, T. L., & Vangelisti, A. (1991). Socioemotional behavior and satisfaction in marital relationships: A longitudinal study. *Journal of Personality and Social Psychology, 61,* 721–733.

Huston, T. L., & Vangelisti, A. (1995). How parenthood affects marriage. In M. Fitzpatrick & A. Vangelisti (Eds.), *Perspectives on family communication* (pp. 147–176). Newbury Park, CA: Sage.

Johnson, M. P. (1991). Commitment to personal relationships. In W. H. Jones & D. Perlman (Eds.), *Advances in personal relationships* (Vol. 3, pp. 117–143). London: Jessica Kingsley.

Johnson, M. P. (1999). Personal, moral, and structural commitment to relationships: Experiences of choice and constraint. In W. H. Jones & J. M. Adams (Eds.), *Handbook of interpersonal commitment and relationship stability* (pp. 73–87). New York: Kluwer Academic-Plenum Press.

Johnson, M. P., Huston, T. L., Gaines, S. O., & Levinger, G. (1992). Patterns of married life among young couples. *Journal of Personal and Social Relationships, 9,* 343–364.

Karney B. R., & Bradbury, T. N. (1995). The longitudinal course of marital quality and stability: A review of theory, method, and research. *Psychology Bulletin, 118,* 3–34.

Kashy, D. A., & Grotevant, H. D. (1999). Methodological and data analytic advances in the study of interpersonal relationships: Introduction to the special issue. *Personal Relationships, 6,* 411–413.

Kayser, K. (1993). *When love dies: The process of marital disaffection.* New York: Guilford Press.

Kelley, H. H. (1979). *Personal relationships: Their structures and processes.* Hillsdale, NJ: Erlbaum.

Kelley, H. H. (1983). Epilogue. In H. H. Kelley, E. Berscheid, A. Christensen, J. H. Harvey, T. L. Huston, G. Levinger, E. McClintock, L. A. Peplau, & D. R. Peterson (Eds.), *Close relationships* (pp. 486–503). New York: Academic Press.

Kelley, H. H., Berscheid, E., Christensen, A., Harvey, J. H., Huston, T. L., Levinger, G., McClintock, E., Peplau, L. A., & Peterson, D. R. (1983). *Close relationships.* New York: Freeman.

Kenny, D. A., & Cook, W. (1999). Partner effects in relationship research: conceptual issues, analytic difficulties, and illustrations. *Personal Relationships, 6,* 433–458.

Kitson, G. C. (1992). *Portrait of divorce: Adjustment to marital breakdown.* New York: Guilford Press.

Kristol, N. D. (1996, February 11). Who needs love? In Japan, many couples don't. *New York Times,* pp. 1, 6.

Lamke, L. K. (1989). Marital adjustment among rural couples: The role of expressiveness. *Sex Roles, 21,* 579–590.

Lamm, H., Wiesmann, U., & Keller, K. (1998). Subjective determinants of attraction: Self-perceived causes of the rise and decline of liking, love, and being in love. *Personal Relationships, 5,* 91–104.

Larson, R., & Almeida, D. (1999). Emotional transmission in the daily lives of families: A new paradigm for studying family process. *Journal of Marriage and the Family, 67,* 5–20.

Larson, R., & Richards, M. H. (1994). *Divergent realities: The emotional lives of mothers, fathers, and adolescents.* New York: Basic Books.

Levinger, G. (1994). Figure versus ground: Micro- and macroperspectives on the social psychology of personal relationships. In R. Ether & R. Gilmour (Eds.), *Theoretical frameworks for personal relationships.* Hillsdale, NJ: Erlbaum.

Levinger, G., & Huston, T. L. (1990). The social psychology of marriage. In E. D. Fincham & T. N. Bradbury (Eds.), *The psychology of marriage: Conceptual, empirical, and applied perspectives* (pp. 19–58). New York: Guilford Press.

Levinger, G., & Rands, M. (1985). Compatibility in marriage and other close relationships. In W. Ickes (Ed.), *Compatible and incompatible relationships* (pp. 309–331). New York: Springer-Verlag.

Lewin, K. (1948). *Field theory in social science.* New York: Harper.

Locke, H. J., & Wallace, K. M. (1959). Short marital adjustment and prediction tests: Their reliability and validity. *Marriage and Family Living, 21,* 251–255.

MacDermid, S., Huston, T. L., & McHale, S. M. (1990). Changes in marriage associated with the transition to parenthood: Individual differences as a function of sex role attitudes and changes in the division of household labor. *Journal of Marriage and the Family, 52,* 475–486.

Malle, B. (1999). How people explain behavior: A new theoretical approach. *Personality and Social Psychology Review, 3,* 23–48.

Markman, H. J. (1981). Prediction of marital distress: A 5-year follow-up. *Journal of Consulting and Clinical Psychology, 49,* 760–762.

Markman, H. J., Floyd, F. J., Stanley, S. M., & Storaasli, R. D. (1988). Prevention of marital distress: A longitudinal investigation. *Journal of Consulting and Clinical Psychology, 56,* 210–217.

Markman, H. J., & Notarius, C. I. (1987). Coding marital and family interaction: Current status. In T. Jacob (Ed.), *Family interaction and psychopathology: Theories, methods, and findings* (pp. 325–390). New York: Plenum Press.

Marks, S. R., & MacDermid, S. M. (1996). Multiple roles and the self: A theory of role balance. *Journal of Marriage and the Family, 58,* 417–432.

McCall, G. J., & Simmons, J. L. (1978). *Identities and interactions* (Rev. ed.). New York: Free Press.

McHale, S. M., & Huston, T. L. (1984). Men and women as parents: Sex role orientations, employment, and parental roles with infants. *Child Development, 55,* 1349–1361.

Medrich, E., Roizen, J. A., Rubin, V., & Buckley, S. (1982). *The serious business of growing up: A study of children's lives outside school.* Berkeley: University of California Press.

Noller, P. (1984). *Nonverbal communication and marital interaction.* Elmsford, NY: Pergamon Press.

Noller, P., & Guthrie, D. (1991). Studying communication in marriage: An integration and critical evaluation. In W. H. Jones & D. Perlman (Eds.), *Advances in personal relationships* (Vol. 3, pp. 37–73). London: Jessica Kingsley.

Ouellette, J. A., & Wood, W. (1998). Habit and intention in everyday life: The multiple processes by which past behavior predicts future behavior. *Psychological Bulletin, 124,* 54–74.

Peplau, L. A. (1983). Roles and gender. In H. H. Kelley et al., *Close relationships* (pp. 220–264). New York: Freeman.

Reis, H. T., & Gable, S. L. (2000). Event sampling and other methods for studying daily experience. In H. T. Reis & C. M. Judd (Eds.), *Handbook of research methods in social and personality psychology* (pp. 190–222). New York: Cambridge University Press.

Robins, E. (1990). The study of interdependence in marriage. In F. D. Fincham & T. N. Bradbury (Eds.), *The psychology of marriage: Basic issues and applications* (pp. 59–86). New York: Guilford Press.

Schwarz, N. (1990). Assessing frequency reports of mundane behaviors: Contributions of cognitive psychology to questionnaire construction. In C. Hendrick & M. S. Clark (Eds.), *Research methods in personality and social psychology* (pp. 98–119). Newbury Park, CA: Sage.

Spanier, G. B. (1976). Measuring dyadic adjustment: New scales for assessing the quality of marriage and similar dyads. *Journal of Marriage and the Family, 38,* 15–38.

Sudman, S., Bradburn, N. M., & Schwarz, N. (1996). *Thinking about answers: The application of cognitive processes to survey methodology.* San Francisco: Jossey-Bass.

Surra, C. A., & Milardo, R. M. (1991). The social psychological context of developing relationships: Interactive and psychological networks. In W. H. Jones & D. Perlman (Eds.), *Advances in personal relationships* (Vol. 3, pp. 1–36). London: Jessica Kingsley.

Tallman, L., Gray, L. M., Kullberg, V., & Henderson, D. (1999). The intergenerational transmission of marital conflict: Testing a process model. *Social Psychology Quarterly, 62,* 219–239.

Terman, L. W., Buttenwieser, P., Ferguson, L. W., Johnson, W. B., & Wilson, D. P. (1938). *Psychological factors in marital happiness.* New York: McGraw-Hill.

Thompson, A., & Bolger, N. (1999). Emotional transmission in couples under emotional distress. *Journal of Marriage and the Family, 61,* 38–48.

Thompson, L., & Walker, A. J. (1982). The dyad as a unit of analysis: Conceptual and methodological issues. *Journal of Marriage and the Family, 44,* 889–900.

Waller, W. W. (1938). *The family: A dynamic interpretation.* New York: The Cordon Company.

Wegner, D. M., & Vallacher, R. R. (1986). Action identification. In R. M. Sorrentino & F. T. Higgins (Eds.), *Handbook of motivation and cognition* (pp. 550–581). New York: Guilford Press.

Wills, T. A., Weiss, R. L., & Patterson, G. R. (1974). A behavioral analysis of the determinants of marital satisfaction. *Journal of Consulting and Clinical Psychology, 42,* 802–811.

Getting Dinosaurs to Dance: Community Collaborations as Applications of Ecological Theory

Daniel F. Perkins, Theresa M. Ferrari,
Martin A. Covey, and Joanne G. Keith

Abstract

This article connects human ecological theory to the practice of collaborative relationships. Findings from a study of community coalitions in Michigan are used to highlight common elements of effective coalitions. The case is made for participation of home economists and human ecologists in collaborative efforts on behalf of children, youth, and families.

Over the last several decades, significant social, economic, and technological changes have affected America's children, youth, and families and have contributed to a fragmentation of community life (Coleman, 1987; Comer, 1984; Gardner, 1989; Hodgkinson, 1989). As a result the naturally occurring networks and linkages—individuals, families, schools, and other social systems within a community—that have traditionally provided a *safety net* may no longer exist. The literature in many fields (i.e., education, business, child care, organizational development, public affairs, health, and human services) suggests that community collaborative efforts are both feasible and desirable as a strategy to improve the status and future well-being of children, youth, and their families (Benard, 1991; Carnegie Council on Adolescent Development, 1992; Dryfoos, 1990; Ellison & Barbour,

1992; Hamburg, 1992; Hodgkinson, 1989; Kagan, 1989; National Commission on Children, 1991; Schorr, 1988; W. T. Grant Foundation, 1988). Collaboration has been around for a long time, in various sectors and in different forms. However, there appears to be a gap in the research base about collaboration. Keith, McPherson, and Smith-Sreen (1992) explain why this may occur:

> From a scientist's point of view, actions taken in communities are often dictated by insufficient data, and a stronger research base is needed. At the same time, research often proceeds too slowly for practitioners and families [who are] facing pressing issues. Recommendations for action, not research, are strongly advocated. (p. 40)

The purpose of this article, therefore, is to connect the theory and the practice of collaborative relationships. The questions "why collaboration" and "why an ecological approach to collaboration" are addressed as well as the relevance of developing collaborative relationships for professionals in home economics/human ecology.

Why Collaboration?

As suggested above, collaboration is not a new idea but perhaps one whose time has come again. The recent upsurge of interest in collaboration (Keith et al., 1993) has prompted Lerner (1993) to refer to the 1990s as "the decade of community coalitions for children" (p. 9). It is generally agreed that comprehensive problem-solving strategies at the local level will yield long-term solutions to complex problems. Therefore, one reason for community collaboration is to bring members of organizations together to systematically solve problems that cannot be solved by one group alone. In other words, the *whole is greater than the sum of the parts.* Although this is easily *said,* experience shows that it is not easily *done.* In fact, it has been described as being as difficult as "teaching dinosaurs to do ballet" (Schlechty in DeBevoise, 1986, p. 12). It may be that collaborating requires a shift in one's value system, from thinking and working individualistically to thinking and working holistically (Astroth, 1991; Kagan, 1989). Successful collaborations are hard work, are time consuming, and require participants to put the needs of children, youth, and families above the needs of institutions (Keith et al., 1993). It is the thesis of this article that communities able to do this are not only making wise investments in the present and the future but also maximizing the diminishing resources that are available.

Leadership in collaborative efforts was a vision of the early leaders of home economics and remains central to the mission of the profession today (Brown & Paolucci, 1979). Home economists can serve as "catalysts to bring together coalitions to build public support for investment in youth" (Meszaros, 1993). The integrative, interdisciplinary nature of the profession provides an organizing framework for establishing collaborative relationships.

Definitions

The terms collaboration and coalition are used in many ways and have a variety of definitions; sometimes they are even used interchangeably. Astroth (1991) suggested a continuum moving from communication at one end, through cooperation and coalition, to collaboration at the other

end. A coalition's intent is to address a specific need and then disband, but collaborations are formalized organizational relationships which involve a long-term commitment to address critical and complex social issues of wide concern. Collaboration/coalition is characterized by formal relationships that exist with commonly defined mission, structure, or planning effort. Whereas, cooperation is characterized by informal relationships without these common characteristics (Mattessich & Monsey, 1992). In addition, collaboration connotes a more durable and pervasive relationship, as it brings previously separated organizations into a new structure with full commitment to a common mission. In order to be more inclusive, this article uses the terms coalition and collaboration interchangeably. Thus, *a coalition or collaboration is broadly defined here as an effort that unites and empowers individuals and organizations to accomplish collectively what they could not accomplish independently* (Kagan & Rivera, 1991).

Why an Ecological Approach?

An ecological model is particularly well-suited to the study of collaborative relationships in the community. This theory looks beyond the individual to the surrounding environment for questions and explanations about human behavior and development. It not only provides a way to describe and explain development but offers a framework for analyzing how to "make the world a better place for children and families" (Garbarino, 1982, p. 31). Studies using an ecological model have shown support for its usefulness in designing programs and in policy formulation (Bubolz & Sontag, 1993).

Human Ecological Theory

Bronfenbrenner (1979, 1986) proposed a model consisting of multiple, interdependent levels that interact with and influence individual behavior and development. The levels are envisioned as a series of concentric circles, with the individual at the center of the model (see Figure 10.3). The microsystem refers to an immediate setting where an individual experiences and creates day-to-day reality, such as the family, the schoolroom, and the neighborhood. The exosystem level influences development because it affects some part of the microsystem (i.e., parents' workplace, school administration, and the community) but does not include individual participation. The macrosystem level is most removed from an individual, yet these external forces influence family life. The macrosystem is the particular culture or subculture (e.g., media, government, and economic conditions) in which the other systems operate. Also, this level would include cultural beliefs and values such as those relating to community collaboration. Values are reflected in policies and regulations regarding issues such as building use, decision making, and funding in communities.

Bronfenbrenner refers to the connection between two microsystems as a *mesosystem.* For example, the overlap of the family and school settings creates a mesosystem. The stronger, more

positive, and more diverse the links between settings, the more powerful and beneficial the resulting mesosystem will be as an influence on the child's development (Garbarino, 1982). The characteristics of the child, family, and the community may operate individually as well as interacting with one another to account for how a particular situation affects a given child, family, or community.

Therefore, the mesosystem, representing the connections between different levels of the environment (beyond microsystems) is shown as a *slice* of the total environment. Just how these levels of the environment exert their influence is complex. Community influences may affect the child indirectly through their impact on the family (Bronfenbrenner, Moen, & Garbarino, 1984). Taken together, these layers recognize the individual and the interconnectedness among, between, and within human systems.

Another dimension, which Bronfenbrenner (1986) refers to as the *chronosystem,* recognizes that development within the person and within the environment occurs over time. Thus, it is necessary to examine specific life transitions as well as the cumulative effects of these changes throughout life. The arrow pointing to the right in the model represents future events, implying the need to examine "the influence on the person's development of changes (and continuities) over time in the environments in which the person is living" (p. 724). These transitions include normative (puberty, school entry, retirement) and non-normative (accidental death, severe illness, receiving an inheritance) changes that occur throughout the life-span of the individual. The left-pointing arrow in the model represents the cumulative element of historical processes. This signifies that present experience is being mediated by history. As Demos (1986) states, "our present [family] arrangements are best construed as a complex and heavily layered precipitate of our entire social history" (p. 38).

While one's disciplinary training may tend to suggest the individual or family as the unit of analysis, these ecological concepts apply to the community level as well. Communities, and community groups, have a history and a life

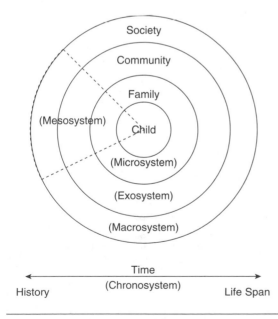

Figure 10.3   Human Ecological Model

SOURCE: Adapted from Bronfenbrenner, 1978, 1986.

course. Societal norms guide group structure, function, and leadership. A community or a group does not exist in isolation but interacts with other players within the community; with individuals, families, and other groups, as well as with other communities. The adage—Think globally, Act locally—captures this concept.

Community Application

Communities are plagued by complex problems that do not respond to "cookbook" solutions. This complexity suggests that it is necessary to have a model that is integrative and interconnected, one that provides the whole picture and a focus on development in context. Community collaboration is about connecting systems at all levels to influence child and family, and consequently, community outcomes. A collaborative effort, therefore, is an ecological approach to problem solving. A coalition is not an end in itself, but rather a *means* of creating community change. The collaboration process empowers communities to address their issues and problems. Thus, in this collaborative process, the community collectively creates its own development. Indeed, if the best programs are created by the community and not superimposed from the outside (Search Institute, 1993), then collaboration is an orientation *every* community must adopt.

Communities do not need fragmented services. Viewing collaborative efforts from an ecological perspective enables community organizations to get an idea where they fit and how their reciprocal relationships affect other sectors, families, and individuals. The collaborative, ecological approach challenges the notion that families must somehow fail before they can receive assistance (Meszaros, 1993). The focus of a human development collaboration would be one of prevention, an expansion of the safety net for children, youth, and their families (Keith et al., 1993). The challenge for America's communities is to create a supportive and nurturing climate that fosters positive development for *all* members of society.

At the community level, a model has been articulated by Hodgkinson (1989) in relation to community services offered to clients. In Hodgkinson's interdependency model (see Figure 10.4), the client is the main focus of service organizations, and there is reciprocal interaction among them. Thus, service providers form coalitions to begin communicating and working with each other.

However, from a human ecological perspective, Hodgkinson omitted several important aspects of the system. First the role that each client, defined as either a family or a child, has to contribute to the process suggests that the arrows in the model need to point in both directions. Interaction between the family or child and the community organizations empowers individuals and allows them to be producers of their own development (Lerner, 1976, 1982). Second, Hodgkinson omits religious institutions and the voluntary sector, including youth-serving organizations and service clubs. Finally, he has also excluded the role of indirect influences such as industry, business, and media. Recognizing these limitations, Keith and her colleagues adapted Hodgkinson's model and created a comprehensive ecological model that demonstrates the interaction of families and/or individuals with a variety of services and organizations, as well as the interactions of these organizations with each other (see Figure 10.5). This model provides the theoretical base for the Community Coalitions in Action project outlined below.

Community Coalitions in Action

Although community-based collaborative efforts on behalf of children, youth, and families have existed for a long time, recent community efforts have arisen to address 1990s circumstances in a variety of ways. Building upon the human ecological model (Bronfenbrenner, 1979, 1986), the Community Coalitions in Action project (CCIA) was established at Michigan State University to conduct research and outreach related to collaboration (Keith et al., 1993). One of the purposes of the project was to identify, document, and evaluate

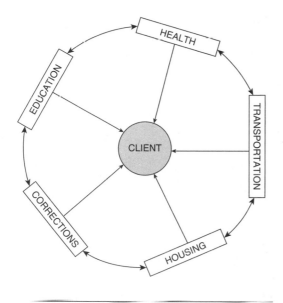

Figure 10.4   Hodgkinson's Interdependency
Model of Service Organizations

SOURCE: Hodgkinson, 1989, Fig. 2, p. 1.

a wide range of collaborative efforts on behalf of Michigan's children, youth, and families. As Bronfenbrenner (1979) suggested, the research was designed to examine the interaction, interdependency, and interconnection among coalitions and coalition members within the natural context of their community.

Procedures

Quantitative and qualitative data were collected using telephone interviews, pilot site visits, a survey questionnaire, and in-depth interviews. First, over 100 coalitions were identified through a brief survey. From this sample, telephone interviews were conducted with contact persons from 35 coalitions. Based upon variability in geographic location, economic status of the community, and the coalition's organizing framework, 13 sites were selected for follow-up visits to gather both quantitative and qualitative data. Qualitative data analyses were conducted on the in-depth interviews of key members from the

13 coalitions using ETHNOGRAPH (Seidel, Kjolseth, & Seymour, 1985). A search/cluster process, which uses keywords to identify similar concepts found across interviews, was used to formulate an analysis and to highlight major themes. In addition to the interviews, simple checklist questionnaires were given to key members of the 13 coalitions. These checklists identified certain key variables that were important to their collaborative efforts. Frequencies and means were calculated on responses from checklists. The results reported in this article represent only a portion of the data gathered by this study. The information presented below was gleaned from the in-depth interviews of coalition members.

Findings

Key members of coalitions were asked to cooperatively draw an ecomap to identify members of the community who were involved in their collaborative efforts (see Figure 10.6). An ecomap is a visual representation of relationships that exist within a larger context (Lauffer, 1982). In this study, the coalition was placed at the center of the ecomap and other individuals, groups, organizations, and agencies were added to represent their direct or indirect involvement with the coalition.

Collaborative Typology. Based upon the community sector which was the motivating force for initiation, leadership, and involvement, the data revealed the following typologies: a) health and human service agency collaborations, b) affiliation group collaborations, c) education collaborations, and d) comprehensive community collaborations with citizen input. Once the typology was identified, the organizational system that characterized its structure was determined by using definitions adapted from Clifford, Bubolz, and Sontag (1992). The type of community sector involvement and the organizational system influenced the focus of collaboratives and how they functioned in carrying out their goals (see Table 10.5).

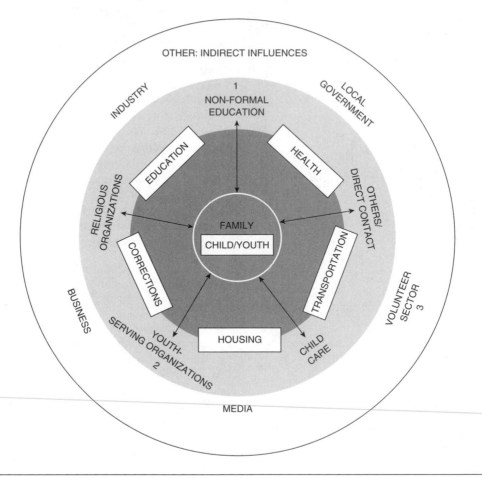

Figure 10.5   Keith's Comprehensive Ecological Model

SOURCE: Keith, Perkins, Zongqing, Clifford, Gilmore, & Townsend, 1993, Fig. 1, p. 6.

Table 10.5   Definitions of Organizational Systems

Formal systems are characterized by the existence of a hierarchical structure, explicitly defined roles, and fixed procedures and rules.

Semiformal systems function with some planned procedures and rules but participants have an equal voice in decisions and may change rules and roles.

Informal systems are characterized by functional exchanges between participants arising from needs, desires, or personal interests; implicit expectations versus formalized rules; and undefined roles.

SOURCE: Community support systems, human values, and resource management in a family-farm ecosystem. In K. Root, J. Heffernan, G. Summers, & J. Stewart (Eds.), *Conference Proceedings of the North Central Regional Conference on the Rural Family, the Rural Community, and Economic Restructuring* (#RRD 159, pp. 193–204). Ames, IA: North Central Regional Center for Rural Development.

These four categories of collaborative efforts are described below.

Health and human service agency collaborations. Groups in this category most frequently began with an initial informal gathering of a small nucleus of representatives from two or three health and human service agencies. Representatives from the religious institutions, courts, and public schools or universities joined forces with health and human service agencies to accomplish mutually agreed-upon goals. These coalitions tended to focus collaborative efforts on developing programs aimed at prevention rather than treatment, on fostering cooperation among agencies to disseminate information, and on preventing duplication of direct services. These collaborations began, for the most part, as informal systems; however, they eventually developed into semiformal frameworks for information dissemination and for service delivery.

Affiliation group collaborations. Either religious or ethnic groups initiated these collaborative efforts and held leadership positions in them. These groups were joined by representatives from the schools, health and human service agencies, the courts, and private businesses. Coalitions in this category were broad-based, encompassing volunteers from various community sectors who were directly involved with children, youth, and families. Many of these volunteers supported the work of the coalition indirectly. This type of coalition had substantial support from the business sector as well as the support of several funding agencies. The focus was toward community service "to promote mutual respect, understanding, dialogue, and cooperation between the minority communities and the non-minority community" (Interview notes, 9/4/91). These coalitions operated as all-inclusive semiformal systems with resources exchanged both among coalition members and members of the community. Appreciation of diversity and personal volunteer involvement at all levels were key components in the effective functioning of affiliation group collaborations.

Education collaborations. Groups in this category were focused on schools and school-age children and youth. This type of coalition was comprised mostly of school personnel and community business people. The major goal of these collaborations was assessment of the needs of students relative to skill development for future employment. These coalitions not only had formal organization characteristics but also characteristics of semiformal systems with respect to decision-making procedures.

Comprehensive community collaborations with citizen input. Members of these coalitions were simply concerned citizens; their volunteer participation was not due to affiliation with any particular group or organization. Their participation was made possible through administrators in the workplace who approved released time for involvement in community activities. Whereas the leadership of these coalitions relied on an existing youth development leader (e.g., Cooperative Extension agents, YMCA staff), perhaps the distinguishing element of this type of coalition was the existence of a committed group of people working to find solutions to critical needs. The focus of these coalitions tended to be based on identified needs from some form of assessment (i.e., town meeting, surveys). The coalition sought funds for specific projects as needs were identified. Programs included such things as substance abuse prevention, education regarding family functions, employment skill development, and parental involvement with children and their communities.

Common Elements of Coalitions

The common elements were derived from in-depth interviews with key members from 13 coalitions. The elements were considered *common* if they were observed in more than three of the coalitions.

Because collaborative efforts depend on people, there is no exact formula for developing an effective coalition (Benard, 1989). However, certain elements were found in a majority of the coalitions examined in this study. More than half

Figure 10.6   Ecomap of Community Coalition Drawn by Coalition Members

SOURCE: Keith, Perkins, Zongqing, Clifford, Gilmore, & Townsend, 1993, Fig. 6, p. 22.

of the coalitions attributed a significant part of their effectiveness in the community to *strong leadership* within their groups. Specific traits of successful leaders included strong determination and optimism. They had the ability to seek resources, to act as a facilitator, and to recruit the right people.

Unity and communication were also important common elements in the overall effectiveness of the coalitions. *Unity* refers to the strong sense of solidarity and togetherness that coalition members felt toward one another; over half of the coalitions assessed this element as an integral part of their effectiveness. Effective *communication*, through informal means, was another common element identified by more than half of the coalitions as important to their functioning. Networking, defined as an informal way of sharing information among coalition members, provided a sense of closeness. Networking was cited as the major means of communication among coalition members.

The *involvement* of *churches and citizen volunteers* was found to be a common element among many of the coalitions. Thus, locality, the sense of connectedness to the people served and commitment to the community, was another element that contributed to coalition effectiveness. Many coalitions agreed that the target group, served by the coalition, must have the final say in defining its own problem. Locality also meant that a coalition must establish itself as an authority on the issues it was attempting to address.

Open-mindedness, trust, enjoyable involvement, personal commitment, and willingness to volunteer were *traits of coalition members* contributing to the effectiveness of the coalition. These characteristics were important because collaboration is a social process and attention to *people* issues can determine success (Benard, 1989).

Distinctive Elements

A *distinctive element* refers to that feature that was not shared by any other coalition. These elements may shed new light on unique factors contributing to the successful development and functioning of collaborative efforts. Three such elements are described below.

Autonomous funding. In most situations outside funding was looked upon favorably and even regarded as essential to a coalition's effectiveness. However, one coalition, formed on behalf of youth at risk, had a different philosophy on outside funding. This group believed that reliance on major outside grants, although assuring the continuation of the work on a year-to-year basis, would reduce volunteer motivation and would encourage dependency on outside money. When outside money runs out,

sometimes programs die even though they were intended to be long-term and sustainable. The coalition members in this case did not want to downplay the importance of outside funding. Rather, they asserted that funding should be sought in such a way that goals and interests of the coalition are not ignored. Funding was considered the means to accomplish the goals of this collaborative effort, not as an end in itself.

Media. The effect of the mass media on the public has long been recognized. In business, intentional use of mass media advertising is considered vital to success. However, in human services, intentional use of mass media to help achieve participation in the formation of goals and objectives is not a common practice. One of the coalitions interviewed in the CCIA project attributed some of its effectiveness to the publicity and support the coalition received from the local media. In one coalition member's words, the local newspaper "played an important role in alerting the community to the goals and efforts of the coalition to work . . . collaboratively in solving problems of youth." The attention received from the media increased awareness among citizens, youth, and families; and, in addition, the publicity established the authority and legitimacy of the coalition's work.

Community problem definition. People *are* aware of their own needs and problems. Thus, using the target audience as a resource to define its own problems is often fundamental to conducting a needs assessment and to building a successful coalition. Moreover, using a community to define its own problems can empower and motivate the members of that community to act. For example, a Native American coalition found that its leadership needed to come from within. A sense of mission and pride generated by leadership was one of the most valuable assets of this collaboration. This was their land, their problem, and their future. In their opinion, "the assistance and the programs that came from outside the community and from outside agencies were doomed to failure" (Interview notes, 6/28/91).

This coalition's strong sentiment demonstrates the fact that mobilization of local people to address their own problems can be crucial to successful collaboration.

Community Application of Research Findings

This study was an initial attempt to document and to understand collaborative efforts as they exist in their own context. Common and unique elements associated with effective collaborative efforts were outlined. Thus, models of community collaboration have evolved from this action research.

Continued research is needed to document the successes and struggles of collaborative relationships but with a new research paradigm—one that adopts an empowerment orientation (Vaines, 1993) where 11 communities are not only receiving information but also conveying to universities their needs and working together to address those needs (Keith, McPherson, & Smith-Sreen, 1992). The CCIA project team used the understanding gained about collaborative efforts to inform community outreach efforts. Two examples of this integration of research and outreach follow.

Coalition training. The Alliance for Community Empowerment (ACE) program was developed to provide community teams with training in the skills that groups need to form and maintain collaborative efforts. The integral involvement of youth in the community team is a distinctive feature that enhances ownership of the process. As a result of this training, teams from four community groups have begun to focus on identified community needs.

Technical assistance. What happens during the initial phase of a collaborative effort can be crucial to its eventual success. CCIA project staff have met directly with community groups to help them clarify their mission and develop strategies for implementing their goals. This assistance is tailored to the needs expressed by the group and to their particular stage of development. The staff members act in concert with coalition group members, not as "experts" who have the answer.

Implications for Home Economics and Human Ecology

Participation in collaborative efforts positions home economists/human ecologists in significant roles for resolving the issues facing children, youth, and families. Brown & Paolucci (1979) stated that home economists need to have "direct involvement in [the process of] seeking needed social and cultural change through participation in social action groups and assisting in the formulation of social policy . . ." (p. 36). The mix of philosophy, theory, and practice suggests a variety of roles for home economists/human ecologists in establishing collaborative relationships. The following suggestions may help get the collaborative *dinosaur* to *dance.*

Learn Some New Steps

Consider using the ecomap as a tool to identify current and potential working relationships in the community. Identify agencies, and specific people within those organizations, that could collaborate on an identified community issue. Professionals can adopt the attitude that community collaboration is a reciprocal relationship: In other words, professionals have as much to learn as they have to offer.

Get Out on the Dance Floor

Although community needs are urgent, careful planning is essential; "instant collaboration may bring instant gratification, . . . [but] it is not likely to bring lasting success" (Guthrie & Guthrie, 1991, p. 22). Home economists and human ecologists can stress the need for comprehensive programs. Guthrie & Guthrie (1991, p. 18) point out that "to move from program-driven to child-centered services, we also need to improve our understanding of children's needs, monitor them over time, and take a broader contextual view of how to help." The interdisciplinary knowledge base of home economics/human ecology relates directly to society's most pressing needs. As professionals who have an understanding of the multiple contexts of human development, we can pinpoint critical developmental transitions, identify potential target audiences, and suggest promising program delivery strategies. Assistance can be given to communities to assess critical needs from an ecological perspective. Although professionals may know what the needs are likely to be, community ownership of the process and, therefore, the results is essential to creating change.

Choose Your Partners

The theory and practice of collaboration has implications for the professional preparation of students in home economics and human ecology. New professionals need to enter the community with the knowledge, attitudes, and skills essential to work with diverse groups. Are faculty and programs geared to educate students according to a collaborative, ecological paradigm? The answer to that question varies, but opportunities can be created for student involvement to bridge the community and the classroom. Certainly the *process* of collaboration is as important as content knowledge. The leadership, communication, decision making, conflict resolution, and social and interpersonal skills that are important for effective collaboration can be facilitated in formal and nonformal learning situations. The process of skill building can continue also through mentoring relationships with experienced collaborators and through ongoing professional development.

The Dance of Collaboration: Putting Theory Into Practice

Human ecology principles must be more widely used as a basis for human action by professionals,

policy makers, and citizens at large in order to achieve changes that are needed for human betterment, [for] realization of universal values, and for improved quality of human life and quality of environment, both locally and globally. (Bubolz & Sontag, 1993, p. 443)

Although dramatic social and economic changes have an impact on society, Bronfenbrenner (1983) maintains that families are still the most powerful and economical units for making and keeping human beings human. Supportive communities are essential for creating systems that nurture families. This ecological relationship is captured by a quote from the W. T. Grant Foundation's report, *The Forgotten Half* (1988):

Responsive communities, along with good schools and strong families, form a triad that supports youth in their passage to work and adult life. Our country has always held that good families create good communities. Now we also need to work on the reverse—that good communities build strong families. (p. 49)

An understanding of ecological theory can lead home economists/human ecologists to form collaborative relationships in the community to prevent problems and to create solutions for the situations facing children, youth, and families.

Responsive professionals can *make a difference; they can help dinosaurs learn to dance.*

Notes

The first three authors are all Ph.D. candidates in the Department of Family and Child Ecology, College of Human Ecology, Michigan State University. Perkins is Project Manager, Community Coalitions in Action. Ferrari is Research Assistant and Extension educator, University of Maine Cooperative Extension. Covey is Research Assistant and Assistant Pastor, Faith Wesleyan Church, Lansing. Dr. Keith is Professor and Extension Specialist, Department of Family and Child Ecology, College of Human Ecology, Michigan State University, and Project Director, Community Coalitions in Action.

The Community Coalitions in Action project is funded by the Michigan Agricultural Experiment Station Project No. 3306 and is housed at the Institute for Children, Youth, and Families, Michigan State University.

The authors would like to acknowledge the many Michigan State University students, Extension educators, and faculty who conducted interviews and provided support to this project. The authors would also like to thank Francisco Villarruel for his review and helpful suggestions during the preparation of this manuscript.

References

Astroth, K. A. (1991, Fall). Getting serious about strategic alliances: Conceptualizing the collaboration process. *Journal of Extension, 29*, 8–10.

Benard, B. (1989). Working together: Principles of effective collaboration. *Illinois Prevention Forum, 10*(2), 4–9.

Benard, B. (1991). *Fostering resiliency in kids: Protective factors in the family, school, and community.* Portland, OR: Northwest Regional Educational Laboratory, Western Regional Center for Drug-Free Schools and Communities, Far West Laboratory.

Bronfenbrenner, U. (1979). *The ecology of human development: Experiments by nature and design.* New York: Cambridge University Press.

Bronfenbrenner, U. (1983). Beyond policies without people: An ecological perspective on child and family policy. In E. Zigler (Ed.), *Children, families, and government. Perspectives on American social policy.* New York: Cambridge University Press.

Bronfenbrenner, U. (1986). Ecology of the family as a context for human development: Research perspectives. *Developmental Psychology, 22,* 723–742.

Bronfenbrenner, U., Moen, P., & Garbarino, J. (1984). Child, family, and community. In R. P. Parke (Ed.), *Review of child development research* (vol. 7, pp. 283–328). Chicago: University of Chicago Press.

Brown, M., & Paolucci, B. (1979). *Home economics: A definition.* Washington, DC: American Home Economics Association.

Bubolz, M. M., & Sontag, M. S. (1993). Human ecology theory. In P. G. Boss, W. J. Doherty, R. LaRossa, W. R. Schumm, & S. K. Steinmetz (Eds.), *Sourcebook of family theory and methods* (pp. 419-448). New York: Plenum.

Carnegie Council on Adolescent Development. (1992). *A matter of time: Risk and opportunity in the nonschool hours.* New York: Carnegie Corporation.

Clifford, M. C., Bubolz, M. M., & Sontag, M. S. (1992). Community support system, human values, and resource management in a family-farm ecosystem. In K. Root, J. Hefferman, G. Summers, & J. Stewart (Eds.), *Conference Proceedings of the North Central Regional Conference on the Rural Family, the Rural Community, and Economic Restructuring (#RRD 159,* pp. 193–204). Ames, IA: North Central Regional Center for Rural Development.

Coleman, J. (1987). Families and schools. *Educational Researcher, 16,* 32–38.

Comer, J. (1984). Home-school relationships as they affect the academic success of children. *Education and Urban Society, 16,* 323–337.

DeBevoise, W. (1986). Collaboration: Some principles of bridgework. *Educational Leadership, 44*(2), 9–12.

Demos, J. (1986). *Past, present, and personal: The family and the life course in American history.* New York: Oxford University Press.

Dryfoos, J. G. (1990). *Adolescents at risk: Prevalence and prevention.* New York: Oxford University Press.

Ellison, C., & Barbour, N. (1992). Changing child care systems through collaborative efforts: Challenges for the 1990s. *Child & Youth Care Forum, 21,* 299–316.

Garbarino, J. (1982). *Children and families in the social environment.* New York: Aldine.

Gardner, S. (1989). Failure by fragmentation. *California Tomorrow, 4*(4), 19–25.

Guthrie, G. P., & Guthrie, L. F. (1991). Streamlining interagency collaboration for youth at risk. *Educational Leadership, 49*(l), 17–22.

Hamburg, D. A. (1992). *Today's children: Creating a future for a generation in crisis.* New York: Times Books.

Hodgkinson, H. L. (1989). *The same client: The demographics of education and service delivery systems.* Washington, DC: Institute for Educational Leadership.

Kagan, S. L. (1989). The care and education of America's young children: At the brink of a paradigm shift? In F. J. Machiarola & A. Gartner (Eds.), *Caring for America's children* (pp. 70–83). New York: Academy of Political Science.

Kagan, S. L., & Rivera, A. M. (1991). Collaboration in early child care and education: What can and should we expect? *Young Children, 47*(1), 51–56.

Keith, J. G., McPherson, M. L., & Smith-Sreen, P. (1992, July). *Shaping the futures of families: The human ecological perspective.* Paper presented at the International Federation for Home Economics, Hanover, Germany.

Keith, J. G., Perkins, D. F., Zongqing, Z., Clifford, M. A., Gilmore, B., & Townsend, M. Z. (1993). *Building and maintaining community coalitions on behalf of children. youth and families.* Research Report 529. East Lansing: Michigan State University Agricultural Experiment Station.

Lauffer, A. (1982). *Assessment tools: For practitioners, managers, and trainers.* Beverly Hills, CA: Sage.

Lerner, R. M. (1976). *Concepts and theories of human development.* Reading: Addison Wesley.

Lerner, R. M. (1982). Children and adolescents as producers of their own development *Developmental Review, 2,* 342–370.

Lerner, R. M. (1993, June). Investment in youth: The role of home economics in enhancing the life chances of America's children. *AHF-4 Monograph Series, 1,* 9–34.

Mattessich, P. W., & Monsey, B. R. (1992). *Collaboration: What makes it work?* St. Paul, MN: Amherst H. Wilder Foundation.

Meszaros, P. S. (1993, June). *The 21st century imperative: A collaborative, ecological investment in youth.* Commemorative lecture delivered at the American Home Economics Association, Orlando, FL.

National Commission on Children. (1991). *Beyond rhetoric: A new American agenda for children and families.* Washington, DC: Author.

Schorr, L. B. (1988). *Within our reach: Breaking the cycle of disadvantage.* New York: Doubleday.

Search Institute. (1993, May). Reaching vulnerable youth: Keys and roadblocks to success. *Strengthening Our Capacity to Care Evaluation Bulletin.* (Available from Search Institute, 700 S. Third St., Suite 210, Minneapolis, MN 55415)

Seidel, J. V., Kjolseth, R., & Seymour, E. (1985). *The ethnograph.* Corvallis, OR: Qualis Research Associates.

Vaines, E. (1993). An empowerment orientation for home economics. *Home Economics FORUM, 6*(2), 21–26, 29.

William T. Grant Foundation Commission on Work, Family, and Citizenship. (1988). *The forgotten half: Pathways to success for America's youth and young families.* Washington, DC: Author.

11

DISCUSSION AND CONCLUSIONS

OVERVIEW OF DEVELOPMENTS IN FAMILY THEORY

In the first chapter of this book, you were introduced to Canon and Judge. As you learned, Canon uses a scientific research process that incorporates the systematic integration and testing of theory into her observations of the world. This process, although similar to the kind of knowledge development process that Judge and all of us use in everyday life, differs from it in a number of important ways. First, the systematic linking of empirical study and theoretical explanation as a way to discover and know the world is characterized by its public nature. Second, clarity in definition and communication of all ideas is fundamental. Third, all concepts and their relationships must be testable in the empirical world. Fourth, there is conscious effort to keep personal and other biases out of the research process, or to state them clearly so that they can be assessed and integrated into the process.

Although other theoretical perspectives exist in the field, the theories described throughout this book are central to the work of researchers such as Canon. Indeed, they describe much of the theoretical landscape in family science and

have much to say about the state of family science as a field of study. As you will recall, theorizing was described as a process of systematically developing and organizing ideas to explain phenomena. In all disciplines, theory development serves the common goal of increasing understanding of the subject matter. With regard to our own disciplines, the theories and readings in this book provide examples of the development and testing of theoretical perspectives on family phenomena.

White and Klein (2002) suggest that theory development occurs in two distinct stages. The first is a formative stage during which basic metaphors, key propositions, and understandings develop. The formative stage is followed by a refinement stage during which theory is tested, applied, criticized, and potentially refined. The ultimate achievement of theoretical concepts may be viewed as their ascendancy to the level of *canonical concept,* which is any construct that comes to consistently guide thinking in a field of knowledge (Silverman, 1993). Canonical concepts are so accepted as to remain largely unchallenged in their fields. For example, evolutionary concepts have risen to such a level in biology, as has the concept of developmental stages in human development. As we have indicated, social learning theory has had a similar level of impact extended across many subdisciplines in the areas of family science and human development.

The scholarship included here clearly suggests that the theories we have been discussing generally lie somewhere between an initial formative stage and existence as canonical concepts within the field of family science. A number of the readings included in this book provide examples of direct tests of theory and include scholars' assessments of the utility of theory in describing family phenomena. Others offer thoughtful reflections on the application of theory to an area of family life. These scholarly activities are at the heart of White and Klein's (2002) concept of a refinement stage of theory development. In general, as a field, we have begun to heed the calls of earlier scholarship to develop research that is theoretically grounded. There is still much to do in this regard, however.

As we consider the status of theory in family science, it is apparent that the field experienced a stage of substantial theory formation in the mid- to late 20th century. Many of our present theories reflect a formative tradition grounded in the work of scholars in the 1950s, 1960s, and 1970s. Those decades may ultimately come to be considered as a "golden age" of theory formation in family science. White and Klein (2002) suggest such periods are characterized by various aspects of theory construction identified by Hill (1971). These include deducing family theories from more general theories, borrowing theoretical constructs from other fields, integrating and expanding theoretical concepts, and combining partial theories into more integrative and complete "whole" theories. For example, family science liberally drew from theory in other fields to develop new and exciting perspectives on family phenomena. Family systems theory, social exchange theory, and social conflict theory are all examples of family theories originally developed during the mid- to late twentieth century that built directly on concepts from sociology, while social learning theory and life-span developmental theory reflect similar progress building on

concepts from psychology. Social conflict theory, feminist theory, and symbolic interactionism dealt directly with political and social issues of interest during this age of theory formation in family science, each moving to a greater focus on family phenomena in more recent decades.

As indicated, the more recent family science scholarship of the late twentieth and early twenty-first century indicates a move to the refinement described by White and Klein (2002). A search of family science scholarship during these years reflects little in the way of new theory formation. Rather, the field has been much more preoccupied with application of previously developed theory to various family issues. Much as children with new toys, family scientists have spent their time playing with the theories that rose to prominence in the earlier period. These theories offered opportunities for new approaches to studying and understanding family phenomena.

In many ways, the state of theory in family science today, then, is clearly reflected in the nature of the readings included here. As a field, we continue to apply theory to individuals and families. As a result, we are developing better understandings of theories themselves and their usefulness to both scholars and practitioners. In the set of readings in this book, several theories have come to be more frequently applied to various issues in family life and, as a result, have guided both academic ruminations and applied practice in those areas. To illustrate, there are countless examples of both researchers and practitioners operating from a social conflict perspective when addressing issues such as family violence. Work on issues such as mate selection and the transition to parenthood demonstrate a strong social exchange perspective. And issues like grandparents raising grandchildren rely heavily on a family life course perspective.

THOUGHTS ON FUTURE DIRECTIONS

Building on our understanding of the current state of theory in family science, we think it is also important to share with you some thoughts on future directions for theory in our field. It is, indeed, difficult to be original with this because the kinds of issues that have been discussed by scholars for many years still need attention (see White & Klein, 2002). In one sense, however, there is an important lesson here (for us, too!). It is that scientific progress is nothing if it is not systematic. It is simply not possible, we have come to learn, to "hurry up" a field of study. As individuals with a high regard and strong respect for the canons of scientific inquiry, this should come as no surprise. In addition, prognostication is always a very iffy enterprise. But, onward and upward we go with a few thoughts about the more immediate future of theory development in family science.

As we mentioned a number of times previously, theory development and application are ongoing processes with extensive implications for future scholars and practitioners. The work included here, as well as countless other pieces worthy of inclusion as exemplars of the various theoretical perspectives, is suggestive of a number of issues family scientists must address in the years to come.

We would first note that despite the indicated impressive growth in theoretical development, it seems fair to conclude that, in general, theory is used more as a framework for investigation rather than in the more sophisticated manner of using empirical research to modify, improve, or jettison theories. This is not really surprising; for example, it took developmental psychologists nearly 40 years to *begin* to question and test Piaget's theoretical formulations on stages of cognitive development with empirical research. Indeed, the nature of the process of scientific knowledge development we describe in the first chapter is generally quite conservative. It takes a lot for someone like Dr. S. Canon to challenge the accumulated wisdom of a field. Another way to say this is that the bulk of the scholarship in family science has been directed toward confirming theory. It is reasonable to assume that the field will eventually move beyond this confirmatory focus, from the period of confirmatory infancy to a more

developmentally advanced stage of testing to inform theory—but we are clearly not there yet.

A second key future direction concerns the issue of theoretical and empirical integration (White & Klein, 2002), or at least more conscious interdisciplinarity. As should be readily apparent, scholarship in our field reflects an essential tension between explorations of individual and family-level phenomena. This is reflected in basic definitions of issues, operationalization of variables, articulation of data collection and analysis procedures, and approaches to testing of key concepts (all aspects of scientific theory development we discussed in Chapter 1 of this book). It seems clear to us that the field will benefit from greater integration between what are often construed to be human development theories and family theories.

Our belief in the potential value of this integration is indicated by our including, in a book of readings on family theory, several theoretical traditions that have largely been identified as human development or individually focused. Some might argue, therefore, that they have little or nothing of relevance to say about *families*. However, although life-span developmental theory, social learning theory, and ecological theory do, indeed, come from an infancy period in which they talked to and about only individual issues, the empirical horse has left the barn and neighs loud and clear on this one. Not only do we believe that these theories offer much of relevance for the field of family science, but they are also being used more and more frequently by family researchers. Of these, perhaps ecological theory has proceeded the furthest on this road to integration. For example, a review of introductory textbooks in marriage and family, child development, and life-span human development shows that ecological theory is frequently included in all three groups. Indeed, research from an ecological perspective is evident in all three areas of knowledge. Because families, at their most basic, are aggregates of individuals, such continued integration of individual and family theoretical concepts will serve to enhance theory in family science as well as theory in human development and, ultimately, will positively impact both scholarship and practice in areas of family life.

We suggest further that future theoretical work should be directed toward exploring possible explicit theoretical links and integrations within the field. We emphasize that what we mean here is not mere borrowing of concepts. (We need to get out of our comfort zones!) Rather, we predict and urge focused development of theoretical and empirical work that uses propositions (you will recall from Chapter 1 that propositions are theoretical statements that relate concepts in the theory, right?) containing both traditional family science concepts and traditional human development concepts in the same theory or empirical work. As you may have noticed from the various readings in this book, the nine perspectives included here are substantially different from one another. Difference does not necessarily mean there is no room for true integration of theory, however. Indeed, a further sign of the maturity of theory in a field is the degree to which integrated theoretical perspectives have been developed. Such integrations should focus on ways in which theories might be combined to better explicate family phenomena. A good example of an ongoing attempt at this kind of true theoretical and empirical integration, and how difficult it can be to carry out, is the development of family life course theory over the last two to three decades.

Elder (1974, 1996) provides a living personal history of this process, which is attempting to integrate broad historical, political, and social concepts with individual human development concepts to explain life course development. White and Klein (2002) talk about this development using concepts from ecological theory—macrosystem and microsystem influences—and point out that the focus of family life course theory still remains on the individual rather than on the family as the unit of analysis. Although this seems to us to be a valid assessment, we would urge that family scholars not look at this matter as an "either-or" (either family or human development) proposition. Why not include both units and levels of analysis under a single theoretical umbrella? Our hypothesis is that scholars

with one or the other theoretical and empirical interest (family or individual) would agree with the proposition that understanding in the other focus informs research in their own area of expertise. We think that there will be more systematic attention to both the theoretical and empirical implications associated with this empirical reality.

Clearly, Canon uses theory to strengthen the focus of her research. But her ability to more fully understand family phenomena would be enhanced by the presence of more focused attention to truly integrating human development and family sciences theoretical perspectives. In addition to the developments in family life course theory discussed above, it is reasonable to assume, for example, that one might employ elements of symbolic interactionism to better explain family interactions that contribute to boundary definitions within a family system. You will have noted in the readings that individual researchers in family science may well use multiple theoretical perspectives rather than just one to guide their work. The reason they do this is that they believe exploring connections between theories provides a better chance to more completely explain and understand the phenomena they study. Such research remains fairly new to the field, however. This suggests that ample opportunities remain for scholars to explore the dynamic ways that theoretical perspectives may be more fully integrated in the future.

We should be clear that we do not think the fuller integration across family and human development areas is a straightforward process—or it would already have happened! Indeed, we believe that the process of systematically integrating theoretical ideas is a very challenging, even daunting, prospect. But, this is only because understanding human families and, indeed, human development is itself an extremely complex endeavor! This is one reason that efforts to systematically pursue theoretical integration have been few and far between. The family science field is in somewhat the same position as the person who looks for lost car keys under a street light at night because "that's where the light is" even though it is believed that the keys were not lost there. Working within a more closely circumscribed theoretical area may be more comfortable because it allows us to see things in that area more clearly. However, narrowing the focus comes at a great cost to overall understanding. We would particularly urge students, to the extent you haven't already done so (and informal, or anecdotal, evidence tells us you are already doing so!), to give some serious thought to what we are suggesting here. Ask your professors about this issue. Read what is available that seems to contradict what we are saying here. And so on.

What do we miss by looking only under the light? It seems to us that the complex phenomena with which researchers in family science and human development deal essentially require expanding the search area. And, by the way, although the focus on this book is on family theory, we mean this comment to apply to life-span developmental theory as well. How does one develop understanding of families without understanding the individuals within? How does one, indeed, develop understanding of individual development without understanding family context? The sooner we in these fields recognize the implications of these kinds of questions, the sooner our ability to explain and understand family behavior will increase. Perhaps this is nowhere more evident than in the nexus of research, practice, and policy, the last arena of families and individuals about which we wish to briefly comment in this book.

Much of the family science research that has been theoretically driven has been of a basic nature: developing knowledge for knowledge's sake. As you now know, basic research finds value in developing essential understandings, and, as we have said, it is essential to developing theory. Far less attention has been paid thus far to theoretical applications that inform practice and policy formation. This is not to say that there is no attention to policy and practice. There is. But many family practitioners and policymakers continue to conduct their work with little attention to family theory. As a result, while there are many examples of theoretically based research, there are far fewer examples of theoretically based policy and

practice. There is a considerable need for research into practical and policy applications of the theories described in this book. In addition to developing theoretical understanding of human development and family science phenomena, we believe it is incumbent on the family science field to more energetically bring its empirical and theoretical work to bear on policy and practice issues.

In closing, we hope that we have contributed to your understanding of theory in family science and in human development. We tried to do that, as we mentioned at the beginning of this book (in the Preface), by communicating with as little jargon as possible and by including readings that we thought you would find to be interesting in the way the authors used theories to form the framework for their approaches and topics of study. We also tried to put a little heat in the discussion by presenting some fairly strong views on a number of important issues that remain debatable in the family science field. We urge you to do some more reading on these issues, to talk them over with professors and fellow students, and to check them out in any way you can imagine—perhaps through some research, policy, or practice activity in your classes or on your own. You can tell from some of the issues we have identified and opined about that discussion of theoretical issues is important to the development of our disciplines. As we said at the beginning, for anyone interested in understanding, helping, or even just talking about families and humans, this is anything but boring stuff. We hope that you develop (or continue to develop) some professional interest in the family and human development fields. Developing real understanding of families and life-span development, with all the intricacies and influences, is one of the most challenging and rewarding fields of endeavor that we can imagine. Scientific theory development is a major tool in that effort to understand. Teaching, doing research, and working in policy or therapeutic areas that have to do with families and humans across the life span is nothing short of a noble endeavor. The fields of family science and human development await new ideas, new approaches, and new commitments to add to the progress that has been made. Are you ready?

References

Akers, R. L. (1996). A longitudinal test of social learning theory: Adolescent smoking. *Journal of Drug Issues, 26*(2), 317–343.

Andersen, M. L. (1991). Feminism and the American family ideal. *Journal of Comparative Family Studies, 22,* 235–246.

Babbie, E. R. (2003). *Practice of social research with Infotrac (Practice of social research)* (10th ed.). Belmont, CA: Wadsworth.

Baber, K. M., & Allen, K. R. (1992). *Women & families: Feminist reconstructions.* New York: Guilford.

Baltes, P. B., Lindenberger, U., & Staudinger, U. M. (1998). Life-span theory in developmental psychology. In W. Damon (Editor-in-Chief) & R. M. Lerner (Vol. Ed.), *Handbook of child psychology: Vol. 1. Theoretical models of human development* (5th ed., pp. 1029–1143). New York: Wiley.

Bandura, A. (1977). *Social learning theory.* Englewood Cliffs, NJ: Prentice-Hall.

Bandura, A. (1986). *Social foundations of thought and action.* Englewood Cliffs, NJ: Prentice-Hall.

Bengston, V. L., & Allen, K. R. (1993). The family life course perspective applied to families over time. In P. G. Boss, W. J. Dougherty, R. LaRossa, W. R. Schumm, & S. K. Steinmetz (Eds.), *Sourcebook of family theories and methods: A contextual approach* (pp. 469–499). New York: Plenum.

Benson, M. J., & Piercy, K. W. (1997). Multiple approaches to developing research: A flexible framework for students and advisors. *Family Science Review, 10,* 121–135.

Berrien, F. L. (1968). *General and social systems.* New Brunswick, NJ: Rutgers University Press.

Bertalanffy, L. (1951). Problems of general systems theory. *Human Biology, 23,* 302–312.

Blau, P. (1964). *Exchange and power in social life.* New York: Wiley.

Blumer, H. (1969). *Symbolic interactionism: Perspective and method.* Englewood Cliffs, NJ: Prentice-Hall.

Broderick, C. B. (1993). *Understanding family process: Basics of family systems theory.* Newbury Park, CA: Sage.

Bronfenbrenner, U. (1979). *The ecology of human development: Experiments by nature and design.* Cambridge, MA: Harvard University Press.

Bronfenbrenner, U., & Ceci, S. J. (1994). Nature-nurture re-conceptualized in developmental perspective: A bioecological model. *Psychological Review, 101,* 568–586.

Bronfenbrenner, U., & Morris, P. A. (1998). The ecology of developmental processes. In W. Damon (Editor-in-Chief) & R. M. Lerner (Vol. Ed.), *Handbook of child psychology: Vol. 1. Theoretical models of human development* (5th ed., pp. 993–1028). New York: Wiley.

Bubolz, M. M., & Sontag, M. S. (1993). Human ecology theory. In P. G. Boss, W. J. Doherty, R. La Rossa, W. R. Schumm, & S. K. Steinmetz (Eds.), *Sourcebook of family theories and methods* (pp. 419–450). New York: Plenum.

Cade, B. (1986). The reality of "reality" (or the "reality" of reality). *The American Journal of Family Therapy, 14,* 49–56.

Chodorow, N. J. (1995). Gender as a personal and cultural construction. *Signs, 20,* 516–544.

Coser, L. (1956). *The functions of social conflict.* Glencoe, IL: Free Press.

Crosbie-Burnett, M., & Lewis, E. A. (1993). Theoretical contributions from social and cognitive-behavioral psychology. In P. G. Boss, W. J. Doherty, R. LaRossa, W. R. Schumm, & S. K. Steinmetz (Eds.), *Sourcebook of family theories and methods: A contextual approach* (pp. 531–558). New York: Plenum.

Doherty, W. J., Boss, P. G., LaRossa, R., Schumm, W. R., & Steinmetz, S. K. (1993). Family theories and methods: A contextual approach. In P. G. Boss, W. J. Doherty, R. LaRossa, W. R. Schumm, & S. K. Steinmetz (Eds.), *Sourcebook of family theories and methods: A contextual approach* (pp. 3–30). New York: Plenum.

Elder, G. H., Jr. (1974). *Children of the Great Depression: Social change in life experience.* Chicago: University of Chicago Press.

Elder, G. H., Jr. (1996). Human lives in changing societies: Life course and developmental insights. In R. B. Cairns, G. H. Elder, Jr., & E. J. Costello (Eds.), *Developmental science* (pp. 31–62). New York: Cambridge University Press.

Ford, D. H., & Lerner, R. M. (1992). *Developmental systems theory: An integrative approach.* Newbury Park, CA: Sage.

Goulet, L. R., & Baltes, P. B. (1970). *Life-span developmental psychology: Research and theory.* New York: Academic Press.

Harter, S. (1999). Symbolic interactionism revisited: Potential liabilities for the self constructed in the crucible of interpersonal relationships. *Merrill-Palmer Quarterly, 45,* 677–703.

Hill, R. (1971). Payoffs and limitations of contemporary strategies for family theory systematization. Paper presented at the annual meeting of the National Council on Family Relations, Estes Park, CO.

Homans, G. C. (1961). *Social behavior: Its elementary forms.* New York: Harcourt Brace & World.

Homans, G. (1974). *Social behavior: Its elementary forms.* New York: Harcourt Brace Jovanovich.

Hook, N., & Paolucci, B. (1970). The family as an ecosystem. *Journal of Home Economics, 62,* 315–318.

Larsen, A., & Olson, D. H. (1990). Capturing the complexity of family systems: Integrating family theory, family scores and family analysis. In T. W. Draper & A. C. Marcos (Eds.), *Family variables: Conceptualization, measurement and use* (pp. 19–47). Newbury Park, CA: Sage.

LaValle, D. (1994). Social exchange and social system: A Parsonian approach. *Sociological Perspectives, 37,* 585–610.

Lewis, R. A., & Spanier, G. B. (1982). Marital quality, marital stability and social exchange. In F. I. Nye (Ed.), *Family relationships: Rewards and costs.* Beverly Hills, CA: Sage.

Litton Fox, G., & Murray, V. (2000). Gender and families: Feminist perspectives and family research. *Journal of Marriage and the Family, 62,* 1160–1172.

Makoba, J. W. (1993). Toward a general theory of social exchange. *Social Behavior and Personality, 21,* 227–240.

Marks, S. R. (1989). Toward a systems theory of marital quality. *Journal of Marriage and the Family, 51,* 15–26.

Marks, S. R., & MacDermid, S. M. (1996). Multiple roles and the self: A theory of role balance. *Journal of Marriage and the Family, 58,* 417–432.

Marrow, A. J. (1977). *The practical theorist: The life and work of Kurt Lewin.* New York: Teachers College Press.

Marx, M. H. (1969). The general nature of theory construction. In M. H. Marx (Ed.), *Theories in contemporary psychology* (pp. 3–46). London: MacMillan.

Miller, N. E. (1992). Introducing and teaching much-needed understanding of the scientific process. *American Psychologist, 47,* 848–850.

Nelson, H. L. (Ed.). (1997). *Feminism and families.* New York: Routledge.

Nimkoff, M. F., & Ogburn, W. F. (1934). *The family.* New York: Houghton Mifflin.

Nosek, B. A., Banaji, M. R., & Greenwald, A. G. (2002). E-research: Ethics, security, design, and control in psychological research on the Internet. *Journal of Social Issues, 58*(1), 161–176.

Ray, M. P. (1988). An ecological model of the family. *Home Economics Forum, 2,* 9–15.

Reiss, D. (1981). *The family's construction of reality.* Cambridge: Harvard University Press.

Sadler, J. Z., & Hulgus, Y. F. (1989). Hypothesizing and evidence-gathering: The nexus of understanding. *Family Process, 28,* 255–267.

Seccombe, K., & Warner, R. L. (2004). *Marriages and families: Relationships in social context.* New York: Thomson Learning.

Silverman, R. J. (1993). Contexts of knowing: Their shape and substance. *Knowledge: Creation, Diffusion, Utilization, 14,* 372–382.

Simmel, G. (1956). *Conflict and the web of group affiliation.* (K. H. Wolff, Trans.). Glencoe, IL: Free Press.

Sprey, J. (1969). The family as a system in conflict. *Journal of Marriage and Family, 31,* 699–706.

Sprey, J. (1979). Conflict theory and the study of marriage and the family. In W. R. Burr, R. Hill, F. I. Nye, & I. L. Reis (Eds.), *Contemporary theories about the family, Vol. 2* (pp. 130–159). New York: Free Press.

Stacey, J. (1996). *In the name of the family: Rethinking family values in the postmodern age.* Boston: Beacon.

Thibaut, J. W., & Kelley, H. H. (1959). *The social psychology of groups.* New York: Wiley.

Thomas, R. M. (2001). *Recent theories of human development.* Thousand Oaks, CA: Sage.

Weis, D. L. (1998). The use of theory in sexuality research. *The Journal of Sex Research, 35,* 1–9.

White, J. M., & Klein, D. M. (2002). *Family theories* (2nd ed.). Thousand Oaks, CA: Sage.

INDEX

Page references followed by *fig* indicates an illustrated figure; followed by *t* indicates a table.

Abbott, E., 15
Abel, G. G., 188
Abel, R. L., 241
Abramovitz, M., 259, 260, 261
Abramowitz, R. H., 308, 313
ACE (Alliance for Community Empowerment)
    program, 354
Ackerman, B. P., 45
Acock, A. C., 167
Acs, G., 271
Adams, J., 140, 142, 143
Adler, J., 313
Adolescent dating/sexual experience, 21–22
AFDC (Aid to Families with Dependent Children), 258,
    259, 262, 263, 264, 266, 268, 270, 272
Affiliation group collaborations, 351
Affleck, M., 228
African Americans
    causes of poverty among, 261
    welfare mothers among, 259, 262, 263,
        264, 265–267, 269
Age differences
    in effect of becoming a parent, 146, 148
    marital status/psychological well-being and, 80*t*–81*t*, 84
Ager, J., 283
Agger, B., 213
Agnew, C. R., 167
Agnostinelli, J., 314
Ahrons, C. R., 240
Alberti, R., 220
Alexander, M. J., 213, 214
Alipuria, L. L., 283
Allen, K., 207
Allen, K. R., 11, 16, 69, 70, 211, 212, 213,
    214, 216, 218, 219, 226
Almeida, D., 325
Altemeier, W. A., 119
Altman, I., 317
Alvarez, F. B., 226

Alvarez, M. D., 243
Alwin, D. F., 143, 225
Amato, P. R., 69, 73, 227
Ambert, A. M., 226
American Peabody Picture Vocabulary Test, 50
Amey, C., 268
Ammons, R. W., 123
Anderson, C. M., 72
Anderson, E. A., 313
Anderson, M., 260
Anderson, S., 13, 14
Anderson, S. A., 290
Andrews, B., 101
Aneshensel, C. S., 86, 142, 143
Arbuckle, J. C., 33, 51
Archer, S. L., 282, 283, 289
Arendell, T., 240, 255
Arnett, J. J., 31, 283, 286, 289
Astroth, K. A., 346
Atkeston, B. M., 121
Atkinson, J., 321, 324, 333
Auerbach, J. G., 120
Auhagen, A. E., 334
Avison, W. R., 144
Axinn, W., 45

Babbie, E. R., 2
Baber, K. M., 214, 216, 219
Babri, K. B., 69
Bailey, C. A., 125
Baj, J., 68
Bakken, L., 283
Baldwin, A., 45
Baldwin, C., 45
Balistreri, E., 284, 285
Ball, J. F., 73
Baltes, P. B., 39, 43, 68, 69, 71, 82, 85
Banaji, M. R., 2
Bandura, A., 96, 98, 99, 114, 123, 142, 188

Banks, M., 46
Barbour, N., 345
Barnett, R. C., 140, 142, 307, 312
Baruch, G. K., 140, 142, 307, 312
Bassin, B., 167
Bates, E. L., 317, 333, 339
Bates, J. E., 45
Baumeister, R., 284
Baumrind, D., 43, 118, 120, 121, 123
Baunach, D., 28
Bazter, J., 197
BCS70 (British Cohort Study), 48–49, 50, 51, 53*t*–58
Beaman, J., 119
Beavers, 297
Becker, B., 44
Becker, G. S., 226, 227, 234
Becker, J. V., 188
Bell, D., 215
Belsky, J., 118, 119, 121, 122, 142
Benard, B., 345, 351, 353
Bengston, V. L., 11, 16, 31, 69, 70
Benin, M. H., 314
Benson, M. J., 2
Bentler, P. M., 52
Bergeman, C. S., 43
Berger, P., 245
Bergin, A., 300
Berg, J. H., 167, 168
Bergmann, B., 259
Berk, S. F., 194
Bernard, J., 320, 327, 328, 329, 331
Berne, L., 18
Berry, J. O., 305, 306, 309, 310, 314
Berscheid, E. D., 165, 317, 327, 331
Besharov, D. J., 271
Best, K. M., 44
Bianchi, S., 161
Biblarz, T. J., 227
Biernat, M., 312
Big Five personality adjective markers, 309
Billingsley, A., 123
Bilsker, D., 289
Birch, H. G., 42
Bird, C. E., 140, 141, 142, 143
Bird, G. W., 307
Blaisure, K. R., 207, 226
Blau, P. M., 42, 137
Blieszner, R., 214
Blood, R., 194, 197
Blumberg, R. L., 194, 206, 207
Blumer, H., 262

Blumstein, P., 245
Bobo, L., 264
Bohannan, P., 241
Bolger, K. E., 42, 45
Bolger, N., 325, 339
Bollen, K. A., 51, 52
Boltwood, A., 28
Bond, J. T., 313
Booth, A., 69, 73, 227
Bor, R., 300
Boss, P. G., 1
Bott, E., 320
Boundaries of family system, 279–280
Bourdieu, P., 273
Bowen, M., 252
Bowlby, J., 69, 121, 241
Bowles, M. K., 282
Boyd, R., 69
Bozdogan, H., 52
Bradbum, N., 82
Bradburn, N. M., 71, 325
Bradbury, T. N., 319, 326, 327, 328, 331, 332, 337, 338
Brailsford, J. C., 280
Branson, M. P., 313
Braver, S. L., 243
Bretherton, I., 69
Briar, S., 272
Brimer, M. A., 50
Brim, O. G., 71, 85, 123
Brody, G., 295
Bronfenbrenner, U., 40, 43, 44, 131, 220, 303, 304, 307, 308, 309, 313, 346, 347, 348
Brook, J. S., 132
Brooks-Gunn, J., 42, 45
Browne, S. F., 98
Brown, M., 346, 354
Brownmiller, S., 218
Bryant, F. B., 69, 71, 82
Buboltz, M. M., 303, 346, 349, 355
Buckley, S., 320
Bui, K. T., 167, 168
Bumpass, L. A., 144
Bumpass, L. L., 68, 71, 74
Burchinal, M. R., 42
Burgess, A. W., 98
Burgess, E., 13, 14
Burgess, E. W., 320, 327, 336
Burgess, R. L., 123
Buri, J. R., 121
Burman, B., 118
Burr, W., 195

Burton, L., 339
Burton, L. M., 31, 36
Burton, R. V., 120
Busch-Rossnagel, N. A., 284
Butler, H., 48
Butler, N. R., 48, 49
Buttenwieser, E., 122
Buunk, B. P., 166, 167, 168, 180
Bynner, J., 42, 46, 48

CAIC (Consistent Akaike Information Criterion), 52
Call, V., 74
Camburn, D., 225
Campbell, D. T., 329
Campbell, F. A., 42
Campbell, J. D., 120
Campbell, L. E. G., 240, 241, 250, 253, 254, 255
Campbell, S. B., 45
Canon, S., 2–4, 5, 359, 361, 362
Carta, J., 42
Casper, A., 42
Caspi, A., 120
Cassidy, J., 119
Castro-Martin, T., 68
Cate, R. M., 166, 167, 168, 169, 188
Caughlin, J. P., 324, 329, 336
CCIA (Community Coalitions in Action)
      project [Michigan State University],
      348–351, 353, 354
Ceci, S. J., 40, 43
Cecil-Pigo, E. F., 166
Celibacy
    consequences of, 24–26
    determining status of, 19–21
    literature review on, 15
    process leading to, 22–24
    See also Involuntary celibacy
CES-D (Center for Epidemiological
    Studies-Depression) index, 75
CFI (comparative fit index), 52
Chalmers, M. A., 122
Chambliss, 240
Chandler, A. L., 325
Change
    family systems, 280
    structural family therapy as model of, 294
Chapman, B. E., 227
Chapman, J. R., 188
Chassin, L., 119, 120
Chen, M. D., 145
Chen, Z.-Y., 97, 118, 121, 122
Cherlin, A., 30, 31, 70

Children
    abstract on costs/rewards of, 140–141
    balancing fatherhood/employment and care of,
        308, 309–310*t*
    cycle of violence and socialization of, 187–189
    discussion on effects of having, 159–161
    gender roles/family formation and intentions to have,
        229, 231*t*–232*t*, 233
    groundwork for theory on violence against, 186–187
    health problems of welfare, 271
    method used to study effects of having, 144–148
    previous research on having, 141–144
    research findings on effects of having, 148–158
    research questions and hypotheses on having, 144
    research summary on effects of having, 158–159
    See also Families; Parents
Chinese Exclusion Act (1882), 216
Chodron, P., 220
Chow, E. N.-L., 216
Christensen, A., 320
Christensen, K., 213, 215, 218
Christiansen, S. L., 313
Chronosystem, 347
Cicchetti, D., 44, 45
Clark, A. L., 268
Clarkberg, M., 226
Clarke, A.D.B., 44, 45
Clarke, A. M., 44, 45
Clark, M. S., 167, 168, 180
Clark, S., 284
Clark, V. A., 143
Cleary, P. D., 140, 143
Clifford, M. C., 349
Cloward, R. A., 259
CMFS (Circumplex Model
    of Family Systems), 285, 290
Cohen, P., 132
Cohen, S., 309
Cohen, T. F., 314
Coleman, D. H., 102, 105
Coleman, J., 345
Collaborative typology, 349
Coll, C. G., 45
Collins, P. H., 212, 213, 214, 215, 216, 221
Collins, R., 195
Coltraine, S., 71, 194
Combrinck-Graham, L., 290
Comer, J., 345
Community collaborations
    abstract on, 345
    applications of research findings on, 354
    common elements of, 351–354

definitions of organizational systems used in, 350*t*

definitions relating to, 346

Ecomap of Community Coalition
(drawn by members), 352*fig*

examining CCIA (Community Coalitions in Action),
348–351, 353, 354

four categories of, 351

interdependency model of service organizations
and, 348, 349*fig*

Keith's comprehensive ecological model of, 348, 350*fig*

procedures used to study, 349

reasons for promoting, 345–346

research findings on, 349, 351

research implications for home economics/human
ecology study of, 354–355

using an ecological approach to, 346–348, 347*fig*

Comprehensive community collaborations with citizen
input, 351

Comstock, G. W., 73

Conger, R. D., 30, 45, 118, 119, 121, 339

Connell, R. W., 207

Constructive parenting

intergenerational transmission of, 118–132

interpersonal relations and, 121–122, 129*t*, 130*t*

psychological disturbance and, 120–121, 129*t*, 130*t*

role-specific modeling and, 123–124

social participation and, 123, 129*t*, 130*t*

See also Families

Cook, J. A., 213

Cook, T. D., 329

Cook, W., 330

Cooley, C., 237

Cooley, C. H., 121, 188

Cooney, T. M., 69, 71

Coontz, S., 16, 217

Cooper, C., 283

Cooper, I., 297

Coppersmith, S., 121

Copy-a-Design test, 49–50

Corbin, J., 18, 19, 262

Coser, L. A., 186, 188

Costa, P. T., Jr., 74

Cote, J. E., 283, 290

Cottrell, L., 327

Covey, M. A., 305, 345

Cowan, C. P., 142, 144, 314

Cowan, P. A., 142

Cox, A. G., 268

Cox, M., 32, 314

Cox, M. J., 119, 121, 142

Cox, R., 314

Coyne, J. C., 121

Crawford, D. W., 324, 339

CR (consciousness-raising) groups, 213, 216–217

Creedon, M. A., 306, 307, 315

Crittenden, P. M., 123

Crohan, S., 142

Crook, T., 121

Crosbie-Burnett, M., 97

Crosnoe, R., 13, 30

Crouter, A. C., 44, 226, 227, 307, 308, 339

CS (Cambridge Scale), 51

CSE (Certificate of Secondary Education)
examination, 50–51

CTS (Conflict Tactics Scale), 103–104

Culp, A. M., 121

Culp, R. E., 121

Dahrendorf, R., 273

Dallas Self-Report Family Inventory, 285

Daniels, D., 43

Daniels, P., 71

Dare, J., 300

Darwin, C., 237

Dating couples equity/social exchange

abstract on, 165

brief overview of investment model research, 167

conclusions of study on, 179–180

discussion of findings on, 176

equity as predictor of
satisfaction/commitment, 176–177

importance of equity relative to other variables in, 177

limitations of study on, 179

method used to study, 168–171

predicting stability of relationship, 174–176

as predictors of change in satisfaction/commitment,
177–178

predictors of change in satisfaction/commitment
in, 173–174

as predictors of relationship stability, 178–179

purposes of investigation on, 167–168

representative research on equity, 166–167

research results on, 171–173

satisfaction/commitment as predictor of changes in, 174

satisfaction/commitment as predictors of change in, 178

theoretical background to study, 166

Dating experiences (adolescents), 21

Davidson, B., 166

Davie, R., 48, 49

Davies, L., 144

Davis, K., 225, 273

Davis, K. B., 123

Davis, L., 259, 272

Davis, M., 140, 216

Davis, M. S., 247
Davis, N. J., 262
Davis, R., 13, 14
Deater-Deckard, K., 45, 314
DeBevoise, W., 346
Decision making (marital), 203–204
DeHart-Mathews, J., 216
Della Fave, R. L., 273, 274
DeLongis, A., 339
D'Emilio, J., 215, 216, 218
Demo, D. H., 142
Demos, J., 191, 347
Depression (nonparents/new parents), 155t, 156t, 159fig
Desmarais, S., 167
Despotidou, S., 48
Deutsch, M., 240
Dewey, J., 237
DIIFO (data/input/information/facts/observations), 2, 3
Dillard, J., 13, 14
Dill, B. T., 216
Dillon, H. A., 240
Diskin, S., 119
Divorce
    abstract on conflict during, 240–242
    claims of "false marriages" and, 251–254
    importance of gender roles for family formation
        and, 225–234
    the other as crazy during, 249–251
    research on conflict during, 242–243
    study conclusions regarding conflict
        during, 254–256
    symbolic origins of conflict in, 240–256
    See also Marriage
Dodge, K. A., 45
Doherty, W. J., 1, 69, 73
Dolan, M., 197
Dombusch, S. M., 120, 123
Domestic labor
    effects of becoming new parents and, 151t–154t
    gender roles and sharing of, 233–234, 306–307
    marital behavior data on sharing of, 325–326
    marital power and division of, 198–200
    See also Fatherhood/employment balance
Donnelly, B. W., 141
Donnelly, D., 13, 14, 16, 17, 22, 26
Dornbusch, S. M., 118, 121, 122, 123, 124
Downey, G., 120, 121, 145
Drigotas, S. M., 166
Dryfoos, J. G., 345
Dual-earner families. See Fatherhood/employment
    balance; Working wives
Duck, S., 178, 246

Duffy, S. M., 167
Duncan, G. J., 42, 44, 45
Duncan, O. D., 42
Dunn, L. M., 50
Durkheim, E., 241, 244, 245
Duvall, E. M., 71

Ebert, T. L., 213, 215, 219
Ecological theory
    Bronfenbrenner's proposed model for,
        346–348, 347fig
    on community collaborations as applications
        of, 345–355
    issues for consideration, 305
    overview of, 303–305
    readings on, 305
    on social ecology of marriage/intimate unions, 317–340
Ecomap of Community Coalition
    (drawn by members), 352fig
Edin, K., 261
Education levels of grandparents,
    31–32, 33t, 34–36t
Edwards, J. N., 167
Egeland, B., 119
EIPQ (Ego Identity Process Questionnaire),
    282, 284–285
Elam, D., 214
Elder, G. H., Jr., 11, 12, 13, 30, 31, 32, 37, 39,
    43, 44, 46, 68, 69, 120, 122, 124, 339, 362
Elias, P., 46
Elifson, K., 28
Eliot, J., 121
Elliot, D., 97, 98
Ellison, C., 345
Ellsworth, E., 214
Ellwood, D. T., 259
Emery, R. E., 240
Engels, F., 260
English Picture Vocabulary Test, 50
Enright, R. D., 283
Equifinality of family systems, 280
Equity
    defining, 166
    importance relative to other social
        exchange variables, 177
    as predictor of change in relationship
        satisfaction/commitment, 173–174, 177–178
    as predictor of relationship satisfaction/commitment,
        176–177
    as predictor of relationship stability, 178–179
    relationship satisfaction/commitment as predictor of
        change in, 174, 178

representative research on, 166–167
status-reversal wives and perceptions of marital, 200
Erel, O., 118
Erikson, E., 142, 282, 283, 289
Erlanger, 240
Essex, M. J., 69, 314
Ethnicity/race
   constructive parenting and, 124
   in effect of becoming a parent, 146, 148
   of families receiving AFDC, 272
   female oppression in context of, 216
   feminism in context of, 218
   of identity formation/family characteristic study
      participants, 286, 287*t*, 288*t*, 289*t*–290
   violence and, 104
   of welfare mothers, 259, 262, 263, 264, 265–267, 269
ETHNOGRAPH search/cluster process, 349

FACES II and III (Family Adaptability and Cohesion
      Evaluation Scales II/III), 282, 285, 290
Faderman, L., 214, 215, 216, 217
Fagan, J. A., 98
Families
   defining, 8–9
   family life course theory definition of, 12
   family systems theory on interdependent
      components of, 279
   feminist visions for transforming, 212–221
   relations between identity formation and characteristics
      of, 282–290
   risk experiences and material conditions of, 49
   social exchange perspective of, 139
   working wives and changes in "traditional," 189–190
   See also Children; Constructive parenting
Families and Family Therapy (Minuchin), 294
Families of the Slums (Minuchin et al.), 294
Family formation/dissolution
   abstract on gender role attitudes and, 225–226
   data and variables on gender roles and, 228–230
   discussion on gender roles and, 232–234
   findings on gender roles and, 230–232
   understanding gender roles and processes of, 226–228
Family Kaleidoscope (Minuchin), 294
Family life course
   defining, 11
   examining involuntary celibacy using perspective of,
      14–28
Family life course theory
   described, 11–12
   examining involuntary celibacy using of, 14–28
   examining life course transitions, grandparent-grandchild
      relationships using, 30–38

four themes of, 12–13
   readings on, 13
Family and Medical Leave Act, 306
Family Support Act (1988), 268
Family systems theory
   issues for consideration, 281
   overview/concepts of, 279–280
   readings on, 280–281
   on structural family therapy, 293–301
Family Therapy Techniques
      (Minuchin & Fishman), 294
Family transformation
   abstract on, 212
   feminist experiments for radical changes and, 216–218
   feminist visions for now and future, 218–221
   love as equals in 19th century, 215–216
   See also Feminism
Family violence
   abstract on, 186
   conflict approach to, 189–192
   groundwork for theory on, 186–187
   introduction to, 186
   socialization and cycle of, 187–189
   summary of explanations on, 192
   See also Marital violence; Violence
Fao, E. B., 169
Farley, S. C., 99
Farnsworth, E. B., 214
Fatherhood/employment balance
   abstract on, 306–308
   conclusions on, 314–315
   discussion of findings on, 311–313
   family stress and, 313–314
   implications of findings on, 313
   method and results of studies on, 308–311*t*
   workplace contribution to, 314
   See also Domestic labor; Parents; Working wives
Feagin, J. R., 259, 260, 261
Featherman, D. L., 43, 68, 69
Feedback mechanisms (family system), 280
Feeley, D., 190
Feeney, J., 121, 122
Feiring, C., 45
Felmlee, D., 167, 168
Felner, R. D., 42
Felstiner, W. L., 241
Female sexual inverts, 216
Feminine Mystique, The (Friedan), 213
Feminism
   CR (consciousness-raising) groups and, 213, 216–217
   defining, 212–214
   ethnicity context of, 216, 217

experiments for radical change in 20th century, 216–218
locating oneself in, 214–215
visions for now/future family transformation, 218–221
See also Family transformation; Women
Feminist theory
comparing different perspectives of, 210
on importance of gender roles for family
formation/dissolution, 225–234
issues for consideration, 211
overview of, 209–211
readings on, 211
Fenstermaker, S., 196, 225
Fergusson, D. M., 45
Fernandez, J. P., 312, 313
Ferrari, T. M., 305, 345
Ferrecuti, F., 186
Ferree, M. M., 194, 226
Ferri, E., 46, 48
FIML (full information maximum likelihood)
approach, 51
Fincham, F. D., 328
Fine, M. A., 167
Finkelhor, D., 98
Finley, B., 226
Fischer, C., 141
Fisher, B., 220
Fish, L. S., 297
Fishman, C., 293
Fitzgerald, H. E., 45
Fletcher, A. C., 219
Fletch, G.J.O., 334
Floyd, F. J., 167, 327
Floyd-Thomas, S. M., 219
Foa, U. O., 169
Fogelman, K., 49, 50
Fogelson, R. D., 241
Folk, K., 196
Foner, A., 70
Fonow, M. M., 213
Fontat, V., 119
Ford, D. H., 40
Forgotten Half, The (W. T. Grant
Foundation report), 355
Forrest, D., 121, 122
Forsstrom, B., 100, 114
Foucault, M., 260, 273
Fox, J. W., 49, 72
Fraleigh, M. J., 118
Frankel, S. A., 71
Frankenberg, R., 214
Freedman, E. B., 215, 216, 218
Freire, P., 215, 217

Frerichs, R. R., 143
Freud, S., 16
Friedan, B., 213
Friederich, W. N., 122
Friedman, D. E., 313
Fujimoto, T., 142
Fullwider-Bush, N., 283, 289
Furstenberg, F. F., Jr., 30, 31, 73, 84

Gable, S. L., 322, 325
Gagnier, R., 214
Gagnon, J. H., 14, 16, 216, 217
Gaines, S. O., 324
Gaint, L., 283
Galinsky, E., 312, 313
Gallagher, S. K., 142, 161
Garbarino, J., 187, 308, 313, 346, 347
Gardner, S., 345
Garfield, S., 300
Garfinkel, H., 246
Garmezy, N., 43, 44, 119, 120
Gaudin, J. M., 123
Gavazzi, S. M., 290
Gay, J., 283
GCE (General Certificate of Education) exam, 50–51
Gecas, V., 121
Geerken, M. R., 143
Geis, G., 324, 328
Geisinger, K. F., 284
Gelles, R. J., 98, 118, 186, 187, 188, 190, 271, 297
Gender
at heart of feminist perspectives, 210
of identity formation/family characteristic study
participants, 286, 287*t*, 288*t*, 289*t*
Gender differences
in dating relationship satisfaction, commitment, stability,
171–176
in effects of becoming a parent, 143–144, 151*t*, 152*t*,
153*t*, 157–158
in identity formation/family characteristic, 288–289
in intergenerational transmission of violence, 100–101
of marital power and status/income resources, 194–207
marital status/psychological well-being and, 80*t*–81*t*
money and power gendered link and, 202–203
sex-role theory on socialization and, 102
See also Men; Women
Gender roles
abstract on family formation/dissolution and, 225–226
data and variables on family formation/dissolution and,
228–230
discussion on family formation/dissolution and, 232–234
domestic labor and sharing of, 233–234, 306–307

findings on family formation/dissolution and, 230–232
as part of family/work role system, 306–307
understanding family processes and, 226–228
Generation X, life/employment expectations of, 46
George, L., 324
Gerson, K., 226, 227
Gerstel, N., 142, 161, 241, 245
Giddens, A., 262
Gilbert, R., 320
Gil, D., 190
Gilder, G., 261
Gillman, L., 219
Ginat, J., 317
Giovannoni, J. M., 123
Given, K., 119
Glaser, B. G., 197, 242, 262
Glass, J., 142, 159
Glenn, N. D., 68, 72, 140, 178, 245
Goals (family system), 280
Goergen, D., 15
Goldberg, E. L., 73
Goldberg, L. R., 309
Goldberg, N., 221
Goldner, V., 297
Goldscheider, C., 226, 234
Goldscheider, F. K., 68, 70, 226, 234
Goldsmith, J., 240
Goldsteen, K., 68, 140, 142
Goldstein, H., 48, 50
Goldstein, M., 300
Gonsiorek, J., 22
Goodban, N., 262
Goode, 241, 246
Goodenough, F., 49
Gordon, L., 259, 261
Gordon, T., 72
Gorell Barnes, G., 298
Gore, S., 72, 140, 142
Gorzalka, B., 23
Gottlieb, G., 43
Gottman, J. M., 320, 326, 327, 332
Gove, W. R., 68, 72, 73, 140, 141, 143, 145
Gramsci, A., 273
Grandparent-grandchild relationships
abstract on, 30
context-specific nature of, 31–32
grandparent level of education, 31–33*t*, 34–36*t*
intergenerational dynamics/human
 life course and, 30–31
method used to examine, 32–33*t*
predicting grandparent mentoring, 34*t*
predicting quality of, 35*t*

research conclusions on, 36–38
results of study on, 33–36
See also Parents
Gravestock, F. M., 339
Gray, J. D., 243
Gray, L. M., 339
Greenbaum, C. W., 120
Greenberger, D., 166
Greenblat, C., 15
Greenwald, A. G., 2
Greenwood, C., 42
Griswold, R. L., 307
Grote, N. K., 167, 168, 180
Grotevant, H. D., 283, 284, 340
GSS (General Social Survey), 72
Gubrium, J. F., 255
Guelzow, M. G., 307, 312
Gully, K. J., 188
Guss, M. B., 227
Gussow, J. D., 42
Guthrie, D., 325
Guthrie, G. P., 354
Guthrie, L. F., 354

Habermas, J., 273
Hagen, J., 259, 272
Hagestad, G. O., 16, 17, 25, 30, 69, 70, 241
Hailer, A. O., 42
Haley, J., 293
Halford, W. K., 339
Hall, D. T., 314
Hamburg, D. A., 345
Hampson, R., 297
Harding-Hidore, M., 72
Harding, S., 213, 214
Hare Mustin, R., 297
Hareven, T. K., 215
Harlow, S. D., 73, 74
Harman, D., 123
Harris, D. B., 49
Harris-Goodenough Test, 49
Harris, K. M., 259
Hart, B., 42
Hartmark, C., 132
Harvey, C. C., 317, 333, 339
Harvey, J. H., 243
Hastings, T. H., 44
Hatfield, E., 166
Hauser, S. T., 282
Haveman, R., 45
Hawkesworth, M. E., 213, 214, 218
Hawkins, A. J., 313, 314

Hazan, C., 121
Health and human service agency
  collaboration, 351
Heath, D. H., 71
Heider, F., 333
Heinicke, C., 119, 121
Heirich, M., 255
Henderson, D., 339
Hendrick, S. S., 170
Henton, J. M., 166
Herbst, P., 324, 333
Hernstein, R., 261
Herrenkohl, E. C., 101
Herrmann, A. C., 213
Hetherington, E. M., 314
Hewlett, S. A., 226
Hierarchy of systems, 280
Hill, C. T., 167, 179
Hill, E. J., 313
Hill, R., 360
Hinde, R., 317, 318
Hinde, R. A., 334
Hochschild, A., 194, 195, 196, 226, 307, 312, 313, 314
Hodgkinson, H. L., 345, 348, 349*fig*
Hoffman, L. W., 43, 141, 142, 293
Holstein, J. A., 255
Homans, G. C., 137, 138
Hook, N., 303
Hopkins, K., 145
Hopper, J., 239, 240, 241, 243, 245, 251, 256
Hornung, C., 195
Horowitz, F. D., 43
Horton, F., 314
Horwood, L. J., 45
Hosie, T. W., 289
Hotaling, G. T., 99, 101, 102, 113
House, J. S., 141, 145
Housework. *See* Domestic labor
Houts, R. M., 324, 329, 331, 336
Huber, J., 140, 143, 195, 226, 227
Huberman, A. M., 262
Huberman, B., 18
Hughes, M., 68
Hulgus, Y. F., 2
Human ecological theory. *See* Ecological theory
Hunt, M. O., 259, 260
Hurley, J. R., 119
Hurst, S., 23
Huston, A. C., 45
Huston, T. L., 141, 142, 305, 307, 317, 320, 321,
  322, 324, 326, 328, 329, 331, 333, 336, 338, 339
Hutchinson, S. A., 262

Hwang, S., 197
Hyde, J. S., 314
Hyden, C., 227

Identity formation/family characteristics link
  abstract on, 282–284
  discussion of findings on, 286–290
  method of studying, 284–285
  research findings on, 285–286
Ihinger-Tallman, M., 70
Income/status differences
  data collection/analyses of marital, 196–198
  findings on marital power and, 206–207
  hiding and avoiding, 205
  managing marital tensions created by, 204–206
  marital division of domestic labor and, 198–200
  marital money management/decision
    making and, 201–204
Indelicato, S., 71
Inputs/outputs (family), 279
Interdependency model of service
  organizations, 348, 349*fig*
Interdependent components concept, 279
Intergenerational relationships.
    See Grandparent-grandchild relationships
Intergenerational transmission
  of constructive parenting, 118–132
  of violence, 99–101
Intergenerational transmission of parenting
  abstract on, 118–119
  background factors of, 124
  discussion of findings on, 129–132
  interpersonal relations and, 121–122
  limitations of previous studies on, 119–120
  measures used during study on, 125–126
  method used to study, 124–125
  psychological state and, 120–121
  research results on, 126–129
  role-specific modeling and, 123–124
  social participation and, 123
  theoretical model used to study, 120
Internet and celibacy, 27
Interpersonal relations/parenting behavior
    link, 121–122, 129*t,* 130*t*
Interpretive feminism, 210
Intimate unions ecology
  abstract on, 317–320
  as behavioral ecosystem, 320–327
  macroenvironmental context of marriage
    and, 338–339
  psychological infrastructure of marriage
    and, 327–338, 329*fig*

three-level model for viewing marriage
and, 318–320, 319*fig*
See also Marriage
Involuntary celibacy
abstract on life course perspective of, 14–15
becoming celibate, 22–26
conclusions reached on, 26–28
descriptive statistics of respondents on, 20*t*
literature review of, 15–16
methods used to study, 17–19
results and discussion on, 19–22
theoretical framework used to examine, 16–17
See also Celibacy
Iowa Youth and Families Project, 32
Isaacs, M. B., 240
Ishii-Kuntz, M., 145
Izard, C. E., 45

Jackson, J. F., 43
Jackson, T., 23
Jacobvitz, D. B., 283, 289
Jaffee, N., 240
Jaggar, A. M., 214
James, D., 239, 258
James, W., 237
Janus, C., 21
Janus, S., 21
Jarrett, R. L., 261, 339
John, D., 146, 225
Johnson, C., 119
Johnson, C. L., 255
Johnson, D. J., 167
Johnson, J. S., 70, 72, 144
Johnson, M. P., 324, 337
Johnson, R. J., 125
Johnson, S., 218
Johnson-Sumerford, D., 195, 207
Johnston, J. R., 240, 241, 250, 253, 254, 255
Joiner, T., 23
Jones, E. E., 274
Jones, R. M., 283
Jones, W. H., 309, 314
Joreskog, K. G., 126
Joshi, H., 42, 46
Josselson, R., 289
Journal of Family Therapy, 301
Judge, H.C.T., 5, 6, 359

Kagan, S. L., 345, 346
Kahn, A., 259
Kalmuss, D., 100, 101, 102, 114
Kamarch, T., 309

Kamerman, S., 259
Kandel, D., 140, 142
Kaplan, A., 269
Kaplan, D. S., 125
Kaplan, H. B., 97, 118, 120, 121, 124, 125
Kaplan, N., 119
Karney, B. R., 326, 327, 331, 337
Kasen, S., 132
Kashy, D. A., 340
Katz, R., 142
Kaufman, G., 211, 225
Kaufman, J., 101
Kayser, K., 338
Keirnan, K., 15, 18
Keith, J. G., 305, 345, 346, 348, 350, 354
Keith's comprehensive ecological model, 348, 350*fig*
Kelley, H. H., 137, 165, 273, 317, 318, 319,
327, 328, 331, 336
Kellner, H., 245
Kennedy, E. L., 216
Kenny, D. A., 330
Kerber, L. K., 216
Kerr, M. E., 241, 252
Kessler, R. C., 69, 73, 307, 339
Kessler, R. D., 140, 142, 143
Keyes, C. L. M., 69, 71, 75
Kidd, K. K., 118
Kim, H., 227
Kingma, D. R., 220
King, V., 31, 32, 36, 37
Kinmouth, L., 334
Kirby, J. B., 30
Kitson, G. C., 69, 74, 241, 246, 336
Kjolseth, R., 349
Klebanov, P. K., 42
Klein, D. M., 1, 4, 7, 9, 11, 39,
40, 359, 360, 361, 362
Kluegel, J. R., 260, 264
Knox, D., 241
Koball, E. H., 307
Komter, A., 194, 195
Koppitz, E. M., 49
Kotelchuck, M., 122
Kressel, K., 240
Krieger, N., 49
Krieger, S., 215, 217
Kristol, N. D., 338
Kroger, J., 283, 284
Krokoff, L. J., 320, 327
Kropp, J. P., 118
Kullberg, V., 339
Kupersmidt, J. B., 42

Kurdek, L. A., 141, 142, 143, 148, 167
Kurz, D., 246, 255
Kutner, M. H., 148
Kuykendall, D. H., 73

Lachenbruch, P. A., 86
Lacombe, A. C., 283
La Gaipa, J. J., 246
Lahey, B. B., 118, 121
Lambert, J. D., 41, 68, 144, 148
Lamke, L. K., 328, 336
Lancaster, J. B., 16
Landis, K. R., 141
Lang, A., 219
Lange, A., 300
Lang, M., 142
Lapsley, D. K., 284
Larner, G., 298
LaRossa, M. M., 142, 144
LaRossa, R., 1, 142, 144, 306
Larson, J. H., 166
Larson, R., 322, 325
Lauffer, A., 349
Laumann, E., 14, 15, 21, 27
LaVee, Y., 142, 285
Lawrence, B. S., 17
Lawton, J. M., 45
Lechner, V. M., 306, 307, 315
Lee, G., 68, 72
Leete, R., 49
Leiderman, P. H., 118
Lein, L., 261
LeMasters, E. F., 142
Lenski, G., 273
Leon, G., 240
Lerner, M. J., 167
Lerner, R. M., 40, 43, 348
Lesbian feminism, 214
Lesbians
    19th century romantic friendship between, 215–216
    CR groups of "emotional," 217
    during the 20th century, 216
    See also Women
Leslie, L. A., 313
Lester, B. M., 45
Letko, C., 190
Letts, D., 121
Levant, R. F., 313
Levinger, G., 317, 318, 321, 324, 331, 333
Levinson, K., 45
Lewin, K., 2, 332, 333
Lewis, E. A., 97

Lewis, M., 45
Lewis, O., 188, 261
Lewis, R., 195
Lew, V., 227
Liazos, A., 189
Liberal feminism, 210
Lickliter, R., 43
Lieberman, M. A., 69, 73, 142
Life cycle concept, 11
Life history, 11
Life span, 11
Life-span development theory
    advantages of approach by, 39–40
    described, 39
    issues for consideration, 41
    on psychological well-being effects of marital
        status, 68–86
    readings on, 40–41
    on risk experiences during childhood
        to midadulthood passage, 42–61
Lindenberger, U., 39
Liu, X., 125
Lloyd, S. A., 166
Locke, H. J., 319, 320
Locke-Wallace scale of marital
    quality/satisfaction, 319–320
Lofland, J., 19
Lofland, L., 19
Long, A. F., 268
Long, E., 166
Long, J. D., 30, 31, 37
Long, J. S., 52
Looking glass self, 121
Lopes, J., 331
Loprest, P., 271
Lorde, A., 213, 218
Lowe, R., 339
Lueptow, L. B., 227
Lugones, M., 219
Lujansky, H., 167, 168
Lukemeyer, A., 271
Lund, M., 170
Luthar, S. S., 44
Lye, D. N., 227
Lyman, S. M., 259
Lynch, J. H., 122
Lynch, S., 142
Lytle, L. J., 283

Maccoby, E. E., 118, 120, 121, 126
MacDermid, S. M., 141, 142, 143, 148, 324, 332
Macrosystem, 307–308

Madge, N., 42
Maheu, M., 27
Main, M., 119, 121
Makepeace, J. M., 188
Mallandain, I., 300
Mangione, T. W., 72, 140, 142
Manis, J. D., 141, 142
Marakovitz, S., 45
Marcia, J. E., 282, 283, 288, 289, 290
Margolin, G., 320
Marital adjustment
    as adaptation process, 328
    changes in spouse's beliefs/attitudes about
        each other and, 335–337
    general model of, 328–335
    marital success/stability and, 337–338
Marital behavior
    additional uses of diary-type data
        to study, 324–325
    as foundation of marriage relationships, 320
    marital success/stability and, 337–338
    microbehavioral, 326–327
    obtaining diary data on, 321–323t, 322t
    patterns of molar, 320–321
    profiling marital lifestyles and, 324
    reflecting spouses' subjective states, 332
    strengths of diary data over other techniques
        to study, 325–326
Marital power
    abstract on, 194
    analytic framework for examining, 195–196
    discussions/conclusions of findings on, 206–207
    division of domestic labor and, 198–200
    insights from past research, 194–195
    managing tensions created in income/status differences
        and, 204–206
    money management/decision making and, 201–204
    research design for study of, 196–198
Marital satisfaction, 204–205
Marital status
    abstract on, 68–69
    age differences and continuity effects of, 82
    age differences in effects of transitions in, 84
    dimensions of psychological health and, 71–72
    discussion and conclusions of study on, 84–86
    effects of becoming a parent and, 144, 151t, 154t, 156t,
        157–158, 160t
    effects on well-being of change in, 82–84
    measures used in study of, 75–77
    methods used to study, 74–75
    psychological well-being and continuity of, 72–73
    research hypotheses and questions on, 74

results of study on continuity and change in, 77–82
    theoretical/empirical background of continuity
        and change in, 69–71
    well-being and transitions in, 73–74
Marital violence
    abstract on, 98
    conflict approach to family and, 186–192
    discussion of social learning theory on, 108–114
    frequency and prevalence of, 105–107, 106t
    generalizability of violence and, 101–102
    hypotheses on exogenous/endogenous
        variables of, 105
    introduction to social learning theory on, 98–99
    literature review on, 99–101
    measures of, 103–105
    methods used to study, 103
    path analyses of, 108, 109fig–112fig
    research findings on, 105–107
    sex-role theory on, 102
    summary of research on, 102–103
    welfare mothers as victims of, 271–272
    See also Family violence; Violence
Markman, H. J., 326, 327
Marks, N. F., 68, 144, 148
Marks, S. R., 41, 218, 332
Markus, E., 300
Marriage
    abstract on ecology of intimate unions
        and, 317–340
    as behavioral ecosystem, 320–327
    defining a well adjusted, 327
    dissolving sacred bonds of, 245–246
    divorce and claims of "false," 251–254
    macroenvironmental context of, 338–339
    meaning of, 243–245
    model of commitment and success/stability
        of, 337–338
    psychological infrastructure of, 327–338, 329fig
    spouses as architects of their, 332–335
    symbolically disassembling, 246–251
    three-level model for viewing, 318–320, 319fig
    See also Divorce; Intimate unions ecology; Spouses
Marrow, A. J., 2
Marshall, C., 18, 19
Marshall, N. L., 307
Marsh, C., 49
Marsiglio, W., 15, 16, 25, 227
Martin, J., 118, 120, 121, 126
Martin, M. W., 167, 168
Martz, J. M., 167
Marx, K., 183, 260
Marx, M. H., 2

Masheter, 240
Mastekaasa, A., 69, 73, 86
Masten, A. S., 44
Mastering Family Therapy
    (Minuchin, Lee, & Simon), 294, 296
Matteson, D. R., 289
Mattessich, P. W., 346
Matthews, F. N., 289
Maughan, B., 50
Mazor, A., 283
McAlpine, D. D., 144
McCall, G. J., 246, 255, 339
McCarthy, J. A., 118
McCartney, K., 307
McClearn, G. E., 43
McCord, J., 98
McCrae, R. R., 74
McCulloch, A., 46
McCullough, C., 195
McHale, S. M., 141, 142, 307, 321, 324, 333
McIntosh, P., 213
McKeering, H., 142
McKnight, A., 46
McLanahan, S. S., 70, 140, 142, 143
McLoyd, V. C., 45
McPherson, J. M., 141
McPherson, M. L., 345, 354
McQuinn, R. D., 167, 168
McRae, J. A., 307
McRae, S., 198
Mead, G. H., 121, 188, 237
Mead, L. M., 261
Mechanic, D., 140, 143
Medicaid, 270
Medlicott, J., 15
Medrich, E., 320
Melli, M. S., 240
Melnick, B., 119
Men
    failure to financially support welfare
        mothers by, 268–269
    family formation/dissolution and gender role
        attitudes by, 225–234
    poverty and image of, 261
    status-reversal wives and, 197–207
    See also Gender differences; Women
Menaghan, E. G., 69, 73, 77, 142, 314
Mermelstein, R., 309
Merton, R. K., 189
Mesosystems, 307, 308, 347
Meston, C., 23
Meszaros, P. S., 346, 348

Methodologies
    details included as part of, 7–8
    value committed, 4–5
Meyer, H. J., 119
Meyer, J. A., 310
Meyers, M. K., 271
Michaels, J. W., 14, 167, 169
Microsystems, 307, 347
Mihalic, S. W., 97, 98
Miklowitz, D., 300
Mikula, G., 167, 168
Milardo, R. M., 320
Miles, M. B., 262
Milkie, M. A., 139, 140
Miller, D., 259
Miller, N. E., 2
Miller, O. C., 259, 260, 261
Mills, C. W., 273
Minuchin, S., 293, 294, 295, 296, 298, 301
Mirowsky, J., 68, 72, 140, 142, 143, 226, 307
Moen, P., 15, 145, 347
Moffitt, T. E., 42
Mohanty, C. T., 213, 214
Money management
    gendered link between marital power and, 202–203
    status-reversal wives and control over, 201–202
Monsey, B. R., 346
Montalvo, B., 293
Moore, G., 45
Moore, W. E., 273
Morgan, R., 215, 216
Morgan, S. P., 226, 227
Morris, A. C., 49
Morrison, T., 214
Morris, P. A., 304
Morrow, G. D., 167
Mortimore, P., 50
Mosier, K. L., 314
Moynihan, D. P., 261
Mulford, H. A., 143
Mullan, J. T., 142
Mulligan, T., 15
Mullis, A. K., 280
Mullis, R. L., 280
Munch, A., 141
Muraven, M., 284
Murray, C., 260, 261
Murray, C. I., 219
Murray, N. P., 220

Nachtscheim, C. J., 148
National Family Violence Surveys, 99

National Medical Expenditures Survey, 268
NCDS (National Child Development Study),
        48, 49, 50, 51, 53*t*–58
Needle, R., 69
Nelligan, J. S., 121
Neter, J., 148
Netting, N., 15
Neugarten, B. L., 16, 69, 70, 85
Nevaldine, A., 243
Newby, K., 45
Newcomb, R., 18
New parents
    abstract on costs/rewards of becoming, 140–141
    differences in depression between nonparents and,
        155*t*, 156*t*, 159*fig*
    discussion on effects of becoming, 159–161
    hours of housework and effects of becoming, 151*t*–154*t*
    marital status and effects of becoming, 144, 151*t*, 154*t*,
        156*t*, 157–158, 160*t*
    method used to study effects of having, 144–148
    previous research on having, 141–144
    research findings on effects of having, 148–158
    research questions and hypotheses on having, 144
    research summary on effects of having, 158–159
    See also Parents
NFER (National Foundation for Educational Research)
        [England and Wales], 50
Ng, C., 243
Nielsen, J. M., 213
Nimkoff, M. F., 9
Nisbett, R. E., 274
Nock, S. L., 226, 227
Noller, P., 121, 122, 320, 325
Nomaguchi, K. M., 139, 140
Nonsummativity, family systems, 280
Nosek, B. A., 2
Notarius, C. I., 320, 326
NSFH (National Survey of Families and Households)
        [1987–1993]
    on effects of becoming a parent, 144–145
    on gender roles and family formation/dissolution,
        225, 228–232*t*
    on marital status and psychological health, 68, 74–75
Nydegger, C. N., 71
NYS (National Youth Survey), 103

Oates, R. K., 121, 122
O'Connor, S., 119
Offord, D. R., 45
Ogburn, W. F., 9
Ohlendorf, G. W., 42
Okun, L., 99

Okun, M. A., 72
O'Leary, Y. D., 100
Oliker, S., 141
Ollman, B., 188
Olson, D. H., 284, 285
Ono, H., 161
Operationalization of proposition, 7
Oppenheimer, V. K., 227, 228
Organizational systems, 350*t*
Orvaschel, H., 118, 121
Osborn, A. F., 49, 50
Osmond, M. W., 214
Ouellette, J. A., 332
Ouston, J., 50
Oyserman, D., 283

Pakenham, K. I., 142
Paley, B., 32
Palguta, R., 15
Palkovitz, R., 71
Pan, H., 46
Paolucci, B., 303, 346, 354
Papini, D. R., 284
Parcel, T. L., 77
Parental Stress Scale, 309
Parents
    constructive parenting by, 118–124, 129*t*, 130*t*
    effects on adults of becoming, 140–161
    See also Children; Fatherhood/employment balance;
        Grandparent-grandchild relationships;
        New parents
Parker, R. G., 216, 217
Parsons, S., 42, 46
Parsons, T., 273
Partnered celibates, 19, 20–21
Partner effects, 330–331
Pasley, K., 70
Patterson, C. J., 42, 217
Patterson, G. R., 122, 320
Pavalko, E. E., 44
Pearlin, L. I., 70, 72, 141, 144
Pederson, F. A., 71
Peplau, L. A., 167, 179
Perceived Stress Scale, 309
Perkins, D. F., 305, 345
Perry, B. D., 122
Perry-Jenkins, M., 196, 226, 227, 307, 339
Personal Mastery Scale, 75
Peterson, R. R., 271
Pettigrew, T., 300
Pettit, G. S., 45
Philliber, W. W., 195, 226

Phillips, D., 307
Phinney, J. S., 282, 283
Piaget, J., 221
Pierce, E. W., 45
Piercy, F. P., 297
Piercy, K. W., 2
Pilling, D., 44
Pinsof, W. M., 300
Piven, F. F., 259
Pizzey, E., 187
Placidi, K. S., 69
Pleck, J. H., 306, 307, 313, 314
Pleck, R., 194
Plomin, R., 43
Polansky, N. A., 122, 123
Popenoe, D., 226
Portner, J., 285
Postmodern feminism, 210
Poverty
    fatalism belief about, 272
    welfare and the culture of, 266
    welfare mothers and perspective on, 260–261
Prandy, K., 51
Prescott, S., 190
Presser, H. B., 268
Press, J., 197
Presson, C. C., 119
Pringle, M. L. K., 50
Problem Arithmetic Test, 50
Protinsky, H., 286, 289
Psychological health
    dimensions of, 71–72
    effects of becoming a parent and resources for,
        142, 149t, 153t, 154t, 156t
    effects of marital status change on, 82–84
    marital status and continuity of, 72–73
    marital status transitions and, 73–74
    parenting and, 120–121, 129t, 130t
    spouses' attitudes/beliefs as distinguished
        from, 334–335
Psychosomatic Families
        (Minuchin, Rosman, & Baker), 294
Pungello, E. P., 42, 45
Putallaz, M., 118, 119, 131

Quadagno, J., 259, 264
Quinnan, S. M., 15, 284

Raceis, V., 140, 142
Race. See Ethnicity/race
Racism against welfare mothers, 269
Radical feminism, 210

Radloff, L. S., 75, 146
Ramey, C. T., 42
Ramey, S. L., 42
Ramsey-Klee, D., 119
Rands, M., 331
Rank, M. R., 259, 260
Rao, J. M., 305, 306
Raschke, H. J., 246
Raskin, A., 121
Raveis, V., 15
Ray, M. P., 304
Reagon, B. J., 218
Referential comparisons, 180
Reflected appraisals concept, 121
Regan, P., 15, 21, 27
Reimers, S., 301
Reinharz, S., 17
Reis, H. T., 322, 325
Rempel, J., 321
Research
    differences between everyday life
        and family, 4–6
    ultimate goal of any discipline, 1
Research process
    example of theory building and, 6–8
    important parts of, 2–4
Reuter, M. A., 339
RGSC (Registrar General's measure
        of social class), 48–49, 51
Rholes, W. S., 121
Rich, A., 214
Richards, M. H., 322, 325
Ricks, M., 119, 131
Riessman, C. D., 241, 243
Riger, S., 213, 214
Riley, M., 70
Rindfuss, R. R., 227
Risk experiences
    abstract on, 42
    assessing socioeconomic risk, 45–46
    described, 42–43
    developmental-contextual model of cumulative
        risk effects, 46–48, 47fig
    development and context of, 43–44
    discussion of results on, 58–61
    effects of wider sociohistorical context, 46
    method of study on, 48
    modeling strategy on, 52–53
    parental social class and, 43–51, 58–61
    results of study on, 53–58
    statistical analysis: modeling cumulative risk
        effects, 51–52

timing and duration of, 44–45
variables/observed indicators
    in both cohorts, 52*t*
Risman, B., 195, 207
Ritter, R. L., 118
Rivera, A. M., 346
Rivers, C., 140
RMSEA (root mean square error
    of approximation), 52
Roach, M. J., 69
Roberto, K. A., 214
Roberts, D. E., 118
Robins, E., 318, 321, 325, 328
Robinson, R. V., 262
Rodgers, 240
Rodgers, W. L., 44
Roizen, J. A., 320
Romantic friendship, 215–216
Romig, C., 283
Rose, J. S., 119
Rosenbaum, A., 100, 114
Rosenberg, M., 75, 145
Rosenfield, S., 142
Rosen, R., 314
Ross, C. E., 68, 70, 72, 77, 86, 143, 226, 307
Ross, C. F., 140, 142, 143
Rosser, S. V., 214
Rossi, A. S., 16, 32
Rossi, P. H., 32
Rossman, G., 18, 19
Rothenberg, P. S., 214
Rowbotham, S., 190
Roy, M., 98
Rubin, V., 320
Rubin, Z., 179
Ruddick, S., 221
Rudolph, J., 22
Ruis, 189
Rules (family system), 280
Rusbult, C. E., 165, 166, 167, 168
Russell, C. S., 284, 285
Russell, S. T., 219
Rutter, C. M., 86
Rutter, M., 42, 43, 44, 45, 50, 131
Ryan, R. M., 122
Ryff, C. D., 69, 71, 72, 75, 82

Sabatelli, R. M., 166
Sacher, J. A., 167
Sacker, A., 42
Sadler, J. Z., 2
Safilios-Rothschild, C., 194

Salisbury, W. W., 143
Sameroff, A. J., 43, 45
Sanchez, L., 142
Sandefur, G. D., 70
Sanders, C. M., 73, 74
Sandler, H., 119
Sarat, A., 241
Sargent, K. P., 313
Sawhney, S., 215
Sayer, L., 161
Scanzoni, J., 194, 226, 227
Scarr, S., 43, 307, 314
Schaie, K. W., 31
Scheldt, S., 339
Schiedel, D. G., 283
Schiller, B., 260
Schoen, R., 68, 70
Schoff, K., 45
Schoon, I., 40, 41, 42, 46
Schorr, L. B., 345
Schulenberg, J., 44
Schumm, W. R., 1
Schwalbe, M. L., 121
Schwartz, P., 170, 179, 194, 195, 207, 245
Schwarz, N., 325
Scott, J., 143
Scott, L. H., 49
Scott, M. B., 259
Sebby, R. A., 284
Seccombe, K., 9, 68, 145, 239, 258, 261, 268, 270
Secondary virgins, 15
Seidel, J. V., 349
Seifer, R., 45
Self construct/concept, 238, 239
Self-efficacy (new parents/nonparents), 158*fig,* 158*t*
Seltzer, J. A., 100
SEMprogram AMOS 4.05, 51
SEM (Structural Equation
    Modeling), 46–48
Serbin, L. A., 123, 132
SES (socioeconomic status)
    individual development and, 43
    risk experiences and, 43–51, 58–61
    SEM (Structural Equation Modeling)
        on influence of, 46–48
    See also Social class
Sewell, W. H., Jr., 42, 245
Sex
    adolescent experiences with, 21–22
    at heart of feminist perspectives, 210
    welfare mothers and peer pressure regarding, 271
Sex-role modeling, 123–124

Sex-role theory, 102
Sexual relationships
    barriers to, 23–24
    becoming celibate in, 22–23
    consequences of celibacy as part of, 24–26
    Internet community to replace, 27
Sexual transitions, 16–17
Seymour, E., 349
Shadish, W., 300
Shannon, H. S., 45
Sharlin, S., 142
Shaver, R., 121
Shehan, C., 68
Shelton, B. A., 146, 225
Shepherd, P., 46, 48
Sherman, S. J., 119
Sherrod, K., 119
Shiedel, D. G., 289
Shilts, L., 286, 289
Shin, H., 68, 72
Shire, K., 197
Sieber, S. D., 141
Siegel, J. M., 73
Siegel, K., 15
*Signs: Journal of Women in Culture
    and Society* (Walby), 213
Silva, P. A., 42
Silverman, R. J., 359
Silver, R. C., 69, 73, 243
Silverstein, L. B., 313
Silverstein, M., 30, 31, 36, 37
Simmel, G., 183, 241
Simmons, J. L., 339
Simon, G., 293, 294
Simon, R. W., 143, 144
Simons, R. L., 118, 119, 120,
    121, 122, 123, 124, 131, 132
Simon, W., 16
Simpson, J. A., 121, 167
Single celibates, 19, 20
Sisterhood Is Powerful (Morgan), 216
Skinner, B. F., 95
Skinnerian conditioning, 95
Slaten, F., 145
Smeeding, T. M., 271
Smith, E. R., 260, 264
Smith, K., 48
Smith, K. B., 259, 260
Smith-Lovin, L., 141
Smith, R. A., 264
Smith-Rosenberg, C., 215
Smith, R. S., 44

Smith, S. E., 324
Smith-Sreen, P., 345, 354
Smyer, M. A., 69, 70, 241
Snarey, S., 120
Social class
    RGSC (Registrar General's measure of social class),
        48–49, 51
    risk experiences and parental, 43–51, 58–61
    See also SES (socioeconomic status)
Social conflict theory
    on family violence, 186–192
    issues for consideration, 185
    on marital power and status/income as gendered
        resources, 194–207
    overview of, 183–185
    readings on, 185
Social exchange
    as predictor of change in satisfaction/commitment,
        173–174, 177–178
    as predictor of relationship stability, 178–179
    relationship satisfaction/commitment as predictor of
        change in, 174, 178
Social exchange theory
    comparison level and behavior according to, 139
    on effects of becoming a parent on adults, 140–161
    on equity/social exchange in dating couples, 165–180
    issues for consideration, 139
    overview of, 137–139
    readings on, 139
Social inequality, 260–261
Socialist feminism, 210
Socialization/violence link, 187–189
Social learning theory
    on intergenerational transmission of constructive
        parenting, 118–132
    issues to consider, 97
    of marital violence, 98–117
    overview of, 95–97
    parental and child behavior explained by, 6–7
    readings on, 97
Social participation/parenting behavior link,
    123, 129t, 130t
Soderlind, A., 23
Sontag, M. S., 303, 346, 349, 355
Sorbom, D., 126
Soulis, J., 121
Southgate Reading Test, 50
Southgate, V., 50
South, S. J., 146, 161
Spanier, G., 195
Spanier, G. B., 73, 84, 319
Spender, D., 214

Spitze, G., 146, 161, 195, 227
Spouses
    as architects of their marriage, 332–335
    changes in beliefs/attitudes about each
        other, 335–337
    marital adjustment by, 328–337
    marital behavior by, 320–338
    model of commitment by, 337–338
    See also Marriage
Sprague, J., 213
Sprecher, S., 15, 21, 27, 139, 165, 166, 167, 170, 171, 179
Sprenkle, D. H., 284, 295
Sprey, J., 184, 241
Stacey, J., 220, 255
Stack, C. B., 261
Stafford, T., 15, 27
Stanley, S. M., 327
Starnes, C. E., 226
Starr, B., 15
Starr, R. H., Jr., 122
Status-reversal wives
    division of domestic labor and, 198–200
    managing marital tensions created
        by resources of, 204–206
    marital power and conventional vs., 197, 198–207
    money management/decision making by, 201–204
    perceptions of marital equity and, 200
Staudinger, U. M., 39, 71, 85
Steinmetz, S. K., 98, 118, 119, 188, 191
Steinmetz, W. K., 1
Stein, P. J., 312
Stewart, A. J., 213
Stewart, S., 72
Stith, S. M., 99
Stock, W. A., 72
Stolzenberg, R. M., 226
Stone, L. H., 259, 260
Storaasli, R. D., 327
Straus, M. A., 98, 99, 101, 102, 103, 105, 113, 114,
    118, 119, 123, 186, 187, 188, 191, 271, 297
Strauss, A. L., 18, 19, 197, 242, 243, 262
Stroebe, M. S., 69, 73
Stroebe, W., 69, 73
Structural family therapy
    abstract on, 293
    an illustration of, 298–300
    applications and efficacy of, 300–301
    assessment for, 296–297
    challenges to, 297–298
    introduction to, 293–294
    as model of change, 294
    principal features of, 294–296

Style, C. B., 68
Sudman, S., 325
Sugarman, D., 99, 102, 113
Suitor, J. J., 226
Surra, C. A., 320
Su, S., 69
Sweet Honey in the Rock (vocal ensemble), 218
Sweet, J. A., 74, 144
Swicegood, G., 227
Symbolic interactionism theory
    issues for consideration, 239
    overview of, 237–239
    readings on, 239
    on social construction of welfare mother, 258–275
    on symbolic origins of conflict in divorce, 240–256
Szatmari, P., 45
Szinovacz, M., 226

Tallman, L., 339
TANF (Temporary Assistance to Needy
    Families), 258, 259
Taylor, H., 18
Terman, L. W., 334
Theory
    concepts and relationships "guts" of, 4
    defining, 1–2
    ecological, 303–355
    example of, 6–8
    family life course, 12–38
    family systems, 279–301
    feminist, 209–234
    life-span development, 39–93
    social conflict, 183–207
    social exchange, 137–180
    social learning, 95–132
    symbolic interactionism, 237–275
Theory building, defining, 2
Thibaut, J. W., 137, 165
Thomas, W. I., 14
Thompson, A., 319, 325
Thompson, L., 213, 218, 219
Thompson, M. S., 143
Thompson, W. W., 42
Thomson, F., 142
Thorne, B., 189
Thornton, A., 16, 21, 22, 45, 70, 225, 228
Tichenor, V. J., 185, 194
Tizard, J., 45
Todd, M., 119
Townsley, E., 197
Trapnell, R., 23
Traupmann, J., 166

Treacher, A., 301
Treas, J., 18
Treiber, F. A., 121
Tsatsas, M., 42, 46
Tuchman, B., 240
Tucker, D., 45
Tudor, J., 72

Uhlenberg, P., 30, 69, 71, 85
Umberson, D., 72, 140, 141, 142, 143,
    144, 145, 161
Urton, W., 68
Utne, M. K., 166

Vaines, E., 354
Valentine, C., 261
Vallacher, R. R., 332
Vangelisti, A., 320, 324
Van Ijzendoorn, M. H., 118, 119, 121, 131
Van Manen, M., 262
Vannoy-Hiller, D., 195, 226
Van Willigen, M., 143
VanYperen, N. W., 167, 168, 180
Vaughan, D., 241, 243, 246, 247, 255
Verette, J., 166
Veroff, J., 69, 71, 82
Vetere, A., 281, 293, 297, 300
Vietze, P., 119
Violence
    CTS (Conflict Tactics Scale) measuring, 103–104
    ethnicity and marital, 104, 106*t*, 107*t*
    generalizability of, 101–102
    intergenerational transmission of, 99–101
    socialization and cycle of, 187–189
    welfare mothers as victims of, 271–272
    See also Family violence; Marital violence
Virginal celibates, 19, 20
Voluntary virgins, 15
Von Bertalanffy, L., 293
Vondracek, F. W., 44
Von Eye, A., 43
Voydanoff, P., 77, 141, 306

Wadsworth, M. E., 120
Wahlsten, D., 43
Waister (Hatfield), E., 166
Waite, L. J., 68, 226
Walby, S., 213
Walker, A. J., 213, 218, 219, 319
Walker, D., 42
Walker, L. R., 98, 102, 113
Wallace, A.F.C., 241

Wallace, K. M., 319
Waller, W. W., 327, 329, 331
Walster, G. W., 165
Walster (Hatfield), E., 165, 179
Walters, K. B., 239, 258
Walters, M., 293
Waltz, D., 15
Waring, J., 70
Warner, R. L., 9
Wasner, G. H., 167
Wasserman, W., 148
Waterman, A. S., 282, 283
Watson, C., 240
Weaver, C. N., 68, 72
Weber, A. L., 247, 252
Weber, M., 183
Webster-Stratton, C., 121
Wegner, D. M., 332
Weiderman, W., 23
Weiner, M., 15
Weingarten, K., 71
Weinick, R. M., 68, 70
Weis, D. L., 2
Weis, J. G., 98
Weiss, H. B., 220
Weiss, K., 23
Weiss, R. L., 320
Weiss, R. S., 240, 241, 243, 246
Weissman, M. M., 118
Weitzman, L. J., 240
Welfare
    AFDC and TANF programs of,
        258–259, 262, 263, 264, 266, 268, 270, 272
    ethnicity/race of families receiving,
        259, 262, 263, 264, 265–267, 269, 272
    fatalism belief about, 272
    perspectives on social inequality, poverty, and, 260–261
    reform efforts to limit benefits of, 274–275
    stigmatization of, 261–262, 263–265
Welfare mothers
    abstract on, 258–259
    conceptual framework for studying, 259–262
    discussion of findings on, 272–275
    ethnicity/race of, 259, 262, 263, 264,
        265–267, 269, 272
    fatalism beliefs of, 272
    marital violence suffered by, 271–272
    methods used to study, 262–263
    racism against, 269
    reasons for being on welfare, 265–272
    research findings on, 263–272
    self-evaluation hypothesis of, 273–274

sexual relationships of, 271
stigmatization of welfare interpreted by,
261–262, 263–265
Wells, G. L., 243
Werner, E. E., 44
West, C., 195, 196, 225
West, J. D., 289
Wethington, E., 140, 142, 325, 339
Wheaton, B., 86
Wheeler, K. K., 122
Whipple, E. E., 121
Whitbeck, L. B., 118, 119, 121
White, C., 15
White, J. M., 1, 4, 7, 9, 11, 39, 40, 359, 360, 361, 362
White, L. K., 73, 227
White, S., 213
Whitley, M., 243
Whittington, F., 28
Whyte, M. K., 194, 244, 245
Widmer, E., 18
Widom, C. W., 102
Wiegman, R., 214
Wiggins, R. D., 42, 46
Wilber, K., 215
Wilcox, K. L., 214
Wille, D. E., 124
Williams, D. P., 122
Williams, D. R., 49
Williams, K., 140, 141, 142, 143, 144
Wills, T. A., 320, 325
Wilson, H. S., 262
Wilson, W. J., 261
Wise, M. J., 71
Witt, D. D., 185, 186, 191
Witter, R. A., 72
Woethke, W., 33
Wolfe, B., 45
Wolfe, D., 194, 197
Wolfgang, M., 186
Women
19th century romantic friendship between, 215–216
Chinese Exclusion Act (1882) prohibiting entry
of Chinese, 216
family formation/dissolution and gender role
attitudes by, 225–234
social construction of welfare mothers, 258–275
status-reversal wives, 197–207
See also Feminism; Gender differences;
Lesbians; Men
Woodrow, K., 68
Wood, W., 332
Work/family stress. *See* Fatherhood/employment
balance
Working wives
changes in traditional families and, 189–190
division of domestic labor and status-reversal, 198–200
managing marital tensions created by resources of
status-reversal, 204–206
marital power and conventional vs.
status-reversal, 197, 198–207
money management/decision making by
status-reversal, 201–204
See also Fatherhood/employment balance
Workplace/Family Stress Scale, 306, 310, 312
Workplace Flexibility Scale, 310
Wortman, C. B., 69, 73, 312
Wright, B. R. E., 42
Wright, E. O., 197
W. T. Grant Foundation, 355
Wu, C., 118, 119
Wyatt, G., 27
Wynne, L. C., 300

Yarrow, M. R., 120, 129
Yeung, W. J., 45
Yllo, K., 188
Youngblade, L. M., 123
Young-DeMarco, L., 70
Young, R. K., 118
Youngstrom, E., 45

Zedeck, S., 314
Zhao, S., 143
Zigler, E., 101
Zimmerman, D., 195, 196, 225
Zuckerman, B. S., 45

ABOUT THE EDITORS

Thomas R. Chibucos has been a Professor of Human Development and Family Studies at Bowling Green State University for 11 years, where he also served as Director of the School of Family and Consumer Sciences for a decade. Previously, he was at Northern Illinois University in the Department of Human and Family Resources for 17 years. He has developed and taught courses on child abuse and neglect, child and family policy, research methodology, and theory at the undergraduate and graduate levels at two universities. He is an active member of numerous professional organizations and his publications include *Serving Children and Families Through Community-University Partnerships* (Kluwer, 1999), which he edited with Richard Lerner.

Randall W. Leite is an Assistant Professor of Human Development and Family Studies at Bowling Green State University. At Bowling Green, he teaches graduate and undergraduate courses in marriage and family, family stress, and family policy. His research largely focuses on aspects of fatherhood, father-child interactions, nonresidential parenthood, and family policy issues. He is also an affiliate of the Center for Family and Demographic Research and the Center for Policy Analysis and Public Service, both located at Bowling Green State University. Prior to his arrival at Bowling Green, he spent several years in various university administrative positions. He lives with his wife Theresa and three children, all of whom provide him on a daily basis with a greater appreciation of the meaning of family life.